THE UMI ANNUAL COMMENTARY 2021–2022

PRECEPTS FOR LIVING®

MISSION STATEMENT

*W*e are called
of God to create, produce, and distribute
quality Christian education products;
to deliver exemplary customer service;
and to provide quality Christian
educational services, which will empower
God's people, especially within the Black
community, to evangelize, disciple,
and equip people for serving Christ,
His kingdom, and church.

UMI

UMI ANNUAL SUNDAY SCHOOL LESSON COMMENTARY
PRECEPTS FOR LIVING® 2021–2022
INTERNATIONAL SUNDAY SCHOOL LESSONS
VOLUME 24
UMI (URBAN MINISTRIES, INC.)

Melvin Banks Sr., LittD, Founder and Chairman

C. Jeffrey Wright, JD, CEO

Bible art: Fred Carter

Item No.: 1-2022. ISBN-13: 978-1-68353-569-0

PFL Large Print Item No.: 1-2622. ISBN-13: 978-1-68353-572-0

Publisher: UMI (Urban Ministries, Inc.), Chicago, IL 60643. To place an order, call us at 1-800-860-8642, or visit our website at www.urbanministries.com.

Get the Precepts for Living® eBook!

Are you among those reading books using a Kindle, iPad, NOOK, or other electronic reader? If so, there's good news for you! UMI (Urban Ministries, Inc.) is keeping up with the latest technology by publishing its annual Sunday School commentary, *Precepts for Living*®, in the leading e-book formats: Kindle (Amazon), NOOK (Barnes & Noble), and iBooks (Apple).

To buy an e-book copy of *Precepts for Living*®, visit our website at urbanministries.com/precepts to find download links and step-by-step instructions.

If you've purchased *Precepts for Living*®, for your e-reader, be sure to leave a rating and a review at the iTunes or Amazon store sites to tell others what you think. Also, spread the word on your favorite social networking sites, and follow *Precepts for Living*® on Facebook @ facebook.com/urbanministriesinc, @umichicago on Twitter, and @umi on Instagram.

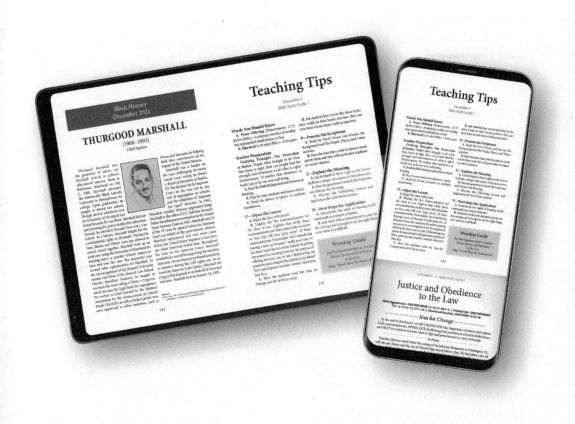

CONTRIBUTORS

Editor
Melvin E. Banks, Sr., LittD

Developmental Editor
Beth Potterveld, MA

Copy Editors
Daschell Phillips
Mary Lewis
Barbara Taylor

Graphic Design
Jennifer Ostman

Bible Illustrations
Fred Carter

Contributing Writers
Essays/In Focus Stories
Luvell Anderson, Jr., PhD
Rodrick Burton
Evangeline Carey
Kelvin Childs
Jacquelyn Donald-Mims, DMin
Whitney M. DuPreé
Hurby Franks
Domeniek Harris, PhD
Angela Lampkin, PhD
Ramon Mayo
Beverly Moore, MS
Daschell Phillips
Maisie Sparks, MA
Jordan Taylor

Bible Study Guide Writers
John Burton, Jr., MDiv
Domeniek Harris, EdD
Wayne C. Hopkins, MA
Karl Hrebik
Angela Lampkin, PhD
Ramon Mayo
Victoria McAfee, MDiv
Beverly Moore, MS
CaReese Mukulu, MA
Eric Redmond, PhD
Allen Reynolds, MA
Maisie Sparks, MA
Charlesetta Watson-Holmes

More Light on the Text
J. Ayodeji Adewuya, PhD
Jamall Calloway, PhD
Norvella Carter, PhD
Moussa et Assita Coulibaly, PhD
Cecilia Dennery, PhD
David Downey, DMin
Ernest Gray, MA
Angela Lampkin, PhD
Cheryl Price, PhD
LaTonya Summers, PhD
Alajemba Reuben Unaegbu, MA
Jamie Viands, PhD
Jeremy Williams, MDiv

Dear Friend,

UMI is blessed because people like you have believed in us and in the work we do. You have trusted us to remain true to our mission of providing biblical content contextualized for the African American community.

We have sought to remain faithful to the mission God gave us. My life mission was impressed upon me as a boy of twelve years of age while living in Birmingham, Alabama. An old man quoted Hosea 4:6 to me: "My people perish for lack of knowledge." After hearing the man quote that Bible verse, I decided to dedicate my life to studying and sharing God's Word with our people.

Through the years since, God has honored this desire so now we can say as Samuel once said, "Thus far the LORD has helped us" (1 Samuel 7:12).

We are immensely grateful for the sustaining grace of God who has guided and provided for us. But, in truth, our eyes are on the future. We strain our eyes to see what God has in store for us in the coming years.

That's because the world keeps changing in the way we receive and process information. When we began, ink on paper and audio were the main modes of communication. Today, digital content is reaching new heights. We will use this and other methods to keep proclaiming the Good News of God's love and forgiveness. We will keep teaching followers of Christ to fully engage in extending His Kingdom agenda.

Melvin Banks, Sr., LittD

Melvin E. Banks Sr., LittD

UMI Founder, Chairman, and Senior Editor

Dr. Melvin E. Banks, Sr. Biography

Dr. Melvin Eugene Banks, Sr. was born on October 15, 1934 in Birmingham, Alabama to the union of Jerry and Survilla Banks. Dr. Banks was the youngest of two children born to this union. Dr. Banks was raised in a blended household with his mother; Aunt, Zerlean Jackson; sister, Margaret Banks; and cousins, Gilbert Williams; Walter Williams; and Martye Jackson.

Dr. Banks was educated in the Birmingham Public School System, and graduated from Parker High School in 1952. In 1955, he graduated from Moody Bible Institute in Chicago.

While attending Moody Bible Institute, Dr. Banks was encouraged by his mentor Dr. B. M. Nottage to find a congregation of Black Christians. At South Side Gospel Chapel he met Beverly and LeRoy Yates. Mrs. Yates suggested he write to her sister Olive. After many letters, he met Olive at a dinner at the Yates home. When he walked in, he said, "The Lord is my Shepherd, I see what I want." November 5, 1955, Dr. Banks married his beautiful wife Olive Perkins. To this union they were blessed with three adorable children, Melvin Eugene, Jr.; Patrice Janene; and Reginald Scott.

Dr. Banks then attended Wheaton College and earned his Bachelor of Arts in Theology and Master of Arts in Biblical Studies. He was later awarded an Honorary Doctorate by Wheaton College and served for many years as a board member of the institution. He was also the Alumnus of the Year in 2008 at Moody Bible Institute.

After graduation, Dr. Banks was employed by Scripture Press Publications, Inc. He left Scripture Press with a blessing and a little financial backing that helped him and his wife, Olive, start Urban Ministries, Inc. in 1970. For the first twelve years, Urban Ministries, Inc. (UMI) operated out of the basement of their home on the South Side of Chicago.

Over the fifty years of leadership of Dr. Banks, UMI has grown to be the largest independent African American -owned and -operated religious publishing company in the nation.

Dr. Banks, along with LeRoy Yates, Sr., and Harvey Rollerson, Jr. were sent to establish Westlawn Gospel Chapel on the west side of Chicago by the elders of Southside Gospel Chapel. He faithfully served there as elder, Sunday School Teacher, Sunday School Superintendent, and Bible Study Leader. Dr. Banks remained in leadership for more than sixty years.

Dr. Banks was involved in the founding of Circle Y Ranch Bible Camp, a Christian camp in Bangor, Michigan, in 1964. He faithfully served in the camp ministry as a counselor, camp director, and board member. Circle Y Ranch has touched more than tens of thousands of urban youth through his teaching and other ministries.

Dr. Banks was awarded the Kenneth N. Taylor Lifetime Achievement Award in 2017. He has also received many other commendations for his work.

Dr. Banks is remembered by his children and grandchildren for making sure family dinners were a time of togetherness. At the dinner table was where he would love to tell Bible stories and he would make them so interesting with his dramatic storytelling.

Dr. Banks made his transition home on February 13, 2021. His parents, Jerry and Survilla, and sister, Margaret, preceded him in death. He leaves to cherish his memory, his loving wife, Olive, of 65 years; three children, Melvin E. Banks, Jr.; Patrice Lee (Tony); and Reginald Banks; two grandchildren, Regis Banks and Antoinette Johnson; two great-grandchildren, Cameron Johnson and Dallas Rogers; sisters-in-law Beverly Yates, Sara Hennings, and Marianne "Kit" Perkins; brother-in-law, William Pannell (Hazel); and a host of nieces, nephews, cousins, and spiritually adopted children.

Christian publisher targets black community

By Deborah Snow
Staff Writer

Photo by David R. Stephens

Grieving with Hope

1 Thessalonians 4:13–14
"Brothers and sisters, we do not want you to be uninformed about those who sleep in death, so that you do not grieve like the rest of mankind, who have no hope. For we believe that Jesus died and rose again, and so we believe that God will bring with Jesus those who have fallen asleep in him."

Dr. Melvin E. Banks, Sr., Founder and Chairman of UMI (Urban Ministries, Inc.) went home to be with the Lord on February 13, 2021 after a month-long illness. Though we are deeply saddened by this loss, we do not grieve like those who have no hope because of the assurance that we have from his own testimony and his life's work that he has indeed fallen asleep in Jesus. He often encouraged all of us to look forward to that future that the Scripture said, "Eye hath not seen, nor ear heard, neither have entered into the heart of man, the things which God hath prepared for them that love him" (Isaiah 64:4 and 1 Corinthians 2:9).

He leaves a legacy of being a dedicated husband to Olive Banks for 65 years; a father to their three children Melvin Jr., Patrice Lee, and Reginald; a church planter of the Westlawn Gospel Chapel; a teacher and leader of leaders as the founder of the Urban Outreach Foundation; a philanthropist with a deep concern for the spiritual formation of our youth as a founder of the Christian camp, Circle Y Ranch; and a Kingdom business entrepreneur as the founder of UMI.

Many of you know him and have testified to the power of his work in bringing the message of the Gospel and the teachings of the Bible to the color and context of the African and African American experience. The affirmation of African identity in biblical exposition, teaching, history, and artwork was sorely needed at a time when our faith was being challenged then, as now, by American injustice and evangelical silence.

We at UMI are blessed to be able to serve and support the efforts of your families and ministries to effectively teach the Word and make disciples during this especially trying season. Following Dr. Banks' example, it is our commitment that we will continue to provide you the best in Christian education resources so that the challenge presented by the verse that inspired our founder will be met:

"My people are destroyed for lack of knowledge" (from Hosea 4:6).

Yours in Christ,

Jeff Wright

Rev. C. Jeffrey Wright
President and Chief Executive Officer

Uncovering the Benefits of Precepts

It is a great privilege to participate in Christian education and play a significant role in the spiritual formation of fellow Christians in our churches. *Precepts for Living®* is a resource that is designed to help you lead others toward greater knowledge and practice of following Jesus Christ. To that end, please take full advantage of the substantive offerings provided to you in this year's commentary.

We want the liberating lesson to help you think about collective application and perspective beyond the individual level and the "Application for Activation" to help you think about personal ways to live out the lessons' themes and draw closer to God.

From the standpoint of your vocation as a teacher, it is very important to be aware of the great responsibility that goes along with your position. James 3:1 reminds us that we have such a great opportunity in front of us that we run the risk of greater judgment if we are derelict in our duties. In the Gospels, Jesus is often referred to as "Teacher." Being a teacher means participating in one of the church's greatest tasks, one that the ancient church called "*catechesis.*"

This is a strong word that helps us understand the great influence we have when we help our students learn about God's Word. It carries with it the idea of imparting the entirety of the faith to Christians. While many teachers might not be familiar with this word, the truth is that every time we help others learn about God's Word and ways, we are participating in this great task of the church that has been with us from the beginning. Unfortunately, this gets lost amid other concerns. As a teacher, you have an opportunity to energize or revitalize this aspect of your church's ministry. Reflect on how you have prepared for the challenge.

What is the goal when you use *Precepts for Living®* to open up the riches of the Bible to your students? It is beyond the mere acquisition of information. We want students to receive revelation that becomes application. Certainly, we want our students to grow in knowledge, but the knowledge we seek to pass on does not solely comprise Bible facts but includes a larger sense of comprehension where the information and doctrine conveyed is oriented toward a faithful life of discipleship. That is why it is called *Precepts for Living®*, and not Precepts for Knowing.

The "People, Places, and Times," "Background," "In Depth," and "More Light on the Text" sections are there to help you provide insight and understanding of the text. But the sections include more than a simple compilation of information. In each lesson, you will also see "In Focus" stories and "Liberating Lesson" and "Application for Activation" sections serving as catalysts for applying the biblical text to life situations. It is very important that we as teachers pass on knowledge that will enable our students to deepen their devotion to God in an upward focus and encourage them to better embody that devotion in a way that makes their lives a living witness to the world. Our hope from every lesson should be to inspire students to become the best living examples of the Scriptures with the understanding that their lives may be the only Bible some people ever read.

To best take advantage of this commentary, utilize the essays to emphasize quarterly themes and enhance the classroom experience.

We believe this commentary is a great tool to help form fully devoted followers of Christ, and we invite you to wholeheartedly partake in all of the resources provided here. May God be glorified as you play your part in this great task of the church!

Creative Teaching

• **Energizing the Class.** If the class does not seem as enthusiastic or energy is low, after you open with prayer, have everyone stretch to the sky or outward. Then tell the class to shake off the low energy, and open up their hands to receive the love of God that is right there. You can always have a 30-second meet and greet time. This usually helps to wake people up so you can begin class on a higher energy level.

• **Two Teachers in One Class—Bring Out the Best in Both.** Taking turns works in some classes, but in others it creates tension and favorites. Encourage teachers to study together, and then divide the segments of the lesson. Perhaps one will teach the introduction while the other teaches a section of the text. Encourage them to also become a true team with each contributing throughout the lesson.

• **Variety.** Everyone cannot read or write on the same level. Use different teaching techniques and styles when teaching. How you learn affects how you teach, so be open and willing to learn and teach through various media.

• **Partner Up.** People often "get it" when they are involved with more than talking about the lesson. Why not allow the class to see the connections themselves? Try using a chart to have adult students work in pairs or groups to compare and contrast Bible people such as David and Solomon or Ruth and Orpah, Naomi's daughters-in-law. To help the students get started, suggest specific categories for comparisons such as lifestyles, families, or public ministry. As class members search the Scriptures, they will learn and remember much more than if you told them about either person individually.

• **Group Studies.** Have the class form groups, and have each group read the Scripture lesson and a section of the Background for the text. Have each group create a two-minute skit about the Scripture to share with the class. Encourage the groups to use their imaginations and energy. You may want to have at least one "leader" in a group if you have more than two or three reserved people in your class.

• **Volunteers.** Many classes begin with reading the lesson. When class members have studied beforehand, this activity is more about bringing minds together than about the actual lesson. Some classes can benefit from dramatic and creative reading of Bible passages at any point in the lesson. As the passage under study lends itself, assign parts to volunteers. This need not be formal—standing up isn't even critical. This strategy works best in passages that have a story such as the conversation between Moses and his father-in-law, Jethro, or Paul confronting the merchants in Thessalonica. Assign one person to each speaking character in the Bible text. Feel free to be creative with giving the class roles as "the crowd." Make sure to assign a narrator who will read the nonspeaking parts. It is fun, it is fast, and it makes for memorable Bible reading.

• **Materials.** You may want to have large sheets of paper, markers, glue or tape, newspapers, and magazines available on a weekly basis for the various activities.

• **Themes.** Write the theme on a large poster board or sheet of paper, and ask each person to write a word or draw a picture that best describes the theme. Read the themes aloud, and discuss any of the pictures before you begin your class discussion or activities. If you have a very large class or time is limited, only select a few words or pictures for discussion. You can either lead the discussion or invite members of the class to do so.

• **Websites.** Connect with us by logging onto www.urbanministries.com. Follow us on social media on Facebook at facebook.com/urbanministriesinc, @umichicago on Twitter, and @UMI on Instagram.

• **Email us** at precepts@urbanministries.com, and send us some of your favorite Teaching Tips for ages 36 and older that you want to share with others. If yours is selected, we will post them under our Teaching Tips sections for Precepts. If you have ice-breaker activities, please submit them as well.

• **Prayer.** Have a Prayer Request Board for people to write their prayer requests on each Sunday. You may want to make this a weekly activity. Have someone read the prayer request and let the class decide which prayer requests they will pray for during the week. One Sunday School teacher has his class write their prayer requests on sheets of paper and place them in the middle of the floor once a year. He then shares with the class that he will write them all down in a prayer journal that he keeps and prays over them at least once a week. Be creative and create your own prayer journal or prayer tradition(s) within your class.

• **Closing.** At the end of the lesson, give your class the assignment of looking for scenes from films or television, advertisements, or parts of songs that either demonstrate the coming week's "In Focus" story, "Liberating Lesson" section, or "Application for Activation" section. Encourage them to be creative and to come up with an explanation of how their contribution helps make the truth of the lesson come to life.

TABLE OF CONTENTS

Contributors..iv
Letter from the Founder.........................v
Remembering Dr. Melvin E. Banks, Sr..................vi
Uncovering the Benefits of Precepts........................x
Creative Teaching...xi
2016–2022 Scope and Sequence-Cycle Spread....xv

Fall Quarter 2021

CELEBRATING GOD

September 2021 Quarter At-A-Glance 1
Engaging the Theme: *We Worship You, O Lord!* ...3
Christian Education in Action:
Christ-Centeredness: The Key to Wisdom 5
Black History: *Paul Laurence Dunbar*....................7

LESSONS
Unit 1: God's People Offer Praise
SEPTEMBER

5   Moses and Miriam Praise God
    Exodus 15:11-21 9
12 David Dances before the Ark
    2 Samuel 6:1-5, 14-19...................................... 20
19 Glorifying God
    Mark 10:46-52 30
26 Believers Praise God
    Acts 2:32-33, 37-47.. 39

Unit 2: Called to Praise God
OCTOBER

3   Make a Joyful Noise
    Psalm 100... 50
10 Praise God for Justice and Righteousness
    Psalm 9:1-12 59
17 Give Thanks for Deliverance
    Psalm 107:1-9, 39-43........................... 68
24 The Joy of Worship
    Psalm 84... 77
31 Praise God with Music
    Psalm 149:1-5; 150:1-6................................... 87

Unit 3: Visions of Praise
NOVEMBER

7   All People Praise God
    Revelation 7:9-17.......................... 97
14 Praise for God's Eternal Reign
    Revelation 11:15-19..................................... 107
21 Rejoicing in Heaven
    Revelation 19:1-8.. 116
28 Good News for All
    Acts 10:34-47 125

Winter Quarter 2021–2022

JUSTICE, LAW, HISTORY

December 2021 Quarter-At-A-Glance 135
Engaging the Theme: *Godliness and Justice:
Two Sides of the Same Coin*..................................137
Christian Education in Action: *Imparting
More than Information* 139
Black History: *Thurgood Marshall* 142

LESSONS
Unit 1: God Requires Justice
DECEMBER

5   Justice and Obedience to the Law
    Deuteronomy 5:1-3; 10:12-13; 27:1-10 143
12 David Administers Justice and Kindness
    2 Samuel 9:1-12 155
19 Justice and Righteousness Reign
    Isaiah 9:2-7.. 166
26 A Just King Is Born
    Matthew 2:1-12... 177

Unit 2: God: The Source of Justice
JANUARY

2   Justice, Vengeance, and Mercy
    Genesis 4:1-16.. 190
9   Hagar and Ishmael Not Forgotten
    Genesis 21:8-20... 202
16 The Laws of Justice and Mercy
    Exodus 23:1-12 213
23 Justice, Judges, and Priests
    Deuteronomy 16:18-20; 17:8-13.................. 225

Unit 3: Justice and Adversity

30 Justice and the Marginalized
    Deuteronomy 24:10-21 235

FEBRUARY

6   Nathan Condemns David
    2 Samuel 12:1-9, 13-15................................. 246
13 Ezra Seeks God's Law
    Ezra 7:1-10, 23-26.. 258
20 Bildad Misunderstands God's Justice
    Job 8:1-10, 20-22.. 271
27 Serving a Just God
    Job 42:1-6, 10-17.. 282

Spring Quarter 2022

GOD FREES AND REDEEMS

March 2022 Quarter At-A-Glance 293
Engaging the Theme: *"I Will Be Your God and You Will Be My People": A Central Theme in Scripture*...295
Christian Education in Action: *Educating Christians on Human Sexuality and Relationships for Holy Living*..............................298
Black History: *Crispus Attucks* 302

LESSONS
Unit 1: Liberating Passover
MARCH
6   Babylonian Captivity Ends
    Ezra 1:1-8, 11; 2:64-70.....................303
13 Freedom to Worship
    Ezra 6:1-12 316
20 Celebrate Passover Liberation
    Ezra 6:13-22 328
27 Lest We Forget
    Deuteronomy 8:1-11 340

Unit 2: Liberating Gospel
APRIL
3   The Passover with the Disciples
    Matthew 26:17-30.........................351
10 Triumphal Entry into Jerusalem
    Matthew 21:1-11............................362
17 The Paschal Lamb Lives!
    Matthew 28:1-10.............................373
24 Freedom in Christ Jesus
    John 8:31-38 384

Unit 3: Liberating Letters
MAY
1   Freedom from Sin
    Romans 6:1-14......................................394
8   Freedom for the Future
    Romans 8:18-30............................406
15 Freedom and the Law
    Galatians 3:18-29..........................418
22 The Nature of Christian Freedom
    Galatians 5:1-15..............................429
29 The Spiritual Fruit of Freedom
    Galatians 5:16-26..............................441

Summer Quarter 2022

PARTNERS IN A NEW CREATION

June 2022 Quarter At-A-Glance..........................452
Engaging the Theme: *"I Do, Lord! I Will!": God Calls His Bride!*..............................454
Christian Education in Action: *Motivating Christ-like Behavior*...............................457
Black History: *Dorothy West*...............................459

LESSONS
Unit 1: God Delivers and Restores
JUNE
5   God Foretells Destruction
    Isaiah 47:10-15..............................460
12 God Foretells Redemption
    Isaiah 49:1-11................................471
19 God's Restored People Shall Prosper
    Isaiah 49:18-23...............................483
26 God Offers Deliverance
    Isaiah 51:1-8...................................494

Unit 2: The Word: The Agent of Creation
JULY
3   The Creating Word Becomes Flesh
    John 1:1-14................................505
10 The Word Heals
    John 4:46-54...............................516
17 The Word Resurrects the Dead
    John 11:17-27, 38-44 527
24 The Word Saves
    John 12:44-50...............................538
31 The Word Gives Peace
    John 14:15-29................................549

Unit 3: The Great Hope of the Saints
AUGUST
7   A New Home
    Revelation 21:1-8............................561
14 A New City
    Revelation 21:9-21.......................572
21 The River of Life
    Revelation 22:1-7......................583
28 Come and Enjoy
    Revelation 22:10-21.....................593

Glossary..604

xiv

2016–2022
SCOPE & SEQUENCE–CYCLE SPREAD

	FALL	WINTER	SPRING	SUMMER
1 YEAR 2016-17	**GOD: SOVEREIGNTY** **Sovereignty of God** Isaiah Matthew Hebrews Revelation	**CREATION** **Creation: A Divine Cycle** Psalms Luke Galatians	**LOVE** **God Loves Us** Psalms Joel Jonah John Romans Ephesians 1 John	**CALL** **God's Urgent Call** Exodus Judges Isaiah Jeremiah Ezekiel Amos Acts
2 YEAR 2017-18	**COVENANT** **Covenant with God** Genesis Exodus Numbers 1 & 2 Samuel Nehemiah Jeremiah Ezekiel 1 Corinthians Hebrews	**FAITH** **Faith in Action** Daniel Matthew Acts Ephesians Colossians 1 Timothy James	**WORSHIP** **Acknowledging God** Genesis Exodus Leviticus 2 Chronicles Psalms Luke John 2 Corinthians Hebrews Revelation	**JUSTICE** **Justice in the New Testament** Matthew Luke Romans 2 Corinthians Colossians
3 YEAR 2018-19	**CREATION** **God's World and God's People** Genesis	**LOVE** **Our Love for God** Exodus Deuteronomy Joshua Psalms Matthew Mark Luke Philippians 2 Thessalonians James 2 John	**CALL** **Discipleship and Mission** Matthew Luke Romans	**COVENANT** **Covenant in God** Ruth 1 Samuel Matthew Luke John Ephesians Hebrews Romans

2016–2022
SCOPE & SEQUENCE–CYCLE SPREAD

	FALL	WINTER	SPRING	SUMMER
4 YEAR 2019-20	**FAITH** **Responding to God's Grace** Genesis Exodus Numbers Deuteronomy 1 Samuel 1 Kings Luke 2 Corinthians 1 Thessalonians 1 & 2 Peter	**WORSHIP** **Honoring God** 1 & 2 Chronicles 1 Kings Ecclesiastes Matthew Luke	**JUSTICE** **Justice and the Prophets** Esther Isaiah Jeremiah Hosea Amos Micah Habakkuk Zephaniah Zachariah Malachi 1 Corinthians	**GOD–WISDOM** **Many Faces of Wisdom** Proverbs Ecclesiastes Matthew Mark Luke John James
5 YEAR 2020-21	**LOVE** **Love for One Another** Genesis 1 & 2 Samuel Luke John Acts 1 Corinthians James 1, 2, & 3 John	**CALL** **Call in the New Testament** Isaiah Matthew Mark Luke John Acts Romans 1 Corinthians Hebrews 2 Timothy	**COVENANT** **Prophets Faithful to God's Covenant** Deuteronomy Joshua 1 & 2 Kings Ezra Nehemiah Isaiah Jeremiah Lamentations Ezekiel Luke	**FAITH** **Confident Hope** Matthew Mark Luke Romans 2 Corinthians Hebrews 1 John
6 YEAR 2021-22	**WORSHIP** **Celebrating God** Exodus 2 Samuel Ecclesiastes Psalms Mark Luke Acts Revelation	**JUSTICE** **Justice, Law, History** Genesis Exodus Deuteronomy 2 Samuel 1 Kings Ezra Job Isaiah Nahum Luke	**GOD–LIBERATION** **God Frees and Redeems** Deuteronomy Ezra Matthew John Romans Galatians	**CREATION** **Partners in a News Creation** Isaiah John Revelation

Celebrating God

This quarter focuses on acts of worship and praise that celebrate both God's divine attributes and God's actions on behalf of the whole created order. The lessons of the Fall quarter draw on several examples of biblical people who celebrate God, psalms that give thanks for God's benevolent actions, and visions of praise for God's work in establishing an eternal realm of justice and righteousness.

UNIT 1 • God's People Offer Praise

This unit has four lessons looking at Moses and Miriam's songs of praise for God's mighty acts, at King David dancing before the ark, at "blind" Bartimaeus glorifying God for healing, and at early believers responding to the Pentecost event by entering into a life of praise for God's redemption through Jesus.

Lesson 1: September 5, 2021
Moses and Miriam Praise God
Exodus 15:11-21

People compose poems and songs for different celebrations. How can songs and poems express thankfulness and rejoicing in victory? After their deliverance from Egyptian slavery, Moses and Miriam composed songs and led the people in praising God.

Lesson 2: September 12, 2021
David Dances before the Ark
2 Samuel 6:1-5, 14-19

Celebrations can be diverse in form and include various actions. How do we celebrate great events in our lives? King David expressed his joy and celebration of God by leading God's people in music and dance.

Lesson 3: September 19, 2021
Glorifying God
Mark 10:46-52

People respond to life challenges and victories differently. How can we respond in ways that are encouraging for ourselves and others? Bartimaeus' boldness and faith in Jesus gave him the courage to ask for and receive his sight from Jesus.

Lesson 4: September 26, 2021
Believers Praise God
Acts 2:32-33, 37-47

Celebrations bring about unity and a new way of seeing and being in the world. How can our celebrations unify a divided community and world? The first Christian community heard the gospel, was inspired by the Holy Spirit to see the world differently, and united to live, worship, and evangelize together.

UNIT 2 • Called to Praise God

This unit has five lessons that explore psalms calling God's people to celebrate what God has done. The psalms speak of making joyful noise to praise God, of praising God for justice and righteousness, of giving thanks for deliverance, of the joy of worship, and of music as a way to celebrate and praise God.

Lesson 5: October 3, 2021
Make A Joyful Noise
Psalm 100

1

Life provides us with many opportunities to praise and find delight in people and things. How do we decide what has more value and is more worthy of our praise? Psalm 100 highlights that God is the object of the earth's praise and joy.

Lesson 6: October 10, 2021
Praise God for Justice and Righteousness
Psalm 9:1-12

People choose to praise and have joy in particular things that may not be the best for them. Why do we choose those things that may harm us or others? Psalm 9 proclaims that God will bring justice and this is cause for our joyful praise.

Lesson 7: October 17, 2021
Give Thanks for Deliverance
Psalm 107:1-9, 39-43

People seek deliverance when they are in trouble. How should we respond when we are delivered? Psalm 107 encourages us to be thankful to God for God's deliverance.

Lesson 8: October 24, 2021
The Joy of Worship
Psalm 84

There are times when the pressures of life are a heavy burden to carry. Where can people go to find the pressures of life lifted and then enjoy a period of celebration? The psalmist recounts a uniquely joyful experience when worshiping in the temple.

Lesson 9: October 31, 2021
Praise God with Music
Psalm 149:1-5; 150:1-6

People choose different ways to express their emotions. What are some of the ways that expressions of victory and joy can be shared? Psalms 149 and 150 share great praise for who God is and the joy of praising God with all of who we are.

UNIT 3 • Visions of Praise

This unit has four lessons that share John's visions of celebration for God's ultimate victory in establishing a realm of peace and justice. In Revelation, people from every nation praise God and all heaven rejoices. In the passage from Acts, believers praise God that the Good News now includes everyone as Gentiles receive the gift of the Holy Spirit.

Lesson 10: November 7, 2021
All People Praise God
Revelation 7:9-17

Celebrations that unite people from all over the world are significant and magnificent. How can we celebrate despite persecution and a hostile world? The writer of Revelation proclaims that God will preserve believers from every nation, tribe, people group, and language who remain faithful to Him despite hardship.

Lesson 11: November 14, 2021
Praise for God's Eternal Reign
Revelation 11:15-19

Celebrations are ways of culminating a unique event and creating new ways of being in the community. How do people celebrate in a hostile world? Revelation helps us to understand that all of the worlds are moving toward the just, eternal reign of God.

Lesson 12: November 21, 2021
Rejoicing in Heaven
Revelation 19:1-8

People want to have victory over the wicked people in their lives and in the world. How will they find victory over the wicked? God has the final judgment of the world, and God is worthy of all praise.

Lesson 13: November 28, 2021
Good News for All
Acts 10:34-47

Barriers often keep people from becoming part of particular groups. How are the barriers removed? God reveals to Peter that the Gospel of Jesus Christ is for all, and the power of the Holy Spirit is God's gift to everyone who accepts Christ.

We Worship You, O Lord!

by Whitney M. DuPreé

When I was 14, I had the opportunity to visit Israel with my church. Even before the plane landed, I knew everything we would see. The tour guide would take us to see Bethlehem, the city where our Lord and Savior was born. We would be baptized in the Jordan River and visit the tomb of Lazarus. We would take a boat ride in the Dead Sea and look upon the Garden of Gethsemane. We would follow the path Jesus took as He carried the cross on His back, which is called the Via Dolorosa, and we would look at what is believed to be the tomb where He was laid but not bound.

I was looking forward to seeing the places I had read about in Sunday School come to life. And even though I knew God to be omnipresent (all-present or present everywhere), I felt there would be a special aura in the birthplace of Christianity. I knew I would experience true worship and peace in Israel. I was eager to be immersed in what I thought would be a spiritually relaxing trip.

While my trip to the Holy Land was emotionally moving, enlightening, and fun, it certainly wasn't spiritually relaxing. The trip challenged me with questions, not of my beliefs, but of my practices and actions. My experience in Israel showed me the importance of disciplined worship.

When I looked upon the Garden of Gethsemane, I was somber. I thought about the enormous pressure that weighed on Jesus' shoulders and His desire to only please His Father. I could not help but stand quietly and honor Him. I stood in awe at the entrance of Lazarus' tomb wondering how a man wrapped in cloth could maneuver through a structure that I, free of binding burial garments, could barely wiggle through. I walked the Via Dolorosa, tired and sore with only a book bag on my back, not the heavy wooden cross our Savior bore. I couldn't imagine the physical pain Jesus must have suffered during that journey, and yet, He continued on. I was moved by the great sacrifice Jesus made and was in awe of God at each of the sacred sites. Later, I learned that this inner feeling was not enough.

It is well known that Israel is home to three of the world's most popular religions: Christianity, Judaism, and Islam. All three claim the Holy Land, and all three are very apparent throughout the land. Every day we would visit a Christian landmark, and we would also see a mosque or a synagogue. The streets were full of Christians, Jews, and Muslims in their traditional religious garbs going about their everyday lives. The juxtaposition of cultures confused me. Initially, my young radical American mind was offended at the sight of seeing so many non-Christians in such a sacred land. I was unable to grasp what I considered disrespect in the Holy Land. I couldn't understand why they didn't believe, even though they walked and lived in the places I could only read about. I could not comprehend why people with so much archeological evidence would refuse to worship correctly.

However, this foolish spiritual arrogance came to an abrupt end when I toured the Old City of

Jerusalem and I came to realize how much I needed to learn about true worship. The Old City is divided into four quarters: the Jewish Quarter, the Armenian Quarter, the Muslim Quarter, and the Christian Quarter. There are no segregation laws, and it is easy to pass from one quarter to another no matter your country of origin or religious beliefs. In fact, most of the Via Dolorosa lies throughout the Muslim Quarter. The Old City reminded me of the markets and bazaars one would see in old Middle Eastern movies. As the group walked through the Old City, merchants were constantly trying to entice us and everyone else who was passing by. I saw people haggling over postcards, jewelry, clothes, and even meat. The streets were made of cobblestone, and it was extremely hot. The air was thick with the stench of human odors, and the high walls made it difficult to feel a breeze.

Suddenly, I heard bells ringing and crowds flooded the marketplace. I was pressed against a wall as crowds and crowds of people rushed passed me. They were all headed in the same direction. As I frantically searched for my church group, I saw a mother rushing through the marketplace with her daughter and young son following closely behind her. Somehow the daughter and son became separated from their mother, and the son began to cry. The mother turned her head to see that her children had fallen back in the crowd. The young son reached toward her, and she did what any devout Muslim trying to get to prayer would do—she kept running toward the mosque. I was shocked and outraged. Why would that mother leave her children! I looked at the daughter and saw her pick up her little brother and run right along with the crowd to prayer. I was amazed.

In less than three minutes, the overcrowded and nearly suffocating marketplace was completely empty. Carts had been abandoned. Shops had been left unattended and open. Everyone was in prayer. Our Jewish tour guide told us this was a regular occurrence, five times a day. He said dedicated Muslims abandoned all tasks so they wouldn't be late to pray and worship. Minutes later, the marketplace was noisy and bustling with activity, but I would never forget what had occurred moments before.

Once a week, Christians across America make their way to praise and worship services. Oftentimes, they pass several churches before arriving at the worship center of their choice. While it can be assumed that few are excited about showing up to church late, tardiness isn't a major concern. If we scan church parking lots, we see congregants casually strutting toward the church, no sense of urgency in the air. Stores are not left unmanned and unlocked simply because a worship service is taking place. If a mother and father rushed ahead of their young teen, chances are that teen would want to hang outside the church instead of following his or her parents into the service. We comfort ourselves by saying we can worship our God any time and any place, but do we have spiritual discipline? We pride ourselves on having a merciful and gracious God, but do we take advantage of our Lord and show a lack of respect in the process?

My trip to the Holy Land showed me what a true yearning to worship looked like, and it encouraged me to be critical of my own life and priorities.

Whitney M. DuPreé was the Market Research Analyst at UMI. After graduating from high school as salutatorian in 2004, she went on to receive a Bachelor of Engineering in civil engineering from Vanderbilt University in 2008. She believes strongly in uplifting the community, and she expresses this through her membership in Alpha Kappa Alpha Sorority Inc., the Jackie Robinson Foundation, the NAACP, and her continued support of her alma mater.

Christ-Centeredness: The Key to Wisdom

by Luvell Anderson, Jr., PhD

If you take a look around, you will undoubtedly see some disturbing things brewing all over the world. Gratuitous wars, legalization of abominable practices, and other such maladies are occurring more and more. Injustice and human atrocities are being committed at the command of those in positions of power and influence. Many are being educated with philosophies that emphasize a concentration on self; it is the Protagorean doctrine "Homo mensura" (man is the measure of all things). This doctrine not only pervades the lives of those in the world, but also has crept into the church in large measure. From televangelists to many of our pulpits, we are told how to easily eliminate our problems. Self-help has supplanted the ministry of the Word of God on Sunday mornings. In a study conducted by Barna Group, 51 percent of Protestants identified having a satisfying family life as their top priority, with understanding and living out the principles of the Christian faith coming in second place.

At the heart of it all, the problem seems to be in the overall philosophy of life that has been adopted. The church has adopted a human-centered philosophy as the way to wisdom. Our actions are motivated more by utilitarianism (i.e., whatever produces the greatest amount of pleasure is the right course of action) than by the Gospel. If we as the church are to recover genuine biblical wisdom, we must reorganize our priorities, placing Jesus Christ at the top of the list,

because our relationship with Him determines how things will go with the rest of the items on the list. In short, we must recover Christ-centered preaching and teaching, Christ-centered thinking, and Christ-centered living.

The obvious place to begin our pursuit of wisdom is the Word of God. The apostle Paul charges Timothy to "preach the word" (from 2 Timothy 4:2). His charge comes after he himself had spent several years faithfully preaching and teaching God's Word. In a letter addressed to the Corinthians, Paul states, "And I, brethren, when I came to you, came not with excellency of speech or of wisdom, declaring unto you the testimony of God. For I determined not to know any thing among you, save Jesus Christ, and him crucified" (1 Corinthians 2:1–2). Paul emphasized the importance of Christ-centered preaching so as not to deliver to the Corinthians a man-centered wisdom that does not have the power to save human beings from their sins. He knew that only a message that was entirely focused on Christ could save them; it alone provides godly wisdom, since Christ is "the wisdom of God" (from 1 Corinthians 1:24).

Furthermore, Paul knew that in order for him to preach from the Scriptures faithfully, his sermons must testify of Jesus. When condemning the Pharisees for their unbelief, Jesus said, "Search the scriptures; for in them ye think ye have eternal life" (from John 5:39). However, Jesus makes it clear that biblical texts are not moralistic stories meant to show us some principle or rule to follow; instead, they testify about Him.

After we have recovered Christ-centered preaching and teaching in our pulpits and churches, we must internalize the message so that it dominates our thinking. There is no greater impediment to attaining wisdom than self-absorption. When we are overconfident in our own abilities, we, in essence, reject God's Word and open ourselves up to perversion and shame. Scripture gives several examples of the consequences of self-absorption. In the book of Genesis, we find Adam and Eve believing that they were wiser than God, defying His command not to eat of the Tree of Knowledge of Good and Evil. As a result, life on Earth was altered for the worse, catapulting humanity into a state of sin and death.

In Daniel, we read about Nebuchadnezzar, king of Babylon, which was the superpower nation in its day. Nebuchadnezzar ponders: "Is not this great Babylon, that I have built for the house of the kingdom by the might of my power, and for the honour of my majesty?" (from Daniel 4:30). Nebuchadnezzar's arrogance brought God's judgment upon him, driving him into the wilderness and reducing him to the level of a wild animal. We also read in Romans how people proclaimed themselves to be wise and instead became fools (Romans 1:22). Paul says that God "gave them up to uncleanness through the lusts of their own hearts" (from v. 24), which led to self-destructive practices. In all of these instances, the thought process of each individual followed the pattern of the world. Each person acted according to the philosophy of the spirit of the age. But God calls us to be transformed by the renewal of our minds (Romans 12:2), by putting off the old nature and putting on the new nature, which is made in the likeness of God (Ephesians 4:22–24; Colossians 3:9–10). The Holy Spirit transforms us, but we must be willing to yield to Him by shedding any self-centered tendencies and submitting to Jesus Christ.

Finally, after absorbing Christ-centered preaching into our minds, we must begin to act upon it by living it out. It is not enough to be able to recall information. In order to claim that we have wisdom, we must evidence wisdom in our everyday lives. Wisdom is demonstrated by our conduct, not by our erudition or articulation. Early twentieth-century Welsh preacher Martyn Lloyd-Jones explains:

The wise man or woman does not merely have knowledge—you can put that into computers; they have the power of appropriating and assimilating that knowledge until it becomes judgment. It becomes part of them, controlling their point of view, and determining their actions and practice. So our wisdom is judged not merely by the number of books we have read or can quote and recite, but by the way we live, the way we use that knowledge. Christ put that in a famous question—"What shall it profit a man, if he shall gain the whole world [of knowledge and of wealth], and lose his own soul?" (Mark 8:36)

We must make Christ the focus of our lives because He is "the wisdom of God." There can be no other focus if we hope to obtain God's wisdom. Christ is also the focus of God's sanctifying work in our lives, "to be conformed to the image of his Son" (from Romans 8:29). God is fashioning us to look like Jesus, and it is our calling as Christians to preach, think, and live in a way that reflects our commitment to being conformed to the image of Christ.

Dr. Luvell Anderson, Jr. is currently an associate professor of philosophy at Syracuse University. His research and teaching interests include philosophy of language, African American philosophy, aesthetics, humor, and social ontology.

Sources:

Barna Group. "What Is a Purpose-Driven Life to Americans?" Barna Group, May 17, 2005. http://www.barna.org/FlexPage. aspx?Page=BarnaUpdate&BarnaUpdateID=188 (accessed February 16, 2006).

Lloyd-Jones, Martyn. "Humanism—The Fifth Woe." Sermon Index. http://www.sermonindex.net/modules/articles/index .php?view=article&aid=533 (accessed February 16, 2006).

PAUL LAURENCE DUNBAR

(1872 – 1906)
Poet and Novelist

In his brief 33-year life, Paul Laurence Dunbar wrote six volumes of poetry, four novels, and several volumes of short stories. Most of the critics of his day attributed the excellence of Dunbar's writing to the mix of European blood in his veins. As a result, Dunbar took advantage of every opportunity to emphasize his "unmixed" or "pure" African ancestry. Dunbar's work was cited as conclusive proof that literary excellence was not limited to those of European ancestry.

In spite of Dunbar's superlative reputation, the author was discouraged with the way his work was popularly received. Although two-thirds of Dunbar's poems were written in standard English that displays skillful manipulation of imagery, masterful rhyme and meter, and expert handling of serious philosophical thought, these are not the works that made him famous. Dunbar's public recognition came primarily from the rhythmic narrative and pleasing description of Black life that characterizes much of his dialect poetry. The white public praised the dialect poems, largely ignoring his more serious works, while he rejected them, and many Black critics were harsh in their judgment of Dunbar because of them.

Dunbar's parents, both former slaves, were the primary influences in his literary life. His father, Joshua Dunbar, was a skilled plasterer who earned his master additional income. Joshua was taught reading and arithmetic by his master to prevent those who purchased his services to cheat him.

Joshua escaped slavery and made his way to Canada. His reading skills allowed him to follow the course of the anti-slavery movement in the United States through Canadian newspapers. When he learned of the imminent Civil War, Joshua returned stateside to fight in the Union Army. After the war, he settled in Dayton, Ohio. In 1871, he married Matilda J. Burton Murphy, a widow 30 years his junior with two boys. Paul was their only child.

Matilda had been a house slave for a white family in Kentucky. After the war she moved to Dayton to be near her mother who had been freed before the war. Joshua and Matilda were divorced five years after they married and Joshua died six years later, when Paul was 12 years old. Dunbar gives this account of his parents in a newspaper article published in March 1902.

My mother, who had no education except what she picked up herself, and who is generally conceded to be a very unusual woman, taught me to read when I was four years old. Both my father and herself were fond of books and used to read to me around the fire at night.

In 1892, at the age of 20, Dunbar's first collection of poetry, *Oak and Ivy*, was published. In 1895, he wrote and published another collection, *Majors and Minors*. William Dean Howell, a critic for *Harper's Weekly*, read and favorably reviewed the books and brought instant fame to Dunbar. Howell arranged for the publication of Dunbar's third volume, *Lyrics of Lowly Life* in 1896 and wrote the book's introduction. In the introduction, Howell described Dunbar as "the only man of pure African blood and of American civilization to feel the Negro life aesthetically and express it lyrically." At first, Dunbar felt honored by Howell's words, but later he regarded them as a mixed blessing. He wrote to a friend, "Mr. Howell has done me irrevocable harm in the dictum he laid down regarding my dialect verse."

After *Lyrics of Lowly Life*, Dunbar published *Lyrics of the Hearthside* in 1899, followed by *Lyrics of Love and Laughter* in 1903 and *Lyrics of Sunshine and Shadow* in 1905. Paul Laurence Dunbar died of an incurable disease in 1906. Seven years later, all his poems were assembled into one volume, *The Complete Poems of Paul Laurence Dunbar*. Dunbar's love of poetry is probably summed up in his poem titled, "A Choice":

> They please me not—these solemn songs
> That hint of sermons covered up.
> 'Tis true the world should heed its wrong,
> But in poem let me sup.
> Not simples brewed to cure or ease
> Humanity's confessed disease,
> But the spirit wine on a singing line,
> Or a dew drop in a honey cup!

(*The Complete Poems of Paul Laurence Dunbar*, 1913, p. 209)

Sources:
Paul Lawrence [sic] Dunbar. Photograph published 1905. https://www.loc.gov/item/93509689/.

Teaching Tips

Words You Should Know

A. Guided (v. 13) *nahal* (Heb.)—To bring to a place of rest

B. Sanctuary (v. 17) *miqdash* (Heb.)—A sacred and holy place, a place that was specially dedicated and consecrated for worship

Teacher Preparation

Unifying Principle—Celebrating with Song. People compose poems and songs for different celebrations. How can songs and poems express thankfulness and rejoicing in victory? After their deliverance from Egyptian slavery, Moses and Miriam composed songs and led the people in praising God.

A. Read the Bible Background and Devotional Reading.

B. Pray for your students and lesson clarity.

C. Read the lesson Scripture in multiple translations.

O—Open the Lesson

A. Begin the class with prayer.

B. Discuss why couples might choose a particular song to be "their song." Why might one particular song be especially meaningful to them? Is there a particular hymn or worship song that could be "their song," reflecting their relationship with God?

C. Have the students read the Aim for Change and the In Focus story.

D. Ask students how events like those in the story weigh on their hearts and how they can view these events from a faith perspective.

P—Present the Scriptures

A. Read the Focal Verses and discuss the Background and The People, Places, and Times sections.

B. Have the class share what Scriptures stand out for them and why, with particular emphasis on today's themes.

E—Explore the Meaning

A. Use In Depth or More Light on the Text to facilitate a deeper discussion of the lesson text.

B. Pose the questions in Search the Scriptures and Discuss the Meaning.

C. Discuss the Liberating Lesson and Application for Activation sections.

N—Next Steps for Application

A. Summarize the value of singing as a vital part of worship.

B. End class with a commitment to praise God both for who He is and what He does.

Worship Guide

For the Superintendent or Teacher
Theme: Moses and Miriam Praise God
Song: "Great Is Thy Faithfulness"

Moses and Miriam Praise God

Bible Background • EXODUS 14:1–15:1–21
Printed Text • EXODUS 15:11–21 | Devotional Reading • PSALM 105:1–2, 37–45

—— Aim for Change ——

By the end of this lesson, we will EXPLORE why and how Moses and Miriam praised God; REFLECT on the actions of God that are celebrated through music, dance, and words; and CELEBRATE God's faithfulness with joy.

—— In Focus ——

"FIRE DEPARTMENT, CALL OUT!"

"Over here!" Ramona cried, coughing.

The smoke stung her eyes and was so thick that she couldn't see where the voice was coming from. The disaster had been sudden. One moment, she was typing away at her desk. The next, there was a quick rumble from the ground that shook the floor and shattered the floor-to-ceiling windows. Part of the ceiling frame fell to the floor, dragging down tiles and light fixtures. Some of the sprinklers came on and drenched everything nearby, but others were broken. The way to the exit stairs was blocked with flaming debris.

Ramona prayed, "Heavenly Father, please bring me to safety." She could hear the firefighters crashing through the wreckage to get to her. "OVER HERE!" she shouted again.

Ramona could see the shapes of the firefighters coming forward in the dark, knocking aside desks and chairs and filing cabinets. The water sprayed from their hoses sizzled and turned to steam as it hit the flames, adding to the chaotic scene. But after a moment, two of them emerged like ghosts and crouched next to her.

"Praise God! I am so grateful to see you!" Ramona cried.

One firefighter said, "Just stay close." The other firefighter slid his arm around her and stood up. "We'll get you out of here. Stick with me."

In between coughs, Ramona said, "Thank you! God is good! God is so good!"

When have you spontaneously praised God after an emotional event?

—— Keep in Mind ——

"Who is like unto thee, O LORD, among the gods? who is like thee, glorious in holiness, fearful in praises, doing wonders?" (Exodus 15:11, KJV)

"Who is like you among the gods, O LORD—glorious in holiness, awesome in splendor, performing great wonders?" (Exodus 15:11, NLT)

Focal Verses

KJV **Exodus 15:11** Who is like unto thee, O LORD, among the gods? who is like thee, glorious in holiness, fearful in praises, doing wonders?

12 Thou stretchedst out thy right hand, the earth swallowed them.

13 Thou in thy mercy hast led forth the people which thou hast redeemed: thou hast guided them in thy strength unto thy holy habitation.

14 The people shall hear, and be afraid: sorrow shall take hold on the inhabitants of Palestina.

15 Then the dukes of Edom shall be amazed; the mighty men of Moab, trembling shall take hold upon them; all the inhabitants of Canaan shall melt away.

16 Fear and dread shall fall upon them; by the greatness of thine arm they shall be as still as a stone; till thy people pass over, O LORD, till the people pass over, which thou hast purchased.

17 Thou shalt bring them in, and plant them in the mountain of thine inheritance, in the place, O LORD, which thou hast made for thee to dwell in, in the Sanctuary, O LORD, which thy hands have established.

18 The LORD shall reign for ever and ever.

19 For the horse of Pharaoh went in with his chariots and with his horsemen into the sea, and the LORD brought again the waters of the sea upon them; but the children of Israel went on dry land in the midst of the sea.

20 And Miriam the prophetess, the sister of Aaron, took a timbrel in her hand; and all the women went out after her with timbrels and with dances.

21 And Miriam answered them, Sing ye to the LORD, for he hath triumphed gloriously; the horse and his rider hath he thrown into the sea.

NLT **Exodus 15:11** "Who is like you among the gods, O LORD—glorious in holiness, awesome in splendor, performing great wonders?

12 You raised your right hand, and the earth swallowed our enemies.

13 With your unfailing love you lead the people you have redeemed. In your might, you guide them to your sacred home.

14 The peoples hear and tremble; anguish grips those who live in Philistia.

15 The leaders of Edom are terrified; the nobles of Moab tremble. All who live in Canaan melt away;

16 terror and dread fall upon them. The power of your arm makes them lifeless as stone until your people pass by, O LORD, until the people you purchased pass by.

17 You will bring them in and plant them on your own mountain—the place, O LORD, reserved for your own dwelling, the sanctuary, O LORD, that your hands have established.

18 The LORD will reign forever and ever!"

19 When Pharaoh's horses, chariots, and charioteers rushed into the sea, the LORD brought the water crashing down on them. But the people of Israel had walked through the middle of the sea on dry ground!

20 Then Miriam the prophet, Aaron's sister, took a tambourine and led all the women as they played their tambourines and danced.

21 And Miriam sang this song: "Sing to the LORD, for he has triumphed gloriously; he has hurled both horse and rider into the sea."

The People, Places, and Times

Miriam. The sister of Aaron and Moses and the daughter of Amram and Jochebed. When Moses is placed in a basket in the Nile as a baby, Miriam watches over her brother and volunteers her mother as a wet-nurse when Pharaoh's daughter decides to keep the child. She is also one of the people sent by God to lead the Israelites. Miriam leads the people in a joyous victory song after they cross the Red Sea out of Egyptian slavery. Much later while journeying through the wilderness, Moses married an Ethiopian woman and Miriam did not approve, rebelling against Moses. She and Aaron spoke against Moses, but God heard them and rebuked them. God struck Miriam with leprosy. Moses prayed for her and she was quickly healed.

Background

Over roughly 400 years, the 70 members of Jacob's family who had moved from Canaan to Egypt had grown to over 600,000 strong (Exodus 12:37). They lived freely in Goshen until a new pharaoh came to power. He was unaware of the life-saving role that Joseph, one of Jacob's sons, had played in saving Egypt and surrounding countries from famine. Threatened by this growing population, Pharaoh tried to decrease their numbers through genocide and enslavement. The people prayed for salvation from oppression. God answered, upholding the promise He had made to Abraham, Isaac, and Jacob, whose name had been changed to Israel. Through a man called Moses, God performed ten mighty acts that forced Pharaoh to end the Israelites' slavery. But Pharaoh couldn't accept the fact that he had been defeated by the God of slaves. He set out to find and kill them. In an epic act of salvation, God walled back the waters of the Red Sea, giving the Israelites safe passage across the final barrier that blocked their exodus. The same waters drowned their oppressors. To memorialize God's phenomenal intervention on their behalf, Moses and Miriam led the Israelites in a song of exuberant praise.

At-A-Glance

1. Sing to Gain Strength
(Exodus 15:11–13)
2. Sing to be Heard (vv. 14–18)
3. Sing to Remember God's Goodness
(vv. 19–21)

In Depth

1. Sing to Gain Strength (Exodus 15:11–13)

The Egyptian culture was known for its numerous gods and goddesses. There was a sun god who was responsible for light and a goddess who was in charge of fertility. Another goddess brought the rain and Pharaoh himself was believed to be the god who had power over all the inhabitants of the land. But for the people who had just experienced deliverance and witnessed the annihilation of their oppressors, no god surpassed their God. He was unrivaled, not only in His power but also in His holiness and His worthiness to be praised. God had wiped out their enemies and that new reality gave them the courage and strength to sing about a future, unlike their past. This song of praise was also a song of hope. They looked forward, confident that their victorious God would guide them and bring them to a place where they would dwell in God's holy presence.

How has a past experience with God shaped your outlook about your future?

2. Sing to be Heard (vv. 14–18)

On their journey, the formerly enslaved people were going to meet people from other nations. News of God's mighty acts would have reached these nations before the Israelites actually arrived. How would the Canaanites respond? Would they realize that God was God? Or would fear lead to violent actions? The fitting response when learning about God's manifested power and goodness is holy reverence. Such an example is Rahab, the prostitute who protected the spies sent to assess Canaan. By the time the Children of Israel reached Jericho years later, she was able to recount the incident at the Red Sea (Joshua 2:9–11). The testimony embedded in this song had proceeded the spies and secured their safety, and the safety of Rahab and her family. The song at the Red Sea was a testimony meant to be shared so that others would hear, trust, and worship God.

Name a time when your faith has been strengthened by someone's testimony.

3. Sing to Remember God's Goodness (vv. 19–21)

Miriam was Moses's sister. She was a courageous woman who, as a child, defied Pharaoh's horrific decree to kill male babies. When her mother, Jochebed, placed her brother, Moses, in a water-tight basket and put him in the Nile River, Miriam kept an eye on the basket and when Pharaoh's daughter found the baby and wanted to keep him, Miriam, with the daughter's consent, ran to get her mother to nurse him. Jochebed was able to rear Moses and share with him his true heritage.

Now years later, Miriam was at her brother's side. She could trace God's deliverance in the past to the joys of freedom she and all Israelites were experiencing that day. Using the unique gifts God had given her as a prophetess, musician, and dancer, Miriam led a chorus of singers and dancers who recounted the triumphant victory of their God.

What are some ways you have celebrated God's liberating grace in your life?

Search the Scriptures

1. Name three ways the Lord God is different from the so-called gods other nations worshiped (Exodus 15:11).

2. What will be the response of other nations when they hear of God's victory for the Israelites (vv. 14–16)?

Discuss the Meaning

Victory for the Israelites also brought about the annihilation of others. Egyptian families lost loved ones that day. In Matthew 5:43, Jesus tells His listeners that they are to love their enemies and pray for those who despitefully use and persecute them.

1. Compare and contrast the context and attitudes toward violence between today's text and Jesus' words in Matthew 5:43-45.

2. In our modern context, how are we to respond when our enemies fall into unfortunate situations?

Liberating Lesson

In *Harriet, the Moses of Her People*, biographer Sarah Hopkins Bradford, states that one of the favorite songs of abolitionist Harriet Tubman was "Swing Low Sweet Chariot." Coded in its verses was a message of salvation from oppression. The Underground Railroad, a network of places and people who helped enslaved African Americans escape the horrors of the South, was the sweet chariot that would be swinging low or coming to the South. It was going to carry home or take to the North, those willing to get on board. Listening with hope, enslaved men, women, and children set out on a journey toward freedom for themselves and their descendants. What songs can you share with others that offer a message of the hope and freedom found in Christ?

Application for Activation

Songs are often used to help shape a people's identity. The song in today's lesson helped formerly enslaved people to see themselves as victors. They could advance, knowing that their unrivaled God would guide them into the land he had promised their forefathers. Another song, "Lift Ev'ry Voice and Sing," had a similar impact. Written in 1900 by James Weldon Johnson and set to music by his brother, John Rosamond Johnson, it helped African Americans to see the gains made despite great adversity. While recognizing the past, it continued in hope, anticipating increased goodness from the God who had brought them thus far on the way.

Consider memorizing all three stanzas of "Lift Ev'ry Voice and Sing," and as a class, perform it at a church service, nursing home, or shelter for formerly incarcerated men or women.

Follow the Spirit

What God wants me to do:

_____

_____

_____

_____

Remember Your Thoughts

Special insights I have learned:

_____

_____

_____

_____

More Light on the Text

Exodus 15:11–21

The Israelites' exit from the land of Egypt was one of the foundational events of the Old Testament. Departing Egypt in this massive exodus were 600,000 men plus their families (Exodus 12:37). Additionally, there were large droves of livestock and various kinds of flocks and herds of animals. The exodus through the Red Sea marked the liberation of God's people from 430 years of oppressive slavery in Egypt and created the powerful gratitude and a desire to celebrate God (Exodus 12:40; Acts 7:6). Exodus 15 is called "The Song of Moses." The song is composed of poetic praise for God's Omnipotence (all power) displayed in the destruction of Egypt's army, and the prophetic promise of God's establishment of Israel and His Kingdom. Moses and the Israelites sang this song to the Lord. Miriam joined him and led the women playing tambourines and dancing (v. 20).

African Americans can relate to this jubilation and celebrate God's liberation from the brutal bonds of slavery in the 1860s. They too sang a song that could be heard across America called "Go Down Moses": "Tell ol' pharaoh to let my people go…" These spirituals that represent freedom from the bondage of slavery are still sung today. The song of Moses is a spiritual song of roaring power and tender feeling, unforgettable for its biblical meaning and enduring poetry.

11 Who is like unto thee, O LORD, among the gods? who is like thee, glorious in holiness, fearful in praises, doing wonders?

Verse 11 is a confession of God's infinite perfection, transcendent and unparalleled. This verse asks the rhetorical question "Who is like God?" and multiple Scriptures respond, "I am God and there is no other" (Isaiah 45:5, 18, 22; 46:9). The term "among the gods" refers to the many false gods and idols the Egyptians and other pagan nations worshiped in vain. Whether the word "gods" referred to mighty giants (cf. Genesis 6:4), or angels (Psalm 29:1), or idols (Isaiah 46:1), no one is like the Lord. The glorious holiness of God cannot be imagined without the deepest reverence and fear, even by angels, who veil their faces before the majesty of God (Isaiah 6:2). It is only through Jesus that we can come boldly before the throne of grace with our prayers (Hebrews 4:16). We cannot fathom the wonders of God, His creation of the universe, and His care of all that exists. Our God is to be worshiped and adored as our only God of infinite perfection. No one is comparable to Him. God is holy and worthy to be praised.

12 Thou stretchedst out thy right hand, the earth swallowed them.

While God does not have a physical body like human beings, the right hand of God is often used figuratively in Scripture to refer to a position of power above all other powers. For example, Jesus is at the right hand of God today, perfectly reigning with God the Father and God the Spirit in community and power (Colossians 3:1; 1 Peter 3:21–22). In this verse, the right hand represents the strength of God. The second part of this verse referred to Pharaoh's army being swallowed up in the mud at the bottom of the sea, by the power of the outstretched, right hand of God.

13 Thou in thy mercy hast led forth the people which thou hast redeemed: thou hast guided them in thy strength unto thy holy habitation.

The next section of the song is prophetic, a prediction of future events (vv. 13–18). This begins with a powerful verse that demonstrates the vastness of God's mercy for His people and what He did to miraculously redeem them (v. 13). It is a reflection of God's love for us and

the extent He will go to (sending Jesus to die for us) to redeem our souls.

As God delivered Israel from Egypt with a strong hand, He would guide and direct them onward in their journey. In the same greatness of His strength, He would bring them to the place chosen for His habitation with them. The word "guided" (Heb. *nahal*, naw-**HALL**) implies guiding to a place of rest. The holy habitation of God was the Promised Land and was consecrated by God as a sacred dwelling place for Jehovah among His people. It was the land promised to the patriarchs (Deuteronomy 26:9; Jeremiah 11:5; 32:22).

God's promise of a specific land for His people was first made to Abraham (Genesis 15:18–21). God also confirmed his promise to Isaac and Jacob (Genesis 26:3; 28:13). The Promised Land spread out wide to house God's people. Today, this land covers modern-day Israel, Palestine, Lebanon, Syria, and Jordan.

This verse is a reflection of how God guides us today, with His strength, mercy, and grace. He provided His holy habitation with us, through the indwelling of God the Holy Spirit in our hearts upon acceptance of Christ.

14 The people shall hear, and be afraid: sorrow shall take hold on the inhabitants of Palestina. 15 Then the dukes of Edom shall be amazed; the mighty men of Moab, trembling shall take hold upon them; all the inhabitants of Canaan shall melt away. 16 Fear and dread shall fall upon them; by the greatness of thine arm they shall be as still as a stone; till thy people pass over, O LORD, till the people pass over, which thou hast purchased.

The people of other nations heard the report of plagues ordered by the God of the Israelites. Word reached every country about the horrified Egyptians who suffered plagues and finally, in pursuit of the Israelites, drowned in the Red Sea. Terror became even greater when they heard about the parting of the Red Sea so the Israelites could cross on dry land (cf. Joshua 2:10; 1 Samuel 4:8). The greatness of Egypt had been destroyed, her land ravished, her army destroyed, and her people left in mourning. These events, orchestrated by God, struck fear into the hearts of everyone, particularly those in the path leading to the Promised Land. Palestina was a land that adjoined Canaan. The Palestinians' location caused them to become some of the first to be panic-stricken.

Edom (southwestern Jordan today) was located south of Canaan. The Edomites are the descendants of Esau, Jacob's brother, so their strife with the descendants of Jacob began as sibling rivalry (see Genesis 25:19–34). The prophesy of this song took place as Moses told them, "Ye are to pass through the coast of your brethren the children of Esau, … they shall be afraid of you" (from Deuteronomy 2:4).

Moab (west-central Jordan today) was immediately to the north of the Promised Land. Moabites were decedents of Moab, the son born to Lot and Lot's oldest daughter in the aftermath of the destruction of Sodom and Gomorrah (Genesis 19:37–38). The Moabites were perpetual enemies of the Israelites.

When the Israelites were faithful to God, their enemies feared them and they were victorious. Moses' triumphal song assured the people that God would bring His people into the Promised Land safely and victoriously.

17 Thou shalt bring them in, and plant them in the mountain of thine inheritance, in the place, O LORD, which thou hast made for thee to dwell in, in the Sanctuary, O LORD, which thy hands have established. 18 The LORD shall reign for ever and ever.

Given the huge population of the Israelites, it took a vast amount of land to form a dwelling place for them, but God in His wisdom created that place for His children as their inheritance. Yahweh will not be limited to the one mountaintop, however, unlike other false gods of the surrounding nations whose power was regional. God created a "Sanctuary," (Heb. *miqdash*, meek-**DOSH**) meaning a sacred and holy place, a place that was specially dedicated and consecrated for communing and fellowshipping with God. God established this Sanctuary with His own hands, not needing any worshipers to make it for Him. Rather, this sanctuary was for His people. It is so important, because it serves as a "example and shadow of heavenly things" (from Hebrews 8:5).

These verses are also prophetic and represent how God will establish a place for us in His Kingdom, He reigns throughout eternity. As Christians, we too are heirs and have an inheritance, that is incorruptible, imperishable, and eternal (1 Peter 1:4). It is waiting in Heaven for us. Jesus said He will go and prepare a place for us, so we may be where He is (John 14:3). This great future is the object of our hope in Christ.

19 For the horse of Pharaoh went in with his chariots and with his horsemen into the sea, and the LORD brought again the waters of the sea upon them; but the children of Israel went on dry land in the midst of the sea.

The event at the Red Sea, when the Egyptian army was drowned, was celebrated as a great military victory achieved by God (Exodus 15:1–12). Given today's powerful weapons of war, we often overlook the magnitude of the mighty chariots and horsemen of that time period. Egyptian war chariots originated about 1500 BC and were heavy vehicles with solid wheels and strong frames. Transportation-type chariots were light and fancy, but weighty military chariots were used to crash into infantry lines of soldiers. The armed chariot runners were equipped with bows and spears. The horsemen of ancient Egypt were muscular soldiers skilled in the art of war. Egypt was a dominant power in the world and used horsemen and chariots to conquer their enemies. Chariots and horsemen were the super-weapons of that day.

This event revealed a new dimension of the nature of God to the Israelites and demonstrated the necessity of forcefully taking possession of the promised land by means of military conquest. Moses described the Egyptian pursuers as being thrown into the sea (Exodus 15:4). The same image describes Pharaoh's earlier order to throw the Hebrew babies into the Nile River (Exodus 1:22). God did to the Egyptians what they had done to the Israelites. This single verse of prose sums up the occasion for the hymn of praise, identifying God's Red Sea Deliverance as both the reason for the song and the occasion of the singing.

20 And Miriam the prophetess, the sister of Aaron, took a timbrel in her hand; and all the women went out after her with timbrels and with dances. 21 And Miriam answered them, Sing ye to the LORD, for he hath triumphed gloriously; the horse and his rider hath he thrown into the sea.

Miriam, the sister of Moses and Aaron, is the first woman mentioned in the Bible as a "prophetess." She is called a prophetess because she received revelations from God (Numbers 12:1–2; Micah 6:4). She also had musical skills. Prophecy and music have been closely related in the Bible (1 Samuel 10:5; 1 Chronicles 25:1). Music played an important part in Israel's worship and celebration. Singing was an expression of love and thanks, and it was a creative way to pass down oral traditions. During the times of African American enslavement, few Black people were allowed to learn how to read, so songs were used to transmit customs, traditions, and even oral history. Some say the Song of Moses is the oldest recorded song in the world; it certainly is the oldest in Scripture. It was a festive, epic poem celebrating God's victory. This song lifted hearts and sent encouragement, in the form of voices, outward to the people, and upward to God.

The mention of dancing refers to the custom of religious dances, also prevalent in the times of David. In many Black churches today, teams of praise dancers lead congregations in song and perform dances as an act of worship to God. They play tambourines (timbrels) and other instruments of music. It should be noted that some Christian denominations view dancing and certain musical instruments as secular and exclude them from worship services. But all Christian churches believe in singing to the Lord. For Christians, the Song of Moses is far more personal than the commemoration of Israel's deliverance, it is a biblical reminder that we too will join in the singing of the song of Moses and the song of the Lamb, as included in the book of Revelation: "And they sing the song of Moses the servant of God, and the song of the Lamb" (15:3).

Thus, when the saints of God gather in God's eternal kingdom, they shall sing both the Song of Moses and the Song of the Lamb. How wonderful that Moses' song gives us a foreshadow of our final and eternal deliverance from sin and continual worship and praise to God.

Sources:
Benson, Joseph. *Benson's Commentary of Old and New Testaments* https://biblehub.com/commentaries/benson/ (Retrieved December 27, 2019)
Bible Commentaries, Adam Clark Commentary, Exodus 15. https://www.studylight.org/commentaries/bcc/exodus-15.html (Retrieved December 20, 2019)
Bible Commentaries, Coffman's Commentaries on the Bible, Exodus 15. https://www.studylight.org/commentaries/bcc/exodus-15.html. (Retrieved December 20, 2019)
Bradford, Sarah Hopkins. *Harriet, the Moses of Her People.* Kindle Edition. 2012.
Healy, Mark. *Armies of the Pharaohs.* Oxford, United Kingdom: Osprey Publishing, 1992.
Henry, Matthew. Exodus 15. https://www.biblestudytools.com/commentaries/matthew-henrycomplete/exodus/15.html. (Retrieved December 22, 2019)
Life Application Study Bible, New Living Translation. Wheaton, IL: Tyndale House Publishers, Inc., 1996.

Lift Every Voice and Sing. PBS.org/black-culture. Black Culture Connection, 2020.

Lockeyer Sr., Herbert, F.F. Bruce, and R.K. Harrison, eds. *The Illustrated Dictionary of the Bible.* Nashville, TN: Thomas Nelson Publishers, 1986.

"A Religious portrait of African-Americans." Pew Research Center: Religion & Public life. (January 30, 2009). https://www.pewforum.org/2009/01/30/a-religious-portrait-of-african-americans/. (Retrieved December 22, 2019)

Shaw, Ian. *Egyptian Warfare and Weapons.* Oxford, United Kingdom: Shire Publications LTD, 1991.

Smith, William. *Smith's Bible Dictionary.* Philadelphia, PA: A.J. Holman Company, 1973.

The Woman's Study Bible, New King James Version. Nashville, TN: Thomas Nelson Publishers. 1995.

Say It Correctly

Philistina. fill-iss-TEE-nah.
Moab. MOE-ab.
Edom. EE-dom.

Daily Bible Readings

MONDAY
God Hardens Pharaoh's Heart
(Exodus 14:1–9)

TUESDAY
Don't Just Do Something; Stand There!
(Exodus 14:10–20)

WEDNESDAY
Victory by the Sea
(Exodus 14:21–31)

THURSDAY
Blessed Be God Our Savior
(Luke 1:67–75)

FRIDAY
Victory in Jesus
(1 Corinthians 15:51–58)

SATURDAY
Moses Sings of God's Triumph
(Exodus 15:1–10)

SUNDAY
Moses and Miriam Praise God
(Exodus 15:11–21)

Notes

_____

_____

_____

_____

Teaching Tips

Words You Should Know

A. Ephod (v. 14) *'ephod* (Heb.)—A priestly garment, usually made of fine linen

B. Flagon (v. 19) *'ashishah* (Heb.)—A measure of wine, or a pressed cake of raisins

Teacher Preparation

Unifying Principle—Celebrating with Enthusiasm. Celebration can be diverse in form and include various actions. How do we celebrate great events in our lives? King David expressed his joy and celebration of God by leading God's people in music and dance.

A. Read the Bible Background and Devotional Reading.

B. Pray for your students and lesson clarity.

C. Read the lesson Scripture in multiple translations.

O—Open the Lesson

A. Begin the class with prayer.

B. Give each participant an index card and instruct them to list the following on it: a favorite song, favorite vacation spot, and favorite holiday. Collect and redistribute cards, and have the group try to match a class member with each list of favorites. Ask: How can our varying preferences help/harm our ability to worship together?

C. Have the students read the Aim for Change and the In Focus story.

D. Ask students how events like those in the story weigh on their hearts and how they can view these events from a faith perspective.

P—Present the Scriptures

A. Read the Focal Verses and discuss the Background and The People, Places, and Times sections.

B. Have the class share what Scriptures stand out for them and why, with particular emphasis on today's themes.

E—Explore the Meaning

A. Use In Depth or More Light on the Text to facilitate a deeper discussion of the lesson text.

B. Pose the questions in Search the Scriptures and Discuss the Meaning.

C. Discuss the Liberating Lesson and Application for Activation sections.

N—Next Steps for Application

A. Summarize the value of celebrating their devotion to God with a variety of musical styles and forms of worship.

B. End class with a commitment to pray for unity and oneness in worship regardless of differences in styles.

Worship Guide

For the Superintendent or Teacher
Theme: David Dances before the Ark
Song: "I Was Glad When They
Said Unto Me"

David Dances Before the Ark

Bible Background • 2 SAMUEL 6
Printed Text • 2 SAMUEL 6:1–5, 14–19 | Devotional Reading • ECCLESIASTES 3:1–9

Aim for Change

By the end of this lesson, we will EXPLORE David's joy and Michal's contempt for him, APPRECIATE many ways to celebrate God's presence, and PLAN celebrations that honor God through praise and worship.

In Focus

Pastor Michael heard some people in his church complaining about the new musicians who wanted to change the service to a more contemporary style. However, he hadn't realized how upset people had become until an after-church meeting got out of control. A discussion on music became more and more heated as people from the two factions argued with each other.

"What are you people doing to our church's music?"

"We want to do something that's more relevant to people today. Is that a problem?"

"I've been playing the organ here for 25 years; you can't just walk in and change it!"

"If we want our church to grow, then we have to play new music. We can't keep doing what we've always done."

"I can't stand these new songs with all those repetitive choruses!"

"Have you ever read Psalm 136?"

Horrified, Pastor Michael stood up and dismissed the meeting. Afterward, he escaped into his study, near tears. "Lord, what have I been doing wrong?" he prayed. "Why is there so much division in my own church? What have we all been missing?" He continued to pray frantically until he took calming breaths and truly focused himself on God. He knew from personal experience when he started by looking at God, everything became clearer.

Even among Christians, selfishness can lead to conflict and disunity. When we focus on God instead of self we can worship in peace. How do you focus on God?

Keep in Mind

"And David and all the house of Israel played before the LORD on all manner of instruments made of fir wood, even on harps, and on psalteries, and on timbrels, and on cornets, and on cymbals." (2 Samuel 6:5, KJV)

"David and all the people of Israel were celebrating before the LORD, singing songs and playing all kinds of musical instruments—lyres, harps, tambourines, castanets, and cymbals." (2 Samuel 6:5, NLT)

Focal Verses

KJV **2 Samuel 6:1** Again, David gathered together all the chosen men of Israel, thirty thousand.

2 And David arose, and went with all the people that were with him from Baale of Judah, to bring up from thence the ark of God, whose name is called by the name of the LORD of hosts that dwelleth between the cherubims.

3 And they set the ark of God upon a new cart, and brought it out of the house of Abinadab that was in Gibeah: and Uzzah and Ahio, the sons of Abinadab, drave the new cart.

4 And they brought it out of the house of Abinadab which was at Gibeah, accompanying the ark of God: and Ahio went before the ark.

5 And David and all the house of Israel played before the LORD on all manner of instruments made of fir wood, even on harps, and on psalteries, and on timbrels, and on cornets, and on cymbals.

14 And David danced before the LORD with all his might; and David was girded with a linen ephod.

15 So David and all the house of Israel brought up the ark of the LORD with shouting, and with the sound of the trumpet.

16 And as the ark of the LORD came into the city of David, Michal Saul's daughter looked through a window, and saw king David leaping and dancing before the LORD; and she despised him in her heart.

17 And they brought in the ark of the LORD, and set it in his place, in the midst of the tabernacle that David had pitched for it: and David offered burnt offerings and peace offerings before the LORD.

18 And as soon as David had made an end of offering burnt offerings and peace offerings, he blessed the people in the name of the LORD of hosts.

NLT **2 Samuel 6:1** Then David again gathered all the elite troops in Israel, 30,000 in all.

2 He led them to Baalah of Judah to bring back the Ark of God, which bears the name of the LORD of Heaven's Armies, who is enthroned between the cherubim.

3 They placed the Ark of God on a new cart and brought it from Abinadab's house, which was on a hill. Uzzah and Ahio, Abinadab's sons, were guiding the cart

4 that carried the Ark of God. Ahio walked in front of the Ark.

5 David and all the people of Israel were celebrating before the LORD, singing songs and playing all kinds of musical instruments—lyres, harps, tambourines, castanets, and cymbals.

14 And David danced before the LORD with all his might, wearing a priestly garment.

15 So David and all the people of Israel brought up the Ark of the LORD with shouts of joy and the blowing of rams' horns.

16 But as the Ark of the LORD entered the City of David, Michal, the daughter of Saul, looked down from her window. When she saw King David leaping and dancing before the LORD, she was filled with contempt for him.

17 They brought the Ark of the LORD and set it in its place inside the special tent David had prepared for it. And David sacrificed burnt offerings and peace offerings to the LORD.

18 When he had finished his sacrifices, David blessed the people in the name of the LORD of Heaven's Armies.

19 Then he gave to every Israelite man and woman in the crowd a loaf of bread, a cake of dates, and a cake of raisins. Then all the people returned to their homes.

19 And he dealt among all the people, even among the whole multitude of Israel, as well to the women as men, to every one a cake of bread, and a good piece of flesh, and a flagon of wine. So all the people departed every one to his house.

The People, Places, and Times

The Ark's Journey. During the wilderness wanderings, the Ark was kept in the Tabernacle wherever the camp moved, but once the Israelites were established in the Promised Land, the Ark and entire Tabernacle complex were kept in Bethel (Judges 20:27). At one point during Samuel's time as a judge, the Philistines captured the Ark in battle (1 Samuel 4). God sent signs and sickness on the Philistines until they returned the sacred object to Israel at Beth-shemesh. God also struck down seventy men of Beth-shemesh who tried to look inside the Ark. The people there called for the priests of Kiriath-jearim to retrieve the Ark. No attempt was made to return it to the Tabernacle, and it remained in Kiriath-jearim for twenty years (1 Samuel 7:2).

Background

As David had been newly crowned King, the relocation of the Ark was a major act. It was significant that one of David's top priorities was related to Israel's spiritual life. David consulted with his officials and his proposal to move the Ark was met with enthusiastic agreement. The Ark had been at Baalah of Judah (also called Kiriath-jearim), according to 1 Chronicles 13:1-8. Before David could execute his plan, he was delayed by two unsuccessful Philistine attacks. He captured the city of Jerusalem and set up a government there. Once established in Jerusalem, David returned his attention to the moving of the Ark.

At-A-Glance

1. Extracting the Ark (2 Samuel 6:1–5)
2. If At First You Don't Succeed
(vv. 14–15)
3. Celebration and Criticism (vv. 16–19)

In Depth

1. Extracting the Ark (2 Samuel 6:1–5)

The Ark of the Lord symbolized God's presence and was the holiest of the items in the Tabernacle. At one point, the Ark had been captured by the Philistines in battle. Even after its return, the Ark of the Lord had been neglected under Saul.

The extraction of the Ark from Kiriath-jearim required extensive planning. David selected a large force of 30,000 men in case they were attacked by the Philistines. This force was accompanied by a large number of Israelites who wanted to be included in the procession.

This was an occasion for great celebration for the people of Israel. They had a new cart to transport the Ark. The sons of Abinadab were selected to guide the cart that would transport the sacred Ark (cf. 1 Samuel 7:1). There was singing and the music of various instruments as they prepared for the successful moving of the Ark.

It is easy to get swept up in all this pomp and celebration, however, even though the Israelites want to do a good thing, they have not discussed the matter with God. Had they taken a moment to do so, they would have known all their preparations were for nothing.

Read Psalms 127:1. How does this advice relate to David's careful preparation to move the Ark the first time?

2. If At First You Don't Succeed (vv. 14–15)

Verses 6-13 describe the tragic death of one of the Israelites in the first attempt to bring the Ark to Jerusalem. While not the focus of this lesson, this knowledge gives crucial insight to the remaining verses. David makes a second attempt to bring the Ark to Jerusalem three months later (vv. 14–15).

The people of Israel did not dwell on past failures. In the three months that passed, David learned that placing the Ark on a cart was forbidden. The Ark and all other sacred items were to be carried on the shoulders of Levite priests (Numbers 7:9). Keeping the Lord's commands in mind, David made a second attempt to move the Ark.

Again, he did so with a great celebration. David wore priestly garments and danced before the Lord with all his might. The people of Israel shouted for joy and offered sacrifices (2 Samuel 6:13) as the instruments played.

When has taking time to consult the Lord charged your plans for the better?

3. Celebration and Criticism (vv. 16–19)

Though his first attempt did not go as planned, David's second attempt to bring the Ark to Jerusalem was a success. After seventy year of neglect, the Ark was again publicly hailed as the sacred object it was. The Ark, symbolizing God's presence with His people, had been brought to Jerusalem, making it the religious and governing center of the nation. After a tragic first attempt, the success of the second attempt must have been that much sweeter. All of Israel celebrated with him.

In the midst of the celebratory entry into the city, Michal, David's wife and the daughter of Saul, looked at David's display of praise with disdain. David, however, was focused on worship, praise and the fellowship of God's people. He offered sacrifices to God and blessed the people, both men and women, with gifts of food and wine to take home with them. It was a joyous day, and David's praise for God's grace was not to be diminished.

How do we articulate doubts without antagonizing others?

Search the Scriptures

1. What are the various forms of worship employed when Israel moved the Ark (2 Samuel 6:5, 14–15, 17)?

2. Once the Ark made it safely to Jerusalem, what did David do (2 Samuel 6:17–18)?

Discuss the Meaning

1. David made both attempts to move the Ark with great praise and celebration. Israel's acts of worship showed great reverence for the ark, which was among the holiest things in the Tabernacle. In a culture that does not value God, how can we maintain reverence and awe for the Lord?

2. Michal had contempt for David based on his demonstrative worship. The church can be a setting in which people from different generations, cultural backgrounds, and socioeconomic status are worshiping together. How can we respect everyone's freedom to worship?

Liberating Lesson

Bringing the ark to Jerusalem was no easy task. It required planning, a tremendous amount of resources, and great effort. David was not deterred by what this endeavor would require. His commitment to Israel's spiritual health was such that he committed himself to bringing the symbol of God's presence to Jerusalem despite the cost.

Similarly, spiritual growth requires effort on our part. We may not need to assemble 30,000 people to take a dangerous journey, but we must be intentional about the things of God. We must actively swim against the pull of modern culture and its endless supply of empty pursuits to live the life that God intends.

Application for Activation

David was intentional about bringing the symbol of God's presence to Jerusalem. Likewise, we must be intentional about cultivating God's presence in our own lives. Do you have a plan for your spiritual growth? Do you have times devoted to prayer, study, and personal worship each week? Are there certain times of the year when you fast or spend an extended period of time alone with God?

When moving the ark, David had the support of Israel. In addition to 30,000 warriors, a large company of Israelites went with him to retrieve the ark. They sang, danced, and offered sacrifices. The church exists as a community to encourage and equip. As a body, let us support one another as we pursue the things of God and create an atmosphere of sincere worship.

Follow the Spirit

What God wants me to do:

_____

_____

_____

Remember Your Thoughts

Special insights I have learned:

_____

_____

_____

More Light on the Text

2 Samuel 6:1-5, 14–19

2 Samuel 6 is the record of an important episode in David's reign. Having restored the political unity of the nation and consolidating it by the establishment of the new political capital in Jerusalem, David's next concern was to make Jerusalem the capital of national worship. With this objective, David prepared to bring out the Ark, which had been neglected in Kiriath-jearim since its return from Philistia (1 Chronicles 13:3). David made its journey to Jerusalem a national affair, as the huge numbers of people present reveals (v. 1). The details given indicate something of the joy and festivity that surrounded the two stages of the Ark's journey from Baale-judah to the capital.

1 Again, David gathered together all the chosen men of Israel, thirty thousand. 2 And David arose, and went with all the people that were with him from Baale of Judah, to bring up from thence the ark of God, whose name is called by the name of the LORD of hosts that dwelleth between the cherubims.

One of the significant themes in 1 and 2 Samuel is the Ark of the Covenant. The Ark was the object most strongly associated with Israel's God, a truth expressed by the writer's notation that the Ark belongs to God "whose name is called the name of the LORD of hosts that dwelleth between the cherubims" (v. 2). An object of overwhelming significance, it contained the covenant between Israel and the Lord (cf. Exodus 25:16; 40:20). It was a place of divine revelation (Exodus 25:22; Numbers 7:89) and was, in fact, the Lord's throne (cf. 1 Samuel 4:4; 2 Kings 19:15; Psalm 99:1; Isaiah 37:16). It was captured by the Philistines but returned to Israelite territory when it became a nightmare to them and proved too embarrassingly powerful and humiliated both them and their god (1 Samuel 5). It stayed in that territory for about seventy years. When David captured Jerusalem, he purposed in his heart that it should be the city where God was to be honored and worshiped. As such, he sought to bring the Ark, the symbol of God's presence there.

3 And they set the ark of God upon a new cart, and brought it out of the house of Abinadab that was in Gibeah: and Uzzah and Ahio, the sons of Abinadab, drave the new cart. 4 And they brought it out of the house of Abinadab which was at Gibeah, accompanying the ark of God: and Ahio went before the ark. 5 And David and all the house of Israel played before the LORD on all manner of instruments made of fir wood, even on harps, and on psalteries, and on timbrels, and on cornets, and on cymbals.

It must be remembered that God had given specific instructions about moving the Ark. It was to be carried with poles (Exodus 25:12–14). The Ark was constructed with rings on the four corners and poles were put through those rings. The Ark was carried on the shoulders of the Levites.

However, although with good intentions and out of zeal, but without due concern for the instruction in Exodus, David made a new cart on which the Ark was to be carried (v. 3). In other words, David did the right thing but in the wrong way. As respectful and well-intended as David's effort was, however, it violated Torah guidelines regarding the transport of the Ark (cf. Numbers 4:15; 7:9). In fact, David's actions in this matter were more like those of the spiritually ignorant Philistines (cf. 1 Samuel 6:7, 10). There was going to be a price to be paid for it. The Philistines transported the Ark contrary to God's instructions and got away with it while David did not, but note that the Philistines were not given any instructions. Added light is added responsibility. This is not to suggest that ignorance is an excuse for not doing things properly. Rather, it is a lesson for God's people to meticulously pay heed to His

commandments and avoid the manifestation of zeal without knowledge.

In conclusion, one must always remember that it is not only important to do the right thing, but also it must be done the right way. This is especially true in the work of the Lord. Nowhere is this principle better illustrated than in the text for this week. The whole notion that the end justifies the means is debunked by the story of David's attempt to bring back the Ark of the Lord to Judah in his own way rather than the one prescribed by the Lord.

14 And David danced before the LORD with all his might; and David was girded with a linen ephod. 15 So David and all the house of Israel brought up the ark of the LORD with shouting, and with the sound of the trumpet.

David had intended to move the Ark to Jerusalem (v. 10), but the tragedy in verses 6-8 caused a detour and David's plan was temporarily shelved. The Ark was transferred to the house of Obed-edom. When David heard that the house of Obed-edom has received signs of God's favor due to the presence of the Ark, he revisited his original plan to bring the ark to Jerusalem.

But there was to be one significant difference between the two attempts to transport the sacred throne; this time Levites carried it on poles (v. 13; cf. Numbers 4:15), not transporting it on a cart (cf. v. 3). The requirements of the law were now duly observed. As soon as the procession started on its way, without any sign of divine displeasure, David offered a sacrifice as a thank-offering for the prosperous commencement, and an intercession for the successful completion of the undertaking.

For the occasion, David had prepared both his capital city and himself. First, he had erected a special tent in Jerusalem that would house the Ark (cf. v. 17).

He also prepared and wore special ritual garments: David was girded with a linen ephod

(v. 14; Heb. *ephod*, ay-**FODE**), a piece of clothing otherwise reserved in Israelite society for priests and Levites (cf. Exodus 28:6; 1 Samuel 2:18; 22:18), and, according to 1 Chronicles 15:27, a "robe of fine linen." He laid aside his royal robes and appeared in the distinctive dress of a priest. As a king and representative of a "kingdom of priests" (Exodus 19:6), the king took on a priestly character; exercising on this particular occasion a priestly function in directing the sacrifices, even if he did not offer them himself (vv. 17–18), and in blessing the people (v. 18).

David's actions were accompanied "with shouting, and with the sound of the trumpet" (v. 15). Trumpets—ones blown by Levitical priests—had also been sounded during a movement of the Ark in the days of Joshua (cf. Joshua 6:4–20). David also danced before the Lord (v. 14). Dances were the usual expression of rejoicing on occasions of thanksgiving (Exodus 15:20; Judges 11:34) and religious festivals (Psalm 199:3).

16 And as the ark of the LORD came into the city of David, Michal Saul's daughter looked through a window, and saw king David leaping and dancing before the LORD; and she despised him in her heart.

At the moment of David's triumph, when the Ark had successfully entered Jerusalem and passed through the royal fortress, David's wife Michal had no interest in all the religious excitement and display. Micah thought that David degraded himself by this public exhibition, which, however it might have become one of his inferior servants, was unsuited to his dignity. As it was, she despised him for the very qualities that made him great, namely devotion to the Lord and spontaneity in worship. David's unbounded enthusiasm for his God expressed itself in "leaping and dancing before the LORD" (v. 16). Michal did not appreciate his enthusiasm.

Although Michal was David's wife, this part of the account calls her Saul's daughter (see also vv. 20, 23). Her designation as Saul's daughter is both to characterize her as lacking in true-hearted piety, as well as distinguish her in comparison with David's other wives, as highest in position. When Michal refers to her husband David as "the king of Israel," she seems to compare him to her father Saul who once bore the title (v. 20). It was Michal's way of telling David, "you are no king," or "my father was a more dignified king!"

Michal holds herself aloof from the procession and criticizes David's conduct with a cold heart which had no part in his and the people's joyous inspiration. She despised him on account of his presumed degradation of himself, to the shame of his royal dignity (v. 20). From her vantage point at the window, Michal saw not a king's triumph but a king exposing himself.

17 And they brought in the ark of the LORD, and set it in his place, in the midst of the tabernacle that David had pitched for it: and David offered burnt offerings and peace offerings before the LORD. 18 And as soon as David had made an end of offering burnt offerings and peace offerings, he blessed the people in the name of the LORD of hosts.

Three worship gestures marked and celebrated the ark's arrival: (1) sacrifice, (2) blessing, and (3) the distribution of food. These rituals are reminiscent of the first sacrifices that were offered before the tent of meeting by the newly ordained Aaron the priest. At that time he blessed the people, offered a burnt offering and a peace offering, entered the tent of meeting, and, upon exiting it blessed the people again (Leviticus 9:22–23). Although the details of David's action here is less elaborate than that of Aaron, its significance is neither diminished nor lost. David offered burnt offerings and peace offerings before the Lord and the offerings being ended, he blessed the people in the name of the Lord of Hosts which was introduced at the beginning of the account (6:2).

19 And he dealt among all the people, even among the whole multitude of Israel, as well to the women as men, to every one a cake of bread, and a good piece of flesh, and a flagon of wine. So all the people departed every one to his house.

In verse 19 the king climaxes the festivities with food gifts. Each one, men and women, received a "cake of bread," a round loaf, such as was baked for sacrificial meals (cf. Exodus 29:23; Leviticus 8:24). The people also each received a measure of meat (KJV: "flesh"), likely from one of the many peace offerings made that day. Meat was not a staple of the commoner's diet then, as it is now. Meat was most commonly eaten as part of a sacrificial meal. While a burnt offering burns up the entire animal to God, a peace offering only burns some of the fat and organs of the sacrificial animal, leaving all of the meat for the people themselves to eat. Lastly, the people receive "a flagon of wine" (Heb. *'ashishah*, ah-shee-**SHAW**) Even though the King James consistently translates this word that way, linguists now believe the word is better translated "raisin cake," a sweet treat of dried grapes that is pressed into shape, rather than baked. Both the meat and the raisin cake would be special treats to help the people celebrate this historic occasion and to show the king's generosity.

Sources:
Baldwin, J. G. *1 and 2 Samuel*. Tyndale Old Testament Commentary. Downers Grove, IL: InterVarsity, 1988.
Bergen, Robert D. *1, 2 Samuel*. The New American Commentary. Vol. 7. Nashville, TN: Broadman & Holman Publishers, 1996.
Brueggemann, W. *First and Second Samuel*. Interpretation: A Bible Commentary for Teaching and Preaching. Louisville, KY: Westminster John Knox Press, 1990.
Edersheim, Alfred. *Bible History: Old Testament*. Grand Rapids, MI: William B. Eerdmans Publishing Company, 1975.
Gordon, R. P. *I and II Samuel*. Grand Rapids, MI: Zondervan, 1986.
Jamieson, Robert, A. R. Fausset, and David Brown. *Commentary Critical and Explanatory on the Whole Bible*. Oak Harbor, WA: Logos Research Systems, Inc., 1997.
Morrison, Craig E. *2 Samuel*. Berit Olam: Studies in Hebrew Narrative & Poetry. Collegeville, MN: Liturgical Press, 2013.
Hubbard, David A. *2 Samuel*. Word Biblical Commentary. Vol. 11. Dallas, TX: Word Incorporated, 1989.
Payne, David F. *I & II Samuel*. The Daily Study Bible Series. Louisville, KY: Westminster John Knox Press, 2001.
Spence-Jones, H. D. M. ed. *2 Samuel*. The Pulpit Commentary. New York: Funk & Wagnalls Company, 1909.

Say It Correctly

Ephod. EE-fode
Kiriath-jeariam. KEAR-ee-ath JEAR-ee-am.
Beth-shemesh. beth SHEH-mesh.
Abinadab. ah-BIN-ah-dab.

Daily Bible Readings

MONDAY
David Prepares to Transport the Ark
(2 Samuel 6:1–5)

TUESDAY
The Holiness of the Sanctuary
(Hebrews 9:1–7)

WEDNESDAY
Uzzah Disregards the Ark's Holiness
(2 Samuel 6:6–11)

THURSDAY
The House of the Lord
(Psalm 122)

FRIDAY
Go to God's Dwelling Place
(Psalm 132:1–12)

SATURDAY
The Ark in the Heavenly Temple
(Revelation 11:15–19)

SUNDAY
David Dances Before the Ark
(2 Samuel 6:12–19)

Teaching Tips

Words You Should Know

A. Cry out (v. 47) *krazo* (Gk.)—To shout out loudly

B. Hold His Peace (v. 48) *siopao* (Gk.)—To keep quiet, stop talking (even though you have something to say)

Teacher Preparation

Unifying Principle—Celebrating Expectantly. People respond to life challenges and victories differently. How can we respond in ways that are encouraging for ourselves and others? Bartimaeus' boldness and faith in Jesus gave him the courage to ask for and receive his sight from Jesus.

A. Read the Bible Background and Devotional Reading.

B. Pray for your students and lesson clarity.

C. Read the lesson Scripture in multiple translations.

O—Open the Lesson

A. Begin the class with prayer.

B. Bring materials from service ministries to class. Allow participants to look through these materials and discuss how they could help bring the physical/spiritual help of Jesus to marginalized members of society.

C. Have the students read the Aim for Change and the In Focus story.

D. Ask students how events like those in the story weigh on their hearts and how they can view these events from a faith perspective.

P—Present the Scriptures

A. Read the Focal Verses and discuss the Background and The People, Places, and Times sections.

B. Have the class share what Scriptures stand out for them and why, with particular emphasis on today's themes.

E—Explore the Meaning

A. Use In Depth or More Light on the Text to facilitate a deeper discussion of the lesson text.

B. Pose the questions in Search the Scriptures and Discuss the Meaning.

C. Discuss the Liberating Lesson and Application for Activation sections.

N—Next Steps for Application

A. Summarize the value of being willing to take risks in order to follow Jesus.

B. End class with a commitment to pray for healing of their spiritual deficiencies as well as for their physical challenges.

Worship Guide

For the Superintendent or Teacher
Theme: Glorifying God
Song: "When I Pray"

Glorifying God

Bible Background • MARK 10:46-52; LUKE 18:35–43
Printed Text • MARK 10:46–52 | Devotional Reading • JAMES 5:13–18

Aim for Change

By the end of this lesson, we will COMPARE and contrast spiritual and physical blindness, APPRECIATE how God is attentive and responds to our needs, and PRACTICE reaching out to those who are marginalized by society.

In Focus

Herman and Shelly Johnson had just moved to the area two months ago. They hadn't even been able to find a church family yet before the tornado hit. The Johnsons had lost so much. Their roof had blown off, drenching everything inside, as Herman and Shelly huddled in the re-enforced basement.

In the immediate aftermath of the storm, the Johnsons prayed for a few things they specifically needed. There was no way they could pay to repair the damages without a steady income, which was proving difficult since both the beauty shop where Shelly had worked and Herman's instruments had been destroyed in the tornado. Daily, they prayed together for a guitar so Herman could perform at gigs again and an open chair where Shelly could continue work as a beautician. God came through with just what they needed. The woman who worked in the chair next to Shelly invited them to her church where the Johnsons were welcomed into the new church family.

Now, a year later, Herman and Shelly were finally finished recovering their losses. It had required persistence with their insurance company to get them to pay all they were supposed to, but the Johnsons had stood up for themselves. They could never replace the exact things the storm had blown away, but they were going to praise God for helping them back to their feet. They would live their lives here on out more thankful for God's blessings.

How has God answered a specific prayer of yours?

Keep in Mind

"And Jesus answered and said unto him, What wilt thou that I should do unto thee? The blind man said unto him, Lord, that I might receive my sight." (Mark 10:51, KJV)

"'What do you want me to do for you?' Jesus asked. 'My Rabbi,' the blind man said, 'I want to see!'" (Mark 10:51, NLT)

Focal Verses

KJV **Mark 10:46** And they came to Jericho: and as he went out of Jericho with his disciples and a great number of people, blind Bartimaeus, the son of Timaeus, sat by the highway side begging.

47 And when he heard that it was Jesus of Nazareth, he began to cry out, and say, Jesus, thou son of David, have mercy on me.

48 And many charged him that he should hold his peace: but he cried the more a great deal, Thou son of David, have mercy on me.

49 And Jesus stood still, and commanded him to be called. And they call the blind man, saying unto him, Be of good comfort, rise; he calleth thee.

50 And he, casting away his garment, rose, and came to Jesus.

51 And Jesus answered and said unto him, What wilt thou that I should do unto thee? The blind man said unto him, Lord, that I might receive my sight.

52 And Jesus said unto him, Go thy way; thy faith hath made thee whole. And immediately he received his sight, and followed Jesus in the way.

NLT **Mark 10:46** Then they reached Jericho, and as Jesus and his disciples left town, a large crowd followed him. A blind beggar named Bartimaeus (son of Timaeus) was sitting beside the road.

47 When Bartimaeus heard that Jesus of Nazareth was nearby, he began to shout, "Jesus, Son of David, have mercy on me!"

48 "Be quiet!" many of the people yelled at him. But he only shouted louder, "Son of David, have mercy on me!"

49 When Jesus heard him, he stopped and said, "Tell him to come here." So they called the blind man. "Cheer up," they said. "Come on, he's calling you!"

50 Bartimaeus threw aside his coat, jumped up, and came to Jesus.

51 "What do you want me to do for you?" Jesus asked. "My Rabbi," the blind man said, "I want to see!"

52 And Jesus said to him, "Go, for your faith has healed you." Instantly the man could see, and he followed Jesus down the road.

The People, Places, and Times

Jericho. A city about fifteen miles east from Jerusalem, near the Jordan River, Jericho was the home of a large population of priests who served the temple in Jerusalem. The tax collector Zacchaeus also lived in Jericho (Luke 19). It was the first city Joshua's forces destroyed as they occupied the Promised Land (Joshua 6:20). Joshua spoke a curse upon anyone who dared to rebuild it, but it was rebuilt anyway, again becoming an important trading center.

Jesus' Titles. The crowd calls Him "Jesus of Nazareth" (v. 47), recognizing His humanity and the city of His upbringing. Bartimaeus calls Him "Son of David" (vv. 47–48), recognizing His Jewish heritage and perhaps His royal lineage. Bartimaeus also calls Jesus "Rabboni" which means "my teacher" (v. 51). Rabbi is the highly respected position of a master spiritual teacher in Jewish society. Bartimaeus calls himself Jesus' pupil, even though they have not met before. The only other time this title is used in Scripture is when Mary Magdalene first recognizes Jesus after the Resurrection.

Which of Jesus' names and titles are striking to you and why?

Background

As He leaves Jericho, Jesus is closing the second phase of His ministry. He is on His way to Jerusalem where, as He has prophesied, He will be condemned by His own people and then handed over to the Roman authorities who will treat Him cruelly and crucify Him. However, Jesus assured His disciples that His death was not His final destiny and that on the third day He would be resurrected (Mark 10:33-34).

In a sense, Bartimaeus' blindness is a metaphor that can be applied to all of Chapter 10. In the discussion of divorce in 10:1–12, the Pharisees and the disciples were blind to God's view of the importance of the family. In 10:13–16, the disciples were blind to the significance of children; in 10:17–31, the rich, young ruler and the disciples were blind to the importance of the kingdom; and in 10:32–34 the disciples were blind to the meaning of Jesus' suffering, death, and resurrection (see Luke 18:34).

Immediately before Bartimaeus' account, the disciples again display their blindness in their desire for supremacy in the kingdom of God (Mark 10:35–45). So the healing of Bartimaeus' blindness is a fitting close to this whole chapter on blindness.

In what ways is spiritual blindness like physical blindness? Where does spiritual blindness leave you?

At-A-Glance

1. Faith Uses Available Resources
(Mark 10:46–47)
2. Faith Answers Objections (vv. 48–50)
3. Faith Makes Specific Requests
(vv. 51–52)

In Depth

1. Faith Uses Available Resources (Mark 10:46–47)

We do not know if Bartimaeus was expecting Jesus or if he just happened to be in the right place at the right time to exercise his faith. It seems obvious that he knew who Jesus was and had probably heard about His healing powers. Jesus was already known to heal diseases with seemingly no cure, like the deaf and mute man from Decapolis (7:31–37). He had even cured the blindness of another man in Bethsaida (8:22–26).

When Bartimaeus heard that Jesus of Nazareth was passing by, he used his available resources to get Jesus' healing. He could not see, but he could hear. So he used his ears. He could not see, but he could think. So he used his brain to recall Jesus' reputation. He could not see, but he could use his voice. So he cried out loudly, "Jesus, thou son of David, have mercy on me" (10:47).

2. Faith Answers Objections (vv. 48–50)

Some people in the crowd tried to quiet Bartimaeus. He was a lowly beggar in their eyes, and Jesus was an important teacher. But Bartimaeus would not be quiet, primarily because he knew that the people who were shushing him could afford to be quiet because they could see! He continued calling until Jesus responded. When Jesus answers by sending Bartimaeus a call of his own, the blind man immediately tosses his outer garment aside, putting away any hindrance or extra baggage that might slow him from rushing to answer the Master's call.

Even though many on the outskirts of society ask for help, we are often too busy to help them. Praise God that He is so grand and important that He can always make time for the lowly.

Bartimaeus boldly ignored the crowd and sought Jesus. How do you do this in your life?

3. Faith Makes Specific Requests (vv. 51–52)

Jesus asked Bartimaeus, "What do you want me to do for you?" (v. 51). Brother Bart didn't hem and haw; he said immediately, "I want to see again." Actually, this was Bartimaeus' second request. His first request was for mercy (v. 48). Now that his cry for mercy had caught Jesus' attention, he proceeded to ask for healing.

When we want Jesus' attention, we should not scream about our virtues, talents, resources, or assets. Ask Him for mercy. If He gives you mercy, as He certainly will, He will surely give you everything that goes along with it.

Search the Scriptures

1. What were Bartimaeus' two requests (vv. 47–48, 51)?

2. What was Bartimaeus' response when he received his sight (v. 52)?

Discuss the Meaning

1. Are you quick to tell others what the Lord has done for you? Practice telling a story about how God blessed you recently.

2. Do you follow Jesus out of gratitude for what He has done or merely out of religious obligation? Is Christianity just an easy path for you or do you follow it with purpose?

Liberating Lesson

Immediately upon receiving his sight, Bartimaeus follows Jesus. People who were once marginalized by society became powerful witnesses for Jesus after an encounter with Him (Mark 1:45; 5:20; John 4:39–42; 20:18). How do we as the Church uplift those in the margins—the learning challenged, the differently-abled, the disadvantaged—so that they can know the love and power of God? Let us seek to introduce people with both physical and spiritual challenges to Jesus, for Jesus says those who have been forgiven much love much.

Application for Activation

Read today's key verse: "And Jesus answered and said unto him, What wilt thou that I should do unto thee? The blind man said unto him, Lord, that I might receive my sight" (Mark 10:51). How would you answer Jesus' question? Pray silently, voicing that desire to God.

Follow the Spirit

What God wants me to do:

_____

_____

_____

_____

Remember Your Thoughts

Special insights I have learned:

_____

_____

_____

_____

More Light on the Text
Mark 10:46–52

The narrative of Bartimaeus and Jesus in Mark's Gospel is one of two healing stories about people who are blind. Both events are reminders of how the disciples were blind as to who Jesus is as the Messiah. They did not understand that Jesus was headed toward Jerusalem that His purpose as the Messiah would be fulfilled. His impending death and resurrection were closer than the disciples knew or could comprehend.

The healing of Bartimaeus' sight occurs during the last three months of Jesus' ministry—between the Festival of the Dedication (John 10:22–28) and his arrival in Jerusalem for Passover. His reputation had been firmly established by that time (vv. 40–42).

Jesus and the disciples had crossed over into Jericho from Perea. Before reaching Jerusalem, Jesus and the disciples walked through Jericho. Jericho was a busy city with many attractions for all who visited and lived there. Jericho is also the setting for the popular and painful story of the Good Samaritan (Luke 10:25-37).

46 And they came to Jericho: and as he went out of Jericho with his disciples and a great number of people, blind Bartimaeus, the son of Timaeus, sat by the highway side begging.

Jesus and the disciples walked along the highway. As they walked along the road, a man named Bartimaeus, who was blind, was sitting there. He was begging for money. In Bartimaeus' day, it was thought blindness represented that you had sinned, and you were cursed by God. Jesus' restoring sight to the blind is contrary to this belief (cf. Matthew 20:34; John 9:2–3).

Three of the four gospels, Matthew (20:29–34), Mark (10:46–52), and Luke (18:35–43), tell the narrative a blind man, Jesus, and the blind man's healing. In Matthew, he states that he was another blind man begging with him, and Luke identifies him only as "the blind man." Mark is the only writer that identifies the man by name. Scholars have noted that Bartimaeus' name is a combination of Greek and Aramaic. His father's name Timaeus is Greek, meaning honorable or worthy, and the added prefix Bar, meaning son. The combination of a Greek name with an Aramaic prefix is not found anywhere else in the Bible.

Bartimaeus is the son of Timaeus and is sitting by the highway, begging for money. Begging was his full-time job. According to some scholars, he was known in the community. The article "the" before "son of Timaeus" highlights that he is a recognized person. Because he was blind, finding a different type of job would be challenging—most jobs required that you be physically able to move and see what you are doing. As a beggar, Bartimaeus was dependent on the gifts and generosity of others to earn a living.

Bartimaeus' status as a blind and begging man was not unusual. Beggars were common in Jericho as well as people who had a debilitating disease or a limiting disability. Seeing beggars on the highways and streets is not a rare experience even today in most cities and towns. What makes Bartimaeus different from the other beggars are his future actions and how others respond.

47 And when he heard that it was Jesus of Nazareth, he began to cry out, and say, Jesus, thou son of David, have mercy on me.

Bartimaeus does not know who is walking in his direction until he hears Jesus of Nazareth. Jesus' popularity had grown because of His healing, teaching, and showing compassion to many. They believed in Him.

Biblical scholars do not know how long Bartimaeus had begged to make a living, but it is clear that he knew about Jesus. Bartimaeus believed that Jesus could change his life if He gave him sight. Although other people were around him, Bartimaeus only wanted Jesus. He cries out (Gk. *krazo*, **KROD**-zo) to Jesus. He does not weep with tears or whimper in worry; this word means he shouts out loudly. Bartimaeus addresses Him using the title, "Son of David," as he asks for mercy (healing). The phrase "Son of David" indicates Jesus is from the royal lineage of David. The title also qualifies Jesus to rule as Messiah (Matthew 9:27; 12:23; 15:22). The title "Son of David" is a title that Matthew uses eleven times for his Jewish readers, while Mark only uses it once, and Luke twice. Both Mark and Luke's Gospels are for Gentile readers. Bartimaeus is clear that Jesus is the Messiah who radically can change his life.

48 And many charged him that he should hold his peace: but he cried the more a great deal, Thou son of David, have mercy on me.

Many people standing near Bartimaeus wanted him to "hold his peace" (Gk. *siopao*, see-oh-**PAH**-oh). The more they told him to keep quiet and stop talking, the louder and more insistent he became. He refused to stop shouting for Jesus. He repeats his desperate outcry to Jesus, "Thou son of David, have mercy on me," to the chagrin and irritation of the people around him. Bartimaeus shows us how to come boldly before God with our requests (Hebrews 4:16), without fear of being ignored or mocked. Christ always has time for us.

Bartimaeus also reminds us that when we want to have a deeper relationship with Jesus, we should give all of who we are. The boldness of Bartimaeus is reflective of the woman who would not leave until the judge granted her request (Luke 18:1–8) or the persistent neighbor who wanted bread to feed his guest (Luke 11:5–8). Giving up on getting Jesus was not Bartimaeus' plan or focus. Crying out to Jesus, and Jesus acknowledging his presence and situation, meant something better than what he was experiencing had to happen.

49 And Jesus stood still, and commanded him to be called. And they call the blind man, saying unto him, Be of good comfort, rise; he calleth thee. 50 And he, casting away his garment, rose, and came to Jesus.

Jesus heard Bartimaeus calling for him and stopped walking. Jesus hears Bartimaeus' pleading for help despite all the noise, people, and activity happening. Next, Jesus asked for him to come to where He was. Jesus wanted to see him. He also wanted everyone else to witness what would happen.

Based on the text, Bartimaeus did not have family or friends helping him. We do not read or hear of any of his friends working together to help Bartimaeus receive his healing. No family or friends, like the courageous friends who tore the roof off of a house so their friend could receive Jesus' healing (Matthew 9:1–8; Mark 2:1–12; Luke 5:17–26). He was again dependent on the people around him. The same people who told him to be quiet were helping him walk to Jesus. They told him some good news so he could "be of good comfort" (Gk. *tharseo*, thar-**SEH**-oh). This word is often used in the Greek translation of the Old Testament to translate the phrase "Do not be afraid." The people who were just telling him to quiet his bold shouts for attention now tell Bartimaeus to be bold and approach Jesus. Nevertheless, he is optimistic because Jesus wants to see him. He needs to get up now and go where Jesus is.

Bartimaeus' determination to call out to Jesus had paid off. He was ready to have Jesus grant him mercy and the healing that only Jesus could give. Bartimaeus throws off his garment (Gk. *himation*, hee-**MAH**-tee-on, a warm outer cloak), jumped to his feet, and went directly to Jesus. He did not procrastinate in going to Jesus. Like Bartimaeus, we need to move when Jesus responds to our calls.

51 And Jesus answered and said unto him, What wilt thou that I should do unto thee? The blind man said unto him, Lord, that I might receive my sight. 52 And Jesus said unto him, Go thy way; thy faith hath made thee whole. And immediately he received his sight, and followed Jesus in the way.

Jesus asks Bartimaeus, "What do you want me to do?" He already knows what Bartimaeus deeply desires and needs; He is the omniscient God. Jesus would sometimes ask questions of people to reveal the truth of what they wanted or their thoughts. For example, Jesus asked the man at the pool of Bethsaida, "Do you want to be whole?" (John 5:16), and the disciples, "Why are you afraid?" during a mighty windstorm (Matthew 8:26). Jesus' questions are questions that we may find ourselves answering today in challenging times. The questions and our answers are prompts to trust and talk to Jesus in our most vulnerable states.

Bartimaeus answers Jesus' question by stating he wants to see. Jesus first responds by giving a direct action to do, "Go" (Gk. *hupago*, hoo-**PAH**-go). Jesus expects nothing in return from Bartimaeus; He fulfills his request and tells him to go on his way. Then, he tells Bartimaeus that his faith has healed him. His eyes are opened, and his vision is perfect. Bartimaeus does not walk away or run to the nearest Temple. Instead, he walks with Jesus along the road.

Bartimaeus' courage and resolve to interact with Jesus represents character strengths; we, too, can develop and exercise toward Jesus. When we cannot see the end of whatever we are going through, we need to believe that Jesus is with us. Bartimaeus is a guide that sometimes we have to wait for Jesus to respond to our questions, our concerns. When Jesus does answer, we should be prepared to say or do what we want in faith and continue following Jesus.

Sources:
African Study Bible, New Living Translation. Oasis International Limited. Carol Stream, IL: Tyndale House Publishers, 2016.
"Biblical Commentary (Bible Study) Mark 10:46-52." Sermonwriter. com. Accessed April 8, 2020.
Life Application Study Bible. Wheaton, IL: Tyndale House Publishers and Zondervan Publishing House, 2005.

Say It Correctly

Bartimaeus. bar-tih-MAY-us.
Perea. peh-RAY-ah.

Daily Bible Readings

MONDAY
Blind Eyes Shall Be Opened
(Isaiah 35:1–6)

TUESDAY
Declare God's Glory Among the Nations!
(Psalm 96)

WEDNESDAY
Glory to God's Name Alone
(Psalm 115:1–3, 9–18)

THURSDAY
Only God Is Good
(Mark 10:17–22)

FRIDAY
Greatness through Servanthood
(Mark 10:42–45)

SATURDAY
Praise the Lord, O My Soul
(Psalm 146)

SUNDAY
Praise God for Healing
(Mark 10:46–52)

Teaching Tips

Words You Should Know

A. Testify (Acts 2:40) *Diamarturomai* (Gk.)—To witness or to bear witness earnestly or repeatedly, attesting to the truth of redemption

B. Wonders and signs (v. 43) *terata kai semeia* (Gk.)—Miracles that point to God's direct activity in the earthly realm

C. Singleness of heart (v. 46) *apheloteti kardias* (Gk.)—Gladness and sincerity of heart

Teacher Preparation

Unifying Principle—Celebrating Unity. Celebrations bring about unity and a new way of seeing and being in the world. How can our celebrations unify a divided community and world? The first Christian community heard the Gospel, was inspired by the Holy Spirit to see the world differently, and united to live, worship, and evangelize together.

A. Read the Bible Background and Devotional Reading.

B. Pray for your students and lesson clarity.

C. Read the lesson Scripture in multiple translations.

O—Open the Lesson

A. Begin the class with prayer.

B. Point out that Acts 2:47 describes the early Christians as "having favour with all the people." Debate whether the same could be said about Christians today and why that might or might not be true.

C. Have the students read the Aim for Change and the In Focus story.

D. Ask students how events like those in the story weigh on their hearts and how they can view these events from a faith perspective.

P—Present the Scriptures

A. Read the Focal Verses and discuss the Background and The People, Places, and Times sections.

B. Have the class share what Scriptures stand out for them and why, with particular emphasis on today's themes.

E—Explore the Meaning

A. Use In Depth or More Light on the Text to facilitate a deeper discussion of the lesson text.

B. Pose the questions in Search the Scriptures and Discuss the Meaning.

C. Discuss the Liberating Lesson and Application for Activation sections.

N—Next Steps for Application

A. Summarize the value of transcending ethnic, national, and socioeconomic barriers in following Jesus.

B. End class with a commitment to pray for the unity of the church in gathering regularly for prayer, the Lord's Supper, and Bible teaching.

Worship Guide

For the Superintendent or Teacher
Theme: Believers Praise God
Song: "Sweet Holy Spirit"

Believers Praise God

Bible Background • ACTS 2:32-33, 37-47
Printed Text • ACTS 2:32-33, 37-47 | Devotional Reading • PSALM 134

Aim for Change

By the end of this lesson, we will UNDERSTAND the role of Christ and the Holy Spirit in our lives, DISCERN how the Holy Spirit inspires believers to share a life of worship, and PLAN opportunities for people to begin a relationship with Jesus through our ministries.

In Focus

For years, the church had prayed for a new building to house a soup kitchen and beds for the homeless in the community. As head of the homeless ministry, Jessica was devastated by the pastor's decision to divert funds from the new building to missions work in India.

"How could you use the building funds like that? Some of them are not even Christians. Pastor, we need a bigger building. This community deserves our help," Jessica stated.

"We are getting a bigger church every time we save a soul or feed a body. It doesn't matter if it's here at home or throughout the world. Come with us next month and see for yourself," said Pastor Whitaker. Jessica agreed.

One month later, Jessica and the members of her church arrived in Mumbai, India. The riverbanks overflowed, and the city was dirty and desperate. Pastor Whitaker shared the Gospel and held prayer meetings. They passed out medication, prepared meals, and sterilized linens and clothing for people left homeless by the monsoons.

When Jessica returned home, the size of the church building was insignificant. She realized that because of the sacrifices she and the rest of the mission team made, God's Church was increased. The community of faith is much larger than the four walls of her local church body. These people needed help, too.

Are you willing to sacrifice and share for the improvement of the entire church body? What are some elements of what makes a great church?

Keep in Mind

"And they continued stedfastly in the apostles' doctrine and fellowship, and in breaking of bread, and in prayers." (Acts 2:42, KJV)

"All the believers devoted themselves to the apostles' teaching, and to fellowship, and to sharing in meals (including the Lord's Supper), and to prayer."
(Acts 2:42, NLT)

Focal Verses

KJV **Acts 2:32** This Jesus hath God raised up, whereof we all are witnesses.

33 Therefore being by the right hand of God exalted, and having received of the Father the promise of the Holy Ghost, he hath shed forth this, which ye now see and hear.

37 Now when they heard this, they were pricked in their heart, and said unto Peter and to the rest of the apostles, Men and brethren, what shall we do?

38 Then Peter said unto them, Repent, and be baptized every one of you in the name of Jesus Christ for the remission of sins, and ye shall receive the gift of the Holy Ghost.

39 For the promise is unto you, and to your children, and to all that are afar off, even as many as the LORD our God shall call.

40 And with many other words did he testify and exhort, saying, Save yourselves from this untoward generation.

41 Then they that gladly received his word were baptized: and the same day there were added unto them about three thousand souls.

42 And they continued stedfastly in the apostles' doctrine and fellowship, and in breaking of bread, and in prayers.

43 And fear came upon every soul: and many wonders and signs were done by the apostles.

44 And all that believed were together, and had all things common;

45 And sold their possessions and goods, and parted them to all men, as every man had need.

46 And they, continuing daily with one accord in the temple, and breaking bread from house to house, did eat their meat with gladness and singleness of heart,

47 Praising God, and having favour with all the people. And the Lord added to the church daily such as should be saved.

NLT **Acts 2:32** "God raised Jesus from the dead, and we are all witnesses of this.

33 Now he is exalted to the place of highest honor in heaven, at God's right hand. And the Father, as he had promised, gave him the Holy Spirit to pour out upon us, just as you see and hear today."

37 Peter's words pierced their hearts, and they said to him and to the other apostles, "Brothers, what should we do?"

38 Peter replied, "Each of you must repent of your sins and turn to God, and be baptized in the name of Jesus Christ for the forgiveness of your sins. Then you will receive the gift of the Holy Spirit.

39 This promise is to you, to your children, and to those far away—all who have been called by the Lord our God."

40 Then Peter continued preaching for a long time, strongly urging all his listeners, "Save yourselves from this crooked generation!"

41 Those who believed what Peter said were baptized and added to the church that day—about 3,000 in all.

42 All the believers devoted themselves to the apostles' teaching, and to fellowship, and to sharing in meals (including the Lord's Supper), and to prayer.

43 A deep sense of awe came over them all, and the apostles performed many miraculous signs and wonders.

44 And all the believers met together in one place and shared everything they had.

45 They sold their property and possessions and shared the money with those in need.

46 They worshiped together at the Temple each day, met in homes for the Lord's Supper, and shared their meals with great joy and generosity—

47 all the while praising God and enjoying the goodwill of all the people. And each day the Lord added to their fellowship those who were being saved.

The People, Places, and Times

Pentecost. The Old Testament Feast of Weeks, which occurred on the fiftieth day (seven weeks) after Passover, is called the Pentecost in Greek (meaning "fifty"). A harvest festival, it marked the beginning of the time when the people brought their offerings of firstfruits. Leviticus 23:15–21 provides the most detailed account of the ritual observed during the feast. The observance is also known as the Feast of Ingathering (Exodus 23:16) and Day of Firstfruits (Numbers 28:26).

For the church, Pentecost has become a time to celebrate God's bestowal of the gift of the Spirit. It celebrates the birth of the New Testament church when thousands were filled with God's Spirit, the Gospel was proclaimed to every nation, and the first missionaries were anointed for service.

Background

The events in our lesson today take place after Jesus had appeared to the apostles and specifically instructed to wait for the promised Holy Spirit, which would be given to them so they might have effective witnessing. In obedience to Jesus' command, the apostles went to the upper room in Jerusalem and devoted themselves to prayer and supplication.

At-A-Glance

1. The Call to Community (Acts 2:32–33)
2. The Community Forms (vv. 37–43)
3. The Community Grows (vv. 44–47)

In Depth

1. The Call to Community (Acts 2:32–33)

Peter has been giving his audience the full story of God's history-spanning plan of salvation. He concludes with the exciting news, only 50 days old: Jesus Christ is risen, and ascended to glory, power, and honor. The Father gave Him the Spirit to pour out on His followers. This is the explanation for the speaking in tongues that had astonished everyone.

In this explanation, we see that the very basis of Christianity is grounded in community between the Persons of the Trinity. Each has a role, each affirms the others' powers. It is a communion of love that naturally calls others to join in its love.

What is your response to hearing the Good News of vv. 32–33?

2. The Community Forms (vv. 37–43)

After listening to Peter's convicting message, the Scriptures affirm that the people were ready for a change in their lives (v. 37). In essence, they tell Peter, "Whatever that is you have, we want it in our lives today." The apostle tells the people that all they have to do to receive God's power is repent of their sins, receive Jesus Christ as their Savior, and they will receive the precious Holy Spirit.

Many people believe that Peter's words were only applicable to the people whom he addressed. But Peter makes it clear that the promise of God's power is available to all who would believe in Jesus Christ throughout this age ("unto you, and to your children") and the age to come ("to all that are afar off, even as many as the LORD our God shall call").

The Holy Spirit's presence and power for the believer did not cease at Pentecost (Acts 8:5; 10:44–46). The Holy Spirit is the birthright of every true born-again believer in Christ (Joel 2:28; Matthew 3:11; Luke 24:49).

Those in the crowd whose hearts had been "pricked" by Peter's words accepted his call to repentance and were baptized that same day. On the birthday of the New Testament church, 3,000 people were converted to Christ and formed the first Christian community. Once the people had received Peter's word, they continued steadfastly in the apostle's doctrine. It is evident that the people needed to be taught how to live for God and how to effect change in the lives of their community, and they were willing to sit at the apostles' feet to feast on the Word of God.

What keeps the modern church from such diligent fellowship and discipleship in Christ?

3. The Community Grows (vv. 44–47)

The 3,000 new converts joined together with the original 120 believers (Acts 1:15) to form a community of believers who "had all things [in] common" (2:44; 4:32). This meant that everyone in the community was ready and willing to sacrifice for the good of the whole. They shared a commonality of participation, prayer, and purpose. They regarded their material blessings as a means of being a blessing to others. All their possessions, talents, and time were dedicated to furthering the mission of the Church and meeting the needs of the brothers and sisters.

The group continued to meet daily in the Temple and at various homes after the services to share meals and companionship. The table of fellowship provided members of the early church with an opportunity to gather together in small groups and discuss the day's teachings.

As the church was faithful in its mission, God demonstrated His faithfulness to the church.

Not only did God continuously provide for the needs of His people, He "added to the church daily such as should be saved" (Acts 2:47). The church did its job, and God did His.

What helped the early church grow so quickly?

Search the Scriptures

1. The church took on the responsibility of meeting the material needs of some of its people. How did they finance this ministry and how did they determine what a person received (Acts 2:45)?

2. What words and/or phrases in Acts 2:47 demonstrate the love and unity among the new Christians?

Discuss the Meaning

1. The church assumed the responsibility of meeting the needs of its less fortunate members. Should our modern-day churches assume this responsibility? If so, how should this ministry be funded? Should this ministry be more than just a "giveaway" program? If so, what programs would you suggest?

2. Lifestyle and active evangelism were key elements of the early church. Do you believe that every Christian is called to active evangelism, or are some people called on just to let the light of their lives shine?

Liberating Lesson

During the reconstruction period and through the period of Jim Crow segregation, the church was the spiritual, social, and political center of the Black community. In modern times, the church has become far less influential. What are some of the social and political factors that may have contributed to this decline? What are some of the implications of the church's decline in influence? What can the church do to improve its relevance to Black society? To society in general?

Application for Activation

Spend some time this week contemplating the lives of the early Christians. Think about their devotion to learning doctrine, their commitment to the church, and the willing sacrifices they made for each other. Ask God to point out areas where you and your church may need to improve. Then determine to work on those areas. Be prepared to share your experiences with the class next week.

Follow the Spirit

What God wants me to do:

_____

_____

_____

_____

Remember Your Thoughts

Special insights I have learned:

_____

_____

_____

_____

More Light on the Text

Acts 2:32–33, 37–47

Acts 2:32 This Jesus hath God raised up, whereof we all are witnesses. 33 Therefore being by the right hand of God exalted, and having received of the Father the promise of the Holy Ghost, he hath shed forth this, which ye now see and hear.

Peter's long discourse (vv. 14–33) has all been to explain "this, which ye now see and hear": the

miracle of the disciples speaking in tongues at the Temple while celebrating the Pentecost with Jews from around the world. When asked what was happening, the outspoken disciple took the opportunity to explain the entire Gospel message to the crowd, culminating in Jesus' resurrection and ascension. Peter remembers Jesus' promise to send the Spirit on them after His ascension and accurately recognizes this as the fulfillment of that promise.

37 Now when they heard this, they were pricked in their heart, and said unto Peter and to the rest of the apostles, Men and brethren, what shall we do?

The audience for Peter's sermon is deeply affected by his message. The Bible reports that "they were pricked in their heart." In Greek, the word *katenugeso* (kah-teh-noo-**GEH**-so) translates as "to sting sharply, stun, or smite." The audience was full of remorse at the gravity of the wickedness committed by the crucifixion of the Messiah, and their blindness and inability to recognize Him. The sin of rejecting and crucifying Jesus was great, yet Peter's words held out hope; so the question, "What shall we do?" undoubtedly means, "What shall we do to be saved?" This is the first time that the most important question ever asked was expressed and the first time it was ever answered so clearly.

38 Then Peter said unto them, Repent, and be baptized every one of you in the name of Jesus Christ for the remission of sins, and ye shall receive the gift of the Holy Ghost.

Peter explains the appropriate response to the Gospel: they must repent of their sins and turn to God. The verb "repent" (Gk. *metanoeo*, meh-tah-no-**EH**-oh) means to change one's mental attitude. The call to repentance, which is Peter's basic and primary demand, requires a complete change of mind and attitude about Jesus. It is an essential element in the proclamation of the

45

Gospel. People have frequently attempted to add additional conditions and works to God's requirements. The fact remains that salvation is a total work of the triune God (Father, Son, and Holy Spirit), and there is no additional effort that we can add to re-make God's plan or provision. Salvation is strictly by grace through faith. The only way to have a personal relationship with God is to accept the provision He offers. There is no "plan B."

Peter called on them to visibly demonstrate their repentance by receiving baptism, the sign of the New Covenant (cf. 13:24; 18:25; 19:3ff; Mark 1:4). They must be baptized in the name of the very person they had previously rejected. This would be a clear token of their repentance and of their faith in Him. Submitting to baptism was a humbling experience since Jews regarded baptism as necessary for Gentile converts only.

Baptism does not add anything to our salvation. It does not wash away sin or help to make us more worthy of the gift God has already given us. Rather, we partake of this ordinance out of love and obedience to Christ. Remember, salvation is a complete and total work of God.

The word "baptize" comes from the Greek word *baptizomai* (bap-**TEED**-zo-my), which means "to dip" or "submerge." When we are baptized, we are indicating to all who witness the event that we identify with Christ in His death, burial, and resurrection. When we go under the water, it represents a death to our old lifestyle independent of Christ. Being raised out of the water is indicative of rising to a new life of submission to Jesus Christ. We are raised to a new way of thinking and being.

Then they would receive two free gifts from God: the remission of their sins and the gift of the Holy Spirit. The "gift" of the Holy Spirit must be distinguished from the "gifts" of the Holy Spirit. The gift of the Holy Spirit is the Spirit Himself given by the Father through the Son. The gifts of the Holy Spirit are the

spiritual abilities that the Spirit distributes as He wills (1 Corinthians 12:11). The Holy Spirit is a gift from God who brings the church to life, furthers its growth, and links its members collectively and individually with Christ and with one another (cf. Acts 2:43–47).

39 For the promise is unto you, and to your children, and to all that are afar off, even as many as the LORD our God shall call.

God had placed no limitations on His offer. Redemption is for all of humanity not just for the 3,000 who responded. Rather, the promise of the Holy Spirit was for them and their children and for all who were far off (Jews and Gentiles included). The promise was extended to those who were present on the Day of Pentecost, to their contemporaries, and to their descendants as well. It was to both the people of Jerusalem and to those of distant lands (cf. Acts 1:8; Isaiah 57:19; Joel 2:32). Everyone God calls to Himself through Christ receives both gifts. Those who call upon the name of the Lord are those whom He has called to Himself (cf. Joel 2:32). God has made His promises available to their descendants and all future generations.

40 And with many other words did he testify and exhort, saying, Save yourselves from this untoward generation.

The phrase "with many other words" indicates that this was not the end of Peter's sermon. Peter both warned and pleaded with his audience. The essence of his warnings and pleadings was, "Save yourselves from this untoward (Gk. *skolios*, sko-lee-**OCE**) generation," a generation that was perverse, and morally crooked (cf. Luke 9:41; 11:29; Deuteronomy 32:5; 1 Thessalonians 1:10). The audience would have to change from a corrupt generation to a new community. By repenting, they would belong to the remnant of the righteous and save themselves from the perverse generation. Peter's words reflect the conviction of the disciples that they formed the faithful remnant of Israel. God's wrath would fall upon the faithless people of Israel (1 Thessalonians 1:10).

Peter exhorts his audience to reject the corruption of those who denied the truth about Jesus. This passage is particularly sobering for our generation, where so many wrong things (abortion, bigotry, homosexuality, pornography, fornication, etc.) are justified as "lifestyle alternatives." As Christians, our attitudes and actions must be consistent with the principles and commandments of God's Word: faithfulness, generosity, justice for the downtrodden.

41 Then they that gladly received his word were baptized: and the same day there were added unto them about three thousand souls.

Large numbers of people gladly received Peter's message, repented, and were baptized. Three thousand were added to their number that day. The growth of the church is regularly noted throughout Acts. Those who received redemption in Christ were baptized. The converts were instant in their obedience to the command to be baptized. Many were travelers visiting Jerusalem for Pentecost. Some returned to their own countries as baptized Christians, thus furthering the spread of the Gospel.

42 And they continued stedfastly in the apostles' doctrine and fellowship, and in breaking of bread, and in prayers.

The four foundations on which the early church was built included the following:

1. The apostles' "doctrine" (Gk. *didache*, dee-dah-**KAY**), or teaching. The apostles were not inventing their own "doctrines," per se, but teaching the facts of Jesus' ministry, His works, and His words as recorded later in the Gospels. They also included constant exposition of Old Testament prophecies as they related to Jesus.

The New Testament is the final form of the teaching of the apostles. We must study it and submit to its authority.

2. "Fellowship" (Gk. *koinonia*, koy-no-**NEE**-ah) comes from the word koinos (koy-**NOCE**), which means "common." It indicates a relation between individuals that involves an active participation in a common interest. It also has the meaning of generous participation or giving of oneself to one another (cf. 2 Corinthians 8:4; 9:13). The early disciples remained constant in fellowship. When the church underwent systematic persecution, fellowship was also a means of solidarity and survival. Their fellowship was not only a sense of belonging to a new community; it was also the practical expression of the fellowship of the Spirit through the sharing of personal possessions. Their fellowship is expressed in what they shared—their common share in God (2 Corinthians 13:14)—and in what they shared—what they gave as well as what they received (cf. Acts 2:44–45; 4:32–37).

3. Their fellowship was expressed not only in caring for one another but in the "breaking of bread." The breaking of bread here denotes something more than the ordinary partaking of meals together. It is a reference to the regular observance of Jesus' breaking of bread at His last meal with the disciples (Luke 24:35; 1 Corinthians 11:23ff; Acts 20:7). Jews saw a religious significance in all meals. Jesus often thanked God while breaking bread (Luke 9:16, 22:19, 24:30); this form of fellowship was also, then, a form of worship.

4. "Prayers" (Gk. *proseuche*, pros-yoo-**KHAY**) are mentioned on equal grammatical footing as doctrine and the others. Praying is just as important to the Christian life as meeting together and learning the Scriptures. Prayer meetings were in homes as well as public prayer services in the Temple court and synagogues (cf. Acts 2:46; 3:1; 12:5, 12).

The new church's collaboration involves cooperating to accomplish the work of the Gospel, ensuring each other's success, praying together, sharing meals, and observing the Lord's Supper. This verse emphasizes the important disciplines of learning, fellowship, prayer, and communion. These disciplines are vital to our spiritual growth and maturity. No Christian should neglect them.

43 And fear came upon every soul: and many wonders and signs were done by the apostles.

The word "fear" (Gk. *phobos*, **FOE**-boce) denotes awe, not terror. A reverential fear of God is critical in helping Christians walk according to godly principles. The verb "came" (Gk. *ginomai*, **GEH**-no-my) is used here to describe something happening again and again (continuously and habitually). The people were in renewed awe of the visible power of God at work through the disciples.

In this situation, the fear was felt by all of Jerusalem, giving the infant Church time to establish a tradition of unity and holiness. Jerusalem was so overwhelmed by the events and acts of the apostles that favor was bestowed, giving the disciples time to multiply and establish themselves before the inevitable tide of opposition from the established Church and Roman Empire. The miracles the apostles performed were done to confirm the Word, and the apostles' teaching, as Jesus had promised (Mark 16:20).

44 And all that believed were together, and had all things common; 45 And sold their possessions and goods, and parted them to all men, as every man had need.

In addition to other expressions of fellowship (v. 42), the disciples were together with a deep sense of their unity in Christ. They gave up their private property and held "all things common." The word "common" (Gk. *koinos*, koy-**NOCE**) denotes sharing their possessions, which was an expression of their fellowship.

These verses give a picture of Christian unity. This was not communism, in the contemporary sense. Nor was it communal living. It was simply Christian charity. All of the apostles and their converts realized the importance of developing and nurturing the faith. Some who were not from Jerusalem ran out of money, so those who were "local" did what they could to make it feasible for these converts to remain nearby. The example and teachings of Jesus made it easy for the believers to share among themselves.

Property was not regarded as private, but as held in trust from God to be donated for the common good. Those with "possessions" (Gk. *ktenos*, **KTAY**-noce, meaning "land") as well as those who had more portable "goods" (Gk. *huparxis*, **HOO**-park-sees, literally meaning "wealth" or "movable" possessions) began to sell their belongings and divide the proceeds among the members of the community according to their individual needs. This voluntary sharing of possessions was based on the deep sense of fellowship and unity of the Spirit that was exceptionally active. The attempt to maintain communal life was plagued with serious difficulties as soon as the flame began to burn a little lower (Acts 4:32–5:11).

46 And they, continuing daily with one accord in the temple, and breaking bread from house to house, did eat their meat with gladness and singleness of heart,

The daily practice of the disciples involved meeting in the Temple for public worship and witness. They also met in each other's homes for fellowship meals and the breaking of bread in accordance with Jesus' ordinance. They were doing these practices regularly. The expression "with one accord" (Gk. *homothumadon*, hoe-moe-**THOO**-mah-**DON**) means in "unanimity," with the same desires.

48

Within the fellowship, there was a spirit of joy and generosity of heart. The believers are described as having "gladness" (Gk. *agalliasis*, ah-gah-**LEE**-ah-sees, which means "extreme joy") and "singleness of heart" (Gk. *aphelotes kardia*, ah-feh-**LOW**-tace kar-**DEE**-ah) literally meaning "in exultation and sincerity of heart" (cf. Galatians 5:22). Their Spirit-filled worship was a joyful celebration of the mighty acts of God through Jesus.

47 Praising God, and having favour with all the people. And the Lord added to the church daily such as should be saved.

The believers enjoyed great popularity and favor with all the people because of the quality of their fellowship, and they ascribed all glory to God. The disciples were not so preoccupied with studying the Word of God and fellowshipping that they forgot about bringing the Gospel to others. The Gospel was spreading through the witness of the disciples by the power of the Holy Spirit. At this juncture, there was no persecution or opposition. Their numbers were constantly increasing as more people were added by the Lord to the new community.

The Lord added to the church, no doubt, through the preaching and the impressive life example of the disciples. The verb "add" (Gk. *prostithemi*, pros-**TEE**-thay-mee) here means "kept adding." The increase was not sporadic; it was continuous and daily. Their worship and proclamation were the natural overflow of hearts full of the Holy Spirit.

Sources:
Henry, Matthew. *Matthew Henry's Commentary on the Whole Bible: New Modern Edition.* Vols. 1-6. Peabody, MA: Hendrickson Publishers, Inc., 2009.
Strong, James. *The New Strong's Exhaustive Concordance of the Bible.* Nashville, TN: Thomas Nelson, 2003.
Thayer, Joseph Henry. *A Greek-English Lexicon of the New Testament.* New York: American Book Company, 1889.

Say It Correctly

Triune. try-YUNE.
Sporadic. spur-AH-dik.

Daily Bible Readings

MONDAY
A Priestly Kingdom, a Holy Nation
(Exodus 19:1–8)

TUESDAY
Worship God Alone
(Exodus 20:1–6)

WEDNESDAY
When Kindred Live in Unity
(Psalms 133)

THURSDAY
Praise in the Heavenly Community
(Revelation 4)

FRIDAY
The Day of Pentecost
(Acts 2:1–12)

SATURDAY
Jesus Is Lord and Messiah
(Acts 2:22–36)

SUNDAY
A Community of Praise
(Acts 2:37–47)

Teaching Tips

Words You Should Know

A. Serve (v. 2) 'abad (Heb.)—To serve or worship

B. Truth (v. 5) 'emunah (Heb.)—Truthfulness, faithfulness

Teacher Preparation

Unifying Principle—Only You. Life provides us with many opportunities to praise and find delight in people and things. How do we decide what has more value and is more worthy of our praise? Psalm 100 highlights that God is the object of the earth's praise and joy.

A. Read the Bible Background and Devotional Reading.

B. Pray for your students and lesson clarity.

C. Read the lesson Scripture in multiple translations.

O—Open the Lesson

A. Begin the class with prayer.

B. Play a song about being devoted to another person such as "Only You," "Hopelessly Devoted," or "Dedicated to the One I Love." Discuss the pros and cons of being totally devoted to another human being.

C. Have the students read the Aim for Change and the In Focus story.

D. Ask students how events like those in the story weigh on their hearts and how they can view these events from a faith perspective.

P—Present the Scriptures

A. Read the Focal Verses and discuss the Background and The People, Places, and Times sections.

B. Have the class share what Scriptures stand out for them and why, with particular emphasis on today's themes.

E—Explore the Meaning

A. Use In Depth or More Light on the Text to facilitate a deeper discussion of the lesson text.

B. Pose the questions in Search the Scriptures and Discuss the Meaning.

C. Discuss the Liberating Lesson and Application for Activation sections.

N—Next Steps for Application

A. Summarize the value of knowing God loves them.

B. End class with a commitment to pray that they continually acknowledge Yahweh as the ultimate authority in their lives.

Worship Guide

For the Superintendent or Teacher
Theme: Make a Joyful Noise
Song: "He Has Made Me Glad"

Make a Joyful Noise

Bible Background • PSALM 100
Printed Text • PSALM 100 | Devotional Reading • PSALM 66:1-7

—————— Aim for Change ——————

By the end of this lesson, we will UNDERSTAND why and how God is to be worshiped, as found in Psalm 100, APPRECIATE that God is worthy to be praised, and CREATE a psalm of praise for the Lord.

—————— In Focus ——————

As Noah strode forward from the stadium tunnel onto the football field, he resisted the urge to look for his parents in the stands. He needed to put his full focus on the choreography and his positioning in the band formations. The crowd was too big for him to be able to spot Mom and Dad anyway.

He knew exactly where they would be, anyway—in tier 2, section 34, their favorite spot. They would be singing and cheering along with the marching band in the halftime show. Proud alums of the school, Mom and Dad never missed a game and were more than thrilled that Noah chose to go to the same college where they had met and married.

Noah's childhood lessons turned his musical interest in into a passion. His college studies broadened his understanding of how music was constructed, but he already knew instinctively how music worked—how it can change one's mood and buoy the spirit. And there was hardly a greater joy than being on the field with over 200 band members, all polished and precise. The visual elements of that week's show dove-tailed perfectly with the songs.

The drum major blew her whistle, and Noah lifted his trumpet. Then the snare drummers tapped out the roll-off for their first number. Noah felt a happy smile welling up inside him as the players strutted across the field and the crowd—40,000 strong—roared with excitement.

Why is music integral to so many public events and celebrations?

—————— Keep in Mind ——————

"Know ye that the LORD he is God: it is he that hath made us, and not we ourselves; we are his people, and the sheep of his pasture." (Psalm 100:3, KJV)

"Acknowledge that the LORD is God! He made us, and we are his. We are his people, the sheep of his pasture." (Psalm 100:3, NLT)

Focal Verses

KJV

Psalm 100:1 Make a joyful noise unto the LORD, all ye lands.

2 Serve the LORD with gladness: come before his presence with singing.

3 Know ye that the LORD he is God: it is he that hath made us, and not we ourselves; we are his people, and the sheep of his pasture.

4 Enter into his gates with thanksgiving, and into his courts with praise: be thankful unto him, and bless his name.

5 For the LORD is good; his mercy is everlasting; and his truth endureth to all generations.

NLT

Psalm 100 A psalm of thanksgiving.

1 Shout with joy to the LORD, all the earth!

2 Worship the LORD with gladness. Come before him, singing with joy.

3 Acknowledge that the LORD is God! He made us, and we are his. We are his people, the sheep of his pasture.

4 Enter his gates with thanksgiving; go into his courts with praise. Give thanks to him and praise his name.

5 For the LORD is good. His unfailing love continues forever, and his faithfulness continues to each generation.

The People, Places, and Times

Gates and Courts. The gates and courts seem to be a reference to the First Temple and its complex built by Solomon (1 Kings 6). Yet there was not a true gate for the complex that could open or close. Instead, the gates seem to be a reference to entering the city of Jerusalem—the city in which the Lord chose to place His name.

Sheep. To this day sheep are a common animal in Israel. They are a commodity for their wool, and lambs are a commodity for their meat.

The simple nature of these flock animals allows them to be a useful analogy for human life in the Scriptures. In Psalm 77:20, the writer recognizes Moses as one who shepherded Israel. False shepherds—false leaders—abounded in Israel and took advantage of God's people (Ezekiel 34:1-6; Jeremiah 23:1-4). The people of Israel are God's flock of sheep who have leaders who fail to tend to them.

In Psalm 23, King David views himself as a sheep before God, his shepherd. More than in any other psalm, one sees here the care the Lord has for His sheep and the great privilege it is to be part of the flock under God's care.

What are some other ways we are like sheep and God is like a shepherd?

Background

Psalm 100 invites God's people to join together in worshiping the Lord. It is both a hymn—a liturgical psalm (or a call to worship)—and a kingship psalm. As is common in such psalms, the people gather in Zion ("gates" are a reference to the city), the city of the Great King.

Three times each year, all of Israel was commanded to gather and feast together (Exodus 34:23; Deuteronomy 16:16). The pilgrimages reminded Israel that they were the people of God united by their worship of the one true God. It also served as a reminder that they were looking forward to a day when they would meet God in Zion (Jerusalem) and enthrone Him as King forever. The pilgrimage made them long for their King, as did each call to come worship inside the gates of the Lord.

In what ways does your worship remind you of God's kingship?

At-A-Glance

1. The Call for All the Earth to Enter the
   Lord's Presence (Psalm 100:1)
2. Scenes of Celebration (vv. 2, 4)
3. Knowledge of the Greatness of God
   (vv. 3, 5)

In Depth

1. The Call for all the Earth to Enter the Lord's Presence (Psalm 100:1)

This psalm begins with a summons to worship: "Make a joyful noise… come … enter into his gates… [and] into his courts with praise." These are commands of exhortation, not imperatives. They are not part of the Law (e.g. "do not steal"). Yet the expectation is that the members of Israel will answer the summons with their presence.

The exhortation goes to Israel and the nations. The full earth receives this summons. No one was excluded from this call, just as no one is excluded from the call of the Gospel. This was an Old Covenant call to all to meet with the one true God. Many other psalms of this type have the same call for a corporate body to worship the Lord (e.g., Psalm 46; 95; 124; 135).

Why is it important to gather as a group to worship God instead of worshiping individually?

2. Scenes of Celebration (vv. 2, 4)

"Joyful noise," "gladness," "singing," "thanksgiving," "praise," "thankful," and "bless." The expectation was that the experience in the Temple would be a celebratory meeting with God. This would be a greater celebration than any post-election party for a winning candidate, or any ticker-tape parade for a national sports championship team. This is a call to celebrate the King of all.

Those coming would not need to wait on any musician or priest to worship. They themselves, having been exhorted to worship with specific commands.

3. Knowledge of the Greatness of God (vv. 3, 5)

"Know" (v. 3) is the motivation for the celebration in verses 1–2. We worship that we might know Him relationally. The call for Israel to worship was not detached from personal intimacy with God.

Likewise, "for" (v. 5) introduces the reason for the celebratory acts of verse 4: The Lord is good, His covenantal love is eternally secure, and He is faithful to His covenant people forever despite themselves. God's love and faithfulness are the most paired traits of God praised in the psalms. It is only in knowing God as Creator and Shepherd, as one always good toward us, that our individual hearts will be stirred to celebrate Him. When everyone who has this knowledge comes together to speak, sing, and learn of Him, a celebration of great magnitude should take place.

What characteristics of God draw you to worship Him?

Search the Scriptures

1. What does the psalm writer mean by "come before his presence" (v. 2)?

2. What is the Lord's "mercy" (v. 5) and what does it mean that this mercy is everlasting?

Discuss the Meaning

The Lord intends for worship of Him to begin before we get to His courts and gates. Yet we often are quite casual in our approach to our corporate worship gathering each week. How does our daily interaction with God contribute to how we approach our weekly gathering to Him?

Liberating Lesson

Because of the culture's emphasis on personal comfort and freedom, we carry a strong sense of personal autonomy with us into both our walk with God and our worship of Him. It is common for us to think worship is something that should be guided by preference or feelings rather than being guided by the Scriptures. However, it should not seem surprising that God would dictate to us how to worship Him. By following God's teachings in the psalms, we will worship in a way that honors Him rather than simply in a way that pleases ourselves.

Application for Activation

Make Saturday evening count by setting aside time to meditate on the Scripture to be preached the following morning (or a few verses of some psalms if the Sunday Scripture passage is unknown). Also try to go to bed early rather than late so that you will be rested enough to get to worship service long before it starts, and so that you can give your fullest bodily attention to worship without fatigue. Pray, too, for the morning service, for all who will participate in making the service honor the Lord, and for you and your family members' hearts to worship in spirit and in truth.

Follow the Spirit

What God wants me to do:

_____

_____

_____

_____

_____

_____

Remember Your Thoughts

Special insights I have learned:

_____

_____

_____

_____

_____

_____

More Light on the Text
Psalm 100

The very first piece of information that the writer gives us for deciphering this psalm occurs before the opening sentence. This psalm's title lets the audience know that this is a psalm of *todah* (Heb. toe-**DAH**), which means praise or thanksgiving. There are various types of psalms. There are psalms of lament like Psalm 42. There are royal psalms like Psalm 2. Psalm 100, however, in no uncertain terms, is a psalm of praise and thanksgiving. The title line sets the tone for how to read the psalm and gives a glimpse into why it is one of the favorite psalms for inviting people to worship God, even in contemporary times. It is a psalm of praise.

1 Make a joyful noise unto the LORD, all ye lands.

"Make a joyful noise" (Heb. *rua'*, roo-**AH**) could insinuate that the psalmist is more interested in sound than substance. That is not the case. *Rua'* can mean to shout in anticipation or in celebration of victory. Only in the Psalms is it translated as "make a joyful noise." In other passages in the Old Testament, the texture of the word is clearer. An example of this is Joshua 6 at the battle of Jericho. After the

Israelites march around the wall seven times on the seventh day, Joshua gives the people instructions to *rua'*, because the Lord has given them the city. This shout was in anticipation of a military victory. It was also in celebration of a victory because Joshua announces in advance that the Lord has already given them the city. (Joshua 6:16). The psalm is saying more than make some noise, but the psalmist is calling the audience to simultaneously celebrate and anticipate God's victory.

2 Serve the LORD with gladness: come before his presence with singing.

The psalmist next exhorts the audience to "serve" (Heb., *'abad*, aw-**BOD**) the Lord with gladness. This Hebrew word is from a root meaning slave or servant. Some translations interpret this term as "worship" (NLT). That is in part because this word is often associated with the Levites and priests who perform service in the Tabernacle and Temple. They were God's property, and their life was committed to doing God's sacred work. The psalmist exhorts people of all lands to commit their whole selves to God, not out of obligation but in gladness.

The language of slavery should not be taken lightly though. Images of slavery and serving must always be considered cautiously in the West, in America, and especially among Black communities whose history involves chattel slavery. In a world where sex trafficking and immigrant exploitation are modern forms of slavery, we cannot be careless when we read or hear words about slaving, serving, and owning human bodies. Christians must reject all forms of humans owning or exploiting other humans for their own benefit.

In this exhortation, the psalmist joins a tradition that juxtaposes the Israelites' cultural heritage of serving the abusive Egyptians against serving Almighty God. Worshipers understand that the only One who owns them is God; they are not responsible to any other authority's demands on their life. The psalmist's call to serve the Lord with gladness is not only a reminder about one's disposition but also of one's position. God's people are not to be subservient to others, whether kings or gods. Rather they are to recognize that they are God's property and are to serve the Lord with gladness.

Hebrew poetry often involves couplets where the second line reemphasizes themes from the first line. The second line of verse two is an invitation to come into God's presence with singing, which reminds worshipers to acknowledge to whom they belong. They are to come before God's "presence," or more literally His "face." When worshipers are faced with God's face they recognize their unworthiness.

At the same time, they can break out into joyful, triumphal "singing" (Heb. *renanah*, ruh-naw-**NAW**), because that radically other, holy God has given God's people victory. They sing a song of victory because they have a relationship with the divine. They are owned by One who cares for them. Often ownership may not seem like something to sing victoriously about. However, when it refers to God, it is worth singing about, because God does not own the worshiper so that God can take advantage of them. God owns the worshiper so that they can share in God's victory, and so that the worshiper has a place to belong even when the world and its exploitative systems want to make them feel like they do not. Belonging to God means triumphing over enemies that attempt to destroy the worshiper. This leads to coming before God's face with a song of victory.

3 Know ye that the LORD he is God: it is he that hath made us, and not we ourselves; we are his people, and the sheep of his pasture.

The word for "know" is *yada'* (Heb. yaw-**DAH**), which can also mean "to recognize."

One recognizing something is not what makes the recognized thing true. It was true even before they recognized. That is the case for the statement that "the LORD he is God."

This statement is particularly powerful because when Lord is rendered in capitals, the Hebrew reads with the sacred name of God: Yahweh. It is the self-existing God's sacred name revealed to Moses at the burning bush when God tells him that "I AM THAT I AM" (Exodus 3:14).

The word for "God" in our psalm here is *'elohim* (Heb. eh-lo-**HEEM**), which is the term used by cultures all around Israel to refer to their "gods." Even though this word is plural, Yahweh is singular. The Israelites have no pantheon, no long list of gods to appease. They only have Yahweh. This is the chief of all doctrinal statements in Judaism, the Shema, found in Deuteronomy 6:4—"Hear O Israel, the LORD is your God."

None of the so-called gods of other nations created humanity. And none of the other gods continue to lovingly care for the world. Many cultures speak of gods who make humans but then do not care for them, and even mistreat them. Yahweh, on the other hand, takes humanity as His own people and gently shepherds them in pleasant pastureland.

Worshipers know that they are God's people because they recognize their sheep-like tendencies: misdirection, vulnerability, and short-sightedness. The Lord, however, provides shepherd-like guidance, protection from enemies, and a pasture that the worshipers do not have to look for. Worshipers know from experience that God has made them and that the Self-existing One has provided for all of their needs. This type of knowledge goes deeper than intellect and resonates with the soul.

4 Enter into his gates with thanksgiving, and into his courts with praise: be thankful unto him, and bless his name.

The themes of victory resurface in this verse and bring us back to the very beginning of this psalm. Entering into God's gates with "thanksgiving" brings us back to the title of the psalm. The same word *todah* is used again here as the gift that the worshipers bring with them through the gates. This reminds us that the war shout was a shout either to anticipate victory or to celebrate victory. It seems that at least by this point in the psalm, the worshipers should be in a place of celebrating God's previous victories. They are implored to give thanks to the Lord. They are not told to wait to praise until they receive special favor while in the court. They are instructed to enter with thanksgiving and to go in with praise to bless God's name.

Their praise or blessing of God involves saying positive things about God. The word *barak* (Heb. baw-**ROCK**) or bless often involves a superior speaking highly of their inferior or gifting their inferior something that they do not have. One may wonder how this can apply to God. The earth is the Lord's and the fullness thereof (Psalm 24). However, what God does not have, until we give it, is our praise and blessing. Hence, the psalmist implores the worshiper to bless God's name.

5 For the LORD is good; his mercy is everlasting; and his truth endureth to all generations.

We bless God by saying about God what God has already said about Himself. This manifests in the two last claims of the final verse. The first statement that "the LORD is good" is elaborated on by the final two statements about God.

The goodness of God is revealed in God's name. When God revealed His glory to Moses (Exodus 34:6), God introduced Himself as, "The LORD, The LORD God, merciful and gracious, longsuffering, and abundant in goodness and truth." Therefore, a portion of the formula for blessing God is to say what God has said about

Himself: God is merciful. God has everlasting mercy or *khesed* (**KHE**-sed), which is often translated as lovingkindness or unfailing love. We can bless God by celebrating God's *khesed* to us, which manifests by God forgiving us when we do not deserve it, or being patient with us when we are taking our time, for being just when we or others need to learn from our mistakes. We are loved unconditionally because God's love is unfailing. We bless God because God has blessed us.

The psalmist also blesses the Lord by saying that God's "truth endureth to all generations." There are parallels to that in Exodus 34 as well. Although the generations change, God remains the same. Some translators interpret *'emunah* (eh-mu-**NAH**) as faithfulness, which attempts to grasp the same notion as "truth." The idea is that God's faithfulness is so sure that it is the ultimate truth. God is so reliable that people do not have to and cannot separate truth from God's faithfulness. It is so trustworthy that it is timeless and universally applicable.

God is faithful. God's faithfulness is not conditional, based on each generation, but it endures. It is not rushing to find others who are more qualified; it is resilient from generation to generation. Worshipers bless God by acknowledging the traits of God that are constant and therefore, bigger, larger, and more superior than they are. Worshipers only have a glimpse because they cannot even comprehend the full view of God's mercy and love, which have existed for generations before us and will exist generations afterward. Saying what God has said about Himself already puts words into worshipers' mouths that they cannot even fully understand. Therefore, it is difficult to say anything higher about God than what He already says about Himself.

Sources:
Henry, Matthew. *Matthew Henry's Commentary on the Whole Bible: New Modern Edition.* Vols. 1-6. Peabody, MA: Hendrickson Publishers, Inc., 2009.
Strong, James. *The New Strong's Exhaustive Concordance of the Bible.* Nashville, TN: Thomas Nelson, 2003.
Thayer, Joseph Henry. *A Greek-English Lexicon of the New Testament.* New York: American Book Company, 1889.

Say It Correctly

Shema. shuh-MAH.

Daily Bible Readings

MONDAY
Praise the Rock of Our Salvation
(Psalm 95)

TUESDAY
Stones Shout Out!
(Luke 19:28, 36-40)

WEDNESDAY
Indescribable and Glorious Joy
(1 Peter 1:3-9)

THURSDAY
Sing to God a New Song
(Psalm 98)

FRIDAY
A Continuous Sacrifice of Praise
(Hebrews 13:12-16)

SATURDAY
Rejoice in God's Mighty Rule
(Psalm 66:1-7)

SUNDAY
Enter God's Courts with Praise
(Psalm 100)

Teaching Tips

Words You Should Know

A. Refuge (Psalm 1:9) *misgab* (Heb.)—A high place, especially a secure height, like a high wall or fortress

B. Humble (v. 12) *'anav* (Heb.)—The poor, needy, and marginalized

Teacher Preparation

Unifying Principle—Ball of Confusion. People choose to praise and find joy in things that may not be the best for them. Why do we choose things that may harm us or others? Psalm 9 proclaims that God will bring justice, and this is cause for our joyful praise.

A. Read the Bible Background and Devotional Reading.

B. Pray for your students and lesson clarity.

C. Read the lesson Scripture in multiple translations.

O—Open the Lesson

A. Begin the class with prayer.

B. Divide the class into teams to debate the proposition, "God's justice is not accomplished in this present age."

C. Have the students read the Aim for Change and the In Focus story.

D. Ask students how events like those in the story weigh on their hearts and how they can view these events from a faith perspective.

P—Present the Scriptures

A. Read the Focal Verses and discuss the Background and The People, Places, and Times sections.

B. Have the class share what Scriptures stand out for them and why, with particular emphasis on today's themes.

E—Explore the Meaning

A. Use In Depth or More Light on the Text to facilitate a deeper discussion of the lesson text.

B. Pose the questions in Search the Scriptures and Discuss the Meaning.

C. Discuss the Liberating Lesson and Application for Activation sections.

N—Next Steps for Application

A. Summarize the value of understanding God's judgment as an ongoing process, not just as an event of the last days.

B. End class with a commitment to pray for God's presence with them when they seek justice for others.

Worship Guide

For the Superintendent or Teacher
Theme: Praise God for Justice and
Righteousness
Song: "We Shall Overcome"

Praise God for Justice and Righteousness

Bible Background • PSALM 9; ECCLESIASTES 3:16–22
Printed Text • PSALM 9:1–12 | Devotional Reading • DEUTERONOMY 10:17–21

Aim for Change

By the end of this lesson, we will CONTRAST God's justice with humanity's injustices, VALUE how God listens and responds to our needs, and PRACTICE God's justice in difficult situations.

In Focus

For years, a group of concerned residents in Rucker Heights fought to remove their complacent village president and his cronies. These officials were re-elected every cycle because no one was willing to put themselves on the line to run against them.

However, this time around, the people had enough. Elder Timothy Shields convened a group of homeowners, generating a groundswell of community engagement and activism. From Elder Shields' example, other leaders emerged so that for the next election cycle, they came together, raised money, and campaigned for change. The president and his cronies had deep pockets, but it was no match for the will of the people. Elder Shields galvanized the community.

As a result, not only did the community rid themselves of an ineffective board of trustees, but they also saw a turnover in leadership for their school boards. The people took back their community, and surrounding communities welcomed the opportunity to partner for the growth of the region.

The media took notice of the change in the Rucker Heights community. In an interview, Elder Shields said, "God is a God of justice. When people with one heart and agenda come together, there is nothing we cannot accomplish with His help. It was a long hard road, but we knew this day would come. We had to be the change we wanted to see."

Why is it important for Christians to lead others in believing God's justice will prevail?

Keep in Mind

"And he shall judge the world in righteousness, he shall minister judgment to the people in uprightness." (Psalm 9:8, KJV)

"He will judge the world with justice and rule the nations with fairness."
(Psalm 9:8, NLT)

Focal Verses

KJV **Psalm 9:1** I will praise thee, O LORD, with my whole heart; I will shew forth all thy marvellous works.

2 I will be glad and rejoice in thee: I will sing praise to thy name, O thou most High.

3 When mine enemies are turned back, they shall fall and perish at thy presence.

4 For thou hast maintained my right and my cause; thou satest in the throne judging right.

5 Thou hast rebuked the heathen, thou hast destroyed the wicked, thou hast put out their name for ever and ever.

6 O thou enemy, destructions are come to a perpetual end: and thou hast destroyed cities; their memorial is perished with them.

7 But the LORD shall endure for ever: he hath prepared his throne for judgment.

8 And he shall judge the world in righteousness, he shall minister judgment to the people in uprightness.

9 The LORD also will be a refuge for the oppressed, a refuge in times of trouble.

10 And they that know thy name will put their trust in thee: for thou, LORD, hast not forsaken them that seek thee.

11 Sing praises to the LORD, which dwelleth in Zion: declare among the people his doings.

12 When he maketh inquisition for blood, he remembereth them: he forgetteth not the cry of the humble.

NLT **Psalm 9** For the choir director: A psalm of David, to be sung to the tune "Death of the Son."

1 I will praise you, LORD, with all my heart; I will tell of all the marvelous things you have done.

2 I will be filled with joy because of you. I will sing praises to your name, O Most High.

3 My enemies retreated; they staggered and died when you appeared.

4 For you have judged in my favor; from your throne you have judged with fairness.

5 You have rebuked the nations and destroyed the wicked; you have erased their names forever.

6 The enemy is finished, in endless ruins; the cities you uprooted are now forgotten.

7 But the LORD reigns forever, executing judgment from his throne.

8 He will judge the world with justice and rule the nations with fairness.

9 The LORD is a shelter for the oppressed, a refuge in times of trouble.

10 Those who know your name trust in you, for you, O LORD, do not abandon those who search for you.

11 Sing praises to the LORD who reigns in Jerusalem. Tell the world about his unforgettable deeds.

12 For he who avenges murder cares for the helpless. He does not ignore the cries of those who suffer.

The People, Places, and Times

Psalms. Music played an important role in the worship practices of ancient Israel. The psalms were Israel's hymns. Unlike most of our modern western poetry and songs which are written in rhyme or meter, Old Testament poetry and songs were based on a parallelism of thought in which the second (or succeeding) line(s) of poetry essentially restates, contrasts with, or progressively completes the first. All three forms of parallelism characterize the psalter.

Concerning authorship of the Psalms, the superscriptions ascribe 73 psalms to David, 12 to Asaph (a musically and prophetically gifted Levite), 10 to the sons of Korah (a musically gifted family), 2 to Solomon, 1 to Heman, 1 to Ethan, and 1 to Moses. Fifty psalms are anonymous. Biblical and historical references suggest that David, Hezekiah, and Ezra were each involved at different stages in collecting the psalms for corporate use in Jerusalem.

Background

The Psalms were the soundtrack of David's life, and he left them for generations to come to laud over the greatness of God (Psalm 145:4). Psalms 9 and 10 are considered one song, a single acrostic poem using every letter of the Hebrew alphabet, which is believed to support memorization. Together these two psalms express the highs, lows, and highs again of David's posture of trust in God's ability to execute power and justice. This particular psalm is not attributed to a specific event in David's life, but he uses it to lead the worship of the Most High God. David provides the tune for the psalm "to be sung to the tune 'Death of the Son,'" which is believed to be a popular composition of his day. This psalm, as several other psalmists also do in 54 other songs throughout the book, is specially dedicated to the choir director.

What songs do you sing to praise God's justice?

At-A-Glance

1. A Reason to Praise (Psalm 9:1–6)
2. A Reason to Believe (vv. 7–12)

In Depth

1. A Reason to Praise (Psalm 9:1–6)

Opening with adoration is a common theme in the psalms of David. David was a skillful musician and writer who spent intimate time in God's presence. In this hymnal expression of thanksgiving and praise, David opens by acknowledging God's power, which is how he ended the previous song (Psalm 8:9; 9:1–2). He will praise with his whole heart, declare all of His wonderful works, and make his boast in Him.

David then illustrates the activity of God on the earth and why God is to be praised. He experienced numerous victories that he declared were given by the hand of the Lord. In David's lifetime, after numerous battles, the nation of Israel gained prominence because of God's defense and David's submission. We can learn from David how God, in His righteous judgment, administers justice and defends what is right. David reminds his hearers that God upholds and defends His people against wickedness. God is so complete in dealing out vindication that He erases the very memory of those who come in opposition to His people.

How can you call to mind the activity of God in your life as an expression of praise and thanksgiving?

2. A Reason to Believe (vv. 7–12)

David magnifies that the Lord sits on the throne and that He is established forever in righteous judgment. As owner and possessor of the heavens and the earth (Psalm 24:1), God is the one qualified to decide how His creations should live. Further, David expresses that God, without partiality, executes justice toward all the people of the earth with honesty and integrity. He is a shelter for those experiencing trouble and oppression. Here is a promise Christians can stand on: God will answer those who seek after Him. We can trust God in His timing to bring an expected end when we come to Him in prayer and a believing heart (Jeremiah 29:12–13).

David calls on those assembled in worship to sing and proclaim God's activity and deeds, for He is tuned into their cry. The Lord vindicates those who are afflicted and will not forget those who caused harm to the ones He loves.

How can you use the Word of God as your reason to believe in God's timing to dispense justice?

Search the Scriptures

1. How does David approach God in worship and why is it important (Psalm 9:1–2)?

2. How does God rule the nations (vv. 7–8)?

3. How does God care for the troubled and oppressed (vv. 9, 12)?

Discuss the Meaning

1. As we reflect on the history of Black people in America, how did enslaved people hope in God's justice and righteousness to persevere through adversity?

2. What artifacts can we pass on to the next generation so that they trust in God's care for the oppressed and troubled?

Liberating Lesson

"Deep in my heart, I do believe, we shall overcome someday" was the mantra of the Civil Rights Movement. To overcome is not a one-time event, but an ongoing process of transformation. To actualize systemic and systematic change, each generation must pick up the mantle to move toward a just society.

David used our text and other psalms to remind the people of God's faithfulness, power, justice, and righteousness to keep them going in the times of opposition. He turns the people's attention to God's ability to deliver, for He sits on the throne administering justice to those who trust Him. The call to action for this generation and generations to come is to be God's hands and feet in fighting injustice for the long haul.

Application for Activation

Seek the heart of God for what He wants to do in your community. How can you, your church, or a team of community members reflect God's heart for the troubled and oppressed? Look for opportunities to provide someone or a group of people with hope in God's ability to administer justice on their behalf. You could meet a need, help solve a problem, or hold those in power accountable to be honorable in their decisions on behalf of many. Get involved in a civic or charitable effort that allows His power to work through you and bring Him glory.

Follow the Spirit

What God wants me to do:

_____

_____

_____

_____

Remember Your Thoughts

Special insights I have learned:

_____

_____

_____

_____

More Light on the Text
Psalm 9

For the choir director: A psalm of David, to be sung to the tune "Death of the Son."

Psalms 9 and 10 were originally one poem with each verse starting with a letter of the Hebrew alphabet. Some Hebrew manuscripts, the Septuagint (Greek translation of the Old Testament) and the Vulgate (Latin translation of the Christian Bible) put them as one single poem in one chapter, whereas the Hebrew text and the Protestant church separate Psalms 9 and 10. It brings a difference in numbering for Psalms 9–146 between translations based on the Vulgate and those based on the Hebrew text.

This psalm, and many others, begins with a title, which provides some information about the context of the song. Even though the information is original to the ancient manuscripts, the King James translation did not include them at first. The line above is from the New Living Translation. The phrase "for the choir director" occurs in 55 psalms and indicates the one the musical direction is intended for. The additional direction "to the tune 'Death of the Son'" is likely a catchphrase to highlight the tune of a popular song in which the psalm should be sung. Other psalms have similarly worded inscriptions presumably noting what tune should be used with the words (e.g., Psalm 22, 45, 60).

1 I will praise thee, O LORD, with my whole heart; I will shew forth all thy marvellous works.

The psalm starts with a thanksgiving to God. The sincerity of the psalmist's gratitude is expressed by the phrase "my whole heart." It indicates that the praise comes from the depth of his being. The Lord would blame some of His people for their lip service: honoring Him with their tongue while their heart is far from Him (Isaiah 29:13). Here David is genuinely expressing his gratefulness to the Lord.

This praise is a result of the wonders God has done for the psalmist. "Marvellous works" is a reference to the extraordinary acts of Yahweh on behalf of His people, Israel. In Exodus 15, the people of Israel sang the mighty deeds of the Lord because He overthrew the army of Pharaoh and parted the Red Sea. These mighty actions, and all other actions the Lord is doing on behalf of His people, must be proclaimed. Failure to do so is nothing other than ungratefulness.

2 I will be glad and rejoice in thee: I will sing praise to thy name, O thou most High.

The Lord's greatness and great works bring David gladness and joy. This leads to an expression of praise. The Hebrew term for "sing praise" means to "sing with accompaniment of instrument." Just like today's most joyous worship, Israel used music, dancing, and playing of instruments in their worship.

"Thy name" stands for God's character and actions, His reputation among the nations. It was used in corporate worship, during the sacrifice, in praise, blessing, court, writing, and war. Calling God "most High" depicts the universal rule of God. He is above all things and therefore above the enemies of the psalmist. And this is the reason for joy.

3 When mine enemies are turned back, they shall fall and perish at thy presence.

The psalmist gives his reasons for praising God (v. 3). The enemies of the psalmist turn their back in defeat after a confrontation. They stagger or stumble and die like soldiers who flee the battlefield confronted with the supremacy of their contender. The enemies must retreat at the presence of the Lord, which is a consuming fire for his enemies and the enemies of his people (Deuteronomy 4:24). They cannot stand His glorious presence for judgment.

4 For thou hast maintained my right and my cause; thou satest in the throne judging right.

Verse 4 is an explanation of verse 3. As a response to the psalmist's plea, God's judgment fell on the enemies who retreated, staggered, and died. They reaped according to their deeds. The verdict was in favor of the psalmist and against his enemies. "Right" (Heb. *mishpat,* meesh-**POT**) is the case lodged against the wicked, and the word "cause" (Heb. *din,* **DEEN**) means judgment.

65

God's right judgment from His throne shows His multifaceted relationship with people. He has full judicial and executive authority. God is not only a judge; He is the King of kings who sits on His throne to judge the world.

5 Thou hast rebuked the heathen, thou hast destroyed the wicked, thou hast put out their name for ever and ever. 6 O thou enemy, destructions are come to a perpetual end: and thou hast destroyed cities; their memorial is perished with them.

The past tense used here is called a "prophetic perfect" which describes future events as if they have already occurred. The Hebrew word used for "heathen" designates people who were not Jews and who were also worshiping other gods. Other translations use the term "nations." These nations who do not know God and worship other gods live in wickedness and oppress God's people.

God's judgment brings destruction on them in such a magnitude that their memory is lost. They are no more remembered. To "rebuke" these nations means to condemn them and bring judgment on them. The rebuke of God is the manifestation of His wrath against the enemy to defend the righteous. To "put out" their name forever is a synonym of total annihilation. The wicked, as well as their cities, were submitted to the same fate. They will no more be remembered.

7 But the LORD shall endure for ever: he hath prepared his throne for judgment. 8 And he shall judge the world in righteousness, he shall minister judgment to the people in uprightness.

The eternal reign of the Lord is contrasted with the ephemeral life of the nations He has utterly destroyed. God is the judge and king forever over the whole universe. This is a source of hope. The knowledge of God's kingship gives two prospects: the conviction that He rules differently from the nations and the assurance of the establishment of His righteousness on earth.

9 The LORD also will be a refuge for the oppressed, a refuge in times of trouble. 10 And they that know thy name will put their trust in thee: for thou, LORD, hast not forsaken them that seek thee.

The word for "refuge" is *misgab* (Heb. mees-GAV), which means a high place, especially a secure height, like a high wall or fortress. It is used in Psalms as a metaphor for God's protection. The protection of the Lord is assured whether one faces individual oppressors or threatening circumstances in life.

Knowledge of the name of the Lord is an expression of the personal relationship established with Him. God does not forsake those who seek Him, but is ever-present for them.

11 Sing praises to the LORD, which dwelleth in Zion: declare among the people his doings.

The psalmist, after praising the Lord for what He has done for him and acknowledging His righteous rule as a source of hope for the oppressed, calls on the people of God to join him in praising the Lord. Zion is a poetic name for Jerusalem, which is called to be an earthly manifestation of God's heavenly rule. He is the Most High who rules over the entire universe though He has chosen Jerusalem to be His dwelling place among His people.

His "doings" and His marvelous deeds (v. 1) are the same. For His people of Israel, He sent plagues in Egypt, He delivered them mightily from the rule of Pharaoh the oppressor, He parted the Red Sea, He conquered nations and led them to the Promised Land in fulfillment of His promise. His rule over the nations is unchallenged. His people must, therefore, proclaim these mighty deeds to the nations. As Christians, we must also sing praises to our Lord Jesus, who delivered us from our oppressors and gave us new life and hope in His kingdom. The world must hear of His wonders.

12 When he maketh inquisition for blood, he remembereth them: he forgetteth not the cry of the humble.

God is equally mindful of the oppressed and the oppressors. To make inquisition for blood is to investigate bloodshed. David has said God sits on His heavenly throne and dispense righteous judgment (vv. 7–8). Now, David gives an example of this: He investigates those who shed innocent blood, a thing which He hates (Proverbs 6:17). We can be sure that these people will suffer the just judgment God hands down to them. Likewise, God knows the cause of the oppressed, here called the "humble" (Heb. *'anav*, aw-**NAV**). This word is used frequently throughout the Old Testament to refer to the poor and needy—the marginalized, as we would say today. He hears their cries and gives righteous judgment to them as well, which will lift them up to flourishing.

Sources:
Attridge, Harold, W. *The Harper Collins Study Bible, New Revised Standard Version.* New York: Harper One, 2006. 740-741.
Bratcher, R. G., and W.N. Reyburn. *A Translator's Handbook on the book of Psalms.* New York: United Bible Society, 1991.
Cabal, Ted, et. al. *The Apologetics Study Bible, Holman Christian Standard.* Nashville, TN: Holman Bible Publishers, 2007. 796-797.
Henry, Matthew. *Matthew Henry's Commentary on the Whole Bible: New Modern Edition.* Vols. 1-6. Peabody, MA: Hendrickson Publishers, Inc., 2009.
Kidner, D. *Tyndale Old Testament Commentaries: Psalms 1-72, An introduction and commentary.* D. J. Wiseman, Ed. Downers Grove, IL: Intervarsity Press, 1973.
Strong, James. *The New Strong's Exhaustive Concordance of the Bible.* Nashville, TN: Thomas Nelson, 2003.
Thayer, Joseph Henry. *A Greek-English Lexicon of the New Testament.* New York: American Book Company, 1889.
Toombs, L. E. *The Interpreter One Volume Commentary of the Bible.* C. M. Laymon, Ed. Nashville, TN: Abingdon Press, 1971.
Van der Mass, Ed M. *Halley's Bible Handbook: Deluxe Edition (25th Edition).* Grand Rapids, MI: Zondervan, 2007. 302.
VanGemeren, W. A. *The Expositor's Bible Commentary: Psalms.* Vol. 5. F. E. Gaebelein, Ed. Grand Rapids, MI: Zondervan, 1991.
Zodhiates, Spiros. *Key Word Study Bible King James Version.* Chattanooga, TN: AMG Publishers, 1991. 1607, 1632, 1652.

Say It Correctly

Satest. SAT-est.
Psalter. SALL-ter.

Daily Bible Readings

MONDAY
Where Is Justice?
(Ecclesiastes 3:16–22)

TUESDAY
A Prayer for Justice
(Psalm 7:8–17)

WEDNESDAY
Let Justice Roll Down
(Amos 5:21–25)

THURSDAY
God's Servant Proclaims Justice
(Matthew 12:14–21)

FRIDAY
God Has Executed Judgment
(Psalm 9:13–20)

SATURDAY
Jesus Pronounces Release and Recovery
(Luke 4:14–21)

SUNDAY
God Judges with Righteousness
(Psalm 9:1–12)

Teaching Tips

Words You Should Know

A. Right (v. 7) *yashar* (Heb.)—Straight, upright, correct

B. Filled (v. 9) *mala'* (Heb.)—Overflowing, made complete

Teacher Preparation

Unifying Principle—I Shall Be Released. People seek deliverance when they are in trouble. How should we respond when we are delivered? Psalm 107 encourages us to be thankful to God for His deliverance.

A. Read the Bible Background and Devotional Reading.

B. Pray for your students and lesson clarity.

C. Read the lesson Scripture in multiple translations.

O—Open the Lesson

A. Begin the class with prayer.

B. Play a pop song about being free such as "I Shall Be Released," "Freedom!" (Pharrell Williams), or "People Get Ready." What do we need to be freed? Who or what is the source of freedom?

C. Have the students read the Aim for Change and the In Focus story.

D. Ask students how events like those in the story weigh on their hearts and how they can view these events from a faith perspective.

P—Present the Scriptures

A. Read the Focal Verses and discuss the Background and The People, Places, and Times sections.

B. Have the class share what Scriptures stand out for them and why, with particular emphasis on today's themes.

E—Explore the Meaning

A. Use In Depth or More Light on the Text to facilitate a deeper discussion of the lesson text.

B. Pose the questions in Search the Scriptures and Discuss the Meaning.

C. Discuss the Liberating Lesson and Application for Activation sections.

N—Next Steps for Application

A. Summarize the value of seeking God's help during hard times and thanking God when He rescues us.

B. End class with a commitment to thank God for His everlasting, unconditional love.

Worship Guide

For the Superintendent or Teacher
Theme: Give Thanks for Deliverance
Song: "I Am Redeemed"

Give Thanks for Deliverance

Bible Background • PSALM 107
Printed Text • PSALM 107:1–9, 39–43 | Devotional Reading • PSALM 68:1–6

——————————— **Aim for Change** ———————————

By the end of this lesson, we will EXPLORE the importance of having a relationship with God, the Deliverer, PLACE value on the role of giving thanks to God, and PRAY for those who need God's deliverance.

——————————— **In Focus** ———————————

"Thank You, Heavenly Father," Dorcas said as she rested on the gurney.

Dorcas was so weak she could barely raise her voice above a whisper, so she whispered. It was difficult to collect her thoughts after the emergency surgery, but the one thing she knew was that she was grateful to be alive. Since that morning, she had been gasping for air as if she had run a marathon, even though she hadn't exerted herself more than she would have at any other time.

Even so, it wasn't until Dorcas had lunch with her best girlfriend Sylvia, and her back started hurting, that she called her doctor. When Dr. Patterson heard her description of how she was feeling—like the air was being squeezed out of her from her upper back—he told her to go to the hospital ASAP! When she came to the hospital, her neck was in terrible pain and she didn't understand why. It seemed like within moments of entering the doors, Dorcas was in an operating room.

Dorcas was woozy now, and could barely focus on what the emergency room physician was telling her—about the cardiac arrest she had suffered, about the symptoms that women can have that men don't, about the arterial blockage that was uncovered and removed, about the stent that was put in. The only thing on Dorcas' mind was "Thank You, Heavenly Father," and she said it again and again.

What stories can you tell about when the Lord has delivered you from great trouble or hardship?

——————————— **Keep in Mind** ———————————

"Then they cried unto the LORD in their trouble, and he delivered them out of their distresses." (Psalm 107:6, KJV)

"'LORD, help!' they cried in their trouble, and he rescued them from their distress."
(Psalm 107:6, NLT)

[handwritten: Sepher Tehillin; Book of Praises]

Focal Verses

[handwritten: Solo backup accompaniment]

KJV **Psalm 107:1** O give thanks unto the LORD, for he is good: for his mercy endureth for ever.

2 Let the redeemed of the LORD say so, whom he hath redeemed from the hand of the enemy;

3 And gathered them out of the lands, from the east, and from the west, from the north, and from the south.

4 They wandered in the wilderness in a solitary way; they found no city to dwell in.

5 Hungry and thirsty, their soul fainted in them.

6 Then they cried unto the LORD in their trouble, and he delivered them out of their distresses.

7 And he led them forth by the right way, that they might go to a city of habitation.

8 Oh that men would praise the LORD for his goodness, and for his wonderful works to the children of men!

9 For he satisfieth the longing soul, and filleth the hungry soul with goodness.

39 Again, they are minished and brought low through oppression, affliction, and sorrow.

40 He poureth contempt upon princes, and causeth them to wander in the wilderness, where there is no way.

41 Yet setteth he the poor on high from affliction, and maketh him families like a flock.

42 The righteous shall see it, and rejoice: and all iniquity shall stop her mouth.

43 Whoso is wise, and will observe these things, even they shall understand the lovingkindness of the LORD.

NLT **Psalm 107:1** Give thanks to the LORD, for he is good! His faithful love endures forever.

2 Has the LORD redeemed you? Then speak out! Tell others he has redeemed you from your enemies.

3 For he has gathered the exiles from many lands, from east and west, from north and south.

4 Some wandered in the wilderness, lost and homeless.

5 Hungry and thirsty, they nearly died.

6 "LORD, help!" they cried in their trouble, and he rescued them from their distress.

7 He led them straight to safety, to a city where they could live.

8 Let them praise the LORD for his great love and for the wonderful things he has done for them.

9 For he satisfies the thirsty and fills the hungry with good things.

39 When they decrease in number and become impoverished through oppression, trouble, and sorrow,

40 the LORD pours contempt on their princes, causing them to wander in trackless wastelands.

41 But he rescues the poor from trouble and increases their families like flocks of sheep.

42 The godly will see these things and be glad, while the wicked are struck silent.

43 Those who are wise will take all this to heart; they will see in our history the faithful love of the LORD.

The People, Places, and Times

Composition of Psalms. The songs in Psalms were written over a period of 1000 years by various authors including prophets (Moses), kings (David and Solomon), and Levites (Asaph and the sons of Korah). The first psalm composed is Psalm 90 and was written by Moses around 1400 BC after leading Israel out of Egyptian bondage. One of the last psalms to be written was Psalm 89, authored by Ethan around

71

400 BC after Israel returned from Babylonian captivity. Psalm 107 is most likely written after the Israelites' return from exile as well (v. 3).

Background

Psalm 107 voices examples of God's steadfastness. Written when the Israelites were permitted to return and resettle in their homelands of Canaan, they were likely filled with excitement, having endured the onerous Babylonian exile. No longer in captivity, the Israelites had been redeemed. They were experiencing true freedom coupled with the ability to finally worship God for His ongoing steadfastness toward them. Some believe the setting of this psalm is at a festival in the Temple in Jerusalem.

What prompted the writing of Psalm 107?

At-A-Glance

1. Praise the Lord (Psalm 107:1–3)
2. Love in Action (vv. 4–9)
3. Recognize God's Steadfastness
(vv. 39–43)

In Depth

1. Praise the Lord (Psalm 107:1–3)

The psalm begins by admonishing everyone to give thanks and praise because their period of exile was finally over. The psalmist extends an invitation for all who have been redeemed to give thanks. His reasoning behind such a praise break: the Lord is good, and His steadfast love endures forever. Even though the Israelites had been in enemy or Babylonian territory, God rescued them. Dispersed throughout the four compass points—north, south, east, and west—now they could reassemble out of those foreign countries and return to Canaan. Therefore the psalmist admonished the Israelites that this was

enough to offer thanks. They know firsthand how good God has been.

Why must we learn to always give thanks to God, regardless of our situation?

2. Love in Action (vv. 4–9)

The psalmist takes the reader on a picturesque journey to showcase God's steadfast love. First, he highlights God's goodness to a group of weary wanderers crossing through the desert. Lost, famished, and parched, they resign to do what costs them nothing: pray. This prayer is spoken four times in the psalm, a refrain that should come more quickly to the lips of all God's people (vv. 6, 13, 19, 28). They cry out to the Lord and He not only hears them, but also delivers them out of their distress. Then, He provides them with a direct route to a safe city where they could settle, Jerusalem. God is good to them. Their every need is supplied. The same God who leads them also feeds them! The Israelites give thanks to the Lord for His steadfast love and His wonderful deeds toward them.

How do we show God we love Him through our actions?

3. Recognize God's Steadfastness (vv. 39–43)

As the old adage goes, "What goes up must come down." The psalmist concentrates on the reverse angle of God's providence. Those who rise despitefully will be humbled. By "oppression, affliction, and sorrow" (v. 39), humiliation is guaranteed. Those who exalt themselves and demean others will be brought low themselves and will wander aimlessly in waste.

Equally, they will see the lowly advance in all ways over them. Those who were once afflicted will be rewarded with deliverance far away from evil's way. God will aid them in establishing families of their own, which is viewed as the ultimate blessing during biblical times (Exodus 1:1–21; Psalm 127:5). The haughty will be made silent and envy their good fortune. This is one example of God's divine providence. He does this to convince the wise to heed and to rely on Him. His steadfast love is for all who are willing to rely upon, repeatedly call on, and abide in Him.

In what ways has God shown His steadfast love in your life?

Search the Scriptures

1. Why should the Israelites offer thanks and praise to God (Psalm 107:1–3)?

2. Why is it important to understand affliction does not last forever (v. 41)?

Discuss the Meaning

Ecclesiastes 1 tells us there is a time for everything. It is important for believers to know that affliction does not last always. After years in exile, the Israelites were delivered. What a reason to praise God! Why is it important to have a relationship with God, the Deliverer?

Liberating Lesson

In a world where confusion and calamity reign, our hopefulness is oftentimes deflated. Imagine spending 30 years in a 5-by-8 foot cell for a crime you did not commit. That was Anthony Ray Hinton's story. With all evidence showing his innocence, Hinton was still jailed for a double-murder. It was not until he connected with Attorney Bryan Stevenson of the Equal Justice Initiative that his plight changed. They were able to prove the evidence against Hinton was incorrect. Hinton persisted in his faith and was awarded complete exoneration. His reunion with his family was filled with shouts of, "Thank you, Lord!" Remain resilient and thankful!

Application for Activation

Prayer is one of the most powerful and effective resources believers have. From a monetary vantage point, though, it costs us nothing to execute. Pray for individuals who need deliverance. Like the Israelites, God can deliver them too, even from self-made troubles. From an addiction, abuse, or an attitude, God can set any form of captive free. If a relationship or re-dedication is required, believe for an encounter with Jesus, the ultimate Deliverer. Identify one person, whether you know their name or not, and pray for God's deliverance.

Follow the Spirit

What God wants me to do:

_____

_____

_____

_____

Remember Your Thoughts

Special insights I have learned:

_____

_____

_____

_____

More Light on the Text

Psalm 107:1–9, 39–43

1 O give thanks unto the LORD, for he is good: for his mercy endureth forever.

Expressing thanks is a popular theme of the Psalms; therefore, it is no surprise that the line "Give thanks unto the LORD" is common throughout the Psalms. However, in Psalm 107, the psalmist begins his song of thanksgiving with the one letter word, "O" that serves as an exclamation to strengthen the following imperative.

As an exclamation, "O" focuses the hearer's attention and elicits excitement as it prepares the worshiper for what is coming next. Further, "O" intensifies the command for the worshiper to "Give thanks unto the LORD." Even though it is a command, the expectation is that the giving of thanks will be voluntary, sung with intensity and intentionality. The thanksgiving is to be expressed equally with lips of praise and with lives of gratitude because of who God is. He is Yahweh, the eternal, covenant-keeping God. The use of the name Yahweh (translated as "the LORD") was this psalm specifically praises God for keeping the covenantal promise: "That after seventy years be accomplished at Babylon I will visit you, and perform my good word toward you, in causing you to return to this place (from Jeremiah 29:10).

Is there a promise from the Lord that you are waiting on? Do not give up! Do not be discouraged! Instead, "Give thanks unto the LORD," in advance, because He is Yahweh, the covenant-keeping God who will surely do all that He has promised. It does not matter how long it has been. You can rest assured that He will fulfill every promise He has ever made. It is indeed sufficient to give thanks just because He is the Lord, but the psalmist is compelled to declare two additional reasons why giving thanks is right and proper: 1) Yahweh is good. *Tov* (**TOVE**) is the Hebrew word for good and means kind and upright; and 2) Yahweh's mercy, His *khesed* (**KHEH**-sed), His compassion and forgiveness, endures forever.

2 Let the redeemed of the LORD say so, whom he hath redeemed from the hand of the enemy;

Next, the psalmist becomes more specific in his call to give thanks. God is a redeemer. To "redeem" (Heb. *ga'al*, gaw-**ALL**) is to buy back property that was sold or a person who was enslaved. In reference to the Lord, the redeemed are those whom God has bought back from bondage and slavery, as He did with His people Israel when He brought them out of Egypt (Exodus 6:6), and when He delivered them from captivity in Babylon.

Because of what the Lord did for Israel, it was mandatory, as the redeemed, not only to sing praises of thanksgiving "unto the LORD," but also to declare it openly so that all nations can know about God's redeeming power. That is exactly what Job did. When he was going through his trials, he declared, "I know that my Redeemer liveth" (Job 19:25). So regardless of the situation you may be going through, you too can declare it, tell it, shout it, and sing with passion: God has redeemed you before and He will again.

3 And gathered them out of the lands, from the east, and from the west, from the north, and from the south.

God redeemed Israel and brought them back to the Promised Land, the holy city, Jerusalem, from the foreign lands where they had been scattered and held in captivity (Psalm 107:3). Christians today can rejoice that the Lord will ultimately bring all of His redeemed people from all the nations, and gather us all together in the place He promised and prepared for us, the New Jerusalem. In that day, this is the song that will be sung: "Thou art worthy... for thou wast slain, and hast redeemed us to God by thy blood out of every kindred, and tongue, and people, and nation" (Revelation 5:9).

4 They wandered in the wilderness in a solitary way; they found no city to dwell in. 5 Hungry and thirsty, their soul fainted in them. 6 Then they cried unto the LORD in their trouble, and he delivered them out of their distresses.

The testimony of Israel's redemption begins with the problems they faced as they traveled, articulating their deep distress. Not only were they lost and homeless, but they were also so hungry and thirsty from wandering in the wilderness, and they almost died (107:4–5). Their distress initiated their prayer (v. 6).

The answer to their dilemma was to cry out to the Lord for help. The phrasing in verse 6 is repeated three other times in the psalm, making a notable refrain (vv. 13, 19, 28). The need for this prayer is the same for us today. Regardless of the situation, the Lord is faithful and trustworthy, so He invites us to "come boldly unto the throne of grace, that we may obtain mercy, and find grace to help in time of need" (Hebrews 4:16). That is the privilege of God's people. Even if the cause of the distress is brought on as a result of disobedience, God remains faithful even when we are not (2 Timothy 2:13). However, if disobedience is the reason for the distress, then repentance is required.

7 And he led them forth by the right way, that they might go to a city of habitation. 8 Oh that men would praise the LORD for his goodness, and for his wonderful works to the children of men! 9 For he satisfieth the longing soul, and filleth the hungry soul with goodness.

Then the psalmist describes the means of their deliverance. God led them forth by the "right" way. That word right is the Hebrew word *yashar* (yaw-**SHAR**) which also means straight. He led them in a straight path, in direct contrast to the aimless wandering that led to their distress. This straight path not only guided them to a place of safety, but to a city and a dwelling place where they could thrive. Imagine the relief this gave them, like a person who had been living on the streets being taken not to a temporary shelter, but to a house for their very own!

The joy of this deliverance bubbles over as praise for what the Lord has done. This verse,

like v. 6, is also found four times in this song and is followed by a statement summarizing the purpose for the praise (vv. 8, 15, 21, 31). In this particular circumstance, the Lord is to be praised "for he satisfieth the longing soul, and filleth the hungry soul with goodness" (107:9). The Hebrew here is deeply poetic. "Satisfieth" (Heb. *saba'*, saw-**BAH**) is often used in the context of food, but it is paired with the "longing" soul rather than the "hungry" soul, a twist making the hearer take greater notice of the words and remember them. The word "longing" (Heb. *shaqaq*, shaw-**KOK**) is sometimes used in connection with food and drink, but more often refers to eagerness, running, and roving. This recalls the Israelites' wandering from which God saves them. He has satisfied their wanderings. The hungry soul is filled (Heb. *mala'*, maw-**LAW**), a word with shades of meaning to show they are filled to overflowing and made complete.

39 Again, they are minished and brought low through oppression, affliction, and sorrow. 40 He poureth contempt upon princes, and causeth them to wander in the wilderness, where there is no way.

In these closing verses of this song of thanksgiving, the psalmist contrasts two groups of people, the rebellious (vv. 39–40), and the redeemed (v. 41). Verse 39 emphatically declares that the rebellious are "brought low" or impoverished through oppression, affliction, and sorrow. Not only that, but they also decrease in number (KJV: "minished"). Even their princes, the wealthy, and upper class are judged by the Lord who causes them to "wander in the wilderness" (v. 40). Here we see a direct reversal of the righteous with the unrighteous. As God's faithful people are brought in from wandering the wilderness, the unjust are forced from their positions of power and sent to wander the same trackless wilderness.

41 Yet setteth he the poor on high from affliction, and maketh him families like a flock.

Next, the psalmist makes the dramatic comparison, declaring how the Lord deals with the redeemed. First, "he setteth the poor on high from affliction" (107:41). In other words, the Lord rescues the poor from their affliction, setting them in high positions of authority and protection so that further trouble cannot reach them. Second, he "maketh him families like a flock," so that the families of the poor increase like flocks of sheep. This is in direct contrast to the rebellious who decrease in number (v. 40).

42 The righteous shall see it, and rejoice: and all iniquity shall stop her mouth. 43 Whoso is wise, and will observe these things, even they shall understand the lovingkindness of the LORD.

In his concluding two verses, the psalmist drives home the fact that because God is faithful and gracious to His people, "the righteous shall see it, and rejoice." They will shout out loud, as they were encouraged to do in the beginning of the psalm (v. 2). On the other hand, the wicked shall "stop her mouth" and be silent (107:42). In their shame and humiliation, they will have nothing to say, neither in their own defense nor in praise to God. They know they cannot argue their case before the righteous God, but they also still do not bend to the will of God.

Finally, if we are among the wise, we "will observe these things" and "shall understand the lovingkindness of the LORD" (107:43), giving Him the praise that is due unto His name.

Sources:
Benson, Joseph. *Commentary on the Old and New Testaments.* Omaha, NE: Patristic Publishing, 2019.
Bruce, F.F. *Zondervan Bible Commentary: One-Volume Illustrated Edition.* Grand Rapids, MI: Zondervan, 2008.
Henry, Matthew. *Matthew Henry's Commentary on the Whole Bible: New Modern Edition.* Vols. 1-6. Peabody, MA: Hendrickson Publishers, Inc., 2009.
Hinton, Linda B. *Basic Bible Commentary.* Nashville, TN: Abingdon Press, 1994.
Limburg, James. *Psalms.* Louisville, KY: Westminster John Known Press, 2000. 370–371.
Spurgeon, Charles H. *The Treasury of David.* Peabody, MA: Hendrickson Publishers. 1876.
Strong, James. *The New Strong's Exhaustive Concordance of the Bible.* Nashville, TN: Thomas Nelson, 2003.
Thayer, Joseph Henry. *A Greek-English Lexicon of the New Testament.* New York: American Book Company, 1889.
Van Harn, Roger. *Psalms for Preaching and Worship: A Lectionary Commentary.* Grand Rapids, MI: Eerdmans, 2009. 281–285.

Say It Correctly

Asaph. AY-saff.
Korah. KORE-ah.

Daily Bible Readings

MONDAY
Delivered from Hunger and Thirst
(Psalm 107:1–9)

TUESDAY
Delivered from Darkness and Gloom
(Psalm 107:10–22)

WEDNESDAY
Delivered from Storms
(Psalm 107:23–32)

THURSDAY
Delivered through Jesus Christ
(Ephesians 1:3–14)

FRIDAY
Delivered from Sin
(Ephesians 2:1–10)

SATURDAY
Delivered and Reconciled
(Ephesians 2:11–22)

SUNDAY
Delivered by God's Steadfast Love
(Psalm 107:33–43)

Teaching Tips

October 24
Bible Study Guide 8

Words You Should Know

A. Amiable (Psalm 84:1) *yedid* (Heb.)—Beloved, lovely

B. Baca (v. 6) *baka'* (Heb.)—Weeping, lamentation

Teacher Preparation

Unifying Principle—Our House. There are times when the pressures of life are a heavy burden to carry. Where can people go to find the pressures of life lifted and then enjoy a period of celebration? The psalmist recounts a uniquely joyful experience when worshiping in the Temple.

A. Read the Bible Background and Devotional Reading.

B. Pray for your students and lesson clarity.

C. Read the lesson Scripture in multiple translations.

O—Open the Lesson

A. Begin the class with prayer.

B. Play a song about going or being at home (e.g. "Our House," "Take Me Home, Country Roads," or "Homeward Bound." What makes being at home different from being anywhere else?

C. Have the students read the Aim for Change and the In Focus story.

D. Ask students how events like those in the story weigh on their hearts and how they can view these events from a faith perspective.

P—Present the Scriptures

A. Read the Focal Verses and discuss the Background and The People, Places, and Times sections.

B. Have the class share what Scriptures stand out for them and why, with particular emphasis on today's themes.

E—Explore the Meaning

A. Use In Depth or More Light on the Text to facilitate a deeper discussion of the lesson text.

B. Pose the questions in Search the Scriptures and Discuss the Meaning.

C. Discuss the Liberating Lesson and Application for Activation sections.

N—Next Steps for Application

A. Summarize the value of feeling truly at home in the presence of God.

B. End class with a commitment to pray for feeling God's presence more and more.

Worship Guide

For the Superintendent or Teacher
Theme: The Joy of Worship
Song: "To Worship You I Live (Away)"

The Joy of Worship

Bible Background • PSALM 84
Printed Text • PSALM 84 | Devotional Reading • 2 CHRONICLES 29:25–30

———— Aim for Change ————

By the end of this lesson, we will DISCOVER why the psalmist expressed joy in worship, FEEL the joy of worship, and PROCLAIM the living presence of God throughout creation.

Bro. Hill / Ann

———— In Focus ————

"Make a left turn up here," Mardelle told the driver.

It had been nearly 40 years since she had been back to the family home in South Carolina. After college, she got married to Theodore, who soon became a Foreign Service Officer for the U.S. State Department.

Over their life together, Theodore had been given multiple postings outside the United States, all over Africa, Central America, and South America. They had only a few short years together after Theodore retired and passed away, Mardelle decided to return to her hometown and live in her parents' house.

She found herself wide-eyed on the way from the airport, taking in all the ways the neighborhoods had changed. But she was happy to see the things that were still standing, unchanged by time—the fountain in the square across from city hall, the restaurant where Theodore had proposed to her, the middle school where she first developed her love of French, which served her well in several of the places they had stayed.

And now, a warm, joyful feeling washed over Mardelle as she heard leaves crunching under the tires as the car made the turn onto the path leading to her family's house. Ahead, she could see the gabled roof, the bay window at the front, and the wide wraparound porch. Mardelle breathed a word of thanks to God for all that had led to this moment, and a happy welcome home.

Where have you felt most at home? Have you ever had that feeling during worship?

———— Keep in Mind ————

"Blessed are they that dwell in thy house: they will be still praising thee. Selah."
(Psalm 84:4, KJV)

"What joy for those who can live in your house, always singing your praises. *Interlude*."
(Psalm 84:4, NLT)

Focal Verses

KJV **Psalm 84:1** How amiable are thy tabernacles, O LORD of hosts!

2 My soul longeth, yea, even fainteth for the courts of the LORD: my heart and my flesh crieth out for the living God.

3 Yea, the sparrow hath found an house, and the swallow a nest for herself, where she may lay her young, even thine altars, O LORD of hosts, my King, and my God.

4 Blessed are they that dwell in thy house: they will be still praising thee. Selah.

5 Blessed is the man whose strength is in thee; in whose heart are the ways of them.

6 Who passing through the valley of Baca make it a well; the rain also filleth the pools.

7 They go from strength to strength, every one of them in Zion appeareth before God.

8 O LORD God of hosts, hear my prayer: give ear, O God of Jacob. Selah.

9 Behold, O God our shield, and look upon the face of thine anointed.

10 For a day in thy courts is better than a thousand. I had rather be a doorkeeper in the house of my God, than to dwell in the tents of wickedness.

11 For the LORD God is a sun and shield: the LORD will give grace and glory: no good thing will he withhold from them that walk uprightly.

12 O LORD of hosts, blessed is the man that trusteth in thee.

NLT **Psalm 84** For the choir director: A psalm of the descendants of Korah, to be accompanied by a stringed instrument.

1 How lovely is your dwelling place, O LORD of Heaven's Armies.

2 I long, yes, I faint with longing to enter the courts of the LORD. With my whole being, body and soul, I will shout joyfully to the living God.

3 Even the sparrow finds a home, and the swallow builds her nest and raises her young at a place near your altar, O LORD of Heaven's Armies, my King and my God!

4 What joy for those who can live in your house, always singing your praises. *Interlude*

5 What joy for those whose strength comes from the LORD, who have set their minds on a pilgrimage to Jerusalem.

6 When they walk through the Valley of Weeping, it will become a place of refreshing springs. The autumn rains will clothe it with blessings.

7 They will continue to grow stronger, and each of them will appear before God in Jerusalem.

8 O LORD God of Heaven's Armies, hear my prayer. Listen, O God of Jacob. *Interlude*

9 O God, look with favor upon the king, our shield! Show favor to the one you have anointed.

10 A single day in your courts is better than a thousand anywhere else! I would rather be a gatekeeper in the house of my God than live the good life in the homes of the wicked.

11 For the LORD God is our sun and our shield. He gives us grace and glory. The LORD will withhold no good thing from those who do what is right.

12 O LORD of Heaven's Armies, what joy for those who trust in you.

Satisfaction in the house of God 3-4

5-7 Finding strength in the journey.

8 Prayer

9. Surpassing greatness in God house

10-12 greatness of God his house

11

The People, Places, and Times *Intro*

Korah. The sons of Korah (who wrote this psalm and others) were the remnant left after their ancestor was destroyed for rebellion against Moses. The rebellion of Korah angered the Lord, and He caused the Earth to open and consume Korah and those that rebelled with him (Numbers 16:1–33). Then fire was sent to consume 250 men. The children of Korah, however, survived the judgment of God (Numbers 26:9–11). This remnant and their descendants proved faithful to God and are listed among their fellow Levites in various positions at the Tabernacle and Temple, often as singers or instrumentalists (1 Chronicles 6, 23–26).

Background *gatekeepers*

The sons of Korah were porters (1 Chronicles 9:17) and musicians (2 Chronicles 20:19) for the priests. These positions meant that they dwelt in God's house. This physical closeness to God's house prompted their love and desire of God in ways that others may not have felt. The sons of Korah long for the Lord's house because they long for the presence of the Lord. Those who can live in God's house should always respond in praise because nothing is better than being in God's presence. There is joy experienced in worship in God's presence, and the benefits of joyfully worshiping God are immeasurable.

At-A-Glance

1. The Tabernacle of Worship
(Psalm 84:1–4)
2. The Valley of Baca (vv. 5–7)
3. Reverential Worship (vv. 8–9)
4. Joy in Worship (vv. 10–12)

In Depth

1. The Tabernacle of Worship (Psalm 84:1–4)

The Tabernacle was a sacred place where God manifested His presence and communicated His will. The physical Tabernacle of God is "amiable" or beloved because God dwells there (v. 1), and the psalmists' souls long to unite with God. They so intently desire the courts of the Lord, that they are weakened. Their committed love for God is passionate, so their flesh cries out for God. There is an insatiable desire to dwell in the house of God, as a bird desires a nest (v. 3). The Tabernacle of God is an honored placed. Those who dwell in the presence of God should perpetually praise, worship, and adore God (v. 4).

How does your desire for the presence of God compare to the psalmists'?

2. The Valley of Baca (vv. 5–7)

Our definition of blessed should align with the Word of God. We are blessed only in God. The valley of Baca is the place of weeping or a valley of tears. Finding strength in God and having a heart fixed on God is the source of greatest blessing (v. 5) Even in sorrow and times of weeping, which we all experience in life, with God those places are made easier (v. 6). Faithful believers in God will experience the journey and grow from strength to strength (cf. 2 Corinthians 3:18). We all become stronger as we grow with God, never weaker (v. 7).

In your valley of tears, how did you keep your heart fixed on God?

3. Reverential Worship (vv. 8–9)

Recognizing God in all of His splendor should dictate how we approach Him. The reverence for God as the "LORD God of hosts" indicates the writers' honor for God being Lord over heaven and earth's armies. God is so vast, yet the psalmists approach God requesting attention to their prayer (v. 8). In the midst of His sovereign rule, they desire God's ear to be attentive to them. They recognize God is their shield and protector (v. 9). We want God to look upon us when we call to Him. We must give humble attention to the majesty of God in the midst of our prayer requests. God is attracted to our reverential worship.

How do you approach God in reverential worship?

4. Joy in Worship (vv. 10–12)

Any day in God's presence is more precious than a thousand days anywhere else (v. 10). Time with God should be the most dedicated and valued of all the time we have. No time on earth is more valuable. Our time should not be more concentrated on temporal moments than moments with eternal significance. The Lord our God is both our guiding light and our protector (v. 11). God gives us both grace and glory. He guarantees that we have grace in difficult times and glory in times of success in Him (v. 11). As God's grace and glory is given to us, we are compelled to walk uprightly. And as we walk uprightly, God bestows wonderful things upon us (v. 11). When we trust God, we are blessed and have everything we need (v. 12).

How have God's grace and glory caused you to walk uprightly?

Search the Scriptures

1. How did your desire for God's presence change at your conversion (Psalm 84:2)?

2. Differentiate the respect for God's Tabernacle and Temple, and the respect for God's house now (v. 4).

Discuss the Meaning

1. How does the reverential worship of the psalmist impact your thoughts of expressing worship currently?

2. How do personal views of God impact how people embrace time spent in the sanctuary?

Liberating Lesson

Churches, worship settings, and liturgical styles are changing. By following what's trending or what might appeal to multiple generations, we can find ourselves compromising the tangible presence of God. Worship is a lifestyle, though, and our lifestyle of worship should be reverential. Time spent with God impacts our lives. Rationed time in God's presence hinders the grace and glory we receive from dwelling in God's presence. When insatiability for God wanes, so does personal worship. We must revive our craving to worship God; it is the catalyst for revival in the global Church.

Application for Activation

Social Media. Family Gatherings. Work and domestic obligations. These often compete with time in the presence of God. The psalmists longed to be in the house of the Lord; the absence of God's presence weakened them. Consider your time. Consider your ways. How much does your soul long for God's presence? Has your longing of worship grown cold? What actions must be taken to return to worship in God's presence?

Follow the Spirit

What God wants me to do:

_____

_____

_____

_____

Remember Your Thoughts

Special insights I have learned:

1 Chronicler 16-22- Psalms 105.15 Do not touch my anointed ones. do my prophets no harm.

add intro

More Light on the Text
Psalm 84

Psalm 84 is a reflection of the desire to worship in God's house. As the superscription indicates, this psalm is one of eleven psalms attributed to the sons of Korah (see 42; 44-49; 84; 85; 87; 88). Korah, the predecessor of musicians from the tribe of Levi, was among 250 conspirators who rebelled against Moses during the exodus to the Promised Land. As a result of this rebellion, God opened up the earth and sent fire from heaven to consume every one of them (Numbers 16:1–40). God preserved Korah's descendants (Numbers 26:11), and they remained faithful serving God as musicians in the Temple. In this psalm, one will feel the sense of joy, safety, and security as one worships the Lord in His tabernacle.

1 How amiable are thy tabernacles, O LORD of hosts! 2 My soul longeth, yea, even fainteth for the courts of the LORD: my heart and my flesh crieth out for the living God.

The psalmist begins this song with a sense of awe and wonder. Addressing the Lord, he expresses how lovely and beautiful it is to be in God's house. The adjective "amiable" is the Hebrew *yedid* (yeh-**DEED**). It expresses how beautiful or delightful it is to be in the house of God. The word "tabernacles" is the Hebrew word *mishkan* (mish-**KAWN'**), and it means a dwelling place, a house, residence, or temple.

The word is in the plural form here, which may suggest that the psalmist is not referring to a particular house or the Temple. Rather it is used metaphorically to express the idea of being in the presence of God.

It has, however, been suggested that the plural is used here to include all the places in or near the Temple complex where acts of divine worship were performed. Since we don't know when the psalm was composed, the idea here could mean being in the presence of the Lord wherever He is worshiped. God does not live in man-made structures (Acts 7:47–50), but He is worshiped anytime and everywhere. Nonetheless, we still have special places dedicated for His worship.

Continuing his excitement about this tabernacle, the psalmist expresses his heartfelt yearning even to the point of exhaustion. His "soul longeth, yea, even fainteth for the courts of the LORD" and his "heart" and "flesh" cry out loud for the living God. We notice here that his whole being—soul, heart, and flesh—is desirous for the court of the Lord for worship. The word "crieth" comes from the Hebrew *ranan* (raw-**NON**); it means "to shout aloud for joy, to sing for joy." This yearning to worship God does not raise a plaintive cry, but a joyful shout. This is a picture of one who once worshiped the Lord in His sanctuary and now is excited to go again. This is significant because only "the living God" alone can satisfy the desires of the soul (Psalm 42:2).

3 Yea, the sparrow hath found an house, and the swallow a nest for herself, where she may lay her young, even thine altars, O LORD of hosts, my King, and my God. 4 Blessed are they that dwell in thy house: they will be still praising thee. Selah.

After expressing his sincere longing to worship in the Lord's house, the psalmist recalls the freedom even birds have to live and have their young in the very house of God. Here he envies the small birds that have unrestricted access to the Tabernacle and even to the altar. There they are able to build their nests and lay their young ones. By this, the psalmist seems to imply that if the little birds could have such freedom and access to the Tabernacle, how much more should he, a child of God. The words "sparrow" and "swallow" seem to represent little birds such as pigeons that often perch and build their nests on house rafters. It is common to see small birds in houses or churches.

In verse 4, the psalmist, still addressing the Lord, tends to move from the envy of the birds that are allowed to nest in the Temple, to the blessedness of those who dwell in the Lord's house, "they will be still praising thee." The word "blessed" comes from the Hebrew 'esher (**EH**-sher); which means happy or happiness. It is best rendered as an interjection, "how happy!" "They that dwell in thy house" would refer to the priests and Levites, who had their permanent dwelling in or near the Tabernacle or Temple and who wholly devoted themselves to serving the Lord continually (see Psalm 65:4).

As Christians, we can meet and praise the Lord anywhere, but going to the house of God—a church building or a cathedral—helps us to step aside from our busy life to focus on, meditate, and worship the Lord with other people. There is an aura of praise, blissfulness, and joy when a Christian enters a sacred place of worship to praise and pray to the Lord, especially with fellow believers (Psalm 133). That is how heaven will be (Revelation 3:12), a perpetual place of worship and praise.

5 Blessed is the man whose strength is in thee; in whose heart are the ways of them. 6 Who passing through the valley of Baca make it a well; the rain also filleth the pools.

The psalmist continues to express how blessed or happy are those who have a relationship with the Lord. Not only are they blessed, but their strength is dependent in the Lord.

The poetic structure of verse 5 is difficult to interpret. The NLT renders the second part of verse 5 as, "who have set their minds on a pilgrimage to Jerusalem." The "ways of them" *mesillah* (meh-seel-**LAH**) means "a thoroughfare, causeway, course, highway." It appears then that what the psalmist has in mind is the Law of Moses, which requires all observant Jews to travel to Jerusalem to celebrate three certain holidays each year.

Making this journey is not an easy task as we can see in the next two verses (6, 7), but the one who relies, not on his or her own strength, but on the Lord's and whose heart is focused on the trip (i.e., set their mind on the pilgrimage) is blessed. What we encounter here is a sense of resolute determination and reliance on God's strength to make the journey because of the expected outcome.

Verse 6 describes the difficulties of this journey and how the pilgrims can overcome them and finally achieve their goal—appearing before God. The word "Baca" or *Baka'* (Heb. baw-**KAW**) is from the word for "weeping," and might refer to an actual valley commonly traveled on the approach to Jerusalem. It is also possible that this name was figuratively used to describe the difficulties people encounter, and how God was with them and provided for them (cf. "the valley of the shadow of death," Psalm 23:4). Finding water in the desert wilderness is a common example and image of how God provides (Exodus 17:1–7; Isaiah 43:19). As believers pass through the wildernesses of life in this world, God promises to open for them fountains in the deserts, and springs in the dry places.

7 They go from strength to strength, every one of them in Zion appeareth before God.

Here we notice a change from singular ("blessed is the man," v. 5) to plural ("they go," v. 7)—which indicates unity and working together to draw strength from one another. The pilgrimage of life is better and best attained in a community. Therefore the more the pilgrims march together, the more their strength grows; they bear their trials better and overcome difficulties more easily. The result is that they succeed in their quest—they will all appear before God in Zion. What a day it will be when all believers are united in love, praise, and worship before the Almighty God. Life here would be more bearable, and in heaven He will be glorified.

8 O LORD God of hosts, hear my prayer: give ear, O God of Jacob. Selah. 9 Behold, O God our shield, and look upon the face of thine anointed.

Continuing the praise, the psalmist calls on the Lord to hear his prayer. Here again, he appeals to God's attributes of authority and power: "O LORD God of hosts." The psalmist also appeals to God's faithfulness as a covenant-keeping God, calling Him the "God of Jacob." As humans, we habitually pay attention (i.e,. give our ears) to only what we want to hear—something that is important or interesting to us. However, we turn away our ears from what we do not want to hear. Thankfully, God is not like us and always hears the prayers of His children.

The psalmist is desperate to be in the house of God; therefore he calls on the Lord to pay attention to his request. The petition continues as he again appeals to God's protective nature—as the "shield." "Shield" translates the Hebrew, *magen* (maw-**GANE**), figuratively used here is a protector or defense. God is our defense; He protects us from all evil.

The author appeals on behalf of God's anointed—that God should "look upon the face of (His) anointed." It is suggested that the psalmist is referring to King David or one of the kings of Israel. The word "anointed" is *mashiach* (maw-**SHEE**-akh), which means a consecrated

person set apart for service as king, prophet, or priest. Mashiach also means "the Messiah" or in Greek, "Christ." Although Christians refer to Jesus as the "Messiah" or the Christ, the allusion here does not seem to refer to Christ.

10 For a day in thy courts is better than a thousand. I had rather be a doorkeeper in the house of my God, than to dwell in the tents of wickedness.

The author's craving for worship in God's house and its splendor reaches its climax as he concludes the psalm. He says that it is better (or more profitable) to spend a day in the Lord's courts than to spend a thousand elsewhere. He continues that he would rather be a "doorkeeper" in the house of God than to live with the wicked. That is how awesome and splendid it is to be part of the Lord's household. The word used here for doorkeeper is not an actual job, but simply denotes someone who stands on the threshold. However, the psalmist and indeed everyone who has relationship with the Lord would prefer to occupy this position in the house of God than to try to dwell comfortably "in the tents of wickedness," where the glory of the Lord is absent.

11 For the LORD God is a sun and shield: the LORD will give grace and glory: no good thing will he withhold from them that walk uprightly.

Verse 11 gives further reasons the house of the Lord is preferable to anywhere else. Firstly, the Lord is sun and shield; He is all that we need to survive on earth. As the sun is the source of life and light to the world, so is the Lord to His people—those who love and adore Him. He is the source of life (Psalm 27:1; Isaiah 10:17, 60:19-20; Malachi 4:2). Without the sun, nothing will survive on earth, life will be extinct. He provides us with divine protection as a shield (vv. 8–9).

Secondly, the Lord is the giving God—He gives grace and glory. Christians, our walk of faith begins with grace and ultimately will end with glory or honor.

Thirdly, the Lord is generous. The Lord may not give us everything we want, but He gives us everything that is good for us, all that we need. The Lord will not withhold any good thing from those who walk uprightly. Remember the implication of this: if God is withholding something from you, it might be because it is not a good thing.

Jesus reinforces this truth of God's generosity and care in the Sermon on the Mount when He says, "If ye then, being evil, know how to give good gifts unto your children, how much more shall your Father which is in heaven give good things to them that ask him?" (Matthew 7:11). Christ's sacrifice of Himself further shows God's character and inspires Paul to write, "He that spared not his own Son, but delivered him up for us all, how shall he not with him also freely give us all things?" (Romans 8:32). Here Paul establishes the unimaginable length and breadth of God's magnanimity to those who put their trust in Him.

12 O LORD of hosts, blessed is the man that trusteth in thee.

This whole psalm describes the God we serve and worship, the God that deserves our praise and honor. The psalmist concludes this song by affirming the pleasure and joy we gain by trusting in the Lord: "O LORD of hosts, blessed is the man that trusteth in thee." This also echoes the joy of the one who does not walk in the counsel of the wicked but puts their trust in Lord in the opening verses of the psalter (Psalm 1:1–3).

Sources:
Henry, Matthew. *Matthew Henry's Commentary on the Whole Bible: New Modern Edition.* Vols. 1-6. Peabody, MA: Hendrickson Publishers, Inc., 2009.

Kidner, Derek. *Psalms 73-150.* Tyndale Old Testament Commentaries. D. J. Wiseman, gen. ed. Downers Grove, IL: InterVarsity Press, 1975.
Radmacher, Earl D., ed. *Nelson's New Illustrated Bible Commentary: Spreading the Light of God's Word into Your Life.* Nashville, TN: Thomas Nelson Publishers, 1999. 1648-1653.
Strong, James. *The New Strong's Exhaustive Concordance of the Bible.* Nashville, TN: Thomas Nelson, 2003.
Thayer, Joseph Henry. *A Greek-English Lexicon of the New Testament.* New York: American Book Company, 1889.

Say It Correctly

Selah. SAY-lah.
Baca. baw-KAW.

Daily Bible Readings

MONDAY
God Has Done Great Things
(Psalm 126)

TUESDAY
Joy Fulfilled in Love
(John 15:9–17)

WEDNESDAY
God's Joy is Your Strength
(Nehemiah 8:9–12)

THURSDAY
Joy Fulfilled in Christ's Sacrifice
(Philippians 2:1–11)

FRIDAY
Rejoice in the Lord Always
(Philippians 4:4–9)

SATURDAY
Fullness of Joy
(Psalm 16)

SUNDAY
How Lovely Is God's Dwelling Place
(Psalm 84)

Teaching Tips

Words You Should Know

A. God (Psalm 150:1) *'el* (Heb.)—God, god, or even a strong human

B. Might acts (v. 2) *geburah* (Heb.)—Works and capabilities that show a particular entity's strength

Teacher Preparation

Unifying Principle—I Just Want to Celebrate. People choose different ways to express their emotions. What are some of the ways that expressions of victory and joy can be shared? Psalms 149 and 150 offer great praise for who God is, and the joy of praising God with all that we are.

A. Read the Bible Background and Devotional Reading.

B. Pray for your students and lesson clarity.

C. Read the lesson Scripture in multiple translations.

O—Open the Lesson

A. Begin the class with prayer.

B. Play a song appropriate for a loud celebration such as "I Just Want to Celebrate" or "Shout!" How do these songs make you feel? When might you play or sing them?

C. Have the students read the Aim for Change and the In Focus story.

D. Ask students how events like those in the story weigh on their hearts and how they can view these events from a faith perspective.

P—Present the Scriptures

A. Read the Focal Verses and discuss the Background and The People, Places, and Times sections.

B. Have the class share what Scriptures stand out for them and why, with particular emphasis on today's themes.

E—Explore the Meaning

A. Use In Depth or More Light on the Text to facilitate a deeper discussion of the lesson text.

B. Pose the questions in Search the Scriptures and Discuss the Meaning.

C. Discuss the Liberating Lesson and Application for Activation sections.

N—Next Steps for Application

A. Summarize the value of using the psalms as sources and examples of worship and praise.

B. End class with a commitment to praise God using a full range of emotional expression.

Worship Guide

For the Superintendent or Teacher
Theme: Praise God with Music
Song: "Hallelujah for the Cross!"

Praise God with Music

Bible Background • PSALMS 147, 148, 149, and 150
Printed Text • PSALMS 149:1–5; 150:1–6 | Devotional Reading • EPHESIANS 5:15–20

—————— Aim for Change ——————

By the end of this lesson, we will COMPARE the reason for and the expressions of praising God in two psalms, GAIN spiritual inspiration by various types of praise music and hymns, and PRAISE God using the psalms.

————————— In Focus —————————

"Now go in there and play one of those pieces by Chopin, Beethoven or Mozart," Mr. Turner told his daughter. "You're a gifted pianist, Lisa. When Dr. Bradley hears you, I know you'll get a scholarship."

"Dad, you're making me nervous," Lisa replied. "I'm not sure what I'll play. I'll see what feels right once I've met him."

Lisa entered the college's recital room. Mr. Turner's daughter loved the piano and could play any musical genre—classical, R&B, folk, jazz. Her joy, however, was playing Negro spirituals. She said it made her feel good in her soul. But today, Mr. Turner was focused on one thing: Lisa playing so well she'd get a scholarship.

Mr. Turner was anxious to know how the audition was going. Suddenly, he heard music coming from the recital room. "What? A Negro spiritual?" he thought.

Several minutes later, Lisa appeared and her father was up in her face. "What were you thinking?" he said. "Why did you play that? Classical pieces win scholarships!"

"Dad," Lisa explained, "Dr. Bradley said I could play whatever I felt like playing, so I did. When I finished, he said it was a refreshing and inspiring choice…said it made him feel good in his soul…said I got a scholarship!"

"Praise the Lord!" Mr. Turner sang out!

God has given us a variety of musical styles to express joy and praise to Him. Name some musical styles, singers, and songs of praise that have enriched your times of worship.

—————— Keep in Mind ——————

"Let every thing that hath breath praise the LORD. Praise ye the LORD."
(Psalm 150:6, KJV)

"Let everything that breathes sing praises to the LORD! Praise the LORD!"
(Psalm 150:6, NLT)

Focal Verses

KJV **Psalm 149:1** Praise ye the LORD. Sing unto the LORD a new song, and his praise in the congregation of saints.

2 Let Israel rejoice in him that made him: let the children of Zion be joyful in their King.

3 Let them praise his name in the dance: let them sing praises unto him with the timbrel and harp.

4 For the LORD taketh pleasure in his people: he will beautify the meek with salvation.

5 Let the saints be joyful in glory: let them sing aloud upon their beds.

150:1 Praise ye the LORD. Praise God in his sanctuary: praise him in the firmament of his power.

2 Praise him for his mighty acts: praise him according to his excellent greatness.

3 Praise him with the sound of the trumpet: praise him with the psaltery and harp.

4 Praise him with the timbrel and dance: praise him with stringed instruments and organs.

5 Praise him upon the loud cymbals: praise him upon the high sounding cymbals.

6 Let every thing that hath breath praise the LORD. Praise ye the LORD.

NLT **Psalm 149:1** Praise the LORD! Sing to the LORD a new song. Sing his praises in the assembly of the faithful.

2 O Israel, rejoice in your Maker. O people of Jerusalem, exult in your King.

3 Praise his name with dancing, accompanied by tambourine and harp.

4 For the LORD delights in his people; he crowns the humble with victory.

5 Let the faithful rejoice that he honors them. Let them sing for joy as they lie on their beds.

150:1 Praise the LORD! Praise God in his sanctuary; praise him in his mighty heaven!

2 Praise him for his mighty works; praise his unequaled greatness!

3 Praise him with a blast of the ram's horn; praise him with the lyre and harp!

4 Praise him with the tambourine and dancing; praise him with strings and flutes!

5 Praise him with a clash of cymbals; praise him with loud clanging cymbals.

6 Let everything that breathes sing praises to the LORD! Praise the LORD!

The People, Places, and Times

Musical Instruments. Just as today's praise ensembles are comprised of many different kinds of instruments, the musicians of David's day had a variety of instruments to call on to use in a worship service. Many are mentioned in today's psalms (Psalm 149:3; 150:3–5). The "trumpet" (Heb. *shofar*, show-**FAR**) was a ram's horn, rather than the modern brass instrument. The "psaltery" (Heb. *nebel*, **NEH**-bell) was similar in shape to a lyre and was probably plucked rather than strummed. The "harp" (Heb. *kinnor*, ki-**NOHR**) was named because of its twanging sound. The "timbrel" (Heb. *toph*, **TOFE**) was closely akin to the modern tambourine. The "cymbals" (Heb. *tselatsal*, tseh-lah-**TSALL**) were probably double cymbals similar to the modern instrument; the Hebrew root means "to clatter."

Other instruments mentioned here are more obscure. "Stringed instruments" (Heb. *men*, **MEHN**) is from a root meaning "parted," as when dividing slender strings or when pressed a string to only play part of it. The word translated "organ" (Heb. *ugab*, oo-**GOB**) is from a root related to "blowing," and likely refers to a wind instrument like a pipe or flute. It is one of the oldest instruments of the Bible (Genesis 4:21).

8487602468

Background

The Book of Psalms can be grouped into five sections which have as their overarching themes: creation, the nation of Israel, God's holiness, the sovereignty of God's kingship over all nations, and thanksgiving and praise. The psalms in today's lesson are from the fifth section. They are a sub-category called the Hallelujah Psalms because these psalms, 146 through 150, begin and end with the Hebrew word, "Hallelujah," meaning "praise the Lord." Songs of joyful praise are a fitting conclusion to Psalms. The Psalms are noted for expressing the full range of human emotions, including deep feelings of praise.

Junction
Conjection

At-A-Glance

1. A Call to Praise (Psalm 149:1–3)
2. God Delights in Praise (vv. 4–5)
3. The Focus of Praise (Psalm 150:1–6)

In Depth

1. A Call to Praise (Psalm 149:1–3)

The call to praise is an invitation to creatively boast, showcase, commend, rave, and celebrate the Creator, who also is the One who gives victory to His people. This celebration is to be embodied through singing, dancing, the use of musical instruments, and the creative art of composing new musical masterpieces. Praise to God lifts us His triumphant ability to deliver, restore, and defend His people from their adversaries. For such feats, not any song will do, but a new song will need to be created.

In what ways should we treat God as a King?

2. God Delights in Praise (vv. 4–5)

The fact that God is both Creator and Victor could be reason enough to honor and praise Him. Yet, the writer gives a third: praise brings delight to God because God finds delight in caring for His people. Those who humbly come to God will find Him a faithful protector and defender. While God's protection does not exempt anyone from the realities of life in a fallen world, it provides an assurance that God is good, and that His peace and presence are eternally with those who trust Him (Psalm 23:4–6).

The history of those who have walked with God is a history of those who have fought, and even died, for Christ. A just God will vindicate those who remain faithful, even when they suffer hardships and cannot understand His ways (Hebrews 11:16). Faith will be rewarded, and that is something to sing about.

What does the phrase, "the LORD taketh pleasure in his people" mean to you?

3. The Focus of Praise (Psalm 150:1–6)

The psalm that concludes the Israelites' songbook concisely sums up the dominant message of the Hallelujah Psalms: God is to be praised. God is to be praised in our homes, our first house of worship; our sanctuaries, where we gather in community; and throughout the vast expanse of God's creation, basically, everywhere we go. God is to be praised for His works—what He does; and for His excellent greatness—who He is. God is to be praised with songs, instruments, and dance. Our creative skills, our bodies, and our musical tools are to be used in praise to God. God is to be praised by everyone who breathes. Each breath we take is part of a thankful rhythm of praise.

From Psalm 150, name two reasons for praising God.

Search the Scriptures

1. Who are the "saints" mentioned in Psalm 149:1 and 5? What are the responsibilities of those who are called saints?

2. What are some of God's mighty acts that have left you in awe of Him?

Discuss the Meaning

From the Hebrew language, Hallelujah is a word whose meaning—praise the Lord—and pronunciation is the same in nearly every language around the world. What might be some benefits to your church to learn and sing songs in different languages?

Liberating Lesson

Gospel music—which gave birth to the blues, jazz, soul, rock, and other styles of music—has in recent years been influenced by the genres it birthed. For some church members, these new sounds are not gospel or what they would call church music. Others feel it is necessary to broaden the church's musical repertoire to appeal to younger audiences. What do you find in today's lesson that would cause you to take a stance on either side of that issue? What makes a musical style fitting for church worship?

Application for Activation

"Praise the Lord" is not an admonition we follow out of duty, but from deep delight. To praise the Lord is an invitation to share our delight in Him, and to tell of His goodness. When we enjoy something, whether it is a cup of coffee, a sports game, or time with a friend, we will verbally and creatively express our pleasure in the thing or person we enjoy. Take a moment to list some things you enjoy about God. Use the items on your list to write a song, poem, or prayer. Share your creation with others.

Follow the Spirit

What God wants me to do:

_____

_____

_____

_____

Remember Your Thoughts

Special insights I have learned:

_____

_____

_____

_____

More Light on the Text

Psalm 149:1–5; 150

1 Praise ye the LORD. Sing unto the LORD a new song, and his praise in the congregation of saints.

Both Psalms 149 and 150 begin with a command, "Praise ye the LORD." The Hebrew term for this phrase is familiar, hallelujah. Hallelujah literally means "praise the Lord." This simple phrase is jam-packed with meaning. First, it is an imperative, compelling the audience to praise. The "jah" part in hallelujah is short for the sacred name of God, which is often transliterated as Yahweh or Jehovah. This name is the personal name of Israel's God.

The psalmist instructs the audience also to sing to the Lord a new song. Singing to the Lord a new song is not novel in this psalm (Psalm 33:3; 96:1; 98:1; 144:9). Each occurrence implies that God's work is so magnificent that old songs, although true, do not fully capture everything about God that is worth singing about. The greatness and faithfulness of God is so inexhaustible that it demands us to compose knew songs to attempt to describe who God is.

The audience is to sing this new song to the assembly of the *chasid* (Heb., khaw-**SEED**). The *chasid* are faithful people who have set themselves apart by choosing to be loyal and faithful to God. Today, we call this people the Church. This passage helps us remember that the church is important not because it is a beautiful building, but because it is where God's praise is sung among people who separate themselves by remaining loyal to God.

2 Let Israel rejoice in him that made him: let the children of Zion be joyful in their King. 3 Let them praise his name in the dance: let them sing praises unto him with the timbrel and harp.

Israel has a special relationship with the God of the universe. They recognize that the God who was their God created everything, including them. God is not just a distant designer of the world, but the people of Israel recognized that God brought the people together out of the land of Egypt when they were not a people. God made them into a people by giving them laws, land, and life. Within this line one can see Israel's history and relationship with the Lord.

The second part of verse 2 hints toward the Israelites' invasion of the Canaanites' land that ends under David's reign. They captured the city of the Jebusites, which becomes Jerusalem also known as Zion. Zion was the hill where the Temple and king's palace resided, while the rest of the city spread around them. The psalmist wants to point the audience to a throne higher than the king's: the true heavenly Temple of which the earthly version was but a replica. The psalmist tells the people to be glad in the Lord, their ultimate King.

4 For the LORD taketh pleasure in his people: he will beautify the meek with salvation. 5 Let the saints be joyful in glory: let them sing aloud upon their beds.

God takes pleasure in His people. The word for "taketh pleasure," *ratzah* (Heb. rat-**ZAH**) can also mean to delight in, accept, or give favor. God finds delight in His people not because they are great, but because they are humble and lowly. The Hebrew for the word "beautify" is *pa'ar* (pah-**ARE**), also translates

as "crown" or "adorn," and ultimately means to make something worth boasting about. God does not take what is conventionally beautiful, but what others overlook. Not only that, but then God also gives them favor.

God grants salvation (Heb. *yeshuah*, **YEH**-shoo-ah) or victory, not because it is deserved, but because God is merciful. "Yeshuah" is the root for the name "Joshua," and its Greek variant "Jesus." God still today beautifies those who are weak, displeasing, unacceptable, and overlooked. God makes them worth boasting about because He adorns them with Jesus.

Being beautified by God leads faithful folks (Heb. *chasid*, see v. 1) to rejoice in such an honor. The praise that erupts from people who are otherwise insignificant keeps those favored believers awake at night. They recognize the unmerited victory that God gives them as His people, and it leads them to sing for joy.

Psalm 150
1 Praise ye the LORD. Praise God in his sanctuary: praise him in the firmament of his power.

As noted above, "hallelujah" means "praise the Lord." This part of the verse contrasts the next part that says, "praise God." The word for "God" in this verse is *'el* (Heb. **ELL**). *'El* means "god" and can refer to other gods and can even refer to a strong human. The psalmist, however, in no uncertain terms, begins the psalm with an instruction and specification. It is an instruction to praise, and the term specifies to whom the praise belongs. The praise does not belong to just any god, the praise belongs to Yahweh, the Self-existing One.

This psalm instructs the audience on the arenas in which to praise God and the abilities for which to praise Him (vv. 1–2). The first arena is God's sanctuary. The word for sanctuary is *qodesh* (Heb. **KOH**-desh), which means holy place. It often refers to the place where God's presence dwelt. Within the Temple, in the Holy of Holies, God's presence dwelt in a special way. In many ways, the holiness of all of Israel radiated from the Holy of Holies. The chamber outside of the Holy of Holies was holy. The room beyond that was holy. The space outside of that where the worshipers offered their sacrifices and prayers was holy, and that holiness filtered out into the entire land.

We are also to praise Him "in the firmament of his power." We can trace the word "firmament" back to Creation, when God made the firmament and called it "sky" (Genesis 1:6–8). The people's praise is to go even beyond the holy place; their praise is to go all the way up into the heavens where God's power is clearly manifested. In this way, their praise is transcendent. It does not focus on the cares of the world, but instead it is exalted to the God of heaven.

The command to praise God in the firmament could also be an instruction to angels who reside in the heavens. It could address God's heavenly court. Many ancient writers believed that the Temple in Jerusalem was a temporary replica based on an eternal heavenly model. The psalmist envisions a worshiping community that does not only include praising on earth, but it also includes praising God in the heavens. The psalmist is inviting all created things on earth and above the earth to give God praise.

2 Praise him for his mighty acts: praise him according to his excellent greatness.

The psalmist moves from the arenas for praising God to reasons to praise God. The first reason is manifested in God's acts of power. The word for "mighty acts" is *geburah* (Heb. geh-boo-**RAH**). It is used to refer to works and capabilities that belong to a particular entity (Judges 5:31; Job 39:19). God's acts of power are works that only God can do. Only God can do what God can do! God's works are

incomparable, inimitable, and innumerable. We cannot truly find any comparison for the way that God acts and moves in the world. Therefore, the psalmist instructs us to praise God for God's acts of power, the type of acts that only God can do!

The psalmist then implores the worshipers to praise God for His "excellent greatness." The phrase suggests that worshipers are to praise God because He surpasses or excels the very concept of greatness. God is so amazing that "great" is insufficient to describe Him. Greatness is anemic in describing God's works. God's activity in the world and in our lives surpasses, exceeds, and goes beyond greatness. God is so great that even God's greatness is excellent. The psalmist invites us to praise a God that the word greatness only begins to describe.

3 Praise him with the sound of the trumpet: praise him with the psaltery and harp. 4 Praise him with the timbrel and dance: praise him with stringed instruments and organs. 5 Praise him upon the loud cymbals: praise him upon the high sounding cymbals.

The psalmist tells the worshipers where to praise, then why to praise, and finally the psalmist says how to praise—with instruments! The psalmist depicts a symphony of praise. Each instrument is mentioned in this lessons' People, Places, and Times section, but there is more to say on two of them.

The "trumpet" (Heb. *shofar*, a ram's horn) was a symbol of three things: 1) God's voice, 2) God's victory, and 3) God's freedom. The shofar was a reminder of God's thundering voice at Mount Sinai (Exodus 19). Later the Israelites blasted the shofar to announce the victory God had given them over the people of Jericho (Joshua 6). Finally, the priests were to blow the shofar on the Day of Atonement (Yom Kippur) and in the fiftieth year in order to proclaim the Year of Jubilee (Leviticus 25). The year of Jubilee occurred every fifty years, and those who were in debt or bondage were set free. The blasting of the horn let all of the bound Israelites know that they were set free. The psalmist picks up on this and commands the worshiper to praise God with a symbol of freedom.

This freedom can also be captured in one of the other instruments mentioned. The psalmist brings in the "harp" (Heb. *kinnor*), which is the instrument that David masterfully used to free Saul from the evil spirits that he had (1 Samuel 16:14–23). The psalmist invites the worshipers to praise God in a way that echoes God's liberating power. This leads to dancing and playing the timbrel or tambourine and stringed instruments. The praise that the psalmist envisions is one founded on, rooted in, and performed with freedom.

6 Let every thing that hath breath praise the LORD. Praise ye the LORD.

We noted above that the psalmist could be inviting the angels into the praise party, and in this verse the psalmist is inviting everything that has breath into the festivities. This creates a low barrier for entry, to say the least. Every breathing, living thing owes God praise if for no other reason than the fact that God is the Creator of every living thing. In the Bible, this is particularly important for the human creature, because God personally took time to craft humans in God's image and then personally breathed in them the breath of life (Genesis 2:7). Life itself then becomes its own reason to praise the Lord.

The repetition of "praise the LORD" could be a statement of emphasis. Often in Hebrew, a writer will repeat a phrase to emphasize it. We do this in English as well. When we really, really mean something, we accentuate the statement by saying it again. Here the psalmist could be saying that everything with breath needs to really praise the Lord. Even if they do not have musical talents or skills and even though they cannot comprehend the excellent greatness of God, worshipers are called praise the Lord, praise the Lord, for real, for real.

Sources:
Barton, John and John Muddiman. *The Oxford Bible Commentary.* New York: Oxford University Press. 2001.
Berlin, Adele, ed., and Marc Zvi Brettler, ed. *The Jewish Study Bible,* second edition. New York: Oxford University Press. 2014.
Fee, Gordon D. and Robert L. Hubbard, Jr. *The Eerdmans Companion to the Bible.* Grand Rapids, MI: Wm. B. Eerdmans Publishing Company, 2011.
Henry, Matthew. *Matthew Henry's Commentary on the Whole Bible: New Modern Edition.* Vols. 1-6. Peabody, MA: Hendrickson Publishers, Inc., 2009.
Life Application Study Bible, New Living Translation. Wheaton, IL: Tyndale House Publishers, Inc., 1996.
Strong, James. *The New Strong's Exhaustive Concordance of the Bible.* Nashville, TN: Thomas Nelson, 2010.
Thayer, Joseph Henry. *A Greek-English Lexicon of the New Testament.* New York: American Book Company, 1889.
Warren, Gwendolin Sims. *Ev'ry Time I Feel The Spirit, 101 Best-Loved Psalms, Gospel Hymns, and Spiritual Songs of the African-American Church.* New York: Henry Holt and Company, Inc. 1997.
Wright, N.T. *The Case for the Psalms.* New York: HarperOne. 2013.

1 2 3 4 5 6 7 8 9 10

12345 678910 11121314

Say It Correctly

Timbrel. TIM-brul.
Yom Kippur. YOM ki-POOR.

Daily Bible Readings

MONDAY
A Song of Praise Is Fitting
(Psalm 147:1–7)

TUESDAY
David's Music Soothes Saul
(1 Samuel 16:14–23)

WEDNESDAY
Paul and Silas Sing in Prison
(Acts 16:23–26)

THURSDAY
Praise the Name of the Lord
(Psalm 148)

FRIDAY
Psalms, Hymns, and Spiritual Songs
(Colossians 3:12–17)

SATURDAY
Making Melody to God
(Psalm 149)

SUNDAY
Praise God with Musical Instruments
(Psalm 150)

Notes

Teaching Tips

Words You Should Know

A. Number (Revelation 7:9) *arithmosai* (Gk.)—An amount, fixed or indefinite

B. Blessing (v. 12) *eulogia* (Gk.)—Speaking well of, commending in eloquent language

Teacher Preparation

Unifying Principle—The Rest of the Story. Celebrations that unite people from all over the world are significant and magnificent. How can we celebrate in spite of persecution and a hostile world? John's revelation proclaims that God will preserve believers from every nation, tribe, people group, and language who remain faithful to him despite hardship.

A. Read the Bible Background and Devotional Reading.

B. Pray for your students and lesson clarity.

C. Read the lesson Scripture in multiple translations.

O—Open the Lesson

A. Begin the class with prayer.

B. Start class by singing a song such as "We Shall Overcome" or "I Shall Not Be Moved." Why are those songs so popular during tough times? What do these songs presuppose about a universal giver of justice?

C. Have the students read the Aim for Change and the In Focus story.

D. Ask students how events like those in the story weigh on their hearts and how they can view these events from a faith perspective.

P—Present the Scriptures

A. Read the Focal Verses and discuss the Background and The People, Places, and Times sections.

B. Have the class share what Scriptures stand out for them and why, with particular emphasis on today's themes.

E—Explore the Meaning

A. Use In Depth or More Light on the Text to facilitate a deeper discussion of the lesson text.

B. Pose the questions in Search the Scriptures and Discuss the Meaning.

C. Discuss the Liberating Lesson and Application for Activation sections.

N—Next Steps for Application

A. Summarize the value of trusting that God is in control, even when situations seem to get out of hand.

B. End class with a commitment to pray to do right, even when circumstances tempt them to take the easy way out.

Worship Guide

For the Superintendent or Teacher
Theme: All People Praise God
Song: "Thank You, Lord"

All People Praise God

Bible Background • REVELATION 7:9–17
Printed Text • REVELATION 7:9–17 | Devotional Reading • REVELATION 1:1–8

Aim for Change

By the end of the lesson, we will UNDERSTAND how God's salvation and justice for all people inspires praise and worship; EMBRACE the significance of praising God in unity; and RESPOND to God's love, goodness, and grace with joy and exaltation.

In Focus

"I hate you, Mom!" Seventeen-year-old Curtis shouted as he slammed the door behind him. Patricia sank down in a kitchen chair, too weary to engage in another battle with her headstrong teenager. Her head was throbbing, and her heart was aching. First, her husband had lost his job. Then, her mother was diagnosed with cancer. And now, her son was rebelling against everything he had been taught.

Whom could she call? Where could she go? In a panic as she paced the floor, she called Sister Gladys from church.

Gladys listened to the whole rant and worry before saying, "Yep. That sounds about right. Have you tried praising God?"

"Oh, I've been praying..." Patricia said.

"No, no, no, not praying. Praising! Praise Him for being with you in these trials."

Patricia stopped in her pacing around the kitchen, and began to think back over the last few years of her life. She had been through many difficult times before. She closed her eyes and took a deep breath. God had been with her, helping her through all of those times. Patricia's heart lifted as she remembered God's faithfulness. She could trust Him to do what He said He would do.

How do we find the faith to trust God in difficult times? When we remember God's track record of grace and mercy, our faith is strengthened, giving us the courage to trust Him again. In times of trouble, we can count on God to keep His promises.

Keep in Mind

"These are they which came out of great tribulation, and have washed their robes, and made them white in the blood of the Lamb."
(from Revelation 7:14, KJV)

"These are the ones who died in the great tribulation. They have washed their robes in the blood of the Lamb and made them white."
(from Revelation 7:14, NLT)

Focal Verses

KJV **Revelation 7:9** After this I beheld, and, lo, a great multitude, which no man could number, of all nations, and kindreds, and people, and tongues, stood before the throne, and before the Lamb, clothed with white robes, and palms in their hands;

10 And cried with a loud voice, saying, Salvation to our God which sitteth upon the throne, and unto the Lamb.

11 And all the angels stood round about the throne, and about the elders and the four beasts, and fell before the throne on their faces, and worshipped God,

12 Saying, Amen: Blessing, and glory, and wisdom, and thanksgiving, and honour, and power, and might, be unto our God for ever and ever. Amen.

13 And one of the elders answered, saying unto me, What are these which are arrayed in white robes? and whence came they?

14 And I said unto him, Sir, thou knowest. And he said to me, These are they which came out of great tribulation, and have washed their robes, and made them white in the blood of the Lamb.

15 Therefore are they before the throne of God, and serve him day and night in his temple: and he that sitteth on the throne shall dwell among them.

16 They shall hunger no more, neither thirst any more; neither shall the sun light on them, nor any heat.

17 For the Lamb which is in the midst of the throne shall feed them, and shall lead them unto living fountains of waters: and God shall wipe away all tears from their eyes.

NLT **Revelation 7:9** After this I saw a vast crowd, too great to count, from every nation and tribe and people and language, standing in front of the throne and before the Lamb. They were clothed in white robes and held palm branches in their hands.

10 And they were shouting with a great roar, "Salvation comes from our God who sits on the throne and from the Lamb!"

11 And all the angels were standing around the throne and around the elders and the four living beings. And they fell before the throne with their faces to the ground and worshiped God.

12 They sang, "Amen! Blessing and glory and wisdom and thanksgiving and honor and power and strength belong to our God forever and ever! Amen."

13 Then one of the twenty-four elders asked me, "Who are these who are clothed in white? Where did they come from?"

14 And I said to him, "Sir, you are the one who knows." Then he said to me, "These are the ones who died in the great tribulation. They have washed their robes in the blood of the Lamb and made them white.

15 "That is why they stand in front of God's throne and serve him day and night in his Temple. And he who sits on the throne will give them shelter.

16 They will never again be hungry or thirsty; they will never be scorched by the heat of the sun.

17 For the Lamb on the throne will be their Shepherd. He will lead them to springs of life-giving water. And God will wipe every tear from their eyes."

The People, Places, and Times

Authorship. The author of Revelation identifies himself as "John" (1:4). Most of the early church scholars identified this "John" as the apostle John, son of Zebedee and brother of James. John, the writer of Revelation, was exiled to the island of Patmos as a consequence for spreading the Word of God and testifying to the existence and ministry of Jesus Christ. It was during this time of exile that he received the vision from God, the "revelation," which he faithfully recorded according to Jesus' instruction and for future generations (1:11).

Living Water. The multitude will enjoy eternal blessings, including "living fountains of waters" (7:17). "Living" water is water that is not stagnant; it is flowing from some source such as a spring or a river. It is constantly being renewed. Spiritually speaking, Jesus is the source of "living water" to those who are believers. When it is the right time, this living water will flow through the world, cleansing it (see Isaiah 35:5–10; Zechariah 14:20–21).

Compare and contrast these "living fountains of waters" (Revelation 7:17) with David's "still waters" (Psalm 23:2).

Background

In Revelation 5, John saw God holding a scroll that was sealed with seven seals. Jesus, "the Lion of the tribe of Judah" was the only one in heaven who was worthy to open the seals (5:5). Each time Jesus opened one of the seals, a corresponding judgment was visited upon the earth. Revelation 7 opens with four angels holding back the wind, signaling an interlude between the opening of the sixth and seventh seals. The events of our text today concerning the "great multitude" (7:9) take place during this lull.

At-A-Glance

1. The Great Multitude
(Revelation 7:9–10)
2. The Great Choir (vv. 11–12)
3. The Great Promises (vv. 13–17)

In Depth

1. The Great Multitude (Revelation 7:9–10)

John sees a new scene before him: a "great multitude" of people—so many that no one could count them (v. 9). They are of all different races, different cultures, and different languages. Nevertheless, all of these people have much in common with one another. All are wearing the white robes of the redeemed, waving the palm branches of the victorious, crying out: "Salvation to our God which sitteth upon the throne, and unto the Lamb" (v. 10).

In ancient times, dusty streets and manual labor mandated sturdy, functional clothing, not something that would show dirt quickly. This meant white garments were reserved for special occasions such as religious ceremonies and celebrations (2 Chronicles 5:12; Ecclesiastes 9:8). Festive palm branches were waved in conjunction with singing hymns and psalms, usually to celebrate a victory, but also during the reading of certain portions of Scripture and during feast days at the Tabernacle.

What would a modern crowd wear or wave to show celebration for God?

2. The Great Choir (vv. 11–12)

Joining in the praises of the great multitude are the rest of God's heavenly inhabitants—the angels, elders, and the "four beasts" (Revelation 7:11). These heavenly beings are constantly around the throne, worshiping and singing praise to God. In response to the worship of the great multitude, this heavenly choir leads the inhabitants of the throne room in a doxology, consisting of seven specific attributes of God and beginning and ending with an "amen" (v. 12). According to some scholars, there being seven items on this list implies their praise is complete or perfect.

3. The Great Promises (vv. 13–17)

During the great praise celebration around the throne, one of the elders explains that these are God's redeemed who have overcome. They have been cleansed by the blood of the Lamb, all of their sin washed away. They remained faithful through great tribulation and trials (vv. 13–14). Because of this, they would now receive eternal rewards.

They forever enjoy the presence of God. Jesus, the Lamb of God, will be our Shepherd. He will lead us to those springs of living water— His very life, flowing through us. And there will be no more cause to mourn (v. 17). God will wipe away every tear from our eyes. What joy! Our God loves us with an everlasting love! And because God keeps His promises, we have the courage to be faithful to a faithful God.

What are some rewards mentioned throughout Scripture for those who overcome trials in God's name?

Search the Scriptures

1. John saw a "great multitude" standing before the throne. What was the multitude doing (Revelation 7:9–10)?

2. Who else was standing around the throne besides the multitude (v. 11)?

Discuss the Meaning

1. The great multitude was enthusiastically worshiping God around the throne after coming through great trials and tribulation. How can their example help us live the life to which God has called each one of us?

2. The angels, elders, and creatures sang a doxology, ascribing praise to God in seven different ways. What are some specific aspects of God's nature for which Christians should praise Him? Why should we do this?

Liberating Lesson

Many people in our world today are concerned about the future. They wonder and worry about the economy, the environment, world peace, and their own families and friends. Christians are not excluded from the troubles and trials of this fallen, flawed world in which we live. But we have what the rest of the world does not—we have hope. Because of God's record of faithfulness in His Word, and to us personally, we have hope to face life's uncertainties.

Application for Activation

We, too, face these same trials in our own lives as believers. Satan wages a war against every person who chooses to follow Jesus Christ as Lord. We may not face an executioner's sword, but we will be tested and tried as we live out our lives of service to God. How can we worship God in the middle of a difficult, pain-filled situation?

The key is this: God is always faithful to His own. When we are faced with an untenable situation, we must look back to what God has already done on our behalf. When we start to meditate on God's faithfulness, we will begin to feel our faith rise to meet the challenge of the day. Keep a journal to aid you in remembering and rejoicing in God's faithfulness to you personally.

Follow the Spirit

What God wants me to do:

_____

_____

_____

_____

Remember Your Thoughts

Special insights I have learned:

_____

_____

_____

_____

More Light on the Text

Revelation 7:9–17

9 After this I beheld, and, lo, a great multitude, which no man could number, of all nations, and kindreds, and people, and tongues, stood before the throne, and before the Lamb, clothed with white robes, and palms in their hands.

The expressions "after this" and "after these things" are familiar time markers moving us forward in the book of Revelation (see 1:19; 4:1; 7:1; 18:1; 19:1). John has just seen a group of 144,000 from the tribes of Israel sealed by God's angel.

Now "after this," John sees a heavenly crowd beyond calculation. These are believing individuals from "all nations (Gk. *ethnos*), and kindreds (Gk. *phule*), and people (Gk. *laos*), and tongues (Gk. *glossa*)." The point of using all four of these synonyms is not to highlight their different shades of meaning, but to emphasize the overwhelming variety of the crowd. Not a single demographic of any kind is overlooked. Placed as it is directly following the election of 144,000 Jews, this multitude assures believers that God cares not just for the nation He chose long ago in Abraham, but for all humans who bear His image.

Having "palms in their hands" reminds us of the festive celebration at Jesus' triumphal entry during the last week of His earthly life (John 12:13). Palm branches were also used regularly at the Jewish annual Feast of Tabernacles (also called the Feast of Booths; Leviticus 23:40).

10 And cried with a loud voice, saying, Salvation to our God which sitteth upon the throne, and unto the Lamb.

"Salvation to our God" means that salvation belongs to God. God is the only source of rescue from the ultimate ruin and judgment to come. Therefore, salvation "is the gift of God" (Ephesians 2:8). This gift of salvation comes to us through the Lamb, Jesus, who sacrificed Himself to work out a way for our salvation.

11 And all the angels stood round about the throne, and about the elders and the four beasts, and fell before the throne on their faces, and worshipped God,

Picture a series of circles around the heavenly throne. The outer ring is composed of all the angels. Nearer are the 24 elders and the four living creatures—the cherubim, each with a face of a different creature and each with six wings completely covered with eyes (Revelation 4:6–8; see also Ezekiel 1:5–16). The inside circle is composed of the throng dressed in white (v. 9). Each group falls prostrate and gives praise to God.

The Greek for "elders" is *presbuteros* (pres-**BOO**-ter-os), which means older or senior persons and can also mean representatives. John first sees them in his heavenly vision dressed in white, wearing crowns, and sitting on thrones (Revelation 4:4). They cast their crowns before the throne of God (v. 10). We also read that they continually worship and praise God (Revelation 5:11, 14; 11:16; 14:3; 19:4); they encourage John when the vision causes him to cry (5:5); they bring to God the prayers of the saints (5:8); and one of them helps John understand the vision (7:13). Their robes and crowns might symbolize how they have remained faithful to God unto death (2:10, 3:4). Many have thought that they represent the 12 tribes of Israel plus the 12 apostles. Jesus promised the apostles 12 thrones for following the Lord (Matthew 19:27–29). Others have seen in them an illusion to the 24 representative priestly leaders (there were too many priests for all to serve) first mentioned in 1 Chronicles 24:1–19.

12 Saying, Amen: Blessing, and glory, and wisdom, and thanksgiving, and honour, and power, and might, be unto our God for ever and ever. Amen.

Now the angels are fallen prostrate before God, saying "amen" to the previous praise of the multitude and then giving their own words of praise, every word of which is meaningful. First they ascribe blessing to God. The Greek for "blessing" is *eulogia* (yoo-log-EE-ah), which is the same root as for "eulogy," the words of praise we offer the dead at a funeral. The Greek word includes the sense of speaking well of, commending in eloquent language, and praising our living God. We should be always blessing God because He both created us and redeemed us.

Next, the angels ascribe "glory" to God. This word refers to God's radiant splendor. His presence physically illumines His surroundings. This is why He will be the light of the New Jerusalem (Revelation 22:5).

The angels also ascribe "wisdom" (Gk. *sophia*, so-FEE-ah) to God. This is wisdom in the spiritual sense as well as in the sense of knowledge. All truth and all knowledge come from God.

Then the angels offer "thanksgiving" to God. We also should be continually thanking God for all the wonderful things He is doing and has done for us.

Fifth, the angels ascribe "honour" to God. God is God and He is worthy to be worshiped. In our prayers, we may forget and focus on the things we want from God, instead of worshiping Him as He deserves.

Then the angels ascribe "power" to God. God's hand is never shortened so that it cannot save us (Isaiah 59:1). In the end, everything will be worked out according to His will. Amazingly, He uses His power to save us.

Finally, the angels ascribe "might," or strength, to God. We often find we do not have the strength in ourselves to do the things we wish to do for our God, but the secret is in drawing upon His strength. As we look at the angels' words of continuous praise, we can meditate upon these words and offer them up to God as well.

13 And one of the elders answered, saying unto me, What are these which are arrayed in white robes? and whence came they? 14 And I said unto him, Sir, thou knowest. And he said to me, These are they which came out of great tribulation, and have washed their robes, and made them white in the blood of the Lamb.

At this juncture, one of the 24 elders speaks up for only the second time in the Book of Revelation. Old Testament visions often involved similar exchanges between a knowledgeable heavenly being and the seer (Zechariah 4:1–6; Jeremiah 1:11–14).

Many read the Bible's uses of the term "tribulation" in one of two ways: (1) to refer to the general trials throughout all the ages (Acts 14:22; Romans 5:3) and (2) to refer to the specific time of tribulation prior to end-time events. Examples of the second usage include one of Daniel's later visions: "there shall be a time of trouble, such as never was since there was a nation even to that same time" (from Daniel 12:1). Hundreds of years later, Jesus also foretells a "great tribulation, such as was not since the beginning of the world to this time, no, nor ever shall be" (Matthew 24:21). This multitude could be comprised of those who have experienced tribulation in both senses.

21 devices

There is a striking irony in the image of washing a garment in blood and it coming out white. However, this whitening or cleansing is like none other on earth, for these people have washed their robes in the blood of the Lamb (cf. Isaiah 1:18). This is why we sing, "What can wash away my sins? Nothing but the blood of Jesus."

15 Therefore are they before the throne of God, and serve him day and night in his temple: and he that sitteth on the throne shall dwell among them.

The last three verses are often read or quoted at funerals because they beautifully depict the current condition of those who are now with the Lord. The afterlife is not a do-nothing time of leisure and laziness. His people "serve him day and night" (v. 15). Of course, there in that perfect environment we will not have any tiredness, drudgery, poor pay, or lack of motivation, for His sinless servants serve Him willingly and joyfully. We will be engaged in wonderful work without any weariness. While our deceased loved ones who belong to God currently enjoy His presence, after the final resurrection we will worship God in this way with our new bodies (1 Corinthians 15:44). No tired muscles or minds then! John's final vision of the New Heaven echoes this truth (Revelation 22:1-5).

God is pictured throughout Revelation as the One who sits upon or occupies the throne. The saints will gather around the throne, so that God will "dwell" among us. The Greek verb _skenoo_ (skay-**NO**-oh) is only used by John in the New Testament. It is used of people who will or do live in heaven, and importantly it is applied to Jesus' incarnation at the beginning of John's Gospel: "The Word [Jesus] became flesh and dwelt among us" (John 1:14). This verb is interesting because it is based on the word _skene_ (Gk. skee-**NAY**), which means "tent." By using this word, John recalls the tent structure of the Tabernacle and the days of God's presence in the wilderness, so overt and caring.

16 They shall hunger no more, neither thirst any more; neither shall the sun light on them, nor any heat.

In contrast to the problems faced by many people in agricultural societies (such as the Israelites of long ago), there will be no hunger, thirst, or heat. John's audience knew an oasis could mean the difference between life and death. Remember how Hagar and Ishmael wandered in the desert until their water ran out and she thought they would die (Genesis 21:14–19). Today, many of us are often strapped with bills that chase us from payday to payday. None of that there! No needs go unmet. No stress or frustration. No more doing without.

17 For the Lamb which is in the midst of the throne shall feed them, and shall lead them unto living fountains of waters: and God shall wipe away all tears from their eyes.

The book of Revelation gives many paradoxical pictures that surprise and baffle us. For example, we see the Lion who is a Lamb (Revelation 5:5–6) who is the light (21:23). Revelation 7:17 reveals another one of these amazing pictures: the Lamb who is our Shepherd (cf. John 10:11) as He feeds and waters His people.

The last benefit in Revelation 7:17 is that "God shall wipe away all tears from their eyes." When drive-by shootings, abandoned newborns, gambled-away money, and hungry children cause us to cry, we have the promise of God that one day He will put all of that away (see also Revelation 22:3). In response to this wonderful truth, His people can only shout, "Hallelujah!" Yes, eventually we will live happily ever after.

Sources:

Henry, Matthew. *Matthew Henry's Commentary on the Whole Bible: New Modern Edition*. Vols. 1-6. Peabody, MA: Hendrickson Publishers, Inc., 2009.

Strong, James. *The New Strong's Exhaustive Concordance of the Bible*. Nashville, TN: Thomas Nelson, 2003.

Thayer, Joseph Henry. *A Greek-English Lexicon of the New Testament*. New York: American Book Company, 1889.

Say It Correctly

Patmos. **PAT**-moce.
Ishmael. **ISH**-may-el.

Daily Bible Readings

MONDAY
May God's Ways Be Known
(Psalm 67)

TUESDAY
The Nations Flock to Mount Zion
(Isaiah 2:1–5)

WEDNESDAY
Make Disciples of All Nations
(Matthew 28:16–20)

THURSDAY
Gentiles Seek the Lord
(Zechariah 8:18–23)

FRIDAY
All the Nations Will Glorify God
(Psalm 86:1–11)

SATURDAY
God's Servants Sealed
(Revelation 7:1–8)

SUNDAY
Multitudes Praise God
(Revelation 7:9–17)

Notes

_____

_____

_____

_____

Teaching Tips

Words You Should Know

A. Sounded (v. 15) *salpizo* (Gk.)—Blast, specifically, blowing a trumpet

B. Destroy (v. 18) *diaphtheiro* (Gk.)—To thoroughly destroy, corrupt, or contaminate

Teacher Preparation

Unifying Principle—Who's in Charge Here? Celebrations are ways of culminating a unique event and creating new ways of being in community. How do people celebrate in a hostile world? Revelation helps us understand that all of the world is moving toward the just, eternal reign of God.

A. Read the Bible Background and Devotional Reading.

B. Pray for your students and lesson clarity.

C. Read the lesson Scripture in multiple translations.

O—Open the Lesson

A. Begin the class with prayer.

B. Read your class a copy of the naturalization oath of allegiance that new US citizens make. Help participants write an oath in which they renounce being a citizen of the kingdom of this world and proclaim allegiance to the kingdom of our Lord.

C. Have the students read the Aim for Change and the In Focus story.

D. Ask students how events like those in the story weigh on their hearts and how they can view these events from a faith perspective.

P—Present the Scriptures

A. Read the Focal Verses and discuss the Background and The People, Places, and Times sections.

B. Have the class share what Scriptures stand out for them and why, with particular emphasis on today's themes.

E—Explore the Meaning

A. Use In Depth or More Light on the Text to facilitate a deeper discussion of the lesson text.

B. Pose the questions in Search the Scriptures and Discuss the Meaning.

C. Discuss the Liberating Lesson and Application for Activation sections.

N—Next Steps for Application

A. Summarize the value of trusting that God is still in control, even though some still wage a losing battle against him.

B. End class with a commitment to pray for the faithfulness of Christ's followers to be rewarded.

Worship Guide

For the Superintendent or Teacher
Theme: Praise for God's Eternal Reign
Song: "Hallelujah"
(further verses: Lord, We Praise You,
Lord, We Love You, etc.)

Praise for God's Eternal Reign

Bible Background • REVELATION 11
Printed Text • REVELATION 11:15–19 | Devotional Reading • REVELATION 1:9–17

—————— Aim for Change ——————

By the end of this lesson, we will DEFINE the nature of God's reign for eternity; REFLECT on how God's eternal reign affects our faith; and ENGAGE in activities that reflect the sovereignty of God in healthy, powerful, and transforming ways.

————— In Focus —————

There was a lot of buzz in the halls; the merger had been publicly announced, and the company's new owner was visiting each of the recently acquired subsidiaries. Today, he was in town to meet the staff at this site.

Phil tried to concentrate on the report he was writing on a looming deadline, but he had to stop. An announcement came instructing everyone to go to the large multipurpose room for a question-and-answer session.

At the front of the room, Phil saw the division vice president looking both grim and relieved. Grim because financial pressures had made the company vulnerable to the takeover, but relieved because the new owning company had a track record of adding resources to help its acquisitions grow.

For his part, Phil liked where he worked; the job fulfilled him professionally and offered time to continue his outside interests, like volunteering at his church's food pantry and singing with the choir. He had left his previous job because it didn't respect his need to devote time to serve the Lord through these activities. But this new company had a reputation for honoring its employees' work-life balance—a directive from the top.

When the new owner entered the room, the vice president stood and applauded, leading the group of employees to do likewise. It was a new day at the company, and Phil smiled with hope that it would be a better one.

When have things worried you, but then turned out for the better?

—————— Keep in Mind ——————

"The kingdoms of this world are become the kingdoms of our Lord, and of his Christ; and he shall reign for ever and ever." (from Revelation 11:15, KJV)

"The world has now become the Kingdom of our Lord and of his Christ, and he will reign forever and ever." (from Revelation 11:15, NLT)

Focal Verses

KJV **Revelation 11:15** And the seventh angel sounded; and there were great voices in heaven, saying, The kingdoms of this world are become the kingdoms of our Lord, and of his Christ; and he shall reign for ever and ever.

16 And the four and twenty elders, which sat before God on their seats, fell upon their faces, and worshipped God,

17 Saying, We give thee thanks, O LORD God Almighty, which art, and wast, and art to come; because thou hast taken to thee thy great power, and hast reigned.

18 And the nations were angry, and thy wrath is come, and the time of the dead, that they should be judged, and that thou shouldest give reward unto thy servants the prophets, and to the saints, and them that fear thy name, small and great; and shouldest destroy them which destroy the earth.

19 And the temple of God was opened in heaven, and there was seen in his temple the ark of his testament: and there were lightnings, and voices, and thunderings, and an earthquake, and great hail.

NLT **Revelation 11:15** Then the seventh angel blew his trumpet, and there were loud voices shouting in heaven: "The world has now become the Kingdom of our Lord and of his Christ, and he will reign forever and ever."

16 The twenty-four elders sitting on their thrones before God fell with their faces to the ground and worshiped him.

17 And they said, "We give thanks to you, Lord God, the Almighty, the one who is and who always was, for now you have assumed your great power and have begun to reign.

18 The nations were filled with wrath, but now the time of your wrath has come. It is time to judge the dead and reward your servants the prophets, as well as your holy people, and all who fear your name, from the least to the greatest. It is time to destroy all who have caused destruction on the earth."

19 Then, in heaven, the Temple of God was opened and the Ark of his covenant could be seen inside the Temple. Lightning flashed, thunder crashed and roared, and there was an earthquake and a terrible hailstorm.

The People, Places, and Times

The Trumpet. In this section of Revelation 11, an angel sounds a trumpet and the ongoing worship around the throne enters a different phase. The sounding of the trumpet first represents God's judgment (Revelation 8:6–13). In ancient times, the trumpet would sound to call the Israelites to order and draw their attention to what may be happening at the Temple. There is even a Feast of Trumpets (Leviticus 23:23–25). The blowing of the trumpet is a signal to draw attention to God. First, His holiness, His victory, His liberty, and His guidance are all acknowledged by the trumpet. Then, of course any time there is an acknowledgment of God, there must be praise!

What are some of the things that we see or hear, that immediately call us to worship?

Background

While many traditions have encouraged a reaction of fear of this book, its actual purpose is not to elicit fear, but rather to incite an unadulterated and unhindered worship to Almighty God. The Book of Revelation largely tells the drama of the completion of God's plan played out in three separate acts: Act I featuring seals being opened, Act II featuring trumpets heralding the arrival of God's eternal kingdom, and Act III featuring bowls of judgment on those who reject God. Each act contains songs celebrating the action. Revelation 11 describes the action ending Act II, the blowing of the seventh trumpet

In verse 16 we see the four and twenty elders giving worship to God, their consecrated purpose. Not only is their position notable for seniority and designation, but the level of their praise is so intent that it sets a high standard for anyone endeavoring to attain position within the contemporary terrestrial church. Leadership is not about the robes, titles, or positions. Leadership is ultimately about worship and providing an example of complete devotion to God.

At-A-Glance

1. The Worship (Revelation 11:15–18)
2. The Wonder (v. 19)

In Depth

1. The Worship (Revelation 11:15–18)

Who are these four and twenty elders? How were they selected for their choice roles in the holiest arena, serving solely to honor, worship and adore God? This is the beauty of the Revelation. While scholars and skeptics alike may dither about the individual identities of each being that is presented here, the point is not who they are, but who God is. Whether beast, elder, or angel, their purpose is to acknowledge God, exemplifying what it means to worship God in spirit and in truth.

Their worship begins with thanksgiving. They honor the eternal God, and they submit themselves as subject to God's judgment. They also recognize that the wicked works of this world may seem to have success for a time, but

they confirm that God has the final say. This worship is not only intense, it is thorough.

Why do the elders praise God for dealing out deadly judgments?

2. The Wonder (v. 19)

In our time, extremes in weather are usually measured for their disruption to the normal flow of activities. The idea of great lightnings, thunder, earthquakes, and hail can be frightening, inconvenient, and might even ultimately prove disastrous to human or financial collateral. Yet, this worship of God precedes an eruption of what appears to be harsh weather. This is not, however, the purpose.

By recognizing God as almighty, eternal, and all powerful, the elders actually have invoked God to demonstrate His authority over all creation. Who can make lightning but God? Who can move the earth and the sky, and wring from them all their treasures? Echoing scenes from the Psalms (Psalm 96–98), John's report covers any questions on whether God is confined to heaven or restricted on earth. He is neither. He alone is God!

When have you seen evidence of God's miraculous power in your life?

Search the Scriptures

1. Why do the elders give thanks to God at this moment (Revelation 11:17)?

2. Who will be rewarded? Who will be destroyed (v. 18)?

Discuss the Meaning

1. What are some examples of the angel's trumpet today, things that draw our attention back to God (Revelation 11:15)?

2. Why did the reveal of the Ark of the Covenant spark such an explosive reaction from the elements of nature (v. 19)?

Liberating Lesson

With so many people trying to fight systemic racism, generational poverty, and mass incarceration, it can be discouraging to see little progress being made. Worry and helplessness can distract us from the good news that in the end, God will bring ultimate justice. Despite what may make noise and distract us from time to time, we can be sure that only God will reign in the end. Better to start our worship now rather than to wait.

Application for Activation

We know that the powers of evil will attempt to subvert the work of God's kingdom, waging a losing battle against Him. However, we also know that only God through Christ can bring eternal peace. Believers await a time at the end of this age when evil will no longer exist, and the faithfulness of Christ's followers will be rewarded. Until that day, we must work to make God's will be done on earth as it is in His heavenly kingdom.

Begin by seeking new ways and reasons to worship God. He has proven Himself worthy in the past, and continues to do so today. If we are truly committed to exercising a lifestyle of praise and adoration to God, this world had better watch out for the worshipers!

Follow the Spirit

What God wants me to do:

Remember Your Thoughts

Special insights I have learned:

_____

_____

_____

_____

More Light on the Text
Revelation 11:15–19

The book of Revelation, written by John, is a prophecy—a biblical message given to God's chosen messenger as a warning or comforting in time of crisis—sent to seven churches in the ancient Roman province of Asia. John begins by telling the church how it ought to live. He tells each church the special reward believers will receive for living holy. Each reward is pulled from the final vision of the marriage of heaven and earth.

John has a vision of God's Heavenly throne room. He describes it with imagery from various Old Testament prophets, which believers of John's day would have recognized and understood immediately. God is surrounded with creatures and elders and they are giving honor and allegiance to the one true creator God who is Holy. The cycles of seven (seals, trumpets, and bowls) depict God's kingdom and justice coming here on earth as in heaven. The Lamb begins to open the scroll's first four seals and John sees four horsemen, an image from the book of Zechariah symbolizing times of war, famine, and death. Later, John sees an angel with a signet ring coming to place a mark of protection on God's servants who are enduring all this hardship and he hears the number of those who are sealed: 144,000 is the military census, like the one in the book of Numbers.

At another point, an angel brings John a scroll. John is told to eat the scroll, then proclaim its message to the nations just as Ezekiel was (Ezekiel 3:3). Then John sees God's Temple and the martyrs by the altar and is told to measure and set them apart. It's an image of protection taken from Zechariah (Zechariah 2).

Directly before today's passage, God appoints two witnesses as prophetic representatives to the nations. John calls them lampstands, clear symbols for the churches. Then suddenly a beast appears and conquers the witnesses, killing them. God brings them back to life and vindicates the witnesses before their persecutors. The end result is that many among the nations finally give glory to the Creator God in the day of the Lord.

15 And the seventh angel sounded; and there were great voices in heaven, saying, The kingdoms of this world are become the kingdoms of our Lord, and of his Christ; and he shall reign for ever and ever.

When the seventh and final trumpet is sounded (i.e. played), all the heavenly host, angels and redeemed human spirits, join to magnify God. God had changed the entire trajectory of the enemy's plan. He is victorious over the enemy, and the voices in Heaven are loud about it. We are not certain who these "great voices in heaven" are or represent, perhaps angels or martyrs or other creatures. What is clear is their announcement.

The time has finally come for Jesus Christ to take the Kingdom. These words are now familiar to many as the "Hallelujah Chorus" from Handel's *Messiah*. This announcement is given with great expectation because we see the completeness of full possession of His authority later in John's vision (Revelation 20). That possession, though it will be fully realized later, has begun now. We are currently living in the kingdom of our Lord and of His Christ.

16 And the four and twenty elders, which sat before God on their seats, fell upon their faces, and worshipped God, 17 Saying, We give thee thanks, O LORD God Almighty, which art, and wast, and art to come; because thou hast taken to thee thy great power and hast reigned.

From the time Jesus took the seven-sealed scroll until this very moment, every step of the way we have seen the expanding consequences. Through all of this, all of the circumstances that are happening, there has been captivating heavenly engagement and intensified enthusiasm. Now, when the seventh trumpet sounds, all that exist in Heaven and all creation breaks out with resounding praises, songs of victory.

The twenty four elders had been seated. They no longer could contain themselves with what had been revealed. In reverence and humility they rise from their seats and fall upon their faces. When Jesus took the seven-sealed scroll, the elders fell down and gave thanks and praises to God (Revelation 5), but now here it was to a much greater level. They do not simply "fall" (Gk. *pipto*, **PEEP**-toe), but fall "to their faces." They humble themselves more sincerely. They do not just bow, they laid themselves on the ground. They praise the God who was and is and is to come, meaning He is forever the same (cf. Hebrews 13:8). The elders recognize and acknowledge God's right to rule and stand supreme over all the world. What a glorious day when our only king is King Jesus!

18 And the nations were angry, and thy wrath is come, and the time of the dead, that they should be judged, and that thou shouldest give reward unto thy servants the prophets, and to the saints, and them that fear thy name, small and great; and shouldest destroy them which destroy the earth.

Here we see all the lands in the world are angry. All will not be joyful, welcoming this sight, for there will be those who will be greeted with God's "wrath" (Gk. *orge*, oar-**GAY**). Wrath is retribution or punishment for an offense or a crime. In the Bible, this wrath can be justified or not, a feeling felt by God or by people (Ephesians 5:6; James 1:20). John is careful with his language reporting his vision, and only uses *orge* to describe God's wrath. Notably, though, the anger of the nations is described with a similar term. While the nations (and the dragon, Revelation 12:17) feel wrathful (Gk. *orgizo*, or-**GEED**-zo), only God has the power and authority to act on His justified wrath.

The wicked are about to get their due justice from God. It is a long time coming, but they are finally about to be judged by God. On the other hand, God is also passing out rewards to His people, His true servants who have been faithful to Him.

People sometimes become angry when others are being rewarded and they are not. We need never question if God is being fair with His judgments, however. The rewards (Gk. *misthos*, meece-**THOCE**) that God is dispensing are the fair wages of work done, whether good or bad. God does not play favorites. He ensures that actions are followed up with their natural, just consequences. He ensures that "small and great" alike have their equal time before the Judge. He sees those that "destroy" (Gk. *diaphtheiro*, dee-aff-theh-**EER**-oh) and enacts the same destruction on them. This is an intensified verb; simply *phtheiro* means "to destroy," but the addition of *dia-* makes it mean "to thoroughly destroy."

19 And the temple of God was opened in heaven, and there was seen in his temple in the ark of his testament: and there were lightnings, and voices, and thunderings, and an earthquake, and great hail.

The Tabernacle and the Temple of the Jews were copies of the actual Temple in Heaven (Exodus 25:40; Hebrews 8:5), which John now sees in his vision. Both the earthly and the heavenly Temple symbolize God's presence, and the Ark is at the very center of that symbol.

As the Jews knew the Temple, God's presence was insulated from unholy mortals by many layers of architecture. Gentiles could only go into the Temple so far; women could only go a little farther. Laymen could not enter the actual Temple building, which only certain priests could do. A priest was allowed in the Holy Place only for certain purposes, and only once a year was anyone allowed into the Holy of Holies. On that day, only the high priest would do, and even then only after he had been rigorously purified. Now, the Temple and even the Holy of Holies are kept are opened, abolishing the divides between God and man, and between the heavenly realm and earthly realm.

The thunder and lightning are reminiscent of when God's presence was on Mt. Sinai, as He communicated His Law to Moses (Exodus 19:16–19). God's kingdom has come (Revelation 11:15), so God is coming to uphold His Law, which is good for the righteous but deadly for the unrighteous. The storms, earthquake, and hail show God's power, which He uses to bless His people and punish His enemies. God used these very tools in the past, when He sent an earthquake to open the prison bars of Paul and Silas (Acts 16:26), and when He sent a plague of hail on Egypt (Exodus 9:18).

Open communication between heaven and earth as John sees it here will be disruptive, but there was a time when fellowship between heaven and earth was perfect. You can see this from God communing with man as early as the Garden of Eden, and many times as He talked and instructed the prophets of old. For example, He walked with Enoch (Genesis 5:21–24), He instructed Noah (Genesis 6:13–15), and God spoke to Moses (Exodus 3:2–6,13–15).

However, because of sin, that perfect fellowship was broken, separating us from the perfect relationship with God (Genesis 3:8–11). Disobedience and sin caused us to be separated from God.

But thank God for the Lamb of God, the second Adam who has redeemed us and brought us back into perfect worship between God and humanity (John 1:12). Those of us who have come into right fellowship with God can rejoice and be glad. We can celebrate and be joyous because we can worship God. We have been given a choice to accept Jesus Christ as our Savior. Once we receive Him, we are put in perfect relationship with Him. Amen.

Sources:
Henry, Matthew. *Matthew Henry's Commentary on the Whole Bible: New Modern Edition.* Vols. 1-6. Peabody, MA: Hendrickson Publishers, Inc., 2009.
Strong, James. *The New Strong's Exhaustive Concordance of the Bible.* Nashville, TN: Thomas Nelson, 2003.
Thayer, Joseph Henry. *A Greek-English Lexicon of the New Testament.* New York: American Book Company, 1889.

Say It Correctly

Terrestrial. tuh-**RESS**-tree-al.
Enoch. **EE**-nok.

Daily Bible Readings

MONDAY
Clap Your Hands, All You Peoples
(Psalm 47)

TUESDAY
An Everlasting Kingdom
(Daniel 4:34–37)

WEDNESDAY
Glory to God Now and Forever
(Jude 1:20–25)

THURSDAY
The Lord Is King Forever
(Psalm 10:12–18)

FRIDAY
God's Faithful Witnesses
(Revelation 11:3–10)

SATURDAY
The Lord Is Robed in Majesty
(Psalm 93)

SUNDAY
A Crescendo of Praise
(Revelation 11:11–19)

Notes

_____

_____

_____

_____

Teaching Tips

Words You Should Know

A. Alleluia (Revelation 19:1) *halleluia* (Gk.)—The Greek spelling of Hallelujah, a Hebrew phrase meaning "Praise Yahweh!"

B. Avenged (v. 2) *ekdikeo* (Gk.)—Meted out righteous justice

Teacher Preparation

Unifying Principle—Family Restored. People want to have victory over the wicked people in their lives and in the world. How will they find victory over the wicked? God has the final judgment of the world, and God is worthy of all praise.

A. Read the Bible Background and Devotional Reading.

B. Pray for your students and lesson clarity.

C. Read the lesson Scripture in multiple translations.

O—Open the Lesson

A. Begin the class with prayer.

B. Allow a few volunteers to tell about the most memorable weddings they have attended.

C. Have the students read the Aim for Change and the In Focus story.

D. Ask students how events like those in the story weigh on their hearts and how they can view these events from a faith perspective.

P—Present the Scriptures

A. Read the Focal Verses and discuss the Background and The People, Places, and Times sections.

B. Have the class share what Scriptures stand out for them and why, with particular emphasis on today's themes.

E—Explore the Meaning

A. Use In Depth or More Light on the Text to facilitate a deeper discussion of the lesson text.

B. Pose the questions in Search the Scriptures and Discuss the Meaning.

C. Discuss the Liberating Lesson and Application for Activation sections.

N—Next Steps for Application

A. Summarize the value of taking the Old and New Testaments together to reveal God's plan for humankind.

B. End class with a commitment to pray for the faithfulness of Christ's followers to be rewarded.

Worship Guide

For the Superintendent or Teacher
Theme: Rejoicing in Heaven
Song: "The Battle Hymn of the Republic"

(handwritten: Loretta 1 / Ann 2 / SisHill 3 / Felicia 4 / Andrea 5-6 / Norma 7-8)

Rejoicing in Heaven

Bible Background • REVELATION 19
Printed Text • REVELATION 19:1–8 | Devotional Reading • REVELATION 5:1–14

—— Aim for Change ——

By the end of this lesson, we will DISCUSS believers' understanding of the implications of God's judgment, BELIEVE that God's judgment is inclusive of God's justice and mercy, and ENJOY the love of Christ for all.

—— In Focus ——

Odetta fingered the prayer beads wrapped around her wrist as she looked at the charging documents one more time. She had read them numerous times over the past several months. Indeed, she had drafted them, meticulously, making certain that each charge was supported by more than enough facts, evidence, and testimony to prove the allegations of a criminal conspiracy. But she remembered something she learned in school about writing, something that had served her well even after she went to college, graduate school, and law school: Explain things well, because the reader can't ask you questions.

Odetta knew the defendant sitting across the courtroom was responsible for a multitude of bad acts. She knew it was her responsibility as state's attorney, representing the people, to bring him to account. Slowly, firmly, deliberately, day after day during this trial, she laid out the state's case, making sure all of the jurors could be as certain in their minds as she was in hers that this danger to the community needed to be removed, for the safety and betterment of all. And as she thumbed through the folder and scanned the charging documents one last time, she breathed a quick prayer, as she always did, for the Lord's justice to be served, quickly and fairly.

"The prosecution rests, your honor."

Can we trust God to propagate justice in the world? Or is His justice primarily to be served at the end of days?

(handwritten: continue reproduce)

—— Keep in Mind ——

"Let us be glad and rejoice, and give honour to him: for the marriage of the Lamb is come, and his wife hath made herself ready." (Revelation 19:7, KJV)

"Let us be glad and rejoice, and let us give honor to him. For the time has come for the wedding feast of the Lamb, and his bride has prepared herself."
(Revelation 19:7, NLT)

Focal Verses

KJV

Revelation 19:1 And after these things I heard a great voice of much people in heaven, saying, Alleluia; Salvation, and glory, and honour, and power, unto the Lord our God:

2 For true and righteous are his judgments: for he hath judged the great whore, which did corrupt the earth with her fornication, and hath avenged the blood of his servants at her hand.

3 And again they said, Alleluia And her smoke rose up for ever and ever.

4 And the four and twenty elders and the four beasts fell down and worshipped God that sat on the throne, saying, Amen; Alleluia.

5 And a voice came out of the throne, saying, Praise our God, all ye his servants, and ye that fear him, both small and great.

6 And I heard as it were the voice of a great multitude, and as the voice of many waters, and as the voice of mighty thunderings, saying, Alleluia: for the Lord God omnipotent reigneth.

7 Let us be glad and rejoice, and give honour to him: for the marriage of the Lamb is come, and his wife hath made herself ready.

8 And to her was granted that she should be arrayed in fine linen, clean and white: for the fine linen is the righteousness of saints.

NLT

Revelation 19:1 After this, I heard what sounded like a vast crowd in heaven shouting, "Praise the LORD! Salvation and glory and power belong to our God.

2 His judgments are true and just. He has punished the great prostitute who corrupted the earth with her immorality. He has avenged the murder of his servants."

3 And again their voices rang out: "Praise the LORD! The smoke from that city ascends forever and ever!"

4 Then the twenty-four elders and the four living beings fell down and worshiped God, who was sitting on the throne. They cried out, "Amen! Praise the LORD!"

5 And from the throne came a voice that said, "Praise our God, all his servants, all who fear him, from the least to the greatest."

6 Then I heard again what sounded like the shout of a vast crowd or the roar of mighty ocean waves or the crash of loud thunder: "Praise the LORD! For the Lord our God, the Almighty, reigns.

7 Let us be glad and rejoice, and let us give honor to him. For the time has come for the wedding feast of the Lamb, and his bride has prepared herself.

8 She has been given the finest of pure white linen to wear." For the fine linen represents the good deeds of God's holy people.

The People, Places, and Times

Bride. The imagery of the bride is used widely in the Bible as a description of the people of God. In the Old Testament, the prophets presented Israel (the Old Testament church) as a bride who had committed repeated adulteries (Jeremiah 3; Ezekiel 16; Hosea 3). The prophets also proclaimed that God was faithful to His unfaithful bride and would restore her (Jeremiah 33:10–11; Isaiah 61:10; 62:5). In the Book of Revelation, bride imagery is used often of the Church (the New Testament Israel) and her relationship to Christ. The bride belongs to Christ, who is the Bridegroom (John 3:29). In Revelation 21, the great wedding is portrayed with the Church prepared for her Bridegroom (vv. 2, 9).

Background

All of Revelation 18 is about the fall and destruction of Babylon. Throughout Revelation, John uses Babylon as emblematic of all evil empires, powers, and people. John's immediate audience in Revelation was the faithful Christ followers of his day, being persecuted and marginalized by the Roman Empire. Here in Revelation 19, John gives us a window into a future event in heaven where a "great multitude" is gathered in worship and praise of God for what He has done for them, and what He has done to those who have done evil.

What systems and empires today act against God's people as Babylon and Rome did?

At-A-Glance

1. The Demise of the Prostitute
(Revelation 19:1–3)
2. The Beautiful Bride (vv. 4–8)

In Depth

1. The Demise of the Prostitute (Revelation 19:1–3)

God's people in heaven praise God and worship Him for having brought judgment and destruction on Babylon, "the great prostitute" (v. 2, NLT). God's justice can be viewed as a two sided coin. God's ultimate judgment of His enemies is one side of God's justice. His mercy and grace toward those who follow Him is the other. His love for all humanity is the common element of His justice.

God warns again and again that all sin must be punished (Ezekiel 18:20; Romans 6:23). Yet God loves all humanity (John 3:16) and desires that all would turn to Him and be saved (1 Timothy 2:4). Each time God declares sinners must die, He follows that with an offer of eternal life if the sinner will turn away from their sins

and follow Him (Ezekiel 18:21–22; John 3:16; Romans 6:23). Those who choose evil, however, who willfully reject Him and choose to persist in their sin, on them He passes the ultimate judgment of eternal death.

Babylon symbolizes all such evil people. That is why the worshiping multitudes are able to say, "true and righteous are his judgments" (v. 2). They, and we, are comforted to know that God will eventually destroy all who oppress His people.

To what extent can human society exact godly judgments?

2. The Beautiful Bride (vv. 4–8)

The next verses describe those same people praising God in worship for what He has done for them, specifically bringing them into His presence for the wedding supper of the Lamb in which they are the bride, holy and spotless. This section shows the other side of the coin of God's justice, His mercy and grace, again because of His great love. John uses familiar imagery to portray the absolute joy of those present at this glorious time of worship. In all cultures, weddings are a time of great joy for all involved. Weddings are also a time of new beginnings, and a time when the couple commit to a permanent joint bond.

Here, the bride is emblematic of the Church, all faithful believers from all time (Ephesians 5:32). A bride who is preparing for her wedding will wash herself carefully and thoroughly and put on a beautiful new white dress. Jesus has done this for His faithful. He has cleansed His Church by taking their sin on Himself. Jesus paid the price of our sin on the Cross, bearing our punishment, so that we could be made holy and blameless in His sight.

God shows mercy (not giving us what we rightly deserve) and grace (giving us what we don't deserve) when we declare our faith in and allegiance to Him. His righteousness is then given to us, and we can be presented to Him in a radiant new white linen gown. Is that not reason for joyful worship and loud hallelujah?

How do you react to the imagery of being a bride to Christ?

Search the Scriptures

1. Read Revelation 19:2–3. How does this affect your understanding of God's justice?

2. Read Revelation 19:7–8. It is important to remember that the bride (the Church) is not made ready by her own actions. How does this contribute to your understanding of the image of the bride in Revelation 19?

Discuss the Meaning

These verses show clearly that God's judgment includes two distinct elements. He will judge, condemn, and destroy all who reject Him and do evil. He also will show mercy and grace to all who follow Him. He is just and right in doing all this. How does knowing this affect your efforts to pray for and show the love of God to others who may not yet know Him?

Liberating Lesson

We often struggle with our desire to get even with those who oppress us. Sometimes it seems that there is no justice for marginalized communities. We must find comfort in the first three verses here where we learn that God will exact vengeance for us in the end. He will judge all the world's evil people and systems. He will deliver on His promise to effect judgment on whose who oppress His people.

Application for Activation

It is so hard to turn the other cheek when we see injustice around us. God's Word and His love should guide our responses to injustice. Our actions should show the world the grace and mercy that have been shown to us. We can show our desire for justice through peaceful protest, not through violence and vengeance. Write a letter this week to an elected official about an injustice close to your heart. Pray for them to use their power to help the most people.

Follow the Spirit

What God wants me to do:

_____

_____

_____

_____

Remember Your Thoughts

Special insights I have learned:

_____

_____

_____

_____

More Light on the Text

Revelation 19:1–8

1 And after these things I heard a great voice of much people in heaven, saying, Alleluia; Salvation, and glory, and honour, and power, unto the Lord our God:

Having just heard the laments of the lords and merchants of sinful Babylon, John's vision now shows how the people on God's side react. God has won a resounding victory over the enemy. Like the final five psalms (see Lesson 9), the victory song in Revelation 19:1–8 is punctuated with cries of "Alleluia!" Both those psalms and this song celebrate the defeat of the world's kingdoms and proclaim the Lord's universal reign. Alleluia (Gk. *halleluia*,

121

hah-lay-loo-ee-**AH**) is the Greek spelling of the Hebrew word hallelujah (*halelu-yah*, hah-leh-loo-**YAH**), which means "Praise Yahweh!" It is used only in this special song in all the New Testament.

The listed praises of salvation, glory, honor, and power recall previous songs of the multitudes of heaven. John has previously heard similar songs from the twenty-four elders and four living creatures when the Lamb comes to open the scroll (Revelation 5:8–10) and when the saints come to heaven out from the great tribulation (7:11–12). Each of those songs proclaimed seven of God's praiseworthy attributes, though this one only mentions four. This does not mean this praise is lesser than the previous songs. God enjoys His creatures' praise, whether it is done with many words or a few.

Notably, each of these three songs contains one unique element. Even though this song does not mention wisdom, strength, or praise as the other two did, this song is the first to mention salvation. Even this close to the end of time, there is still a new song to sing for God.

2 For true and righteous are his judgments: for he hath judged the great whore, which did corrupt the earth with her fornication, and hath avenged the blood of his servants at her hand.

The kingdom of Satan and the kingdom of God are both represented by women. The kingdom of this world is pictured as a great prostitute (Revelation 17–18), and the kingdom of Christ is pictured as a bride prepared for her husband (19:7–8). The image of being faithful to God as a pure bride, while being unfaithful is likened to prostitution is common in Scripture. The bond that God offers His people is holy, complete, exacting, and intimate. To willingly enter such a relationship with God is a joyous event (19:7), but to break that oath is a shocking, repugnant betrayal.

The character of the whore is seen earlier in John's vision. She is extravagantly wealthy, and exerts influence over ten kingdoms, even though they hate her (17:12, 16). She is called Babylon (v. 5), commits adultery (v. 2) with the ten kings—likely a reference to idolatry—and is drunk with the blood of God's prophets and holy ones (v. 6, 18:24).

John does not mean to shock his audience or heap extra shame on the unfaithful by using crass language, calling Babylon a "whore" (Gk. *porne*, **POOR**-nay). The Greek word is the term for a prostitute, with no additional crudeness about the word itself.

As God is the very source of justice, He alone has the right to exact vengeance against those who have wronged Him or His people. The word for "avenged" (Gk. *ekdikeo*, ek-dee-**KEH**-oh) is related to the word for "righteous" (Gk. *dikaios*, **DEE**-keye-oce) from earlier in the verse. They both include the root *dike* (Gk. **DEE**-kay), which means just or righteous. The idea in the word *ekdikeo* is that of one meting out righteous justice.

3 And again they said, Alleluia And her smoke rose up for ever and ever.

Babylon's burning rubble gives off eternal smoke. The word "smoke" (Gk. *kapnos*, kop-**NOCE**) is the same used of the prayers of the saints rising like the smoke of burned incense. This word, used almost exclusively in Scripture by John, can be positive or negative. This is the same smoldering fate that awaits those who worship the Beast (Revelation 14:11). John has already seen the effect this continuous smoke trail will have: kings will see it and weep for Babylon (18:18). God will leave the smoking remains of Babylon as an example of what happens to those who set themselves against His righteousness.

4 And the four and twenty elders and the four beasts fell down and worshipped

God that sat on the throne, saying, Amen; Alleluia.

The twenty-four elders join in praise as celebration songs are sung throughout the three acts of Revelation (7:9–17; 11:15–19; 19:1–9). The twenty-four are thought to represent various groups, like the twelve tribes of Israel and the twelve apostles (21:12–14). Here, they add their alleluia to those of the "great voice in heaven" (v. 1), praying, "amen," that all the voice has said will happen to Babylon and affirming the wonderful traits of God that were just mentioned.

andrea

5 And a voice came out of the throne, saying, Praise our God, all ye his servants, and ye that fear him, both small and great. 6 And I heard as it were the voice of a great multitude, and as the voice of many waters, and as the voice of mighty thunderings, saying, Alleluia: for the Lord God omnipotent reigneth.

John heard a voice come from the throne before, when an angel poured out the seventh bowl of wrath. That loud voice was also accompanied with thundering (16:17–18). Now the voice calls all of heaven to praise God. If you consider yourself God's servant, or hold Him in reverence, whether you are important or not, praise God!

The answering alleluia to this call is extreme. John has heard many loud sounds in this vision so far. The sound of a "great multitude" recalls the crowd from every tribe, nation, and tongue who praised God when they come to heaven out from the great tribulation (Revelation 7:9). The sound of "many waters" recalls the sound of the voice of Jesus (1:15). Finally, the "mighty thunderings" recalls God's presence on many occasions throughout Scripture, but recently a voice like seven thunders prophesied (10:3–4) and the revelation of God's heavenly Temple caused thunderings (11:19). The singing of the 144,000 standing on Mount Zion with the Lamb was like both many waters and mighty thunderings (14:2), but this new shout is even louder than anything before. It requires a three-fold description of its decibel level.

The words they sing are familiar from the "Hallelujah Chorus." No longer do we have to worry about our leaders being corrupt, debauched, stupid, cruel, or militant. God Himself reigns with all power.

7 Let us be glad and rejoice, and give honour to him: for the marriage of the Lamb is come, and his wife hath made herself ready.

No my

When tragedy occurred in a family in Israel, a kinsman redeemer could make things right again. A widow left childless would quickly fall into bankruptcy and possibly servitude. A kinsman redeemer would clear the widow's debt (Leviticus 25:25; 47–49), remove the threat of a harassing enemy by being the avenger of blood (Deuteronomy 19:12), and finally marry the widow back into the family (25:5–6). Revelation shows Jesus as humankind's redeemer who pays our debt (Revelation 5:6), takes vengeance upon Satan (Revelation 6–18), and announces his intention to marry us back into God's family (19:7–8).

After much darkness and struggle, the story of God's revelation of Himself to His people approaches its end with a joyous wedding. The faithful believers are finally with their Lord, joined in a permanent relationship in His heavenly home!

We as the Church are not just waiting until that glorious day comes, and we can reap at least some of the benefits now. John's apocalypse, like most divine prophecy, is full of an already/not yet theology. For example, the kingdom of God is come even now, but not fully come until the end. Here, John calls the Church Christ's "wife," even though the marriage has not yet happened. The woman is just now getting ready for the wedding feast, and will be presented after the final judgment (Revelation 20:14–21:2). Even though John will later call the Church Christ's "bride" (Gk. *numphos*, **NOOM**-foce, 21:9), in verse 7 she is already called His "wife" (Gk. *gune*, goo-**NAY**). Christ already cares for His Church as a man would care for his wife, faithfully sacrificing for her so that she can grow more wonderful.

8 And to her was granted that she should be arrayed in fine linen, clean and white: for the fine linen is the righteousness of saints.

God's servants are often depicted as dressed in white, for example the angels at the tomb and Jesus during His transfiguration. John has also seen the 24 elders dressed in white (Revelation 4:4), and the martyrs of the tribulation as well (7:9).

Fine linen was an expensive import from Egypt. Babylon had pridefully dressed herself in fine linen and other expensive clothes and jewelry (Revelation 18:16), contrasting with the simple purity of Christ's true Church.

Few fibers, even linen, are naturally white. To get white linen, it must be bleached and processed. This purification process is not gentle to the fabric. Neither is the purification process to attain righteousness. Thankfully, Christ's bride has not had to undergo this harsh process. The righteousness, instead, "was granted" to her (Gk. *didomi*, **DEE**-doe-me, to give), the passive voice grammatically curtailing any involvement on her part toward earning this beautiful garment. Her betrothed, her avenger, her omnipotent judge has taken the process on Himself, and given His bride righteousness as a gift.

Sources:
Henry, Matthew. *Matthew Henry's Commentary on the Whole Bible: New Modern Edition*. Vols. 1-6. Peabody, MA: Hendrickson Publishers, Inc., 2009.
Strong, James. *The New Strong's Exhaustive Concordance of the Bible*. Nashville, TN: Thomas Nelson, 2003.
Thayer, Joseph Henry. *A Greek-English Lexicon of the New Testament*. New York: American Book Company, 1889.

Say It Correctly

Debauched. deh-BOCH-t.
Curtailing. cur-TALE-ing.

Daily Bible Readings

MONDAY
A Vision of Praise
(Isaiah 6:1–8)

TUESDAY
Let the Heavens Be Glad
(1 Chronicles 16:23–34)

WEDNESDAY
Let All God's Angels Worship Him
(Hebrews 1:5–14)

THURSDAY
King of Kings, Lord of Lords
(Revelation 19:9–16)

FRIDAY
God Judges the Wicked
(Revelation 19:17–21)

SATURDAY
The Lord Rejoices Over You
(Zephaniah 3:14–20)

SUNDAY
The Lord Almighty Reigns
(Revelation 19:1–8)

Teaching Tips

Words You Should Know

A. Preach (Acts 10:42) Gk. *kerusso*—To act as a herald, proclaiming the message of a king or lord

B. Baptized (v. 47) Gk. *baptizo*—A ceremonial ordinance of Christianity; practiced as a public testimony to identify new believers

Teacher Preparation

Unifying Principle—No Difference. Barriers often keep people from becoming part of particular groups. How are barriers removed? God reveals to Peter that the Gospel of Jesus Christ is for all, and the power of the Holy Spirit is God's gift to everyone who accepts Christ.

A. Read the Bible Background and Devotional Reading.

B. Pray for your students and lesson clarity.

C. Read the lesson Scripture in multiple translations.

O—Open the Lesson

A. Begin the class with prayer.

B. Read Acts 1:8 aloud. Use it as an outline to trace the history of the church in the first ten chapters of the Book of Acts (origins in Jerusalem, expansion into Judea and Samaria, introduction of the gospel to Gentiles).

C. Have the students read the Aim for Change and the In Focus story.

D. Ask students how events like those in the story weigh on their hearts and how they can view these events from a faith perspective.

P—Present the Scriptures

A. Read the Focal Verses and discuss the Background and The People, Places, and Times sections.

B. Have the class share what Scriptures stand out for them and why, with particular emphasis on today's themes.

E—Explore the Meaning

A. Use In Depth or More Light on the Text to facilitate a deeper discussion of the lesson text.

B. Pose the questions in Search the Scriptures and Discuss the Meaning.

C. Discuss the Liberating Lesson and Application for Activation sections.

N—Next Steps for Application

A. Summarize the value of unity in the church.

B. End class with a commitment to pray that the Holy Spirit will lead them into all truth and to shape their character so that they are more like Jesus.

Worship Guide

For the Superintendent or Teacher
Theme: Good News for All
Song: "Sweet, Sweet, Spirit"

Good News for All

Bible Background • ACTS 10:34–47
Printed Text • ACTS 10:34–47 | Devotional Reading • ACTS 15:6–18

—————————— Aim for Change ——————————

By the end of the lesson, we will EXPLORE the gift of the Holy Spirit in our lives, VALUE the leadership of Peter in the early church and his relationship with Christ, and SPREAD the Good News that Christ is for all who want to know Him.

—————————— In Focus ——————————

One evening Aisha and Malik hosted their career adult Bible study group at their house to watch Mel Gibson's movie *The Passion of the Christ*. Their son Damon was home from college for the weekend and asked if he could join them with a teammate of his, Kyle, whom Damon had been trying to witness to. Kyle would be the only white guy there, but he liked movies, so it seemed like a good way to spark a spiritual conversation with him. Afterward the group ordered pizza and discussed the movie's emotional impact.

Kyle had really appreciated the movie's cinematography, but raised a question about the casting. "I wonder if it would have been as successful if Mel Gibson had portrayed Jesus as a brown-skinned Jewish Israeli instead of a white guy. What do you think?"

Malik chose his words carefully as he answered the question. "No doubt it would have made a difference for Mel Gibson's bank account. But personally, I have a problem with any portrayal of deity. Scripture states that we are not to create a graven image of God because images can divide and cause confusion. Yet since Jesus is both God and man, portraying Him based on His Jewish, non-White ethnicity is justified."

Aisha nodded and said, "God is no respecter of persons. He knows the differences in gender and race and utilizes those differences to His glory, but He limits no one because of it! If we dwell on things like the skin color of Jesus, it limits the message of Christ."

Are you constrained by culture or can you witness to someone regardless of race or ethnicity?

—————————— Keep in Mind ——————————

> "Then Peter opened his mouth, and said, Of a truth I perceive that God is no respecter of persons: But in every nation he that feareth him, and worketh righteousness, is accepted with him." (Acts 10:34–35, KJV)

"Then Peter replied, 'I see very clearly that God shows no favoritism. In every nation he accepts those who fear him and do what is right.'" (Acts 10:34–35, NLT)

Focal Verses

KJV **Acts 10:34** Then Peter opened his mouth, and said, Of a truth I perceive that God is no respecter of persons:

35 But in every nation he that feareth him, and worketh righteousness, is accepted with him.

36 The word which God sent unto the children of Israel, preaching peace by Jesus Christ: (he is Lord of all:)

37 That word, I say, ye know, which was published throughout all Judaea, and began from Galilee, after the baptism which John preached;

38 How God anointed Jesus of Nazareth with the Holy Ghost and with power: who went about doing good, and healing all that were oppressed of the devil; for God was with him.

39 And we are witnesses of all things which he did both in the land of the Jews, and in Jerusalem; whom they slew and hanged on a tree:

40 Him God raised up the third day, and shewed him openly;

41 Not to all the people, but unto witnesses chosen before God, even to us, who did eat and drink with him after he rose from the dead.

42 And he commanded us to preach unto the people, and to testify that it is he which was ordained of God to be the Judge of quick and dead.

43 To him give all the prophets witness, that through his name whosoever believeth in him shall receive remission of sins.

44 While Peter yet spake these words, the Holy Ghost fell on all them which heard the word.

45 And they of the circumcision which believed were astonished, as many as came with Peter, because that on the Gentiles also was poured out the gift of the Holy Ghost.

46 For they heard them speak with tongues, and magnify God. Then answered Peter,

NLT **Acts 10:34** Then Peter replied, "I see very clearly that God shows no favoritism.

35 In every nation he accepts those who fear him and do what is right.

36 This is the message of Good News for the people of Israel—that there is peace with God through Jesus Christ, who is Lord of all.

37 You know what happened throughout Judea, beginning in Galilee, after John began preaching his message of baptism.

38 And you know that God anointed Jesus of Nazareth with the Holy Spirit and with power. Then Jesus went around doing good and healing all who were oppressed by the devil, for God was with him.

39 And we apostles are witnesses of all he did throughout Judea and in Jerusalem. They put him to death by hanging him on a cross,

40 but God raised him to life on the third day. Then God allowed him to appear,

41 not to the general public, but to us whom God had chosen in advance to be his witnesses. We were those who ate and drank with him after he rose from the dead.

42 And he ordered us to preach everywhere and to testify that Jesus is the one appointed by God to be the judge of all—the living and the dead.

43 He is the one all the prophets testified about, saying that everyone who believes in him will have their sins forgiven through his name."

44 Even as Peter was saying these things, the Holy Spirit fell upon all who were listening to the message.

45 The Jewish believers who came with Peter were amazed that the gift of the Holy Spirit had been poured out on the Gentiles, too.

46 For they heard them speaking in other tongues and praising God. Then Peter asked,

47 Can any man forbid water, that these should not be baptized, which have received the Holy Ghost as well as we?

47 "Can anyone object to their being baptized, now that they have received the Holy Spirit just as we did?"

The People, Places, and Times

Cornelius. With the possible exception of the Ethiopian eunuch (Acts 8:26–39), Cornelius was the first Gentile cited in Scripture to hear the Gospel, receive salvation, and influence many to believe. Cornelius adhered to Jewish customs but was a Roman centurion, a high-ranking army official. Evidence of his piety was in the conversion of his whole household, giving alms to the poor, and praying to God in accordance with the Jewish ritual. However, because he was not a circumcised Jew, he could not worship in the inner sanctuary of the Jewish synagogue. He worshiped God on the fringes of his religious culture, but he still worshiped God, and God heard his prayers (v. 4).

Peter's Vision. In a vision at a time of fasting and prayer, the Lord spoke to Peter. After showing Peter animals given for food of all species, God commands Peter to rise, kill, and eat. However, as a devout Jew, Peter refuses to eat that which his culture has deemed common and unclean. The Lord rebukes Peter, declaring that which God calls clean is no longer subject to being called unclean. Peter did not immediately understand the meaning of the vision; but as he thought about it more, the Spirit of the Lord gave him revelation.

Background

God used Cornelius to minister to Peter, one of Jesus' disciples. Peter was surrounded by the cultural divisions between the Jews and Gentiles. Although he had heard Jesus preach salvation to all nations, Peter struggled to think outside the boundaries of exclusion and inclusion. The contrast between Jew and Gentile was great and buttressed by many barriers—culture, language, prejudicial hatred, and geography.

Through a vision and instructions to join Cornelius's entourage, the Lord helps Peter understand that His gift of salvation is available to the Jews, the Greeks, and all who believe. From this revelation, Peter vows never again to call any man common, unclean, or unworthy of the Gospel.

Why are all people—Jew, Gentile, male, female, any race—equal before God?

At-A-Glance

1. The Witnesses (Acts 10:34–39)
2. The Facts (vv. 40–43)
3. The Baptisms (vv. 44–48)

In Depth

1. The Witnesses (Acts 10:34–39)

Peter declares that God shows no partiality but accepts all people who revere Him and do what is right (vv. 34–35). The same Peter who considered non-Jews, and especially Greeks, as unclean now stands preaching the Gospel to a Greek congregation. He confesses the truth that God does not play cultural favorites, but that He favors people from any nation who reverence Him in righteousness.

Peter preaches the Good News of Christ to the people gathered with Cornelius (vv. 36–39). He tells them of the Gospel, John's water baptism, Jesus' anointing of the Holy Spirit and of the good works, healings, and crucifixion which would follow.

2. The Facts (vv. 40–43)

But praise God, the crucifixion is not the end of the story. Peter affirms himself as an eyewitness to the truth that Jesus came to life again. Following Christ's command, he preaches that Jesus "was ordained of God to be the Judge" (v. 42). The Good News does not consist of judgment only, though. Peter further affirms that Jesus—in fulfillment of prophecy—takes away the sin of those who believe Him, who submit to His leadership. The simple message, based on then recent historical facts, must have immediately moved the hearers to belief, because the next thing that happens is a sign of such.

How would you present a simple Gospel message to someone who had not heard it before?

3. The Baptisms (vv. 44–48)

While Peter was preaching, the Holy Spirit came upon the people who heard him (v. 44). As the Word was preached, the hearers believed and were filled with the Holy Spirit. The Jewish believers were amazed as they watched the Gentiles speak in tongues and worship God (vv. 45–46). This evidence of the presence of the Holy Spirit being poured out on the Gentiles could not be denied.

The Jewish believers had questioned the possibility of regarding the Gentiles as full members of the Christian church—namely, including them in the ceremony of baptism. Peter settles the questions, saying that any who received baptism in the Holy Spirit could not be denied the baptism by water. The baptism in the Spirit was indicative of an inward conversion; the baptism by water was indicative of an outward inclusion into the family of God. Therefore, Peter commanded that Cornelius, his family, and his friends—the Gentile converts—be baptized with water in the name of Jesus as they had been baptized by the Holy Spirit.

Recall and share the story of your own baptism. Was it joyous? Bittersweet? Solemn?

Search the Scriptures

1. What happened as the people listened to Peter preach? (vv. 44–45)

2. After the Gentiles were baptized in the Holy Spirit, evidenced with speaking in tongues and magnifying God, what question arose among the believers? (vv. 47–48)

Discuss the Meaning

Divisions in the Church have led to the formation of new denominations, or worse, schisms within the professing Body of Christ that dilute our unified testimony and preaching of the Gospel. The circumcised Jewish believers questioned the extension of water baptism to Gentile believers who had been baptized in the Holy Spirit. What do you believe are the purposes of the water baptism and baptism in the Holy Spirit? What does your church or denomination practice regarding them both?

Liberating Lesson

Like trees in a forest, Christians need to support one another. When we find Christians of dissimilar races, cultures, classes, genders, callings, and expressions of worship, we should become like a forest of trees and link up to nourish one another in the faith. Through our inclusion of all believers, the Church is fortified and God is glorified. Instead of excluding Christians who do not look like us or worship like us, we must extend our roots of righteousness to give what we have and get what we need to grow as the church until Christ returns.

Application for Activation

When was the last time you or your church had worship or fellowship with another body of Christian believers that you know has doctrinal differences? A good place to begin to know others in the body of Christ is through neighborly relationships. If someone in your family, workplace, or neighborhood belongs to a different church or denomination, ask them if you might accompany them to a fellowship or worship service, and extend a reciprocal invitation. Resist the temptation to rank or condemn the various styles of expressions of worship; but rather, seek to experience God through the eyes of another.

Follow the Spirit

What God wants me to do:

Mat 3 16-17
And Jesus, when he was baptized went up Straightway out of the water; and, lo the heavens like a dove and lighting upon him

Remember Your Thoughts

Special insights I have learned:

And lo a voice from heaven, saying, This is my beloved Son, in whom I am well pleased.

More Light on the Text

Acts 10:34-47

34 Then Peter opened his mouth, and said, Of a truth I perceive that God is no respecter of persons. 35 But in every nation he that feareth him, and worketh righteousness, is accepted with him.

Peter knew why he was where he was, so he went right to work. He began by acknowledging the truth which God had shown him in his own vision.

The truth is that Jesus was not kidding when He told Peter and the other original disciples to take the Gospel to "all nations" and to "the uttermost part of the earth" (see Matthew 28:19; Acts 1:8). The truth of God is that He does not care what color a person is nor what language they speak. God sent Jesus to die on the Cross for "whosoever" would believe (John 3:16). As a result of believing in Christ, God said that "whosoever" would not perish but have everlasting life (cf. Romans 10:13). In the event at Cornelius's house, God was using a formerly prejudiced Peter to initiate opening up the Church's Gospel invitation to Gentiles everywhere.

36 The word which God sent unto the children of Israel, preaching peace by Jesus Christ: (he is Lord of all:) 37 That word, I say, ye know, which was published throughout all Judaea, and began from Galilee, after the baptism which John preached.

Peter began to lay out the chronological progression of the Gospel. He told his audience that God started by sending Jesus (who is "Lord of all") to preach first to the "children of Israel," that is, the Jews (Romans 1:16).

Peter encouraged them by saying that they already knew about some aspects of the message which had been spread to areas beyond Jerusalem. He indicated that the ministry of Jesus began in Galilee after His baptism by John the Baptist. John preached a message of repentance from sin and water baptism (Mark 1:4). Peter is sure that those in Cornelius' house have heard at least that much of the amazing events of Judea in the past few years.

38 How God anointed Jesus of Nazareth with the Holy Ghost and with power: who went about doing good, and healing all that were oppressed of the devil; for God was with Him.

131

Peter then tells his audience about the earthly ministry of Jesus, which might not have been as known to them. He says that Jesus was "anointed… with the Holy Ghost and with power" (v. 38; cf. Matthew 3:16). This phrasing recalls the very beginning of Jesus' ministry as Luke records it: "Jesus returned in the power of the Spirit into Galilee" (Luke 4:14). Then Jesus did good and miraculous works, such as healing people with all sorts of ailments (Matthew 8:2–3; 12:10–13; John 9:1–7).

Peter says Jesus was able to do these things "for God was with Him" (Acts 10:38). In Jesus' time, some confronted Him with the accusation that He cast out demons by the power of demons (Luke 11:15). Jesus flatly and powerfully denied this (vv. 18–20), and Peter does not want his hearers to have any doubts as to where Jesus' power came from.

39 And we are witnesses of all things which he did both in the land of the Jews, and in Jerusalem; whom they slew and hanged on a tree.

Next, Peter gives verification of all the events in Jesus' ministry by asserting his own presence on those occasions, saying, "We are witnesses of all things which he did." Peter gives eyewitness testimony of Jesus' ministry. Finally, Peter indicates that Christ was killed and took on our sin, saying Jesus is He "whom they slew and hanged on a tree." Under Mosaic Law anyone who died that way was "accursed," so Christ became "accursed" for us (Deuteronomy 21:22–23; Galatians 3:13).

40 Him God raised up the third day, and shewed him openly; 41 Not to all the people, but unto witnesses chosen before God, even to us, who did eat and drink with him after he rose from the dead.

"Him God raised up." Hallelujah! The odd word order is a reflection of the Greek, which places words that the beginning of the phrase to give them emphasis. Peter has been discussing Jesus and emphasizes this same man is the one God raised from the dead. After this miracle, God made Jesus' Resurrection public knowledge. In an epistle, Paul speaks of over 500 eyewitnesses to the Risen Savior, most of whom were still alive at the time (1 Corinthians 15:6).

The detail that the witnesses ate and drank with the risen Jesus serves two purposes. First, consuming physical food seemed to allay fears among the Twelve that post-crucifixion that Jesus was a ghost or spirit of some sort (Luke 24:37–43). He was raised as a flesh and blood human again. Second, sharing a meal is a way to express and maintain deep connection among the people gathered, especially for the Jews of that day. Saying that Peter himself ate and drank with the risen Lord acts as a strong proof of the truth of his account.

42 And he commanded us to preach unto the people, and to testify that it is he which was ordained of God to be the Judge of quick and dead.

Peter stands before the assembled household of Cornelius, proclaiming that he is doing just as his Master has commanded him: preaching and testifying. The verb "preach" (Gk. *kerusso*, kay-**ROOS**-so) means to act as a herald, proclaiming the message of a king or lord. We all act as royal ambassadors when we widely proclaim the salvation that our King provides. The verb "testify" (Gk. *diamarturomai*, dee-ah-mar-**TER**-oh-my) means to be a thorough, fervent, and solemn witness. It is used widely in Acts to describe Christ's early followers' diligent and sometimes antagonizing work spreading the news of the Kingdom.

Peter is a solemn witness to the fact that God appointed Christ as Judge over the living (KJV: "quick") and the dead. In recent lessons, we have discussed the implications of Christ as Judge, both the blessing He bestows upon His righteous followers and the destruction He imposes on those who do not follow His will. These righteous judgments may fall on those either living or dead, for Christ rules the present earthly kingdom just as much as He rules the heavenly realm. Christ acts as Judge for all, not just once in the end-times, but every day. One may also interpret the phrase spiritually to refer to Jesus' judgment between those who are spiritually alive or spiritually dead. The spiritually alive will continue in abundant life with Christ, whereas the dead will continue in separation from our living, life-giving God.

43 To him give all the prophets witness, that through his name whosoever believeth in him shall receive remission of sins.

Besides the historical miracle of the Resurrection, we can trust that Jesus is the Messiah because He fulfilled the prophecies. His lineage, His birthplace and the events surrounding His early years, His healings, His base of missions, and many details of His manner of death—all of these were spoken to God's people as signs to distinguish the Messiah. Jesus fulfilled them all, and explained how He had to His disciples soon after His resurrection (Luke 24:25–27).

Peter lastly shares the final piece of salvation: believe the truth about Jesus (which will naturally place you under His Lordship, and drive you to lead a holy life), and you will receive remission (Gk. *aphesis*, **AH**-feh-sees) of your sins. This is a compound verb simply meaning "to go away from." It is used in the New Testament to speak almost exclusively of the removal of sin (Matthew 26:28; Hebrews 9:22), and is most often used by the author Luke, who wrote both the Gospel bearing his name and the Book of Acts. Remission of sins means the sin is removed from the believer, sent away so that they are left blameless and righteous in God's sight.

44 While Peter yet spake these words, the Holy Ghost fell on all them which heard the word.

When Peter mentions that salvation came from belief in Christ (v. 43), "the Holy Ghost fell on all them which heard the word." Apparently, the Gentile audience of Cornelius' household believed on Jesus at that moment, because the Holy Spirit came (1 Corinthians 12:3). When the Spirit comes on them, they speak in tongues and praise God (v. 46). This is exactly how the Spirit made His presence known on the day of Pentecost (Acts 2:4). Peter had also personally witnessed many Samaritans receiving the Holy Spirit (8:14–17), and knew it was a sign of true belief. Now the Church has spread to the Gentiles with the Spirit falling on the household of Cornelius.

45 And they of the circumcision which believed were astonished, as many as came with Peter, because that on the Gentiles also was poured out the gift of the Holy Ghost.

Six of the Jewish believers from Joppa had gone with Peter to Cornelius' house (Acts 10:23; 11:12). There is no doubt that they were Jewish because they were "of the circumcision." Though Peter had confronted and resolved his own prejudice through a vision from God, apparently these other Jews still felt a modicum of superiority. They were "astonished" at the Spirit's radical acceptance.

God is "no respecter of persons" (v. 34), playing no favorites. Since God was opening up salvation to "every nation," this inaugural event with the Gentiles of the world was to have all the signs which the Jews experienced at Pentecost (Acts 2:1-4). The Jews could not say that Gentiles had a lesser salvation and, thus, not be as close to God. All receive the Spirit equally because all have received forgiveness equally.

46 For they heard them speak with tongues, and magnify God. Then answered Peter, 47 Can any man forbid water, that these should not be baptized, which have received the Holy Ghost as well as we?

These verses show the completion of God's stamp of authenticity on the Gentiles' conversion to Christ. They spoke in tongues just like the Jews at Pentecost (Acts 2:4). The first thing they do when they receive the Spirit is "magnify" (Gk. *megaluno*, meh-gah-**LOO**-no) God. This is another word used often in Luke and Acts, and means "to make great or praise." It is the same word Mary uses in her joyous song to Elizabeth: "My soul doth magnify the Lord" (Luke 1:46). Of course, there is no way to make God greater than He already is, but when we magnify Him, we make a big deal out of Him. We talk about Him all the time. We think deeply about His Word. Our first thought is to live our lives by His principles.

Seeing this obvious outpouring of the Holy Spirit, Peter challenges his Jewish brethren to give a reason that the Gentiles should not be baptized. Many churches have deeply held beliefs about the exact order a believer must experience the aspects of salvation. Peter had just witnessed the order of belief, then baptism, and then receiving the Spirit after a prayer with the apostles (Acts 8:14–17). Here he sees belief and the immediate coming of the Spirit. Following this, these new believers will be baptized to show their initiation into Christian fellowship, but this event seals in Peter's mind that no special lineage, no special prayer, no special baptism is necessary for salvation. He knows better than to second guess the obvious seal of Spirit.

Sources:
Henry, Matthew. *Matthew Henry's Commentary on the Whole Bible: New Modern Edition.* Vols. 1-6. Peabody, MA: Hendrickson Publishers, Inc., 2009.
Strong, James. *The New Strong's Exhaustive Concordance of the Bible.* Nashville, TN: Thomas Nelson, 2003.
Thayer, Joseph Henry. *A Greek-English Lexicon of the New Testament.* New York: American Book Company, 1889.

Say It Correctly

Cornelius. core-NEE-lee-us.
Centurion. sin-TUR-ee-on.

Daily Bible Readings

MONDAY
God Speaks to a Pagan King
(Genesis 20:1–7, 14–16)

TUESDAY
An Angel Speaks to Cornelius
(Acts 10:1–8)

WEDNESDAY
A Vision of Inclusion
(Acts 10:9–22)

THURSDAY
The Queen of Sheba Blesses God
(1 Kings 10:1–9)

FRIDAY
A Centurion Comes to Jesus
(Luke 7:1–10)

SATURDAY
Peter Enters Cornelius' House
(Acts 10:23–33)

SUNDAY
God Shows No Partiality
(Acts 10:34–47)

Justice, Law, History

The study this quarter focuses on justice as presented in a variety of Old Testament Scriptures. Justice originates in the nature of God and is given to God's people as a gift under the Law. The history of God's covenant people shows that kings who exercised God's justice according to God's Law were considered good kings. Over time, adverse circumstances caused God's people to raise questions about God's justice.

UNIT 1 • God Requires Justice

This unit has four lessons that explore how leaders of God's people must rely on God's Law as they administer justice. Deuteronomy demands that God's people be just and equitable. In 2 Samuel, King David demonstrates justice by showing kindness to Mephibosheth. Isaiah describes a reign of justice and righteousness. The Christmas lesson shows foreign "kings" respecting God's justice more than Israel's own king.

Lesson 1: December 5, 2021
Justice and Obedience to the Law
Deuteronomy 5:1–3; 10:12–13; 27:1–10
People often struggle to do what they know is right. How can people find the strength and motivation to do what is right? Deuteronomy 10 teaches that obedience to God's Law is for our own well-being.

Lesson 2: December 12, 2021
David Administers Justice and Kindness
2 Samuel 9:1–12
People rely on the kindness and support of others. How can people show radical kindness to one another? King David acted justly, remembered his promise to Jonathan, and was kind to Jonathan's son.

Lesson 3: December 19, 2021
Justice and Righteousness Reign
Isaiah 9:2–7
People suffer injustices and ill treatment. Will there be a time when people can count on being treated fairly? God's kingdom will be one of justice and righteousness.

Lesson 4: December 26, 2021
A Just King Is Born
Matthew 2:1–12
People look for someone to bring justice in spite of injustice. To whom can people turn to address issues of injustice? The wise men searched and found the King of Justice, Jesus, and worshiped Him.

UNIT 2 • God: The Source of Justice

In this unit, four lessons focus on God's justice in the lives of God's people and in the gift of the Law. Stories in Genesis reveal God's justice in the face of human injustice. Included are stories of Cain's murder of his brother Abel, as well as Hagar and Ishmael being cast out of Abraham's household. Exodus demands justice for all people, including one's enemies. In Deuteronomy, judges, officials, and priests work together to administer justice for God's people; in particular, Deuteronomy demands justice for marginalized people.

Lesson 5: January 2, 2022
Justice, Vengeance, and Mercy
Genesis 4:1–16

Some people become angry when their best efforts don't result in the anticipated outcome. How do people deal with their anger and disappointment? God punished Cain because he allowed his anger to turn to rage and then to murder.

Lesson 6: January 9, 2022
Hagar and Ishmael Not Forgotten
Genesis 21:8–20

People sometimes face situations that feel hopeless. How can people find assurance when their circumstances change? Genesis shows that, even though Hagar and Ishmael's circumstances changed, God was still with them.

Lesson 7: January 16, 2022
The Laws of Justice and Mercy
Exodus 23:1–12

It can be tempting to treat friends with more leniency and enemies with more harshness than they deserve. How can people treat others justly? Exodus demands justice for all people, including one's enemies.

Lesson 8: January 23, 2022
Justice, Judges, and Priests
Deuteronomy 16:18–20; 17:8–13

People sometimes distort justice. What actions can we take to prevent manipulations of justice? In Deuteronomy, judges, officials, and priests work together to administer justice for God's people.

UNIT 3 • Justice and Adversity

This unit has five lessons that deal with situations in which justice seems absent. In 2 Samuel, Nathan condemns David for his acts of injustice toward Uriah the Hittite, Bathsheba's husband. In Ezra, after years of exile in Babylon, Ezra returns to Jerusalem and determines to restore respect for God's Law. Lesson 3 tells the story of Job's faithfulness to God after several tragic events in his life. The Scriptures in Job question the presence of God's justice when Job has suffered greatly.

Lesson 9: January 30, 2022
Justice and the Marginalized
Deuteronomy 24:10–21

Some people are poor and marginalized. How can their dignity and worth be respected? Deuteronomy demands justice for all who are poor or marginalized.

Lesson 10: February 6, 2022
Nathan Condemns David
2 Samuel 12:1–9, 13–15

People often see acts of injustice being committed. How are we called to respond when we witness unjust acts? Nathan sought God's guidance and received wisdom for how to address David's sin.

Lesson 11: February 13, 2022
Ezra Seeks God's Law
Ezra 7:1–10, 23–26

People sometimes face situations in which they fear others will oppose their efforts. What motivates people to behave benevolently toward others? God's hand was on Ezra, and he was able to return to Jerusalem in an effort to restore respect for God's Law.

Lesson 12: February 20, 2022
Bildad Misunderstands God's Justice
Job 8:1–10, 20–22

People tend to rationalize why bad things happen. How do people respond when they are faced with tragedy—natural disasters, birth defects, atrocious crimes, etc.? Job remained faithful to God after several tragic events in his life, even while his friends questioned God's justice and Job's innocence.

Lesson 13: February 27, 2022
Serving a Just God
Job 42:1–6, 10–17

Even the most downcast people can still have hope. How does our hope keep us focused on what is important? Job had an honest, heart-to-heart conversation with God, and God blessed Job's faithfulness.

Godliness and Justice: Two Sides of the Same Coin

by Rodrick Burton

Justice means many things to many people. For African Americans, justice often brings thoughts of historic injustice inflicted on us. To the patron in the barbershop or beauty shop, justice may mean "just us." To others, justice means punishing the guilty. But what does justice mean as defined by the Bible? Shouldn't Christians speak with absolute clarity concerning justice? In short, how is justice connected to godliness?

For the average person, justice is usually associated with the court system. Popular courtroom television shows capitalize on this association, and media coverage of popular court cases reinforce this view. Similarly, the average person associates the term "godliness" with the church and religion.

God's love is manifested in these three things: godliness, mercy, and justice. To the Christian, godliness should mean a lifelong effort to conform to God's laws and wishes as they are manifested in Jesus Christ and His teachings. This conformity must not be the hollow piety that the prophets warned about, but a devoutness flowing from fellowship with God through Christ. God did not create us as robots with a default setting for love; He made us mentally free to accept or reject Him. Yet, as we study the Scriptures and meditate on the love shown to us through the sacrifice of Jesus, our desire to respond to this unmerited love should manifest itself in a lifestyle that is characterized by godliness.

What does godliness entail? Worship, of course, and praise, absolutely. These dispositions are aimed at God vertically, but what of our fellows with whom we coexist on a horizontal plane? How does justice come into play? Jesus called us to love all humanity as He did, including our enemies. To do this, we must follow God's example of both mercy and justice.

God's mercy was manifested as Jesus allowed Himself to be put to death for crimes He did not commit. In so doing, He abated the eternal death penalty we deserved as convicted sinners. It cannot be emphasized enough that, although we all deserved death, Christ secured our full pardon in the divine supreme court. This transaction leads to fidelity. The promise of eternal life is good because God's faithfulness is exhibited in His covenant with Abraham, which extends to all believers through Christ. This is faithfulness indeed! God fills us with this faithfulness through the indwelling of the Holy Spirit.

Lastly, God's love is manifested in justice. Outlaws and evildoers must pay. Wrongs committed are not forgotten but dealt with. Why is this? God knows His creation. He set boundaries out of love, and crossing these boundaries has consequences. God's rules and laws are typically viewed negatively because they are limiting; in reality, however, they protect us because sin has inclined us as humans to abuse our freedom. This is especially relevant in our society, where the cult of individuality trumps everything, even common sense. The new American mantra is that anything should be permitted as long as it breaks no laws. God knows us better than we know ourselves, and the contortion of justice into "just us" is an injustice to God, the owner and dispenser of true justice.

So what does justice look like for those proponents of godliness? For some it means reaching out to members of our communities who are trapped in cycles of oppression. Just as the prophets Amos and Micah warned Israel that God was disgusted with the exploitation of the poor, He must also be disgusted as individuals are seduced into lifestyles of sexual exploitation and oppression. As proponents of godliness, Christians must strive to liberate our culture from the toxic embrace of an oppressive iconography. As proponents of godliness we must challenge our culture and expose the vile wickedness that it involves. To leave this ideology unchallenged is to deny justice to the weak and vulnerable in our society.

Godliness includes a relentless drive to extend fairness, truth, and mercy to all who enter our sphere of influence in order to ensure that justice is not for just us, but for everyone, believer and nonbeliever alike. It means looking at the crime in our communities and working with the police to see that offenders will not perpetuate their crimes. We must work harder to rehabilitate offenders, mentoring them as they return to our communities so that they can be transformed from purveyors of injustice into champions of justice.

Justice is not about just us. It is about God's world, redeemed by the sacrifice of His Son. Because of His love for a fallen humanity, God sees that justice exists to repel the walls of inhumanity, which, without Him, would collapse on top of us. To exhibit godliness is to show God's love to all people. Therefore, when we act justly, we are exhibiting godliness—the love God wants all His children to exhibit.

Imparting More Than Information

by Hurby Franks

We are in the midst of a postmodern generation. Though very difficult to define, essentially, postmodernism is the questioning or outright rejection of accepted "modern" thought in the areas of culture, architecture, philosophy, and religion. In other words, postmodernists redefine or regard as more complex truth in these areas. Beginning in the mid to late 1970s, people began to define truth as a personal concept instead of a universal one. It becomes harder for us as Christians to present the Gospel as truth when some postmodernists feel that everyone has his or her own truth. In order to combat this problem, we need to impart the application as well as the information of the Gospel.

I have seen examples of this need in my own Christian walk. For four years, I was a college campus minister. Over that four-year period, I noticed that, in the Bible Belt (an area of the United States typically associated with the southern states), almost everyone claimed to be a Christian. However, the truth of the Gospel did not always have an effect on how college students lived their lives. Students tended to apply the parts of Scripture they felt were "true" for them, while discarding the parts that did not agree with their lifestyles, labeling those verses as "untrue" for them. As I talked with my colleagues in other parts of the country, they informed me that the prevailing theory for students in their areas was

that the Gospel, as well as all of Christianity, is just another "truth" in a long list of possible "truths." In order for this perspective to change, Christianity needs to be shown as not only true, but relevant for everyone.

The issue of justice is just one example of how the Lord has shared His universal truth. The Lord speaks of the justice that He will bring. The Lord requires His people to care about justice in every area. However, there are some areas in which we do not have the ability to make immediate changes. In such areas, we are required to pursue justice and trust God to bring it to pass in His time. Repeatedly in these passages, the Lord declares that He will bring justice. For example, in Zephaniah 3:8–9, the Lord requires us to wait on Him, and He will allow His people to call on His name and to serve Him in the end. All those who are opposed to God will be dealt with by Him in the end.

In the meantime, we as Christians are called to live justly, be merciful to others, and keep walking with God. God's prophets were always insisting that God's people follow His example of justice.

Isaiah warns of the Lord not accepting Israel's offerings (Isaiah 1); however, he also says the Lord offers restoration. If God's people put away evil, seek justice, and plead for the poor, the land will be restored. In other words, if they (and we) commit to doing right, restoration will take place.

Jeremiah announces that the disobedient and the unjust will answer to the Lord of hosts. Added into the equation is the need to keep our hope in God, be responsible for ourselves, and repent. In Lamentations, Jeremiah continues to encourage his audience to wait on the Lord and seek Him. We are encouraged to place our hope in God, even in hard times.

Ezekiel informs us that we are not to blame our sins on our fathers or our predecessors, but to take full responsibility for our own actions. The Lord says that He will judge each individual according to his or her own ways.

Hosea also rebukes God's people, pointing out how the sin of Israel has affected the land. Because of the lying, stealing, adultery, and more of God's people, the land literally suffers. God says that when He would have healed the land, more iniquity was discovered (Hosea 7).

Amos calls for God's people not just to care about but actually to deal with issues of injustice. He points out how the people of God have taken advantage of the poor and have committed other sins that afflict the just. Amos says that as a result of the mistreatment of the poor and the just, the Lord God of hosts will not accept the sacrificial offerings of His people. The greater concern of the Lord God of hosts is that "judgment run down as waters, and righteousness as a mighty stream" (from Amos 5:24, KJV).

The prophet Micah continues to highlight the need for the people of Israel to act justly. Micah challenges us "to do justly, and to love mercy, and to walk humbly with [our] God" (Micah 6:8, KJV).

Habakkuk announces that the unrighteous who have built their cities with the blood and labor of others will be doomed by the Lord of hosts.

Zephaniah declares that God's justice will ultimately triumph over evil.

Zechariah calls for all of us to return to God, a turning that once again includes taking care of the poor and overcoming evil. Zechariah says, "oppress not the widow, nor the fatherless, the stranger, nor the poor; and let none of you imagine evil against his brother in your heart" (Zechariah 7:10, KJV).

Malachi reiterates how just God is in His judgment. The prophet uses vivid imagery to describe what will happen to those who have been unjust.

Today, non-Christians need to see how much Christians are committed to justice and righteousness. One complaint from non-Christians that I heard quite often on the college campus was that Christians care only about themselves and about adding to their numbers, instead of being concerned with issues that everyone should care about. However, as we can see from Scripture, the Lord mandates that we not only care about injustices, but that we also repent and rid ourselves of any injustices that we commit. The Lord challenges us to start with ourselves when it comes to righting injustices; when we do, He will bring change to the environment and to the people around us.

According to God's prophets, what are we as Christians being called to do? The prophet Micah says it best: "He hath shewed thee, O man, what is good; and what doth the Lord require of thee, but to do justly, and to love mercy, and to walk humbly with thy God?" (Micah 6:8, KJV). First, we are called to seek justice. Injustices are happening all around us. Our call is to be just to others, to pursue and pray for justice, and to place our hope and trust in God that He will bring about ultimate justice. God also calls Christians to love mercy. As much as we are to pursue justice, we are also to be merciful to those who need to be shown mercy. Finally, Christians are to walk continuously with God, and He will show us when and how to pursue justice and mercy. Also, because God is our guide, He will convict us when we do wrong and show us when we need to ask for forgiveness and mercy from others.

As previously mentioned, we are in the midst of a postmodern generation. There are many theories in the Christian world as to the best way to minister in a postmodern society. In *Christian Apologetics in the Postmodern World*, three possible responses to postmodernity are given. One possible response is to continue to provide evidence of the truth of the Gospel. Although some postmodernists tend to pursue other "truths," Christians can provide evidence that the Gospel is the ultimate truth. Another possible response is to attack the critiques of Christianity and Western culture. Finally, the book argues that the key aspects of postmodernity can be used to support and defend orthodox Christianity. Postmodernists believe that "the truth" should have a positive impact on society. If we Christians pursue justice and mercy the way we should,

postmodernists will come to understand that justice and mercy are parts of the main purpose of the Gospel. Also, seeing our mercy toward others will introduce non-Christians to the mercy and restorative power of Jesus Christ. It will help them see the kingdom of God as more than a club looking for new recruits. They will see it as a society of people who have been changed by God and want to see others changed as well. In other words, imparting the application of the Gospel to our lives as Christians will allow non-Christian postmodernists to hear the information of the Gospel.

Source:
Phillips, Timothy, and Dennis Okholm, eds. *Christian Apologetics in the Postmodern World*. Westmont, Ill.: InterVarsity Press, 1995.

THURGOOD MARSHALL
(1908–1993)
Chief Justice

Thurgood Marshall was the grandson of slaves, yet Marshall strived to achieve educational success. Born in Baltimore, Maryland on July 2, 1908, Marshall attended the historically Black Lincoln University in Pennsylvania for college. Upon graduation, he sought to attend law school. Though denied admission into the University of Maryland Law School because he was Black, Marshall did not quit pursuing his goal to further his education. Instead, he attended Howard University Law School. As a lawyer, Marshall fought for the constitutional rights of all people. During his time, Blacks and Whites were not allowed to attend school together. Marshall took up an early case suing the University of Maryland for denying entry to another African American man and won the case. The successful case created other opportunities for Marshall. At the encouragement of his Howard University mentor and Dean of Howard Law School, Charles Hamilton Houston, he sought to overturn the court ruling of *Plessy v. Ferguson*, which became the legal basis for segregation. He worked as Chief Counsel for the National Association for the Advancement of Colored People (NAACP), as well as helped people who were oppressed in other countries, such as Ghana and Tanzania, by helping draft their constitutions at the request of the United Nations.

Marshall was a leader on the case challenging the lower circuit court ruling on *Brown v. Board of Education of Topeka*. The decision by the Supreme Court on the case led to the end of segregation in schools and the refutation of "separate but equal" doctrine. In 1965, President Lyndon Johnson appointed Judge Marshall to the office of U.S. Solicitor General. Before his subsequent nomination to the United States Supreme Court in 1967, Marshall won 14 of the 19 cases he argued before the Supreme Court on behalf of the government. Indeed, Marshall represented and won more cases before the United States Supreme Court than any other American before him. Throughout his time on the Supreme Court, Marshall established a record for supporting the voiceless American. He developed a profound sensitivity to injustice during the civil rights era. As an Associate Supreme Court Justice, Marshall left a legacy that expands to include all of America's voiceless. Marshall died on January 24, 1993.

Sources:
Inteen Sept. 2017 & Thurgood Marshall College http://marshall.ucsd.edu/about-us/about-our-namesake.html

Teaching Tips

Words You Should Know

A. Peace Offering (Deuteronomy 27:7) *shelem* (Heb.)—A voluntary sacrifice of worship that represented thankfulness to God

B. Take heed (v. 9) *sakat* (Heb.)—To be quiet

Teacher Preparation

Unifying Principle—The Protection of Justice. People often struggle to do what they know is right. How can people find the strength and motivation to do what is right? Deuteronomy 10 teaches that obedience to God's Law is for our own well-being.

A. Read the Bible Background and Devotional Reading.

B. Pray for your students and lesson clarity.

C. Read the lesson Scripture in multiple translations.

O—Open the Lesson

A. Begin the class with prayer.

B. Display the Ten Commandments for the class to see. Explain that while these commandments are clear, some of the decisions we face may fall into "gray areas" of these commandments. For example: Am I considering buying a new car because I really need one, or because I covet the cars of my friends? Is putting my parent in a nursing home for the purpose of offering the best care, or am I dishonoring my parent by not caring for that parent in my home? Have participants consider similar dilemmas they face.

C. Have the students read the Aim for Change and the In Focus story.

D. Ask students how events like those in the story weigh on their hearts and how they can view these events from a faith perspective.

P—Present the Scriptures

A. Read the Focal Verses and discuss the Background and The People, Places, and Times sections.

B. Have the class share what Scriptures stand out for them and why, with particular emphasis on today's themes.

E—Explore the Meaning

A. Use In Depth or More Light on the Text to facilitate a deeper discussion of the lesson text.

B. Pose the questions in Search the Scriptures and Discuss the Meaning.

C. Discuss the Liberating Lesson and Application for Activation sections.

N—Next Steps for Application

A. Summarize the value of trusting God's commands as a source of justice.

B. End class with a commitment to pray for the courage and strength to do the right thing, even when it is difficult.

Worship Guide

For the Superintendent or Teacher
Theme: Justice and Obedience
to the Law
Song: "Break Thou the Bread of Life"

Justice and Obedience to the Law

Bible Background • DEUTERONOMY 5; 10; 27; 28:1–2 | Printed Text • DEUTERONOMY 5:1–3; 10:12–13; 27:1–10 | Devotional Reading • MATTHEW 22:36–40

Aim for Change

By the end of this lesson, we will UNDERSTAND the importance of justice and explore God's commandments, APPRECIATE the blessing God promises as a benefit of obedience, and PRAY for wisdom to know what is right and perseverance to carry it through. ·

In Focus

Brandon Johnson stood under the canopy of the Jefferson Monument in Washington, DC, with his son Trevor and the rest of Trevor's high school history class. He had taken a day off work so that he could chaperon his son's field trip to the National Mall and nearby monuments. Brandon knew his son would have questions about the nation's heritage and his own.

The tour guide pointed out the famous words inscribed around the top of the rotunda: "We hold these truths to be self-evident that all men are created equal."

Trevor loudly remarked, "And that's why Jefferson recognized Sally Hemings's equal status with himself, right? And allowed her the full freedoms of life, liberty, and the pursuit of happiness?" Trevor's teacher gave him a look to check his attitude.

As the group continued on their way, passing the Japanese cherry trees to the FDR memorial, Brandon put his arm around his son. "I'm glad you brought up Hemings, son. What do you think that means for us today that a man like Jefferson kept one of his slaves as his mistress?"

"That the people who think they're the best and most enlightened people are still full of it," Trevor replied. "You just can't trust anything," he said, full of teenage cynicism.

"Not anything, huh?" Brandon asked. "Not anything we humans make, you mean. Trevor, that's why I'm so glad to be a Christian. America is nice enough; sure is nicer now than when my pops had to fight tooth and nail just to vote. But it still ain't the way it oughta be. That's why I'm glad I follow God's Law. It's always been and will always be perfect and just, and so is the God who administers it."

How do we respond when our country's laws are not in line with God's law of justice?

Keep in Mind

> "And now, Israel, what doth the LORD thy God require of thee, but to fear the LORD thy God, to walk in all his ways, and to love him, and to serve the LORD thy God with all thy heart and with all thy soul, To keep the commandments of the LORD, and his statutes, which I command thee this day for thy good?" (Deuteronomy 10:12–13, KJV)

"And now, Israel, what does the LORD your God require of you? He requires only that you fear the LORD your God, and live in a way that pleases him, and love him and serve him with all your heart and soul. And you must always obey the LORD's commands and decrees that I am giving you today for your own good." (Deuteronomy 10:12–13, NLT)

Focal Verses

KJV **Deuteronomy 5:1** And Moses called all Israel, and said unto them, Hear, O Israel, the statutes and judgments which I speak in your ears this day, that ye may learn them, and keep, and do them.

2 The LORD our God made a covenant with us in Horeb.

3 The LORD made not this covenant with our fathers, but with us, even us, who are all of us here alive this day.

10:12 And now, Israel, what doth the LORD thy God require of thee, but to fear the LORD thy God, to walk in all his ways, and to love him, and to serve the LORD thy God with all thy heart and with all thy soul,

13 To keep the commandments of the LORD, and his statutes, which I command thee this day for thy good?

27:1 And Moses with the elders of Israel commanded the people, saying, Keep all the commandments which I command you this day.

2 And it shall be on the day when ye shall pass over Jordan unto the land which the LORD thy God giveth thee, that thou shalt set thee up great stones, and plaister them with plaister:

3 And thou shalt write upon them all the words of this law, when thou art passed over, that thou mayest go in unto the land which the LORD thy God giveth thee, a land that floweth with milk and honey; as the LORD God of thy fathers hath promised thee.

4 Therefore it shall be when ye be gone over Jordan, that ye shall set up these stones, which I command you this day, in mount Ebal, and thou shalt plaister them with plaister.

5 And there shalt thou build an altar unto the LORD thy God, an altar of stones: thou shalt not lift up any iron tool upon them.

6 Thou shalt build the altar of the LORD thy God of whole stones: and thou shalt offer burnt offerings thereon unto the LORD thy God:

NLT **Deuteronomy 5:1** Moses called all the people of Israel together and said, "Listen carefully, Israel. Hear the decrees and regulations I am giving you today, so you may learn them and obey them!

2 The LORD our God made a covenant with us at Mount Sinai.

3 The LORD did not make this covenant with our ancestors, but with all of us who are alive today."

10:12 "And now, Israel, what does the LORD your God require of you? He requires only that you fear the LORD your God, and live in a way that pleases him, and love him and serve him with all your heart and soul.

13 And you must always obey the LORD's commands and decrees that I am giving you today for your own good."

27:1 Then Moses and the leaders of Israel gave this charge to the people: "Obey all these commands that I am giving you today.

2 When you cross the Jordan River and enter the land the LORD your God is giving you, set up some large stones and coat them with plaster.

3 Write this whole body of instruction on them when you cross the river to enter the land the LORD your God is giving you—a land flowing with milk and honey, just as the LORD, the God of your ancestors, promised you.

4 When you cross the Jordan, set up these stones at Mount Ebal and coat them with plaster, as I am commanding you today.

5 Then build an altar there to the LORD your God, using natural, uncut stones. You must not shape the stones with an iron tool.

6 Build the altar of uncut stones, and use it to offer burnt offerings to the LORD your God.

7 Also sacrifice peace offerings on it, and celebrate by feasting there before the LORD your God.

7 And thou shalt offer peace offerings, and shalt eat there, and rejoice before the LORD thy God.

8 And thou shalt write upon the stones all the words of this law very plainly.

9 And Moses and the priests the Levites spake unto all Israel, saying, Take heed, and hearken, O Israel; this day thou art become the people of the LORD thy God.

10 Thou shalt therefore obey the voice of the LORD thy God, and do his commandments and his statutes, which I command thee this day.

8 You must clearly write all these instructions on the stones coated with plaster."

9 Then Moses and the Levitical priests addressed all Israel as follows: "O Israel, be quiet and listen! Today you have become the people of the LORD your God.

10 So you must obey the LORD your God by keeping all these commands and decrees that I am giving you today."

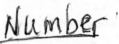

The People, Places, and Times

Burnt Offering. A sacrifice that was burned entirely to God was called a burnt offering. One might sacrifice a bull, goat, lamb, or dove, but it had to be a male animal without defect. As you entered the Tabernacle, you had to lay your hand on the animal's head and dedicate it as a burnt offering (Leviticus 1:1–17). The Israelites were to perform these offerings with certain purification rituals, and the priests were to administer them daily, weekly, monthly, and during festivals. This was the most common form of sacrifice and was meant to show one's complete devotion to God.

Peace Offering. A peace offering proceeded much like a burnt offering, but the animal could be male or female, and instead of the entire animal being burned up on the altar, only the animal's entrails were burned (Leviticus 3:1–17). Sacrificing the animal's liver and kidneys to God was indeed a sacrifice at the time, as those organs are dense with fats and nutrients. At the time, the liver (and often the kidneys, too) were used regularly in divination, as they had sacred significance in Egypt and Babylon. Israelites set themselves apart by simply disposing of these organs. The meat of the animal would then be distributed to the priests and those bringing the offering (Deuteronomy 12:27).

Background

The people of Israel—who had been eyewitnesses to the ten plagues that visited their oppressors, seen God part the Red Sea so that they could escape an advancing army, heard God's voice at Mount Sinai, received His commandments, dined on food from heaven, and drank water from a rock—failed to believe that God could take them into the land He had promised them. Fearful, they believed it was better to die in a wilderness than enter God's Promised Land. God gave them what they wanted. Instead of moving forward, they wandered in a wilderness for 40 years until unbelief died out and a new generation was at the threshold of actualizing God's promise. Moses, knowing that he would not be going into the promised homeland, used a farewell address to remind this new generation of God's greatness and holiness. Moses conveyed God's desire for them to have just relationships with each other and foreigners, and the need to remember their history so they would not repeat it.

At-A-Glance

1. A Promise to Everyone
(Deuteronomy 5:1–3)
2. A Promise to Live By (10:12–13)
3. A Promise to Remember (27:1–10)

In Depth

1. A Promise to Everyone (Deuteronomy 5:1–3)

The people who listened to Moses speak from a hilltop in Moab were very young, or perhaps not even born, when their parents camped at Mount Sinai and agreed to obey God's commandments. Sadly, that former generation failed to trust God's ability to secure the promised homeland. Now, a new generation was on the threshold of receiving God's promise. Moses wanted them to understand that God's promise was made, not only to the previous generation, but also to all who had been delivered from Egypt, even those who were yet to be born. The people standing before Moses were heirs of a promise that God had made to Abraham and then passed on to Isaac, Jacob, and his descendants. Now the promise was theirs. They were within sight of the homeland, and Moses wanted them to know they would experience the blessings of God's promise as they trusted and loved God and lived with each other according to the just ways God had ordained.

What did Moses want his listeners to do with the message they heard?

2. A Promise to Live By (10:12–13)

To prepare the people to live in their homeland, Moses detailed God's design for a good relationship with God and others. They were to love God with their whole hearts, avoiding idolatry. They were to follow God's commandments for living with each other. Though they were free, following God's just laws would keep them from actions and behaviors that would harm the well-being of the entire community. After a time of speaking, Moses summarized God's desire in the form of a question. *What did God want?* The answer was uncomplicated: God wanted a loving relationship with His people and for His people to have just relationships with each other. The laws Moses shared were to be seen as protections, not prohibitions. God knew the way to a blessed life was to follow His loving and just instructions. The defining characteristic of God's people was their love for God and each other.

Name the five requirements God expected from the people listening to Moses' speech.

3. A Promise to Remember (27:1–10)

When the Israelites would finally enter the land of Canaan, Moses did not want the land's abundance to distract them from their relationship with God. Their first priority was to write the commandments on whitewashed stones and build an altar at Mount Ebal. The city of Shechem was at the base of Mount Ebal. This was where the Lord had appeared to Abraham, promising him that his descendants would have a land they could call their own (Genesis 12:6–7). Those entering Canaan would be fulfilling that promise. Writing the commandments for all to see would be a reminder that they had agreed to have a loving relationship with God and had chosen to obey God's just laws.

What does public display of the law mean for the common citizen?

Search the Scriptures

1. What are the responsibilities and benefits of following God's commandments? (Deuteronomy 5:1–21, 32)

2. Why did Moses say that the people of Israel were supposed to treat foreigners fairly? (Deuteronomy 10:19)

Discuss the Meaning

Words like commandments, laws, and decrees can leave some readers with the opinion that God is more concerned about people following rules than having an abundant life based on a relationship with Him. Yet, from the time of God's visits with Adam and Eve in the cool of the evening to His embodiment in Jesus Christ, God has desired a loving relationship with people. One reason the laws were given was for the people's good, to uphold justice in relationship with others and with God.

1. What are some examples from the lesson's Background and Focal Verses that indicate God's desire for a loving relationship with people?

2. What is the role of God's commandments, laws, and decrees in the lives of individuals who desire to develop a loving and just relationship with God and with other people?

Liberating Lesson

When a middle-aged woman refused to give up her seat on a public bus in Montgomery, Alabama, she was agreeing with God that her life possessed intrinsic value. No longer would Rosa Parks allow herself to be unfairly treated. On December 1, 1955, she began a journey that secured for herself and countless descendants of African slaves the freedoms promised in the Constitution of the country which was now their homeland. Her lived experience was going to align with the truth that all people were created by God with equal worth. Justice, she believed, was to be evenly dispersed. What can you do to help ensure more people experience the benefits of a just society?

Application for Activation

For each generation, there are justice issues that selfless men and women need to address on the behalf of others. Some of our current issues include mass incarceration, child and senior care, affordable health care, adequate education, and immigration pathways. Make a commitment to visit, talk with, or serve with a local organization that ministers to people who are impacted by inequitable systems.

Follow the Spirit

What God wants me to do:

_____

_____

_____

_____

Remember Your Thoughts

Special insights I have learned:

_____

_____

_____

_____

More Light on the Text

Deuteronomy 5:1–3; 10:12–13; 27:1–10

1 And Moses called all Israel, and said unto them, Hear, O Israel, the statutes and judgments which I speak in your ears this day, that ye may learn them, and keep, and do them.

Moses, leader of the Hebrew people and messenger of God, consistently communicated commands, laws, instructions, guidance, judgments, and information to everyone in Israel. Here, Moses ensures everyone receives God's communication of statutes and judgments. Statutes and judgments are formally written enactments of an authority that legally governs a people, city, state, or country. Statutes and judgments are laws, commands, and decrees whether moral, ceremonial, or judicial. The authority in this chapter, without question, is God. Moses calls Israel together to hear a restatement of the Ten Commandments, which had already been given to the people of Israel. In His commandments, God cited what was just and His children promised obedience.

Restatement of the Law is significant for three major reasons. First, the original call to hear the statutes was for the generation of Israelites who went through the Red Sea. The sins of that generation caused them to wander and die in the wilderness before reaching the promised land of Canaan. Their children, the survivors, were a new generation of people, and Moses needed to share the statutes and judgments with them before entering the Promised Land. Secondly, the restatement of the statutes shows the significance of hearing, learning, keeping, and doing the requirements of God. The statutes are worthy of repeating, so they will become embedded in the hearts of the people that would enter the Promised Land. Finally and most importantly, the current people of Israel need to understand how to live, prosper, and prolong their days in the land they are to possess (Deuteronomy 5:33).

2 The LORD our God made a covenant with us in Horeb. 3 The LORD made not this covenant with our fathers, but with us, even us, who are all of us here alive this day.

A covenant is a contract or agreement between God and His people. In the covenant, God makes promises to His people either unconditionally or based on a certain conduct from them. There are many covenants throughout the Bible. For example, God made covenants with Noah, Abraham, the Israelites through Moses, David, and all people through Jesus Christ.

The Noahic Covenant, given to Noah, was unconditional and promised that God would never again destroy the world with water. He created the rainbow as a sign of this covenant (Genesis 9:12–17). The Abrahamic Covenant was a promise made by God to Abraham, that Abraham's descendants would inherit the Promised Land and from his lineage, all the nations of the earth would be blessed (Genesis 13:14–16; 15:18–21; 17:7; 22:18). Circumcision was used as a sign of the covenant between Abraham and God. The Mosaic Covenant was a conditional covenant of Law. God promised Israel that He would make them a chosen people, a holy nation, and His treasured possession. He promised to bless them abundantly in every way, but only if they kept His Law (Exodus 19:5–8). The Davidic Covenant was a promise by God to establish David's dynasty forever. David's descendants would be kings, including King Jesus.

The word Horeb (Heb. *khoreb*, khor–**ABE**) means waste or desert, and was a general name for the whole mountain range of which Mount Sinai was one of the summits. This mountain range formed a huge mountain block in the southern Sinai peninsula and had a very spacious plain at its northeast end where the Israelites camped. This is where Moses originally came down the mountain with the revelation of God's Law. In verse 3, Moses emphasizes that he was speaking to the current generation of living Israelites. Even though this group's parents were the adults making covenant vows at that time, Moses reminds the current generation of Israelites that they are bound to the same covenant. Their parents had sworn for themselves, but this oath covered both the adults and the children of the household.

Deuteronomy 10:12–13
12 And now, Israel, what doth the LORD thy God require of thee, but to fear the LORD

thy God, to walk in all his ways, and to love him, and to serve the LORD thy God with all thy heart and with all thy soul, 13 To keep the commandments of the LORD, and his statutes, which I command thee this day for thy good?

These verses ask the question, "What does God require of you?" The Israelites knew quite well that God commanded many things in the Book of Leviticus and the Mosaic Law. There were purity laws, rules for daily living, and regulations for family responsibilities, sexual conduct, and relationships. All of which were external observances that could be monitored and enforced. But respect and true love for God must come from the heart and can only be discerned by God. He and He alone can look into the motives and intent of the mind, soul, and spirit. God, in His love for us, deposited a free will in our spirits and then asked us to love Him, the Creator and lover of our soul. How astonishing that God requested our love. He did not make us robots or mechanical beings that were forced to love Him. He made us independent human beings who must choose to love Him as an act of our will. Moses exhorted God's people to love, serve, and obey Him with every inch of their being, for their own good. God's laws were not designed to spoil their fun or make life difficult for them. They were designed for the people's good, to protect them from their own evil inclinations and to uphold justice within the community of faith.

God has the same desires and requirements for us today. How amazing that we can have the forgiveness of our sins and eternal life with God as a free gift from Jesus Christ our Lord. What a joy to show our gratitude by loving, serving, and obeying God with all our heart, mind, and spirit.

Deuteronomy 27:1–10

1 And Moses with the elders of Israel commanded the people, saying, Keep all the commandments which I command you this day. 2 And it shall be on the day when ye shall pass over Jordan unto the land which the LORD thy God giveth thee, that thou shalt set thee up great stones, and plaister them with plaister:

In this verse, the elders joined Moses in exhortation for the first time in this book. Seventy elders formed the council of the Israelite nation. They were serious in their commands to the people to obey God's Law. The people deemed God as their King and vowed allegiance to Him. The people heard their command: as soon as the people took possession of the Promised Land, they were to set up an altar and erect a stone monument on which the Law would be inscribed. The stone monuments were plastered to ensure a smooth surface so the inscription would be more easily read.

3 And thou shalt write upon them all the words of this law, when thou art passed over, that thou mayest go in unto the land which the LORD thy God giveth thee, a land that floweth with milk and honey; as the LORD God of thy fathers hath promised thee.

The engraved monument would serve as a reminder to the Israelites and all others that the land of Canaan was dedicated to God's service. Repeatedly in the Old Testament, the Promised Land is described as the land of milk and honey (Exodus 3:8; Numbers 14:8; Deuteronomy 31:20; Ezekiel 20:15). This poetic description the Promised Land as "a land flowing with milk and honey" is a beautifully picturesque way of highlighting the agricultural richness of the land that awaited God's chosen people. The reference to "milk" suggests that many livestock could find pasture there, and the mention of "honey" suggests the vast farmland available, where bees had plenty of plants to draw nectar from. God brought His people out of slavery in Egypt to a prosperous land of freedom, blessings, and the knowledge of the Lord. However, the land flowing with milk and honey was home to the Canaanites, Hittites, Amorites, Perizzites, Hivites and Jebusites, all of whom were great in number and valued the land high enough to fight and die for it.

4 Therefore it shall be when ye be gone over Jordan, that ye shall set up these stones, which I command you this day, in mount Ebal, and thou shalt plaister them with plaister.

Once the Israelites passed over the Jordan River, they were to erect the stone monument and plaster the surface for easy inscribing. Years later, Joshua followed all of Moses' instructions from God (Joshua 8:30–35). He wrote all the laws and had them plastered as Moses ordered. Half of the people stood at Mount Gerizim and half of them in front of Mount Ebal. Joshua read all the words of the Law. He read the blessings at Mount Gerizim and the curses at Mount Ebal, written in the Book of the Law. God wanted to show His people the stark contrast between the blessings for those who obeyed His commands, and the curses for those who disobeyed His Law. The key point is that God is just, whether one decides to obey or disobey. His justice stands forever, but we, like the Children of Israel, decide if we want to be showered with His blessings or suffer His wrath for disobedience. Either way, God is just.

5 And there shalt thou build an altar unto the LORD thy God, an altar of stones: thou shalt not lift up any iron tool upon them. 6 Thou shalt build the altar of the LORD thy God of whole stones: and thou shalt offer burnt offerings thereon unto the LORD thy God:

God required an altar of stones and had previously explained why iron tools should not be used on them: "for if thou lift up thy tool upon it, thou hast polluted it" (from Exodus 20:25). The Lord also required "whole stones" that were not broken, or hewed out, but rough as they were when taken out of the quarry, because carved stones with figures and ornaments might lead to superstition. God knew His people were prone to making graven images and idolatry. He wanted sincere worship of Him without distractions.

This command was given during their temporary wilderness state and stayed in force until the Tabernacle was built. As the Israelites traveled, they had altars that were erected quickly and taken down with speed, designed for when circumstances required a hasty move. Some altars were even made of turf from the earth or dirt. The Israelites did not leave behind their altars when they moved camp. The altars they made either traveled with them or were destroyed to avoid abuse and superstitious uses. Although future altars in the Tabernacle and Temple were exquisite, durable, and majestic, they were still in stark contrast to the altars of idolaters, which were gaudy spectacles.

Jesus Christ, our altar, is a stone cut out of the mountain without hands (Daniel 2:34–35). He became our chief cornerstone (Matthew 21:42). Jesus made it possible for Christians to worship God in any place, as long as our worship is in spirit and truth. Our altar is present each time we pray and come boldly before the throne of grace, in Jesus' name (Hebrews 4:16).

7 And thou shalt offer peace offerings, and shalt eat there, and rejoice before the LORD thy God.

The Hebrew word for "peace offering" is *shelem* (**SHEH**–lem), which is from the same root as *shalom*, meaning peace, prosperity, and longevity. The peace offering was a voluntary sacrifice of worship and contribution given to God that represented thankfulness and gratitude in three specific instances: 1) blessings received; 2) the fulfillment of a vow; or 3) God's unsought generosity. The contribution was bread for thanksgiving or meat for a vow or freewill gift. The peace offering is described in detail in Leviticus 3 and 7:11–21.

Those who gave peace offerings had regard for God as the giver of all good things. The peace offerings were offered by way of prayer. If a person were in pursuit of mercy, a peace offering would be added to their prayer. The offerings were divided among the altar (for God), the priest, and the person bringing the sacrifice, including his family and friends. The peace offering represented God and His people feasting together, in love and friendship. This is why *shelem* is sometimes translated as "fellowship offering." The peace offerings were times of feasting, drinking, talking, singing, and enjoying salvation as a great gift from God. The peace offerings were the only kind that allowed the worshiper and his family and friends to participate. How wonderful that God included the family in this festive time of rejoicing and thanksgiving. On this occasion, the passage of Jordan and the arrival of Israel in the heart of the country, would be solid reasons for giving thanks to God. Certainly, a peace offering was warranted.

God's Law required a "burnt offering" in order that a peace offering could follow. Being in alignment with God's will, as represented by the burnt offering, meant the worshiper would be in a position to fellowship with God and with family in sharing the peace offering. Details about the burnt offering are found in the People, Places, and Times section of this lesson. Today, Christ, our Prince of Peace, is our "burnt offering," having made peace through His blood, shed on the Cross (Isaiah 9:6; Colossians 1:20). Isaiah prophesied about Jesus' taking our sins to satisfy the wrath of our just God against us, "He shall see the travail of his soul, and shall be satisfied" (from Isaiah 53:11). Through Jesus, the believer is reconciled to God; and having the peace of God in our hearts, we are disposed to pursue peace with all people. Through Jesus alone, we can obtain an answer of peace to our prayers. As we offer God our worship, praise, and fellowship, we too can engage in peace offerings.

8 And thou shalt write upon the stones all the words of this law very plainly. 9 And Moses and the priests the Levites spake unto all Israel, saying, Take heed, and hearken, O Israel; this day thou art become the people of the LORD thy God. 10 Thou shalt therefore obey the voice of the LORD thy God, and do his commandments and his statutes, which I command thee this day.

The laws on the stones were written clearly so everyone could read and understand them. The priest assisted Moses in urging the people to pay attention and seriously internalize the meaning of God's words and the solemn renewing of their covenant with Him. They were charged with attending to and executing God's plan for them. The Israelites are ordered to "take heed" (Heb. *sakat*, saw-**KOT**)—which means to be quiet—so that they can follow the second command here, "hearken" (Heb. *shama*, shaw-**MAW**), which means not only to listen, but also to obey.

The importance of this day had to be articulated. This day was the official, ceremonial day that Israel became God's people. Of course, they were His people before. He had chosen them to be His special people above everyone else; He had redeemed and delivered them out of Egypt; He led them through the wilderness, and provided and protected them; He gave them just laws and statutes to live by; all of which showed them to be His peculiar people. But now, in a very formal and solemn manner they were officially declared by God to be His people, and they had solemnly vowed and declared that He was their God and King.

This event was comparable to the day they entered into covenant with Him. God provided justice and His children promised obedience. Such power and privilege are overwhelming to the believer. Certainly, they were compelled to obey the voice of the Lord, just as we are urged by the Holy Spirit to follow Jesus' example.

Sources:

Annus, Amar, ed. *Divination and Interpretation of Signs in the Ancient World.* Oriental Institute Seminars, No. 6. The Oriental Institute of the University of Chicago. 2010. https://oi.uchicago.edu/sites/oi.uchicago.edu/files/uploads/shared/docs/ois6.pdf. Retrieved June 14, 2020.

Bartleby Research. *The Old Testament: The Five Covenants Essay.* https://www.bartleby.com/essay/The–Old–Testament–The–Five–Covenants–F3CG8P9YTC Retrieved January 7, 2020.

Constable, Thomas. *Expository Notes of Dr. Thomas Constable.* Exodus Overview. https://www.studylight.org/commentaries/dcc/deuteronomy.html. Retrieved January 6, 2020.

Easton's Illustrated Bible Dictionary. https://www.biblestudytools.com/dictionary/horeb/ Retrieved January 7, 2020.

Ellicott, Benson. *Exodus 5, 10 and 27.* Bible Hub Commentary. https://biblehub.com/commentaries/deuteronomy/5–3.htm Retrieved January 4, 2020.

Gill, John. *Gill's Exposition of the Whole Bible, Online Study.* Deuteronomy 5, 10 and 27. https://www.studylight.org/commentaries/geb/deuteronomy-5.html. Retrieved January 6, 2020.

Henry, Matthew. *Deuteronomy 5, 10 and 27.* https://www.biblestudytools.com/commentaries/matthew–henrycomplete/exodus/15.html. Retrieved December 28, 2019.

Henry, Matthew. *Commentary on the Whole Bible.* Kindle Edition.

Jamieson, R., Robert Fausset, and Robert Brown. *Jamieson, Fausset, and Brown's Commentary on the Whole Bible.* Grand Rapids, MI: Zondervan, 1961.

Jastrow, Jr., Morris, J. Frederic McCurdy, Kaufmann Kohler, and Louis Ginzberg. "BURNT OFFERING." *The Jewish Encyclopedia.* 1906. http://www.jewishencyclopedia.com/articles/3847–burnt–offering. Retrieved June 14, 2020.

Life Application Study Bible, New Living Translation. Wheaton, IL: Tyndale House Publishers, Inc., 1996.

Norwood, Arlisha. "Rosa Parks." National Women's History Museum. 2017. www.womenshistory.org/education–resources/biographies/rosa–parks. Retrieved April 6, 2020.

Park, Rosalind. "Kidneys in Ancient Egypt." DE 29 (1994). 125–129. https://www.academia.edu/227484/Kidneys_in_Ancient_Egypt. Retrieved June 14, 2020.

Poole, Matthew. *Commentary on Deuteronomy.* https://biblehub.com/commentaries/deuteronomy/5–3.htm. Retrieved January 7, 2020.

The Pulpit Commentary, 2010. https://biblehub.com/sermons/auth/orr/the_covenant_at_horeb.htm. Retrieved December 27, 2019.

Towns, Elmer, L. *Bible Answers for Almost All Your Questions.* Nashville, TN: Thomas Nelson, 2003.

Smith, William. *Smith's Bible Dictionary.* Philadelphia, PA: A.J. Holman Company, 1973.

The Woman's Study Bible, New King James Version. Nashville, TN: Thomas Nelson

Say It Correctly

Horeb. HOAR–ebb.
Ebal. EE–ball.

Daily Bible Readings

MONDAY
The Law of Justice
(Deuteronomy 5:6–21)

TUESDAY
Follow the Path of God's Law
(Deuteronomy 5:23–33)

WEDNESDAY
Discern the Good, Acceptable, and Perfect
(Romans 12:1–2, 9–21)

THURSDAY
The Written Law and the Ark of Wood
(Deuteronomy 10:1–11)

FRIDAY
Jesus Fulfills the Law
(Matthew 5:17–20)

SATURDAY
Curses upon Disobedience
(Deuteronomy 27:14–26)

SUNDAY
Obey the Statutes and Ordinances
(Deuteronomy 5:1–3; 10:12–13; 28:1–10)

Teaching Tips

December 12
Bible Study Guide 2

Words You Should Know

A. Kindness (2 Samuel 9:1) *chesed* (Heb.)—Love, grace, mercy

B. Father (v. 7) *ab* (Heb.)—Male parent or ancestor

Teacher Preparation

Unifying Principle—The Mercy of Justice. People rely on the kindness and support of others. How can people show radical kindness to one another? King David acted justly, remembered his promise to Jonathan, and was kind to Jonathan's son.

A. Read the Bible Background and Devotional Reading.

B. Pray for your students and lesson clarity.

C. Read the lesson Scripture in multiple translations.

O—Open the Lesson

A. Begin the class with prayer.

B. Search online for examples of Medieval and Renaissance art depicting the relationship between David and Mephibosheth. Select and display the art and invite students to respond to them.

C. Have the students read the Aim for Change and the In Focus story.

D. Ask students how events like those in the story weigh on their hearts and how they can view these events from a faith perspective.

P—Present the Scriptures

A. Read the Focal Verses and discuss the Background and The People, Places, and Times sections.

B. Have the class share what Scriptures stand out for them and why, with particular emphasis on today's themes.

E—Explore the Meaning

A. Use In Depth or More Light on the Text to facilitate a deeper discussion of the lesson text.

B. Pose the questions in Search the Scriptures and Discuss the Meaning.

C. Discuss the Liberating Lesson and Application for Activation sections.

N—Next Steps for Application

A. Summarize the value of keeping promises.

B. End class with a commitment to pray for breaking down artificial barriers that separate people.

Worship Guide

For the Superintendent or Teacher
Theme: David Administers Justice and Kindness
Song: "There Is a Wideness in God's Mercy"

David Administers Justice and Kindness

Bible Background • 2 SAMUEL 9
Printed Text • 2 SAMUEL 9:1–12 | Devotional Reading • PROVERBS 18:24

Aim for Change

By the end of this lesson, we will EXPLORE David's kindness toward Mephibosheth as an act of justice and equity, REFLECT on the value of keeping our word, and SHOW radical kindness to someone in need.

In Focus

Carl and Eddie had been best friends since seventh grade, when they were the only two Black kids in their suburban junior high. They stuck together through high stakes tests, team try–outs, and asking out the prettiest girls. The boys promised they would always look out for each other. Always.

After high school, Eddie joined the Navy like his dad had. Carl earned an academic scholarship to a good college, where he studied robotics. As they entered adulthood, it was harder and harder for Carl and Eddie to stay connected, but they would send each other birthday and Christmas cards at least.

Just as Carl had established himself in a good company, tragedy struck. Both Eddie and his wife died in a car wreck as she picked him up to come home after a long deployment. Eddie's young son, Junior, was suddenly orphaned. Carl was heartbroken and prayed to God asking what he should do. God moved him to show his friend's child the most kindness he could.

"Junior," Carl said to the youngster. "I want you to come home with me. I'll adopt you and raise you as best I can."

Junior was having trouble sorting it all out. "Why would you do that? You have your own kids to raise."

"I made a promise to your father," Carl said. "We were always going to look out for each other. I couldn't help much before. No way I could stop that truck from hitting them. But I can help now. I can help you. It's the least I could do for Eddie."

How has God ever moved you to show great kindness?

Keep in Mind

"And David said, Is there yet any that is left of the house of Saul, that I may shew him kindness for Jonathan's sake?" (2 Samuel 9:1, KJV)

"One day David asked, 'Is anyone in Saul's family still alive—anyone to whom I can show kindness for Jonathan's sake?'" (2 Samuel 9:1, NLT)

Focal Verses

KJV 2 Samuel 9:1 And David said, Is there yet any that is left of the house of Saul, that I may shew him kindness for Jonathan's sake?

2 And there was of the house of Saul a servant whose name was Ziba. And when they had called him unto David, the king said unto him, Art thou Ziba? And he said, Thy servant is he.

3 And the king said, Is there not yet any of the house of Saul, that I may shew the kindness of God unto him? And Ziba said unto the king, Jonathan hath yet a son, which is lame on his feet.

4 And the king said unto him, Where is he? And Ziba said unto the king, Behold, he is in the house of Machir, the son of Ammiel, in Lodebar.

5 Then king David sent, and fetched him out of the house of Machir, the son of Ammiel, from Lodebar.

6 Now when Mephibosheth, the son of Jonathan, the son of Saul, was come unto David, he fell on his face, and did reverence. And David said, Mephibosheth. And he answered, Behold thy servant!

7 And David said unto him, Fear not: for I will surely shew thee kindness for Jonathan thy father's sake, and will restore thee all the land of Saul thy father; and thou shalt eat bread at my table continually.

8 And he bowed himself, and said, What is thy servant, that thou shouldest look upon such a dead dog as I am?

9 Then the king called to Ziba, Saul's servant, and said unto him, I have given unto thy master's son all that pertained to Saul and to all his house.

10 Thou therefore, and thy sons, and thy servants, shall till the land for him, and thou shalt bring in the fruits, that thy master's son

NLT 2 Samuel 9:1 One day David asked, "Is anyone in Saul's family still alive—anyone to whom I can show kindness for Jonathan's sake?"

2 He summoned a man named Ziba, who had been one of Saul's servants. "Are you Ziba?" the king asked. "Yes sir, I am," Ziba replied.

3 The king then asked him, "Is anyone still alive from Saul's family? If so, I want to show God's kindness to them." Ziba replied, "Yes, one of Jonathan's sons is still alive. He is crippled in both feet."

4 "Where is he?" the king asked. "In Lo-debar," Ziba told him, "at the home of Makir son of Ammiel."

5 So David sent for him and brought him from Makir's home.

6 His name was Mephibosheth; he was Jonathan's son and Saul's grandson. When he came to David, he bowed low to the ground in deep respect. David said, "Greetings, Mephibosheth." Mephibosheth replied, "I am your servant."

7 "Don't be afraid!" David said. "I intend to show kindness to you because of my promise to your father, Jonathan. I will give you all the property that once belonged to your grandfather Saul, and you will eat here with me at the king's table!"

8 Mephibosheth bowed respectfully and exclaimed, "Who is your servant, that you should show such kindness to a dead dog like me?"

9 Then the king summoned Saul's servant Ziba and said, "I have given your master's grandson everything that belonged to Saul and his family.

10 You and your sons and servants are to farm the land for him to produce food for your master's household. But Mephibosheth, your master's grandson, will eat here at my table." (Ziba had fifteen sons and twenty servants.)

may have food to eat: but Mephibosheth thy master's son shall eat bread alway at my table. Now Ziba had fifteen sons and twenty servants.

11 Then said Ziba unto the king, According to all that my lord the king hath commanded his servant, so shall thy servant do. As for Mephibosheth, said the king, he shall eat at my table, as one of the king's sons.

12 And Mephibosheth had a young son, whose name was Micha. And all that dwelt in the house of Ziba were servants unto Mephibosheth.

11 Ziba replied, "Yes, my lord the king; I am your servant, and I will do all that you have commanded." And from that time on, Mephibosheth ate regularly at David's table, like one of the king's own sons.

12 Mephibosheth had a young son named Mica. From then on, all the members of Ziba's household were Mephibosheth's servants.

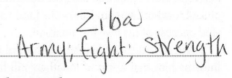

Ziba
Army, fight, strength

The People, Places, and Times

Lameness. People who did not have able bodies in David's day would almost always become beggars. Families would not have the resources to care for them properly, and they could not do most kinds of work that was available, which was usually agricultural work. Even though today we know to care for those who need physical accommodations, in David's day any physical abnormality was seen as a mark of shame. In neighboring cultures, they would be laughed at and ridiculed just for being differently abled. Even in Israel, the Law prohibited people with some forms of disfigurement from acting as priests (Leviticus 21:16–23), or even worshiping in the assembly (Deuteronomy 23:1). Other kings might not even allow differently able people into their presence. By welcoming Mephibosheth to his own table, David is showing conspicuous kindness to this young man whose feet never supported him.

Dogs. In David's day, there were some breeds of hunting hounds that people kept, but most of the dogs were strays. These animals were nearly feral, and might surround and attack people (Psalm 22:16, Jeremiah 15:3). Dogs were considered extremely unclean (Isaiah 66:3), and were thought to be especially stupid animals (Proverbs 26:11). Calling someone a dog was a supreme insult.

Background

After returning the Ark of the Covenant to Jerusalem, and establishing himself as king over Israel, David set about subjugating his enemies. David conquered the Philistines, the Moabites, the Syrians, and the Edomites, giving Israel control of land as far as the Euphrates (2 Samuel 8). David was at the height of his power. Still, he remembered his close friend, Jonathan.

David and Jonathan had grown to be the closest of friends. Though Jonathan was Saul's biological heir, he recognized that God's hand was on David to be the next ruler. Jonathan even stopped his father Saul from taking David's life (1 Samuel 19:1–7). Jonathan had been fully devoted to David, and David was fully devoted to Jonathan in return. This devotion continued even after Jonathan's death.

At-A-Glance

1. David Inquires (2 Samuel 9:1–3)
2. Mephibosheth Appears before David (2 Samuel 9:4–7)
3. David Establishes Saul's Legacy (2 Samuel 9:8–12)

In Depth

1. David Inquires (2 Samuel 9:1–3)

In addition to being a fierce warrior and a capable administrator, David proved himself to be a kind and just king. He sought to honor the pledge he made to Jonathan (1 Samuel 20:14–15), where he agreed to treat Jonathan's family with faithful love. Once established in his reign, David inquired after the descendants of Saul to whom he could show the kindness of God because of his love for Jonathan.

David consults with Saul's land steward who informs him that a son of Jonathan still lives. His name was Mephibosheth. Unfortunately, Mephibosheth was crippled and living in the obscure village of Lo-debar. The name Lo-debar is thought to mean "without pasture." This was not choice land by any means. Mephibosheth was only five when his father Jonathan was killed. David was in exile during that time and knew nothing of Mephibosheth.

David's inquiry about the descendants of Saul demonstrates a profound devotion to Jonathan and his memory. It also reveals something about David personally. He had achieved great success, and he still felt it important to show kindness.

Is it always best to withhold the fulfillment of a promise until you are able to do so in a big way?

2. Mephibosheth Appears before David (2 Samuel 9:4–7)

Upon learning Mephibosheth whereabouts, David sends for him at once. Mephibosheth appears before David bowing low to show him utmost respect. Mephibosheth is afraid when he approaches David, and with good reason. It was customary for a new king to wipe out any remnants of rival dynasties. David acts quickly to allay his fears, however (v. 7).

David tells Mephibosheth not to be afraid because David intends to show him kindness to honor the memory of Jonathan. Saul's family estate had fallen to David either through Michal, his wife, or the rebellion of Ish-bosheth. David intends to restore Saul's property to Mephibosheth and offers him a place at the king's table.

Mephibosheth responds with great humility. He had been afraid of finding his own destruction, but now Mephibosheth realizes that David had summoned him so he could honor him and restore his family's land. He became the stunned beneficiary of a pact David had made with his father years before.

How do you react when showered with unexpected praise or reward?

3. David Establishes Saul's Legacy (2 Samuel 9:8–12)

Restoring Saul's family estate was an act of extreme kindness. Saul's ancestral lands would become Mephibosheth's. David then goes even further, establishing a means for Mephibosheth to collect an income for years to come.

Ziba, the land steward, is appointed to manage the land for Mephibosheth. In exchange, he would receive half of the proceeds of the land. The rest would go to Mephibosheth. Ziba himself has fifteen sons and twenty servants. This is mentioned to show that Mephibosheth would be honored like one of the king's sons.

Finally, Mephibosheth also had a son. This son would carry on the name and preserve the memory of David's dear friend Jonathan.

How is your legacy protected for future generations?

Search the Scriptures

1. Why does David inquire after Saul's descendants (2 Samuel 9:1, 3)?

2. How does Mephibosheth respond when he learns that David intends to restore his ancestral lands instead of killing him, as dictated by custom (v. 8)?

Discuss the Meaning

This passage describes an extraordinary turn of events for Mephibosheth. He was the recipient of restoration so profound that it forever changed his life and that of his descendants. As illustrated in this passage, God is the God of radical restoration. God seeks to restore individuals, communities, and the world. How can we ask God to restore us so that we may show His love and kindness to others?

Liberating Lesson

The story of David and Mephibosheth is a story about kindness, restoration, and justice. However, at its core, it is a story about relationship. David had a very close friendship with Jonathan. Years after Jonathan's death, David was still devoted to him. Upon hearing about Mephibosheth, David restored Saul's family estate. In addition, David offered Mephibosheth a place at his own table. Instead of passing his days in Lo–debar, he ate at the table as if he were David's own son.

Similarly, we can show God's kindness and justice to the world around us. David's kindness to Mephibosheth was rooted in relationship. We should demonstrate kindness and justice to those around us, bringing them into a right relationship with us and pointing them toward a right relationship with God.

Application for Activation

The church provides a number of opportunities to grow in community and to form meaningful relationships. Look for someone to disciple and grow in friendship.

The church also provides opportunities to work together to serve as agents of God's love. Also look for opportunities to show the kindness and justice of God to the wider community at large.

God cares deeply for the poor and marginalized. Mephibosheth was physically impaired, but there are several people groups that are marginalized.

Women, ethnic minorities, the elderly, the poor, people suffering from mental illness, and people in numerous other groups can be marginalized, as well. They need to receive God's kindness and justice, just as Mephibosheth did.

Follow the Spirit

What God wants me to do:

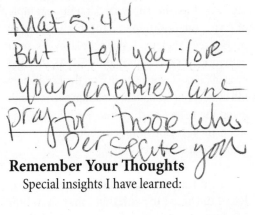

Mat 5:44
But I tell you, love your enemies and pray for those who persecute you

Remember Your Thoughts

Special insights I have learned:

_____

_____

_____

_____

More Light on the Text

2 Samuel 9:1–12

"Out of sight, out of mind," so goes a common saying. Not so with David. After all the injustice and persecution he had suffered at the hands of Saul, it would have been understandable if David had conveniently forgotten his promise to Jonathan (1 Samuel 20:14–16, 42). However, the passage of time has not relieved him of faithfulness to the oath he swore to Jonathan. As such, it was one of David's strengths that he did not forget what he had undertaken, even though many years had passed since that covenant had been made. Mephibosheth, who now has a young son himself (v. 12), was five years old at the death of his father Jonathan (2 Samuel 4:4). He probably was not aware of the covenant between David and Jonathan.

David had seen his enemies defeated, his throne secured, and his capital established. He was therefore in a position to fulfill the obligation he had undertaken to show loyalty to Jonathan's descendants. In this chapter, we see David as the supreme Israelite example of covenant faithfulness, the highest virtue in Hebrew society. Judged by David's own demanding criteria (cf. Psalm 15:1, 4), the king proved himself worthy to live on the Lord's holy hill by keeping his oath to Jonathan even though it ran the risk of hurting his own dynasty. The story, then, is not so much about undeserved charity as it is about loyalty.

1 And David said, Is there yet any that is left of the house of Saul, that I may shew him kindness for Jonathan's sake? 2 And there was of the house of Saul a servant whose name was Ziba. And when they had called him unto David, the king said unto him, Art thou Ziba? And he said, Thy servant is he. 3 And the king said, Is there not yet any of the house of Saul, that I may shew the kindness of God unto him? And Ziba said unto the king, Jonathan hath yet a son, which is lame on his feet.

Established on the throne in Jerusalem after having effectively put down both internal and external opposition, David was now in a position to fulfill his commitment to "the house of Saul" (v. 1). He casts the net wider than his promise to Jonathan demanded, extending his generosity to any of Saul's surviving sons or grandsons. His sole motive is to show kindness (Heb. _khesed_, **KHEH**–sed) for Jonathan's sake, for he remembered how much he had owed to Jonathan. The word _khesed_ means more than a charitable deed; it is love and faithfulness. David's inquiry shows his uncertainty or lack of awareness of whether Jonathan had left behind him a son. However, there was a servant who had information. Ziba had probably taken care of Saul's property in the tribe of Benjamin. He had been a steward for Saul, and after his master's death, he had continued in possession of the estate. He was a man of some standing, with twenty servants of his own (v. 10).

David sends for him not because he expected to hear of a son of his dear friend Jonathan, but because he was ready to show kindness to any representative of the fallen monarch. The repetition of David's question in verse 3 (cf. v. 1) is in fact significant in establishing the theme of this chapter. It underscores that David was not an enemy of "the house of Saul" (v. 3); in fact, he was an agent of God's kindness (_khesed_) working to benefit Israel's former dynastic family.

Mephibosheth's condition was caused when he was a five–year–old child. News of Saul and Jonathan's death in battle reached Saul's household, and everyone scrambled to flee the turmoil of an uncertain royal succession. In her haste, Mephibosheth's nurse dropped him. This twisted his feet in such a way that he was "lame" (Heb. _nakeh_, naw–**KEH**), meaning smitten, the rest of his life. This might have referred to a stumbling or limping gait, since Mephibosheth is also described as "lame" (Heb. _pasakh_, paw–**SOKH**), meaning halting or wavering (2 Samuel 4:4).

4 And the king said unto him, Where is he? And Ziba said unto the king, Behold, he is in the house of Machir, the son of Ammiel, in Lodebar. 5 Then king David sent, and fetched him out of the house of Machir, the son of Ammiel, from Lodebar. 6 Now when Mephibosheth, the son of Jonathan, the son of Saul, was come unto David, he fell on his face, and did reverence. And David said, Mephibosheth. And he answered, Behold thy servant!

Through his inquiry, David learns that there was "still a son of Jonathan" (v. 4) apparently living with a wife and son (cf. v. 12) in a self-imposed seclusion "in the house of Machir, son of Ammiel, in Lodebar." Not much is known of Lo-debar; it is only mentioned here and in 2 Samuel 27:17, both times only as the abode of Machir. The name probably means "no pasture," which does not sound like a likely place to settle in an agrarian economy. Machir, mentioned here for the first time, was a wealthy and powerful individual living east of the Jordan in the river valley of Gilead. Later he proved to be one of David's most loyal supporters (cf. 17:27–29). He provided for the needs of David and his followers at a crucial time, during the rebellion of Absalom. He may have taken charge of Mephibosheth at Jonathan's death. His name suggests that he was from the tribe of Manasseh (Numbers 32:39, 40).

Mephibosheth was "crippled in both feet" (v. 3) as a result of an accident in early childhood (1 Samuel 4:4). David summoned him for appearance at the royal court. In a manner befitting a king but nonetheless awkward due to his condition, Mephibosheth bowed before the king. In the customary manner of communication between a social superior and an inferior, David calls out Mephibosheth's name. Mephibosheth, in turn, refers to himself as "your servant."

7 And David said unto him, Fear not: for I will surely shew thee kindness for Jonathan thy father's sake, and will restore thee all the land of Saul thy father; and thou shalt eat bread at my table continually. 8 And he bowed himself, and said, What is thy servant, that thou shouldest look upon such a dead dog as I am?

Despite the close relationship between his father and David, Mephibosheth had never before been to the court of the king, and it would hardly be surprising if he felt both fear and resentment at the summons he had received. Mephibosheth probably expected the typical fate for members of a dethroned dynasty in the region. In other words, he might have been afraid that David hunted him out to put the previous king's relatives to death. Later in the Northern Kingdom of Israel, each new line of usurpers put to death every male relative of its predecessor (1 Kings 15:29, 16:11; 2 Kings 10:17, 15:25). Mephibosheth seems to have lived in hiding in Lo-debar.

But David tells him not to fear this fate. The king called him there to show him kindness on behalf of Jonathan, his "father" (Heb. *'ab*, **AV**) and to restore to him lands that had belonged to Saul, his "father" (Heb. *'ab*, **AV**). In a single sentence, David uses the same word to refer to a father and a grandfather. Here we see how fluidly the Hebrew word *'ab* is used for one's direct male parent or for an ancestor one or several generations back.

In addition, David promised to turn over Saul's private estate in Gibeah, which passed to David's possession when he came to the throne (12:8). The property of the previous regime would have come into David's possession, and to restore that property to a member of his predecessor's family was to run the risk of encouraging thoughts of usurping the throne. In returning the possession to Mephibosheth, David was not only magnanimous, but also taking a risk because what was intended as a generous gesture without any ulterior motive could in this way backfire.

Here we find a reversal of fortunes indeed, and that in a positive way. Mephibosheth—who had apparently been dependent up to this point on the hospitality of a generous individual—suddenly became a rich man, the owner of wealth-producing property. David probably restored to Mephibosheth not only the lands at Gibeah, which Ziba had managed to hold, but Saul's estates generally. David's promise that Mephibosheth would eat at his table ensured not only a place of honor at court, but also access to those who were directing the affairs of state. He would now be in the know.

His reference to himself as a dead dog is unnecessarily disparaging, and reflects what would now be regarded as a morbid self–image, induced perhaps by his disability. It is interesting to note that Mephibosheth described himself in terms similar to those used by David of himself to Saul (1 Samuel 24:14). However, he probably meant no more than to express great gratitude, and also to acknowledge the disparity of rank between himself and the king.

9 Then the king called to Ziba, Saul's servant, and said unto him, I have given unto thy master's son all that pertained to Saul and to all his house. 10 Thou therefore, and thy sons, and thy servants, shall till the land for him, and thou shalt bring in the fruits, that thy master's son may have food to eat: but Mephibosheth thy master's son shall eat bread alway at my table. Now Ziba had fifteen sons and twenty servants.

It was all very well to bestow property on Mephibosheth, but it required management, hence the involvement of Ziba as chief steward, a man of substance who would realize what was required. Ziba had evidently thrived, for, beginning as a slave in Saul's household, he had now several sons and many slaves of his own, and had become a person of considerable importance. He would still remain so, now serving his former master's grandson.

Though Mephibosheth ate at the king's table, he would have a household to maintain—for he had a wife and son—and other expenses. His having "food to eat" (v. 10) includes everything necessary, as does our prayer for "daily bread." He would live in Jerusalem as a nobleman, and Ziba would cultivate his estates, paying (as is usual at the time) a fixed proportion of the produce's value to his master.

11 Then said Ziba unto the king, According to all that my lord the king hath commanded his servant, so shall thy servant do. As for Mephibosheth, said the king, he shall eat at my table, as one of the king's sons. 12 And Mephibosheth had a young son, whose name was Micha. And all that dwelt in the house of Ziba were servants unto Mephibosheth.

Ziba took over this responsibility as requested, and Mephibosheth lived at court like one of the royal princes, for whom the arrangement could have proved irksome. By sheer repetition, the account lays stress on Mephibosheth's lameness, his place at the king's table, and on the servants he needed. David's kindness involved a cost, to others as well as to himself. There was one other relevant factor: Mephibosheth had a young son, whose name was Micha. This son of Mephibosheth became the representative of the house of Saul, and had a numerous offspring, who were leading men in the tribe of Benjamin until the Babylonian Captivity (see 1 Chronicles 8:35–40; 9:40–44).

In Christian preaching, this story has often been used as an illustration of unmerited grace. The great king goes out of his way to bring even a lowly cripple to eat at his table, granting the marginalized great honor. Mephibosheth's name even means "dispelling shame." Although that application may be correct, that is not the thrust or core of the story. It is about covenant faithfulness. The story neither begins nor ends with this chapter. David's act of kindness arose from his friendship with Jonathan; more than that, he was fulfilling a promise made long before to Jonathan (cf. 1 Samuel 20:15). To "show kindness" (v. 1) is not precisely what the Hebrew phrase means; the noun includes the idea of loyalty, and so picks up the theme of the covenant between David and Jonathan. So the chapter begins by recalling David's duty to his dead friend; and it ends with Mephibosheth in an honored position at court. The story, then, is not so much about undeserved charity as about loyalty.

Sources:
Baldwin, J. G. *1 and 2 Samuel*. TOTC. Downers Grove: InterVarsity, 1988.
Bergen, Robert D. *1, 2 Samuel, vol. 7*. The New American Commentary. Nashville: Broadman & Holman Publishers, 1996.
Brueggemann, W. First and Second Samuel. IBC. Louisville: John Knox, 1990.
Darby, J. N. *Synopsis of the Books of the Bible: Genesis to 2 Chronicles*. Bellingham, WA: Logos Research Systems, Inc., 2008.
Edersheim, Alfred. *Bible History: Old Testament*. Grand Rapids, MI: William B. Eerdmans Publishing Company, 1975.
Gordon, R. P. *I and II Samuel*. Grand Rapids: Zondervan, 1986.
Hubbard, David A. *2 Samuel, vol. 11*. Word Biblical Commentary Dallas: Word, Incorporated, 1989.
Jamieson, Robert, A. R. Fausset, and David Brown. *Commentary Critical and Explanatory on the Whole Bible*. Oak Harbor, WA: Logos Research Systems, Inc., 1997.
Mathews, Kenneth A. "The Historical Books." In *Holman Concise Bible Commentary*, edited by David S. Dockery. Nashville, TN: Broadman & Holman Publishers, 1998.
Morrison, Craig E. *2 Samuel*. Berit Olam: Studies in Hebrew Narrative & Poetry. Collegeville, MN: Liturgical Press, 2013.
Payne, David F. *I & II Samuel*. The Daily Study Bible Series. Louisville, KY: Westminster John Knox Press, 2001.
Spence–Jones, H. D. M. ed. *2 Samuel*. The Pulpit Commentary. New York: Funk & Wagnalls Company, 1909.

Say It Correctly

Ammiel. AM–ee–uhl.
Lo–debar. loh–DEE–bar.
Mephibosheth. muh–FIH–bo–sheth.

Daily Bible Readings

MONDAY
Death of Saul and Jonathan Mourned
(2 Samuel 1:1–12)

TUESDAY
A Lament from a Just Heart
(2 Samuel 1:17–27)

WEDNESDAY
A Cry for Justice
(Luke 18:1–8)

THURSDAY
Mercy from the Son of David
(Matthew 20:29–34)

FRIDAY
David Made King Over All Israel
(2 Samuel 3:1–5; 5:1–5)

SATURDAY
The King Rejoices in God
(Psalm 21)

SUNDAY
David Shows Kindness
to Saul's Descendant
(2 Samuel 9:1–7, 9–12)

Notes

Teaching Tips

Words You Should Know

A. Shadow of Death (Isaiah 9:2) *tsalmaveth* (Heb.)—Distress or extreme danger

B. Yoke (v. 4) *'ol* (Heb.)—A condition of servitude or slavery

Teacher Preparation

Unifying Principle—The Source of Justice. People suffer injustices and ill treatment. Will there be a time when people can count on being treated fairly? God's kingdom will be one of justice and righteousness.

A. Read the Bible Background and Devotional Reading.

B. Pray for your students and lesson clarity.

C. Read the lesson Scripture in multiple translations.

O—Open the Lesson

A. Begin the class with prayer.

B. Open class by playing the song "[I Need a] Hero" by Gloria Estefan. Discuss the attributes we look for in a true hero. How many of those qualities will we find in our text today?

C. Have the students read the Aim for Change and the In Focus story.

D. Ask students how events like those in the story weigh on their hearts and how they can view these events from a faith perspective.

P—Present the Scriptures

A. Read the Focal Verses and discuss the Background and The People, Places, and Times sections.

B. Have the class share what Scriptures stand out for them and why, with particular emphasis on today's themes.

E—Explore the Meaning

A. Use In Depth or More Light on the Text to facilitate a deeper discussion of the lesson text.

B. Pose the questions in Search the Scriptures and Discuss the Meaning.

C. Discuss the Liberating Lesson and Application for Activation sections.

N—Next Steps for Application

A. Summarize the value of trusting that troubles are temporary but Jesus is eternal.

B. End class with a commitment to pray for a deep sense of peace because of Jesus' presence, even when their world seems to be in turmoil.

Worship Guide

For the Superintendent or Teacher
Theme: Justice and Righteousness Reign
Song: "Prince of Peace, Control My Will"

Justice and Righteousness Reign

Bible Background • ISAIAH 9:1–7
Printed Text • ISAIAH 9:2–7 | Devotional Reading • MICAH 6:1–8

Aim for Change

By the end of this lesson, we will ANALYZE the importance of this prophecy for the people of God in Isaiah's time and today; CELEBRATE the justice, righteousness, and peace that Jesus brings to God's people; and SHARE with others the hope of eternal peace and justice found in Jesus' reign.

In Focus

Maxine's teenage daughter Taneisha was excited because they were leaving Detroit for Christmas to spend time with her grandmother in Memphis. Taneisha had never been on a plane before. When they arrived at Detroit's Metro International Airport, Maxine had to all but threaten Taneisha to calm down so they could hear their flight being announced.

Later, as Northwest Airlines flight #743 took off from Detroit, Taneisha became a chatterbox. She talked to Maxine all the way to Memphis. A few hours later, when Maxine and Taneisha stepped off the plane, Maxine's mother was there to meet them. Taneisha ran and jumped into her grandmother's arms, laughing and squealing all the way.

After Maxine had unpacked and settled in front of the fireplace and Christmas tree with a cup of cocoa, she thought about her daughter's excitement and the day's events. Maxine truly loved Taneisha. But as the girl slept soundly in bed, Maxine valued the peace and quiet she now enjoyed while she sat looking at the fire dance around the logs. Now that they were with their family for Christmas, she could slow down and thank God for sending His blessing of peace on earth.

Peace was a treasured commodity that Maxine did not often get to enjoy. Her fast-paced job and Taneisha's full school schedule created tension and fatigue in their lives. However, Maxine also knew they needed to take time out to enjoy the simple things in life, so that they could experience tranquility and peace in the midst of the chaos.

How does Jesus help you experience true and lasting peace in your personal life?

Keep in Mind

"Of the increase of his government and peace there shall be no end, upon the throne of David, and upon his kingdom, to order it, and to establish it with judgment and with justice from henceforth even for ever. The zeal of the LORD of hosts will perform this." (Isaiah 9:7, KJV)

"His government and its peace will never end. He will rule with fairness and justice from the throne of his ancestor David for all eternity. The passionate commitment of the LORD of Heaven's Armies will make this happen!" (Isaiah 9:7, NLT)

Focal Verses

KJV **Isaiah 9:2** The people that walked in darkness have seen a great light: they that dwell in the land of the shadow of death, upon them hath the light shined.

3 Thou hast multiplied the nation, and not increased the joy: they joy before thee according to the joy in harvest, and as men rejoice when they divide the spoil.

4 For thou hast broken the yoke of his burden, and the staff of his shoulder, the rod of his oppressor, as in the day of Midian.

5 For every battle of the warrior is with confused noise, and garments rolled in blood; but this shall be with burning and fuel of fire.

6 For unto us a child is born, unto us a son is given: and the government shall be upon his shoulder: and his name shall be called Wonderful, Counsellor, The mighty God, The everlasting Father, The Prince of Peace.

7 Of the increase of his government and peace there shall be no end, upon the throne of David, and upon his kingdom, to order it, and to establish it with judgment and with justice from henceforth even for ever. The zeal of the LORD of hosts will perform this.

NLT **Isaiah 9:2** The people who walk in darkness will see a great light. For those who live in a land of deep darkness, a light will shine.

3 You will enlarge the nation of Israel, and its people will rejoice. They will rejoice before you as people rejoice at the harvest and like warriors dividing the plunder.

4 For you will break the yoke of their slavery and lift the heavy burden from their shoulders. You will break the oppressor's rod, just as you did when you destroyed the army of Midian.

5 The boots of the warrior and the uniforms bloodstained by war will all be burned. They will be fuel for the fire.

6 For a child is born to us, a son is given to us. The government will rest on his shoulders. And he will be called: Wonderful Counselor, Mighty God, Everlasting Father, Prince of Peace.

7 His government and its peace will never end. He will rule with fairness and justice from the throne of his ancestor David for all eternity. The passionate commitment of the LORD of Heaven's Armies will make this happen!

The People, Places, and Times

Isaiah. One of the most influential Old Testament prophets, Isaiah lived and ministered in the Southern Kingdom of Judah for 58 years. Isaiah lived through one of his nation's most turbulent periods, during which he witnessed Judah's defeat by the Babylonian Empire and actually saw his fellow citizens taken into captivity. He prophesies during the reigns of five kings: Uzziah, Jotham, Ahaz, Hezekiah, and Manasseh. His free access to the palace in Jerusalem and his familiarity with court life imply that Isaiah belonged to Judah's wealthy class and may have been related to the ruling family. However, this did not keep Isaiah from verbally attacking the aristocracy in defense of the common people. Scripture refers to his wife as a "prophetess" and identifies him as the father of at least two sons: Shear–jashub and Maher–shalal–hash–baz (Isaiah 7:1–3; 8:1–3).

Background

Much of Isaiah's writings strongly criticizes the people of Judah for their sinfulness and unwillingness to be faithful to the one true God. During the reign of King Ahaz of Judah, the kings of Israel and Damascus waged war against him. Instead of looking to God for support, Ahaz foolishly allied himself with the Assyrian king, Tiglath–pileser. Judah soon found itself a vassal state under the Assyrians. Later, the Assyrians invaded Judah and demanded great amounts of tribute. Ahaz's successor and son, King Hezekiah, rebelled, but his revolt was squashed out. Isaiah warned that their continued refusal to be faithful to God would result in disaster for the entire nation. King Hezekiah refused to heed the prophet, and Judah was almost destroyed before the people turned back to God and begged Him to come to their aide.

Throughout his ministry, Isaiah repeatedly called on the nation to rely on God, rather than military strength or political alliances. The Northern Kingdom had refused to listen to their prophets, Amos and Hosea. Instead, Israel had resorted to military might to assert their nationhood, and as a result had been soundly defeated and no longer existed as a nation. By the grace of God, Judah was for a time spared.

How does Isaiah's prophecy show that God's plans are better than a king's plans?

At-A-Glance

1. End of the Darkness (Isaiah 9:2–5)
2. Gift of Forthcoming Peace (v. 6–7)

In Depth

1. End of the Darkness (Isaiah 9:2–5)

During the time Isaiah lived, Assyria was a major military force that was defeating many countries. It is understandable that the future appeared foreboding and hopeless to the people of Judah. Judah was in a state of spiritual darkness and political distress as it helplessly watched the scorched earth policy of the invading Assyrians.

It is onto this scene that the prophet Isaiah introduces a wonderful prophecy of hope. Isaiah makes it clear that he is addressing Judah, the people who had walked in "darkness" and dwelled "in the land of the shadow of death" (Isaiah 9:2). This kind of darkness is a frightening but apt description of sin. This spiritual darkness contributes to the encompassing sense of hopelessness and helplessness.

Conversely, God's presence is equated with light. God declares that Israel will receive His light—His life and wisdom—in the midst of chaos and confusion. The great light that will appear is Jesus Christ, the Messiah. Seven hundred years later, Jesus would begin His ministry and bring light into this very land that is now plunged into darkness (John 8:12). Isaiah insists that because a Messiah is coming, there will be "joy" instead of the gloom (Isaiah 9:3). The hope of the people is to be placed in the Lord, not in reliance on military strength or political savvy.

Present–day saints should be reminded that we are not bound by our present circumstances; we can rejoice in our hope in the only One who can remove the gloom from our lives. From a Roman prison, the Apostle Paul rejoiced in his chains: "Rejoice in the Lord always: and again I say, Rejoice" (Philippians 4:4).

Isaiah likens the time of Israel's ultimate deliverance to the time when God used Gideon to free Israel from the Midianites (see Judges 7:1–25). Like Gideon, the Deliverer will lead God's people from the battle with their enemies with full assurance of victory on their side. Isaiah also states that the "warrior's garments" would be "rolled in blood" (v. 5). Jesus would pay the highest price for our freedom from darkness and bondage: His death on the Cross.

Whom do you see today standing against the darkness and helping shine God's light?

2. Gift of Forthcoming Peace (v. 6–7)

How wonderful it is to Christians to note that the birth of this Child, introduced by Isaiah, is a gift to us from God Himself. Isaiah stresses that He will "be given" (Isaiah 9:6). Here, Isaiah's prophecy recognizes that the Messiah will be a legitimate heir to the Davidic throne, a point of paramount importance to the people living in the time of this writing.

When Jesus came to redeem Israel, He became the focal point of a new and better "government" (v. 6). His kingdom is eternal, and all who come to God through Him in humble submission will be a part of His government, of which He is the head (Ephesians 5:23). When we read "the government will rest on his shoulders" (9:6, NLT), we see Isaiah's poetic description of the Messiah as a capable and sovereign ruler, not to be confused with a mere human king.

Isaiah further identifies the Messiah as "Wonderful, Counsellor" (v. 6). Here, we are assured that the Messiah will rule with infinite wisdom that exceeds human limitations. He will be efficient and effective in the planning and implementation of His divine plans. When we affirm Jesus as our greatest counselor, we will cease our desire to lean on human understanding and reasoning for solutions to life's problems.

The prophet's description of the Messiah as "Mighty God" recognizes the full omnipotence and absolute deity of the Savior (v. 6). The qualities of eternal tenderness and protection are evoked with the title "Everlasting Father." Jesus offers us the same compassion and provision that the loving and caring Father shows toward His children who love, fear, and obey Him.

Finally, Isaiah declares that the Messiah is the "Prince of Peace" (v. 6). Not only will He bring peace, but He will rule with peace. As the Prince of Peace, He will provide His children with eternal rest and joy that will be an integral part of His kingdom. Christians have the blessed assurance that at the very moment we place our trust in Jesus, He gives us His perfect peace. This does not mean that all of our problems will go away. Professing Christ will sometimes bring strife as Paul found. However, because he was so steadfast in preaching and believing Christ, Paul also found God's peace to "passeth all understanding" (Philippians 4:7). Today too, we can have confidence that we will never face our problems alone—He will always be with us, guiding and providing protection through our darkest hours.

Why does Isaiah use so many different expressions to describe the Messiah?

Search the Scriptures

1. According to Isaiah, where will the government of God reside (v. 6)?

2. How will God's government increase (v. 7)?

Discuss the Meaning

Do you think that our society is suffering from the effects of spiritual darkness? In what ways? How does God's just kingdom lead us out of and protect us from this spiritual darkness?

Liberating Lesson

The growing number of global military conflicts and economic meltdowns that have left millions jobless and homeless only add to a growing sense of helplessness throughout the world. Alarming crime rates have also left many frightened and insecure. Few, if any, leave their doors unlocked, and many are afraid to travel. Every day we see examples of people with money, power, and position afforded one form of treatment within the judicial system, while the poor and disadvantaged are treated radically different. There are some rich people who steal millions and get away with little more than a slap on the wrist, and there are poor individuals sentenced to prison for stealing a pair of shoes.

What can we learn from today's lesson that can help people whose lives are unsettled and dysfunctional because of unjust systems? Develop a specific plan that you can share with people, especially during the holiday season.

Application for Activation

The prophet Isaiah lived in a time of political turmoil and spiritual confusion. The people of Judah were understandably anxious as the powerful Assyrian army gathered at the gates of Jerusalem. Their world was similar to ours in some ways. Many people are stressed and feel powerless, hopeless, and helpless. Similar to Isaiah, reach out to someone this week and let them know that God is still in control. Speak words of comfort to them and let them know that God knows and He cares.

Follow the Spirit

What God wants me to do:

_____

_____

_____

_____

_____

Remember Your Thoughts

Special insights I have learned:

_____

_____

_____

_____

_____

More Light on the Text

Isaiah 9:2–7

In Isaiah 9:1, God's initial treatment of Zebulun and Napthali ("he lightly afflicted" them) referred to the first invasion by Assyria's King Tiglath–pileser in 733 or 732 BC, during which the king annexed a large part of the Northern Kingdom of Israel (2 Kings 15:29). Only a decade later, in 722 BC, the Assyrians would return to capture the entire Northern Kingdom. The situation will be so hopeless that they will not be able to find any help. They will be surrounded by utter darkness, and they will even curse their king and their God. Over against this awful situation, Isaiah comes with a message of hope and joy in place of despair; their darkness would be turned to light. This change is figuratively described in the following verses.

2 The people that walked in darkness have seen a great light: they that dwell in the land of the shadow of death, upon them hath the light shined.

Although Israel rejected God, directly and through His prophets, He still planned redemption for them—in due time. Matthew did not miss the glorious reality that, in his day, Jesus fulfilled God's promises delivered through Isaiah, even quoting the prophet's words (Matthew 4:15–16; see also Luke 1:79; John 8:12).

The Hebrew word for "darkness" here is *khoshek* (kho-**SHEK**), and it is the same term used at Creation (Genesis 1:2). Isaiah used the term frequently (5:20, 30; 42:7; 60:2); the meaning is clear that this is not just nighttime, but rather dangerous spiritual obscurity at best and the definition of evil at worst. It can refer to misery, destruction, death, ignorance, or sorrow. This darkness is framed in stark contrast with the brightness of God's glory. The Hebrew here for "light" is *'or* (**ORE**), which also is the same word used in Creation (Genesis

1:3–5). Just as He did at the beginning of time, God will bring order to chaos, peace to strife, and justice to problematic systems.

Note how this prophecy is cast in what is called prophetic perfect tense; Isaiah can prophesy in the present tense because God shows him future events with such certainty.

3 Thou hast multiplied the nation, and not increased the joy: they joy before thee according to the joy in harvest, and as men rejoice when they divide the spoil.

The prophet now addresses God directly. The translation and interpretation of the first part of verse 3 pose some difficulty. While the NLT translates this phrase as "its people will rejoice," the KJV has that God has "not increased the joy" of the people. Many commentators believe that the word "not" should be omitted in the text since it is out of harmony with the rest of the verse, which says that the people do rejoice. If this is the correct reading, then the reason for this joy is made clear in verses 4–5, where the oppressor is defeated and driven out of the land. However, if the word "not" is retained in the text, then we must look at the phrase as referring to the past history of Israel. In this case, the text may be understood, "In the past, Thou hast multiplied this nation's numbers, but not its joy," and the next part of the verse would mean that things will change in the future. Despite the former sorrow, the coming joy will be great. This latter idea is defensible, but the former makes more sense.

In ancient times, the enlarging of a nation and the goods both from crops and spoils of war were considered signs of God's blessing. Compare this with Isaiah's messianic reference to Jesus' "spoils" (Isaiah 53:12).

4 For thou hast broken the yoke of his burden, and the staff of his shoulder, the rod of his oppressor, as in the day of Midian.

Multiple comparisons can be made between Isaiah's reference to the Messiah and Gideon's victory over the Midianites. The yoke, staff, and rod are images of oppression (Isaiah 10:5, 24, 27), which in Gideon's case came from an opposing army of 120,000 (Judges 8:10). God reduced the Israelite army from 32,000 to a mere 300, making them outnumbered 400 to one. The whole purpose was so there was no way the Israelites would receive the glory. Clearly, the sovereign God secured the victory (Judges 7:2).

The lesson of Gideon is a lesson of trust and faith in God (Judges 7). God overcame the Midianites and delivered Israel with Gideon's tiny army—in the same way He would ultimately break the power of sin and bring redemption to the world through a tiny infant.

This infant would grow to be the One who took everyone's sin and shame. The One who was beaten would deliver humankind from the rod of injustice; the one who bore the yoke of the Cross would deliver people from their impossible burdens.

5 For every battle of the warrior is with confused noise, and garments rolled in blood; but this shall be with burning and fuel of fire.

Along with the theme of light versus darkness, another major theme of Isaiah is the end of war or end of hostilities—the advent of peace. Indeed, "they shall beat their swords into plowshares" (Isaiah 2:4) and "the wolf also shall dwell with the lamb" (11:6) are among the prophet's best-loved passages. It must be noted that the end of hostilities is a precondition of peace, but peace is not limited to putting down arms (see 32:17).

The first clause of verse 5 refers to the method of deliverance, which, as in the case of the Midianites, will be achieved through confusion and noise (Judges 7:18ff.). The second part of the verse refers to the future, when there will be no more wars, battles, and violence in the land. The boots and blood-drenched uniforms of the last soldiers will be burned. They are only good for kindling, for the prophesied kingdom of peace has come (see 2:4 and Micah 4:3).

6 For unto us a child is born, unto us a son is given: and the government shall be upon his shoulder: and his name shall be called Wonderful, Counsellor, The mighty God, The everlasting Father, The Prince of Peace.

The promise of a child named Immanuel (Isaiah 7:14) is fulfilled by the promised birth in 9:6 of the Son, who was both God and King. It is beyond question that both prophecies foretell Jesus. Isaiah goes on to describe the nature, name, and being of our Messiah. The descriptive words present Him as the great King and Conqueror who has crushed all His enemies, and has liberated His people from the yoke of oppression.

The Child who would bear the righteous rule on His shoulders would remove the burden from the shoulders of the oppressed (v. 4). The phrase "the government shall be upon his shoulder" speaks of Him as the King who is clad with authority (cf. Isaiah 22:22–24). The phrase "upon His shoulder" is similar to how we might say today that someone felt "the weight of the world on their shoulders." In contrast to the burden and staff that Israel bore on their shoulders under the dominion of their oppressors, this time the staff of power will rest on the Messiah, and He will have dominion. To do this, He is given a five–fold (or four–fold depending on the translation) name that describes the nature and mode of His kingship.

First, He will be called "Wonderful" (Heb. *pele'*, **PEH**–leh), meaning "marvelous, or a miracle or wonder." Second, He is called "Counselor" (Heb. *ya'ats*, yaw–**OTS**), which means "to devise, consult, plan, or advise." The

idea is that He will be the Supreme Counselor—the One qualified to give advice and direction to all creation. We should note the difference in translations. While the KJV and NKJV separate "Wonderful" and Counselor" with a comma, many other modern translations string the two words together (to be parallel with the other two word descriptors of the Messiah). Whether together or separate, these are attributes of Yahweh (see Isaiah 5:19; 25:1). There is a supernatural, extraordinary overtone of divine wisdom and power (see Isaiah 11:2).

"Mighty God"—in Hebrew this is *gibbor 'el* (gee–**BORE EL**), a divine title (see Nehemiah 9:32; Isaiah 10:21; Jeremiah 32:18). This is one of the many places in Scripture where the Messiah is called God (see John 1:1; 20:28; Romans 9:5; Hebrews 1:8; 1 John 5:20). A *gibbor* is a "strong, valiant champion." Many people throughout the Hebrew Bible are called *'ish gibbor* (**EESH** gee–**BOR**), a mighty man. The Messiah, however, is the only *gibbor 'el*, mighty God.

"Everlasting Father"—in Hebrew this is *'ad 'ab* (**ODD AWB**), a simple phrase with much poetry in its repeated and similar sounds. Yahweh, the divine Father, cares for the orphans and widows (Psalm 68:5) and also loves and cares for all His people (103:13). Isaiah uses similar language later: "thou, O LORD, art our father, our redeemer; thy name is from everlasting" (Isaiah 63:16). He is the unchangeable Father, both in character, exhibiting the true fatherhood and in existence, living from eternity to eternity.

"Prince of Peace"—in Hebrew this is *sar shalom* (**SAR** shaw–**LOME**), another alliterative phrase. This name is the culmination of other names. The word "Prince" is translated from the Hebrew word *sar*, which is used for military and official terms such as "captain, general, ruler, or governor." It also means "steward" or "keeper." He is therefore the chief or captain who is the custodian and keeper of peace. "Peace" here does not necessarily only mean absence or cessation of hostility and violence, but as derived from the Hebrew *shalom* (shaw-**LOME**) which speaks of "complete salvation, rest, welfare, happiness, and tranquility." Shalom can mean many things: contentment or fulfillment (Genesis 15:15); health and well-being (29:6); confidence and freedom from anxiety (1 Samuel 1:17); goodwill, harmony, or tranquility (Exodus 4:18); and favor or peace with God (see Numbers 6:26; also Isaiah 53:5, prophetically speaking of Jesus creating this peace).

7 Of the increase of his government and peace there shall be no end, upon the throne of David, and upon his kingdom, to order it, and to establish it with judgment and with justice from henceforth even for ever. The zeal of the LORD of hosts will perform this.

As an elaboration of the divine names of the Child, the implications also are nothing short of supernatural. A king might enlarge a kingdom (e.g., David, 2 Samuel 8), but only a divine king can enlarge His kingdom infinitely— this kingdom will be so much greater than the kingdom of Israel. His government will continue to increase until one day it fills the entire earth. Likewise, the increase of His peace will be limitless; it will stretch to all parts of the earth. This increase will also have no end in time; when the Messiah returns in His glory to sit on His throne, it will last for eternity.

By sitting on the throne of David and ruling in His kingdom, the Messiah completes a promise made earlier to David (2 Samuel 7:12ff.) and fulfilled in Christ Jesus (Luke 1:32). He will "order it" (Heb. *kun*, **KOON**), i.e., set it up or establish it firmly. He will uphold or sustain it with "judgment" (Heb. *mishpat*, meesh-**POT**, lawful orders) and with "justice" (Heb. *tsedaqah*, tseh–daw–**KAH**, righteousness). Not only that, everything will be built on judgment and justice (see again Isaiah 11:1–9). In other words, He will rule by God's own set standards, with equity and fairness (1:17) in contrast to the reign of the Jewish rulers both past and present (3:14; 5:7, 23). The prophet again reiterates the permanency of the Messiah's kingdom, characterized by justice and righteousness, and says that it will be different "from henceforth even for ever."

All that Isaiah foresees here will be accomplished through the all-powerful and loving zeal of the Lord Almighty. This last phrase removes even the slightest doubt regarding the fulfillment of this prophecy. The last sentence of verse 7 changes the prior prophetic perfect tense to simple future tense: It will happen— God Himself will make sure of it.

Sources:

Barker Bible Pronunciation Chart. Better Days Are Coming.com. http://www.betterdaysarecoming/bible/pronunciation.html (accessed January 29, 2011).

Blenkinsopp, Joseph. Isaiah 1–39: A New Translation with Introduction and Commentary. The Anchor Bible, vol. 19. New York: Doubleday, 2000. 245–51.

Grogan, Geoffrey W. Isaiah–Ezekiel. The Expositor's Bible Commentary, vol. 6. Edited by Frank E. Gaebelein. Grand Rapids, MI: Zondervan, 1986. 73–75.

"Isaiah." Biblical Resources. www.biblicalresources.info/pages/isaiah/biography.html (accessed June 24, 2010).

Old and New Testament Concordances, Lexicons, Dictionaries, Commentaries, Images, and Bible Versions. Blue Letter Bible. org. http://www.blueletterbible.org/ (accessed November 17, 2010).

Passage Lookup. Bible Gateway.com. http://www.biblegateway.com/passage (accessed January 24, 2011).

Seitz, Christopher R. Isaiah 1–39. Interpretation: A Bible Commentary for Teaching and Preaching. Louisville, KY: John Knox Press, 1993. 84–87.

Say It Correctly

Gideon. GID–ee–uhn.
Hezekiah. heh-zuh–KI–uh.
Jotham. JOH–thuhm.
Midian. MID–ee–uhn.
Tiglath-pileser. TI–glath puh–LEE–zuhr.
Zebulun. ZEB–yuh–luhn.

Daily Bible Readings

MONDAY
God's Holy People Live Justly
(Leviticus 19:1–2, 11–18)

TUESDAY
Enthroned upon Righteousness
and Justice
(Psalm 89:14–21)

WEDNESDAY
Be Content; Pursue Righteousness
(1 Timothy 6:6–12)

THURSDAY
Do Justice, Love Kindness, Walk Humbly
(Micah 6:1–8)

FRIDAY
Seek God's Kingdom and Righteousness
(Matthew 6:25–34)

SATURDAY
God's King Will Judge with Righteousness
(Isaiah 11:1–9)

SUNDAY
God's Light Has Shined
(Isaiah 9:1–7)

Notes

_____

_____

_____

_____

Teaching Tips

Words You Should Know

A. Wiseman (Matthew 2:7) *magos* (Gk.)—Name for an important courtly astrologer, seers, etc., from the Persian or Babylonian area

B. Worship (v. 8) *proskuneo* (Gk.)—To adore or reverence; to bow down or even lie down on the ground before the object of our worship

Teacher Preparation

Unifying Principle—The King of the World Calls for Justice. People look for someone to bring justice in spite of injustice. To whom can people turn to address issues of injustice? The Wise Men searched for and found the King of Justice, Jesus, and worshiped Him.

A. Read the Bible Background and Devotional Reading.

B. Pray for your students and lesson clarity.

C. Read the lesson Scripture in multiple translations.

O—Open the Lesson

A. Begin the class with prayer.

B. Before the session, ask a class member to prepare a short report about Herod the Great. After the class member presents their findings, ask how these findings compare to the depiction of Herod in Matthew 2.

C. Have the students read the Aim for Change and the In Focus story.

D. Ask students how events like those in the story weigh on their hearts and how they can view these events from a faith perspective.

P—Present the Scriptures

A. Read the Focal Verses and discuss the Background and The People, Places, and Times sections.

B. Have the class share what Scriptures stand out for them and why, with particular emphasis on today's themes.

E—Explore the Meaning

A. Use In Depth or More Light on the Text to facilitate a deeper discussion of the lesson text.

B. Pose the questions in Search the Scriptures and Discuss the Meaning.

C. Discuss the Liberating Lesson and Application for Activation sections.

N—Next Steps for Application

A. Summarize the value of stepping back for our own cultural lens to view others'.

B. End class with a commitment to pray for those who risk upsetting the powerful to uphold justice.

Worship Guide

For the Superintendent or Teacher
Theme: A Just King Is Born
Song: "We Three Kings"

A Just King Is Born

Bible Background • MATTHEW 2
Printed Text • MATTHEW 2:1–12 | Devotional Reading • EXODUS 34:1–10

Aim for Change

By the end of this lesson, we will EXPLAIN how the wise men point to the inclusion of the marginalized, GRIEVE for those who suffer innocently due to the world's brokenness and sin, and IDENTIFY with the wise men's decision to perform an act of civil disobedience.

In Focus

Edward had been living in El Paso, Texas, for about a year after he moved from Washington, DC. The cost of living had gotten too high for him to maintain in DC, so he saved up, found an apartment, and got a part-time job at a small restaurant while he looked for a better position. One day while he was at the restaurant, a lady came in carrying a small child who was probably about 2 years old. She looked like she hadn't bathed in days and the baby was crying. Edward tried speaking to her and realized she didn't speak English.

Edward felt moved to offer her something to eat, so he went to the kitchen to check with his manager about giving her some food and some oatmeal for the child. His manager replied that he didn't like to give away free food, but he would make an exception since Edward seemed so moved.

Then Edward heard sirens outside as he walked back to the front of the restaurant. He figured it was police, but then he saw the immigration van. His heart sank. What should he do?

The laws of the land often seem to least protect the lives of the most vulnerable people. Widows, children, and immigrants can easily be overlooked or even opposed by those with power and authority who see the actions of the vulnerable as threats to order instead of cries for help. How do we discern God's justice when the innocent are in danger?

Keep in Mind

"And when they were come into the house, they saw the young child with Mary his mother, and fell down, and worshipped him: and when they had opened their treasures, they presented unto him gifts; gold, and frankincense and myrrh." (Matthew 2:11, KJV)

"They entered the house and saw the child with his mother, Mary, and they bowed down and worshiped him. Then they opened their treasure chests and gave him gifts of gold, frankincense, and myrrh." (Matthew 2:11, NLT)

Focal Verses

KJV **Matthew 2:1** Now when Jesus was born in Bethlehem of Judaea in the days of Herod the king, behold, there came wise men from the east to Jerusalem,

2 Saying, Where is he that is born King of the Jews? for we have seen his star in the east, and are come to worship him.

3 When Herod the king had heard these things, he was troubled, and all Jerusalem with him.

4 And when he had gathered all the chief priests and scribes of the people together, he demanded of them where Christ should be born.

5 And they said unto him, In Bethlehem of Judaea: for thus it is written by the prophet,

6 And thou Bethlehem, in the land of Juda, art not the least among the princes of Juda: for out of thee shall come a Governor, that shall rule my people Israel.

7 Then Herod, when he had privily called the wise men, enquired of them diligently what time the star appeared.

8 And he sent them to Bethlehem, and said, Go and search diligently for the young child; and when ye have found him, bring me word again, that I may come and worship him also.

9 When they had heard the king, they departed; and, lo, the star, which they saw in the east, went before them, till it came and stood over where the young child was.

10 When they saw the star, they rejoiced with exceeding great joy.

11 And when they were come into the house, they saw the young child with Mary his mother, and fell down, and worshipped him: and when they had opened their treasures, they presented unto him gifts; gold, and frankincense and myrrh.

12 And being warned of God in a dream that they should not return to Herod, they departed into their own country another way.

NLT **Matthew 2:1** Jesus was born in Bethlehem in Judea, during the reign of King Herod. About that time some wise men from eastern lands arrived in Jerusalem, asking,

2 "Where is the newborn king of the Jews? We saw his star as it rose, and we have come to worship him."

3 King Herod was deeply disturbed when he heard this, as was everyone in Jerusalem.

4 He called a meeting of the leading priests and teachers of religious law and asked, "Where is the Messiah supposed to be born?"

5 "In Bethlehem in Judea," they said, "for this is what the prophet wrote:

6 'And you, O Bethlehem in the land of Judah, are not least among the ruling cities of Judah, for a ruler will come from you who will be the shepherd for my people Israel.'"

7 Then Herod called for a private meeting with the wise men, and he learned from them the time when the star first appeared.

8 Then he told them, "Go to Bethlehem and search carefully for the child. And when you find him, come back and tell me so that I can go and worship him, too!"

9 After this interview the wise men went their way. And the star they had seen in the east guided them to Bethlehem. It went ahead of them and stopped over the place where the child was.

10 When they saw the star, they were filled with joy!

11 They entered the house and saw the child with his mother, Mary, and they bowed down and worshiped him. Then they opened their treasure chests and gave him gifts of gold, frankincense, and myrrh.

12 When it was time to leave, they returned to their own country by another route, for God had warned them in a dream not to return to Herod.

The People, Places, and Times

Magi. Matthew 2 opens with wise men coming from "the East." To people of New Testament days, that would probably have been from Persia, modern–day Iran. This was a center of much belief in astrology. The Bible makes very clear that the study of horoscopes is wrong (Deuteronomy 4:19; 18:9–14; Isaiah 47:11–14), but sometimes God uses the unexpected to bring people to Himself. God most fully revealed Himself to humans through Jesus, but He also uses nature to reveal Himself to all people—not just Judeans of the first century AD. These Magi seem to be responding to "general revelation" that God provided for them in the stars (Deuteronomy 4:19). In calling these Gentiles from far away, God showed that Christ came for us all.

The wise men were astrologers and saw some sort of unusual star (possibly a conjunction of planets) that indicated to them that a new king of the Jews was born; and so they traveled to Jerusalem, the Jewish capital, where they expected to see this baby. They almost certainly arrived in a great caravan with many servants. Scripture mentions three gifts (Matthew 2:11), but it does not say how many wise men there were, nor does it say they came riding on camels—it may have been horses. Their arrival caused quite a stir in Jerusalem, especially as they were asking about the birth of a king.

Background

Herod the Great was the provincial king of Judea who governed from 37 BC until his death around 4 BC. He was a Jewish king, but worked on behalf of the Roman Empire that actually ruled the region. He was known for his tremendous architectural feats, supervising construction and design of many Romanized cities in Judea and most famously the renovating of the Second Temple in Jerusalem. Herod the Great was also known for his terrible violence that was fueled by paranoia. He is said to be responsible for the murders of not only enemies, but also several of his own children and wives that he felt threatened his position. By the first century AD, the oppressive rule of the Romans—who were known for executing anyone who questioned their rule and allowing Herod and his colleagues to charge the Judeans excessive taxes—had led to a height of expectation that the Messiah would come to liberate Judah from its oppressors. It was into this environment that Jesus was born, not as the king that was expected, but as a baby boy born to a poor and faithful woman and her new husband from a small village.

Why is it important to hold people accountable in weak areas even when they are gifted in other areas?

At-A-Glance

1. Revelation from Outsiders (Matthew 2:1–3)
2. Information from Insiders (vv. 4–8)
3. The Savior at His Mother's Side (vv. 9–12)

In Depth

1. Revelation from Outsiders (Matthew 2:1–3)

Jesus was born just a few years after the Second Temple in Jerusalem was completed. His mother Mary and her husband Joseph were from Nazareth, which was a little village near the Sea of Galilee, north of the big city Jerusalem. They had come to Bethlehem to be counted in Caesar Augustus' census because Joseph's family was from Bethlehem. Matthew 1 traces Joseph's lineage, which puts him firmly in the line of King David, and Jesus as the son of David born in the hometown of David.

The Wise Men, also called Magi, were eastern experts in sacred texts and astrologers who were likely from the former Persian Empire. They were apparently familiar with Jewish traditions about the Messiah, and came to Jerusalem as men who did not know the Lord, but were interested in prophecies about the Savior King of the Jews. They were probably wealthy and influential, which is why they sought direction directly from King Herod to properly identify the Messiah and worship Him. They may have assumed that the prophesied king of the Jews would be easily found at the palace in the capital of Jerusalem. They were likely surprised to find out that the King of Judea did not know where the new king of the Jews was to be found.

The king and his subjects were surprised that there was another king of the Jews they hadn't heard about! This was the ultimate threat to King Herod. Influential foreigners knew about a Jewish prophesy that he was not aware of and had come to worship a newborn that was meant to take the throne of Judea from King Herod.

How can someone's rules, assumptions, and behaviors keep other people from encountering Jesus?

2. Information from Insiders (vv. 4–8)

Herod moves to get more information and form a response to this news. This was Good News—Gospel for the world—but was taken as bad news for Herod and the elite. He gathers together the religious leaders in Jerusalem and inquires of them. The question he asks was reasonable and shows something about the culture. An expert in religious texts in that society could be expected to know where the Messiah would be born. The average person would not be able to recall that kind of information from casual study. It is both telling and can be criticized that the king of Judea did not know that information but had just

finished rebuilding the most important place in the Jewish faith. He had centered his faith in outward appearances rather than inward devotion.

The religious leaders inform him that the Messiah was supposed be born in Bethlehem. How do they know? They knew because they had meticulously studied the Scriptures and knew of the verse from Micah 5:2 (quoted in Matthew 2:6) that revealed the Ruler/Shepherd would come from Bethlehem. But they also knew it because the Messiah had to be from the line of David, and David was raised in Bethlehem.

Then Herod goes and speaks privately with the Wise Men. He did not want his plan foiled or his ignorance exposed to any outsiders. He gathers more information about when the star they had followed arose. Then he tells them to go find the Messiah and let him know where he is. Herod was clearly trying to use the Wise Men to get to the newborn Savior. Herod did not want to worship Him as he stated. He wanted to eliminate Him so he could stay in power. This powerful man was intimidated and willing to murder an innocent baby in order to maintain his position.

What are some ways leaders need to learn from those they lead?

3. The Savior at His Mother's Side (vv. 9–12)

The Magi followed the star from Jerusalem to Bethlehem. The star led them right to the house where Mary was staying with her baby Jesus. They rejoiced to see the star rest over a particular place where they knew they would find the Savior. Their hope was rewarded as they saw the child with his mother and they were able to worship Him as they desired. They not only brought gestures of honor, but they also brought very expensive gifts. These wealthy and influential men bowed to worship the Son of a poor girl from an unpopular village who was pregnant before she was married.

We do not know how many wise men were there, but three gifts are described: gold, frankincense, and myrrh. Frankincense and myrrh were both powerful perfumes that were costly in Jesus' day. Myrrh was more commonly used for burials and the other for anointing kings. The Magi honored the Savior King who was born to die for the sins of the world. They were influential outsiders who were some of the first people to recognize, humble themselves, and worship the King of Israel. They represented—from the very beginning of the Gospel—that Jesus Christ was not simply Savior of the Jews, but the Savior of the world.

They could have gone from that place and followed Herod's directions, which would have led to an attack on Jesus by Herod. But God was at work in the lives of these non–Jews. These religious outsiders, who did not have the background to follow God as the Jews did, were able to hear God clearly because they had humbled themselves to listen. The Lord warned them in a dream not to return to Herod and so they went back to their own country another way, disobeying King Herod to protect the King of Kings.

What is the importance of Christmas in your life? How does God speak to you this season?

Search the Scriptures

1. How did the priests and religious leaders know Bethlehem was the place where the Messiah was born (Matthew 2:5–6)?

2. How did God communicate with the wise men even though they weren't Israelites (Matthew 2:9, 12)?

Discuss the Meaning

1. There are a variety of reactions to the birth of Jesus in our Scripture today, ranging from fear and anger to excitement and worship. Why do people react so differently to Jesus? How do you react to Jesus' birth? Do you react differently knowing that following Jesus may cost your comfort and put you at odds with influential people?

2. The Magi remind us that it is not always the religious insiders who recognize God's work in the world. How can we create room and be open to people whom we may not expect in church to come to know Jesus? How can we invite them to worship with us, learn with us, and work with us for Kingdom-impact in our communities?

Liberating Lesson

The story of Christmas and the Magi invites us to consider standing in solidarity with the most vulnerable among us. The Savior of the world was born as an innocent baby instead of descending from the heavens with angels. The Son of God, who had all glory, chose to be the Son of Man who was rejected by His own people. Our Savior King chose to give up heaven to love us and live with us on Earth.

The Magi were influential outsiders who were willing to leave their places of comfort and familiarity to find a newborn King who could be Savior of the world. They did not worry about being rejected because they weren't born into the chosen people; they humbled themselves to worship the Messiah. They were willing to risk upsetting the violent King Herod to protect the innocent King Jesus and His family. They were willing to follow a God they just met and disobey the laws of a liar to show their devotion to the Light of the world.

We are called to follow the example of the Magi, and ultimately of Jesus. Will we give up or use our positions, our influence, our resources, our time, our reputations to worship God and protect the vulnerable? Will we risk upsetting unjust leaders to pursue true righteousness before God? Will we stand in humble solidarity with those at risk of being hurt the most? Will we care for the widow, the orphan, the foreigner, the prisoner, the vulnerable, and the innocent by giving of ourselves? Think about how you can challenge yourself and your church to live more into these calls of Jesus' birth and example this holiday season.

Application for Activation

We are entering a new year next week, and often people make New Year's resolutions. But as we remember Jesus' birth and the Magi's worship of the Savior, let's make sure we put seeking God as the top priority of the New Year. How can we worship God in new ways in the New Year? How can we make seeking justice part of our worship? Take some time to pray and write down a person or group of people you want to advocate for, extend hospitality toward, or share Jesus with in the New Year. Spend the week praying for yourself and that person or group so that you can turn that compassion into Spirit-led action in the New Year.

Follow the Spirit

What God wants me to do:

_____

_____

_____

_____

Remember Your Thoughts

Special insights I have learned:

_____

_____

_____

_____

More Light on the Text

Matthew 2:1–12

1 Now when Jesus was born in Bethlehem of Judaea in the days of Herod the king, behold, there came wise men from the east to Jerusalem.

Matthew sets the stage in this introductory verse by identifying the place as Bethlehem and the time as the days of Herod the King. The specific historical context of Bethlehem tells the reader some things about Jesus. It reminds us that He is of the line of David, since Bethlehem was the city of David (1 Samuel 16:18). The name of the town means "house of bread," implying the area's agricultural bounty, an appropriate birthplace for the Bread of Life.

"In the days of Herod" refers to the time period when Herod and his sons ruled over a section of Judea (Matthew 2:1–3). By all accounts, this period was marked by political subjugation, religious interference, and conflict within the territories of Israel. According to scholars, Rome gave Herod the title "King of the Jews." He was a psychologically troubled man who was so suspicious and paranoid that he executed one of his wives and two of his sons. The entire Herod family, including Herod the Great, was wicked and murderous (see Luke 13:31–32; 23:6–12; Acts 4:27). Herod had three surviving sons who divided up the kingdom and ruled after his death: Herod Archelaus, Herod Philip, and Herod Antipas (who executed John the Baptist, Luke 9:9, and participated in Jesus' trial, Luke 23:11).

In the midst of Herod's folly, wise men came. There were still people looking for the good. There were still human beings who were wise enough to seek out the good, not to kill and destroy, but to acknowledge good and give thanks. The wise men (Gk. *magos*, **MAH–GOS**) were men of rank who more than likely had wealth in abundance; they were considered by some early scholars to be kings. Origen, a third century theologian, identified three wise men, probably because of the three gifts, even though no definite number is mentioned in the biblical text.

2 Saying, Where is he that is born King of the Jews? for we have seen his star in the east, and are come to worship him.

These wise men were usually knowledgeable in astrological analysis. We now know that African people were familiar with the constellations, and with that knowledge came the ability to interpret the effect of what was happening in the solar systems. The Dogon and Ibos people of West Africa exemplify such knowledge among African peoples. Of course, the ancient Egyptians knew the movement of heavenly bodies as well. Scholars debate whether these wise men came from Babylon, Persia, or Arabia, as the term "East" could mean any of these locations. Herodotus, an ancient historian, uses the term Magi for a class of priests in Persia.

They ask a question that changed the mindset of many throughout history and brought the people of God out of their sleepwalking. No longer would the people of Israel and their pretend king be able to avoid the divine interrogative. By asking this question, these wise ones were forcing Herod and his court to think about the promise of the everlasting God.

Imagine, they were foreigners, but still the first to understand that the Messiah had come—they had seen His star! Not only did they see the sign, but they also came to worship. Remember, these men were deeply learned, but with all of their learning and wealth, they still came to worship. The word "worship" is the Greek word *proskuneo* (proce-koo-**NEH**-oh), meaning "to prostrate oneself in homage." They came to give reverence and to adore this newborn King.

3 When Herod the king had heard these things, he was troubled, and all Jerusalem with him.

Herod, who perceived himself to be the foundation of power and sovereignty in Judah, heard this news and was troubled. The implication is that a king of Israelite descent had been born to replace the mean, destructive ruler Herod. The word translated "was troubled" is from the Greek word *tarasso* (ta-ra-**SO**), which means to "stir or to agitate." Simply stated, Herod was angry. This man, who had worked so hard to be accepted by the people of Israel, now realized this threat could usurp his title.

This stirring was not just for Herod, but for all of Jerusalem. This is a city of peace gripped in fear, not because of an army, but because God has just arrived in the flesh. Herod represents the resistance of the world to the divine kingship represented by Jesus. Jerusalem shows the tendency of God's people to let the fear of the world become their fear in the midst of the divine revelation.

4 And when he had gathered all the chief priests and scribes of the people together, he demanded of them where Christ should be born.

In this verse, we see Herod's strategy for dealing with his troubled heart. First, he calls the very people who were guardians of the promise—the chief priests. Even though the word here (Gk. *archieras*, are-**KIE**-air-oss) can be translated as "high priest," the word is clearly plural. There was only one high priest at a time, so this translation "chief priests" must refer to some elite group of priests, chief among the Levite clan. We also read here that Herod brought together the scribes (Gk. *grammateus*, gram-mah-teh-**OOSE**), referring to people vastly learned in linguistic and grammatical processes. They were also interpretive writers of divine proclamations who recorded various occurrences in relation to the Word of God. The idea here is that Herod gathered them together as God would have gathered them. They convened in response to what God was doing, but not with joy.

5 And they said unto him, In Bethlehem of Judaea: for thus it is written by the prophet.

Those who study God's revelation have a ready answer for Herod's question: Bethlehem. We find Matthew using his signature phrase: "thus it is written." The Israelites always looked at what God spoke through the prophets to determine what was happening in the present. This passage states "the prophet," yet has no name attached to it. For the Israelites, the prophet's identity (though known) was not important because the prophet simply acted as a foreteller. What is important to remember is that they saw the Scripture as being inspired by God. To them, these things were not mere poetic verses, but divine insight into the future.

6 And thou Bethlehem, in the land of Juda, art not the least among the princes of Juda: for out of thee shall come a Governor, that shall rule my people Israel.

Verse 6 is a paraphrase of Micah 5:2. This prophecy gave the religious leaders and the people hope that the promises made to their ancestors, via the prophets, would be fulfilled. This religious assembly had no problem stating that the Messiah would be born in Bethlehem. Yet, all their belief, knowledge, and hope did not keep them from joining Herod in his paranoia. Bethlehem was the birthplace of their beloved king of Israel, David, who was the monarchical ancestor of the Messiah. The promise is made specifically to include the Israelites who were a part of Judah.

This verse features a correlation to the story of David. The Greek word *elachistos* (eh–LACK–see–toce) is translated "least"; it is the superlative form of the word *elachus*, which means "short." It also means least in terms of size, quantity, or dignity. Recall that David, who was considered the "least," was appointed king, and this event took place in Bethlehem (1 Samuel 16). Even the prophet Samuel was misled by David's size (1 Samuel 16:7). Here the prophet Micah is emphatic: "thou Bethlehem … art not the least."

Implicit is the understanding that people might have considered Bethlehem to be of no consequence, just as David's father considered him to be of no consequence. Yet, in God's eyes, neither David nor Bethlehem were by any means "the least." Economically, Bethlehem did not have the power to rival Jerusalem or Bethel. Yet God was about to do something great with it. Just as God looked beyond David's stature and anointed him king, so it would be with the city of the coming Messiah's birth. The passage states that something substantial—someone of importance—was going to come out of this city. Someone considered to be a nobody would emerge as a chief among leaders.

Verse 6 also describes what the leader will do. The Greek word used here for "rule" is *poimaino* (poy–MY–no), which means "to tend as a shepherd and to feed the sheep." It was a common idiom from the time of Homer to call leaders the "shepherds" of their people, so this verb for ruling is etymologically descended from the word for shepherd.

7 Then Herod, when he had privily called the wise men, enquired of them diligently what time the star appeared. 8 And he sent them to Bethlehem, and said, Go and search diligently for the young child; and when ye have found him, bring me word again, that I may come and worship him also.

Having discovered that this King would be born among a people he thought inferior, Herod called the wise men privately (KJV: privily), to ask them when the Child was to be born. The verb phrase "enquired … diligently" is translated from the Greek word *akriboo* (ah–kree-**BOH**–oh), meaning that he wanted the wise men to provide the exact or specific time of the star's appearance.

Herod attempts to use these men of wisdom to lead him to the Christ child before any other news of the Messiah could spread. Herod lets them depart for the purpose of accomplishing an objective different from what he states. He hopes they will recognize the kingship of Herod as opposed to the King who had been divinely revealed to them. Again, they are to search for the child "diligently," which is the adverbial form of the verb from the previous verse (Gk. *akribos*, ah–kree–**BOCE**). This highlights the determination of Herod as he sought to undermine the work of God.

9 When they had heard the king, they departed; and, lo, the star, which they saw in the east, went before them, till it came and stood over where the young child was.

The wise men did follow a number of the king's suggestions. They did indeed traverse the land. They removed themselves from Herod's presence. They did not stop their journey; they kept on walking in the light of the star. They were led by divine light, not by their own wisdom.

An important word here is the Greek word *proago* (pro–**AH**–go), which is translated as "go before." The star is now seen as a princely messenger leading an audience into the presence of a powerful king. They were preceded by this divine messenger, which announced to them the place where God, in meekness, now lay.

Similarly, the light of God's Word will lead us until we come to the time and place that He intends for us. The light of God's presence will lead us to fulfill His purpose in our lives.

10 When they saw the star, they rejoiced with exceeding great joy.

Here we read the wise men's response. As you recall, when they were talking with Herod, the star was hidden from their sight. Now, "they saw the star" (v. 10). This second sight affirmed the experience they had back in their home town. Their knowledge was now confirmed by seeing the star again.

We are told that they "rejoiced with exceeding great joy." The Greek word *sphodra* (**SFODE**–rah) translated as "exceeding," can mean violently or vehemently. They might have burst into ecstatic dancing. Not only does Matthew use the word *sphodra*, he also adds another word, *megas* (Gk. **MEH**–gas) which literally means big. Translated, they were high in the spirit or they became loud in a mighty way.

11 And when they were come into the house, they saw the young child with Mary his mother, and fell down, and worshipped him: and when they had opened their treasures, they presented unto him gifts; gold, and frankincense and myrrh.

The star guided the magi to the exact location in Bethlehem. They entered the house (Gk. *oikia*, oy–**KEY**–ah), which means residence. Note that the wise men are not at the stable; they are in the abode of the family. The Greek word *heurisko* (hyoo–**REES**–ko), translated here as "saw," is more literally translated "found." They found what they were looking for, as will any who truly seek Him (cf. Matthew 7:7).

They brought three gifts: gold, for Jesus as King; sweet–smelling frankincense, for burning in worship and prayer for Jesus the divine; and the embalming spice myrrh, for Jesus the crucified Savior. Much has been made of the symbolism of the gifts. Gold was a sign of wealth representing the king's or queen's ability to provide for his or her subjects. It was also used for religious ornamentation. The word "frankincense" (Gk. *libanos*, **LEE**–bah–**NOCE**) is taken from the Hebrew *lebonah*, which refers to the incense tree, as well as to incense itself. Myrrh (Gk. *smurna*, sm–**EARN**–ah) was an ointment used for burial in many African traditions. The perfumed or scented oil is still used in many parts of Africa and Asia today.

These wise ones had saved their treasures so they would able to give. In fact, the word "treasure" (Gk. *thesauros*, theh–sow–**ROCE**) could also mean a deposit of wealth. We are told that they offered gifts to Him. The word for "gifts" is *doron* (Gk. doe–**ROAN**), which refers to "a present," but can specifically imply the sense of making a sacrifice.

12 And being warned of God in a dream that they should not return to Herod, they departed into their own country another way.

This verse deals with divine intervention to save the wise men from serving as instruments for Herod's work. We are told that God appeared and spoke to them in a dream (Gk. *onar*, **OH**–nar), which means an utterance similar to what occurred in oracles. For the first time in all of these conversations and in their long journeying, God speaks to the wise ones.

The word translated "warned" (Gk. *chrematizo*, kray–mah–**TEED**–zo) means that they were called or admonished. God revealed something to them. This dream was so authoritative that they did not return to Herod. After they had seen the Lord, they could not bear to think of Herod and his request. Instead, they went back to their homeland another way.

The Greek word translated "departed" (*anachoreo*, ah–nah–kho–**REH**–oh) means

that they turned aside; in this case they turned aside from the way of Herod. They withdrew themselves from their commitment to Herod. By doing this, God gave them divine progress. They thought they knew the way; or they may have thought that the only way back was through Herod's house. But God shows them that there is always another way to get out of a deal with the devil. He opens their eyes and shows them the divine highway leading to the will of God.

The wise men could have tried to excuse themselves from following God's message to them. After all, they were foreigners, only there by the grace of the host country. They did not follow the God of this area. They had made a promise to the nation's king that they would do as he asked. Should they lose their honor by breaking a promise? It was not their fault what the king did with the knowledge they gave him. But the wise men chose to rise above and uphold true justice. Likewise, we always have a choice to obey the just and righteous commands of God whenever they contradict unjust laws of our land.

Sources:
Blainey, Geoffrey. A Short History of Christianity. Lamham, MD: First Rowman & Littlefield, 2014.
Comay, Joan, and Ronald Brownrigg. Who's Who in the Bible. Vol. 1. New York: Bonanza Books, 1980.
Chadwick, Owen. A History of Christianity. New York: St. Martin's Press, 1995.
Edwards, David L. Christianity: The First Two Thousand Years. Maryknoll, NY: Orbus Books, 1997.
France, R. T. The Gospel According To Matthew: An Introduction and Commentary. Grand Rapids, MI: Eerdmans Publishing, 1985.
Latourette, Kenneth Scott. History of Christianity. New York: Harper Brothers Publishers, 1953.
Morris, Leon. The Gospel According to Matthew. Grand Rapids, MI: Eerdmans Publishing, 1992.
Tasker, R.V.G., ed. The Gospel According to St. Matthew: An Introduction and Commentary. Grand Rapids, MI: Eerdmans Publishing, 1977.

Say It Correctly

Magi. MAH–jie.
Archelaus. AR–keh–LAY–us.

Daily Bible Readings

MONDAY
God's Chosen Nation
(Psalm 33:1–12)

TUESDAY
A People Whom God Has Blessed
(Isaiah 61:4–9)

WEDNESDAY
Mary, the Servant of the Lord
(Luke 1:26–37)

THURSDAY
May God's King Rule Justly
(Psalm 72:1–8, 11–14)

FRIDAY
God Lifts Up the Lowly
(Luke 1:46–55)

SATURDAY
Jesus Born Into an Unjust World
(Luke 2:1–7)

SUNDAY
God Avenges God's People
(Matthew 2:1–12)

Notes

_____

_____

_____

_____

Teaching Tips

Words You Should Know

A. Offering (Genesis 4:5) *minkha* (Heb.)—An offering, usually of agricultural produce, especially a grain offering

B. Slew (v. 8) *harag* (Heb.)—To kill, smite, or slay

Teacher Preparation

Unifying Principle—Undeserved Mercy. Some people become angry when their best efforts don't result in the anticipated outcome. How do people deal with their anger and disappointment? God punished Cain because he allowed his anger to turn to rage and then to murder.

A. Read the Bible Background and Devotional Reading.

B. Pray for your students and lesson clarity.

C. Read the lesson Scripture in multiple translations.

O—Open the Lesson

A. Begin the class with prayer.

B. Discuss ways that people use to keep from acting out of anger, whether participants use them themselves or have seen others use them.

C. Have the students read the Aim for Change and the In Focus story.

D. Ask students how events like those in the story weigh on their hearts and how they can view these events from a faith perspective.

P—Present the Scriptures

A. Read the Focal Verses and discuss the Background and The People, Places, and Times sections.

B. Have the class share what Scriptures stand out for them and why, with particular emphasis on today's themes.

E—Explore the Meaning

A. Use In Depth or More Light on the Text to facilitate a deeper discussion of the lesson text.

B. Pose the questions in Search the Scriptures and Discuss the Meaning.

C. Discuss the Liberating Lesson and Application for Activation sections.

N—Next Steps for Application

A. Summarize the value of accepting their role as being their brother's keeper rather than their brother's rival.

B. End class with a commitment to pray to be rid of unchecked sin that can lead to hatred and violence.

Worship Guide

For the Superintendent or Teacher
Theme: Justice, Vengeance, and Mercy
Song: "Standing in the Need of Prayer"

Justice, Vengeance, and Mercy

Bible Background • GENESIS 4
Printed Text • GENESIS 4:1–16 | Devotional Reading • HEBREWS 2:14–18

Aim for Change

By the end of this lesson, we will EXPLORE God's justice in the face of human sinfulness; REFLECT on the dangers of allowing sin to control us; and REPENT of thoughts and actions that could harm others and ask for God's mercy and forgiveness.

In Focus

Reginald remembered the anger that once burned like a hot coal in his heart. He had spent most of his life as a troubled person. By the age of 37, he had not held a job for longer than a couple of years and was about to be fired from his present job.

He was in a terrible state back then. His wife had just left him, taking their only child, a son he adored. She was no longer willing to bear the brunt of his angry outbursts. He had lost all that was dear to him because of his bad temper.

Reginald's life probably would have remained unchanged had it not been for his coworker Cheryl who sat down with him during lunch one day. They got to chatting about their families, and Reginald ended up admitting that he was having troubles. Cheryl prayed for him right then and there, and told him, "God has a better way for you." That message of hope started Reginald on the road to the righteous life that God desires for everyone.

After a time of working through his anger and committing his life to Christ, Reginald's family was reunited. As he thinks about the peaceful life he enjoys today, he wonders how different things would be if his former coworker had not had the courage to confront his negative behavior.

How do you react when someone confronts you about your harmful actions? Ask members to share periods in their lives when they felt deluged by tragic events. Invite them to share how God's grace sustained them.

Keep in Mind

"And he said, What hast thou done? the voice of thy brother's blood crieth unto me from the ground." (Genesis 4:10, KJV)

"But the LORD said, 'What have you done? Listen! Your brother's blood cries out to me from the ground!'" (Genesis 4:10, NLT)

Focal Verses

KJV **Genesis 4:1** And Adam knew Eve his wife; and she conceived, and bare Cain, and said, I have gotten a man from the LORD.

2 And she again bare his brother Abel. And Abel was a keeper of sheep, but Cain was a tiller of the ground.

3 And in process of time it came to pass, that Cain brought of the fruit of the ground an offering unto the LORD.

4 And Abel, he also brought of the firstlings of his flock and of the fat thereof. And the LORD had respect unto Abel and to his offering:

5 But unto Cain and to his offering he had not respect. And Cain was very wroth, and his countenance fell.

6 And the LORD said unto Cain, Why art thou wroth? and why is thy countenance fallen?

7 If thou doest well, shalt thou not be accepted? and if thou doest not well, sin lieth at the door. And unto thee shall be his desire, and thou shalt rule over him.

8 And Cain talked with Abel his brother: and it came to pass, when they were in the field, that Cain rose up against Abel his brother, and slew him.

9 And the LORD said unto Cain, Where is Abel thy brother? And he said, I know not: Am I my brother's keeper?

10 And he said, What hast thou done? the voice of thy brother's blood crieth unto me from the ground.

11 And now art thou cursed from the earth, which hath opened her mouth to receive thy brother's blood from thy hand;

12 When thou tillest the ground, it shall not henceforth yield unto thee her strength; a fugitive and a vagabond shalt thou be in the earth.

13 And Cain said unto the LORD, My punishment is greater than I can bear.

NLT **Genesis 4:1** Now Adam had sexual relations with his wife, Eve, and she became pregnant. When she gave birth to Cain, she said, "With the LORD's help, I have produced a man!"

2 Later she gave birth to his brother and named him Abel. When they grew up, Abel became a shepherd, while Cain cultivated the ground.

3 When it was time for the harvest, Cain presented some of his crops as a gift to the LORD.

4 Abel also brought a gift—the best portions of the firstborn lambs from his flock. The LORD accepted Abel and his gift,

5 but he did not accept Cain and his gift. This made Cain very angry, and he looked dejected.

6 "Why are you so angry?" the LORD asked Cain. "Why do you look so dejected?

7 You will be accepted if you do what is right. But if you refuse to do what is right, then watch out! Sin is crouching at the door, eager to control you. But you must subdue it and be its master."

8 One day Cain suggested to his brother, "Let's go out into the fields." And while they were in the field, Cain attacked his brother, Abel, and killed him.

9 Afterward the LORD asked Cain, "Where is your brother? Where is Abel?" "I don't know," Cain responded. "Am I my brother's guardian?"

10 But the LORD said, "What have you done? Listen! Your brother's blood cries out to me from the ground!

11 Now you are cursed and banished from the ground, which has swallowed your brother's blood.

12 No longer will the ground yield good crops for you, no matter how hard you work! From now on you will be a homeless wanderer on the earth."

14 Behold, thou hast driven me out this day from the face of the earth; and from thy face shall I be hid; and I shall be a fugitive and a vagabond in the earth; and it shall come to pass, that every one that findeth me shall slay me.

15 And the LORD said unto him, Therefore whosoever slayeth Cain, vengeance shall be taken on him sevenfold. And the LORD set a mark upon Cain, lest any finding him should kill him.

16 And Cain went out from the presence of the LORD, and dwelt in the land of Nod, on the east of Eden.

13 Cain replied to the LORD, "My punishment is too great for me to bear!

14 You have banished me from the land and from your presence; you have made me a homeless wanderer. Anyone who finds me will kill me!"

15 The LORD replied, "No, for I will give a sevenfold punishment to anyone who kills you." Then the LORD put a mark on Cain to warn anyone who might try to kill him.

16 So Cain left the LORD's presence and settled in the land of Nod, east of Eden.

The People, Places, and Times

Firstfruits. This word was used in reference to the choicest examples of the harvest that should be dedicated to God. According to Mosaic Law, individual Israelites brought the best of the firstfruits of the land to Yahweh (Exodus 23:19; 34:26). The Book of Proverbs promises prosperity to those who honor God with their firstfruits (Proverbs 3:9).

The term is also used figuratively for a person or group that represents a special, preeminent treasure. Israel was described as God's "firstfruits" (Jeremiah 2:3). Christ, in His Resurrection, was described as the "firstfruits" of those who have died (1 Corinthians 15:20, 23). The Holy Spirit is referred to as a "firstfruits" in Romans 8:23. Believers are a "kind of firstfruits," according to James 1:18.

Firstborn. A couple's first born son was required to be dedicated to Yahweh, in remembrance of the Passover when God claimed all the firstborns. The firstborn of a newly married couple, according to tradition, was believed to represent the prime of human vitality (Genesis 49:3).

The birthright of a firstborn son included a double portion of the family estate and leadership of the family. The firstborn would become head of the household upon his father's death. He could sell his birthright, as Esau did (Genesis 25:29–34) or forfeit it due to misconduct, as Reuben did (Genesis 35:22; 49:3, 4).

How do you give the first and the best to God in your offerings, including time, talent, and money?

Background

Sons were important to the Hebrew people for a variety of reasons. The ability to farm and herd animals was vital to their survival, a task well–performed by strong, young men. Fathers who had sons gained a measure of respect from the community.

The birth of Adam and Eve's sons was the beginning of the fulfillment of God's directive to them that they "be fruitful and multiply" (see Genesis 1:22). Some Bible scholars believe that the phrase "and she again bare" (v. 2) suggests that Cain and Abel were twins. The text is not explicit, however, as it is with the birth of later twins (Genesis 25:24; 38:27).

The story of these two brothers is deeper than that of sibling rivalry. It reflects the willingness and desire of one faithful steward to give his best to please the Lord. Another steward, his own brother, wanted God's favor, yet, did not want to give his best in order to obtain it. The jealousy and anger which Cain held for his brother led him to take Abel's life.

What actions have you taken in jealousy or anger that you regretted later?

At-A-Glance

1. The First Brothers (Genesis 4:1–7)
2. Jealousy Leads to Sin (vv. 8–9)
3. God Deals with Cain (vv. 10–16)

In Depth

1. The First Brothers (Genesis 4:1–7)

Eve readily acknowledges that the birth of her first son is the work of the Lord. She also gives birth to another son, Abel. The brothers assume occupations vital to their survival and well-being. These brothers were comparably employed, and each makes an offering of their wares to the Lord. God looks with favor upon Abel's offering, but not Cain's.

When God does not look upon Cain's offering with favor, Cain becomes very angry. No different than any of us, Cain wants God to approve of him. Instead of examining himself to find any hidden sin, however, Cain chose to direct his anger toward Abel.

Not all gifts are equal before God. He weighs both what we give as well as our attitude about our gift. Anger, envy, and self-pity can twist our minds and lay the foundation for trouble. God knew that if Cain did not examine his own shortcomings and try to do right, Cain would fall to sin. Anger's sinful fruit was perched at Cain's door. God makes it clear to Cain that he has to master the sin. When we become angry, we must learn to control and channel it into positive results.

What are positive, constructive channels for your anger?

2. Jealousy Leads to Sin (vv. 8–9)

The fact that Cain invites Abel to go out into the field indicates possible premeditation of his deed. However, it is equally possible that Cain led his brother into the field simply to scare or bully him. Either way, Cain's anger ruled the moment. Anger can provoke us to do things we would not do normally. In this case, anger took control of Cain, and in the end, his brother was dead. Cain refused to feel any sense of responsibility for what happened. Instead of focusing on doing what was right, as God had told him to do, Cain chose to make his brother the problem.

God questioned the whereabouts of Cain's brother: "Where is Abel thy brother?" Cain's unrepentant guilt prompted him to answer the Lord's question with a question (v. 9), "Am I my brother's keeper?" Apparently, God's answer to Cain's question was "Yes" as He continued to query the guilty firstborn about his younger brother.

3. God Deals with Cain (vv. 10–16)

The expression used in verse 10 concerning the earth "which hath opened her mouth to receive thy brother's blood," is consistent with an Old Testament concern that the depths of the earth (Sheol, hell) have an insatiable appetite for human beings, wanting to devour them at every opportunity. Sheol is not so deep, however, that God did not hear the cry of Abel's blood.

Cain is punished with a nomadic lifestyle because the earth, now holding his brother's blood, will no longer yield crops for him. Life as he knew it as a farmer would be no more. At this point, Cain finally exhibits sorrow, but it is because of his punishment and not for his misdeed, complaining that his punishment was more that he can bear.

In His grace, God places a mark (v. 15) of protection upon Cain to prevent harm from coming to him. Cain then leaves the presence of the Lord because there was no longer fellowship between him and Yahweh. His sin was unpardonable because Cain displays no desire to repent or reconcile with the Lord. The broken bond between Cain and God was the result of Cain's lack of faith, not God's lack of mercy.

Is Cain's punishment and protection fair?

Search the Scriptures

1. What was Eve's comment concerning her first born (v. 1)?

2. What advice did the Lord give to Cain concerning his offering (vv. 6–7)?

3. What punishment and what mercy did Cain receive for his misdeed (vv. 12–14)?

Discuss the Meaning

1. Why was it easier for Cain to focus on Abel rather than on himself and his own offerings to the Lord?

2. How is it possible that Cain felt no responsibility for Abel's whereabouts, yet he felt Abel had been responsible for the poor reception of his own offerings?

3. Are you your "brother's" keeper? Look for biblical references to support the fact that believers do bear some responsibility for one another.

Liberating Lesson

The term "rageaholic" describes those who appear to be addicted to anger. Such people have rampant anger that may often be directed at unsuspecting, innocent people. Anger can lead us to commit acts that we later regret, including acts of violence. Even though our anger may only last for a moment, like a bomb, anger's momentary explosion can cause widespread damage. Discuss possible ways that people become addicted to anger. How can Christians be rageaholics? How can rage affect a person's ability to be an effective witness for Christ?

Application for Activation

Consider times when you have chosen to focus on another person's ability or dedication, rather than on your own shortcomings? What factors influenced your actions? How, if at all, did you resolve the issue? Take an honest assessment of yourself to determine whether you have feelings of anger or jealously toward someone because you do not want to take responsibility for your own behavior. Share with the class what you feel the root causes of anger and jealousy are. Prayerfully consider feelings of anger or jealousy you may harbor which have shattered one or more relationships.

Follow the Spirit

What God wants me to do:

_____

_____

_____

_____

_____

Remember Your Thoughts

Special insights I have learned:

_____

_____

_____

_____

_____

More Light on the Text

Genesis 4:1–16

1 And Adam knew Eve his wife; and she conceived, and bare Cain, and said, I have gotten a man from the LORD.

The word "knew" is the Hebrew *yada* (yaw–DAH). It is used throughout Scripture in various ways: figuratively, literally, euphemistically, and inferentially. Thus, it includes keen observation for the purpose of understanding. It means bringing careful attention to bear on something, especially an idea. It could also mean recognition or awareness, especially as it relates to the will of God. It represents a comprehensive form of knowing. Here, it is used as the Hebrew figure of speech representing intimate sexual relations between Adam and his wife Eve. One could actually interpret this as meaning that the man and the woman shared intellectual, spiritual, and emotional depth, which is why the Hebrew use of the word "know" is so appropriate. If this is so, then, there is nothing casual about sexual intimacy, as the Bible teaches.

When Eve bares her first child, she recognizes that he comes from God. Eve goes further than just saying, "I have gotten a man." She says "I have gotten a man *from the LORD*." Remembering her part of the curse, Eve has experienced the pain of bringing children into the world. She knows it was only by help from the Lord that she survived. Even though modern medicine has eased some of the effects of this part of the curse, the experience remains physically and emotionally draining. Many still die in childbirth even in the developed world. It truly still is only from the Lord that children are born.

2 And she again bare his brother Abel. And Abel was a keeper of sheep, but Cain was a tiller of the ground.

Eve gives birth to another child and calls him Abel. Here a distinction is made between the two brothers, based on the meanings of their names. While Cain means "acquired," Abel means "transitoriness" or vanity. The celebration and thankfulness of Cain's birth is followed by the acknowledgment of brevity in Abel's. It may be that Eve was now becoming aware of the effect of the curse, especially as it relates to human finitude.

When they are grown, the brothers engage in two of the oldest professions known to humanity: keeping the flocks, and keeping the fields. While even nomadic cultures may herd cattle, the fact that Cain works the ground shows that their family stays in a relatively small area. Only when a family puts down roots figuratively can they put down roots literally. Farmers must stay by their fields to tend and harvest them. A stable place to live and call home gives a person a sense of safety and belonging that little else can match.

3 And in process of time it came to pass, that Cain brought of the fruit of the ground an offering unto the LORD. 4 And Abel, he also brought of the firstlings of his flock and of the fat thereof. And the LORD had respect unto Abel and to his offering: 5 But unto Cain and to his offering he had not respect. And Cain was very wroth, and his countenance fell.

When the two brothers came to offer sacrifices to Yahweh, we find a contrast between the worshiping attitudes of the two brothers. In many traditions the sacrifice of animals was a way to bring thanks to God, and also a way to express one's gratitude to God as the One who owns all. As the Igbos say, He is "the One who owns the world." We know the brothers knew that their sacrifice was either accepted by God or rejected. God respected Abel's offering. To "have respect unto" simply means when God looked over the sacrifice, Abel's offering was acceptable, which resulted in God's favor being bestowed upon him.

197

We know from the Law that there was nothing inherently wrong with the material that Cain brought. Food offerings like Cain's and fatty offerings like Abel's were both common. In fact, the word used of the offering the brothers brought (Heb. *minkha*, meen–**KHAH**) usually refers to agricultural produce. It is often translated "grain offering" (Leviticus 2). So God's rejection of Cain's sacrifice could mean, as is common among ancient religions, that Cain's offering was done in the wrong way. In the religion of Israel, the correct method was emphasized in the offering of sacrifice. Not conducting the sacrificial process in the proper way could lead to rejection and divine displeasure (see Leviticus 10:1–2). Some Jewish interpreters have argued that it was Cain's passivity against the curse which made his offering displeasing. They suggest that by continuing to farm the ground that suffers thorns and weeds from the curse, Cain is dejectedly accepting his fate, but Abel understood how to use sheep to his advantage for farming and other purposes. In this reading, Cain simply accepts the curse, while Abel tries to build something beautiful from it. Whatever the case might have been, the point of the narrative is not to specify why Cain's offering was rejected but to focus on Cain's reaction to God's disapproval.

Cain knew that his offering was not acceptable to God. Instead of correcting his attitude, he became angry. This anger could have been the continuation of the improper attitude that Cain brought to the place of sacrifice. The prophets record that sacrifice without inner righteousness is not pleasing to God. Cain's animosity toward his brother led him to murder.

6 And the LORD said unto Cain, Why art thou wroth? and why is thy countenance fallen? 7 If thou doest well, shalt thou not be accepted? and if thou doest not well, sin lieth at the door. And unto thee shall be his desire, and thou shalt rule over him.

God engaged Cain in a conversation in order to save him from trouble. Note however, that Cain does not enter into dialogue with God. Maybe a dialogue with God would have saved him, as it did later. God focused on Cain's anger and his hot temper. The Hebrew word for wrath or anger is *kharah* (khaw–**RAW**), which means to glow red hot. Though the smoke of his sacrifice could not move heaven, the stench of his anger burning inside him did reach up to heaven. How different it would have been were he burning with the love of God. What a difference it would have been had the smoke of repentance and the sacrifice of a broken heart reached heaven, instead of the stench of his unrighteous anger.

God's point to Cain was, "if you do well, will you not be accepted?"(v. 7). From the passage, it would seem that Cain's anger was not directed at God, but at his brother. This statement speaks to the impartiality of God. If Cain had done well, God would not have refused him. Cain's major problem was his desire for a righteous reward, without the demonstration of righteousness.

The statement, "and if you do not well, sin lies at your door" is a warning, denoting that refusal to listen to God often leads to sinful action. God's words envision sin as a demon crouching in a doorway, ready to pounce on any passing victim. However, God not only says that sin is near, but also says that Cain "must rule over it." From God's perspective it was not Cain's destiny to kill Abel. With help "from the Lord," as his mother affirmed at his birth, Cain could have mastered his sinful anger. Sadly, since we do not find that he confessed, it is safe to assume that Cain continued to carry the bitterness toward his brother in his heart.

8 And Cain talked with Abel his brother: and it came to pass, when they were in the

field, that Cain rose up against Abel his brother, and slew him.

God attempted to draw Cain into talking about the source and reason for his bitterness. Cain refused to enter into dialogue. Cain refused to listen to the wisdom of God. Instead, he talks with his brother, continuing to focus on Abel instead of God's instructions.

When they were in the field, Cain rose up against his brother. Since Cain could not rise to Abel's spiritual level, he seems to believe that the only way to deal with Abel was to kill him. So we read that Cain murdered his brother. The Hebrew word used in this passage is *harag* (haw-**ROG**), which means "to smite, or to kill." In the legal text portions of Numbers and Deuteronomy, some distinction might be made between *harag* to refer to manslaughter (unintentional killing) and *ratsakh* to refer to premeditated murder. However, throughout the many uses of *harag* in Genesis and the narrative portions of Exodus, *harag* is used exclusively for premeditated murders. No doubt, Cain intended to kill Abel. Here we see two brothers who, because of some sibling rivalry, let bitterness get between them resulting in death.

9 And the LORD said unto Cain, Where is Abel thy brother? And he said, I know not: Am I my brother's keeper? 10 And he said, What hast thou done? the voice of thy brother's blood crieth unto me from the ground.

This passage represents the second dialogue between God and Cain. As with Adam and Eve's fall, the focus of the narrative is on the conversations with the adversary and God surrounding the sin, rather than on the specifics of the sin itself, which is mentioned in a single, quick line. Cain has just killed his brother and apparently buried him.

God's question to Cain, "Where is thy brother?" does not mean that God is unaware of the plight of the deceased brother. Similarly,

God asked Adam where he was after the Fall in the Garden. Here we see God's desire to call Cain to a righteous consciousness. Cain's response is simply to remind God that he was not his brother's "keeper." This could also mean Cain was saying to God that he was not his brother's attendant or guardian. The Hebrew word *shamar* (shaw-**MAR**) is used, meaning, "to keep, observe, or guard."

In many discussions, the one asking the questions is in control of the conversation. Cain does not like where God's first question is leading, so he counters with his own question: "Am I my brother's keeper?" However, God does not take the rhetorical bait. He retains control of the conversation and asks another question, deep and penetrating: "What hast thou done?" This again echoes the dreadful questioning Adam and Eve endured after their sin.

God expected Cain to act differently. God knew he could act differently. He told Cain so in the first dialogue. Now, however, Abel's blood "crieth unto" God. This word (Heb. *tsa'aq*, tsaw-**OCK**) is usually used of calling out for help, whether from God or another leader. Abel's blood asks God to help administer the justice that he did not receive in life.

11 And now art thou cursed from the earth, which hath opened her mouth to receive thy brother's blood from thy hand; 12 When thou tillest the ground, it shall not henceforth yield unto thee her strength; a fugitive and a vagabond shalt thou be in the earth.

The consequence of Cain's sin comes swiftly from God. This is the first time a curse is placed directly on a human being. In Genesis 3, only the serpent receives such deadly judgment. Though God definitely judged Adam and Eve, God refrained from cursing them, rather cursing the ground because of Adam and warning Eve of her future anxieties and pains concerning children. Here, God does use the word to define the state of Cain's relation to the ground he used to till. In Genesis 3, God told Adam and Eve that the earth shall yield freely for them as it did in the garden, but they must now sweat to bring forth the yield. Now Cain is cut off completely from the fruit of the earth. Instead of the stable home he used to enjoy, he must be a hunter-gather: "fugitive and vagabond … upon the face of the earth." His parents had lost the garden; now he loses a sense of being at home anywhere in the world.

Cain became a person of no significance and was doomed to stagger. In fact, he was going to be one who wandered with no purpose in mind. By murdering his brother, Cain had taken away all of his remaining sense of human dignity. The word "vagabond" (Heb. *nood*, **NOOD**) puts further weight on the curse, as it means "to run scared." These words God spoke to Cain show how grievous the sin of murder is in the sight of God.

13 And Cain said unto the LORD, My punishment is greater than I can bear. 14 Behold, thou hast driven me out this day from the face of the earth; and from thy face shall I be hid; and I shall be a fugitive and a vagabond in the earth; and it shall come to pass, that every one that findeth me shall slay me.

Cain finally gets the message. He enters into a dialogue with God. This time, he communicates humbly instead of defiantly, as had been characteristic of him. He acknowledges his dependence on the Lord. Cain accepts the nature of his heinous sin. He does not say that the punishment is not justified, but that it is more than he can bear.

Cain then summarizes his understanding of the judgment: (a) it included alienation from the land. In many ancient cultures, including Israel, removal from the land by exile was punishment for some crimes. One of the most important principles of ancient life is the principle of connection to the land. In Israel, God's covenant was always connected to the land. To be alienated from the land was to be in disfavor with God. Taking people away from the land was also one way in which oppressive rulers and conquerors asserted their power. Both the Assyrians and Babylonians did this. (b) It included alienation from God. "And from thy face shall I be hid" implies that God was turning away His face, and thereby withdrawing His favor. Cain worries that anyone who finds him will "slay" (Heb. *harag*) him, just as he did Abel.

15 And the LORD said unto him, Therefore whosoever slayeth Cain, vengeance shall be taken on him sevenfold. And the LORD set a mark upon Cain, lest any finding him should kill him. 16 And Cain went out from the presence of the LORD, and dwelt in the land of Nod, on the east of Eden.

Here we find God showing mercy to Cain even though Cain showed no mercy to his brother. God's ways are not our ways. God heard Cain's plea. Though God does not take back the curse of the earth and the driving of Cain from the land, God takes away capital punishment, which would be the fair judgment. God made a promise to Cain to preserve his life from the severe judgment by making it an even greater sin to kill Cain. Anyone who killed Cain out of hatred would suffer sevenfold. God placed a mark on Cain that would broadcast this protection, though it is not clear what form this mark took.

Even after receiving some mercy from God, Cain still must leave the face of the Lord. He must depart from the presence and covenant circle of God. This is ultimately what any sin does. By disregarding the place of God before all creation or disregarding the place of our neighbors (who bear God's image), we shun the proper place of God in our lives. In doing so, we remove ourselves from His divine, holy presence, which is the only place to find true justice or mercy.

Sources:

Butler, Trent, gen. ed. *Holman Bible Dictionary*. Nashville, TN: Broadman & Holman Publishers, 1991.

Walton, John H. *The NIV Application Commentary: Genesis*. Grand Rapids, MI: Zondervan, 2001.

Say It Correctly

Sheol. SHEE–ole.
Euphemistically.
YOU–feh–MISS–tih–kal–lee.

Daily Bible Readings

MONDAY
Stephen Prays for Mercy
for His Persecutors
(Acts 7:54–60)

TUESDAY
Herod's Vengeance
(Matthew 2:1–8, 16–18)

WEDNESDAY
Martyrs Long for Justice
(Revelation 6:9–17)

THURSDAY
Shine Forth, God of Vengeance!
(Psalm 94:1–10)

FRIDAY
God's Just Acts
(Psalm 94:11–23)

SATURDAY
Love One Another
(1 John 3:4–13)

SUNDAY
Abel's Blood Cries Out for Vengeance
(Genesis 4:1–13)

Notes

_____

_____

_____

_____

Teaching Tips

Words You Should Know

A. Cast Out (Genesis 21:10) *garash* (Heb.)—To drive out forcibly, as an enemy; to separate in divorce

B. Grievous (v. 11) *yara* (Heb.)—Causing shaking or trembling; being greatly displeased

Teacher Preparation

Unifying Principle—Improbably Hope. People sometimes face situations that feel hopeless. How can people find assurance when their circumstances change? Genesis shows that even though Hagar and Ishmael's circumstances changed, God was still with them.

A. Read the Bible Background and Devotional Reading.

B. Pray for your students and lesson clarity.

C. Read the lesson Scripture in multiple translations.

O—Open the Lesson

A. Begin the class with prayer.

B. Search the Internet for rags to riches stories—accounts of famous people who rose from seemingly hopeless situations to positions of prominence. What do these imply?

C. Have the students read the Aim for Change and the In Focus story.

D. Ask students how events like those in the story weigh on their hearts and how they can view these events from a faith perspective.

P—Present the Scriptures

A. Read the Focal Verses and discuss the Background and The People, Places, and Times sections.

B. Have the class share what Scriptures stand out for them and why, with particular emphasis on today's themes.

E—Explore the Meaning

A. Use In Depth or More Light on the Text to facilitate a deeper discussion of the lesson text.

B. Pose the questions in Search the Scriptures and Discuss the Meaning.

C. Discuss the Liberating Lesson and Application for Activation sections.

N—Next Steps for Application

A. Summarize the value of holding themselves accountable to God's, not human, standards of justice.

B. End class with a commitment to stand up for oppressed and exploited people.

Worship Guide

For the Superintendent or Teacher
Theme: Hagar and Ishmael
Not Forgotten
Song: "He Hideth My Soul"

Hagar and Ishmael Not Forgotten

Bible Background • GENESIS 21:8–21
Printed Text • GENESIS 21:8–20 | Devotional Reading • LUKE 2:52

Aim for Change

By the end of this lesson, we will DISCOVER how God was with Hagar and Ishmael; BELIEVE that God is at work, even in the midst of hopeless situations; and TRUST in God's presence and provision, even when experiencing injustice.

In Focus

Carol slowly opened the envelope. She already knew what was inside: the same birthday card and $100 check that her father sent her every year since she had turned thirteen.

Her father had never really been a part of her life. Carol prayed often that he would take more of an interest in her, maybe even attend church with her. She tried to wait patiently for God's timing, but a part of her resented this annual token "gift" from him. Carol's father and mother had dated in high school and married shortly after that. When Carol's mother became pregnant, her father had broken all ties. Not long after, he married again, and now lived a happy little life with his new wife, their two daughters, and a dog in the suburbs.

He sent regular child support payments, but rarely visited Carol, even though they lived in the same city. If they happened to bump into one another at stores or on the street, he would say hello and then claim to have to hurry off somewhere. When she graduated from high school, he had sent a note congratulating her and a check. Friends had told her that he attended the graduations of both of his other daughters and had showered them with floral bouquets.

After years of scraping together enough for tuition, Carol was one semester away from finishing college and graduating with honors. She already knew that her father would have some excuse for not attending. She knew there would probably be another note and a check.

How do you avoid bitterness while looking forward to God's timing?

Keep in Mind PS 68:5 Father of the fatherless

"And God heard the voice of the lad; and the angel of God called to Hagar out of heaven, and said unto her, What aileth thee, Hagar? fear not; for God hath heard the voice of the lad where he is. Arise, lift up the lad, and hold him in thine hand; for I will make him a great nation." (Genesis 21:17–18, KJV)

"But God heard the boy crying, and the angel of God called to Hagar from heaven,
'Hagar, what's wrong? Do not be afraid! God has heard the boy crying as he lies there.
Go to him and comfort him, for I will make a great nation from his descendants.'"
(Genesis 21:17–18, NLT)

Focal Verses

KJV **Genesis 21:8** And the child grew, and was weaned: and Abraham made a great feast the same day that Isaac was weaned.

9 And Sarah saw the son of Hagar the Egyptian, which she had born unto Abraham, mocking.

10 Wherefore she said unto Abraham, Cast out this bondwoman and her son: for the son of this bondwoman shall not be heir with my son, even with Isaac.

11 And the thing was very grievous in Abraham's sight because of his son.

12 And God said unto Abraham, Let it not be grievous in thy sight because of the lad, and because of thy bondwoman; in all that Sarah hath said unto thee, hearken unto her voice; for in Isaac shall thy seed be called.

13 And also of the son of the bondwoman will I make a nation, because he is thy seed.

14 And Abraham rose up early in the morning, and took bread, and a bottle of water, and gave it unto Hagar, putting it on her shoulder, and the child, and sent her away: and she departed, and wandered in the wilderness of Beersheba.

15 And the water was spent in the bottle, and she cast the child under one of the shrubs.

16 And she went, and sat her down over against him a good way off, as it were a bow shot: for she said, Let me not see the death of the child. And she sat over against him, and lift up her voice, and wept.

17 And God heard the voice of the lad; and the angel of God called to Hagar out of heaven, and said unto her, What aileth thee, Hagar? fear not; for God hath heard the voice of the lad where he is.

18 Arise, lift up the lad, and hold him in thine hand; for I will make him a great nation.

19 And God opened her eyes, and she saw a well of water; and she went, and filled the bottle with water, and gave the lad drink.

NLT **Genesis 21:8** When Isaac grew up and was about to be weaned, Abraham prepared a huge feast to celebrate the occasion.

9 But Sarah saw Ishmael—the son of Abraham and her Egyptian servant Hagar—making fun of her son, Isaac.

10 So she turned to Abraham and demanded, "Get rid of that slave woman and her son. He is not going to share the inheritance with my son, Isaac. I won't have it!"

11 This upset Abraham very much because Ishmael was his son.

12 But God told Abraham, "Do not be upset over the boy and your servant. Do whatever Sarah tells you, for Isaac is the son through whom your descendants will be counted.

13 But I will also make a nation of the descendants of Hagar's son because he is your son, too."

14 So Abraham got up early the next morning, prepared food and a container of water, and strapped them on Hagar's shoulders. Then he sent her away with their son, and she wandered aimlessly in the wilderness of Beersheba.

15 When the water was gone, she put the boy in the shade of a bush.

16 Then she went and sat down by herself about a hundred yards away. "I don't want to watch the boy die," she said, as she burst into tears.

17 But God heard the boy crying, and the angel of God called to Hagar from heaven, "Hagar, what's wrong? Do not be afraid! God has heard the boy crying as he lies there.

18 Go to him and comfort him, for I will make a great nation from his descendants."

19 Then God opened Hagar's eyes, and she saw a well full of water. She quickly filled her water container and gave the boy a drink.

20 And God was with the lad; and he grew, and dwelt in the wilderness, and became an archer.

20 And God was with the boy as he grew up in the wilderness. He became a skillful archer.

The People, Places, and Times

The Wilderness of Paran. Paran is a desert area located in the northeastern section of the Sinai Peninsula, with the Arabah on the east and the wilderness of Shur on the west. The region experiences very little rainfall (fewer than 10 inches per year). The Wilderness or Desert of Paran was one of the places where the Israelites spent part of their 40 years of wandering. It was from Kadesh, in Paran, that the twelve scouts were sent into the Promised Land to gather information prior to what would have been the Israelites' entry just a little more than two years after the Exodus from Egypt (Numbers 10:11). King David spent some time in the wilderness of Paran after Samuel died (1 Samuel 25:1). This region is part of modern–day Egypt and Saudi Arabia.

Background

The incident in today's lesson is not the first time Hagar left Abraham's household because of Ishmael. When Hagar first became pregnant, jealousy, hostility, and turmoil ruled the day too. Even though it was Sarah's idea to have her servant Hagar bear a child for her by Abraham, Sarah treated the pregnant Hagar so harshly that the Egyptian girl ran away into the wilderness. There, an angel of the Lord appeared to the abused Hagar and instructed her not only to return, but to also submit herself to Sarah! The angel promised Hagar that from her seed would come countless descendants. Hagar was told she would have a son, and was instructed: "Call his name Ishmael; because the LORD hath heard thy affliction" (Genesis 16:11).

God's instructions challenge Hagar. She was instructed to return to the very same abusive and painful situation that sent her to the wilderness in the first place. God's direction, while uncomfortable for the young girl, held the promise of wonderful blessings from the God who heard and responded to her crying in the middle of the desert. When Hagar is again in a desperate situation in the desert, God again hears her.

When and how has God unexpectedly shown up for you?

At-A-Glance

1. The Cause of the Conflict (Genesis 21:8–10)
2. The Comfort in the Conflict (vv. 11–13)
3. The Cost in the Conflict (vv. 14–16)
4. The Provision in the Conflict (vv. 17–20)

In Depth

1. The Cause of the Conflict (Genesis 21:8–10)

When Genesis 21 opens, a feast is being held to celebrate the weaning of Isaac. Children tended to nurse longer in those days, so Isaac may have been as old as three or four years old when he was finally weaned. The enjoyment of the day was interrupted when Sarah observed Ishmael mocking his little brother. Though Ishmael's behavior seemed questionable, we must recognize that for the past 13 years he had been the only child of an aging man who desperately wanted children. Abraham was a very wealthy and very powerful man, and Ishmael had enjoyed a privileged childhood that he now had to share with a brother.

Sarah demanded that Abraham "cast out this bondwoman and her son: for the son of this bondwoman shall not be heir with my son" (v. 10). Though her motivation was wrong, Sarah was absolutely right on one key point—Ishmael was not the child of promise! It was Isaac whom God had promised would bring Abraham a line of descendants more numerous than the stars in the sky. Ishmael was not the result of God's supernatural movement in the life of Abraham; he was the result of underpatience and self-indulgence on the part of Sarah and Abraham. Isaac, not Ishmael, was God's choice.

2. The Comfort in the Conflict (vv. 11–13)

Sarah's request that Abraham expel Hagar and Ishmael is heartbreaking to Abraham. However, God reminded Abraham of His promise, telling him to do as Sarah said and to send both Hagar and Ishmael away. In the face of this heart-wrenching pronouncement, God comforted Abraham by assuring him that His blessing toward Ishmael would mirror the blessing He had in store for Isaac.

What a powerful reminder that the God we serve is in control of everything. We must develop a spirit of obedience—even when we don't understand what lies ahead. We must trust that God knows and that He cares. He requires that each of us commit to obediently trusting and following His Word. Even in the midst of our anguish, our comfort lies in knowing God loves us and wants what is best for us. God's will, not our immediate comfort, must reign supreme if we are to triumph.

What is something difficult God has asked you to do? Did you do it?

3. The Cost of the Conflict (vv. 14–16)

After receiving provisions from Abraham—bread and water—Hagar and her son left the safety of the tents of Abraham and headed off into the desert. Instead of heading west into Egypt, Hagar and Ishmael traveled east into the wilderness of Beersheba. Soon enough, the water Hagar received from Abraham ran out, and she and Ishmael faced a slow and agonizing death by dehydration. Unwilling to watch her son die, Hagar moved a "bowshot" away from her son and began to cry.

4. The Provision in the Conflict (vv. 17–20)

God had not abandoned Hagar or her son. Through His angel, God addresses Hagar by name. He knows her, and He knows all about her troubles. She is called to trust God. "Fear not," she is told, "God hath heard the voice of the lad." The same God who heard her voice years ago assures her that He now hears Ishmael's voice. God responds when someone cries out from a situation of helplessness and hopelessness.

God renews His promise regarding Ishmael's descendants becoming a nation. It is only when Hagar obeys God that she sees a well from which she can draw the water to sustain both of them. God's blessing to her was made evident in a real and needed way.

The account ends with the indication that God's promise had been fulfilled. Ishmael's future had been accurately prophesied: his descendants, the Arabian nomads or Bedouins, indeed roamed the wilds of the desert. Ishmael himself becomes an archer and a skilled hunter who would be more than able to kill game for food and be a formidable opponent to any human enemy.

Discuss a time God when provided for your immediate and long-term needs at once.

Search the Scriptures

1. How did Abraham feel about Sarah's demand (Genesis 21:11)?

2. What provisions did Abraham make for Hagar and Ishmael (v. 14)?

3. What promise was made to Hagar in the desert (v. 18)?

Discuss the Meaning

1. In verse 9, it appears that Sarah wanted Hagar and Ishmael cast out because Ishmael posed a threat to Isaac's inheritance. Do you think there may have been other factors that caused Sarah to demand the eviction of Hagar and Ishmael? Are these types of issues still faced by families today? How are Christians expected to deal with these types of issues?

2. Do you think that Hagar's Egyptian ethnicity contributed to her victimization? If you do, why do you believe this?

Liberating Lesson

Very often when we are feeling isolated, hurt, or even victimized, it is difficult to remember that the God we serve is omniscient, omnipresent, and omnipotent. He knows everything that is going on in our lives. He knows when we are hurt, and He knows who is hurting us. Our faith demands that we trust Him to reconcile every situation in His appointed time. God is everywhere all of the time. There is no situation that we endure alone. He is available to comfort us if we ask Him. God is all-powerful. When present trials make us anxious or fearful, we must remember that the provision for all we need rests in His hands. Christians are not immune from tests, trials, and tribulations, nor are Christian families immune from dysfunctions. Through these hardships, we must hold on to the promise and the hope that only God can provide.

Application for Activation

It is often difficult for us to recollect abusive incidents that have occurred in our families. It is much easier to maintain a safe distance between us and the offending relative. This week, ask God to provide an opportunity for you to be reconciled with someone in your family and begin the healing process that will allow you to fully embrace, rather than just tolerate, that family member. Spend time in prayer and Scripture study so that you may be prepared when this opportunity presents itself. If you are not presently at odds with a family member, think of what other types of families (or communities) you are a part of; think of someone you might be at odds with and reconcile your differences with that person.

Follow the Spirit

What God wants me to do:

_____

_____

_____

_____

Remember Your Thoughts

Special insights I have learned:

_____

_____

_____

_____

More Light on the Text
Genesis 21:8–20

Ishmael was the elder son of the Hebrew patriarch Abraham, and the reputed ancestor of a group of Arabian tribes. The Ishmaelites, who lived as nomadic traders, are his descendants. The twelve sons of Ishmael and his Egyptian wife became princes and progenitors of as many tribes, just as Isaac's son Jacob did (Genesis 25:12–18). The region occupied by these Ishmaelites included most of central and northern Arabia. The Ishmaelite people are frequently mentioned in the Bible (see Genesis 37:25; Judges 8:24).

It may be a revelation to some that the current conflict in the Middle East goes all the way back to these passages in Genesis, in particular the heartrending conflict in Abraham and Sarah's family regarding their oldest son, Ishmael, born of Sarah's Egyptian handmaiden Hagar, and Isaac, the long-awaited son of promise. Many consider Ishmael the father of the Arabian nations, and Muslims universally claim religious descent from him. Jews and Arab Muslims claim Abraham as their founding patriarch, a historical fact. The vast differences between their religions began with Ishmael, claimed by the Arabs, and Isaac, claimed by the Jews. Thus, the conflict that started in Genesis continues to this day.

What seems plain in Scripture to Christians, a Muslim would consider distorted. According to the Muslims' account, Abraham took Ishmael to Mecca to sacrifice him, rather than taking Isaac to Mount Moriah (where the Jewish Temple would be built). Moreover, the Koran (Qur'an) claims that Ishmael then inherited the land of Israel, and not Isaac. However, Christians must remember to trust to our sacred Scriptures over any other religious writings. Through many hands and many years, God protected His Word and caused it to be handed down through the generations. That is a much more solid foundation than the Qur'an, which is a record from single so-called prophet of a single supposed revelation which he had, that outright contradicts much of God's previous revelation of Himself to His people.

One of many practical applications can be made here in a call for peace among families, for we never know how far our family disputes may travel, or what long-term consequences may result. Further, we always need to be alert for God's voice and His guidance, and to be obedient to Him when He speaks to us.

Genesis 21:8 And the child grew, and was weaned: and Abraham made a great feast the same day that Isaac was weaned. 9 And Sarah saw the son of Hagar the Egyptian, which she had born unto Abraham, mocking.

This event is part of the various types of laughter that surrounded Isaac's life, which God foresaw when He selected his name. Still, we aren't told exactly why Ishmael, who was thirteen or fourteen years older than Isaac, would act this way toward his baby brother. In Hebrew the term "mocking" is *tsachaq* (tsaw–**KHAK**). It is used thirteen times in the Old Testament and means "to make fun of, or repeated laughing," as contrasted with a gentle teasing. Seemingly, in Hebrew, the word itself sounded like laughter. Isaac here was about three to four years old, which most scholars agree was the age when children in ancient times were weaned. One could only imagine that with such a difference in their ages, nothing justified a teenager mocking a toddler, especially a family member. The greater reality of the events, however, is much more significant than what appears on the surface to be just another case of normal sibling rivalry.

10 Wherefore she said unto Abraham, Cast out this bondwoman and her son: for the son of this bondwoman shall not be heir with my son, even with Isaac.

As Sarah previously had done with Hagar (16:3–4), she complains to Abraham once again to resolve the issue for her, this time by casting Hagar out. In Hebrew, the phrase "cast out" is *garash* (gaw–**RASH**); it is used in the sense of driving out forcibly, as in driving out an enemy (see Joshua 24:12, 18) or the separation from a divorce (see Leviticus 21:14). Abraham had previously told Sarah that since Hagar was her handmaiden, she was free to do with her as she pleased. This time Sarah was asking her husband to cast out both Hagar and Ishmael, his son. This was a much weightier matter and was not within Sarah's sole discretion as before. Things had come to a head for Sarah, just as in our lives we often come to a point where a hard decision must be made regarding a sinful desire, which continually works against the Spirit (cf. Romans 7:19; Galatians 5:17). An even closer parallel is when we must come to terms with a family member who interferes or conflicts somehow with our pursuit of God, a case for which this lesson is very instructive.

A female servant serving as a surrogate mother, such as Hagar, was an accepted cultural practice of the day. According to this practice, Hagar should have been accorded the same privileges as a wife, privileges Sarah asks Abraham to ignore by sending her away. Sarah knows that she is the primary wife and her child is the one whom God has chosen, so she uses her power to expel any rivals. Sarah could have used her position of power to aide Hagar, a fellow woman from an underprivileged social class. Instead, Sarah uses her power to lord it over her servant and tries to disinherit her. Today too, we still see many mistreated by people in positions of power, even if that person should have learned better from their own trials. While we should respect those in authority, we must also stand up for oppressed and exploited people, and trust that God will ultimately hold those with such authority culpable for their actions.

11 And the thing was very grievous in Abraham's sight because of his son. 12 And God said unto Abraham, Let it not be grievous in thy sight because of the lad, and because of thy bondwoman; in all that Sarah hath said unto thee, hearken unto her voice; for in Isaac shall thy seed be called.

Even though he was well aware by now that Ishmael was not the promised heir, Abraham struggled with the difficult decision to cast out his own son. "Grievous" in Hebrew is *yara'* (yaw–**RAH**); it signifies shaking or trembling. It is used during times when God is greatly displeased with Israel (1 Chronicles 21:7). Abraham was visibly shaken to consider such a drastic measure. Abraham has had many years to get to know and love Ishmael; he understandably was torn.

As any person of faith would do in the throes of a serious conflict, Abraham apparently prayed, because God responded during his struggle. Now the decision was God's, and by trusting God's wisdom, Abraham found the peace and courage to carry out even the most difficult of decisions, to cast out both his firstborn son and the boy's mother. Surely it was God's reminder of His previous promise, repeated several times now, that made Abraham realize what was at stake. Sarah had previously made a mistake in encouraging her husband to have a child with Hagar; this time she was not wrong in wanting to protect the child of promise from the child of flesh, of whom God had not approved. By obeying, Abraham opened the door for God's higher purpose for all who would follow.

13 And also of the son of the bondwoman will I make a nation, because he is thy seed.

With this repeated pronouncement (see Genesis 17:20), God essentially created the Arab nations of the world. Though Muslims correctly claim their most ancient descendants are Ishmael and Abraham, they incorrectly believe Ishmael, rather than Isaac, originated the bloodline of the world's Savior (and so deny that Jesus Christ is that Savior). They attribute their prophet Muhammad's ancestry to one of Ishmael's sons (either Nabut or Kedar), and through Muhammad came the Twelve Imams.

Out of respect for the seed of Abraham, God did make a nation of Ishmael as promised, but it was a nation born in conflict, destined to wage war with Israel throughout much of both biblical and modern history.

14 And Abraham rose up early in the morning, and took bread, and a bottle of water, and gave it unto Hagar, putting it on her shoulder, and the child, and sent her away: and she departed, and wandered in the wilderness of Beersheba.

It must be remembered that while Sarah asked Abraham to cast Hagar and Ishmael out, his love for Ishmael would have stopped him from doing it had God not instructed him to do what Sarah asked. Abraham already had learned the rewards of faith, trust, and obedience. Little did he know, however, that even though this was a very difficult trial for him, he was to face a much greater trial when God would ask him later to sacrifice Isaac, the son of promise (Genesis 22:1–19). Abraham would obey God then, and he also obeys God in this instance by sending Hagar and Ishmael out. Since he does still care for Ishmael, he does not close his heart entirely to them, but sends them with a few provisions: bread and water.

Both mother and child were humbled at the hand of God for His purposes, an experience with which many are familiar. When we learn to be thankful for God's humbling and trust His hand even in the worst trials, we are truly growing in understanding (Deuteronomy 8:2, 16; 2 Chronicles 34:17; Daniel 4:37). Christians must wait patiently on the Lord when we face a seemingly hopeless situation, knowing that God knows what is best for us.

15 And the water was spent in the bottle, and she cast the child under one of the shrubs. 16 And she went, and sat her down over against him a good way off, as it were a bow shot: for she said, Let me not see the death of the child. And she sat over against him, and lift up her voice, and wept. 17

And God heard the voice of the lad; and the angel of God called Hagar out of heaven, and said unto her, What aileth thee, Hagar? fear not; for God hath heard the voice of the lad where he is. 18 Arise, lift up the lad, and hold him in thine hand; for I will make him a great nation.

Had Hagar remembered God's words to her the first time she was cast out (see Genesis 16:7–14), she might not have been so quick to despair. Hagar was comforted not in response to her faith, but solely out of God's mercy and grace. God responded to the voice of Ishmael, demonstrating the reason for God naming the child as He did, "God hears." God heard the cries of the child of flesh and responded with mercy. Christians must trust this promise, that God hears, is not empty piety but powerful reality for us today, too. The Lord hears us, and—as Hagar realized her first time lost in the desert—the Lord sees us (Genesis 16:13).

Even though we are born into the slavery of sin, God still hears our cries when we call out to Him and responds with His forgiving love and merciful grace. Like Hagar, though, we often fail to see God's providence, and we also easily forget His promises to us. Even a tiny amount of faith can make it easy to simply listen for God's voice and see His provision!

Ultimately however, Scripture is not a list of case studies of people we should or should not emulate, but a revelation of God about Himself to His people. More important than learning to be more faith-sighted than Hagar, is to learn to be merciful and just like God. He assures Hagar that He will keep His promise and provides for her needs. The Christian life is to be one of integrity and of standing up for the dispossessed *deprive* and abandoned. We hold ourselves accountable not to human standards of justice, but to God's. God knew it was just to separate Ishmael from his father so that Isaac could inherit as the child of promise. However, God also knew that Hagar and Ishmael would then need a new source of provision, which He willingly became.

19 And God opened her eyes, and she saw a well of water; and she went, and filled the bottle with water, and gave the lad drink. 20 And God was with the lad; and he grew, and dwelt in the wilderness, and became an archer.

In God's care for Ishmael in the desert, even though it was by His command that Abraham cast them out, He fulfilled His promise to Abraham to make a nation of Ishmael (Genesis 17:20). God preserved Ishmael's life, but that did not mean that Ishmael's character would change; God had also told Hagar that her child would be a "wild man" and would live a life of hostility "against every man" (16:12). This part of God's Word also came to fulfillment as promised, even as Ishmael became a huge nation. Ishmael's descendants were antagonistic throughout history toward Israel (God's chosen people), and to this very day they continue to cause dissension within the family by persecuting both Christians and Jews.

Sources:

Landman, Isaac, ed. "Ishmaelites." In *The Universal Jewish Encyclopedia*. Vol. 5. New York: The Universal Jewish Encyclopedia, Inc., 1941. 609–10.

Packer, J. I., and M. C. Tenney, eds. Illustrated Manners and Customs of the Bible. Nashville, TN: Thomas Nelson Publishers, 1980. 592–94.

Tenney, Merrill C., ed. "Ishmaelite." In *The Zondervan Pictorial Bible Dictionary*. Grand Rapids, MI: Zondervan Publishing House, 1963. 387.

Say It Correctly

Arabah. AIR–uh–buh.
Paran. pah–RON.
Kadesh. KAY–desh.

Daily Bible Readings

MONDAY
The Lord Blesses Hagar and Ishmael
(Genesis 16:1–15)

TUESDAY
Hear My Prayer, O God
(Psalm 5)

WEDNESDAY
The Pure in Heart Will See God
(Matthew 5:3–12)

THURSDAY
Abraham and Ishmael Are Circumcised
(Genesis 17:23–27)

FRIDAY
The Twelve Tribes of Ishmael
(Genesis 25:12–18)

SATURDAY
Remember Me, O Lord
(Psalm 106:1–5)

SUNDAY
God Hears Ishmael's Voice
(Genesis 21:8–21)

Teaching Tips

Words You Should Know

A. Countenance (Exodus 23:3) *hadar* (Heb.)—To turn one's face toward or honor

B. Enemy (v. 4) *'oyeb* (Heb.)—One who hates another

Teacher Preparation

Unifying Principle—Unbiased Actions. It can be tempting to treat friends with more leniency and enemies with more harshness than they deserve. How can people treat others justly? Exodus demands justice for all people, including one's enemies.

A. Read the Bible Background and Devotional Reading.

B. Pray for your students and lesson clarity.

C. Read the lesson Scripture in multiple translations.

O—Open the Lesson

A. Begin the class with prayer.

B. Write the following quip on the board: "We know all people are equal—but some are just more equal than others!" Discuss the meaning of the quip. How have we seen people act that way? How can we avoid acting that way?

C. Have the students read the Aim for Change and the In Focus story.

D. Ask students how events like those in the story weigh on their hearts and how they can view these events from a faith perspective.

P—Present the Scriptures

A. Read the Focal Verses and discuss the Background and The People, Places, and Times sections.

B. Have the class share what Scriptures stand out for them and why, with particular emphasis on today's themes.

E—Explore the Meaning

A. Use In Depth or More Light on the Text to facilitate a deeper discussion of the lesson text.

B. Pose the questions in Search the Scriptures and Discuss the Meaning.

C. Discuss the Liberating Lesson and Application for Activation sections.

N—Next Steps for Application

A. Summarize the value of seeing all people as special creations of God.

B. End class with a commitment to pray for courage to take risks in loving others, knowing that God commands them to do so.

Worship Guide

For the Superintendent or Teacher
Theme: The Laws of Justice and Mercy
Song: "Holy Bible, Book Divine"

The Laws of Justice and Mercy

Bible Background • EXODUS 23
Printed Text • EXODUS 23:1–12 | Devotional Reading • 2 JOHN 1:4–6

Aim for Change

By the end of this lesson, we will REMEMBER that God expects believers to care for others, ASPIRE to be impartial in showing justice and mercy, and PRACTICE helping those who are in need.

In Focus

Toni had lived in her neighborhood for ten years. She tried to take an active role in helping the neighborhood be a safe and welcoming place. One afternoon while resting on her front porch, Toni's neighbor Binta stopped by to chat.

"When are you going to bring your family over for dinner with us?" Toni asked. "We really do need to return the favor for that delicious ablo and grilled chicken you made for us last week!"

Binta smiled. "I hope we can join you soon, my friend. But this week I am too busy with business troubles."

Binta explained she was planning to rent a local storefront to sell furniture and antiques. However, she was a little uncomfortable with the contract for the lease agreement. English wasn't Binta's first language, so some of the contract wording was difficult for her to understand. Toni agreed to take a look at the lease paperwork.

After reviewing Binta's paperwork, Toni discovered that several of the rules in the lease were unusual and seemed to favor the landlord. She suspected that the landlord was trying to take advantage of Binta. Tony worked with Binta to renegotiate the lease so that the terms were reasonable. The following week, Binta happily reported that the landlord had agreed to the new terms. She thanked Toni with a big hug. "Thanks for looking out! You're a true friend!"

How do you help those around you who are new to the area or to the country?

Keep in Mind

"Thou shalt not follow a multitude to do evil; neither shalt thou speak in a cause to decline after many to wrest judgment: Neither shalt thou countenance a poor man in his cause."
(Exodus 23:2–3, KJV)

"You must not follow the crowd in doing wrong. When you are called to testify in a dispute, do not be swayed by the crowd to twist justice. And do not slant your testimony in favor of a person just because that person is poor." (Exodus 23:2–3, NLT)

Focal Verses

KJV **Exodus 23:1** Thou shalt not raise a false report: put not thine hand with the wicked to be an unrighteous witness.

2 Thou shalt not follow a multitude to do evil; neither shalt thou speak in a cause to decline after many to wrest judgment:

3 Neither shalt thou countenance a poor man in his cause.

4 If thou meet thine enemy's ox or his ass going astray, thou shalt surely bring it back to him again.

5 If thou see the ass of him that hateth thee lying under his burden, and wouldest forbear to help him, thou shalt surely help with him.

6 Thou shalt not wrest the judgment of thy poor in his cause.

7 Keep thee far from a false matter; and the innocent and righteous slay thou not: for I will not justify the wicked.

8 And thou shalt take no gift: for the gift blindeth the wise, and perverteth the words of the righteous.

9 Also thou shalt not oppress a stranger: for ye know the heart of a stranger, seeing ye were strangers in the land of Egypt.

10 And six years thou shalt sow thy land, and shalt gather in the fruits thereof:

11 But the seventh year thou shalt let it rest and lie still; that the poor of thy people may eat: and what they leave the beasts of the field shall eat. In like manner thou shalt deal with thy vineyard, and with thy oliveyard.

12 Six days thou shalt do thy work, and on the seventh day thou shalt rest: that thine ox and thine ass may rest, and the son of thy handmaid, and the stranger, may be refreshed.

NLT **Exodus 23:1** You must not pass along false rumors. You must not cooperate with evil people by lying on the witness stand.

2 You must not follow the crowd in doing wrong. When you are called to testify in a dispute, do not be swayed by the crowd to twist justice.

3 And do not slant your testimony in favor of a person just because that person is poor.

4 If you come upon your enemy's ox or donkey that has strayed away, take it back to its owner.

5 If you see that the donkey of someone who hates you has collapsed under its load, do not walk by. Instead, stop and help.

6 In a lawsuit, you must not deny justice to the poor.

7 Be sure never to charge anyone falsely with evil. Never sentence an innocent or blameless person to death, for I never declare a guilty person to be innocent.

8 Take no bribes, for a bribe makes you ignore something that you clearly see. A bribe makes even a righteous person twist the truth.

9 You must not oppress foreigners. You know what it's like to be a foreigner, for you yourselves were once foreigners in the land of Egypt.

10 Plant and harvest your crops for six years,

11 but let the land be renewed and lie uncultivated during the seventh year. Then let the poor among you harvest whatever grows on its own. Leave the rest for wild animals to eat. The same applies to your vineyards and olive groves.

12 You have six days each week for your ordinary work, but on the seventh day you must stop working. This gives your ox and your donkey a chance to rest. It also allows your slaves and the foreigners living among you to be refreshed.

The People, Places, and Times

Perjury. The Ten Commandments clearly state God's law against "false witness." Elaborating from this, the Law of Moses often reiterates how negatively God feels toward lying. A lying tongue is one of the few things God hates (Proverbs 6:17). Today, before witnesses may testify during a trial, they must swear to "tell the truth, the whole truth, and nothing but the truth." This reinforces the law of perjury, and if violated and proven that one has lied under oath, it carries a serious penalty. In non-legal settings, the justice principle of speaking truthfully about others extends to gossip and slander.

Law Codes. Today's Scriptures focus on the arena of law called "social justice" legislation. The first set of judicial imperatives is addressed to witnesses in a legal proceeding. These are given as examples of the types of things that constitute injustice, which are to be avoided under penalty of judgment. The list was not meant to be exhaustive, and there are many other similar situations that would involve the same principles of not only avoiding injustice, but also doing justice. Most ancient law codes, including the Law of Moses, should not be read as a full listing of society's dos and don'ts. They are examples of wise standards of justice. Judges would familiarize themselves with all these laws and extrapolate from them what verdict to give in a particular situation.

Background

The Covenant Code of Exodus 20:22–23:33, also known as "The Book of the Covenant," follows and expands on the Decalogue (the Ten Commandments) that God gave to Moses on Mount Sinai. This was not a one-way relationship, because Israel had readily agreed to obey God's laws (Exodus 19:2–8). It was their voluntary agreement to follow and obey God that caused Israel to suffer God's judgment when they disobeyed the covenant laws. Implicit in any law forbidding something is a judgment for disobedience. Because of the justice and mercy infusing God's character and His Covenant Code, God's anger was kindled when His people engaged in injustice and did not show mercy to others.

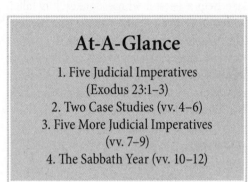

At-A-Glance

1. Five Judicial Imperatives (Exodus 23:1–3)
2. Two Case Studies (vv. 4–6)
3. Five More Judicial Imperatives (vv. 7–9)
4. The Sabbath Year (vv. 10–12)

In Depth

1. Five Judicial Imperatives (Exodus 23:1–3)

Lying is forbidden in two legal situations: in bringing a false accusation (KJV: "a false report," v. 1) and while acting as a witness in a trial. This is reiterated in the case of popular opinion, too. Going along with a "multitude" does not protect you if you do evil, especially if it causes you to lie and pervert justice. Not only must a just person not follow the crowd, but also he or she must be willing to speak out against it.

While many Old Testament laws encourage the Israelites to show kindness to the poor, God also cautions them to not automatically show partiality for a poor person, just because he or she is poor. A normal, flawed human system might not give the poor a fair shake, but the pendulum should not swing the other way. The just child of God must be equitable to all, whether poor or wealthy.

How do your stereotypes of the poor and the wealthy affect how you view them?

2. Two Case Studies (vv. 4–6)

The just person is to help a man whose donkey has strayed, even if that person is an enemy. Through the ages, this has been the testimony that often has won converts because they saw God's people being kind and just, even to their enemies. Similarly, the just person must also help a person whose donkey has fallen with a load, even if that person is an enemy. The parable of the Good Samaritan is a perfect New Testament parallel to this Old Testament injunction. The just person must offer help in all situations, whether the person needing help is a friend or foe.

When have you had an opportunity to help your enemy?

3. Five More Judicial Imperatives (vv. 7–9)

Just as one should not deny justice to a rich person just because he or she is rich (v. 3), so the just person must not deny justice to a poor person just because he or she is poor. A judge must never falsely charge anyone and must never put an innocent person to death. Particularly when it comes to matters of life and death, God specifically will not excuse any with innocent blood on their hands, but will Himself judge the unjust judge.

Sadly, bribing judges and other officials is a sin that continues to this day. No one in a position of authority should take a bribe. Bribes blind judges to justice, when instead judges are to be blind to partiality.

As the Israelites were once oppressed as strangers in Egypt, they are not to oppress strangers (e.g., foreigners and travelers) in their own land. While this injunction is likely spoken specifically to judges, the guideline applies to any just God-follower. No one, especial a person on trial, should be judged in light of their nationality or ethnicity.

How have you seen justice perverted because of bribes?

4. The Sabbath Year (vv. 10–12)

Finally, God institutes the practice of a Sabbath year that provides many righteous outcomes. Besides the obvious rest for the farmer, a Sabbath year also allows the animals and the land itself to rest, showing them respect. During this rest time, the farmers are compelled to rely on the grace of God to get by, which strengthens their faith. The Sabbath year also provides food for the poor, who are allowed to reap freely of the vineyards, olive groves, and fields during that time. A Sabbath year is to proceed much as a Sabbath day would. God's just provision provides rest for all: His people, their land, their animals, their servants, and even the foreigners among them.

What would a Sabbath Year look like among God's people today?

Search the Scriptures

1. How do popular opinions and bribes affect the administration of justice (Exodus 23:2, 8)?

2. What steps does God's Law take to systemically protect the poor?

Discuss the Meaning

1. Compare the examples of injustice given in the Covenant Code. Try to find modern examples that would parallel the same principles. Have you ever witnessed injustice firsthand or participated in it?

2. How can Christians protect their hearts from wanting to see their enemies suffer? How do Christians ensure they will stop and help their enemies when the chance arises?

Liberating Lesson

One hears a lot about social justice in the news, and it is only natural for victims of injustice to cry out for justice in every aspect of society. Studying the Scriptures that pertain to social justice presents a clear picture of what it means for God's people to embody justice in society—how they are to both avoid injustice and exercise justice. This clear picture must be preserved in a world where so many believe that only political solutions or new laws will fulfill God's requirements for justice. Governments are capable of doing things that individuals cannot, as they enact sweeping laws that shape our perspectives and begin to change the way we treat each other. But according to God's Word, individuals are always responsible for their own actions and decisions. Even governments are made up of individuals, and each will give an account of every decision, whether it was just or unjust. Ultimately, no one will be excused for inflicting or enabling injustice.

Application for Activation

Even though today's believers live in the New Covenant, God's holy character and standards have not changed. He still does not tolerate injustice among His people. He still calls His people to be holy and to come out from among those in the world who commit such evil, as stated in 1 Peter 2:9, "But ye are a chosen generation, a royal priesthood, an holy nation, a peculiar people; that ye should shew forth the praises of him who hath called you out of darkness into his marvelous light." The challenge for believers today is to correct injustices when they are found and to act justly, even when there is compelling reason or temptation to do otherwise.

Follow the Spirit

What God wants me to do:

_____

_____

_____

_____

Remember Your Thoughts

Special insights I have learned:

_____

_____

_____

_____

More Light on the Text
Exodus 23:1–12

The Covenant Code of Exodus (20:18–23:33) immediately follows the Decalogue in 20:1–17. This portion of that code addresses behavior toward others, focusing on the arenas of justice and mercy. Earlier sections of the covenant code stress love and compassion toward the disenfranchised widow, orphan, and stranger. This section now begins to exhort another virtue: justice.

1 Thou shalt not raise a false report: put not thine hand with the wicked to be an unrighteous witness.

This verse adds detail to the ninth commandment (20:13; see also Leviticus 19:11; Deuteronomy 19:15–21) and indicates a courtroom situation, but it is not limited to that context. Any "raising up" of an "unrighteous" witness or testimony in any context is to be avoided. This includes even telling the truth in an unrighteous way (i.e., bringing harm to a person or damaging them in any way). Rather, Christians are called to speak the truth in love. It is common knowledge that there are countless scenarios where gossip has caused great injury and injustice. The entire spectrum of gossip—from inappropriate truth telling, to minor exaggerations, to outright fabrications— is to be avoided by God's people.

Exodus 23:1 also specifically addresses giving false testimony about someone who is guilty, which would include helping cover up an evil person's deeds. Doing so enables the wicked person to continue in his or her evil and directly contributes to any future harm that comes to others as a result of the false testimony. According to Old Testament Law, any false or unrighteous report (also in v. 8, "perverteth the words of the righteous") deserves the same punishment that was intended for the other (see Deuteronomy 19:15–21). To put one's hand with the wicked, as said in the second part of the verse, refers to working together with another to pervert the course of justice and deprive an innocent individual of his rights.

2 Thou shalt not follow a multitude to do evil; neither shalt thou speak in a cause to decline after many to wrest judgment:

Justifications such as "majority rule" or "popular consensus" do not relieve a child of God from the responsibility of speaking out against evil. When it comes to the weighty matter of injustice, God expects His people to take a stand—even if it means swimming against the current or enduring the pressure of the crowd attempting to pervert justice. "Multitude" in Hebrew is *rab* (**ROV**) and means "many," but also can mean "mighty" or "chief," which is a sharp contrast to the plight of the vulnerable poor person whose welfare is at stake. "To decline after" (Heb. *natah*, naw–**TAW**) the crowd means to turn aside toward their opinion. The word is similarly used in the time of the judges when Abimelech convinces his relatives to make him their king, and they "inclined to follow" him (Judges 9:3). Simply following the majority opinion is not wrong in itself. The problem comes when the crowd wants to "wrest" (Heb. *natah*) judgment. In other words, we must not turn aside to the crowd when the crowd wants to turn aside justice.

In verse 1, the prohibition was against personally engaging in the evil; verse 2 prohibits hiding the truth even when one's opinion is outnumbered. Again, the verse implies primarily a courtroom setting, but can extend universally. These injunctions are amplifications of the Decalogue, but do not and cannot cover all possible cases for doing evil and committing injustice. In a modern application, even if the other eleven jurors are tired and want to throw the accused under the bus so they can be done with him or her, God's people are held to a higher standard and must uphold justice, no matter how unpopular.

3 Neither shalt thou countenance a poor man in his cause.

"Countenance" in the Hebrew is *hadar* (ha–DAR) and means to honor. This verse can be viewed with the illumination of Leviticus 19:15, which addresses the same matter of partiality or favoritism—which perverts justice—but specifies both rich and poor. Sympathy for a poor person should not be allowed to influence justice any more than partiality for the rich might subvert justice. The message, especially for judges, is simply to never show partiality.

4 If thou meet thine enemy's ox or his ass going astray, thou shalt surely bring it back to him again. 5 If thou see the ass of him that hateth thee lying under his burden, and wouldest forbear to help him, thou shalt surely help with him.

Verses 4 and 5 are two case laws showing examples of impartiality, which specifically address justice for one's enemies. Apparently, it was a common misunderstanding—and still is—to think that the Old Testament taught people to hate their enemies. On the contrary, benevolence and mercy were frequent themes (see 2 Kings 6:18–23; Proverbs 25:21–22; Jeremiah 29:7). Even the famous "eye for an eye" assertion (Exodus 21:24) was a matter of upholding straight justice rather than revenge or hatred. In reality, vengeance often far exceeds the original incident. What Jesus clarified and overruled in the Sermon on the Mount was a misinterpreted oral tradition and not a matter of actual law (Matthew 5:38–39). These verses are examples of the practical application of justice, a dominant and explicit theological theme of the Old Testament.

Even when the circumstance involves an "enemy," which in Hebrew is 'oyeb (oh–**YABE**)—a common word which can also mean one who hates you—God's standards clearly are to dispense justice for all. In today's world, helping someone with his or her donkey that has strayed or fallen with a load would be like helping someone change a tire. In this case, it would be helping someone who perhaps had mistreated you, or flat out despised you. Doing a good thing for him or her would heap coals of shame on his or her head for hating you (Proverbs 25:22). Jesus illustrated the principle with the parable of the Good Samaritan. An act of compassion or kindness, even for those who hate you, is what Jesus meant when He refuted the mistaken oral tradition of hatred toward one's enemies, and instead embraced the greater and also explicit commands for justice and mercy, even for enemies (Matthew 5:43–45; 23:23; Luke 6:27–38).

6 Thou shalt not wrest the judgment of thy poor in his cause. 7 Keep thee far from a false matter; and the innocent and righteous slay thou not: for I will not justify the wicked.

The injunction now returns to courtroom procedural laws, this time addressing corrupt judges who put vulnerable people at a great disadvantage. There are two types of poor in this section: "poor" in Exodus 23:3 in Hebrew is *dal* (**DAL**), a basic term, while "poor" in verse 6 in Hebrew is 'ebyon (eb–**YONE**) and refers

to an extremely needy person, in danger of oppression and abuse; someone who is destitute or indigent. Verse 9 works together with verse 3 showing that while judges should not skew justice toward the poor just for being poor, neither should they pervert (KJV: "wrest," as in verse 1) justice away from the poor just for being poor. Again, God's people are called to a higher standard, and even the poorest of the poor must be treated fairly and justly. Since such matters frequently fall to judges to determine, they are singled out for these holy proscriptions.

Even more specific is the injunction to see to it that no innocent person ("innocent or honest," NLT) is ever put to death, which begins by staying far away from anything false or evil. In this case, God warns that He will not spare judgment on the judge. The warning is transcultural on principle to all who occupy positions of power or influence, not only judges, but any who abuse their positions by acting unjustly. No matter how high their offices— even Supreme Court judges—they are not the ultimate authorities.

8 And thou shalt take no gift: for the gift blindeth the wise, and perverteth the words of the righteous. 9 Also thou shalt not oppress a stranger: for ye know the heart of a stranger, seeing ye were strangers in the land of Egypt.

As if the above is still not explicit enough against favoring the rich, verse 8 specifically discusses taking bribes. In verse 8, the word "gift" in Hebrew is *shakhad* (**SHAW**–khad), and means a bribe or present for a corrupt official, that is, a gift with the intent of gaining some kind of favor. The Old Testament has many such warnings (see the close parallel in Deuteronomy 16:19, "a gift doth blind the eyes of the wise, and pervert the words of the righteous"; see also Proverbs 17:8, 23; 21:14). In some countries and agencies, bribes are a routine order of business.

Christians must fight against this wherever it is seen. In a society and economy so tied up with monetary wealth, it is easy to be tempted to go with the highest bidder, the one who will pay the most for your services, or the one who promises you the best deal. We must be careful, however, to make sure that the benefits being offered are offered fairly and that our final decision is just.

The rule to be kind to the stranger is important to God. Therefore, there are several passages nearly identical to this one, for example Exodus 22:21; Leviticus 19:34; and Deuteronomy 10:19. The latter verse in the list goes far above and beyond not oppressing and extols the Israelite to "love ye therefore the stranger: for ye were strangers in the land of Egypt." To "oppress" (Heb. *lakhats*, law–**KHOTS**) a stranger means to take advantage of them, pervert justice for them, or treat them cruelly. The Israelites are often led to remember their time in Egypt as the time when they were dispossessed as foreigners at the whims of a cruel power. Even though the Israelites lived in Egypt comfortably for many years, when their numbers swelled and the Egyptians feared them, they became oppressed and enslaved. That cultural memory of suffering is meant to remind them not to despise Egyptians for oppressing them, but to rise above the temptation to oppress those that come under their power.

Ultimately, why should Israel exercise justice, even for enemies and aliens? The greater truth is that justice is the embodiment of God's holiness within His people. God did not simply deliver His Law to His people, and then leave them to their own devices to interpret and apply it. Rather, He is personally involved with the lives of His people, even judging individual cases, and He hears the cries of the oppressed (see also Exodus 22:22–24; Judges 2:18; Nehemiah 9:27).

10 And six years thou shalt sow thy land, and shalt gather in the fruits thereof: 11 But the seventh year thou shalt let it rest and lie still; that the poor of thy people may eat: and what they leave the beasts of the field shall eat. In like manner thou shalt deal with thy vineyard, and with thy oliveyard.

One reason George Washington Carver so avidly researched peanuts and sweet potatoes is that he understood the agricultural importance of crop rotation. Here, baked into the Law of God, we also have the importance of allowing the land to lie fallow for a year, so that its nutrients are not continuously depleted. Just like everything else in God's creation, the land itself needs to rest periodically. This law is important for more than just the ground, however.

The poor are entitled to the entire harvest once every seven years. The poor are usually allowed to glean just what the harvesters leave behind, giving them just enough to scrape by until next harvest. On the Sabbath Year, however, they themselves are the harvesters. They are allowed to take the entire crop of whatever grows naturally from what the plants dropped the year before. This is just the kind of economic boost that many of them would need to get the capital to get back on their feet financially. They will be food secure and perhaps have some to spare. This process is true not just for the grain fields, but also for the vineyards and olive groves.

As a point of comparison, in ancient Rome, the government gave a free daily grain dole to its needy citizens, and offered reduced prices for other food. It is estimated that this daily amount of food did not keep them well nourished, but did at least keep them from starving. However, this food was distributed only to citizens living in cities. If you were not a citizen, or lived in the country, you would not receive this handout. God's people, on the other hand, allowed the poor free access to all crops, vineyards, and olive groves regularly throughout the land. The Law does not clearly state that foreigners are allowed the same access to the fields as the poor are during the Sabbath Year (v. 11). It can be assumed, however, that they do have such access, since the poor and the foreigners are grouped together so often in laws like this (v. 12).

12 Six days thou shalt do thy work, and on the seventh day thou shalt rest: that thine ox and thine ass may rest, and the son of thy handmaid, and the stranger, may be refreshed.

Lastly, the Commandment to observe the Sabbath is reiterated. The scope of the law is once again expansive: including not just citizens but also the foreigner, not just people but also animals, not just employers but also employees, not just adults but also children. All of God's creation is allowed to rest and refresh themselves. The three words used for resting in this verse have similar, but nuanced meanings. The first is that the Hebrews shall "rest" (Heb. *shabat*, shaw–**BOT**), or cease from labor. The second is that the ox and ass shall "rest" (Heb. *nuakh*, NOO–**akh**), or settle down and enjoy a quiet repose. The third is that the handmaid and foreigner may be "refreshed" (Heb. *nafash*, naw–**FOSH**), or allowed to take a breather. This word is from the same root as the Hebrew word for breath or spirit. It is a pause to catch your breath, and perhaps to see to the rejuvenation of your soul rather than just your body.

Ultimately, the Sabbath day and Sabbath year are both supposed to be soulful practices for all those living among God's people. It is a time to trust God's provision for your physical needs, rather than getting hung up on providing for yourself or worrying if you are living up to your role as a provider for your family. God is the ultimate provider and will see to His children with even more vigor than you see to yours. During this time of rest from our usual labors, when we embrace the peace that comes from knowing God will cover our body's needs, we have time to focus on our soul's needs. It is a time to reorient ourselves toward God, remember His goals for our lives, and reset our households to start living out God's community of faith in the week or year to come.

Sources:
Brown, Peter. *Through the Eye of a Needle: Wealth, the Fall of Rome, and the Making of Christianity in the West, 350–550 AD.* Princeton, NJ: Princeton University Press, 2013. 68–71.
Bruckner, James K. *Exodus.* Old Testament Series. New International Biblical Commentary. Peabody, MA: Hendrickson Publishers, 2008. 216–17.
Brueggemann, Walter. *An Introduction to the Old Testament: The Canon and Christian Imagination.* Louisville, KY: Westminster John Knox Press, 2003. 60–66.
Kaiser, Walter C. *Genesis, Exodus, Leviticus, Numbers.* The Expositor's Bible Commentary, vol. 2. Edited by Frank E. Gaebelein. Grand Rapids, MI: Zondervan, 1990. 442–43.
Mackay, John L. *Exodus: A Mentor Commentary.* Ross-Shire, Great Britain: Christian Focus Publications, 2001. 398–401.
Rogerson, John, and Philip Davies. *The Old Testament World.* Englewood Cliffs, NJ: Prentice Hall, 1989. 238–42.

Say It Correctly

Decalogue. DEH–kah–log.

Daily Bible Readings

MONDAY
Serve God Alone
(Exodus 23:13–19)

TUESDAY
Blessings for the Obedient
(Exodus 23:20–33)

WEDNESDAY
Mercy Triumphs Over Judgment
(James 2:1–13)

THURSDAY
Faith Without Works Is Dead
(James 2:14–26)

FRIDAY
Seek the Advantage of Others
(1 Corinthians 10:23–33)

SATURDAY
Steadfast Love and Faithfulness
(Psalm 85)

SUNDAY
Treat Others Justly
(Exodus 23:1–12)

Notes

_____

_____

_____

_____

Teaching Tips

Words You Should Know

A. Judges (Deuteronomy 16:18) *shafat* (Heb.)—A position not unlike today's judges; leaders of the local council of elders known for availability, impartiality, uprightness, and dedication

B. Officials (v. 18) *shoter* (Heb.)—Writers of documents and a kind of police that enforced decisions of the judges

Teacher Preparation

Unifying Principle—Incorruptible Leaders. People sometimes distort justice. What actions can we take to prevent manipulations of justice? In Deuteronomy, judges, officials, and priests work together to administer justice for God's people.

A. Read the Bible Background and Devotional Reading.

B. Pray for your students and lesson clarity.

C. Read the lesson Scripture in multiple translations.

O—Open the Lesson

A. Begin the class with prayer.

B. Find and play a video of Franklin Delano Roosevelt's "Four Freedoms" speech from 1941. What are the four freedoms he lists? Are they achievable? If so, how? If not, why not?

C. Have the students read the Aim for Change and the In Focus story.

D. Ask students how events like those in the story weigh on their hearts and how they can view these events from a faith perspective.

P—Present the Scriptures

A. Read the Focal Verses and discuss the Background and The People, Places, and Times sections.

B. Have the class share what Scriptures stand out for them and why, with particular emphasis on today's themes.

E—Explore the Meaning

A. Use In Depth or More Light on the Text to facilitate a deeper discussion of the lesson text.

B. Pose the questions in Search the Scriptures and Discuss the Meaning.

C. Discuss the Liberating Lesson and Application for Activation sections.

N—Next Steps for Application

A. Summarize the value of civil authority for keeping order.

B. End class with a commitment to pray for a truly just society.

Worship Guide

For the Superintendent or Teacher
Theme: Justice, Judges, and Priests
Song: "We Are Called to Be God's People"

225

Justice, Judges, and Priests

Bible Background • DEUTERONOMY 16:18–20; 17:8–13; 19:15–21 | Printed Text • DEU-TERONOMY 16:18–20; 17:8–13 | Devotional Reading • PROVERBS 15:25–26

Aim for Change

By the end of this lesson, we will DISCOVER why God established the roles of judges, officials, and priests and what those roles entailed; VALUE people who make decisions based on God's justice; and PRACTICE justice in our roles as leaders.

In Focus

Rev. Dr. James Sheldon was the newly appointed pastor of a historic church. He spent much of his life and ministry focused on being a bridge between elected officials and the people. He was sought after to speak to critical issues affecting communities of color. He did not live in the neighborhood of his new church, and so he met with church officials to get their input. The church leaders advised him to, of course, meet with the alderman, statehouse and congressional representatives.

He personally called each and invited them to the church for a private luncheon with his church leaders. "I want to ensure a collaborative environment where we all work together for the good of the community," Dr. Sheldon said to the chair of his board of deacons. As the party came together, the elected officials said how honored they were to meet him because of his reputation to galvanize people.

Alderman Johnson was also new, and as a Christ-follower, he wanted to make sure he served the community with integrity. As he spoke to Dr. Sheldon, he expressed his desire to work with him to get the best resources for the people. "Dr. Sheldon, I grew up in this neighborhood. When I finished my law degree and passed the bar, I promised God that I would give back to those who invested in me. There are a lot of good people here, and I believe with God's guidance and your help, we can make a difference."

Dr. Sheldon was relieved to have an ally who aligned with his values. For him, it was the start of a God-ordained relationship.

How important is it for church and civic leaders to work together in partnership?

Keep in Mind

"Judges and officers shalt thou make thee in all thy gates, which the LORD thy God giveth thee, throughout thy tribes: and they shall judge the people with just judgment." (Deuteronomy 16:18, KJV)

"Appoint judges and officials for yourselves from each of your tribes in all the towns the LORD your God is giving you. They must judge the people fairly." (Deuteronomy 16:18, NLT)

Focal Verses

KJV **Deuteronomy 16:18** Judges and officers shalt thou make thee in all thy gates, which the LORD thy God giveth thee, throughout thy tribes: and they shall judge the people with just judgment. *Snatch/fore*

19 Thou shalt not wrest judgment; thou shalt not respect persons, neither take a gift: for a gift doth blind the eyes of the wise, and pervert the words of the righteous.

20 That which is altogether just shalt thou follow, that thou mayest live, and inherit the land which the LORD thy God giveth thee.

17:8 If there arise a matter too hard for thee in judgment, between blood and blood, between plea and plea, and between stroke and stroke, being matters of controversy within thy gates: then shalt thou arise, and get thee up into the place which the LORD thy God shall choose;

9 And thou shalt come unto the priests the Levites, and unto the judge that shall be in those days, and enquire; and they shall shew thee the sentence of judgment:

10 And thou shalt do according to the sentence, which they of that place which the LORD shall choose shall shew thee; and thou shalt observe to do according to all that they inform thee:

11 According to the sentence of the law which they shall teach thee, and according to the judgment which they shall tell thee, thou shalt do: thou shalt not decline from the sentence which they shall shew thee, to the right hand, nor to the left.

12 And the man that will do presumptuously, and will not hearken unto the priest that standeth to minister there before the LORD thy God, or unto the judge, even that man shall die: and thou shalt put away the evil from Israel.

13 And all the people shall hear, and fear, and do no more presumptuously.

NLT **Deuteronomy 16:18** Appoint judges and officials for yourselves from each of your tribes in all the towns the LORD your God is giving you. They must judge the people fairly.

19 You must never twist justice or show partiality. Never accept a bribe, for bribes blind the eyes of the wise and corrupt the decisions of the godly.

20 Let true justice prevail, so you may live and occupy the land that the LORD your God is giving you.

17:8 Suppose a case arises in a local court that is too hard for you to decide—for instance, whether someone is guilty of murder or only of manslaughter, or a difficult lawsuit, or a case involving different kinds of assault. Take such legal cases to the place the LORD your God will choose,

9 and present them to the Levitical priests or the judge on duty at that time. They will hear the case and declare the verdict.

10 You must carry out the verdict they announce and the sentence they prescribe at the place the LORD chooses. You must do exactly what they say.

11 After they have interpreted the law and declared their verdict, the sentence they impose must be fully executed; do not modify it in any way.

12 Anyone arrogant enough to reject the verdict of the judge or of the priest who represents the LORD your God must die. In this way you will purge the evil from Israel.

13 Then everyone else will hear about it and be afraid to act so arrogantly.

The People, Places, and Times

The Place the Lord Your God Will Choose. This cumbersome phrase is found often throughout Deuteronomy. It refers to the location of God's holy shrine. The Tabernacle would be set up in several places throughout the period of the judges and kings until Solomon finally finished the Temple in Jerusalem. God did not want to limit His guidance to one shrine location and leave His people confused as to how to obey His laws when the shrine was moved to another location. God chose not to say "the Tabernacle" either, knowing He would later be worshiped in the Temple. This ambiguity later gave the Samaritans an excuse not to worship at Jerusalem as tensions between them and the Israelites rose. The Samaritans believed the place the Lord chose was their own local Mt. Gerizim, rather than the Israelites' Mt. Zion. This was still an object of tension in Jesus' day (John 4:20–21).

Background

After forty years of wandering in the wilderness, the children of Israel were ready to become a nation. God wanted Israel to be a theocracy, where His people would live in a manner that would reflect His government. In this transfer of power, Moses stood as the intermediary serving as prophet and judge. In the book of Deuteronomy, God restates and reaffirms to a new generation the decrees and ordinances given to Israel, starting in Exodus with the Ten Commandments to the laws written in the books of Leviticus and Numbers. The descendants of Israel are instructed throughout the book of Deuteronomy to be careful that they do as the Lord has commanded so that they would live long and prosper in the land. They were to be an example to the other nations of God's power and blessing by administering justice as a civil society (Deuteronomy 5:32, 6:17–19, 7:12–22, 8:11). God, through His ordinances, decrees, and precepts, set the culture for Israel as the mark of His presence. His handprint makes Israel a peculiar nation that worshiped the true and living God.

What is mark of God's presence in our culture?

At-A-Glance

1. Just Officials (Deuteronomy 16:18–20)
2. Civil Obedience
(Deuteronomy 17:8–13)

In Depth

1. Just Officials (Deuteronomy 16:18–20)

God, through His prophet Moses, instructs Israel as they become a nation to be governed by His standard of right and wrong. God is righteous, just, and upright in all His ways. He sets the expectation through His commands that those placed in civil authority among the tribes and towns be submitted to God as the highest authority. He directs that leaders be chosen from among the people to administer justice just as Jethro, Moses' father-in-law, had advised him soon after escaping Egypt (Exodus 18:13–26). Those chosen were to be people who feared God, were considered trustworthy among the people, wise, impartial, had integrity, able to discern between right and wrong, and not subject to bribery. Justice is at the heart of God's character, and He hates imbalanced scales (Proverbs 11:1).

Moses implores the judges and officers among the tribes to have an unwavering commitment to justice and truth above all in representing the people and making decisions when upholding the Law. God recognizes that when people accept bribes and partiality, it is unjust to the righteous. People living in community will have disputes and disagreements, but there must be a representative who can listen to the facts, review the rule of law, and with the wisdom of God administer fair judgment. Leaders must seek God's heart in mediating a peaceful resolution to conflicts and upholding the rights of all people, seeing them as God's creation.

What is the evidence of a godly leader?

2. Civil Obedience (Deuteronomy 17:8–13)

In establishing civil order for Israel, Moses further instructs the officials on how to handle difficult cases such as murder, assault, or lawsuits. They are told to seek the Lord and go to the Tabernacle to seek the counsel of the Levitical priest and the judge. The Levitical priests were to be in lockstep with God to hear His voice. The priests were to serve as spiritual advisors to judges to support their discernment in interpreting the Law. The judge was in charge of rendering a decision on the matter, like the Supreme Court in our time. The judge's decision under the auspices of godly wisdom was to be final, and once the decision was announced, it could not be overruled or overturned. Moses gives God's command that if the person should not abide by the judge's decision, they would be put to death. It was considered evil before the Lord to not adhere to godly authority, and God expected swift justice so that others would not follow that example.

Further, God expected the judges and priests to be fully submitted to His authority and display excellent moral character so that the people will view them as His representatives. When leaders fail in exhibiting godly character, people lose faith in authority and the result is social disorder.

How can those in authority change the narrative on leadership to reflect God's heart for justice?

Search the Scriptures

1. What roles did God through Moses command the people to establish to lead their communities (Deuteronomy 16:18)?

2. What was God's warning to those who failed to heed the priest or judge's decision (Deuteronomy 17:12–13)?

Discuss the Meaning

1. What was the significance of God's command to appoint leaders in the land? Why was it important for these leaders to exhibit excellent moral character and sound judgment?

2. Why do you think God established an order to deal with difficult cases? Why was God stern on the consequences of disobedience to the judge's decision?

Liberating Lesson

Our world needs authority in every realm, and there should be healthy respect and honor for those in leadership. However, when power is misused, it erodes trust and systems break. God provided instructions to safeguard against broken trust, and He also established that when those leaders are proven trustworthy, their word is bond. Leaders and the people under their authority must work as partners in progress; one should not oppress the other. A just society is when all are equal under the law, and people are judged fairly. The people have to be able to trust the integrity of leaders. People must receive due process and have their voices heard for the fair resolution of conflicts. Further, as citizens, we must hold leaders accountable to guide us under the protection of God's authority.

Application for Activation

Imagine what families, churches, communities, schools, businesses, and justice systems would be like with people who took seriously the God's mandate to lead with integrity? Imagine the impact if people were engaged, involved, and held leaders accountable in a respectful way. Imagine the exchange of ideas if people actively participated in the processes needed to make society just. An essential activity to start living in a just society is to listen with an empathetic ear, to reflect on how an individual can bring forth change, and then take action. Look for opportunities in your spheres of influence to attend town hall meetings or to even host one. These meetings should be places where people can speak with respectful candor, and leaders can give and receive feedback. The lively discussion can usher in a renewed level of engagement.

Follow the Spirit

What God wants me to do:

_____

_____

_____

_____

Remember Your Thoughts

Special insights I have learned:

_____

_____

_____

_____

More Light on the Text

Deuteronomy 16:18–20; 17:8–13

18 Judges and officers shalt thou make thee in all thy gates, which the LORD thy God giveth thee, throughout thy tribes: and they shall judge the people with just judgment.

The judges (Heb. *shafat*, shaw–**FOT**) are different from the elders. Their role was not very different from that of today's judges. Four characteristics were required of them;

namely availability, impartiality, uprightness, and dedication. They were the leaders among the local council of elders. The officers (Heb. *shotar*, sho–**TAR**) on the other hand, were probably assisting the judges. This word means a writer of documents. However they were not mere scribes because both "official" and "scribe" are also used distinctly from one another (2 Chronicles 34:13). The official's role is similar to that of the modern police where they represent the executive branch of the judiciary.

Although there is no particular method of selection of the judges, the use of the second person suggests that the people themselves were to select their judges either directly or through the council of elders. In that case, the judges would have the required legitimacy to carry out their duties. The more experienced and upright people among them were to be chosen, or they were picked up among the members of the council of elders. The judge could be the local chief chosen from among the elders.

These appointed judges would limit their jurisdiction to a local community. Each tribe and each town in Israel was to appoint judges for their community. For matters that are not too complex, the local judges have the authority and the legitimacy to give a verdict. The availability of judges in every town of each tribe was God's provision for the people to have easy access to judges, even in stressful or urgent cases. They were to hold their trials publicly at the city gate, where most legal matters were discussed and decided in the ancient Near East. The judges were to exhibit high moral and ethical standards and carry their duty with fairness, showing no favoritism.

19 Thou shalt not wrest judgment; thou shalt not respect persons, neither take a gift: for a gift doth blind the eyes of the wise, and pervert the words of the righteous.

The many important aspects to delivering justice discussed in this verse could be required either of the judges or the whole assembly because verse 19 is in the second person. The KJV uses the second personal pronoun "you," while the NLT put it in the third to assume that the judges must fulfill the below requirements. Although it was the primary duty for the judges to ensure the equity of each case brought before them, it was also a requirement for the entire population to ensure the fair delivery of justice. It therefore makes the judges accountable to the people who appointed them.

This warning against twisting justice appeared in Exodus 23:6 as a provision to protect the poor in judgment. Poor people should not be condemned simply because of their social status. The warning is basically against overturning the verdict of a case in favor of the guilty.

The idiom translated as "respecting persons," here alludes to avoiding miscarriage of justice in favor of rich and powerful people against weak and poor people. But it also means that weak or poor people should likewise not be favored. God's Law also states that there should be no favoritism for the poor nor consideration for the rich (Leviticus 19:15). Fair judgment should be applied to all irrespective of social status.

The Hebrew word used for bribe here is *shahad* (**SHAW**–hodd), which means a gift for which something is expected in return. Isaiah curses those who justify the wicked for a reward and take away the righteousness of the righteous (Isaiah 5:23). A judge would not accept a fee from a party in a trial against another. God's word warns that a gift corrupts the heart (Ecclesiastes 7:7), and a bribe hurts the cause of the innocent (Exodus 23:8).

20 That which is altogether just shalt thou follow, that thou mayest live, and inherit the land which the LORD thy God giveth thee.

The necessary condition for the people of Israel to live peaceful and prosper in the Promised Land was the application of true justice. The Lord's blessing for His people is enjoyed as long as the people live in accordance with the requirements laid down for them. The absence of justice will incur not only the curse of God in the land but will also generate disorder that will make life challenging. True justice will protect the vulnerable from oppression by the strong, but above all, it will grant everyone the possibility to enjoy a peaceful life where their rights are protected.

17:8 If there arise a matter too hard for thee in judgment, between blood and blood, between plea and plea, and between stroke and stroke, being matters of controversy within thy gates: then shalt thou arise, and get thee up into the place which the LORD thy God shall choose.

With cases that are above their ability to rule, the local judges had to refer them to a higher court. It is not a court of appeal for the ruling in the lower court, but a court of referral which handles cases where guilt or innocence cannot be determined or the application of justice is unclear. This could have been the seventy-one member Sanhedrin (Numbers 11:16–17).

In the wilderness, Moses was the last resort for justice. Difficult cases were brought to him to settle (Deuteronomy 1:17). But once in the Promised Land, a place was designated by God to be the capital city of the nation, the center of their political, religious, social, and judicial life. The higher court was therefore to be located at the Tabernacle (and later the Temple) complex. The appeal to the court of referral is made by the local judges and not the parties involved in the trial.

The three kinds of cases beyond local judge's knowledge or ability that require referral was murder (KJV: "between blood and blood"), lawsuit (KJV: "between plea and plea"), and assault (KJV: "between stroke and stroke"). Murder is a case in which it is difficult to determine whether the act was intentional or accidental or whether the accused person is really guilty. The lawsuit probably refers here to criminal law such as theft or damage. The assault could be bodily injury or property damage done by accident or on purpose.

9 And thou shalt come unto the priests the Levites, and unto the judge that shall be in those days, and enquire; and they shall shew thee the sentence of judgment:

All the priests were descendants of Levi. The priest might have judged the court in religious matters and a layman chief judge in secular matters, similar to the court set up by Jehoshaphat in the 9th century BC (2 Chronicles 19:4–11). In Jehoshaphat's time, priests and laymen presided in the high court depending on the issue. The matters related to the worship were sorted out by the priest, while the other matters were solved by the lay judge.

10 And thou shalt do according to the sentence, which they of that place which the LORD shall choose shall shew thee; and thou shalt observe to do according to all that they inform thee: 11 According to the sentence of the law which they shall teach thee, and according to the judgment which they shall tell thee, thou shalt do: thou shalt not decline from the sentence which they shall shew thee, to the right hand, nor to the left.

The sentence of the high court of referral was final and did not call for any other appeal. No stroke should be removed from their verdict. Two reasons account for the impossibility to appeal to the decision of the high court. First, its decisions were divinely sanctioned. Secondly, the judges at the higher court were men of experience and knowledge above those of the local courts. The local judges were responsible for the application of the ruling of the high court, because they brought the case before it. They were forbidden to amend it.

12 And the man that will do presumptuously, and will not hearken unto the priest that standeth to minister there before the LORD thy God, or unto the judge, even that man shall die: and thou shalt put away the evil from Israel. 13 And all the people shall hear, and fear, and do no more presumptuously.

Any contempt to the ruling of the high court leads to the death penalty. This verse suggests that the high court included priests who could inquire of the Lord for the difficult cases. The act of contempt is a seed of rebellion and should be treated as such.

Capital punishment for contempt of court serves as a deterrent from any subsequent attempt of contempt. Purging the evil from Israel, as stated in the last part of verse 12, appears nine times with slight variations throughout Deuteronomy, all in explaining a law that calls for the death penalty. Paul quotes this verse when he exhorts the Corinthian church to expel the evil of an incestuous relationship from among them (1 Corinthians 5:13). In our present generation, the debate is still going on about outlawing capital punishment, so it is difficult to read about our loving God demanding the death penalty. The view presented in these verses is that a harsh penalty will deter others from imitating the crime. Much of the cause to abolish the modern death penalty is also due to the possibility of errors in judgment. Here however, God Himself is consulted, so we can trust His judgment as to someone's guilt. Because the priest is consulted in the matter, disregarding the decision is tantamount to disregarding God's word. Therefore, this crime is punished as seriously as other crimes of idolatry and direct defiance of God.

Remember also, that these laws were meant to display God to the nations. Other nations at this time used the death penalty for much lesser crimes. The Code of Hammurabi, for example, calls for the death penalty for various kinds of theft or for harboring a fugitive slave. Across the ancient world, only the most serious offenses called for the death penalty but many other non-lethal punishments existed. In other contemporary cultures, criminals who did not earn death might instead have their hands, noses, or genitals cut off. These mutilations might themselves lead to death by infection or would at least leave the person unable to financially support themselves for the rest of their lives. In God's Law, however, almost all non-lethal punishments were merely fines.

Further, from what scholars can tell, few other ancient cultures troubled themselves with how to uphold the integrity of their legal system. Those guilty of perjury in ancient Egypt would be sentenced to death, but no other law can be found similar to this Israelite law about upholding a judge's decision. God's justice system was to be obeyed to distribute justice to every citizen, no matter their wealth or class. Contempt of the court system was penalized as a serious offense so that the system could make a difference, not just for those who could afford fines and long legal battles, but for everyone.

Sources:
Attridge, Harold, W. *The Harper Collins Study Bible, New Revised Standard Version*. New York: Harper One, 2006. 282–283.
Bratcher, R. G., and H.A. Hatton. *A Handbook on Deuteronomy*. New York: United Bible Society, 2000.
Brown, R. *The Message of Deuteronomy*. J. A. Motyer, Ed. Leicester, England: Intervarsity Press, 1993.
Cabal, Ted et. al. *The Apologetics Study Bible, Holman Christian Standard*. Nashville, TN: Holman Bible Publishers, 2007. 290–291.
Craigie, P. C. *The New International Commentary on the Old Testament: The Book of Deuteronomy*. R. K. Harrison, Ed. Grand Rapids, MI: Wm Eerdmans, 1976.
Kalland, E. S. *The Expositor's Bible Commentary: Deuteronomy–2 Samuel* (Vol. III). F. E. Gaebelein, Ed. Grand Rapids, MI: Zondervan, 1992.

Miller, P. D. *Interpretation: A Bible Commentary for Teaching and Preaching*. Louisville, KY: Jonh Knox Press, 1990.
Thompson, J. A. *Tyndale Old Testament Commentaries: Deuteronomy*. D. J. Wiseman, Ed. London, England: Intervarsity Press, 1974.
Tigay, J. H. *The Jewish Publication Society Torah Commentary: Deuteronomy*. N. M. Sarna, Ed. Philadelphia: The Jewish Publication Society, 1990.

Say It Correctly

Sanhedrin. San–HEE–drin.

Daily Bible Readings

MONDAY
True and False Witnesses
(Deuteronomy 19:15–21)

TUESDAY
Addressing Church Conflicts
(Matthew 18:15–20)

WEDNESDAY
The Duty to Forgive
(Matthew 18:21–35)

THURSDAY
Moses' Court of Appeal
(Exodus 18:13–26)

FRIDAY
Speak Truth and Act on It
(Ephesians 4:25–32)

SATURDAY
God Is an Impartial Judge
(Deuteronomy 10:14–22)

SUNDAY
Appoint Leaders to Administer Justice
(Deuteronomy 16:18–20, 17:8–13)

Teaching Tips

Words You Should Know

A. Hired Servant (Deuteronomy 24:14) *sakir* (Heb.)—A paid employee, contracted for a certain number of years

B. Pervert (v. 17) *natah* (Heb.)—Turn aside, repel, or decline

Teacher Preparation

Unifying Principle—Countercultural Compassion. Some people are poor and marginalized. How can their dignity and worth be respected? Deuteronomy demands justice for all who are poor or marginalized.

A. Read the Bible Background and Devotional Reading.

B. Pray for your students and lesson clarity.

C. Read the lesson Scripture in multiple translations.

O—Open the Lesson

A. Begin the class with prayer.

B. Before class, ask a participant to prepare a brief report on the legislation called War on Poverty introduced by Lyndon Johnson in the 1960s. What was it? How effective has it been? What are obstacles that have prevented the total elimination of poverty? Move from there to looking at what the Bible prescribed for alleviating poverty.

C. Have the students read the Aim for Change and the In Focus story.

D. Ask students how events like those in the story weigh on their hearts and how they can view these events from a faith perspective.

P—Present the Scriptures

A. Read the Focal Verses and discuss the Background and The People, Places, and Times sections.

B. Have the class share what Scriptures stand out for them and why, with particular emphasis on today's themes.

E—Explore the Meaning

A. Use In Depth or More Light on the Text to facilitate a deeper discussion of the lesson text.

B. Pose the questions in Search the Scriptures and Discuss the Meaning.

C. Discuss the Liberating Lesson and Application for Activation sections.

N—Next Steps for Application

A. Summarize the value of trusting God to supply their needs.

B. End class with a commitment to stand against business practices that hurt the most marginalized among us.

Worship Guide

For the Superintendent or Teacher
Theme: Justice and the Marginalized
Song: "Christ Is Our King"

Justice and the Marginalized

(handwritten: Insignificant above "Marginalized")

Bible Background • DEUTERONOMY 24:10–21
Printed Text • DEUTERONOMY 24:10–21 | Devotional Reading • 3 JOHN 1:2–8

—————————— **Aim for Change** ——————————

By the end of this lesson, we will EXPLORE God's standards for justice, APPRECIATE how God loves those who are poor and marginalized, and SHARE love with those who are rejected by others.

————————————— **In Focus** —————————————

Melissa couldn't believe her bad luck. She had been laid off three times in the past two years. Every time she was financially stable, her company announced plans to downsize, or shut down. That evening, Melissa needed time alone, but then her phone rang.

"Brandy told me about the cutbacks," her brother Adam said sympathetically.

Melissa said, "That wasn't her news to tell. And you need to mind your own business!"

Adam quickly said, "Don't shut me out again! God has a purpose. He is your provider, not the company. He's always got your back!"

Melissa hated when her brother got all preachy. His religion was fine for him, but it wasn't her thing. "Adam, my dinner's getting cold. I've got to go."

"Sis, wait!" Adam said. "I know you don't care for Jesus, but He gave His church some very specific instructions about what to do when people hit hard times. I want to help, and my church has a program that might be just right for your current situation."

"I'm not some charity case, Adam" Melissa said.

"I know, Sis," Adam said. "Just give this a bit of a chance. It can't hurt. Can I come by and talk with you about it tomorrow?"

Melissa hated that her brother wouldn't take no for an answer. She hated her situation. But she also hated feeling so much hate at it all. "Tomorrow, then." Melissa hung up the phone as tears ran down her face.

What programs does your church support to help the disenfranchised and marginalized in your community?

(handwritten: Outreach)

———————————— **Keep in Mind** ————————————

> "But thou shalt remember that thou wast a bondman in Egypt, and the LORD
> thy God redeemed thee thence: therefore I command thee to do this thing."
> (Deuteronomy 24:18, KJV)

"Always remember that you were slaves in Egypt and that the LORD your God redeemed you from your slavery. That is why I have given you this command." (Deuteronomy 24:18, NLT)

Focal Verses

KJV **Deuteronomy 24:10** When thou dost lend thy brother any thing, thou shalt not go into his house to fetch his pledge.

11 Thou shalt stand abroad, and the man to whom thou dost lend shall bring out the pledge abroad unto thee.

12 And if the man be poor, thou shalt not sleep with his pledge:

13 In any case thou shalt deliver him the pledge again when the sun goeth down, that he may sleep in his own raiment, and bless thee: and it shall be righteousness unto thee before the LORD thy God.

14 Thou shalt not oppress an hired servant that is poor and needy, whether he be of thy brethren, or of thy strangers that are in thy land within thy gates:

15 At his day thou shalt give him his hire, neither shall the sun go down upon it; for he is poor, and setteth his heart upon it: lest he cry against thee unto the LORD, and it be sin unto thee.

16 The fathers shall not be put to death for the children, neither shall the children be put to death for the fathers: every man shall be put to death for his own sin.

17 Thou shalt not pervert the judgment of the stranger, nor of the fatherless; nor take a widow's raiment to pledge:

18 But thou shalt remember that thou wast a bondman in Egypt, and the LORD thy God redeemed thee thence: therefore I command thee to do this thing.

19 When thou cuttest down thine harvest in thy field, and hast forgot a sheaf in the field, thou shalt not go again to fetch it: it shall be for the stranger, for the fatherless, and for the widow: that the LORD thy God may bless thee in all the work of thine hands.

20 When thou beatest thine olive tree, thou shalt not go over the boughs again: it shall

NLT **Deuteronomy 24:10** If you lend anything to your neighbor, do not enter his house to pick up the item he is giving as security.

11 You must wait outside while he goes in and brings it out to you.

12 If your neighbor is poor and gives you his cloak as security for a loan, do not keep the cloak overnight.

13 Return the cloak to its owner by sunset so he can stay warm through the night and bless you, and the LORD your God will count you as righteous.

14 Never take advantage of poor and destitute laborers, whether they are fellow Israelites or foreigners living in your towns.

15 You must pay them their wages each day before sunset because they are poor and are counting on it. If you don't, they might cry out to the LORD against you, and it would be counted against you as sin.

16 Parents must not be put to death for the sins of their children, nor children for the sins of their parents. Those deserving to die must be put to death for their own crimes.

17 True justice must be given to foreigners living among you and to orphans, and you must never accept a widow's garment as security for her debt.

18 Always remember that you were slaves in Egypt and that the LORD your God redeemed you from your slavery. That is why I have given you this command.

19 When you are harvesting your crops and forget to bring in a bundle of grain from your field, don't go back to get it. Leave it for the foreigners, orphans, and widows. Then the LORD your God will bless you in all you do.

20 When you beat the olives from your olive trees, don't go over the boughs twice. Leave the be for the stranger, for the fatherless, and for the widow.

21 When thou gatherest the grapes of thy vineyard, thou shalt not glean it afterward: it shall be for the stranger, for the fatherless, and for the widow.

remaining olives for the foreigners, orphans, and widows.

21 When you gather the grapes in your vineyard, don't glean the vines after they are picked. Leave the remaining grapes for the foreigners, orphans, and widows.

The People, Places, and Times

Deuteronomy. Deuteronomy is one of the most significant books in the Old Testament. It is directly quoted over 40 times in the New Testament, exceeded only by Psalms (quoted 68 times), and Isaiah (quoted 55 times). In fact, Jesus Himself quoted from Deuteronomy each time He was tempted by Satan during His forty days and nights in the wilderness (Deuteronomy 6:13, 16; 8:3). When a lawyer asked Jesus which is the greatest commandment in the Law (Matthew 22:36), Deuteronomy again provided the answer, "Thou shalt love the Lord thy God with all thy heart, and with all thy soul, and with all thy mind" (6:5). Verse 6 goes on to say, "These words, which I command thee this day, shall be in thine heart." It was obvious Jesus had obeyed the command and hidden the Word in His heart so that He would not sin against God (Psalm 119:11). We can do the same if we memorize the Word, meditating on it day and night in order to obey it and be blessed by it (Joshua 1:8).

Are you able to follow Jesus' example to use the power of God's Word to defend yourself against the attacks of the enemy?

Background

In chapter 24, the Israelites are introduced to a set of miscellaneous laws. It speaks to the understanding of marital commitments for grounds for divorce and remarrying after divorce (vv. 1–4). Verse 5 explains why newly married men are absolved of military duty for one year. The understanding of loan and collateral is interpreted in verse 6. If a person

borrows anything, he is expected to provide collateral of his choosing, as a sign of good faith for the loan. Kidnapping to sell someone as a slave was forbidden (v. 7). Verses 8–9 are not laws, but reminders of the priestly directives on how to deal with those who have leprosy (Leviticus 13–14). This assortment of laws for the Israelites is presented in concert with previous laws framing a clear expectation of how to govern themselves. Their understanding and their ability, or inability, to appropriately practice these laws would have societal and divine consequences (Deuteronomy 24:15). These laws are not directed only to those who were wealthy, but are equally important for those who were poor. The remaining portion of chapter 24 is fixed on the dignity of the poor.

Why was there such an emphasis on the dignity of the marginalized?

At-A-Glance

1. The Debtors (Deuteronomy 24:10–15)
2. The Disassociation (v. 16)
3. The Destitute (vv. 17–21)

In Depth

1. The Debtors (Deuteronomy 24:10–15)

The theme of loans and collateral, initially sketched in verse 6, resurfaces in more detail in verse 10. Most often, debtors are viewed as being at the disadvantage of the loaner. Although in debt, the debtor should not lose their dignity or self-respect. The loaner oppressing the debtor or ignoring the debtor's family's needs is outlawed. God cares just as much for the well being of the debtor as He cares for the creditor's. Each person, regardless of status, is viewed equally in the sight of God. The loaner's job was not to intimidate or humiliate because someone owed a debt. As a symbol of good faith, the debtor was to initiate their repayment methods. Conversely, the loaner could not dictate what was to be used as collateral or payment. Further, he was not permitted to enter the debtor's home to demand his preferred method of payment.

If the only thing the debtor could afford to render were his sleeping clothes, then that should be deemed to be an acceptable form of payment. However, those were to be returned to the debtor by evening. The same courtesy is to be given to workers who live hand to mouth. They cannot wait overnight to receive their day's wages, so the employer must not force them to do so.

This was all enveloped with respect. Mutual respect was to be provided by both parties. The debtor knows he owes the debt and shows his willingness to pay. The creditor recognizes he is owed funds but trusts the fidelity of the debtor. It creates loving-kindness to treat your neighbor as you would also want to be treated (Mark 12:31).

Should acts of kindness reciprocate kindness?

2. The Disassociation (v. 16)

Moses reiterates that each person is to be treated individually. This means there is no generational penalty, where the children pay for the crimes of the parent or vice versa (Jeremiah 31:29; Ezekiel 18). Imposing a cumulative punishment would present unjust repercussions and unfair retaliation for offenses not committed by the person receiving the punishment. If this were to be allowed, families or villages could potentially be obliterated, all

because of the offenses of another. Verse 16 seeks to eliminate such retaliatory actions.

What would happen if families had to pay for previous family members' delinquencies?

3. The Destitute (vv. 17–21)

Moses continues his dissection of the have and the have nots. He goes into further detail on how one must handle the disadvantaged. Regardless of one's social or economic class, each person must be treated the same. The imagery and remembrance of Israel being slaves are brought into focus. In Moses' use of the word slave, he does not want Israel to never forget how they too were disenfranchised in Egypt, classless and poor. Still, God chose to redeem them. Now freed, Israel is supposed to see the powerful and powerless as equal. They are so similar, we should consider the lowly as our neighbors. Taking care of your neighbors is something we should all do, especially the privileged. Gleaning—the process of sharing with the poor—is not only appropriate, but showcases true love for humanity. Their surplus is to serve as manna from heaven for the needy. Everyone has something to give.

Do you think the poor have anything to give?

Search the Scriptures

1. Why is God concerned about protecting people's dignity (Deuteronomy 24:10–13)?

2. Why don't we have to pay for the sins of our ancestors (v. 16)?

3. By calling them slaves, what did Moses want the Israelites to remember (v.18)?

Discuss the Meaning

It is easy to think that if we have money or status that we are more important than others. In God's eyes, each of us is considered the same and we should believe we are equal. How does God seek to deal with our ego and classism? How does Jesus' bodily sacrifice coincide with an unredeemable debt?

Liberating Lesson

The Urban Institute's Well–Being and Basic Needs Survey found that nearly 40 percent of non-elderly adults report difficulty meeting basic needs such as food, healthcare, housing, and utilities. We are one of the wealthiest nations in the world, so why is this statistic still true? God blesses us so that we can be blessings to our neighbors. It is not a matter of the privileged and the underprivileged in the sight of God. It is never about lauding privilege, but being generous enough to share it knowing that we should love our neighbors as ourselves.

Application for Activation

Daily, we have seen people on streets or near freeways holding signs that in essence say, "I need help." Often we ignore their concern or don't think we have enough to help them in their time of need. Yet our help, regardless of the increment, could be the assistance they need. Many of us have the privilege of going to a home, changing clothes, and having a meal. It may not be exactly what we want, but we have something. Maybe enough to share. Let's do something! Look for ways to assist the underprivileged, whether providing for their needs, or advocating for their rights.

Follow the Spirit

What God wants me to do:

_____

_____

_____

_____

_____

Remember Your Thoughts

Special insights I have learned:

_____

_____

_____

_____

More Light on the Text
Deuteronomy 24:10–21

The book of Deuteronomy reveals many attributes of God: He is jealous (4:24), faithful (7:9), loving (7:13), holy (26:15), merciful (4:31), and yet angered by sin (6:15). Indeed, it is these very attributes of God that makes Him concerned about His people and especially the marginalized. Deuteronomy 24:10–21 records some of the laws God established to protect the disenfranchised.

24:10 When thou dost lend thy brother anything, thou shalt not go into his house to fetch his pledge. 11 Thou shalt stand abroad, and the man to whom thou dost lend shall bring out the pledge abroad unto thee. 12 And if the man be poor, thou shalt not sleep with his pledge: 13 In any case thou shalt deliver him the pledge again when the sun goeth down, that he may sleep in his own raiment, and bless thee: and it shall be righteousness unto thee before the LORD thy God.

This law stipulates just dealings when making loans. If a pledge or security for the loan was required, the lender cannot go into the borrower's house and take anything he might want as security. He is required to wait outside the home for the borrower to bring the pledge to him. In this way the dignity of the borrower is preserved.

But God gives an additional stipulation to the lender. If the borrower is so poor that the only item he can give for security is his cloak, the lender must return the cloak by sunset. The borrower's cloak also served as his blanket at night, and he would need it to keep warm. However, this was not a new command. It was also given to the previous generation at Mt. Sinai in Exodus 22:26–27. "If thou at all take thy neighbour's raiment to pledge, thou shalt deliver it unto him by that the sun goeth down: For that is his covering only, it is his raiment for his skin: wherein shall he sleep? and it shall come to pass, when he crieth unto me, that I will hear; for I am gracious."

In other words, God takes note of what is done to the poor. If they cry out to the Lord due to an injustice, He firmly declares, "I will hear." Hear is the Hebrew word *shama'* (shaw–**MAH**). It does not only mean that God listens to the complaint with attention and interest, but that He will take action. The Lord is gracious, full of divine grace. This same gracious God will also "hear" us when we cry out to Him. In fact, He bids us to come boldly to His throne of grace to obtain mercy and help in the time of need (Hebrews 4:16). When the lender does what is commanded and returns the poor man's cloak, he will be blessed by the debtor, and approved by God as righteous.

14 Thou shalt not oppress an hired servant that is poor and needy, whether he be of thy brethren, or of thy strangers that are in thy land within thy gates: 15 At his day thou shalt give him his hire, neither shall the sun go down upon it; for he is poor, and setteth his heart upon it: lest he cry against thee unto the LORD, and it be sin unto thee.

Once again, Yahweh appears as the protector of the poor and the needy, this time on behalf of the destitute person who works as a laborer. It does not matter if the person is a fellow Jew or a resident alien, the day laborer must be paid his wages daily before sunset. The reason is that the poor "setteth his heart upon it," depending on the money to provide the daily necessities for himself and his family. As the word is commonly used elsewhere in Scripture, a "hired servant" (Heb. *sakir*, saw–**KEAR**) is usually with an employer for an appointed time of several years (Deuteronomy 15:18; Job 7:1; Isaiah 16:14). If that is the case in this verse, it seems reasonable to withhold wages from such a person and only pay them weekly, monthly, or even just at the end of their hiring period. They are not like day workers who might or might not be there the next day to collect accumulated wages. However, God instructs His people that even hired servants who will be there for years need to be paid daily if they are living hand to mouth.

Consistent with the previous command, there is a warning to the employer. If denied his daily wages, the poor man's recourse was to cry to God, who will take appropriate action against the employer. Indeed, when Israel cried out to the Lord (Exodus 2:23, 3:9), God took action against Pharaoh through ten devastating plagues, and through drowning the entire army in the Red Sea (Exodus 14:28, 15:4). In like manner, the employer might find himself judged for withholding a poor man's wages.

Kindness to the poor was not only for employers. Proverbs provides this wise advice: "He that hath a bountiful eye shall be blessed; for he giveth of his bread to the poor" (Proverbs 22:9), and "He that hath pity upon the poor lendeth unto the Lord; and that which he hath given will he pay him again" (Proverbs 19:17). There are needy people today in similar situations that we can either give to personally or through donations to food banks, benevolence ministries, charities, etc. God's promise is to "bless" and to "repay" those who graciously give to the poor.

16 The fathers shall not be put to death for the children, neither shall the children be put to death for the fathers: every man shall be put to death for his own sin.

This law regarding personal responsibility was straightforward: the person who sins is the one who should die for his sin. However, this law was necessary because in some nations, a son might be executed if his father's negligence caused the death of another man's son. For example, by the laws of Hammurabi (an 18th century BC Babylonian ruler), if a builder constructed a shabby house that fell and killed the son of the person who lived in the house, then the builder's son would be killed.

God wanted to ensure that Israel did not adopt that practice. Nevertheless, in spite of this law, the Jews sometimes used a proverb to excuse their sin: "The fathers have eaten sour grapes, and the children's teeth are set on edge" (Ezekiel 18:2). In other words, their forefathers were the ones that sinned (i.e., ate sour grapes), but now they were the ones unfairly enduring the bitter punishment (i.e., teeth set on edge). However, they were dishonest for they too had followed in the sinful footsteps of their ancestors; therefore, the Babylonian invasion and captivity they were enduring was just punishment for their own sins.

So God was reiterating to the people, through the prophet Ezekiel, the basic principle of this law by asserting, "the soul that sinneth, it shall die" (Ezekiel 18:4, 20). Then Ezekiel summarized some of the sins a person must pay for. "If a man has a son that is a robber... that has oppressed the poor and needy... has not restored the pledge... has given forth upon usury... he shall surely die; his blood shall be upon him" (Ezekiel 18:10–13). Not surprisingly, among the offenses listed are sins against the marginalized, emphasizing once again God's concern for the poor and needy.

Although God's command is "the soul that sinneth, it shall die," yet He graciously announces that He takes no pleasure in the death of the wicked, but desires that they should turn from their sin and live (Ezekiel 18:23, 32). It is for this reason that the plan of salvation is so extraordinary. After declaring that "all have sinned" (Romans 3:23), that "there is none righteous" (Romans 3:10), that "the wages of that sin is death" (Romans 6:23), God then upends His own Law. He sent His sinless Son to die on Calvary, the innocent in place of the guilty, paying the penalty so that the soul that sins but repents and "believes in Him shall not perish, but have everlasting life" (John 3:16). If you have not yet accepted this incredibly gracious gift, today is your day of salvation (Hebrews 3:15), your day to choose to live and not die and declare the works of the Lord (Psalm 118:17).

17 Thou shalt not pervert the judgment of the stranger, nor of the fatherless; nor take a widow's raiment to pledge: 18 But thou shalt remember that thou wast a bondman in Egypt, and the LORD thy God redeemed thee thence: therefore I command thee to do this thing.

The focus on the less fortunate continues and now the attention is turned to assuring that the foreigner, the fatherless, and the widow—those who are particularly vulnerable—are treated justly and with love and respect (10:18). The righteous judgments given the marginalized in the courts should not be "pervert[ed]" (Heb. *natah*, naw–**TAW**), meaning turned aside, repelled, or declined. The judgment they receive must be enacted and not simply ignored. God is so serious about this that He issues this severe warning if His command is not followed. "Cursed be he that perverteth the judgment of the stranger, fatherless, and widow" (27:19), and "my wrath shall wax hot, and I will kill you with the sword; and your wives shall be widows, and your children fatherless" (Exodus 22:23–24). Mistreating the poor was a grave sin, and God would administer punishment accordingly.

Israel was to treat foreigners with love, remembering they were oppressed as "bondmen" (Heb. *ebed*, EH–bed, "slaves") in Egypt and how God punished the Egyptians as a result, delivering them with a mighty hand (15:15, 24:22). Israelites should have pity for those experiencing economic hardship, because they have the cultural memory of experiencing the same hardship. They also saw what happened to the nation that oppressed such people. Egypt was thoroughly destroyed, so they know God is powerful enough to visit a similar fate on them if they mistreated the needy.

19 When thou cuttest down thine harvest in thy field, and hast forgot a sheaf in the field, thou shalt not go again to fetch it: it shall be for the stranger, for the fatherless, and for the widow: that the LORD thy God may bless thee in all the work of thine hands. 20 When thou beatest thine olive tree, thou shalt not go over the boughs again: it shall be for the stranger, for the fatherless, and for the widow. 21 When thou gatherest the grapes of thy vineyard, thou shalt not glean it afterward: it shall be for the stranger, for the fatherless, and for the widow.

The focus of this particular law is again on the marginalized: foreigners (strangers), the fatherless (orphans), and widows. It deals with the principle for providing food for the poor during harvest. The first of the three main crops mentioned was the "harvest in the field" which was either barley or wheat, both commonly referred to as grain. The overlooked sheaf (bundle) of grain was to be left for the underprivileged so that the Lord would bless the owner. Leviticus 23:22 gives this additional detail: "When ye reap the harvest of your land,

thou shalt not make clean riddance of the corners of thy field…, neither shalt thou gather any gleaning of thy harvest: thou shalt leave them unto the poor, and to the stranger." Gleaning is the act of collecting leftover crops from the fields after they have been harvested by the owner. This was the privilege of the poor so that they were not reduced to the humiliation of begging or seeking welfare. In so doing, they could still preserve their dignity by working for their food.

Such was the case with Ruth who went to glean in the fields of Boaz (Ruth 2:3). Ruth is three times over the kind of person this law was written for: she is foreign, not protected by a father, and widowed. For his generosity toward Ruth and Naomi, the Lord blessed Boaz indeed and he was honored as the progenitor of King David and ultimately Jesus, the Messiah (Ruth 4:17; Matthew 1:5). *anaestor*

A similar procedure was to be followed for harvesting the other staple two crops, olives and grapes. Olives were harvested by laying down a sheet under the tree and sending a small person up the tree to hit its branches with a hard stick. The ripe olives would then fall to the sheet and be gathered up. This law instructs that only once were the olive trees to be beaten with poles to harvest olives. The remaining olives were for the alien, the widow, and the orphan. During grape harvest, the vines were gone over only once so that the needy could have the remainder.

Sources:
Barker, K.L. and J.R. Kohlenberger. *Expositor's Bible Commentary (Abridged Edition): Old Testament.* Grand Rapids, MI: Zondervan, 2004.
Bruce, F.F. *Zondervan Bible Commentary: One–Volume Illustrated Edition.* Grand Rapids, MI: Zondervan, 2008.
Bruggemann, Walter. *Deuteronomy.* Nashville, TN: Abingdon Press, 2008. 235–241.
Payne, David. *Deuteronomy.* Louisville, KY: Westminster Press. 1985. 135–135.
Hinton, Linda B. *Basic Bible Commentary Numbers and Deuteronomy.* Nashville, TN: Abingdon Press, 1994.
Interpreter's One–Volume Commentary on the Bible: Introduction and Commentary for Each Book of the Bible Including the Apocrypha. Nashville, TN: Abingdon Press, 1971. 136–137.
Walvoord, J.F. and Zuck, R.B. *The Bible Knowledge Commentary: Old Testament.* Wheaton, IL: Victor Books, 1985.

Psalm 23.

Say It Correctly

Pentateuch. PEN–tuh–took.
Hammurabi. hah–muh–RAW–bee.

Daily Bible Readings

MONDAY
God Executes Justice for the Poor
(Psalm 140)

TUESDAY
Remembering Our
Marginalized Ancestors
(Deuteronomy 26:1–11)

WEDNESDAY
Woe to Those Who Mistreat Workers
(James 5:1–11)

THURSDAY
Justice for the Weak and Orphaned
(Psalm 82)

FRIDAY
Jesus' Compassion for the Helpless
(Matthew 9:27–38)

SATURDAY
Do Not Oppress the Alien
(Leviticus 19:32–37)

SUNDAY
Justice for the Poor
(Deuteronomy 24:10–21)

Notes   8,810

7,487 promises made by
God to humankind

Teaching Tips

Words You Should Know

A. Anger (2 Samuel 12:5) *'aph* (Heb)— Wrath; flared nostrils

B. Sinned (v. 13) *khata* (Heb.)—To miss the mark; to incur guilt

Teacher Preparation

Unifying Principle—Speaking Truth to Power. People often see acts of injustice being committed. How are we called to respond when we witness unjust acts? Nathan sought God's guidance and received wisdom for how to address David's sin.

A. Read the Bible Background and Devotional Reading.

B. Pray for your students and lesson clarity.

C. Read the lesson Scripture in multiple translations.

O—Open the Lesson

A. Begin the class with prayer.

B. Create a checklist with participants to help them evaluate their fitness for wielding power. Some questions might be: In what way(s) might I be tempted to abuse power? How well do I take correction? Who among my closest friends would be willing to hold me accountable?

C. Have the students read the Aim for Change and the In Focus story.

D. Ask students how events like those in the story weigh on their hearts and how they can view these events from a faith perspective.

P—Present the Scriptures

A. Read the Focal Verses and discuss the Background and The People, Places, and Times sections.

B. Have the class share what Scriptures stand out for them and why, with particular emphasis on today's themes.

E—Explore the Meaning

A. Use In Depth or More Light on the Text to facilitate a deeper discussion of the lesson text.

B. Pose the questions in Search the Scriptures and Discuss the Meaning.

C. Discuss the Liberating Lesson and Application for Activation sections.

N—Next Steps for Application

A. Summarize the value of differentiating between ignoring a moral lapse and forgiving a moral lapse after remediation.

B. End class with a commitment to pray for godly, prophetic voices that challenge evil in high places.

Worship Guide

For the Superintendent or Teacher
Theme: Nathan Condemns David
Song: "Give Me a Clean Heart"

Nathan Condemns David

Bible Background • 2 SAMUEL 12
Printed Text • 2 SAMUEL 12:1–9, 13–15 | Devotional Reading • JOHN 7:40–47

—————— Aim for Change ——————

By the end of this lesson, we will EXPLORE how sins' consequences extend beyond the individual and bring hurt to God and others; ADDRESS sin and the injustices that occur as a result; and ADMIT our sins, ask God's forgiveness, and make godly choices.

—————— In Focus ——————

Carlton was a proud eight-and-a-half year old. He was his mother's pride and joy. He was a capable student with good grades, good behavior, and he often was known as the center of activity at his school. Though he was surrounded by friends at school, he was the youngest child in the family, and his older siblings had moved out on their own. Yes, Carlton was clearly a special kid, but he was still a kid.

One evening while goofing around in his mother's living room—an area that had always been off-limits to kids—he realized his jumping and bouncing had gone too far when he heard a crash. After searching for something large to be broken, he realized he had actually caused a tiny, delicate glass vase to topple over. It was one of his mom's newest decorations, and she had chosen it because it was so uniquely designed. As it happened, Carlton was able to put the pieces together and prop them up against a lamp so that it appeared to still be in one piece. Oddly, Mom never heard the crash and never came running.

After going to bed, Carlton soon forgot about his little incident. Months later, Carlton was in his room doing homework. He'd had a good day at school and even made an A on a test. Suddenly his great day was ruined when he heard his mother yell in that unmistakable tone of voice:

"CARLTON!" Right then, he remembered the vase, put down his pen, took a deep breath, and went to answer his mom's call. It was now time to face the truth.

We try to teach the younger generation that sometimes even though people are allowed grace, they still have to face the consequences. Where have you seen this in your life?

—————— Keep in Mind ——————

"And Nathan said to David, Thou art the man." (from 2 Samuel 12:7, KJV)

"Then Nathan said to David, 'You are that man!'" (from 2 Samuel 12:7, NLT)

Focal Verses

KJV **2 Samuel 12:1** And the LORD sent Nathan unto David. And he came unto him, and said unto him, There were two men in one city; the one rich, and the other poor.

2 The rich man had exceeding many flocks and herds:

3 But the poor man had nothing, save one little ewe lamb, which he had bought and nourished up: and it grew up together with him, and with his children; it did eat of his own meat, and drank of his own cup, and lay in his bosom, and was unto him as a daughter.

4 And there came a traveller unto the rich man, and he spared to take of his own flock and of his own herd, to dress for the wayfaring man that was come unto him; but took the poor man's lamb, and dressed it for the man that was come to him.

5 And David's anger was greatly kindled against the man; and he said to Nathan, As the LORD liveth, the man that hath done this thing shall surely die:

6 And he shall restore the lamb fourfold, because he did this thing, and because he had no pity.

7 And Nathan said to David, Thou art the man. Thus saith the LORD God of Israel, I anointed thee king over Israel, and I delivered thee out of the hand of Saul;

8 And I gave thee thy master's house, and thy master's wives into thy bosom, and gave thee the house of Israel and of Judah; and if that had been too little, I would moreover have given unto thee such and such things.

9 Wherefore hast thou despised the commandment of the LORD, to do evil in his sight? thou hast killed Uriah the Hittite with the sword, and hast taken his wife to be thy wife, and hast slain him with the sword of the children of Ammon.

13 And David said unto Nathan, I have sinned against the LORD. And Nathan said

NLT **2 Samuel 12:1** So the LORD sent Nathan the prophet to tell David this story: "There were two men in a certain town. One was rich, and one was poor.

2 The rich man owned a great many sheep and cattle.

3 The poor man owned nothing but one little lamb he had bought. He raised that little lamb, and it grew up with his children. It ate from the man's own plate and drank from his cup. He cuddled it in his arms like a baby daughter.

4 One day a guest arrived at the home of the rich man. But instead of killing an animal from his own flock or herd, he took the poor man's lamb and killed it and prepared it for his guest."

5 David was furious. "As surely as the LORD lives," he vowed, "any man who would do such a thing deserves to die!

6 He must repay four lambs to the poor man for the one he stole and for having no pity."

7 Then Nathan said to David, "You are that man! The LORD, the God of Israel, says: I anointed you king of Israel and saved you from the power of Saul.

8 I gave you your master's house and his wives and the kingdoms of Israel and Judah. And if that had not been enough, I would have given you much, much more.

9 Why, then, have you despised the word of the LORD and done this horrible deed? For you have murdered Uriah the Hittite with the sword of the Ammonites and stolen his wife.

13 Then David confessed to Nathan, "I have sinned against the LORD." Nathan replied, "Yes, but the LORD has forgiven you, and you won't die for this sin.

14 Nevertheless, because you have shown utter contempt for the word of the LORD by doing this, your child will die."

unto David, The LORD also hath put away thy sin; thou shalt not die.

14 Howbeit, because by this deed thou hast given great occasion to the enemies of the LORD to blaspheme, the child also that is born unto thee shall surely die.

15 And Nathan departed unto his house. And the LORD struck the child that Uriah's wife bare unto David, and it was very sick.

15 After Nathan returned to his home, the LORD sent a deadly illness to the child of David and Uriah's wife.

The People, Places, and Times

David. David is one of the Bible's great heroes, in part because his story covers such a wide range of human experience. Born the youngest of eight sons, David had few, if any, expectations on his life, beyond shepherding and following the orders of others. David would rise quickly from the moment of his anointing, through great victories in battle, and ultimately succeed Saul as king. Like many who rise to power, David was not exempt from temptation, nor was he innocent of yielding, particularly as his life changed upon encountering Bathsheba. Just like the rest of us, David was not exempt from the consequences of his actions, nor was he able to sin outside of God's omniscient view.

Nathan. Nathan was a faithful prophet and a trusted advisor. Unlike others who hover close to the seat of power, he maintained his faithfulness to God first, and the king next. While many people fear losing their place if they do not enable a misguided leader, Nathan shows that it is more important to trust and obey God. Nathan utilized his creativity to instruct and correct David, retaining respect as a man of God. Nathan was aware of many of David's sins, but he intervened before David made the mistake of thinking he was invincible. Many of us need genuine friends who will tell us the truth, versus what we want to hear.

What friend or mentor do you have in your life who will hold you accountable?

Background

The imagery of the innocent lamb should resonate with Christians. David is now king, but many years ago, he had been a shepherd, No doubt, Nathan was able to relate to David at this core place in his personal history. While most are quite separate from our agricultural origins today, we do not have to look far to see how God has brought us from humility to glory, all because of His grace and mercy.

Nathan's story of the beloved sheep may be expanded to represent God's love for His people. The enemy is certainly seeking to devour and destroy us, while God loves us to the point He holds us close to His bosom. While Nathan's story holds a tragic end for the lamb, our truth is that God promises nothing and no one can pluck us from God's hand. Although David was guilty of taking Bathsheba wrongly, God's grace and mercy spared David's life and allowed him to continue to fulfill the call upon his life. There were still consequences, but Nathan's intervention on God's instructions saved David from utter catastrophe.

At-A-Glance

1. God Reveals (2 Samuel 12:1–7)
2. God Reforms (vv. 7–9)
3. God Redeems (vv. 13–15)

In Depth

1. God Reveals (2 Samuel 12:1–7)

God used Nathan to reveal to David the truth of his own actions. Similarly, Christ would use many parables during His ministry. Preaching and teaching by illustration can actually lead to greater revelation in some cases.

In verse 5, David's anger reached its highest point, as he was insulted on behalf of the poor man and his beloved lamb. Sin causes us to be arrogant and to become blind to the reality that we have caused damage by our actions. David had not just damaged Uriah, he had taken his life in order to take his wife. This extremity was no secret—yet God used Nathan to reveal the horror of this behavior to David so that he could see himself from another perspective.

In this moment of revelation, David went from being royal to wrong, and the anger he demonstrated would soon be turned toward himself. God reveals our wrongs to us so that we can take corrective action. David was no stranger to repentance, but he had let this practice lapse. Revelation has a way of rerouting us from disaster.

If God were to reveal your sins to the public, what could you stand to lose? Friendships? Respect? Livelihood?

2. God Reforms (vv. 7–9)

"Thou art the man!" These words ring from the voice of Nathan, and David stands accused in his own royal chamber. His guilt is inescapable, and his accuser is not the prophet, but Almighty God Himself. Truly there can be no remission of sin without repentance, and there can be no repentance without an acknowledgment of guilt.

God's reform is thorough. God is not interested in temporary remedies that will spare our feelings or compromise right and wrong. Instead, God can only reform us when we yield to Him, acknowledge His righteousness and admit our wrong.

After the initial shock of the revelation of David's guilt, Nathan continues by prophetically declaring all the many reasons David had no excuse for what he had done. Again, revelation leads to reformation, as we all must account for our wrongdoings, and evaluate how to make better choices in the future. David had been blessed to accomplish great things. He had absolutely no reason to take his soldier's life and seduce his wife. He did so simply because he could.

What privileges have we abused, knowing that it would displease God and harm ourselves in the long run?

3. God Redeems (vv. 13–15)

The beauty of the grace of God is that it covers a multitude of sins. David's confession is refreshing, considering our political climate which finds many powerful leaders quite unrepentant and indignant at the notion that they may be wrong. In David's case, he had the power as a king to command right and wrong to be precisely what he chose. Yet, by recognizing God's revelation and accepting God's reformation, he could now fully receive God's redemption.

"I have sinned against the LORD." These simple words are very difficult to say sometimes, but they are no less vital to the quality of our Christian life. We are not capable of living a sin-free life. However, we are entirely free from sin because of God's redeeming grace.

In yet another parallel similar to the poor man's lamb, God used Bathsheba's child as an example for our faith. While the child had committed no sin in being conceived, it was still conceived in sin, and would no doubt have lived a life of scorn, shame, and mistreatment. While the loss of the child was incredibly painful, it is a reminder that God Himself sacrificed His own Son so that the sins of the entire world may be forgiven. David and

Bathsheba's child died as punishment for sin, but he was still not to be the propitiation for all sin. David is a perfect example of God's ability to expose, admonish, and forgive those He loves.

Has God ever taken something from you, then provided something even better than what you lost?

Search the Scriptures

1. What was Nathan risking when he went to speak to David (2 Samuel 12:1)?

2. How do we know David was truly repentant for his sin (v. 13)?

Discuss the Meaning

1. Why did Nathan risk his own safety by confronting David?

2. Although David had been warned that this son would die, he begged God to spare the child's life. Why did God allow the child to die anyway?

Liberating Lesson

Although David eventually was restored to favor with God, he had to endure the consequences of his sin. Here, we have an example of what it means to be humble before God, even as we retain prominence in other areas. The fact is that no one is exempt from the truth. Right is right and wrong is wrong, regardless of our station in life. Fortunately, God so loved the entire world that He gave His Son, so that those who believe shall not perish in their sin, but shall have everlasting life.

Application for Activation

In our litigious society, there is often a price tag placed on forgiveness. While we can perhaps repay some debts with money or time, true repentance requires humility, admission, and acceptance of our need for God's redeeming power. How should this understanding of forgiveness be applied to the questions of reparations or restorative justice?

Follow the Spirit

What God wants me to do:

_____

_____

_____

_____

Remember Your Thoughts

Special insights I have learned:

_____

_____

_____

_____

More Light on the Text
2 Samuel 12:1–9, 13–15

Scripture unabashedly chronicles King David's absolute disregard to God's Law and ordinances by coveting and committing adultery and murder (2 Samuel 11). David lusted for Bathsheba, the wife of Uriah, one of his top fighters (2 Samuel 23:39). He has sex with her while Uriah is in the battlefield fighting to defend David and Israel. Since David abused his position of king to have sex with Bathsheba when she had no power to deny him, this is rape. To cover up his crime, David invites Uriah home from the battle. He tries to entice Uriah to go home and sleep with Bathsheba. His plan fails. Then David orders Uriah killed in battle by putting him in a position where he would not escape. His orders are carried out—Uriah is killed with enemy weapons. Following Uriah's death, King David takes Bathsheba as his wife and bears him a son. The concluding sentence of the last verse of the chapter sets up the stage for the dramatic saga that would follow, which is the basis of our discussion "…But the LORD was displeased with what David had done" (11:27). The drama that follows demonstrates certain aspects of God's attribute: a righteous and a just God; a merciful and gracious God, and a God who never winks at sin no matter who commits it.

1 And the LORD sent Nathan unto David. And he came unto him, and said unto him, There were two men in one city; the one rich, and the other poor. 2 The rich man had exceeding many flocks and herds: 3 But the poor man had nothing, save one little ewe lamb, which he had bought and nourished up: and it grew up together with him, and with his children; it did eat of his own meat, and drank of his own cup, and lay in his bosom, and was unto him as a daughter.

The author brings another character into the unfolding drama, Nathan, a prophet of God. After the birth of Bathsheba's son, the Lord sends Nathan to David. David is familiar with Nathan as God's prophet. Earlier, God had used Nathan to deliver a message of God's covenant relationship with David and his descendants (2 Samuel 7; 1 Chronicles 17:1–15). It is not unusual for the prophet to visit the king. However, unbeknownst to David, the prophet has come this time not with praise, but with rebuke.

Probably David thought that he has succeeded in concealing his sin because no one challenged him or confronted him about it. It is likely that no one had the courage to challenge him because of his position as king. It should be noted that David's sin against Uriah was not a secret. The people in the kingdom knew about it—from the servant he sent to call Bathsheba, to the servants who stayed with Uriah when he refused to go his house, to the general who positioned Uriah at the frontlines to be murdered. Finally, taking Bathsheba to be his wife was not hidden. People must have gossiped about it, but no one dared challenge him.

As chapter 11 reveals, David started little by little until he was overtaken by sin and injustice. Like most people in a high position who think they can do anything and go free, especially against the poor and the less privileged, David thought he could do anything without challenge. We may hide our sin from humans and shield ourselves in injustice, but not with God. He sees and knows everything—nothing can be hidden from Him. David is familiar with this God, but self-indulgence and sinful pleasures (adultery, covetousness, injustice) cloud his judgment. God sends Nathan to David to challenge him with his sin.

Nathan begins with a story of a rich man who, in spite of having everything, steals a poor neighbor's only ewe to entertain his guest. Using a story or a parable to reveal a truth is customary in the Jewish culture (Ezekiel 17:1–4; 24:3–5). Jesus often used parables to illustrate the truth of the Gospel (Matthew 13; Mark 4; Luke 15; 18 etc.). It is common among the Igbo people of Nigeria to use parables in their conversation or to illustrate a point. Here Nathan employs the same method to illustrate the severity of David's sin. However, David is unaware that he is the person being described in the story.

The narrator presents an extreme contrast between the rich and the poor man. The Jewish economy had always been agriculturally based. Therefore, wealth in the Jewish culture was determined by the number of flocks or herds one possessed. David was a shepherd before he became king. "Flocks" and "herds" can be used synonymously; however specifically "flocks" (Heb. *tso'n*, **TSONE**) refers mainly to a fleet of sheep and goats, while "herds" (Heb. *baqar*, baw-**KAWR**) refer to cattle and horses. The rich man had "exceeding many" of them. In contrast, the poor man had nothing except "one little ewe lamb, which he bought and nourished up." The lamb grew in the family with his children; it ate with them and even drank from the same cup and "lay in his bosom." To the poor man this lamb was more than a pet, it "was unto him as a daughter." It was all he had; he cherished and loved it.

4 And there came a traveller unto the rich man, and he spared to take of his own flock and of his own herd, to dress for the wayfaring man that was unto him; but took the poor man's lamb, and dressed it for the man that was come to him. 5 And David's anger was greatly kindled against the man; and he said to Nathan, As the LORD liveth, the man that hath done this thing shall surely die: 6 And he shall restore the lamb fourfold, because he did this thing, and because he had no pity.

As a shepherd, David must have been very interested in the story. Nonetheless, Nathan had a purpose in mind to catch David off guard in his own words in order to present his case. Jews are known for their hospitality, especially to visitors. It is common practice for a Jew to attend to guests, expected or unexpected, by feeding them. Abraham entertained the three visitors who turned to be angels by taking from his flock (Genesis 18:1–8). The writer of Hebrews instructs, "Be not forgetful to entertain strangers: for thereby some have entertained angels unawares" (Hebrews 13:2). In this story, according to Nathan, the rich man has a guest. Instead of taking from his numerous flocks and herds, he takes the poor man's only ewe to entertain his visitor.

On hearing the story, David is very angry against the rich man for committing such a heinous act. As a king, David was obligated to see that the poor receive justice. Enraged by such despicable behavior, David exclaims that the death penalty is fitting for a man who would do such a wicked thing. The phrase "David's anger was greatly kindled..." describes the enormity of David's anger against the rich man. The word "kindled" (Heb. *kharah*, khaw-**RAW**) means that his anger was ignited as in a flame of fire. He burned with anger. He then swears that this wicked man must die. The phrase "as the Lord liveth" is the most solemn oath pronounced in the name of the reigning king (Genesis 42:15), a deity (Psalm 16:4), or the Lord Himself as we have here (Judges 8:19; 14:39; Deuteronomy 6:13). It is often used to show the importance of the statement or an irrevocable oath or pledge.

David avows that the rich man must pay a restitution of four lambs for the one he stole from the poor man according to the Law (Exodus 22:1). Further, however, he also demands the rich man's life. The Mosaic Law does not provide such hash penalty for property theft, though it does for kidnapping (Exodus 21:16). However, David probably saw this offence in that light—it is equivalent to kidnapping and murder. To David, the poor man deserved justice, and the rich man's behavior deserved restitution and death.

David then gives the reason the rich should pay with his life, "because he had no pity." This Hebrew word for having pity (*khamal*, khaw-**MALL**) also means showing compassion or sparing (from death). Even though David says the rich man had no *khamal*, that is exactly the word Nathan used for the man's action earlier in the story when he "spared" (v. 4) the animals from his own flock and instead took from the poor man. The rich man has pity for himself and his own possessions, but none for his neighbor. This is exactly David's offense. Not only did he take Uriah's wife; he also ordered Uriah killed and showed no compassion to spare him from David's snowballing sin. Ironically, David was pronouncing his own punishment not realizing he was the person the story was about. Indeed, what he did to Bathsheba and to Uriah deserved death (Leviticus 20:10; Deuteronomy 22:22–24).

It is interesting to note that things have not changed or improved much since Biblical times. The axiom, "the rich get richer, the poor gets poorer" is very much alive today. Injustice is still a common occurrence; the rich stealing from the poor is still a common phenomenon in our society. The rich still extort the poor and the needy; people in positions of authority use their office and position to steal from those who are less rich, and they are even celebrated. There is uninhibited injustice all over the world.

7 And Nathan said to David, Thou art the man. Thus saith the LORD God of Israel, I anointed thee king over Israel, and I delivered thee out of the hand of Saul; 8 And I gave thee thy master's house, and thy master's wives into thy bosom, and gave thee the house of Israel and of Judah; and if that had been too little, I would moreover have given unto thee such and such things.

The story reaches its climax when Nathan tells David, "Thou art the man." Through Nathan, the Lord states His case against David. The phrase "Thus saith the LORD God of Israel" signifies the authenticity of Nathan's message— the charge is directly from the very God whom David is familiar with—the Lord God of Israel. Nathan uses the Jewish personal name of God, Yahweh, who is also the God of Israel referring to the Lord's covenant relationship with Israel.

The Lord lays His charges against David. He reminds him of the Lord's goodness to him— He gave him everything he possessed and would have given more. The Lord anointed him king of Israel in place of Saul; the Lord protected

him when Saul sought his life. The Lord gave David Saul's palace, including his wives, as was the custom of the day. So David was at liberty to take his predecessor's wives. Scripture does not indicate this was a large harem to inherit as Saul had only one wife (1 Samuel 14:50) and one concubine (2 Samuel 3:7), but it was still more than was usual, especially since David already had two wives of his own by this point (1 Samuel 25:42–44).

In addition, the Lord has placed him over the house of Israel and Judah. As the king, David has everything in Israel and Judah at his disposal; he is given the whole nation. He has power to choose from among the daughters of Judah and Israel to take young virgins as wives if he wishes. If all this isn't enough, the Lord continues, "I would have given you more." Therefore, it doesn't make sense to steal and murder in order to cover sin.

9 Wherefore hast thou despised the commandment of the LORD, to do evil in his sight? thou hast killed Uriah the Hittite with the sword, and hast taken his wife to be thy wife, and hast slain him with the sword of the children of Ammon.

David is guilty of all charges. After stating His case, the Lord asks David a conscience–piercing question, "why?"—"Wherefore (why) hast thou despised the commandment of the LORD, to do evil in his sight?" The word "despised" is the Hebrew word *bazah* (baw-**ZAW**), which means to disesteem, disdain, contempt, or disrespect. By this, David had committed two serious sins.

First, he had forgotten the goodness of the Lord who gave him everything he had and would have given him more (vv. 7–8). Second, David had disrespected the Lord's commandment and treated it with contempt instead of upholding it, which means disregarding the Lord. This was the same sin Saul committed, which forced the Lord to take the kingdom from him and give to

David, whom the Lord called "a man after his own heart" (1 Samuel 13:14; Acts 13:22). David showed no regard for the Lord's commandment by coveting, committing adultery, bearing false witness, and committing murder. David had broken four of the Ten Commandants and thought he could get away with it. Notice that God lays the blame for Uriah's death at David's hand, even though another person held the sword that slew the Hittite.

Verses 10 to 12 contain the consequences of David's sin. There, the Lord shows that He is a just God, that every sin has its consequences, and that He is not a respecter of persons, whether a king or a commoner. Each one of the consequences pronounced against David for his sin against Uriah comes to pass. Because David murdered Uriah and took his wife: 1) Murder was constant in his household (2 Samuel 13:26–30; 1 Kings 2:23–25); 2) There was constant rebellion against him by his family (2 Samuel 15:13); 3) His wives were given to another in public (2 Samuel 16:20–23); and 4) David's first child by Bathsheba died (2 Samuel 12:18).

13 And David said unto Nathan, I have sinned against the LORD. And Nathan said unto David, The LORD also hath put away thy sin; thou shalt not die. 14 Howbeit, because by this deed thou hast given great occasion to the enemies of the LORD to blaspheme, the child also that is born unto thee shall surely die. 15 And Nathan departed unto his house. And the LORD struck the child that Uriah's wife bare unto David, and it was very sick.

After Nathan confronted David with his sin and its consequences, David confessed and said to Nathan, "I have sinned against the LORD." Unlike Saul who tried to give excuses for his disregard for the Law of the Lord (1 Samuel 13:22ff.), David did not try to justify his sin or blame anyone else. He readily admits his sin and confesses right away, acknowledging that it is the Lord he has sinned against. The substance of the confession is recorded as Psalm 51.

After David confesses, Nathan can tell him of God's forgiveness. David's sin is not only forgiven, but the Lord gracefully releases him from the customary death penalty for adultery and murder (Leviticus 20:10; 24:17, 21), the penalty which David himself pronounced on the "rich man" (v. 5). David experienced the joy of knowing his sin is forgiven (Psalm 23:1, 5; 51:8, 12). God shows here how He is gracious and shows mercy to those who genuinely repent of their sin.

Although, David is totally forgiven, he still has to bear the consequences for his action. Therefore, this firstborn son of David and Bathsheba shall die, Nathan pronounces. Here we encounter the essence of God's nature and attributes. He is gracious and merciful, yet He is still a righteous and just God. He executes justice and equity to all people, irrespective of who they are or the position they occupy. Every sin committed is against the Lord, as David acknowledges (Psalm 51:4). By his action, David has given God's enemies an occasion to blaspheme the Lord's name. Some have suggested that had the child lived, God's name would have been dishonored among Israel's pagan neighbors.

Even though David does not die for his sin, the child born to Bathsheba from David's sinful encounter does die. As we wrestle with this difficult event, we must remember two facts about God's involvement in David's life. Firstly, the Lord spared David's life because of His covenant promise to establish David's kingdom from his offspring (2 Samuel 7:11–12; 12:24–25). Secondly, the death of the child was not a judgment on the child being born out of wedlock, but a judgment against David for his sin. Every sin has its consequences. While God forgave David's sin, He did not negate its consequences.

Sources:

Keil and Delitzsch Commentary on the Old Testament: New Updated Edition. Electronic Database. Hendrickson Publishers, Inc., 1996.

Life Application Study Bible NIV. Carol Stream, Illinois: Tyndale House Publishers, Inc

New Exhaustive Strong's Numbers and Concordance with Expanded Greek–Hebrew Dictionary. Nashville, TN: Thomas Nelson, 2006.

Wiersbe, Warren W. *The Bible Exposition Commentary: Old Testament.* Elgin, IL: David C. Cook, 2004.

Say It Correctly

Uriah. yur–EYE–uh
Bathsheba. bath–SHEE–buh

Daily Bible Readings

MONDAY
David's Sin with Bathsheba
(2 Samuel 11:1–13)

TUESDAY
David Murders Bathsheba's Husband
(2 Samuel 11:14–27)

WEDNESDAY
Walk in the Light
(1 John 1:5–10)

THURSDAY
Create in Me a Clean Heart
(Psalm 51:1–14)

FRIDAY
Redemption Through Repentance
(Psalm 32)

SATURDAY
Christ, the Sacrifice for Our Sins
(1 John 2:1–11)

SUNDAY
Nathan Tells a Pointed Parable
(2 Samuel 12:1–9, 13–15)

Notes

Teaching Tips

Words You Should Know

A. Prepared (Ezra 7:10) *kun* (Heb.)—Established, firmly fixed, made ready

B. Seek (v. 10) *darash* (Heb.)—To ask or inquire of someone or something; to diligently study

Teacher Preparation

Unifying Principle—Restoring Law and Order. People sometimes face situations in which they fear others will oppose their efforts. What motivates people to behave benevolently toward others? God's hand was on Ezra, and he was able to return to Jerusalem in an effort to restore respect for God's Law.

A. Read the Bible Background and Devotional Reading.

B. Pray for your students and lesson clarity.

C. Read the lesson Scripture in multiple translations.

O—Open the Lesson

A. Begin the class with prayer.

B. Ask participants to recount a time they had to be a leader. Were they bold or timid? Did they have the backing of their superiors? Was the group they were leading prone to hostility or indifference? How did these factors affect their time as leader?

C. Have the students read the Aim for Change and the In Focus story.

D. Ask students how events like those in the story weigh on their hearts and how they can view these events from a faith perspective.

P—Present the Scriptures

A. Read the Focal Verses and discuss the Background and The People, Places, and Times sections.

B. Have the class share what Scriptures stand out for them and why, with particular emphasis on today's themes.

E—Explore the Meaning

A. Use In Depth or More Light on the Text to facilitate a deeper discussion of the lesson text.

B. Pose the questions in Search the Scriptures and Discuss the Meaning.

C. Discuss the Liberating Lesson and Application for Activation sections.

N—Next Steps for Application

A. Summarize the value of Bible education in church.

B. End class with a commitment to pray for church leaders who care for the daily practical matters of the church.

Worship Guide

For the Superintendent or Teacher
Theme: Ezra Seeks God's Law
Song: "How Firm a Foundation"

Ezra Seeks God's Law

Bible Background • EZRA 7:1–26
Printed Text • EZRA 7:1–10, 23–26 | Devotional Reading • 2 TIMOTHY 3:14–17

——————— Aim for Change ———————

By the end of this lesson, we will UNDERSTAND the historical and spiritual significance of Ezra's return to Jerusalem, VALUE how God works through various types of people to bring His plan to fruition, and THANK local leaders and teachers of God's Word.

——————— In Focus ———————

"Pastor, our church is gone," cried Deacon Jenkins. "The hurricane swept everything away; there's nothing left but the foundation."

Pastor Joel looked around. He saw what Deacon Jenkins saw: piles of rubble to the south of the building, furniture soaked by hammering rains, and plans for the church's 100th anniversary celebration put on an indefinite pause.

"Then, Deacon, let's get ready to rebuild. And I'm not talking about the building," said Pastor Joel. "I'm talking about rebuilding the faith of our community. We've got to build up everyone's faith in the goodness of God, despite what we see around us."

Deacon Jenkins could hardly see how. "Well, the school on Pine Hill was hardly touched," began Pastor Joel. "Let's see if we can have services there. We'll use the classrooms for Sunday School and have Wednesday Bible class and Friday prayer meeting there, too. But first, let's see if we can organize a community-wide prayer of thanksgiving in the school's auditorium soon. We must thank God that no lives were lost. One day, Deacon Jenkins, we'll not only have a church on this site, but a school where we can study God's Word and learn how to live it out in our lives."

"That's a pretty big vision," Deacon Jenkins observed.

"Yes, and we worship a pretty big God," Pastor Joel proclaimed.

Churches, communities, and families can experience losses that seem insurmountable to overcome. Name a Bible verse, spiritual song, or a sermon that offered encouragement, strength, and hope during a difficult life experience.

——————— Keep in Mind ———————

"For Ezra had prepared his heart to seek the law of the LORD, and to do it, and to teach in Israel statutes and judgments." (Ezra 7:10, KJV)

"This was because Ezra had determined to study and obey the Law of the LORD and to teach those decrees and regulations to the people of Israel." (Ezra 7:10, NLT)

Focal Verses

KJV **Ezra 7:1** Now after these things, in the reign of Artaxerxes king of Persia, Ezra the son of Seraiah, the son of Azariah, the son of Hilkiah,

2 The son of Shallum, the son of Zadok, the son of Ahitub,

3 The son of Amariah, the son of Azariah, the son of Meraioth,

4 The son of Zerahiah, the son of Uzzi, the son of Bukki,

5 The son of Abishua, the son of Phinehas, the son of Eleazar, the son of Aaron the chief priest:

6 This Ezra went up from Babylon; and he was a ready scribe in the law of Moses, which the LORD God of Israel had given: and the king granted him all his request, according to the hand of the LORD his God upon him.

7 And there went up some of the children of Israel, and of the priests, and the Levites, and the singers, and the porters, and the Nethinims, unto Jerusalem, in the seventh year of Artaxerxes the king.

8 And he came to Jerusalem in the fifth month, which was in the seventh year of the king.

9 For upon the first day of the first month began he to go up from Babylon, and on the first day of the fifth month came he to Jerusalem, according to the good hand of his God upon him.

10 For Ezra had prepared his heart to seek the law of the LORD, and to do it, and to teach in Israel statutes and judgments.

23 Whatsoever is commanded by the God of heaven, let it be diligently done for the house of the God of heaven: for why should there be wrath against the realm of the king and his sons?

24 Also we certify you, that touching any of the priests and Levites, singers, porters, Nethinims, or ministers of this house of God, it shall not be lawful to impose toll, tribute, or custom, upon them.

NLT **Ezra 7:1** Many years later, during the reign of King Artaxerxes of Persia, there was a man named Ezra. He was the son of Seraiah, son of Azariah, son of Hilkiah,

2 son of Shallum, son of Zadok, son of Ahitub,

3 son of Amariah, son of Azariah, son of Meraioth,

4 son of Zerahiah, son of Uzzi, son of Bukki,

5 son of Abishua, son of Phinehas, son of Eleazar, son of Aaron the high priest.

6 This Ezra was a scribe who was well versed in the Law of Moses, which the LORD, the God of Israel, had given to the people of Israel. He came up to Jerusalem from Babylon, and the king gave him everything he asked for, because the gracious hand of the LORD his God was on him.

7 Some of the people of Israel, as well as some of the priests, Levites, singers, gatekeepers, and Temple servants, traveled up to Jerusalem with him in the seventh year of King Artaxerxes' reign.

8 Ezra arrived in Jerusalem in August of that year.

9 He had arranged to leave Babylon on April 8, the first day of the new year, and he arrived at Jerusalem on August 4, for the gracious hand of his God was on him.

10 This was because Ezra had determined to study and obey the Law of the LORD and to teach those decrees and regulations to the people of Israel.

23 "Be careful to provide whatever the God of heaven demands for his Temple, for why should we risk bringing God's anger against the realm of the king and his sons?

24 I also decree that no priest, Levite, singer, gatekeeper, Temple servant, or other worker in this Temple of God will be required to pay tribute, customs, or tolls of any kind.

25 And thou, Ezra, after the wisdom of thy God, that is in thine hand, set magistrates and judges, which may judge all the people that are beyond the river, all such as know the laws of thy God; and teach ye them that know them not.

26 And whosoever will not do the law of thy God, and the law of the king, let judgment be executed speedily upon him, whether it be unto death, or to banishment, or to confiscation of goods, or to imprisonment.

25 And you, Ezra, are to use the wisdom your God has given you to appoint magistrates and judges who know your God's laws to govern all the people in the province west of the Euphrates River. Teach the law to anyone who does not know it.

26 Anyone who refuses to obey the law of your God and the law of the king will be punished immediately, either by death, banishment, confiscation of goods, or imprisonment."

The People, Places, and Times

Rebuilding Jerusalem. Ezra and Nehemiah both chronicle the rebuilding of Jerusalem after the return from exile. The book of Ezra starts with those returning under the leadership of Zerubbabel with the patronage of King Cyrus the Great (Ezra 1:5–7). Their first order of business was to rebuild the altar at the site of the ruined Temple (3:3). Soon after, they began rebuilding the Temple itself (3:8). Outside agitators, however, kept them from this work for the rest of Cyrus' reign (4:5). During the reign of the next king, Darius, the prophets Haggai and Zachariah (whose books contain their calls to work) encouraged the people to work on the Temple again (5:1–2). Agitators again tried to stop them, but Zerubbabel insisted Cyrus had sanctioned the rebuilding efforts (5:17). Darius was convinced and again put imperial funds and patronage behind rebuilding the Temple (6:14). It was completed in time to celebrate the Passover that year (6:15, 19).

Having completed the altar and the Temple, the work in Jerusalem turned to the walls. In reign of Darius' successor, Xerxes, little could be accomplished again because of Israel's enemies (Ezra 4:6). When Artaxerxes succeeded Xerxes, however, they began to build the walls again. Leaders in the other people groups surrounding Israel warned Artaxerxes that if Jerusalem's walls were restored, there would

surely be rebellion (vv. 12–16). Artaxerxes did not want to take that chance, and the half-built walls were destroyed (v. 23). This is where Nehemiah's account begins. He is distraught about Jerusalem's lack of walls and convinces the king to send him with men and money to see to the protection of the Israelite's renewed capital city (Nehemiah 2:2–8). Through many setbacks and much opposition, Nehemiah leads the people to finish rebuilding Jerusalem's walls. Once that is accomplished, Ezra himself reads the Law to the assembled people, and they rededicate themselves to honoring the full commands of God (Nehemiah 8:2–3).

Background

The Babylonian captivity of the people of Israel ended with the defeat of the Babylonian Empire by King Cyrus of Persia in 539 BC. Cyrus allowed many conquered people to return to their homelands and to their forms of worship. This was a strategic move by the Persian Empire meant to gain loyalty from formerly exiled peoples, and it established imperial outposts that buffered the empire's capital from invaders. In 538 BC, a group of exiles, led by Zerubbabel, returned to Jerusalem. They entered a demolished city and started to put the pieces of their city and their heritage back together. This group rebuilt the Temple. A second major group arrived from Babylon in

458 BC, led by Ezra. With the backing of the next Persian king, Artaxerxes, Ezra set out to return the people to the laws found in the Torah, the first five books of the Hebrew Scriptures. Ezra was a contemporary of Nehemiah who led the rebuilding of the walls around Jerusalem. Ezra's focus was on establishing the Torah as the governing laws that would inform how this re-emerging city would conduct their daily lives.

What are some reasons people give for returning to places of devastation and loss and deciding to rebuild?

At-A-Glance

1. Godly Heritage (Ezra 7:1–5)
2. Personal Commitment (vv. 6–10)
3. The Favor of God and Man (vv. 23–26)

In Depth

1. Godly Heritage (Ezra 7:1–5)

Ezra had a priestly pedigree. He could fill in the names on his family tree all the way down to its roots in Aaron, the first high priest. Handed down to him would have been the history, religious instructions and cultural practices of his people. He learned of the Promised Land and of God's promise to return the exiled to that land.

His heritage inspired him, and his occupation as a scribe educated him. He could reproduce texts, those of the Babylonians as well as the narratives of his own people. Being a scribe called for more than merely copying words. A scribe also had to have a profound understanding of the words he copied and become qualified to interpret and teach what was written. Ezra was just such a scribe and became an important link in the long line of individuals who preserved the history and religious life of a people and the works and ways of their God.

What are the benefits and responsibilities of having a godly heritage?

2. Personal Commitment (vv. 6–10)

Though Ezra came from an impressive lineage and had a noteworthy occupation, he possessed something that was far more significant. Ezra had an abiding love for God's Word. He was an ardent student of the Torah and wanted to bring to his people a greater understanding of and obedience to the teachings of God's Law. It wasn't enough that the Temple had been rebuilt. From his studies, Ezra realized that the hearts of his people needed to return to God's Word.

Ezra's passion for God's Word rallied the support of others to join him in the journey. These individuals would be part of the leadership team that would conduct worship and praise to God. The risks inherent in the four-month journey did not deter the travelers, especially Ezra. Ezra desired that the Word of God would once again flow from the Temple and into the lives of God's people so they would love, know, and follow the ways of God.

In what ways could your occupation be used to spread God's Word?

3. The Favor of God and Man (vv. 23–26)

God honored the desire of Ezra's heart, giving him favor with Artaxerxes, the king. A royal decree helped to secure safe passage. It also ordered the leaders of the provinces that Ezra would travel through to supply all of Ezra's material needs. The king exhibited a holy reverence for the laws of God and the person who taught them, Ezra. The king also noticed that God's laws gave Ezra wisdom, making him a person of integrity. Such a leader would govern well and make just laws. Ezra's devotion to studying, obeying, and teaching God's Word made him a person with godly influence.

How might your knowledge of Scripture influence your community, nation, or the world?

Search the Scriptures

1. Why did the king show such generous favor to Ezra (Ezra 7:6)?

2. Name the individuals who would work in the Temple. Why did the king exempt them from paying taxes (Ezra 7:24)?

Discuss the Meaning

Before the people of Israel were exiled to Babylon, their nation was a sovereign theocracy, the Law of God was the law of the land. On Ezra's return to his homeland, it was a small portion of the Persian Empire. While Ezra was charged with restoring the laws of the forebearers in his ancestral home, he also had a mandate to institute the rules of the Persian Empire (Ezra 7:26).

1. Did Ezra face any conflicts because of this dual responsibility? Explain.

2. What are some challenges that people of faith can face if their faith and the laws of the land are in conflict?

Liberating Lesson

The First African Baptist Church in Savannah, Georgia, was one of the first congregations formed by the enslaved people brought to America from Africa. This church dates back to 1773, its members witnessed the Revolutionary and Civil Wars, it was a stop on the Underground Railroad, and it organized the first Sunday School for African Americans in 1826. In 1930, it had more than 2,000 members. Its commitment to its location and its people has been an inspiration to all who have visited this National Historic Landmark.

How is your family or church recording its history and its godly legacy in your community? In what ways can the history of your family or church be an inspiration to your community and nation?

Application for Activation

Having a working knowledge of biblical themes, narratives, and history is crucial to understanding world history, and more specifically an understanding of the people who founded our country. The American countryside is dotted with the names of places pulled from the Bible. The motivations of early European and African American settlers were often based on whom they identified with in biblical stories. What are some ways a church can help to enhance the biblical literacy of the children and adults in its congregation? How can congregations make biblical literacy available outside the doors of their churches?

Follow the Spirit

What God wants me to do:

_____

_____

_____

_____

_____

Remember Your Thoughts

Special insights I have learned:

_____

_____

_____

_____

_____

More Light on the Text
Ezra 7:1–10, 23–26

1 Now after these things, in the reign of Artaxerxes king of Persia, Ezra the son of Seraiah, the son of Azariah, the son of Hilkiah, 2 The son of Shallum, the son of Zadok, the son of Ahitub,

Ezra 7 picks up after the returning exiles under Zerubbabel's leadership have rebuilt the altar and the Temple. After that, Ezra knows it is time to reestablish clear teachings from God's Law. He decides to leave Babylon (now the capital of the Persian Empire), and King Artaxerxes gives him permission to go with anyone who wishes to go with him, to appoint leadership positions within Israel, and also gives him funds to pay for sacrifices to God at the new Temple in Jerusalem.

This is the reader's first introduction to Ezra himself, and the first thing we learn about him is his impressive priestly heritage. Ezra begins his family tree with the last priestly ancestor who had lived in Israel. Each of Ezra's grandfathers and great-grandfathers listed here served as high priests in Israel before the Exile. They were men who helped guide Israel back to God during the reforms of Hezekiah's and Josiah's reigns.

Hilkiah (v. 1) was the high priest who found the copy of the Law in the Temple that launched Josiah's heartfelt reforms. This is likely the same text that Ezra would read before the people during his own reforms. This Hilkiah was also likely the father of the famous prophet Jeremiah, who wept for his nation's neglect of God. Shallum is possibly the husband of the prophetess Huldah, who foresaw that Israel would fall after the time of Josiah.

3 The son of Amariah, the son of Azariah, the son of Meraioth, 4 The son of Zerahiah, the son of Uzzi, the son of Bukki, 5 The son of Abishua, the son of Phinehas, the son of Eleazar, the son of Aaron the chief priest:

Between Meraioth, son of Zerahiah and Azariah, who fathers Amariah, Ezra seems to skip back six generations. This is made easier by the fact that the names Amariah, Ahitub, Zadok, and Azariah are all repeated in this section of the family list (1 Chronicles 6:7–14). Just as families do today, Ezra's family named their children after previous generations. Even though modern genealogists would never make a practice of leaving out any generations, the Hebrew language allowed the words "son" and "father" to mean "descendant" or "ancestor" as freely as they mean relations within one generation (cf. 2 Samuel 9:7).

Ezra is the likely author of both this genealogy and the genealogy in 1 Chronicles 6, and he makes different records for different literary purposes. In 1 Chronicles, he is making a full list of all the members of the priestly families. This means he must include every generation. Here in Ezra 7, he is introducing himself and giving his priestly pedigree. His audience does not need all 24 generations between him and Aaron to know Ezra is a trustworthy source. He only recounts those famous for reforms in the late Israelite monarchy, and those famous for establishing correct worship at Sinai and in the Promised Land.

Phinehas is famous for stopping a plague that was ravishing Israel because of their disobedience (Numbers 25:7–13). This deed is even remembered in holy song (Psalm 106:30). As reward for Phinehas' zeal, God promised that his line would forever be priests. A thousand years later, Ezra is part of the fulfillment of that promise.

Eleazar is Aaron's third son, but after God kills the older sons, Nadab and Abihu, for making an improper sacrifice, Eleazar rises to be Aaron's heir (Leviticus 10). He helps purify Israel after the rebellion of the sons of Korah (Numbers 16) and continues to work closely with his uncle, Moses, to lead the people during their forty years in the wilderness. God appoints Eleazar to work with Joshua to divide the land of Canaan fairly among the Israelites (Numbers 34:17).

All of Ezra's famous priestly ancestry of course goes back to Aaron, the first priest of Yahweh, who stood alongside Moses as he confronted Pharaoh, guided the people out of Israel, led the people in worship at Mt. Sinai, and ministered to them throughout the forty years in the wilderness. Aaron, like his brother Moses, did not get to enter the Promised Land, but is forever remembered as one of the most influential leaders in Israelite history.

6 This Ezra went up from Babylon; and he was a ready scribe in the law of Moses, which the LORD God of Israel had given: and the king granted him all his request, according to the hand of the LORD his God upon him.

Ezra is a scribe (Heb. *safar*, saw–**FAR**), a word with roots meaning to number or recount. Scribes would be charged with keeping exact records of censuses, tallies, or events, and with reporting on the same. To be a scribe of the Law meant that Ezra could be trusted to flawlessly reproduce a Torah manuscript. Such an extremely intimate knowledge of the text meant he could also help explain and teach the meaning of the Law to others. Ezra is further described as a "ready" (Heb. *mahir*, maw–**HERE**) scribe, meaning he was quick and skillful in his role, working efficiently and effectively with his deep knowledge of the Torah.

Ezra comments on the hand of the Lord being upon him or upon Nehemiah many times as he recounts their resettlement of Jerusalem (Ezra 8:18, 31; Nehemiah 2:8, 18). When the hand of the Lord is on them, they are successful in all they do. Ezra explains to the king why God sets His hand on people: "The hand of our God is upon all them for good that seek him" (from

Ezra 8:22). Those who seek (Heb. *baqash*, baw–**KOSH**) for something are not always physically searching their query, but are requesting or asking for it to be where they are, often as a matter of life and death. The Lord places His almighty hand on those who are asking to receive God's presence.

Often in Scripture, the hand of the Lord being on someone means they are being punished (Exodus 9:3; Deuteronomy 2:15). This is perhaps why sometimes Ezra clarifies that it is the "good hand" of the Lord at work (see verse 9 below). The hand of God is at all times supremely powerful, and will not be put off. Whether we are joyful about our divine work or not, the hand of the Lord guides us, pushing His followers into action and clearing obstacles from their path.

7 And there went up some of the children of Israel, and of the priests, and the Levites, and the singers, and the porters, and the Nethinims, unto Jerusalem, in the seventh year of Artaxerxes the king.

Ezra made the 900-mile journey from Babylon to Jerusalem with a large company of people, as was usual for the day. The road between major capitals would be watched by brigands, so large groups provided protection. Additionally, travel would be faster with fewer stops at oases or settlements along the way, and large groups can carry more supplies with them.

In this caravan were common folk ("some of the children of Israel") and many Temple workers. All priests were Levites (from the tribe of Levi), but not all Levites were priests. Some Levites' jobs were more in the administration of the Temple, guarding the gates, or caring for Temple furnishings. Nethinims (from Heb. *natan*, naw–**TON**, "to give") were a servant class "given" to service at the Temple. This word is only used in Ezra, Nehemiah, and 1 and 2 Chronicles, implying it was a position only established after the return from exile (when Ezra wrote those books).

Persian records tell us Artaxerxes began his rule in the year 465 BC by our modern calendar, so the seventh year of his reign would be 458 BC. However, sometimes nations in the ancient Near East counted a king's first year as his "ascension year" and did not start numbering the years of his reign until the second year. If this tabulation includes an ascension year, Ezra's journey was in 457 BC.

8 And he came to Jerusalem in the fifth month, which was in the seventh year of the king. 9 For upon the first day of the first month began he to go up from Babylon, and on the first day of the fifth month came he to Jerusalem, according to the good hand of his God upon him.

"The first day of the first month" here does not refer to January 1 on our calendar. The "first month" as reckoned by the Jewish calendar is called Nisan and corresponds to our March or April. By combining surviving information about Artaxerxes' reign and the year Ezra notes (v. 7), scholars can deduce that the dates of Ezra's travels were April 8, 458 (or 457 as noted above) BC through August 4 of the same year.

Figuring out dates on ancient calendars can easily get confusing or boring. However, these specific dates can help the modern reader remember that our sacred texts are historical documents. The Bible is not based on a single revelation from a single self-proclaimed prophet. It is the cultural history of God's people, written down over the course of a thousand years, from the Exodus from Egypt to the return from Babylon. The various books of Scripture were written down because the events they relate really took place at a particular time and in a particular place. This particular event of Ezra departing from Babylon took place on April 8, 458 BC.

10 For Ezra had prepared his heart to seek the law of the LORD, and to do it, and to teach in Israel statutes and judgments.

Ezra is so revered in Jewish history that he is considered a second Moses for the people of Israel, since he introduced the Law to them again as they reentered the Promised Land, just as Moses had instructed the people before they entered the Promised Land for the first time. He is not celebrated solely because of his parentage, nor because of his high position in the Persian court. He does not do all he does for Israel simply because he figured it would be a good idea. He is deeply moved in his soul to establish God's holy Law again at the newly reconstructed Temple because he is prepared (Heb. *kun*, **KOON**), meaning firmly fixed in his mind, to do three things: to seek God's Law, to do it, and to teach it to God's people.

To "seek" (Heb. *darash*, daw-**ROSH**) the Lord's Law means to study it diligently, to inquire of it how one should act. It is a close synonym to *baqash*, discussed above. In fact, the two words are often paired (Psalm 105:4; Jeremiah 29:13) to intensify the notion of a person doggedly seeking out what they wish to find. The thing Ezra seeks with such passion is the will of God as revealed in His Law. When he finds it, he will also "do" it (Heb. *'ashah*, aw-**SHAW**). It is no good simply to know God's Word; we must act on it. James, the half-brother of Jesus, makes this clear when he says, "be ye doers of the word, and not hearers only, deceiving your own selves" (James 1:22). Ezra is not content to merely study the Word. Nor is he content to simply do it himself. Ezra has also firmly fixed his mind to "teach" (Heb. *lamad*, law-**MOD**) the Law to the people. Ezra knows, as all Christians should know, that God's way is not just a nice way for him to follow, but the best way for anyone to follow. Today, we ought not to be content to let people practice whatever spirituality they wish as long as we are allowed to practice Christianity in peace. We know Jesus is the Way—the only Way, and the best Way. Like Ezra, we should teach others the Way of God, with gentleness and wisdom.

23 Whatsoever is commanded by the God of heaven, let it be diligently done for the house of the God of heaven: for why should there be wrath against the realm of the king and his sons? 24 Also we certify you, that touching any of the priests and Levites, singers, porters, Nethinims, or ministers of this house of God, it shall not be lawful to impose toll, tribute, or custom, upon them.

Here we read the words of King Artaxerxes to Ezra in a letter he gave to the scribe granting him permission to return to Jerusalem with any Israelites who wished to join him, and granting him large sums of money to beautify the Temple and make sacrifices once he got there. Artaxerxes' interest in sacrificing in Jerusalem is a clear indication of the differences between Babylonia and Persia. While the Babylonians saw conquering other nations as a sign of their gods conquering the other nation's gods (or God), the Persians were happy to let cultural groups within their empire practice their native religions. The Persians hoped this would foster good relations between the Persian government and the foreign gods, or at least between the government and the foreign people they now ruled.

Babylonian policy of dealing with conquered nations and cultures is seen in the book of Daniel. Babylonians took the wealthiest and the aristocrats (who would have the most means and inclination to rebel) from their newly conquered territory and forced them to assimilate into Babylonian culture. This is what happens to Daniel and his three friends and why it is so noteworthy that they refuse to eat the king's food (Daniel 1). The rest of the population, however, was left alone in their original land with either no leadership or with Babylonian leadership enforcing Babylonian culture and religion. The Babylonians saw their ability to conquer another nation as proof that their god was superior, and so they discouraged worship of the gods of conquered territories, including Israel's Yahweh.

The Persian Empire worked differently. They preferred to conquer a nation and when their people were in charge, allow the conquered nations to be fairly unchanged. Persia still required tribute and military support from the new territory, but they allowed local religions to continue. This made the people less inclined to insurrection and helped the Persian nation flourish for many more years than the Babylonians did. The polytheism of the Persians figured it was better to assimilate and not anger the gods of foreign nations rather than try to conquer them and their people. Even though Artaxerxes did not honor or follow Yahweh, he did not want to anger Him against his country, asking "Why should there be wrath?" between them.

To show how he was humoring the Israelites and their religion, the king did not exact taxes from those who worked at the Temple. Neither "toll, tribute, or custom" would be taken from them (v. 24). Artaxerxes wanted the Israelites to be happy by practicing their own ancestral religion so that they would be less likely to rise up against him. He did this with tax breaks, just as a modern politician would bargain to obtain tax breaks for their special interest groups.

25 And thou, Ezra, after the wisdom of thy God, that is in thine hand, set magistrates and judges, which may judge all the people that are beyond the river, all such as know the laws of thy God; and teach ye them that know them not.

As was Persian practice, they let conquered nations retain much of their usual command structure. The Persian king had hand-selected both Ezra and Nehemiah to be their regents in Israel, so he feels safe in letting these formerly suppressed people select their own leadership. Artaxerxes also stipulates that these new magistrates and judges should be those who "know the laws of thy God," even going so far as to order Ezra to "teach ye them that know them not." While many Jewish citizens were living in Babylon, it is possible King Artaxerxes familiarized himself with Jewish Law and found it to be a good set of instructions for a people group. If he did not have a favorable opinion of Moses' Law code, he would have ordered that the Jews adopt the Persian laws even when in their old land.

It is also possible Artaxerxes did not know the Law of Moses himself, but only knew Ezra for the wise teacher he was. If that was the case, Artaxerxes' entire outlook on Jewish Law was based on the upstanding conduct of one of his administrators. Christians must remember this possibility today. As the saying goes, "You might be the only Bible your neighbor ever reads."

Readers must remember that Artaxerxes himself does not practice Judaism. He has not given himself to belief in Yahweh. Still, sometimes even pagans following their own pagan laws and traditions can be used to the glory of God. He who makes "all things work together for good to them that love Him" (Romans 8:28) protects and prospers His people by all means, even the actions of unbelievers.

26 And whosoever will not do the law of thy God, and the law of the king, let judgment be executed speedily upon him, whether it be unto death, or to banishment, or to confiscation of goods, or to imprisonment.

Artaxerxes stipulates that the Israelites should abide not only by "the law of thy God" but also by "the law of the king" as well. This is where problems are bound to arise. God's laws are not human laws. What do we do when our country's laws are at odds with Scripture? Daniel and his friends show us two examples of how to hold onto God's Law without compromising. First, they refuse to eat the king's food, but negotiate an alternative that is pleasing all around. Second, in the case of Nebuchadnezzar's gold idol, the friends boldly proclaim they will follow God's Law even unto death. Their dedication and salvation from the fiery furnace deeply effect the foreign king, forcing him to recognize the power of God.

The king of Persia lets the Israelites practice their religion, even to the point of executions. Some empires did not give that right to their client states. This is why the Jewish leaders needed Pontius Pilate to order Jesus' execution rather than just stoning Him by themselves when they accused Him of blasphemy. King Artaxerxes trusts Ezra enough that he will even allow Israel a full exercise of their own laws. Again we see the benefit of Christians being citizens of excellent repute, especially among non-Christians. Daniel and his friends would not have had the chances the Babylonian king gave them if they had been rabble-rousers. Today, whether they be our boss, landlady, or elected official, Christians will be given more latitude from the unbelievers who command us if they know us to be people of good, honest, and wise character.

Sources:
Brenner, Michael. *A Short History of the Jews*. Princeton, NJ: Princeton University Press, 2010.
Brueggemann, Walter. *An Introduction to the Old Testament, The Canon and Christian Imagination*. Louisville, KY: Westminster John Knox Press, 2003.
Comfort, Philip, ed. and Elwell, Walter A., ed. *The Complete Book of Who's Who in the Bible*. Castle Books, New York, NY: 2014.
Life Application Study Bible, New Living Translation. Wheaton, IL: Tyndale House Publishers, Inc., 1988 – 1991, 1993, 1996.
The Jesus Bible NIV Edition, Grand Rapids, MI: Zondervan, 2016.
Puchner, Martin. *The Written World, The Power of Stories to Shape People, History, Civilization*. New York, NY: Random House. 2017.

Say It Correctly

Artaxerxes. ARE–tah–ZERK–zees.
Zerubbabel. zeh–ROO–bah–bell.
Nethinims. NEH–thin–eems.

Daily Bible Readings

MONDAY
God's Law Is Perfect
(Psalm 19)

TUESDAY
Meditate Continuously on the Law
(Joshua 1:1–9)

WEDNESDAY
Obey God's Commandments
(1 John 3:18–24)

THURSDAY
Teach Me Your Statues
(Psalm 119:1–16)

FRIDAY
How I Love Your Law!
(Psalm 119:97–112)

SATURDAY
The King's Letter to Ezra
(Ezra 7:11–22)

SUNDAY
Ezra Leads the Exiles Home
(Ezra 7:1–10, 23–26)

Notes

Black History

Teaching Tips

Words You Should Know

A. Pervert (Job 8:3) *'avath* (Heb.)—To falsify, bend, subvert, or make crooked

B. Evil doer (v. 20) *hanep* (Heb.)—A hypocrite

Teacher Preparation

Unifying Principle—Enduring False Charges. People tend to rationalize why bad things happen. How do people respond when they are faced with tragedy—natural disasters, birth defects, atrocious crimes, etc.? Job remained faithful to God after several tragic events in his life, even while his friends questioned God's justice and Job's innocence.

A. Read the Bible Background and Devotional Reading.

B. Pray for your students and lesson clarity.

C. Read the lesson Scripture in multiple translations.

O—Open the Lesson

A. Begin the class with prayer.

B. Discuss the view of the church held by unbelievers participants know. Are they more likely to view the church as a place of condemnation or a place of restoration? What can we do to be seen as the latter?

C. Have the students read Aim for Change and the In Focus story.

D. Ask students how events like those in the story weigh on their hearts and how they can view these events from a faith perspective.

P—Present the Scriptures

A. Read the Focal Verses and discuss the Background and The People, Places, and Times sections.

B. Have the class share what Scriptures stand out for them and why, with particular emphasis on today's themes.

E—Explore the Meaning

A. Use In Depth or More Light on the Text to facilitate a deeper discussion of the lesson text.

B. Pose the questions in Search the Scriptures and Discuss the Meaning.

C. Discuss the Liberating Lesson and Application for Activation sections.

N—Next Steps for Application

A. Summarize the value of avoiding easy explanations of every instance of suffering.

B. End class with a commitment to pray for empathy when encountering others' suffering.

Worship Guide

For the Superintendent or Teacher
Theme: Bildad Misunderstands
God's Justice
Song: "Jesus, Friend of Sinners"

271

Bildad Misunderstands God's Justice

Bible Background • JOB 8
Printed Text • JOB 8:1–10, 20–22 | Devotional Reading • JOB 37:5–7

—————— Aim for Change ——————

By the end of this lesson, we will UNDERSTAND Bildad's response to Job's suffering, DISCERN carefully when others misinterpret God's ways, and GROW closer to God and live faithfully in God's just ways.

————— In Focus —————

Angela had been battling cancer for over six months. After so many sessions of chemotherapy, she was a shell of her former self. Her husband, Tim, could barely hold himself together as he watched his wife suffer. He often looked at her and wondered how she continued to be optimistic and keep her faith in God. She still prayed and thanked God every day. Since the diagnosis, they had not missed one Sunday morning church service. Tim endured it, although the hope and optimism that he experienced from Angela and the people at church grated on him. How could God do this to my wife? he asked himself.

One day while driving home, Angela began quietly humming a praise and worship song they had heard in church. Tim couldn't take it anymore. Frustrated, he asked her, "How can you sing a song like that in a time like this? Why praise a God who does this to you?"

Angela was shocked by his question but then calmly collected herself. "Songs like that were made for times like this," she responded. "I know I've followed the Lord as best I can. I know I've seen His blessings in my life. I'm not fond of this cancer, but if that's how God chooses to take me home, so be it. I've still seen Him do plenty of good, and I'm still going to praise Him for it."

How do you respond when you don't understand God's plan?

—————— Keep in Mind ——————

"Then answered Bildad the Shuhite, and said, How long wilt thou speak these things? and how long shall the words of thy mouth be like a strong wind?" (Job 8:1–2, KJV)

"Then Bildad the Shuhite replied to Job: 'How long will you go on like this? You sound like a blustering wind.'" (Job 8:1–2, NLT)

Focal Verses

KJV **Job 8:1** Then answered Bildad the Shuhite, and said,

2 How long wilt thou speak these things? and how long shall the words of thy mouth be like a strong wind?

3 Doth God pervert judgment? or doth the Almighty pervert justice?

4 If thy children have sinned against him, and he have cast them away for their transgression;

5 If thou wouldest seek unto God betimes, and make thy supplication to the Almighty;

6 If thou wert pure and upright; surely now he would awake for thee, and make the habitation of thy righteousness prosperous.

7 Though thy beginning was small, yet thy latter end should greatly increase.

8 For enquire, I pray thee, of the former age, and prepare thyself to the search of their fathers:

9 (For we are but of yesterday, and know nothing, because our days upon earth are a shadow:)

10 Shall not they teach thee, and tell thee, and utter words out of their heart?

20 Behold, God will not cast away a perfect man, neither will he help the evil doers:

21 Till he fill thy mouth with laughing, and thy lips with rejoicing.

22 They that hate thee shall be clothed with shame; and the dwelling place of the wicked shall come to nought.

NLT **Job 8:1** Then Bildad the Shuhite replied to Job:

2 "How long will you go on like this? You sound like a blustering wind.

3 Does God twist justice? Does the Almighty twist what is right?

4 Your children must have sinned against him, so their punishment was well deserved.

5 But if you pray to God and seek the favor of the Almighty,

6 and if you are pure and live with integrity, he will surely rise up and restore your happy home.

7 And though you started with little, you will end with much.

8 Just ask the previous generation. Pay attention to the experience of our ancestors.

9 For we were born but yesterday and know nothing. Our days on earth are as fleeting as a shadow.

10 But those who came before us will teach you. They will teach you the wisdom of old.

20 But look, God will not reject a person of integrity, nor will he lend a hand to the wicked.

21 He will once again fill your mouth with laughter and your lips with shouts of joy.

22 Those who hate you will be clothed with shame, and the home of the wicked will be destroyed."

[handwritten: Is. 59: 4]

[handwritten: parallizism 2 questions same meaning]

The People, Places, and Times

Theodicy. Why do bad things happen to good people? Does God not care enough to help people? If He cares, why can't He stop the bad things? Is God not just? Does He not have enough power to uphold His justice? These questions have long plagued humanity. When discussed in philosophical or theological circles, the topic is called theodicy (from Greek *theos*, God and *dike*, justice).

Some cultures in Job's time believed their gods simply did not care about the doings of lowly mortals. Others held that people would often anger a god without knowing it, but the proper catchall atonement sacrifice would appease them. Job insists that Yahweh cares for His people and has revealed Himself to His people. We can honestly examine our minds and our actions and know for certain if we have sinned against God. Job is confident that his friend is wrong, but he still does not understand God's actions fully.

Background

Job was a man of great wealth who suddenly found himself losing everything, even his children. This sudden loss was perplexing to Job because he had always been upright and blameless, a God-fearing man (Job 1:1). He continued to worship and praise God even after such a great loss (Job 1:20–22). Rather than blame God for his suffering, Job simply mourns and seeks the council of friends. But his friends just couldn't figure out what Job might have done that was so terrible that God had brought all this suffering down on him.

At-A-Glance

1. God Is Perfectly Just
(Job 8:1–3)
2. A Just God Will Punish Sin (v. 4)
3. A Just God Will Bless the Obedient
(vv. 5–10)
4. A Just God Will Restore the Repentant
(vv. 20–22)

In Depth

1. God Is Perfectly Just (Job 8:1–3)

Chapter 8 opens with Job's friend Bildad expressing exasperation at Job's insistence of his innocence (Job 6:24) and questioning God's justice (Job 6:29). Bildad pleads with Job to acknowledge that God is perfectly just and would never do anything that is unjust (v. 1–3). To this point Bildad is absolutely correct in his arguments. God is perfectly just in all He does.

This truth is affirmed dozens of times in Scripture. Although Job did not have a Bible, he apparently had been taught by his forefathers that this just God rewarded those who are faithful and obedient with many blessings, large families, land and wealth. Since Job had all those things, he thought he had favor with God. We can empathize with Job for questioning how a just God could have taken all those blessings away! God's justice is difficult to see or comprehend when we feel that we have been wronged and when we suffer loss. Job turned to his friends at this difficult time.

Where do you turn when things go wrong?

2. A Just God Will Punish Sin (v. 4)

As was common in Old Testament times, Job's friends all seemed to firmly believe a certain theology which we now call retribution theology. This theology, which is partially upheld in Scripture (Deuteronomy 30:16–18; Proverbs 3:33, 13:25; Psalm 35:17), holds that God deals with people immediately based on their behaviors. If you obey God, you will be blessed. If you sin, you will suffer. Sin was the only logical explanation for all suffering. Job agonized over what he had done to deserve his suffering. His friends weren't much help. They insisted he must have done something really terrible. Bildad didn't stop there. In verse 4 he says that even Job's children must have sinned and got what they deserved! Imagine how Job must have felt hearing that!

Was Bildad being helpful to his hurting friend? Was Job right in thinking that God was punishing him and his children for their sin?

3. A Just God Will Bless the Obedient (vv. 5–10)

Bildad reminds Job that God will restore Job to his former blessed state if he will return to his life of integrity and purity. Retributive theology says that God's justice is immediate, and goes both ways. If you are suffering, you must have sinned. If you stop sinning and return to God, you will be blessed again. For Bildad, the explanation of Job's suffering was simple, and the solution was just as simple. Job must have sinned, and Job needed to turn away from his sin and turn back to God.

Do you understand from Scripture that God's justice is immediate yet reversible?

4. A Just God Will Restore the Repentant (vv. 20–22)

Bildad continues his argument that Job just needs to repent and return to God, and God will immediately restore his good fortunes. By reading the rest of the book of Job, we find that this is exactly what happened! Even though Job's initial suffering is not from sin, Job does eventually sin by haughtily demanding an explanation from God. When he repents of this and submits himself to God's wisdom, he is blessed. Does this story teach us that God is truly a God of retributive and immediate justice? This is the challenge of Job. From Job we learn that God means what He says, that the wages of sin is death, but obedience leads to blessings. But it does not explain all suffering. Sometimes bad things happen to good people and we never learn why. God never told Job why He had allowed the man to suffer.

How often do we cry out, "Why me, Lord?" How should we respond to suffering or what we perceive as injustice?

Search the Scriptures

Read Job 8:4, John 9:1–3, and Romans 6:23. What singular message do we take away from these verses? Discuss how the penalty of sin has not changed, but the way God deals with the sinner has. Read Job 8:20–21 and Romans 3:21–26. How does the promise of Job's restoration, and the gift of salvation by faith demonstrate God's justice?

Discuss the Meaning

It is easy to fall into thinking that God blesses us because we're good and punishment comes for some specific sin. However, this understanding does not allow for God's grace. Because of Jesus' completed work of redemption, namely His paying the price for our sins (death), we now live in the age of grace. The wages of sin is still death, but by grace through faith, we can all receive the gift of eternal life. How does this knowledge affect your attitude toward sin?

Liberating Lesson

The book of Job does not explain the reason for all suffering. Nor does Jesus' explanation of why the man was born blind in John 9:3. What Jesus seems to be telling us is that sometimes we just won't understand, yet we have to trust that all things will somehow work to His glory and our good. While we are tempted to seek answers for the reason for suffering, what things should we ask of God instead when faced with suffering or injustice?

Application for Activation

While reading the book of Job, we immediately feel empathy for Job. When we see someone sick or hurting, as Christians we want to comfort them and help them. But we don't always know what to say or do. We can learn a lot from Job's three friends. They started out doing the thing that is often needed most. They spent seven days with him, not saying a word (Job 2:11–13). This may be the greatest lesson we can learn from this wisdom book of Job. Often this is what is needed most by those who are suffering. They just need a friend who will sit with them, mourn with them, comfort them. This week look for a chance to just give love, consolation, and physical comfort such as a warm meal, rather than unwelcomed advice, judgment, and opinions.

Follow the Spirit

What God wants me to do:

_____

_____

_____

_____

Remember Your Thoughts

Special insights I have learned:

_____

_____

_____

_____

_____

More Light on the Text

Job 8:1–10, 20–22

Speaking the truth is important, but saying it in love is most important. Criticism should always be given to help the other person, not harm them. In this chapter, Job's friend Bildad, a traditionalist, did not understand that. Not only did he offer lousy advice to his suffering companion, but he did it in the most unloving way possible. He reacts in anger to what he considers complete irreverence on Job's part. He takes hold of the general trend of Job's arguments and attempts to contradict the conclusions to which Job had come.

1 Then answered Bildad the Shuhite, and said, 2 How long wilt thou speak these things? and how long shall the words of thy mouth be like a strong wind?

Job has just finished responding to the rebuke of Eliphaz, one of his friends. Job had asserted

that right was on his side (6:29–30). Job also had bitterly charged that the life of man is cruelly shaped by the unbearable pressures brought upon him by an unrelenting and inescapable God (7:1–7, 17–18). Bildad, another friend of Job, now speaks. He confronts Job for his denunciation of Eliphaz, who had previously scolded Job. Whereas Eliphaz had shown a little kindness in his remarks, Bildad is not afraid to be blunt and dismisses Job's defense as a "strong wind" that is, only noise and empty content. We might say Bildad thinks Job is just full of hot air. The tactlessness of Bildad is astounding. With none of the courtliness characteristic of Eliphaz, Bildad leaps into the fray. He has been driven into a fury by Job's denial of God's justice. There is not a word of apology or any touch of friendly sympathy. He does not attempt to soothe and calm a suffering friend.

3 Doth God pervert judgment? or doth the Almighty pervert justice?

Like Eliphaz, Bildad shows no compassion whatsoever for his friend. He simply ignores Job's plea for understanding and sympathy. High on Bildad's order of priorities is to defend God's just character. Bildad detected in Job's outburst a criticism of God's handling of affairs, and he is incensed. Bildad appeals to tradition to defend his position. Bildad cares more for doctrine and theology than he does for Job. He feels his theology threatened, but fails to see Job is the one actually in danger—his integrity, self-esteem, and personhood. Bildad's question conveys surprise and dismay: How could it ever be thought that the Almighty could pervert justice? The Hebrew word 'avath (aw-**VATH**) means to falsify, bend, subvert, or make crooked. Bildad's main argument is that God never twists or bends justice, never makes its path crooked (8:3). In sum, Bildad implies that God allows no one to suffer who does not deserve it. God and injustice are incompatible terms.

277

The moral universe, in Bildad's theology, is founded upon the principle of retribution. Bildad does not accept Job's claims of innocence. "There is no smoke without fire" is Bildad's working hypothesis. Job's miserable condition speaks of a crime, and if Job only searched his conscience, he will discover what it is. Suffering is punishment, and the death of Job's children is proof of it! Bildad is a traditionalist, entirely wedded to the past, a moralist for whom everything is either black or white. For Bildad, everything is so utterly simple and straightforward: we get what we deserve. Sounding like the "prosperity gospel" of today, Bildad suggests those who prosper in this world do so because they are righteous. Those who suffer do so because they are wicked. There appear to be no exceptions to this simple rule.

Nothing is further from the truth, and the inadequacy of such a view is evident in the world today. There are evil people who do very well in this world. The same problem bothered David to no end as he wrote, "For I envied the arrogant when I saw the prosperity of the wicked" (Psalm 73:3).

4 If thy children have sinned against him, and he has cast them away for their transgression;

Bildad's argument proceeds from the result to the cause: if there was premature death, there must have been prior sin. So wedded is he to the sufficiency of the doctrine of retribution as an explanation for all human fortune or misfortune that he even states the result in terms of the cause. So, as Bildad reasoned, God has "cast away," that is, abandoned Job's children to the power of their guilt. If that is the result, the cause is already apparent—they have sinned against God. The doctrine of retribution is so fundamental to Bildad's worldview that he has perceived the death of Job's sons and daughters as God's punishment. Bildad assumes

or expects Job himself to have drawn the same conclusion, and have seen in the death of his children further proof of the reliability of the doctrine of retribution.

Bildad brings up the matter of Job's children simply to remind him of the contrast between their fate and his. However, the initial narrative does not in any way suggest or insinuate that the fate of Job's sons and daughters was the result of their behavior (Job 1–2); for Job, his children's fate and his own are equally inexplicable. Although Bildad nowhere in this speech expressly says that Job is a sinner, the inference is clear. A consequence of Bildad's equation of justice with divine power is that he can tell Job in complete seriousness and with absolute certainty that even though Job is suffering, he is experiencing divine mercy: he is still alive. He must therefore have sinned less than his children, who are dead. It is difficult to imagine a less comforting or more insensitive response to Job's plight.

5 If thou wouldest seek unto God betimes, and make thy supplication to the Almighty; 6 If thou wert pure and upright; surely now he would awake for thee, and make the habitation of thy righteousness prosperous.

Nevertheless, Bildad will argue, all hope is not lost for Job if he does two things. First, he must seek the face of God and call unto the Almighty (v. 5). The word "betimes" means "sometimes" or "early" and translates the Hebrew word *shachar* (shaw-**KHAR**) that refers to "dawn," thus suggesting getting up early for a task with the implication of earnestness. Here, Bildad picks up Job's word in 7:21. Whereas Job had spoken of God seeking him, Bildad says it would be more fitting if Job would seek God. Job should go early to seek God, and with earnestness. If Job were to rise up early and plead for mercy, God "would awake" that is, rouse Himself as He would the dawn (Psalm 57:9) and restore Job to his former condition.

Second, he must be pure and upright (v. 6). Bildad seems to be asking Job to demonstrate virtues that God already affirmed (1:8; 2:3). While Bildad does not explicitly deny that Job possesses these qualities, he seems far less certain than God seemed that Job is who he claims to be. If Job meets this double condition, linking devoutness and moral purity, Bildad's dogma of retribution, in the positive sense now, assures him that God cannot fail to respond to Job's behavior with signs of favor.

Bildad contends for an unbending doctrine of retribution, which makes the sinner the victim of his or her guilt (v. 4), which then chains God also, and compels Him to respond with favor to any human merit (v. 6). We must learn a lesson from the utterances of Bildad that a rigid application of a truth—to the exclusion of any possible exceptions or broader analyses of the situation—is a dangerous and cruel line to take. Bildad is a man who has got hold of half of the truth and has made it into the whole truth. It is always a mistake to do that, and always damaging.

7 Though thy beginning was small, yet thy latter end should greatly increase.

In verse 7, Bildad, in the same manner as Eliphaz (5:19–26), holds out before Job hopes of a prosperous future. However, unlike Eliphaz, Bildad does not elaborate the details of such a future. Rather he devotes a larger portion of his speech to an elaboration of the fate of the wicked (vv. 11–19) by way of warning to Job. Nevertheless, he offers Job a hope that he believes to be real. Bildad speaks more truly than he knows, for God will bless Job's end more than his beginning (42:12).

8 For enquire, I pray thee, of the former age, and prepare thyself to the search of their

fathers: 9 (For we are but of yesterday, and know nothing, because our days upon earth are a shadow:) 10 Shall not they teach thee, and tell thee, and utter words out of their heart?

Bildad appeals to ancient tradition to prove his assertion that God always acts justly (vv. 8–10). His rationale for appealing to the original generation of the fathers is the ephemeral nature of mortals (7:1–3, 9) and the capacity of the fathers to instruct in wisdom from the depth of their knowledge. In this regard one may think of people like Enoch and Noah who lived extremely long lives and acquired a lot of wisdom. The reason for the relative ignorance of present generation is the relative brevity of life in Bildad's day (Job 14:1–2). Wickedness inherits its own reward (Job 8:9–13; cf. Eliphaz's perception in 4:8: "You reap what you sow"). Bildad contends that his teaching was in harmony with traditional teaching and human experience. Eliphaz based his thinking on observation and experience, but Bildad is a traditionalist who looks for wisdom in the past. "What do the ancients say about it?" was his key question.

To be sure, we can learn from the past. In an age which idolizes the latest fashions, an appeal to tradition is no bad thing. To say "it has always been this way," can often be a means of introducing sanity into an otherwise disorientated, confused jungle of ideas. The case for the supremacy of tradition could not be more crisply put. However, it is important to see the past something to learn from—a rudder to guide us and not an anchor to hold us back, a launching pad, and not a parking lot.

Truth about human existence, according to Bildad, is to be learned, specifically from others. The truth is knowledge, not experience. As creatures of yesterday whose whole lifespan can be likened to a fleeting "shadow," humans cannot hope to acquire for themselves the wisdom and experience accumulated over the ages. In a positive sense the Hebrew word, *sel* (**TSALE**) translated "shadow" conveys the ideas of shade, protection, and defense. However, the word serves as a negative metaphor when it is viewed as ephemeral and fleeting. Man's life is compared to a shadow, for it has no permanence and flees quickly away (1 Chronicles 29:15). Shadow also describes the failing condition of one who is enduring a sickness (Job 17:7).

Comparisons of life's brief span to a shadow are made elsewhere are common in the Old Testament (1 Chronicles 29:15; Psalm 102:11; Ecclesiastes 6:12; 8:13). While former generations have passed away, their accumulated wisdom remains, and to that old wisdom Bildad made his appeal. Job and Bildad share the same sense of the extreme brevity of life (cf. 7:7, 16). Still, while it wrings from Job an elemental cry to God, Bildad experiences it intellectually, as a ground for adherence to traditional wisdom.

Bildad's respect for the wisdom of the past is admirable, as is his conviction that God does not pervert justice (v. 3). The way he allows the doctrine of retribution to fill the whole horizon both of human wisdom and divine justice, though, makes him both unappealing and unconvincing. He insists on absolutizing the doctrine so much that he must be both unjust and unkind to Job.

20 Behold, God will not cast away a perfect man, neither will he help the evil doers: 21 Till he fill thy mouth with laughing, and thy lips with rejoicing. 22 They that hate thee shall be clothed with shame; and the dwelling place of the wicked shall come to nought.

Bildad's recapitulation of his teaching drawn for ancient tradition embraces God's attitude toward the blameless and evil doers—God will not abandon the blameless in times of disaster, and evil doers will not be sustained by their sin. Bildad thinks he heard Job say that God perverts justice (v. 3). It seemed that Job has problems concerning divine justice; but he has not yet blatantly accused God of being unjust, though he has come close to it (6:20). Job finds it difficult, if not impossible, to understand God's justice. Although Job does not claim perfection (6:21), he considers himself a "perfect" or blameless man (Heb. *tam*, **TAWM**). This is also God's view of him in the prologue (1:8; 2:3), but Bildad is sure that God has rejected Job. Since God accepts blameless men (8:20), Job cannot be one. So, he must be an "evil doer" (Heb. *hanep*, ha–**NEP**), a hypocrite. The situation, however, can be remedied: if only he would turn to God, Job's lips might laugh again.

Bildad ends his discourse with a strong word of assurance directed to Job personally (vv. 21–22). He does not preface this happy conclusion that he predicts for Job's suffering with conditions (see v. 5). He allows the promise of salvation itself to carry its own reminder of the necessary condition—if such a reminder is necessary. His final message to Job is an affirming restitution promise analogous to the closing of Eliphaz (5:19–26). Job can expect to rejoice and celebrate the fall of his foes.

Sources:

Balentine, Samuel E. *Job*. Smyth & Helwys Bible Commentary. Macon, GA: Smyth & Helwys Publishing Inc., 2006.

Clines, David J. A. *Job 1–20*, vol. 17, Word Biblical Commentary. Dallas, TX: Word, Incorporated, 1989.

Estes, Daniel J. *Job*. Teach The Text Commentaries. Grand Rapids, MI: Baker Publishing House, 2013.

Habel, *The Book of Job: A Commentary*. Old Testament Library. Philadelphia: The Westminster Press, 1985.

Rowley, H. H. *The Book of Job*. The New Century Bible Commentary. Grand Rapids, MI: Wm. B. Eerdmans, Publishing Company, 1980.

Smick, Elmer B. "Job" in *The Expositor's Bible Commentary: 1 Chronicles–Job* (Revised Edition), ed. Tremper Longman III and David E. Garland, vol. 4. Grand Rapids, MI: Zondervan, 2010.

Thomas, Derek. *Job: The Streams Breaks*. Welwyn Garden City, UK: EP Books, 2015.

Say It Correctly

Theodicy. thee–ODD–ih–see.
Bildad. BILL–dad.

Daily Bible Readings

MONDAY
Job Suffers Sinlessly
(Job 1:8–11, 13–22)

TUESDAY
Habakkuk Struggles to See Justice
(Habakkuk 1:12–17)

WEDNESDAY
Suffering for Doing Right
(1 Peter 2:20–25)

THURSDAY
God Is in the Storm
(Psalm 29)

FRIDAY
Remove This Cup from Me
(Mark 14:32–42)

SATURDAY
God Speaks from the Whirlwind
(Job 38:1–11)

SUNDAY
God's Justice Is Unfathomable
(Job 8:1–10, 20–22)

Notes

_____

_____

_____

_____

Teaching Tips

Words You Should Know

A. Abhor (Job 42:6) *ma'ac* (Heb.)—Despise, reject

B. Bemoaned (v. 11) *nud* (Heb.)—Show grief, have compassion on

Teacher Preparation

Unifying Principle—Hope for Justice. Even the most downcast people can still have hope. How does our hope keep us focused on what is important? Job had a frank, heart-to-heart conversation with God, and God blessed Job's faithfulness.

A. Read the Bible Background and Devotional Reading.

B. Pray for your students and lesson clarity.

C. Read the lesson Scripture in multiple translations.

O—Open the Lesson

A. Begin the class with prayer.

B. Give each participant an index card on which they will write the title of their favorite novel or movie. Collect and shuffle the cards and redistribute them. Have the person with the new card guess who wrote it. The person should then identify himself or herself and tell why they liked the ending of the book or movie chosen. Lead into Bible study by noting that Job's tragic story had a happy ending.

C. Have the students read the Aim for Change and the In Focus story.

D. Ask students how events like those in the story weigh on their hearts and how they can view these events from a faith perspective.

P—Present the Scriptures

A. Read the Focal Verses and discuss the Background and The People, Places, and Times sections.

B. Have the class share what Scriptures stand out for them and why, with particular emphasis on today's themes.

E—Explore the Meaning

A. Use In Depth or More Light on the Text to facilitate a deeper discussion of the lesson text.

B. Pose the questions in Search the Scriptures and Discuss the Meaning.

C. Discuss the Liberating Lesson and Application for Activation sections.

N—Next Steps for Application

A. Summarize the value of waiting on the Lord.

B. End class with a commitment to pray for those who cause them pain.

Worship Guide

For the Superintendent or Teacher
Theme: Serving a Just God
Song: "Waymaker"

Serving a Just God

Bible Background • JOB 42
Printed Text • JOB 42:1–6, 10–17 | Devotional Reading • JOB 37:14–24

────────── **Aim for Change** ──────────

By the end of this lesson, we will UNDERSTAND the necessity of being humble before God, APPRECIATE how God listens to our thoughts and responds with justice, and HELP others see the justice of God in difficult situations.

────────── **In Focus** *Job a man* ──────────

A woman named Carrie had finally been released from jail. She was happy to get out, but Carrie was also fearful and anxious about returning to society. How would she take care of herself? How would she be able to get hired with a felony on her record? The odds were stacked against her.

On top of that, she still felt anger and frustration at the events that one night long ago. Carrie had not done anything wrong except be in the wrong place at the wrong time. While she and her friends were hanging out in front of their apartment building, police officers came by and frisked them for drugs. One of the officers planted drugs in Carrie's jacket. She had no record or any history of being affiliated with drugs or dealers, but she had no voice in the courtroom. She ended up spending 6 years in prison for a crime she did not commit.

Carrie happened to walk past her old church while a Wednesday night Bible Study was going on. She went in without really knowing why. The pastor immediately recognized and embraced Carrie. In the weeks that followed, Pastor Jackson helped Carrie find a job and a place to stay. Carrie also began to go back to school to be a lawyer so she could be an advocate for those who needed a voice against injustice.

Where do you find hope, and how do you share it when you have it?

────────── **Keep in Mind** ──────────

"Who is he that hideth counsel without knowledge? therefore have I uttered that I understood not; things too wonderful for me, which I knew not." (Job 42:3, KJV)

"You asked, 'Who is this that questions my wisdom with such ignorance?' It is I—and I was talking about things I knew nothing about, things far too wonderful for me." (Job 42:3, NLT)

38, 39, 40 1-26 6-24

Focal Verses

proselyte-convert

April 17, 2022

KJV **Job 42:1** Then Job answered the LORD, and said,

2 I know that thou canst do every thing, and that no thought can be withholden from thee.

3 Who is he that hideth counsel without knowledge? therefore have I uttered that I understood not; things too wonderful for me, which I knew not.

4 Hear, I beseech thee, and I will speak: I will demand of thee, and declare thou unto me.

5 I have heard of thee by the hearing of the ear: but now mine eye seeth thee.

6 Wherefore I abhor myself, and repent in dust and ashes. *despise / hate loathe*

10 And the LORD turned the captivity of Job, when he prayed for his friends: also the LORD gave Job twice as much as he had before.

11 Then came there unto him all his brethren, and all his sisters, and all they that had been of his acquaintance before, and did eat bread with him in his house: and they bemoaned him, and comforted him over all the evil that the LORD had brought upon him: every man also gave him a piece of money, and every one an earring of gold.

12 So the LORD blessed the latter end of Job more than his beginning: for he had fourteen thousand sheep, and six thousand camels, and a thousand yoke of oxen, and a thousand she asses.

13 He had also seven sons and three daughters.

14 And he called the name of the first, Jemima; and the name of the second, Kezia; and the name of the third, Kerenhappuch.

15 And in all the land were no women found so fair as the daughters of Job: and their father gave them inheritance among their brethren.

16 After this lived Job an hundred and forty years, and saw his sons, and his sons' sons, even four generations.

17 So Job died, being old and full of days.

NLT **Job 42:1** Then Job replied to the LORD:

2 "I know that you can do anything, and no one can stop you.

3 You asked, 'Who is this that questions my wisdom with such ignorance?' It is I—and I was talking about things I knew nothing about, things far too wonderful for me.

4 You said, 'Listen and I will speak! I have some questions for you, and you must answer them.'

5 I had only heard about you before, but now I have seen you with my own eyes.

6 I take back everything I said, and I sit in dust and ashes to show my repentance."

10 When Job prayed for his friends, the LORD restored his fortunes. In fact, the LORD gave him twice as much as before!

God justice

11 Then all his brothers, sisters, and former friends came and feasted with him in his home. And they consoled him and comforted him because of all the trials the LORD had brought against him. And each of them brought him a gift of money and a gold ring.

12 So the LORD blessed Job in the second half of his life even more than in the beginning. For now he had 14,000 sheep, 6,000 camels, 1,000 teams of oxen, and 1,000 female donkeys.

13 He also gave Job seven more sons and three more daughters.

14 He named his first daughter Jemimah, the second Keziah, and the third Keren-happuch.

15 In all the land no women were as lovely as the daughters of Job. And their father put them into his will along with their brothers.

16 Job lived 140 years after that, living to see four generations of his children and grandchildren.

17 Then he died, an old man who had lived a long, full life.

The People, Places, and Times

The Book of Job. This book was written late compared to other Scriptures. Its Hebrew is oddly archaic, but its theological questions ring throughout the ages. The setup of Job's misfortunes provides a reason for a lengthy discussion of theology. The poetry of the book is organized into cycles, with a narrative, prologue, and epilogue. First Job sets out the scope of his misery (Job 3), then his friends try to convince him what he needs to do to appease God and have his blessings restored. Three times, Eliphaz speaks, then Bildad, then Zophar, with Job answering after each (Job 4–31), although in the last cycle, Job is so frustrated that he preempts anything Zophar wanted to say and speaks for much longer than usual. In chapters 32–37, another of Job's friends, Elihu, tries to offer a more nuanced answer to both Job and the other friends, but this is ultimately rejected as well. Finally, God answers them all from out of a storm (Job 38–41), overwhelming Job into awe at God's amazing breadth of insight and control. Job is humble in his reply, and God blesses him again (Job 42).

Background

Job is the first poetic book of the Old Testament. Job is a book of wisdom, it answers the soul-aching questions of godly sufferers. Job grapples with the question, "If God is loving and just, why did he allow such pain and degradation in the life of a righteous man?" Job essentially exposes three distinct scriptural truths. First, God allowed Job to be tested as he was perfect and upright, feared God and eschewed evil. God's omniscience is evident. Satan was granted permission to test Job. Secondly, human frailty and limited thinking stumbles to understand the counsel of God. The awesomeness of God is too wide for human understanding and comprehension without the illumination of God's grace. Finally, the reality of faith is not in blessing, favor, humanistic understanding and answers, but in the revelation of God Himself. Faith is God being revealed to us, in us, and through us. Job conveys that testing purifies character and integrity. God never initiates pain and suffering without benevolence and grace. God makes full restitution and can be fully trusted.

At-A-Glance

1. God's Wisdom and Counsel
(Job 42:1–3)
2. Job's Humanity (vv. 4–6)
3. God's Justice (vv. 10–11)
4. God's Faithfulness in Adversity
(vv. 12–17)

In Depth

1. God's Wisdom and Counsel (Job 42:1–3)

God is wisdom and His understanding is infinite (Romans 16:27; Psalm 147:5). Job tried rationalizing God's counsel and wisdom through his own understanding, and it was fruitless. It is foolish to believe we understand God's counsel and wisdom at work in our lives. God's wisdom annihilates humanistic wisdom, and knowledge falters in gaining access to the mind and counsel of God. God's wisdom and counsel exposes secret and hidden things, even thoughts. Job confesses that God can do anything, including discern thoughts (v. 2). God is revealed as omniscient and His counsel powerful (v. 3). God's counsel is great, mighty in works, and stands forever. Our purposes are worked out through the counsel of God's will. God's wisdom and counsel will cause human utterings that are too wonderful to understand. Job recognizes the abundance of God's wisdom and his own frailty and fragility in the illumination of God's counsel.

How does interpreting God's wisdom and counsel impact how we see God's wisdom and counsel at work in the adversity of your own life?

2. Job's Humanity (vv. 4–6)

Job has a head knowledge of God, but a limited understanding of the operation of God's involvement in our suffering and adversity (v. 5). Job proclaims that the personal revelation of God is far more excellent than the perception of God.

Thoughts are personal, yet never hidden from God. The revelation of God in Job's anguish and calamity produced disgust within Job, and he relegated himself to dust, ashes, and repentance. As our eyes see God's wisdom and counsel in suffering and adversity, rejection of personal wisdom and repentance is the only response (v. 6). When humans are absent from the presence and reality of God, they grow in pride toward Him, which hinders them from seeing the justice and faithfulness of God in suffering.

What hinders us so that we do not see the reality of God in our deepest pain and misfortunes?

3. God's Justice (vv. 10–11)

God's justice is evident in Job's life. As Job vindicated his friends, God vindicated Job (v. 10). Earnest prayers of forgiveness for those who hurt and abandon us demonstrates God's justice in us. The turning of Job's captivity just as he prayed for his friends indicates God's expectation of us when we are wronged by loved ones. God expects us to see through His eyes in their failure, just as God sees us when we fail. All who abandoned Job returned, comforted, and blessed him. Job received them without reservation and celebrated with them (v.11). Job was blessed with words of comfort and the restoration of relationships. God's justice always prevails.

How might restoration of personal suffering and adversity reside within your power? How can you reconcile in your mind that God's justice might be dependent on us?

4. God's Faithfulness in Adversity (vv. 12–17)

God is faithful in not tempting us beyond our capacity (1 Corinthians 10:13). Despite the trouble we walk through, God preserves us (Job 42:16). Our life's preservation is God's demonstrated faithfulness in adversity. Job suffered a while, then God restored, confirmed, strengthen, and established him (v. 17). Adversity tests faith and commitment to God, but as faith is fortified and commitment solidified, our blessings are verified. Surviving adversity is an indication that God's faithfulness is operating in your life. God always blesses us with more than we had as we remain faithful (v. 12). With God, the ending of a thing is always better than the beginning (v. 12). God's faithfulness can always be fully trusted in adversity.

During adverse circumstances of your life, how did you show your faithfulness to God? Where has God demonstrated faithfulness toward you?

Search the Scriptures

1. What does knowing that "no thought can be witholden from thee" cause you to think? Why? How can you adjust what you think about God and His ways (Job 42:2)?

2. Reread Job 42:11. What does this passage suggest about the heart of Job concerning his brethren, sisters, and his acquaintances? Should boundaries be given in these relationships because they abandoned and rejected him in his most vulnerable state? How do you handle relationships when people hurt you?

3. Read Job 42:1–6 (for more details read the entire passage). What does this passage suggest about Job's relationship with God? What can you

infer about the faithfulness of God in adversity? How should we respond when we experience Job-like circumstances?

Discuss the Meaning

1. What are the attributes of God that can be seen in Job? What character traits does Job possess? Are there any adjustments that you need to make to your character?

2. Job repented for not understanding or respecting the counsel and wisdom of God. Is there any place where you have discounted the wisdom and counsel of God? Why? How can we ensure that we always embrace the counsel and wisdom of God especially in adversity?

Liberating Lesson

Adversity comes to all of us, but many of us view adversity as punishment. How could a loving and just God allow devastation? Like Job, these questions are too wonderful for us. In our humanity, we struggle with the realities of adversity and God's allowing of the adversity. The outcomes of adversity are up to God; we are responsible for our responses. God allows specific circumstances because He desires specific outcomes. God's justice always prevails. From slavery to "Black Lives Matter" the circumstances have been adverse, yet God is faithful. God executes justice in His faithfulness. God selected Job, and He may select you as an active part of His justice. Like Job, we must pray purely and forgive simultaneously.

Application for Activation

Consider your own life. How might things have worked out differently had you showed faithfulness to God in the area instead of rejecting His counsel and wisdom? We know that "If we believe not, yet he abideth faithful: he cannot deny himself" (2 Timothy 2:13). Has God been faithful in your life, when you were not? We see the faithfulness of both Job and God. Can we see

your faithfulness to God in personal adversity? Ask God to bring to mind those you need restoration with during your times of adversity. Seek forgiveness for rejecting God's counsel and wisdom in your life.

Follow the Spirit

What God wants me to do:

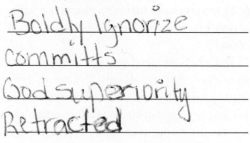

Boldly Ignorize
committs
God superiority
Retracted

Remember Your Thoughts

Special insights I have learned:

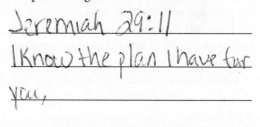

Jeremiah 29:11
I Know the plan I have for
you,

Job 1:12 Don't touch his

More Light on the Text

Job 42 comes after two speeches of God addressed to Job (Job 8:1–40:2; 40:6–41:34). In those speeches, God addressed Himself to the fact that Job had been presumptuous in his desire to dispute with God. The display from creation put Job in his place, but it has not yet dealt with Job's flagrantly impious attitude. Job had levied a charged. In his reply to the first divine speech (40:3–5), Job has said that he stands by what he has previously argued, and he will not reiterate his case. Job's response to the second divine speech is our text for today (42:1–6). Job is convinced of God's majesty and wisdom. Job has three crucial remarks to make in the address. First, he acknowledges the omnipotence of God (v. 2). Second, Job accepts that he has intruded into the area of wonders in which he has no competence (v. 3). Third, now that Job has heard the utterances God has addressed personally to him (v. 5), he abandons his complaints against God together with his mourning, and he intends to resume his everyday life (v. 6).

1 Then Job answered the LORD, and said, 2 I know that thou canst do every thing, and that no thought can be withholden from thee. 3 Who is he that hideth counsel without knowledge? therefore have I uttered that I understood not; things too wonderful for me, which I knew not. 4 Hear, I beseech thee, and I will speak: I will demand of thee, and declare thou unto me.

Starting his response to God's second speech, Job does not immediately retract what he has said; Job does not admit that God is in the right or that he is in the wrong. He does not confess to any sins or apologize for what he has said. He simply begins by affirming God's omnipotence, something which, curiously, he had acknowledged all along. He accepts the argument of the divine speeches: he is a mere mortal, unfitted by capacity or knowledge for the management of the universe; as he has said already, in comparison with Yahweh, he is of little account (40:4). Nothing is beyond God's ability. He also asserts that no purpose (KJV: thought) of God can be thwarted.

Job's second remark (v. 3) is a paraphrase of God's question, "Who is this that darkeneth counsel by words without knowledge?" (Job 38:2) followed by his response to it, making it quite explicit that he is responding formally to the challenge which God posted against him. By doing so, Job admits that he is guilty as charged. He has spoken about things that are far beyond his knowledge and experience.

Job again references God's words: "I will question you, and you shall answer me" has been spoken by Yahweh at the beginning of both his speeches (v. 4; cf. 38:3; 40:7). Obviously Job has been listening intently, as we all should when God speaks.

5 I have heard of thee by the hearing of the ear: but now mine eye seeth thee.

"I have heard of thee" (v. 5) indicates that Job's knowledge of God has been far too limited. He had been academic. His friends and religious teaching had told Job about God. He had passed this information to others—probably including his children—and engaged in a great deal of theoretical discussion about the nature of God. But the conceptions held by his friends were inadequate to meet his needs or fit his present circumstances. Those held by himself led him to make rebellious and blasphemous charges against God. Job had longed that he might see God in order to receive some kind of vindication of his position (19:24–27). That vision has been partly fulfilled in the visions of God that Job has now seen in the storm.

Already, Job has come to appreciate something about God that he had not known before. Through this trial, Job has come in some way face-to-face with God. What Job had known of God in the past was secondhand. Even so, Job had believed in God and lived for Him. But he had now been changed—"but now mine eye seeth thee." It is as if Job is saying that, through his experience of loss, abiding uncertainty, and unrelieved suffering—and his relentless turning toward God—he has come to "see" in a new way. It is this kind of seeing generated by way of anguished turning toward God that forms the basis of his repentance. Now Job has received personal experience of God. What Job saw physically is not essential. Like the crowd that followed Jesus due to the initial proclamation of the Samaritan woman (John

4:39–42), it is no longer hearsay truth that Job relies upon. He has been confronted by God on a Person-to-person basis.

hate

6 Wherefore I abhor myself, and repent in dust and ashes. *despise*

Then comes the climax of the whole dispute between Job and God (v. 6). Job has definitely learned something about himself. Thus, he says, "Wherefore I abhor myself, and repent in dust and ashes." The Hebrew word, *ma'as* (maw–**OS**) translated as abhor also means to spurn, contemn, or become loathsome. However, this is not the abject self-loathing of radical repentance that requires admitting known sins. Job never says: "Now, at last, I concede that I deserved that punishment." Connected with verse 3, Job here expresses regret at his foolish words, uttered hastily and in ignorance—a fault deserving correction, but not a wickedness deserving punishment. If he is sorry about what he said, repentance from that could be the spiritual growth and character formation Job's catastrophe was intended to promote, and Job now recognizes this.

From the very start, Job had erred in his response to his trial. He repents of his arrogance in impugning God's justice. He repents of the attitude whereby he simply demanded an answer as if such were owed him.

Job's reference to dust and ashes reminds us of Abraham's words when he was praying to God (Genesis 18:27). The expression "dust and ashes" shows that, as a humble suppliant, he knows his status. The words dust and ashes are very similar in Hebrew and they both refer to matters which so much resemble each other. Dust (Heb. *aphar*, aw-**FAR**) is the lightest particle of earth. Ashes (Heb. *epher*, **EH**·fer) are the residue of consumed substances. By these expressions he shows how deeply his soul was humbled in the presence of God. He who has high thoughts of himself must have low thoughts of the dignity of the divine nature, of the majesty of God, and the sinfulness of sin.

Andrew

10 And the LORD turned the captivity of Job, when he prayed for his friends: also the LORD gave Job twice as much as he had before.

Verses 7–9 show God was displeased with Job's friends. God is concerned only with the false things they had said about Him. They had declared that Job's sufferings proved he had offended God and brought them on himself. This was not the right thing to say about God. Therefore, God told Job to make intercession for his friends, so that God does not punish them for their terrible advice and flawed theology. Job does so.

In verse 10, Job is restored. The word "captivity" translates the Hebrew word *shebuth*, (sheh–**BOOTH**) which commonly means "exile." However, it also has the meaning "to restore someone to his or her former state of prosperity," welfare, and happiness. Job's fortunes are restored—his possessions are doubled, and his friends bring presents to him.

Job's restored divine blessings are not contingent on Job's confession of his own sins, contrary to what Bildad predicted (8:7), but are granted by God after he obediently prayed for his friends. One could imagine how hard and painful it was for Job to pray for his friends after their harsh words to him. Nevertheless, Job overcomes evil with good (cf. Romans 12:21). Job was not motivated by self-interest as the adversary charged to begin with (1:9–11). He cares for his friends, even when they have not taken good care of him.

11 Then came there unto him all his brethren, and all his sisters, and all they that had been of his acquaintance before, and did eat bread with him in his house: and they bemoaned him, and comforted him

over all the evil that the LORD had brought upon him: every man also gave him a piece of money, and every one an earring of gold.

God has now restored the vertical relationship between Himself and Job, and He has healed the horizontal relationships between Job and other people who were once close to him. During this time of need, Job's family and friends abandoned him (19:13–19), but now they return to fellowship with him. Job does not seem to begrudge these fair weather friends. He welcomes them to his house and dines with them. Even though Job's crisis is over, he still has to deal with the considerable loss that he has incurred, especially the death of his children. His solitude and pain are replaced by community and rejoicing, as Job receives belated consolation and encouragement. Job's wide circle of family and friends also give him a bit of money to help him back to his feet. No one feels obligated to give lots, but each is able to give a piece of the funds Job lacks.

Felicia

12 So the LORD blessed the latter end of Job more than his beginning: for he had fourteen thousand sheep, and six thousand camels, and a thousand yoke of oxen, and a thousand she asses.

Job was tested to the limit, but now God restores his fortune twofold, doubling the number of Job's flocks and herds from before his affliction (1:3). It is as though he has to be given some consolation for an unwarranted trial initiated as a wager between God and his adversary in the council of heaven (1:6–12). Yet this act of restoration is an act of God's grace, not a reward for Job's goodness, integrity, or honesty with God. Job now enjoys greater blessings in the post-disaster period of his life.

Felicia

13 He had also seven sons and three daughters. 14 And he called the name of the first, Jemima; and the name of the

second, Kezia; and the name of the third, Kerenhappuch. **15 And in all the land were no women found so fair as the daughters of Job: and their father gave them inheritance among their brethren.**

The number of Job's children is not doubled, though the beauty of his daughters is mentioned probably as a public indication of special blessing. By giving his daughters an inheritance with their brothers, Job demonstrates that he continued a policy of justice and equity in his life, which went beyond the practice of the ancient world (cf. Job 31) and even some contemporary societies. In Israel, for example a daughter would only inherit the property of her father if there was no male heir (cf. Numbers 21:7–8).

The names of Job's three daughters probably represent a symbol of beauty and love. Jemimah means "turtle dove." The dove was a symbol of beauty and love. Keziah is cassia, an intensely aromatic spice made from the cassia tree (most commercial cinnamon is cassia). Cassia is one of the perfumes scenting the clothes of the queen (Psalm 45:8). Keren–happuch seems to indicate "horn of antimony," a black powder used as an eye cosmetic (or as anointing oil, 1 Samuel 16:1, 13; 1 Kings 1:39). The three names invoke three of the senses: Jemimah the hearing, Keziah the taste or the smell, and Keren–happuch the sight.

Joyce

16 After this lived Job an hundred and forty years, and saw his sons, and his sons' sons, even four generations. 17 So Job died, being old and full of days.

The total length of Job's life marks him a patriarchal figure from that heroic era when people survived at least twice an average life span. Thus, Job is to be compared with Abraham, who lived 175 years and, like Job, died an old man sated with days. The precise expression "full of days" is used elsewhere

Susann

only of Isaac (Genesis 35:29) and of David (1 Chronicles 29:28); Abraham died in a "good old age, an old man, and full of years" (Genesis 25:8); Jehoiada the priest "waxed old, and was full of days" (2 Chronicles 24:15). Job's death, at such an age, is no calamity, but the natural and even desired end of a full and satisfying life. There will be ritual lamenting over him, of course, as on every occasion of death. Still, this last little sentence in the story of Job has its profundity: death is the completion of Job, as it is of his story, and the end of his life is not a failing or a fading or a weakening but a filling up to the brim, a fullness, even satiation of days.

Sources:

Balentine, Samuel E. *Job.* Smyth & Helwys Bible Commentary. Macon, GA.: Smyth & Helwys Publishing Inc. 2006

Clines, David J. A. *Job 1–20,* vol. 17, Word Biblical Commentary. Dallas, TX: Word, Incorporated, 1989.

Estes, Daniel J. *Job.* Teach The Text Commentaries. Grand Rapids, MI: Baker Publishing House, 2013.

Habel, *The Book of Job: A Commentary.* Old Testament Library. Philadelphia: The Westminster Press, 1985.

Rowley, H. H. *The Book of Job.* The New Century Bible Commentary. Grand Rapids, MI: Wm. B. Eerdmans, Publishing Company, 1980.

Smick, Elmer B. "Job" in *The Expositor's Bible Commentary: 1 Chronicles–Job* (Revised Edition), ed. Tremper Longman III and David E. Garland, vol. 4. Grand Rapids, MI: Zondervan, 2010.

Thomas, Derek. *Job: The Streams Breaks.* Welwyn Garden City, UK.: EP Books, 2015.

Facilitator

liberating

Freeing

Say It Correctly

Eliphaz. ELL–uh–fazz.
Zophar. ZOH–far.
Elihu. ee–LIE–who.
Jemimah. jeh–MY–muh.
Keziah. keh–ZIE–uh.
Keren–happuch. KER–en–HA–pook.

Daily Bible Readings

MONDAY
Abraham Pleads for Justice
(Genesis 18:20–33)

TUESDAY
Trust in God's Coming Justice
(Psalm 37:1–11)

WEDNESDAY
The Lord Loves Justice
(Psalm 37:21–28, 34–40)

THURSDAY
Righteousness, Peace, and Joy
(Romans 14:13–23)

FRIDAY
Jesus Demonstrates God's Justice
(Matthew 12:1–13)

SATURDAY
Job Cries Out for a Redeemer
(Job 19:23–29)

SUNDAY
Job's Fortunes Are Restored
(Job 42:1–11)

God Frees and Redeems ✓

This quarter uses the lens of liberation, Christian freedom, to examine and experience the nature of God who acts to deliver and free people in different situations. This liberation is experienced in the story of the Passover and in the good news of Easter. Liberation is experienced in God's new covenant community.

UNIT 1 • Liberating Passover

In this unit, four lessons explore the memory of the liberating event of the Exodus. The memory of the Exodus, relived in the Passover liturgy, cultivated a desire for restoration and liberation for the Hebrew people as told in the books of Ezra and Deuteronomy. *– Second ritual Law*

Lesson 1: March 6, 2022
Babylonian Captivity Ends
Ezra 1:1-8, 11; 2:64-70

Sometimes people are given a challenging job, which requires a change or risk. Where can we find resources to meet these challenges? Israel's release from Babylonian captivity reveals that we can have faith that God will provide persons and resources to fulfill God's purposes.

Lesson 2: March 13, 2022
Freedom to Worship
Ezra 6:1-12

Sometimes people focus on their own adverse situations rather than seeking guidance. Why do we act and speak according to our situations rather than seeking liberation from them? Ezra shows us that when we recognize and confess our failings God is ready to listen and support us, even in unexpected ways.

Lesson 3: March 20, 2022
Celebrate Passover Liberation
Ezra 6:13-22

Celebrations provide opportunities for persons to rejoice after a difficult task. How can we celebrate and show thanksgiving to the person who made the victory possible? After the Temple was completed, the Israelites celebrated God by sharing the Passover together.

Lesson 4: March 27, 2022
Lest We Forget
Deuteronomy 8:1-11

Humility can be thought of as a weakness in today's society. Why do people forget the road they traveled in life and who helped them in their accomplishments? Deuteronomy extols humility as liberating and explains its purpose.

UNIT 2 • Liberating Gospels

This unit offers four lessons that explore the liberating freedom found in events beginning with Jesus' triumphal entry into Jerusalem and continuing through His death and resurrection. These lessons are drawn from the Gospel of Matthew. The text from John describes the liberating freedom found by following Jesus.

Lesson 5: April 3, 2022
The Passover with the Disciples
Matthew 26:17-30

People need reminders of times of liberation in history. How do people deal with the burdens of daily life? In celebrating the Passover with His disciples, Jesus reminded them of the freedom He gave from fear and want.

Lesson 6: April 10, 2022
Triumphal Entry into Jerusalem
Matthew 21:1-11

People long for leaders who can liberate them from tyranny and be worthy of their praise. What does humility teach us about leadership? Matthew describes Jesus' humility and the crowds blessing Him.

Lesson 7: April 17, 2022
The Paschal Lamb Lives!
Matthew 28:1-10

The world is full of sadness and despair. How can we find hope in the midst of our anguish? In Matthew, Jesus allays our fears and gives courage to face the future.

Lesson 8: April 24, 2022
Freedom in Christ Jesus
John 8:31-38

Many people are bound by bad habits and vices. How can one experience deliverance? Jesus is the truth that sets us free and enables us to be His disciples.

UNIT 3 • Liberating Letters

This unit contains five lessons based on the letters to the Romans and Galatians that explore Paul's understanding of the radical nature of Christian freedom. The final lesson in the unit focuses on the fruit of the Spirit emanating from Christian freedom.

Lesson 9: May 1, 2022
Freedom from Sin
Romans 6:1-14

In life, we are constantly struggling to do what is morally right. How can we overcome temptations? Through Jesus' death and resurrection, we become dead to sin and instruments of righteousness.

Lesson 10: May 8, 2022
Freedom for the Future
Romans 8:18-30

Living in the world we sometimes suffer because of evildoers. Where can one find inspiration and hope for the future? God promises to bring good out of our suffering and give us a blessed future.

Lesson 11: May 15, 2022
Freedom and the Law
Galatians 3:18-29

Laws are provided to govern and ensure a functioning society. If there were no laws, what would guide human behavior? Paul taught that God's Law served a purpose, but when Christ came grace made it possible for all people to become children of God and heirs of God's promises.

Lesson 12: May 22, 2022
The Nature of Christian Freedom
Galatians 5:1-15

Sometimes people feel bound by laws and desires that keep them in chains. Where can we find freedom to experience life in transforming ways? According to Galatians, God calls us to a freedom that is guided by love for others.

Lesson 13: May 29, 2022
The Spiritual Fruit of Freedom
Galatians 5:16-26

In the world many opposing forces influence our lives. When we feel conflicted, what can we do? Paul reminds us that choosing to be guided by the Spirit will result in good fruit.

"I Will Be Your God and You Will Be My People": A Central Theme in Scripture

by Evangeline Carey

Scholars tell us that, "It took some 40 men a period of approximately 1,600 years to produce the 66 books that compose the Bible" (Thiessen 267). God inspired these men to record His inerrant Word in their original documents "for doctrine, for reproof, for correction, for instruction in righteousness" (2 Timothy 3:16). It should be noted that the central theme, or thread, that runs throughout the collage of Scriptures from Genesis to Revelation is God's desire that the people He created to be in relationship with Him.

Five Historical Books Called the "Pentateuch" (Genesis, Exodus, Leviticus, Numbers, and Deuteronomy)—the Books of the Law

In the Pentateuch, God's great love for humanity and His desire for relationship can be readily seen through (1) His creation of man and woman, (2) His hands-on involvement with Adam and Eve in the Garden of Eden, and (3) the binding agreements He made with His people under the Mosaic Law.

God desired to have a people who would love, honor, respect, and worship Him. He wanted a people who would walk with Him in obedience. When we explore the 66 books of the canon, we find God reaching out to humanity in unconditional love, salvation, and fellowship.

God's chosen people (the Israelites) were to be the channel through which the world would come to know the true and living God. He became the Israelites' God, but the Israelites were a complaining, hardheaded, rebellious people who disobeyed God at every turn.

The Additional 12 Historical Books (Joshua, Judges, Ruth, 1 and 2 Samuel, 1 and 2 Kings, 1 and 2 Chronicles, Ezra, Nehemiah, and Esther)

From these historical books, we also come to appreciate God's character and know Him more intimately as we look at how He dealt with the Israelites. These books further explain how God tried to help His chosen people understand and obey His commands and remain in relationship with Him. He raised up priests, judges, and kings to help them stay on His path, but they still broke their covenant–relationship with Him. They perpetuated a cycle of sin or disobedience, captivity (God's punishment for their sins), remorse, repentance, and deliverance.

The Five Poetry Books (Job, Psalms, Proverbs, Ecclesiastes, and Song of Solomon)

These books extol God's unconditional love for His people. They also share how He punishes sin.

The whole range of human emotion is expressed in these accounts. We learn how to walk with a holy God in confession. We also learn how to focus on Him and lift our hearts in praise and worship to our God, who is more than enough in our times of need.

Job, the central character of the book of Job, is a model of trust in and obedience to God. From his life, we learn that God is completely and eternally good, in spite of our suffering in a fallen world. We also learn that the Almighty God is awesome, that the covenant–relationship with Him still exists, and that Satan cannot do anything to God's children that God does not allow. We learn that Satan had to ask God for permission to afflict Job (1:12).

Psalms, Proverbs, Ecclesiastes, and Song of Solomon also help us picture the unconditional love of God for His sheep. These books show us that if we are going to let God be our God and if we are going to be His people, we should honor our daily commitment to Him by applying godly morals and wisdom.

The 17 Prophetic Books (Isaiah, Jeremiah, Lamentations, Ezekiel, Daniel, Hosea, Joel, Amos, Obadiah, Jonah, Micah, Nahum, Habakkuk, Zephaniah, Haggai, Zechariah, and Malachi)

These books continue to illustrate how God takes His covenant relationship with His people very seriously. God rose up these spokesmen to warn His chosen people (Israel) to turn from their sinful ways and turn back to Him. He wanted them to honor their agreement with Him. The prophets then called the people back to God and proclaimed His future provision of salvation through the coming Messiah, Jesus. They taught that God is love, God is merciful, but God is also Judge.

The Four Gospels (Matthew, Mark, Luke, and John)

Whereas the 39 books of the Old Testament foretold the coming of the Messiah, who is the eternal King, the four Gospels declare that Jesus has come and He is the Word of God to man. Jesus has revealed Himself to a lost and dying world as the only way back to a holy God. The gap or gulf between sinful humanity and a holy God can be closed when sinners believe on the Lord Jesus Christ (John 3:16). With true belief and repentance, Jesus becomes our Lord and Savior.

The Acts of the Apostles

The book of Acts, a sequel to the Gospel of Luke, covers the 30 years after Jesus' ascension into heaven. From the book of Acts, again we see that God stresses to believers He will be their God and they will be His people. He uses His promised Holy Spirit (the Comforter, Counselor, and Guide) to advance and direct His church outward "from Jerusalem to Judea, in Samaria, and to the uttermost part of the earth" (Acts 1:8).

The 21 Epistles or Letters (Romans, 1 and 2 Corinthians, Galatians, Ephesians, Philippians, Colossians, 1 and 2 Thessalonians, 1 and 2 Timothy, Titus, Philemon, Hebrews, James, 1 and 2 Peter, 1, 2, and 3 John, and Jude)

The epistles, or letters, definitely demonstrate a loving, merciful Father's desire for relationship with His people and His concern for their wellbeing. Under the anointing of the Holy Spirit, Peter, James, John, and Jude wrote some of the letters, but Paul wrote most of them to the infant churches that he helped establish on three missionary journeys (which are chronicled in Acts).

Paul presented his case for the Good News of the Gospel of Jesus Christ. Often, these letters were written from prison, in chains, after beatings with wooden rods, and in the midst of other perils. In them, Paul explained that God was and is still saying to His followers, "I will be your God and you will be my people."

Revelation—The Book of Hope

God used the apostle John, while he was exiled on the island of Patmos in the Aegean Sea, to spell out the hope that believers have of a life beyond the grave in God's kingdom. John had a vision or revelation from Jesus Christ, which unveiled the victorious Lord Jesus' Second Coming. Jesus is coming back to rule the earth! He will no longer be a suffering Servant, but a Judge who vindicates the righteous and judges the wicked.

God, who is Creator, Redeemer, Sustainer, and Judge, gave His revelation to the apostle John nearly 2,000 years ago. This unveiling agrees with what the other 65 books of the Bible proclaim to all believers: that God says and means, "I will be your God and you will be my people forever and ever and ever!"

———

Evangeline Carey was a staff writer for UMI and had been an adult Sunday School teacher for more than 25 years.

Sources:

Boer, Harry R. *Pentecost and Missions*. Grand Rapids, Mich.: Eerdmans, 1961, 161.

Thiessen, Henry C. *Lectures in Systematic Theology*. Grand Rapids, Mich.: Eerdmans, 2000, 67–255.

Educating Christians on Human Sexuality and Relationships for Holy Living

by Jacquelyn Donald-Mims, DMin

The quarter's lesson on Nathan confronting David can bring up a lot of issues about Christian sexuality. Consider taking time to have an open and honest discussion with learners about what God expects of His people on the subject of physical desires and spiritual union.

The landscape of Christian education, as we once knew it, has made dramatic shifts—shifts that embellish teaching on new topics that the church rarely addresses, yet the believer persistently encounters them in situations. Helpful teaching fosters holistic living. Over the recent years, America has witnessed more Bible study classes inaugurated by non-church groups. In the past these classes were largely unilaterally church-based Sunday School division initiatives. Even when launched by a church, many Bible study discussion groups today are taught in venues dispersed across the community in homes, school buildings, libraries, community centers, apartment complex clubhouses, and in local bookstore atrium areas, just as the Apostle Paul taught—both "publicly and from house to house" (Acts 20:20). The influence of high tech tools has made private studies on any issue possible, even with interactive Bible study lessons and quizzes using the computer and Internet. With these movements in the logistics of Christian education detached from the church building, has come concomitant relaxation in the standard rigor of the curriculum offerings. People have become more comfortable discussing biblical content with direct, personal, and intimate life application. Reality-based teaching on prevalent subjects like human sexuality has evolved to centrality in our lives.

Reality-based Bible study, especially the topic of human sexuality, captivates the interests of students of all ages in a new way. Real issues that are so practical and fundamental to daily living are explored in a Christian context for life application. When Bible study content is converged around a topic that is serious, challenging, interesting, and applicable to life, its popularity soars. Sex—in the life of singles, dating, engaged, and married couples—is a serious aspect of life. People have experienced the emptiness and feeling being used (or some other negative effect) that results from the misuse of sex, but God meant it to be a wonderful act of intimate creation. Christian education becomes highly applicable to the troublesome questions of coexistence in a relationship.

Just who is the most appropriate authority to teach human sexuality is still a controversy. Who can be trusted to deliver the full truth, candor, and the requisite spirituality among the contenders: the parent, the public education system, or the church? Preoccupation with this debate is no good justification to delay the education of our youth. Yet long delays in orthodox training now account for so many who have grown to adulthood who have still, today, never soaked up a complete discussion of value teachings on the matter of sex. Youth, mystified by the mystery surrounding the discussion, view participation in sex as a necessary rite of passage to adulthood and are unprepared for the seriousness of parenthood or the potential for sexually transmitted diseases (STDs). The answer lies in satisfying the need for knowledge-based discussions to be delivered by an authority that embraces a strong value standard. For the Christian, that value standard is the Bible–our most trusted source. Teachers, then, must dig deeply into the trusted biblical text for true and balanced interpretations of God's meaning and intent. Teachers must avoid relying upon those easy philosophies or pat answers that have been based upon little or no theological reflection or truth.

Principal in every educational endeavor is the Christian's supreme knowledge of the Person of Jesus Christ, including how one views their own sexuality, theologically. Though the Gospels reveal nothing about Jesus and human sexuality—that is, Jesus' own involvement in dating, courtship, sex, or marriage—certain important precepts are gleaned from His life and useful in predicting how He would respond in certain situations. We can learn much from Jesus' profound teachings, His startling miracles, His many parables, through His ministry of redemption of others, and in His leadership of His disciples. Thus, how do these biblical principles compare with the Christian's life and sphere of influence? Popular culture advocates that sex is both *good to us* and it seems to be *good for us*

in our quest for enjoyment and feelings of well-being. The church should respond at the outset, affirming that sex is not wrong, dirty, or sinful, but that it is good and is a beautiful gift from God meant to be enjoyed within the context of marriage.

The Christian is called to decipher the truth of the Gospel for their lives amid the myriad of world messages. The very glamorous, large, public, and glorified image of sex tends to influence the teaching about it by popular culture. The world's view, unfortunately, has delivered enigmas on the topic of sex in an unbalanced mixture of conjecture, hype, braggadocio, fantasy, outright lies, frenzy, miseducation and hazardous misconceptions, intertwined with small facts that keep everyone talking about it. In fact, there are so many people involved in talking about what they are doing today that it is spreading misconception and influencing the behavior of others who will listen and try it.

Hearing all of the talk about sex makes the Christian believer feel left out. It is as if the whole world is having fun except us! According to the results of the random sampling of respondents, the real truth is that within any given 12 months of a year, from 11 to 14 percent of men and women have experienced *no* sex partners at all, and more than 75 percent of the active population had sex with an exclusive, monogamous partner. However, the proliferation of sex myths do more than create harmful, false expectations, low self-esteem, and dangerous attempts to mimic misbehavior, they discourage the Christian believer, who is also a sexual being, from seeking a higher moral ground. The great conundrums of intimate relationships in practical life need to be demystified so that humans can emerge powerful and capable of analyzing truth amid massive amounts of information—such as data and sex preferences and patterns—and enable them to make healthy choices more effectively.

Real love requires a sound foundation of good intentions and commitment for goodness, respect, and well-being towards the other in the hearts, minds, actions, and wills of each party. The three integral components of such a soundly built love are friendship, unconditional love, and sex—all as God intended within marriage. One component of love is sex, viewed by most as harmless, enormously fun, and a recreational aspect of love. This erotica side of sex is pleasure-seeking, intended for a good physical feeling, aesthetic love, and romance between two people. *Eros* is the base for the word "erotica," which is an external stimuli with the objective of arousal of the sexual desire. The characteristics of *eros*, or erotic love, is conceitedness, since it seeks to please itself rather than others, though it has an *appearance* of being an outward love, or self-giving love. Erotic passion is the physicality, the feeling, and the gratification of wants. Its objective is its own; thus it makes no claim to fulfill needs other than intrinsic sensuality, romance, and passion. Erotic love, alone, is not strong enough to sustain a relationship of quality.

Secondly, basic friendship is a positive component of loving relationships which can contribute to the balance one should seek. The love embodied in a friendship, often characterized as the Greek, *philia*, is often love that is reciprocal between personal friends.

Finally, a fundamental, unconditional caring and compassion is the core foundational basis of a real relationship. This quality of the relationship is *agape* love. Love, care, compassion, prayer, praise, forgiveness towards the other, these are unconditional love attributes. Finally, agape is that love which is without condition. Its distinctive quality is that it is 'self-giving love' not 'recipient love.' Agape love's major characteristic is that people who love this way are understanding, considerate, forgiving, patient, redemptive and ever-kind to their partners. Agape love is exceptional because it gives without the expectation of a gift in return. This high quality love is never vindictive or angry. God's love is infinite, and therefore indescribable. For humans, the concept of agape asymptotically approaches what God's love is like. It never matches God's perfect love, because God is infinitely perfect, and we are finitely imperfect. The closest earthly model of love with the agape attribute is that kind of love that a good mother or a good father conveys which is unfailing.

The virtues modeled by Jesus of unconditional love become more demonstrative and understandable for which students can readily relate. Thus, the human sexuality Bible study lesson will become more than just sex talk when it is the focus of a Christian discussion. The function of caring for the souls of adults in a relationship is real. Adults occasionally feel depressed in relationships. Jesus modeled compassion, the virtue of "suffering with" another and feeling the other person's pain. Jesus' Great Commandment (Mark 12:30-31) is to love our God and neighbor just as we love ourselves. Upright living is the ultimate model that will provide happiness to those who meditate and delight on God's law (Psalm 1:1-2). Following the masses can be detrimental for the Christian believer, because the crowd very often has diverse objectives with little moral compass. The result of vulnerability is to be susceptible to the wind and blown away as chaff (Psalm 1:4).

God's people are called to be holy and to seek transformation. Our Judeo-Christian rootedness in the Old Testament emphasizes God's intention for us to be holy people. In the Pentateuch Books of Deuteronomy and Leviticus, the Hebrew term "holy," originally *qadah*, meant "set apart" specifically for religious purposes. Yahweh intended for all humans of all generations to respond to God's miraculous acts of salvation and deliverance as seen in Israel's rescue from

Egyptian bondage and in our own African American recovery from the cruelty of slavery and separation in America. Remaining central to our faith is our reverence and closeness to pleasing God, the final arbiter of our salvation, happiness, and eternal life. Yahweh's moral excellence became part of the concept of holiness, and God's demand that the people of God's covenant be holy was bound up by the law. The New Testament writer of 1 Peter 2:9 affirms the role of the Christian believer, "But you are a chosen race, a royal priesthood, a holy nation, God's own people, in order that you may proclaim the mighty acts of him who called you out of darkness into his marvelous light" (NSRV). It is not just the priests and pastors, but the whole of the Christian community that is meant to be a "holy nation" and to live an exemplary life in the world.

Paul reminds us as he taught in his letter to the church at Rome, "I beseech you therefore, brethren, by the mercies of God, that ye present your bodies a living sacrifice, holy, acceptable unto God, which is your reasonable service. And be not conformed to this world: but be ye transformed by the renewing of your mind, that ye may prove what is that good, and acceptable, and perfect, will of God" (Romans 12:1-2). We, therefore, resist the waves of sexual indulgence and living based upon pure fleshly content. Ours is a pursuit of high fidelity and spiritual union with God as we establish relationships of unconditional love with another.

The point is fairly simple—we must protect the human spirit. In the interest of protecting one's spirit from hurt, pain, exploitation, and exposure to carelessness, a fuller, deeper, committed relationship is needed. For serious couples who have learned by experience to take such care, this kind of a commitment comes with marriage between two who share agape love. Our ability to wait for sex, to develop a sound relationship based upon unconditional love and marriage, undergirded by real love is transformative. We live in the Spirit and we draw upon a strength that is not our own, but a strength that is from God to empower us. In this way, we, as Christians, become the reflectors of the light that Jesus brought into the world. We become positive examples that are conformed to the way of Christ in building our relationships and in our approach to sexuality and counterbalancing forces to the world's view.

Sources:

Michael, Robert T., John H. Gagnon, Edward O. Laumann, and Gina Kolata. *Sex in America: A Definitive Study*. Boston, MA: Little, Brown and Company, 1994. 35.

Donald-Mims, Jacquelyn. *Obsessive Sex: Resolving the Conflict of Loving Sex and Loving God*. Austin, TX: Devon Publishing, 2001. 94.

La Sor, William Sanford, David Allan Hubbard, and Frederic William Bush. *Old Testament Survey: The Message Form and Background of the Old Testament*. Grand Rapids, MI: Eerdmans, 1982. 152.

CRISPUS ATTUCKS

(1723-1770)

Sailor, Patriot

There are many details about the life of Crispus Attucks before the events in Boston that are not documented. It was believed that Attucks' father was an African and his mother a Natick or Nantucket Indian.

He was born during the time when African Americans and their descendants were enslaved. As a slave in Framingham, he had been known for his skill in buying and selling cattle. His owner was William Brown. William Brown described Attucks as a runaway.

Attucks was carried off on many vessels over the next 20 years. As a sailor, he worked on whaling crew that constantly sailed out of Boston harbor. He was also thought to be a rope maker in Boston. Attucks' occupation made him particularly vulnerable to the presence of the British.

In the fall of 1768, British soldiers were sent to Boston to help control growing colonial unrest. A fight between Boston rope makers and three British soldiers on Friday, March 2, 1770, set the stage for a later confrontation.

One story says that after dusk on March 5, 1770, a crowd of colonists confronted a sentry who had struck a boy for complaining that an officer was late in paying a barber bill. Both townspeople and the British soldiers of the 29th Regiment of Foot gathered.

Five Americans were killed and six were mortally wounded. Attucks took two bullets in the chest and was the first to die. Coroners Robert Pierpoint and Thomas Crafts, Jr., conducted an autopsy on Attucks. Attucks' body was carried to Faneuil Hall, where it lay in state until Thursday, March 8, when he and the other victims were buried together. Attucks became a hero to the colonials during the American Revolution. They saw him as gallantly standing up to abusive British soldiers.

Attucks also became a hero to African Americans. In the mid-nineteenth century, African-American Bostonians celebrated "Crispus Attucks Day" every year on March 5.

Crispus Attucks is an important figure in African-American history because he was a hero not only for his own race but for oppressed people everywhere. He is a reminder that the African-American heritage began with the beginning of America.

There may be many things still unsure about Crispus Attucks, but one thing for certain is that his faith, courage, and act of bravery changed history.

Sources:
http://www.biography.com/articles/Crispus-Attucks-9191864 accessed 6/9/11 http://afroamhistory.about.com/od/biographies/a/A-Biography-Of-Crispus-Attucks.htm-accessed 6/9/11
http://www.pbs.org/wgbh/aia/part2/2p24.html accessed 6/9/11

Teaching Tips

Words You Should Know

A. Stir (Ezra 1:1) *'ur* (Heb.)—To open up one's eyes; to arouse

B. Willingly Offered (v. 6) *nadab* (Heb.)—To give freely or spontaneously

Teacher Preparation

Unifying Principle—The Resources to Rebuild. Sometimes people are given a challenging job, which requires a change or risk. Where can we find resources to meet these challenges? Israel's release from Babylonian captivity reveals that we can have faith that God will provide the people and resources to fulfill His purposes.

A. Read the Bible Background and Devotional Reading.

B. Pray for your students and lesson clarity.

C. Read the lesson Scripture in multiple translations.

O—Open the Lesson

A. Begin the class with prayer.

B. Brainstorm a list of societal needs and write them on the board. Ask the class to consider items on the list and debate whether the needs should be met by government funds, private contributions, or a combination of both. Lead into the Bible lesson about how the rebuilding of the Temple was financed.

C. Have the students read the Aim for Change and the In Focus story.

D. Ask students how events like those in the story weigh on their hearts and how they can view these events from a faith perspective.

P—Present the Scriptures

A. Read the Focal Verses and discuss the Background and The People, Places, and Times sections.

B. Have the class share what Scriptures stand out for them and why, with particular emphasis on today's themes.

E—Explore the Meaning

A. Use In Depth or More Light on the Text to facilitate a deeper discussion of the lesson text.

B. Pose the questions in Search the Scriptures and Discuss the Meaning.

C. Discuss the Liberating Lesson and Application for Activation sections.

N—Next Steps for Application

A. Summarize the value of trusting God to supply what is needed to complete God's work.

B. End class with a commitment to pray for those who do not believe but may nonetheless accomplish God's purposes.

Worship Guide

For the Superintendent or Teacher
Theme: Babylonian Captivity Ends
Song: "We'll Work 'Til Jesus Comes"

[handwritten notes: prayer Line Intercessory, 213 338 8477 Thursday 7:30 PM, CODE 893 5948 4624]

Babylonian Captivity Ends

Bible Background • EZRA 1; 2:64-70
Printed Text • EZRA 1:1-8, 11; 2:64-70 | Devotional Reading • AMOS 5:14-15

Aim for Change

By the end of this lesson, we will EXAMINE the rebuilding plan for the Temple in Jerusalem that God gave to King Cyrus, BELIEVE and TRUST that God provides resources for the tasks God asks us to do, and SHARE situations in which believers will trust God's provision and act in faith.

In Focus

After 27 years of ministry to the community, the leaders of the Samaritan Evangelistic Center knew it was time for them to move out of their old facility. The walls were crumbling, the foundation was shifting, and the stairs had begun cracking. Plus, Samaritan Evangelistic Center was ministering to more people than they could possibly hold in the old building, which made the facility a fire hazard.

The executive committee of the center began looking for an existing structure in the community close to their present location. But after months of searching and talking with prospective realtors, the committee couldn't find a suitable building which would meet their needs and give them greater opportunities to expand their ministry to domestic abuse survivors. So, the committee decided to buy a parcel of land right next door to their present location and build a new facility from the ground up. Said executive director Brenda Charles, "Given the circumstance, it was the most feasible and logical thing to do."

The committee's accountant said, "Building projects are never easy to accomplish. Not only are there finances to be raised, but also material to buy, construction crews to hire, and deadlines to meet in order to finish the goal in a timely manner. Any wrinkle in the schedule can hinder the process."

The committee knew the most important thing to do: PRAY!

Sometimes we remember to rely on God's provision and guidance from the start. When have you forgotten to plan with God? What happened?

Keep in Mind

"And some of the chief of the fathers, when they came to the house of the LORD which is at Jerusalem, offered freely for the house of God to set it up in his place." (Ezra 2:68, KJV)

April 17 Easter

"When they arrived at the Temple of the LORD in Jerusalem, some of the family leaders made voluntary offerings toward the rebuilding of God's Temple on its original site." (Ezra 2:68, NLT)

Focal Verses

KJV **Ezra 1:1** Now in the first year of Cyrus king of Persia, that the word of the LORD by the mouth of Jeremiah might be fulfilled, the LORD stirred up the spirit of Cyrus king of Persia, that he made a proclamation throughout all his kingdom, and put it also in writing, saying,

2 Thus saith Cyrus king of Persia, The LORD God of heaven hath given me all the kingdoms of the earth; and he hath charged me to build him an house at Jerusalem, which is in Judah.

3 Who is there among you of all his people? his God be with him, and let him go up to Jerusalem, which is in Judah, and build the house of the LORD God of Israel, (he is the God,) which is in Jerusalem.

4 And whosoever remaineth in any place where he sojourneth, let the men of his place help him with silver, and with gold, and with goods, and with beasts, beside the freewill offering for the house of God that is in Jerusalem.

5 Then rose up the chief of the fathers of Judah and Benjamin, and the priests, and the Levites, with all them whose spirit God had raised, to go up to build the house of the LORD which is in Jerusalem.

6 And all they that were about them strengthened their hands with vessels of silver, with gold, with goods, and with beasts, and with precious things, beside all that was willingly offered.

7 Also Cyrus the king brought forth the vessels of the house of the LORD, which Nebuchadnezzar had brought forth out of Jerusalem, and had put them in the house of his gods;

8 Even those did Cyrus king of Persia bring forth by the hand of Mithredath the treasurer, and numbered them unto Sheshbazzar, the prince of Judah.

11 All the vessels of gold and of silver were five thousand and four hundred. All these

NLT **Ezra 1:1** In the first year of King Cyrus of Persia, the LORD fulfilled the prophecy he had given through Jeremiah. He stirred the heart of Cyrus to put this proclamation in writing and to send it throughout his kingdom:

2 "This is what King Cyrus of Persia says: 'The LORD, the God of heaven, has given me all the kingdoms of the earth. He has appointed me to build him a Temple at Jerusalem, which is in Judah.

3 Any of you who are his people may go to Jerusalem in Judah to rebuild this Temple of the LORD, the God of Israel, who lives in Jerusalem. And may your God be with you!

4 Wherever this Jewish remnant is found, let their neighbors contribute toward their expenses by giving them silver and gold, supplies for the journey, and livestock, as well as a voluntary offering for the Temple of God in Jerusalem."

5 Then God stirred the hearts of the priests and Levites and the leaders of the tribes of Judah and Benjamin to go to Jerusalem to rebuild the Temple of the LORD.

6 And all their neighbors assisted by giving them articles of silver and gold, supplies for the journey, and livestock. They gave them many valuable gifts in addition to all the voluntary offerings.

7 King Cyrus himself brought out the articles that King Nebuchadnezzar had taken from the LORD's Temple in Jerusalem and had placed in the temple of his own gods.

8 Cyrus directed Mithredath, the treasurer of Persia, to count these items and present them to Sheshbazzar, the leader of the exiles returning to Judah.

11 In all, there were 5,400 articles of gold and silver. Sheshbazzar brought all of these along when the exiles went from Babylon to Jerusalem.

did Sheshbazzar bring up with them of the captivity that were brought up from Babylon unto Jerusalem.

2:64 The whole congregation together was forty and two thousand three hundred and threescore,

65 Beside their servants and their maids, of whom there were seven thousand three hundred thirty and seven: and there were among them two hundred singing men and singing women.

66 Their horses were seven hundred thirty and six; their mules, two hundred forty and five;

67 Their camels, four hundred thirty and five; their asses, six thousand seven hundred and twenty.

68 And some of the chief of the fathers, when they came to the house of the LORD which is at Jerusalem, offered freely for the house of God to set it up in his place:

69 They gave after their ability unto the treasure of the work threescore and one thousand drams of gold, and five thousand pound of silver, and one hundred priests' garments.

70 So the priests, and the Levites, and some of the people, and the singers, and the porters, and the Nethinims, dwelt in their cities, and all Israel in their cities.

2:64 So a total of 42,360 people returned to Judah,

65 in addition to 7,337 servants and 200 singers, both men and women.

66 They took with them 736 horses, 245 mules,

67 435 camels, and 6,720 donkeys.

68 When they arrived at the Temple of the LORD in Jerusalem, some of the family leaders made voluntary offerings toward the rebuilding of God's Temple on its original site,

69 and each leader gave as much as he could. The total of their gifts came to 61,000 gold coins, 6,250 pounds of silver, and 100 robes for the priests.

70 So the priests, the Levites, the singers, the gatekeepers, the Temple servants, and some of the common people settled in villages near Jerusalem. The rest of the people returned to their own towns throughout Israel.

Jeremiah 1:5
Before I formed you in the womb I knew you.

The People, Places, and Times

Nebuchadnezzar, King of Babylon from 605 to 562 BC. King Nebuchadnezzar enters the biblical narrative when he besieges Jerusalem in 597 BC. That siege ended with Nebuchadnezzar taking many elites as captives back to Babylon, and setting up a puppet king in Jerusalem. When that king rebelled, Nebuchadnezzar and his army returned to Jerusalem and destroyed the city, taking all the inhabitants captive, and sacking the many valuables in the Temple. Besides the gold-plated fixtures used in actual worship at the Temple, the building also stored

many expensive items people had given as dedications to God. King Nebuchadnezzar took all of these sacred objects as plunder and displayed them in temples in his own country, thinking this showed that his gods were more powerful than the Jewish God.

Cyrus, King of Persia from 559 to 530 BC. King Cyrus captured the city of Babylon from the Babylonian king Belshazzar. Cyrus had a policy of allowing conquered people to return to their homelands. This policy set the stage for the return of the Hebrew people to Jerusalem following their long period of captivity under the Babylonians. As a result of the Persian conquest of Babylonia, the Jews were free to return to Jerusalem and rebuild the Temple. Cyrus is remembered in the Old Testament as a heroic figure and messenger of God who redeemed Israel.

Discuss a time when a change in leadership allowed you to return to older, better ways.

Background

The Children of Israel had experienced a period of sheer rebellion against God. Because God is merciful, He sent His prophets to speak to them concerning their ways, but "they mocked the messengers of God, and despised his words, and misused his prophets until the wrath of the LORD arose against his people, till there was no remedy" (2 Chronicles 36:16). As a result the young, old, male, female, rich, and poor were led into captivity. Many died in Nebuchadnezzar's attacks, and those who lived were taken away to Babylon "where they were servants" to Nebuchadnezzar and to Belshazzar after him (v. 20).

Ezra 1 begins with God fulfilling His promise to return His people to the land of promise after 70 years of exile. Some call this Israel's "second exodus."

At-A-Glance

1. The Revelation of a Stirred Heart
(Ezra 1:1)
2. The Proclamation of a Stirred Heart
(vv. 2-4)
3. The Response of a Stirred Heart
(vv. 5-11)
4. The Gifts of Stirred Hearts
(Ezra 2:64-70)

In Depth

1. The Revelation of a Stirred Heart (Ezra 1:1)

Jeremiah prophesied that God would deliver His people after a period of bondage. At the appointed time God began to move. No matter how long one may be held in captivity by the devil or by sinister human machinations, God has promised deliverance. When God wants to change a situation, the divine Spirit searches for those whose hearts are malleable to the stirring of God.

He stirred Cyrus's spirit. We need for God to stir our spirit for the plight of others. Many of us wish to end suffering, but are we willing to put our names or personal kingdoms on the line, to stand for "the least of these"? We thank God that Cyrus did not just get stirred by the Spirit, but he followed through with an obedient spirit.

How does God stir hearts today?

2. The Proclamation of a Stirred Heart (vv. 2–4)

God wanted His people and Temple again, and He was going to use King Cyrus to put things in motion. Cyrus proclaimed (v. 2) that God had given him all the kingdoms of the earth and appointed him to build a Temple in Jerusalem. Cyrus is clear that he was not speaking about just any god, but of the God who is at Jerusalem. The proclamation was also a challenge directed at the people of God. It was a time for rebuilding and refreshing. Cyrus is here calling on not just those who claim to belong to God, but those who have faith in God's ability to protect and keep those who step out for God.

3. The Response of a Stirred Heart (vv. 5–11)

The family heads of Judah and Benjamin with the priests and Levites were preparing to "go up to build the house of the Lord" (v. 5). They needed silver, gold, goods, livestock, and freewill offerings for the house of God. This was costly, but God made a way.

All that the Babylonians stole—valuable vessels, candlesticks, incense burners, linens—were now returned. The inventory of the vessels listed (vv. 9-10) is not so much about material things as it is about the possibility of again worshiping God in a space worthy of His glory. It also signifies the power of the God of Israel over the gods and kings who laid claim to what belonged to the people of God.

4. The Gifts of Stirred Hearts (Ezra 2:64–70)

Ezra's precise history writing is on display in the exact numbers recorded here. A total of 42,360 Israelites compose the huge caravan. They require hundreds of all kinds of pack animals. Ezra is not interested in giving a detailed travel log of their journey. The destination is the only focus: Jerusalem and the Temple of God.

As soon as they arrive, the returning exiles rejoice by giving gifts toward the construction of the Temple. All gave something, not trying to one-up each other to show off how much they could give, but giving as they could.

After these gifts were given, they could settle into their ancestral lands. The Jewish nation managed to retain its identity through the exile. Therefore, they knew which lands God had appointed to which tribe. There was no need to fight and bicker over where anyone would live.

How have you celebrated the end of a long journey, or a long-anticipated journey?

Search the Scriptures

1. What did the Lord do to the spirit of Cyrus king of Persia (Ezra 1:1)?

2. What was Cyrus the king charged to do (v. 2)?

Discuss the Meaning

1. Why did the Temple need to be rebuilt with so much grandeur? Costly building fixtures and flourishes could have paid for many meals for the hungry or homes for the homeless. Why do we even today want to beautify our sanctuaries?

2. Why do you think God thought it was so important not to send the captives out empty-handed? What does this reveal about God?

Liberating Lesson

There are people in our society who have been cast aside because of some unfortunate event in their lives. Their possessions may even have been taken away from them as well. The individual may have placed himself or herself in a position that caused these misfortunes to occur. But when God shows mercy, we must show mercy and lend a helping hand and strengthen these individuals to stand on their own two feet again.

In this lesson God supplied His people with a portion of gold, silver, and cattle to get them started again. How can we help someone who was once in jail and now has served that sentence?

Application for Activation

This week think of someone who needs your help. What kind of people may have lost their job, house, and possessions due to disobedience to God and His ways? They may be recovering drug addicts, alcoholics, or prisoners. They are trying their best to get back on track. How can you help right now? Ask God to guide you.

Follow the Spirit

What God wants me to do:

_____

_____

_____

_____

Remember Your Thoughts

Special insights I have learned:

_____

_____

_____

_____

More Light on the Text

Ezra 1:1-8, 11; 2:64-70

1:1 Now in the first year of Cyrus king of Persia, that the word of the LORD by the mouth of Jeremiah might be fulfilled, the LORD stirred up the spirit of Cyrus king of Persia, that he made a proclamation throughout all his kingdom, and put it also in writing, saying,

"The first year of Cyrus king of Persia" refers to the first year that Cyrus ruled over Babylon, which would have been 538 BC. Cyrus's reign partly began in 559 BC when he succeeded his father as king of Anshan. Cyrus defeated the king of Media and melded the empires into a dual monarchy called Medo-Persia. In 539 BC Cyrus's army marched into the city of Babylon, bringing the Babylonian empire to a close. A few years later in 536 BC, the newly named Persian Empire would include Persia, Media, Babylonia, and Chaldea, with many smaller dependencies.

For many years the Children of Israel had been in captivity while their land laid in waste. But deep in the mind of the Israelites was the promise of God from his prophets. Before the fall of Judah, the prophet Jeremiah predicted that Judah would be taken into Babylonian captivity and the land would remain desolate for 70 years. After 70 years God would punish the Babylonians for their cruelty and sinfulness (Jeremiah 25:12). The prophet further predicted that at that time

He would cause the Jews to return to Judah (29:10). The 70-year captivity began with the first of the Jews taken into captivity in 605 BC during the reign of Jehoiakim (2 Kings 24:1; Daniel 1:1). The period ended when the captives began their return in 538 BC, approximately 70 years later.

Note Ezra's careful wording. The message is the word of the Lord, even though it came through Jeremiah's mouth. When the prophets spoke, they were only passing on God's message. In fulfillment of the word which God had spoken through Jeremiah and through Isaiah, God began to move.

Ezra tells us that "the LORD stirred up the spirit of Cyrus king of Persia" to issue the proclamation. "Stirred" is from the Hebrew word 'ur (**OOR**) meaning to "arouse from sleep." "Spirit" is a translation of the Hebrew *ruakh* (**ROO**-okh). In this case the word refers to the seat of human will and intellect and emotion. By stirring Cyrus's heart to be kind toward these exiled people, God enabled the word of His promise to Jeremiah to be fulfilled.

The LORD God of Israel caused Cyrus to figuratively wake up to the group of people in his kingdom who had borne the brunt of many prejudices and injustices. The great thing about the word "stir" is that it implies that God is saying to Cyrus: "get up from your complacency; lift up yourself and do something for me." Cyrus follows through this stirring with an obedient spirit and a listening ear to hear "thus saith God."

The result of God's stirring is that Cyrus "made a proclamation" (Heb. literally, "caused to send out a voice") throughout the kingdom. The idea here is not mere talk. The Hebrew verb form used here for "made" is causative. Cyrus puts effort into pushing out this call and making sure everyone hears or reads it. In this context the king did not just talk; he actively works to bring about God's will. People like King Cyrus who hear the word of the Lord let it be known that God has spoken to them.

2 Thus saith Cyrus king of Persia, The LORD God of heaven hath given me all the kingdoms of the earth; and he hath charged me to build him an house at Jerusalem, which is in Judah.

Cyrus' proclamation begins by establishing his own power and naming the power that backs him. Saying God gave him "all the kingdoms of the earth" is hyperbole (accepted exaggeration), but it was literally true that the Persian Empire was the greatest ruling power in the Western world at that time. "God" in this case is a translation of the Hebrew *el* (**ELL**), which in the ancient Near East was the most widespread word for God. But Cyrus makes certain to specify which God he means: this God is in heaven, and wants a house in Jerusalem in Judah. "Heaven" from the Hebrew *shamayim* (shah-**MY**-eem) refers to the abode of God, a higher realm where celestial beings dwell. This God is the "LORD," a common stand-in instead of translating the true name of God written in the Hebrew: Yahweh.

Cyrus recognizes that his task to rebuild the Temple in Jerusalem is something God "hath charged" (Heb. *paqad*, paw-**KOD**) him with. The word means that God has placed it in his care to see to its completion. Even though Cyrus worked this great task in full acknowledgment of God, the Bible student ought not to think Cyrus had converted to worshiping only Yahweh. Although Cyrus acknowledged the Lord, Scripture clearly states that he was an unbeliever (Isaiah 45:4). In the current verse, as well as the next, Cyrus is clear he was not speaking about just a god, but of the God who is at Jerusalem. Since Cyrus understands that the Jewish Yahweh is over in Jerusalem, he sees no reason to exclusively worship Him from all the way over in Babylon.

3 Who is there among you of all his people? his God be with him, and let him go up to Jerusalem, which is in Judah, and build the house of the LORD God of Israel, (he is the God,) which is in Jerusalem. 4 And whosoever remaineth in any place where he sojourneth, let the men of his place help him with silver, and with gold, and with goods, and with beasts, beside the freewill offering for the house of God that is in Jerusalem.

The question "who" is not about identity. This "who" is meant to draw out the willing. Who is he among you who is willing? Why will the people not be willing? Just because people are God's people does not always mean that they will go when God calls.

The purpose of Cyrus's proclamation was to grant full permission to Jewish exiles to return to their own country if they so chose. No prominent person and certainly no large people-group under a monarch was allow to pick up stakes whenever they wished. Cyrus needed to grant them permission to move to another part of his territory. Also, this charge recommended to those of their countrymen who chose to remain to aid the returnees on their way by contributing liberally toward the rebuilding of the Temple. Whether they are able to give money, goods, or livestock, any gift from those staying behind is accepted.

Today still, ambitious building projects require large budgets, and it is difficult for many to afford them. This is especially true of people who have experienced times when they did not know how their own bills would be paid. Our God works miracles, though, and makes a way. Just as today projects are completed with public funds, private funds, and a combination of both, so the Temple in Jerusalem was to be funded by Cyrus' public contributions and the private contributions of those who were unable or unwilling to make the trek themselves.

5 Then rose up the chief of the fathers of Judah and Benjamin, and the priests, and the Levites, with all them whose spirit God had raised, to go up to build the house of the LORD which is in Jerusalem. 6 And all they that were about them strengthened their hands with vessels of silver, with gold, with goods, and with beasts, and with precious things, beside all that was willingly offered.

The tribes of Judah and Benjamin are mentioned here because they were the most numerous of those that went into Babylonian exile. When the nation of Israel split after Solomon died, the only tribes that remained with the Southern Kingdom were Judah and Benjamin, which is why that nation was called Judah. The Northern Kingdom, Israel, with the majority of the other 10 tribes had been conquered and disbursed earlier by the Assyrians.

"The chief of the fathers" is a reference to the paternal and ecclesiastical leaders during the captivity. By Cyrus's day, these leaders were primarily elders of the tribes of Judah and Benjamin, but members of the other 10 tribes who retained the pure worship of God were also represented (1 Chronicles 9:3). These elders naturally took the lead in this movement. They were followed by all those Jews whose love for God and patriotism were strong enough to leave the comforts of a foreign land for the hardships of the repatriation.

Many of the Jews who had been born in Babylonia or had comfortably established themselves decided to stay behind. Although they would remain behind, they generously contributed to the venture. It also appears that some of their international friends and neighbors displayed hearty goodwill and great liberality in aiding and promoting the views of the emigrants. The phrase "willingly offered" is a translation of the Hebrew *nadab* (naw-**DOV**) which means "to give freely." The word denotes

the inward attitude of those who spontaneously gave to the construction of the Temple.

What a glorious time this must have been! A form of jubilee. God had a remnant of people to fulfill the next phase of Israel's spiritual journey. The leaders were preparing to go forth in the power and might of God's promise to His people. They were strengthened to do the work of the Lord. Generations had been in bondage and now there was release!

7 Also Cyrus the king brought forth the vessels of the house of the LORD, which Nebuchadnezzar had brought forth out of Jerusalem, and had put them in the house of his gods;

Nebuchadnezzar had looted the Temple of God and taken the vessels of the house of the Lord as prizes and proof of the power of the Babylonian gods. Some of the vessels had been taken in 605 BC (Daniel 1:2), others in 597 BC (2 Kings 24:13), and the rest in final deportation in 586 BC (2 Kings 25:13-15). These items were placed in the temples of the Babylonian gods.

God wanted His people and Temple again, and He was going to use King Cyrus to put things in motion. No matter how long it takes, God can bring His people back to the place of true worship and restore all that has been lost. In this sense Cyrus is a type (or picture) of the Messiah who seeks by Word and work to restore humanity to the place of true worship and celebration. Cyrus is even called God's "anointed" (Heb. *mashiakh*, maw-**SHE**-okh), which is what "messiah" means (Isaiah 45:1). The term "anointed" is used for various people in the Old Testament. They were all God's agents, working out His plan of salvation. They all prefigured the true Messiah, who could provide true and lasting salvation.

8 Even those did Cyrus king of Persia bring forth by the hand of Mithredath the treasurer,

and numbered them unto Sheshbazzar, the prince of Judah.

11 All the vessels of gold and of silver were five thousand and four hundred. All these did Sheshbazzar bring up with them of the captivity that were brought up from Babylon unto Jerusalem.

Many believe that Sheshbazzar and Zerubbabel are two different people, but it is more likely that they were the same person. The name Sheshbazzar is Babylonian in origin, but Zerubbabel is Hebrew. The Babylonian name indicates that Sheshbazzar may have served in the royal court where Babylonian names were given to young men chosen to serve to make them more Babylonian. The most famous case of Babylonian renaming is that of Daniel's friends (Daniel 1:7; also see Esther 2:7). The element that ties the names together is the office of Judah's governor. Ezra records that Sheshbazzar was governor of Judah (Ezra 5:14), while Haggai records the name Zerubbabel as the governor at the same time (Haggai 1:1). It is likely that Ezra simply used both names. "Numbered" is from the Hebrew *safar* (sah-**FAHR**) meaning to enumerate or count, usually through a written record. These expensive gold and silver vessels were inventoried and a written record was given.

Verses 9 and 10 list specific objects that were part of this written record. This itemized list only tallies to 2,499, but is totaled to 5,400 in verse 11. It is probable that the larger, most valuable vessels are mentioned, while the inventory of the whole, including great and small, came to the gross sum stated in the text.

As Sheshbazzar, a Babylonian official, this man has little to do in Ezra's account. However, as Zerubbabel, the Jewish prince, he is well remembered. Zerubbabel was the son of Shealtiel who was the son of Jeconiah and an ancestor of Christ (Matthew 1:12). Because of his royal bloodline, he was recognized among

the exiles as a hereditary "prince of Judah." He led the exiles in their return to Judah from their Babylonian captivity (Ezra 2:1–64). In the ruined city of Jerusalem, Zerubbabel and Jeshua, the high priest, led the people in the restoration of the Temple (3:1–9).

2:64 The whole congregation together was forty and two thousand three hundred and threescore, 65 Beside their servants and their maids, of whom there were seven thousand three hundred thirty and seven: and there were among them two hundred singing men and singing women. 66 Their horses were seven hundred thirty and six; their mules, two hundred forty and five; 67 Their camels, four hundred thirty and five; their asses, six thousand seven hundred and twenty.

Not all the Jewish exiles embraced the privilege which the Persian king granted them. The great proportion of Jews, born in Babylon, preferred continuing in their comfortable homes instead of undertaking a long, expensive, and hazardous journey to a desolate land. Mordecai and Esther are examples of these. Nor did the returning exiles all go at once. This first band of 42,360 went with Zerubbabel, others afterwards with Ezra (7:1–10:44), and a large number with Nehemiah at a still later period (Nehemiah 1:1–2:20). Note that the 42,360 number is only those of the official Jewish congregation; when their entourage is added, the caravan number swells to almost 50,000.

The 8,136 animals mentioned in verses 66-67 obviously are not enough to carry the 42,360 citizens of the expedition. These animals were likely used for carrying the people's many belongings and all the treasure that Cyrus was returning to the Temple. The people would have walked or ridden in carts.

68 And some of the chief of the fathers, when they came to the house of the LORD

which is at Jerusalem, offered freely for the house of God to set it up in his place: 69 They gave after their ability unto the treasure of the work threescore and one thousand drams of gold, and five thousand pound of silver, and one hundred priests' garments.

Ezra records that once the group finally arrived in Jerusalem, they immediately gave offerings to God. What a celebration it must have been for this formerly oppressed people to be free to rebuild their culture. The very first step, they knew, had to be the Temple. Many gave freely to the project, perhaps depositing the gifts that were given to them by those who could not make the journey (vv. 4, 6).

A dram is an ancient unit of currency, one of the oldest we have in the archaeological record. Though a single dram is not a significant sum, 1,060 of them would be worth close to $5,300 today. While the cost of silver currently (2020) is over $200 per pound, one could assume the silver mentioned here was in a form of currency rather than pure silver. Still, it is a princely sum by itself. Textiles were a valuable commodity in pre-industrial societies as well. Priestly garments were even more highly prized, as they included many pieces of fine linen and richly dyed and embroidered fabric (Exodus 39).

70 So the priests, and the Levites, and some of the people, and the singers, and the porters, and the Nethinims, dwelt in their cities, and all Israel in their cities.

Now that the people have arrived and taken their first steps toward building the Temple, they can settle in to building back up their nation. They return to their ancestral lands, which God appointed for each tribe in the Promised Land. The Levites, who were charged with populating the priesthood for the nation, were a special case, though. Unlike the other tribes, the Levites were not granted a specific territory in the Promised Land. Rather, the other tribes were to give the Levites several towns in their territories (Numbers 35:2-8). These are "their cities" (v. 70) in which the Levites and all the worship leaders dwell as the other Israelites return to their own cities.

There was much rebuilding still to do. But the returning Jews were willing to accept all these life-altering challenges when they were convinced that God wanted them to do so. They trusted that, while difficult times had come, such times were temporary. The prophets had told them the exile would only be 70 years, and that afterward, they would return and rebuild. May we too trust God's promises as we venture out to fulfill His will.

Sources:

Henry, Matthew. *Matthew Henry's Commentary on the Whole Bible: New Modern Edition*. Vols. 1-6. Peabody, MA: Hendrickson Publishers, Inc., 2009.

Strong, James. *The New Strong's Exhaustive Concordance of the Bible*. Nashville, TN: Thomas Nelson, 2003.

Thayer, Joseph Henry. *A Greek-English Lexicon of the New Testament*. New York: American Book Company, 1889.

Say It Correctly

Nebuchadnezzar.
neh-buh-kad-NEZZ-zer.
Belshazzar. bell-SHAZZ-zar.
Mithredath. MYTH-reh-dath.
Sheshbazzar. SHESH-bazz-zar.
Nethinims. NEH-thee-neems.
Zerubbabel. zeh-ROO-bah-bell.

Daily Bible Readings

MONDAY
Prepare the Way of the Lord
(Isaiah 40:1-11)

TUESDAY
Being God's Instrument
(Isaiah 45:1-10)

WEDNESDAY
God Will Provide for Every Need
(Philippians 4:10-19)

THURSDAY
Lift Up Your Eyes to God
(Isaiah 40:12-15, 21-31)

FRIDAY
Live Freely but Responsibly
(1 Peter 2:13-17)

SATURDAY
Light Dawns for the Righteous
(Psalm 97)

SUNDAY
Cyrus Permits Jews to Return Home
(Ezra 1:1-8, 11; 2:64-70)

Notes

Teaching Tips

March 13
Bible Study Guide 2

Words You Should Know

A. Hindered (Ezra 6:8) *betel* (Aram.)—To cease; to cause to stop

B. Destroy (v. 12) *khabal* (Aram.)—To corrupt or despoil with impurity

Teacher Preparation

Unifying Principle—Support for Needed Projects. Sometimes people focus on their own adverse situations rather than seeking guidance. Why do we act and speak according to our situations rather than seeking liberation from them? Ezra shows us that when we recognize and confess our failings God is ready to listen and support us, even in unexpected ways.

A. Read the Bible Background and Devotional Reading.

B. Pray for your students and lesson clarity.

C. Read the lesson Scripture in multiple translations.

O—Open the Lesson

A. Begin the class with prayer.

B. Begin class by writing on the board: "Dear Representative _____: I am writing to urge you to _____." Ask participants to bring up ways that this letter might be continued. Lead into Bible study by explaining that our lesson text deals with a request made to a government official and his response.

C. Have the students read the Aim for Change and the In Focus story.

D. Ask students how events like those in the story weigh on their hearts and how they can view these events from a faith perspective.

P—Present the Scriptures

A. Read the Focal Verses and discuss the Background and The People, Places, and Times sections.

B. Have the class share what Scriptures stand out for them and why, with particular emphasis on today's themes.

E—Explore the Meaning

A. Use In Depth or More Light on the Text to facilitate a deeper discussion of the lesson text.

B. Pose the questions in Search the Scriptures and Discuss the Meaning.

C. Discuss the Liberating Lesson and Application for Activation sections.

N—Next Steps for Application

A. Summarize the value of seeking God's guidance during difficult times.

B. End class with a commitment to pray for forgiveness for letting fears paralyze them.

Worship Guide

For the Superintendent or Teacher
Theme: Freedom to Worship
Song: "The Church's One Foundation"

Freedom to Worship

Bible Background • EZRA 5, 6:1-12; 10:1-5
Printed Text • EZRA 6:1-12 | Devotional Reading • 1 CORINTHIANS 6:19-20

Aim for Change

By the end of this lesson, we will REVIEW the pivotal role of Darius in getting the new Temple built in Jerusalem; PONDER excuses we offer for failing to act in accord with God's will; and CONFESS our failings before God, receive the joy of forgiveness, and get on with the task at hand.

In Focus

Maddie and Erica had been best friends since college. They were there for the other through all the highs and lows. Every breakup and promotion both women knew they could count on their sister to be in their corner praying, celebrating, and comforting them.

Erica was having another low in her life after the birth of her and her husband Ryan's first daughter. Having her little mini-me was one of the happiest moments of her life, but since they came home from the hospital two months ago, Erica's emotions were all over the place. She didn't feel like herself anymore. She thought no one would understand.

One day Maddie stopped by Erica's to visit. Maddie hadn't heard from Erica since the baby was born, but Maddie figured Erica was just getting adjusted to being a mom.

Maddie was shocked to see her best friend's state. "Girl, what is wrong?" Maddie asked holding the baby for Erica.

"Everything! All she does is cry. All Ryan does is work. I never get a moment to myself. My body isn't the same. I just need a break from everything."

"Erica, why didn't you call me? It sounds like this might be postpartum depression," Maddie explained. "We may need to make you an appointment to see what's wrong."

"I didn't think you'd understand," Erica said.

"We are sisters. You can come to me about anything, and I'll be by your side. I can ask my sister who she went to about her postpartum," said Maddie hugging Erica.

How do you know when it's time to ask for help?

Keep in Mind

"And the God that hath caused his name to dwell there destroy all kings and people, that shall put to their hand to alter and to destroy this house of God which is at Jerusalem. I Darius have made a decree; let it be done with speed." (Ezra 6:12, KJV)

"May the God who has chosen the city of Jerusalem as the place to honor his name destroy any king or nation that violates this command and destroys this Temple. I, Darius, have issued this decree. Let it be obeyed with all diligence." (Ezra 6:12, NLT)

Focal Verses

KJV **Ezra 6:1** Then Darius the king made a decree, and search was made in the house of the rolls, where the treasures were laid up in Babylon.

2 And there was found at Achmetha, in the palace that is in the province of the Medes, a roll, and therein was a record thus written:

3 In the first year of Cyrus the king the same Cyrus the king made a decree concerning the house of God at Jerusalem, Let the house be builded, the place where they offered sacrifices, and let the foundations thereof be strongly laid; the height thereof threescore cubits, and the breadth thereof threescore cubits;

4 With three rows of great stones, and a row of new timber: and let the expenses be given out of the king's house:

5 And also let the golden and silver vessels of the house of God, which Nebuchadnezzar took forth out of the temple which is at Jerusalem, and brought unto Babylon, be restored, and brought again unto the temple which is at Jerusalem, every one to his place, and place them in the house of God.

6 Now therefore, Tatnai, governor beyond the river, Shetharboznai, and your companions the Apharsachites, which are beyond the river, be ye far from thence:

7 Let the work of this house of God alone; let the governor of the Jews and the elders of the Jews build this house of God in his place.

8 Moreover I make a decree what ye shall do to the elders of these Jews for the building of this house of God: that of the king's goods, even of the tribute beyond the river, forthwith expenses be given unto these men, that they be not hindered.

9 And that which they have need of, both young bullocks, and rams, and lambs, for the burnt offerings of the God of heaven, wheat, salt, wine, and oil, according to the appointment of

NLT **Ezra 6:1** So King Darius issued orders that a search be made in the Babylonian archives, which were stored in the treasury.

2 But it was at the fortress at Ecbatana in the province of Media that a scroll was found. This is what it said: "Memorandum:

3 In the first year of King Cyrus's reign, a decree was sent out concerning the Temple of God at Jerusalem. Let the Temple be rebuilt on the site where Jews used to offer their sacrifices, using the original foundations. Its height will be ninety feet, and its width will be ninety feet.

4 Every three layers of specially prepared stones will be topped by a layer of timber. All expenses will be paid by the royal treasury.

5 Furthermore, the gold and silver cups, which were taken to Babylon by Nebuchadnezzar from the Temple of God in Jerusalem, must be returned to Jerusalem and put back where they belong. Let them be taken back to the Temple of God."

6 So King Darius sent this message: "Now therefore, Tattenai, governor of the province west of the Euphrates River, and Shethar-bozenai, and your colleagues and other officials west of the Euphrates River—stay away from there!

7 Do not disturb the construction of the Temple of God. Let it be rebuilt on its original site, and do not hinder the governor of Judah and the elders of the Jews in their work.

8 Moreover, I hereby decree that you are to help these elders of the Jews as they rebuild this Temple of God. You must pay the full construction costs, without delay, from my taxes collected in the province west of the Euphrates River so that the work will not be interrupted.

9 Give the priests in Jerusalem whatever is needed in the way of young bulls, rams, and male lambs for the burnt offerings presented the priests which are at Jerusalem, let it be given them day by day without fail:

10 That they may offer sacrifices of sweet savours unto the God of heaven, and pray for the life of the king, and of his sons.

11 Also I have made a decree, that whosoever shall alter this word, let timber be pulled down from his house, and being set up, let him be hanged thereon; and let his house be made a dunghill for this.

12 And the God that hath caused his name to dwell there destroy all kings and people, that shall put to their hand to alter and to destroy this house of God which is at Jerusalem. I Darius have made a decree; let it be done with speed.

to the God of heaven. And without fail, provide them with as much wheat, salt, wine, and olive oil as they need each day.

10 Then they will be able to offer acceptable sacrifices to the God of heaven and pray for the welfare of the king and his sons.

11 Those who violate this decree in any way will have a beam pulled from their house. Then they will be lifted up and impaled on it, and their house will be reduced to a pile of rubble.

12 May the God who has chosen the city of Jerusalem as the place to honor his name destroy any king or nation that violates this command and destroys this Temple. I, Darius, have issued this decree. Let it be obeyed with all diligence."

The People, Places, and Times

Darius's Law. Reigning between 522-486 BC, Darius the Great was an effective legislator, interested in policy. During his reign, the most important of these policies for biblical history was the revival of the decree of King Cyrus the Great allowing the Jews to return to Judah, rebuild their Temple, and write down their laws. The Persian kings functioned differently from their Babylonian predecessors in that they did not mind their subjects worshiping their own gods and having their own laws, which made them popular with their subjects. They also wanted the laws written down and codified so they could be followed and information on them held in the capital.

Tatnai. As the governor of the region that included Samaria and Judah during the reign of King Darius, Tatnai (NLT: Tattennai) was responsible for allowing the returned exiles to rebuild the Temple in Jerusalem. Tatnai initially took issue with this project, feeling as though it was an act of rebellion that undermined his authority, but after speaking with the leaders of the returned exiles, he sought to clear up the matter and receive official instruction from King Darius on how to proceed.

Background

The book of Ezra is not written in a clear chronological order even though the events it describes are telling a historical account. Between chapters 2-6, Ezra traces the history of rebuilding the Temple and restoring worship under King Cyrus the Great of Persia and then the interruption of the rebuilding process. There was resistance to rebuilding the Temple at Jerusalem from many sides: people who were left in the city during exile, Samaritans who lived nearby, and enemies of Judah who did not want them restored to the land. In addition, the people had gotten distracted, focusing on rebuilding their own homes and assimilating to the culture around them, rather than restoring worship at the Temple.

Within this messy context of building, then stopping, then facing continued resistance, we come to Ezra 6 when the rebuilding continues with renewed fervor.

What sorts of things keep people from following through on projects? Are they different or similar to things that keep people from obeying God? Why or why not?

At-A-Glance

1. Resurrected Decree (Ezra 6:1–4)
2. Restored Protection (vv. 5–7)
3. Renewed Resources (vv. 8–12)

In Depth

1. Resurrected Decree (Ezra 6:1–4)

King Darius investigates his imperial records after he receives an inquiry from his governor Tatnai about whether or not the Jews could rebuild their Temple. It is a sign of wisdom and humility that the king looked for the decision of his predecessor rather than simply dismissing prior history and making a new decree himself. The information was not found in the place he expected, but in a fortress in a completely different city.

The original decree from Cyrus the Great was for the Jews to rebuild their Temple in the same place it had been, and to have it paid for from the royal treasury of the Persian Empire. This was an incredible set of circumstances that led to incredible news. God's will to have the Jews rebuild the Temple was being carried out, and He was using the wisdom, authority, and resources of a conquering king to do it.

What documentation methods do your church and local governments use to make sure they stand by previous decisions?

2. Restored Protection (vv. 5–7)

King Darius adds to this decree that the materials that were stolen from the Temple by King Nebuchadnezzar of Babylon are to be restored to the Temple in Jerusalem. Further, in addition to restoring precious treasures, the king restores the protection of Judah. He commands his governor to leave the Jews alone as they rebuild the Temple, and to command all of his other officials in the region to leave the Jews alone as well. This would not only protect the peace of the people of Judah as they rebuilt, but would mean the king was protecting the rebuilding project.

How has God protected you or a loved one in the past?

3. Renewed Resources (vv. 8–12)

The final portion of these verses instructs the governor to help the people of Judah rebuild the Temple and make sure they have all of the resources they need to finish. This goes a step beyond leaving them alone, to actively helping them. What a testimony of God's power, that those who were (and still are) enemies are used as servants and helpers.

King Darius doesn't stop there. He wants to make sure the priests have everything they need to give proper sacrifices to the Lord, not just once, but consistently. He asks that they honor the Lord on his behalf as well. He is an unbeliever who wants to help God's people worship and add his own worship as well. Lastly, the king adds that anyone who tries to stop the Jews from rebuilding their Temple will be executed and their houses destroyed. The king had spoken, and his decree would not be broken!

What resources are needed to accomplish the things God has called you to do as a believer? What resources are needed to accomplish the mission of your local church?

Search the Scriptures

1. Who were the people who needed to authorize the rebuilding of the Temple in Jerusalem (Ezra 6:1, 6)?

2. What would be supplied by the king to help the Temple be rebuilt (vv. 8-9)?

Discuss the Meaning

1. The people of Judah had returned to the land with a commission from God, and yet faced resistance and distraction that caused them not to follow through. How can we resist temptation that distracts us from God's will? How can we work to follow through on what God has called us to do?

2. What are some obstacles that keep us from trying again if we haven't finished something? How can we overcome those obstacles?

Liberating Lesson

During political campaigns we often hear campaign promises and policy proposals that would be beneficial to our communities, yet often we do not see them come to pass. It can be easy to grow cynical and believe that all politicians are bad, and feel hopeless about what we can do to help our neighbors and ourselves. But in our democratic society, the government is built to serve the people, and often the policies that get enacted are in response to the people who engage the most with government, whether it be lobbyists or just actively engaged citizens.

How can we as individuals and churches be more actively engaged to make sure our government leaders respect our values and implement policies that benefit our communities? This is especially important to lift up concerns for marginalized groups such as immigrants, children, those returning from prison, and those who face homelessness or discrimination. If we stay engaged collectively, we can get far more accomplished than people with the loudest voices or largest donations and then see more of the changes we want. What policy proposals would your community benefit from seeing implemented? How can you work with your church and others to convince government officials to enact those policies?

Application for Activation

There are a diversity of ways to worship God, and everyone should be free to worship God in the ways that feel most meaningful and authentic to them. There are some people who worship loudly and expressively and some people who worship quietly or in silence. Some people love to dance, others love to sing, others love to lay down, and some stand with their hands raised. Some people feel most worshipful when they are reading the Word of God, others when they are listening to Scripture, and others praying or reciting Scripture. Some write, some walk or run, and some meditate, some give to others, and some even cook.

But often when we attend worship services, check social media, or see someone else in worship we may feel pressure to worship like those around us. This week consider how you feel most connected to God in worship. Is there anything that makes you feel restricted in your worship? How can you spend time with God alone and with others in ways that feel meaningful to you?

Follow the Spirit

What God wants me to do:

_____

_____

_____

Remember Your Thoughts

Special insights I have learned:

_____

_____

_____

More Light on the Text
Ezra 6:1–12

This section of Scripture is recorded in Aramaic, rather than the Hebrew that is used in the majority of the Hebrew Bible. Aramaic is a language closely related to Hebrew, and was originally spoken in Upper Mesopotamia and became the most widely used language in the Babylonian and subsequent Persian Empire. Jews returning from exile spoke both Hebrew and Aramaic, but by Jesus' day Hebrew was mostly only spoken in the synagogue, while Aramaic was used in daily conversation. Both the books of Daniel and Ezra contain sections of text in Aramaic (Daniel 2:4-7:28; Ezra 4:8-6:18) while the rest is in Hebrew.

1 Then Darius the king made a decree, and search was made in the house of the rolls, where the treasures were laid up in Babylon.

When Tatnai and others asked Darius to look into whether or not the Jews actually had permission to rebuild their Temple, the king sent out a decree to search for any records of such an order. A "house of the rolls" is an archive made to store royal decrees. Caches of records found from this time period detail such things as judgments, offerings, and economic allotments for subjects. The Aramaic word used here translated "rolls" corresponds to the Hebrew for scroll (Heb. *sephar*, she-**FAR**). Etymologically, the word refers simply to "writing" no matter the form this media is transcribed in. We are used to thinking of Hebrew records as made on scrolls of vellum (calf skin), but Persian records were more likely to be stamped on clay tablets or cylinders. The writing was done in cuneiform, which is made by stamping the triangle tip of a stylus into clay, making signs for various words, syllables, or letters. These tablets would then be fired to harden the clay. The Persian Empire developed archives to store their laws, decrees, records of offerings, or anything else that would be important for the administration of such a large, long-lived empire.

2 And there was found at Achmetha, in the palace that is in the province of the Medes, a roll, and therein was a record thus written:

Achmetha, also called Ecbatana, was a city Cyrus captured in 550 BC and then established as his summer residence. Its historical site now stands in western Iran. The "province of the Medes" covered the area that is now mostly northern Iran, including the southern coast of the Caspian Sea. Darius' administration must have searched far and wide indeed to see if the Israelites' claim was true, since Achmetha was 420 miles from Babylon, where they first started looking.

The word here for "roll" is different from that used in verse 1. This word, corresponding to the Hebrew *megillah* (meh-geel-**LAW**), actually does refer to a rolled up document. This was likely made of either papyrus (made from the Egyptian reed) or vellum (made from calf skin). Not only did they end up finding the decree in another city than they started, they also eventually found what they were looking for in a different format than they expected.

3 In the first year of Cyrus the king the same Cyrus the king made a decree concerning the house of God at Jerusalem, Let the house be builded, the place where they offered sacrifices, and let the foundations thereof be strongly laid; the height thereof threescore cubits, and the breadth thereof threescore cubits; 4 With three rows of great stones, and a row of new timber: and let the expenses be given out of the king's house:

Cyrus generously provides for the building out of his own excessive wealth. This can be seen as kindness to the exiles, since they likely did not have enough wealth of their own to rebuild the Temple to the majesty that it deserved. It can also be seen as King Cyrus making a show of wealth so as to impress other nations and his own people. The three rows of stone and row of timber would be for constructing the Temple's inner courtyard as Solomon had (1 Kings 6:36). It is odd to list only the dimensions for height and width here, omitting length. Also the height of 60 cubits (90 ft) is taller than Solomon's Temple, which was only 45 feet high.

5 And also let the golden and silver vessels of the house of God, which Nebuchadnezzar took forth out of the temple which is at Jerusalem, and brought unto Babylon, be restored, and brought again unto the temple which is at Jerusalem, every one to his place, and place them in the house of God.

Here we see an event astoundingly rare in colonial history: the repatriation of stolen cultural artifacts. Repatriation is when an item is returned to its original country after having been stolen or otherwise taken away. Showing a stark difference from Babylonia's imperial dominion, the Persian Empire allows their conquered people to reestablish their cultural pillar of worship with all its previous splendor. Modern empires often irreverently steal art from indigenous peoples, caring about them simply as precious materials (e.g., gold or silver) or as a pretty trinket. To the indigenous people, however, these art pieces are cultural touchstones that strongly represent their identity as a cohesive people. Stealing such items away from their native lands disrupts the nation's ability to remember and pass down who they are and what they value. Many artifacts, like the Rosetta Stone and the Benin Bronzes, are centerpieces of the British Museum in London to this very day even though they were stolen from their original African lands.

Working against Babylonia's previous colonialist repression of native culture, Persia wonderfully returns Israel's Temple vessels. The reason behind this will be explained in v. 10.

6 Now therefore, Tatnai, governor beyond the river, Shetharboznai, and your companions the Apharsachites, which are beyond the river, be ye far from thence: 7 Let the work of this house of God alone; let the governor of the Jews and the elders of the Jews build this house of God in his place.

Having decided in the favor of the Israelites, Darius also decrees against the governor who brought this issue to him. The king warns Tatnai and his associates to leave the Israelites alone. To "be ye far from thence" means to give them a wide berth and not invade or insinuate themselves in Israelite territory. Until recently, Tatnai's governance likely included the Israelite's territory. The boundaries only recently were redrawn to set aside the province of Israel, with its governor Zerubbabel. While Tatnai used to have control over this land, the king must remind him that the Jews now have jurisdiction over their own province. They are in fact allowed to continue rebuilding their Temple, and should not be hindered.

"Beyond the river" is a common directional phrase in Babylonian records. The river in question is the Euphrates, and from the perspective of the Babylonian capital, beyond the Euphrates is to the west, including all the lands from that part of modern Iraq to the Mediterranean Sea. The phrase is used as the name of Tatnai's province, which covered most of modern Syria and Jordan.

Shetharboznai is only known from the four verses in Ezra 5 and 6 that mention his name alongside Tatnai's suite against Israel. The Apharsachites are only mentioned in this interchange and in an earlier suite (Ezra 4:9) when they and people from many other Persian cities and provinces brought a successful legal case against the Israelites being allowed to rebuild Jerusalem's walls. Scholars are not certain where in the empire they lived.

8 Moreover I make a decree what ye shall do to the elders of these Jews for the building of this house of God: that of the king's goods, even of the tribute beyond the river, forthwith expenses be given unto these men, that they be not hindered. 9 And that which they have need of, both young bullocks, and rams, and lambs, for the burnt offerings of the God of heaven, wheat, salt, wine, and oil, according to the appointment of the priests which are at Jerusalem, let it be given them day by day without fail:

Darius also provides funds for the building project and offerings for the priests to give daily once the altar and Temple are built. Funds are requisitioned from the "king's goods," i.e., his personal wealth, and from the "tribute beyond the river," i.e., the taxes that would have been collected from the area. Darius gives the people a tax break so that the funds that would have been siphoned off of the Israelites and given over to a far off imperial capital can stay in the land and help rebuild the Temple.

Darius makes sure they have these funds so that their building will not be "hindered" (Aram. beh-**TALL**). This word is also used when the Samaritans cause the building of Jerusalem's walls to cease. The word does not simply mean to impede and make something harder to do; it means to be stopped. After learning that the Israelites should have been allowed to rebuild their Temple since the time of Cyrus, Darius does not want the process to stop again. Once the Jews have their Temple again, it will be good not only for them, but for the Persian Empire as well. After the Temple is finished, other nations will be able to hear and see how benevolent a ruler the Persian king is, how wealthy he is, and how generous with that wealth.

The word for "burnt offering" corresponds to the *'olah* (Heb. oh-**LAW**), which refers to an offering that was completely burned up for God. A whole burnt offering of a lamb was supposed to be offered at the Temple each morning and each night, besides any others that the people needed to make to cover their misdeeds (Leviticus 1:1–17; 6:8–13). These sacrifices could be of a young bull, or male goat or sheep, and Darius provides for all these options. The wheat, oil, and salt were all used in grain offerings (2:4, 13), and wine was often poured out as a supplement to offerings, especially on festival days (Leviticus 23; Numbers 15). Some scholars suggest Cyrus had a Jewish advisor when drafting this decree, since it provides specifically for details of correct Jewish sacrificial practice.

10 That they may offer sacrifices of sweet savours unto the God of heaven, and pray for the life of the king, and of his sons.

Here we see the reasoning behind Darius' kindness. He hopes the priests of Israel will pray for him and his descendants. Darius' interest in providing animals for sacrificing and prayers on his behalf in Jerusalem is a clear indication of the differences between Babylonia and Persia. While the Babylonians saw conquering other nations as a sign of their gods conquering the other nation's gods (or God), the Persians were happy to let cultural groups within their empire practice their native religions. The polytheism of the Persians figured it was better to assimilate all gods into their pantheon and not anger the gods of foreign nations rather than try to conquer them and their people. This leniency is seen in other Persian kings too, like Cyrus (6:5) to Artaxerxes (7:23). The Persians hoped this would foster good relations between the Persian government and the foreign gods, or at least between the government and the foreign people they now ruled. Persia still required tribute and military support from the new territory, but they allowed local religions to continue. This made the people less inclined to insurrection and helped the Persian nation flourish for many more years than the Babylonians did.

Readers must remember that none of the Persian kings truly converted to Judaism. As mentioned in the previous lesson concerning Cyrus, it must not be thought that all this favor toward the Israelites means that Darius became a devotee of Yahweh. Sometimes even pagans following their own pagan laws and traditions can be used to the glory of God.

The Aramaic term translated "sweet savours" corresponds to the Hebrew word *nikhoakh* (nee-**KHOE**-akh) of the same meaning. It is frequently used to describe the purpose of a sacrifice to God. It was thought that the smoke and smell of an offering rose up from the altar all the way to heaven where it reached God's nose. Anyone who has heard and smelled the bacon frying in the pan knows the sweet, savory smell of roasting fat. The phrase is common throughout Leviticus and Numbers, another indication that perhaps a Persian official who was Jewish was helping draft this decree.

11 Also I have made a decree, that whosoever shall alter this word, let timber be pulled down from his house, and being set up, let him be hanged thereon; and let his house be made a dunghill for this.

The word used here for "word" refers not to the substance of the law, but the document itself. The warning here is against tampering with the wording of this law, whether as a scribal error or as an intentional change. Without this part of the decree, an official might try to add something to the regal decree to give himself a political or economic boost, like is done today with riders on bills and earmarked funds.

The word translated "hanged" comes from the Aramaic *mekha'* (meh-**KHAW**), which

comes from roots meaning break apart and destroy. Rather than being hanged from a gallows, this likely refers to the execution method of impalement. The person who tried to change Darius' decree would have their house disassembled and a timber from their house used as an impaling spike. Then the whole house would be condemned as a dung heap.

This seems a harsh punishment to the modern reader, but the punishment of one's house being turned into a "dunghill" is also used twice by King Nebuchadnezzar (Daniel 2:5; 3:29). Impaling as a form of execution was not uncommon in Persian society. Since public distribution of copies of this decree are the only way for Darius to rule his vast empire, it must be considered a capital offense to alter the king's word.

12 And the God that hath caused his name to dwell there destroy all kings and people, that shall put to their hand to alter and to destroy this house of God which is at Jerusalem. I Darius have made a decree; let it be done with speed.

Note that Darius simply refers to God as "the God that hath caused his name to dwell there." This allows room for other gods to dwell in other lands. Yahweh is just the one who dwells in Jerusalem. Darius lays down his law as to what will happen to those who disregard his own words. He also warns what will happen to those who disregard this God's words. He calls down God's own wrath to destroy those who seek to destroy the Temple. These two words for destroy are tellingly different however. Those who seek to "destroy" (Aram. *khabal*, **KHAH**-ball) the Temple would corrupt or spoil it with impurity. In response to this, God would "destroy" (Aram. *megar*, meh-**GAR**) them by casting them down into ruin.

With a final dictum of imperial authority, Darius ends his decree, calling for it to be done without delay. This call for speed repeats what was already translated as "forthwith" (v. 8), and is indeed obeyed (v. 13).

Sources:
Breneman, Mervin. *Commentary on Ezra-Nehemiah.* Baker Illustrated Bible Commentary. Grand Rapids, MI: Baker Books, 2012.
Collins, John J. *Introduction to the Hebrew Bible.* Minneapolis, MN: Augsburg Fortress Press. 2004. 427-437.
Lester, L. Grabbe. *Eerdmans Commentary on the Bible: Ezra and Nehemiah.* Grand Rapids, MI: Wm. B. Eerdmans Publishing Co., 2003.

Say It Correctly

Achmetha. ak-MEE-tha.
Tatnai. tat-NIE.
Shetharboznai. sheh-THAR-boze-nie.
Apharsachites. ah-FAR-sah-kites.
Ecbatana. ek-bah-TAH-nah.
Aramaic. air-ah-MAY-ik.
Akkadian. ah-KAY-dee-an.

Daily Bible Readings

MONDAY
Rebuilding the Temple and Praising God
(Ezra 3:8–13)

TUESDAY
Jews Discouraged from Rebuilding
(Ezra 4:1–5)

WEDNESDAY
Worship in the Heavenly Sanctuary
(Revelation 5)

THURSDAY
Bowing in Thanksgiving
(Psalm 138)

FRIDAY
The Time to Rebuild Has Come
(Haggai 1)

SATURDAY
The Temple's Foundation Laid
(Haggai 2:1–9, 15–19)

SUNDAY
God Provides through King Darius
(Ezra 6:1–12)

Notes

God created us, sin almost destroyed us, Jesus christ restored us. God freely gave us a generous grant his only son to save us A told satan to leave us for the rebuilding of the 327 Kingdom.

Teaching Tips

Words You Should Know

A. Captivity (Ezra 6:19) *golah* (Heb.)—Anyone who has been deported as a slave or taken into captivity

B. Purified (v. 20) *taher* (Heb.)—To be clean, whether from a disease or from sin

Teacher Preparation

Unifying Principle—The Celebration of Completion. Celebrations provide opportunities for people to rejoice after a difficult task. How can we celebrate and show thanksgiving to the person who made the victory possible? After the Temple was completed, the Israelites celebrated God by sharing the Passover together.

A. Read the Bible Background and Devotional Reading.

B. Pray for your students and lesson clarity.

C. Read the lesson Scripture in multiple translations.

O—Open the Lesson

A. Begin the class with prayer.

B. Ask class members with smartphones to find a list of federal holidays that are celebrated each year. Discuss the history behind the holidays that make them so significant. Lead into Bible study noting that Israel celebrated to commemorate significant historical events.

C. Have the students read the Aim for Change and the In Focus story.

D. Ask students how events like those in the story weigh on their hearts and how they can view these events from a faith perspective.

P—Present the Scriptures

A. Read the Focal Verses and discuss the Background and The People, Places, and Times sections.

B. Have the class share what Scriptures stand out for them and why, with particular emphasis on today's themes.

E—Explore the Meaning

A. Use In Depth or More Light on the Text to facilitate a deeper discussion of the lesson text.

B. Pose the questions in Search the Scriptures and Discuss the Meaning.

C. Discuss the Liberating Lesson and Application for Activation sections.

N—Next Steps for Application

A. Summarize the value of taking pride in the building of houses of worship and their sacred dedication.

B. End class with a commitment to pray for courage to contribute liberally to God from their financial resources in order to celebrate God's goodness.

Celebrate Passover Liberation

Bible Background • EZRA 6:13-22; LEVITICUS 23:4-8
Printed Text • EZRA 6:13-22 | Devotional Reading • EXODUS 2:23-25

Aim for Change

[handwritten: Examine] *[handwritten: inspire]*

By the end of this lesson, we will EXPLORE the celebration prompted by the completion of the new Temple, IDENTIFY reasons to celebrate God's goodness, and JOIN TOGETHER as believers in celebrating and sharing the Good News of God's love.

In Focus *[handwritten: Psalm 145:7]*

Pastor Perry in Illinois was called of God to build a church, both the congregation and the building. Neighbors came to hear Pastor Perry share the Word encouragingly, and the congregation soon tied together in bonds of love. Then, Perry purchased land with cash and the next step was to build the church. But that process would prove to be difficult. Before any construction could begin, the village had to approve a church building being constructed on the land. Did it have the correct zoning codes? Did the village really need another church? Was there a way to use the land that would get the village more capital? After several village meetings the board voted against a church structure being constructed.

There were times when the pastor became discouraged and wondered if God really told him to build a church for His glory. The congregation would try one more time to get the village to approve the construction of the church building. Seeing such a groundswell of local support, the village finally approved the building project. Everyone rejoiced. Even after the village approved the construction, the church faced other obstacles. But the will of God prevailed! Finally, the construction was completed and a dedication service was held. The people rejoiced, and felt in their hearts that God was pleased.

How have you seen a large project, like this building project, bring people together?

[handwritten: Jo] *[handwritten: I can do all]* *[handwritten: rise]*
[handwritten: things through] *[handwritten: outpouring]*
[handwritten: Phil. 4:13]

Keep in Mind

[handwritten: him who strengthen me]

"And the children of Israel, the priests, and the Levites, and the rest of the children of the captivity, kept the dedication of this house of God with joy." (Ezra 6:16, KJV)

"The Temple of God was then dedicated with great joy by the people of Israel, the priests, the Levites, and the rest of the people who had returned from exile." (Ezra 6:16, NLT)

Focal Verses

KJV Ezra 6:13 Then Tatnai, governor on this side the river, Shetharboznai, and their companions, according to that which Darius the king had sent, so they did speedily.

14 And the elders of the Jews builded, and they prospered through the prophesying of Haggai the prophet and Zechariah the son of Iddo. And they builded, and finished it, according to the commandment of the God of Israel, and according to the commandment of Cyrus, and Darius, and Artaxerxes king of Persia.

15 And this house was finished on the third day of the month Adar, which was in the sixth year of the reign of Darius the king.

16 And the children of Israel, the priests, and the Levites, and the rest of the children of the captivity, kept the dedication of this house of God with joy.

17 And offered at the dedication of this house of God an hundred bullocks, two hundred rams, four hundred lambs; and for a sin offering for all Israel, twelve he goats, according to the number of the tribes of Israel.

18 And they set the priests in their divisions, and the Levites in their courses, for the service of God, which is at Jerusalem; as it is written in the book of Moses.

19 And the children of the captivity kept the passover upon the fourteenth day of the first month.

20 For the priests and the Levites were purified together, all of them were pure, and killed the passover for all the children of the captivity, and for their brethren the priests, and for themselves.

21 And the children of Israel, which were come again out of captivity, and all such as had separated themselves unto them from the filthiness of the heathen of the land, to seek the LORD God of Israel, did eat,

NLT Ezra 6:13 Tattenai, governor of the province west of the Euphrates River, and Shethar-bozenai and their colleagues complied at once with the command of King Darius.

14 So the Jewish elders continued their work, and they were greatly encouraged by the preaching of the prophets Haggai and Zechariah son of Iddo. The Temple was finally finished, as had been commanded by the God of Israel and decreed by Cyrus, Darius, and Artaxerxes, the kings of Persia.

15 The Temple was completed on March 12, during the sixth year of King Darius's reign.

16 The Temple of God was then dedicated with great joy by the people of Israel, the priests, the Levites, and the rest of the people who had returned from exile.

17 During the dedication ceremony for the Temple of God, 100 young bulls, 200 rams, and 400 male lambs were sacrificed. And 12 male goats were presented as a sin offering for the twelve tribes of Israel.

18 Then the priests and Levites were divided into their various divisions to serve at the Temple of God in Jerusalem, as prescribed in the Book of Moses.

19 On April 21 the returned exiles celebrated Passover.

20 The priests and Levites had purified themselves and were ceremonially clean. So they slaughtered the Passover lamb for all the returned exiles, for their fellow priests, and for themselves.

21 The Passover meal was eaten by the people of Israel who had returned from exile and by the others in the land who had turned from their corrupt practices to worship the LORD, the God of Israel.

22 Then they celebrated the Festival of Unleavened Bread for seven days. There was

22 And kept the feast of unleavened bread seven days with joy: for the LORD had made them joyful, and turned the heart of the king of Assyria unto them, to strengthen their hands in the work of the house of God, the God of Israel.

great joy throughout the land because the LORD had caused the king of Assyria to be favorable to them, so that he helped them to rebuild the Temple of God, the God of Israel.

The People, Places, and Times

Sin Offering. This offering is also known as a guilt offering. It was presented for unconscious or conscious sins for which there was no possible restitution. This offering signified repentance and a search for divine forgiveness. For example, if one did not give his servants their due, such a person could make a sin offering. Usually this offering was also accompanied by a fine.

Darius's Building. An effective organizer and administrator, Darius I of Persia developed trade; built a network of roads; established a postal system; standardized a system of coinage, weights, and measures; and initiated fabulous building projects such as Persepolis, Achmetha, and Babylon. Darius continued Cyrus the Great's policy of restoring the Jewish people to their homeland. In 520 BC, Darius's second year as king, the Jews resumed work on the still-unfinished Temple in Jerusalem. Darius assisted with the project by ordering it to continue and even sending a generous subsidy to help restore worship in the Temple. The Temple was completed in 515 BC, in the sixth year of Darius's reign.

Think of the stories from the prophet Daniel. How else did God influence Darius during his reign in Persia?

Background

The decree had gone forth from King Cyrus for the Children of Israel to rebuild the Temple after their captivity in Babylon. Unfortunately the job was not completed under Cyrus's reign. Because of this, when the Jews were trying to complete the Temple later on, local leaders

raised concerns about who told them to rebuild it. Darius was king at the time, and he issued an order that the archives be searched for the decree made by King Cyrus. The decree was discovered. King Darius in turn issued his own decree to finish the work (Ezra 6:8).

The expenses of this project were to be fully paid out of the royal treasury, from the revenues of Trans-Euphrates, so that the work would not stop. Whatever was needed—young bulls, rams, male lambs for burnt offerings to the God, wheat, salt, wine, and oil, as requested by the priests in Jerusalem—must be given to them daily without fail, so that they could offer sacrifices pleasing to the God of heaven and pray for the well-being of the king and his sons. Thus begins today's lesson.

At-A-Glance

1. The People Finish and Rejoice
(Ezra 6:13–16)
2. The People of Israel Offer Sacrifices
(vv. 17–18)
3. The Feasts Celebrated (vv. 19–22)

In Depth

1. The People Finish and Rejoice (Ezra 6:13–16)

The Temple was finally completed! God's people had been through so much. They had endured many obstacles, but the finished product was now visible and they rejoiced! They rejoiced because the favor of the Lord had been upon them as they sought to honor God by re-instituting worship at the Temple. To start a work and see it to completion is a sign of the grace of the Most High. Israel knew this.

The Temple was completed, but not by human powers. From the touching of the hearts of Cyrus and Darius, to providing funds to complete the work, it was all of God. It was God who initiated the project by His Spirit. It was God who guided their hands to its completion. The house belonged to God. It was therefore logical to dedicate the building back to God. All our victories and accomplishments are because God has favored us.

How many times do we complete a task after many struggles and then get it in our head that it was by our own strength?

2. The People of Israel Offer Sacrifices (vv. 17–18)

The Children of Israel did not just sing and dance and shout; they brought an offering. They could have said, "We have already worked. We gave our time and we gave our talent; we do not need to give any more sacrifices." But they went a step further and offered sacrifices.

The Children of Israel were doing things in order and according to what was written in the books of Moses. During the dedication of the new Temple, they offered sacrifices. Sacrificial offerings in the Old Testament were a means to atone for human sins and restore people back to God. Jesus, the perfect sacrifice, did away with all of that when He died for us once and for all on the Cross. The Children of Israel offered what is called a sin offering. This included the blood from bulls, rams, lambs, and goats.

3. The Feasts Celebrated (vv. 19–22)

In a sense this was a second exodus. The freed captives had just been delivered from the house of exile. The Passover, as celebrated by Hebrew people, is the archetype (or pattern) of

divine intervention in the life of God's people. It is not a coincidence that the Temple's dedication occurred just before Passover. What better time to declare the glorious grace of the Most High who rescues the lonely and restores those who are accounted dead?

It was the 14th day of the first month, and everyone was ceremonially clean. The Levites slaughtered the Passover lamb for all the exiles, for their brothers, the priests, and for themselves. They separated themselves from the unclean practices of their Gentile neighbors in order to seek the Lord, the God of Israel. For seven days they celebrated the Feast of Unleavened Bread joyfully because the Lord had filled them with joy by changing the attitude of the king of Persia, so that he assisted them in the work on the house of God, the God of Israel. When the Lord blesses us to complete a task, may we rejoice in hope and rededicate ourselves to God.

Why were purification rites important before celebrating Passover?

Search the Scriptures

1. When was the Temple completed (v. 15)?

2. What was offered during the dedication (v. 17)?

Discuss the Meaning

1. Why was it important for those returning from exile to celebrate the Passover?

2. God used three pagan kings to do His will in rebuilding Jerusalem. What does this reveal about God and His plans for His nation?

Liberating Lesson

Often we start projects and do not complete them in a speedy manner. If God gives us a command, we must complete the job speedily. A lot of our obstacles can be avoided if we do things in a timely manner and not procrastinate. In today's lesson we see that the Temple was completed, but what obstacles could have been avoided if the elders had moved swiftly after they received the first command from King Cyrus? What are you procrastinating?

Application for Activation

Examine your own life. Think of some projects you are currently working on that you can speed up the process. Pray for God to make a way to finish the project.

Follow the Spirit

What God wants me to do:

_____

_____

_____

_____

Remember Your Thoughts

Special insights I have learned:

_____

_____

_____

_____

More Light on the Text

Ezra 6:13–22

When the Jews originally started work on rebuilding the Temple, their Samaritan neighbors opposed them. The Samaritans brought court cases to Persian officials and were able to halt the Israelites' work on the Temple (Ezra 4:5) and Jerusalem's walls (vv. 6–24). Work on the Temple stopped for 16 years until God sent His prophets Haggai and Zechariah, during

the second year of the reign of Darius of Persia, to encourage the Jews to resume rebuilding the Temple (Haggai 1:1–3; Zechariah 1:1). Under the leadership of Zerubbabel (governor) and Jeshua (the high priest), the people immediately went back to work rebuilding the Temple (Ezra 5:1–2).

When word of the rebuilding reached Tatnai, the Persian governor west of the Euphrates River, and Shethar-boznai his aide, they sent a letter to King Darius informing him of the Jewish activities and asking if there was any legal basis for the work. Darius had his officials search the royal archives in Babylon to find Cyrus's original decree without success. The order was finally found in the city of Achmetha (or Ecbatana) in the province of Media (6:1–2). When Darius read the decree, he allowed the rebuilding work to continue and added his own order to it. The Persian officials were not only ordered not to interfere with the Jews but to help finance the operation from their treasury and to supply the Jews with any animals they needed for sacrifice (vv. 8–9).

13 Then Tatnai, governor on this side the river, Shethar-boznai, and their companions, according to that which Darius the king had sent, so they did speedily. 14 And the elders of the Jews builded, and they prospered through the prophesying of Haggai the prophet and Zechariah the son of Iddo. And they builded, and finished it, according to the commandment of the God of Israel, and according to the commandment of Cyrus, and Darius, and Artaxerxes king of Persia.

Tatnai and Shethar-boznai had been opposed to building the Temple previously, but once they received the orders from King Darius, they helped the Jews instead of hindering them. They complied with the king's decree, and work on the Temple continued and prospered through the prophesying of Haggai and Zechariah.

"Prophesying" refers to preaching, teaching, or predicting the future. The word written here is *nebuah* (neh-voo-**AH**), and is in Aramaic, rather than Hebrew. Aramaic is a language closely related to Hebrew, and was originally spoken in Upper Mesopotamia and became the most widely used language in the Babylonian and subsequent Persian Empire. Jews returning from exile spoke both Hebrew and Aramaic. The books of Daniel and Ezra contain both Hebrew and Aramaic sections of text.

Ezra asserts that their prosperity was "through the prophesying," not to be credited to chance or to King Darius's kindness but to God alone. It was God acting through His prophets who had required and encouraged the people to proceed in the work, and it was His mighty power that moved Darius's heart to allow the work to continue.

In the end, the Jews were following various decrees to build the Temple, but there is an order to Ezra's list of whose commandment they were following. First and most importantly, they built "according to the commandments of the God of Israel." God had given instructions as to how His sanctuary should be built, with specific dimensions and materials. These commandments had to be obeyed. Secondarily, they also chose to obey the commandments of the earthly rulers, the kings of Persia. Here Ezra reviews all three different rulers who favored the Jews in their return from captivity and the rebuilding of the Temple.

15 And this house was finished on the third day of the month Adar, which was in the sixth year of the reign of Darius the king. 16 And the children of Israel, the priests, and the Levites, and the rest of the children of the captivity, kept the dedication of this house of God with joy.

On March 12, 515 BC in the sixth year of the reign of Darius, the Temple was completed—20 years after the foundation had been laid during under the reign of Cyrus. When they completed the Temple, which became known as Zerubbabel's Temple, it was 90 feet high and 90 feet wide (6:3). This was much smaller and far less grand than Solomon's original Temple. However, this Temple would stand for 100 years longer than Solomon's Temple did.

The Israelites celebrated the dedication of the Temple with a great feast similar to the one that Solomon had when he dedicated the original Temple (1 Kings 8:23). The reference to the "children of Israel" affirms that there were members of the Northern Kingdom of Israel who returned from Babylonian captivity along with the vast majority from the Southern Kingdom of Judah. This is also likely given that one goat for each tribe is given as a sin offering during the dedication (v. 17). The priests and the Levites led the Temple dedication. Of the 12 tribes, the tribe of Levi, was set aside for ritual religious service. Within the tribe of Levi, only those descended from the bloodline of Aaron could serve as priests. Other families from the tribe were assigned various duties linked with Tabernacle or Temple worship.

The priesthood was vital to the practice of Old Testament faith. The Aramaic word for priest is the same as the Hebrew word: *kohen* (koh-**HANE**), which occurs over 700 times in the Old Testament. The priest had a trifold ministry of (1) watching over and guarding the covenant, (2) teaching God's precepts and law, and (3) offering incense and offerings at God's altar (Deuteronomy 33:9–10).

The high priest had two mediatorial functions which summed up the role of the priesthood. In his vestments the high priest had the Urim and Thummim (Deuteronomy 33:8). God spoke to the people through these twin instruments to provide guidance for His people and to communicate His will. The second function of the high priest involved a unique sacrifice. Once a year on the Day of Atonement the high priest would enter the Holy of Holies in the Tabernacle or Temple, carrying the blood of the sacrifice and sprinkling it on the cover of the Ark. This was done to atone for all the sins of all of God's people (Leviticus 16).

17 And offered at the dedication of this house of God an hundred bullocks, two hundred rams, four hundred lambs; and for a sin offering for all Israel, twelve he goats, according to the number of the tribes of Israel.

The Aramaic word for "dedication" is *hannukkah* (**KHAN**-nuh-kah). Jews today have a different holiday called Hanukkah, honoring the re-dedication of the Temple after a political revolt in 160 BC, hundreds of years after this. The word *hannukkah*, however, is simply the word for dedication and is used in the Old Testament to describe a kind of sacrifice. The Old Testament emphasizes the dedication ceremonies that inaugurated the use of something for God's service. The joyful offerings at this dedication consisted of 100 male bulls, 200 rams, and 400 male lambs. Solomon offered 200 times more animals at the dedication of the original Temple, but because of the poor circumstances, this offering was limited. Their hundreds meant just as much to them as Solomon's thousands.

The Aramaic word for sin offering is the equivalent of the Hebrew *khata'ah* (chah-taw-**AW**). The sin offering, as explained in Leviticus 4–5, was sacrificed for those who committed a sin unintentionally or out of weakness or negligence as opposed to outright rebellion against God. The person sacrificing the animal would lay their hand on the animal's head to symbolize passing the person's sins onto the sacrifice. The animal would then die instead of the person. Blood would be sprinkled before the Temple's inner sanctuary and on the altar. Then all the animal's entrails and fat would be

burned on the altar. The remaining carcass was taken outside of the camp to the dump heap and burned. This sacrifice showed blood covering sin, a pleasant smell of repentance rising to God, and the rest of our efforts being only worthy of burning with the rest of the trash. Different animals were sacrificed as sin offerings for different people: a young bull for a priest or for the entire congregation, a male goat for a leader, a female goat or lamb for any other individual, or two doves for those too poor for a lamb.

At this dedication celebration, they sacrificed one male goat for each tribe. This could mean that a leader from each tribe was present to lay his head on the goat's head as part of the sacrificial rite. Note also that purifying the entire congregation with a sin offering could have been done with a single young bull. The returning exiles, however, chose to show their devotion by selecting 12 goats, a more costly sacrifice and one that was more personal as each individual tribe was represented with its own goat.

18 And they set the priests in their divisions, and the Levites in their courses, for the service of God, which is at Jerusalem; as it is written in the book of Moses.

King David divided the descendants of Aaron who served as priest into 24 classes as the basis for rotating priestly duties (1 Chronicles 24:3, 7–19). Some of the classes died out or had to be consolidated with others, and new ones were formed to take their places. In the return from exile only four registered classes were represented (Ezra 2:36–39). By the time of Nehemiah's return, 22 classes had been reinstated (Nehemiah 10:2–8). The Levites were also divided into groups, or courses, corresponding to the bloodlines of Gershon, Kohath, and Merari (Exodus 6:16). The duty of the Levites was to assist Aaron's descendants in the service of the Temple (Exodus 38:21; Numbers 3:6–7).

19 And the children of the captivity kept the passover upon the fourteenth day of the first month.

With this verse Ezra's text switches back to Hebrew from Aramaic. The switch is abrupt, but relevant. While the language of the Empire was used to discuss the building and completion of the Temple with imperial funds, the native language of the Hebrews is used to recount the celebration of this most formative of Jewish holidays: the Passover.

The "children of captivity" is a translation of the Hebrew *ben golah* (ben go-**LAW**). In this case *ben* is used idiomatically to denote children or descendants. *Golah* refers to anyone who has been deported as a slave or taken into captivity. In this case the phrase describes the descendants of those carried into Babylonian captivity. It is also a telling name for the Jews to use just before observing Passover, when they remember their freedom from captivity in Egypt.

The Passover is called *pasakh* (**PEH**-sakh) in Hebrew. This Hebrew verb means "to skip or pass over; to grant exemption from penalty or calamity." The Passover is an annual feast that celebrates the day when the Lord selectively passed over the homes of those who put lambs' blood over the door frames of their homes. On that night the firstborn male of every household who did not have the blood over the door frame was killed. This event precipitated Israel's deliverance from Egyptian bondage. The Passover lamb and its saving blood point to Jesus Christ, the Lamb of God, whose blood takes away the sins of the world (John 1:29; 1 Corinthians 5:7).

The Israelites are faithfully observing the feast on the correct day, as recorded in Exodus, which they knew as one of the books of Moses.

There are recorded God's instructions to always celebrate the Passover on the 14th day of the first month, which corresponds to the beginning of spring. Even though the Jewish "New Year" Rosh Hashanah is celebrated in the autumn, the month of Passover is also remembered as the "first" month, because of its religious prominence. The month of Tishri is the first month on the calendar, but Adar is the "first" and most important month religiously. Similarly, in Christian liturgical calendars, the year begins with Advent on the first Sunday in December, even though more broadly speaking, January is the first month.

20 For the priests and the Levites were purified together, all of them were pure, and killed the passover for all the children of the captivity, and for their brethren the priests, and for themselves.

"The Levites were purified together" means that they were all ready at one time to observe the proper rites and ceremonies. There was no need to postpone the celebration as was prescribed by law. If circumstances made it necessary, the Passover could be postponed from the first month to the second (Numbers 9:10–11; cf. 2 Chronicles 30:3).

"Purified" is a translation of the Hebrew *taher* (taw-**HAYR**) and literally means to be clean, whether from a disease or from sin. Outward cleanliness was used to remind priests of their need for inward cleanliness. Those who were considered unclean were not permitted to participate in Temple rituals until they were purified. The ritual for becoming cleansed in this way is recorded in Numbers 19:17–21. The process involves the person (along with all his possessions and household) being sprinkled with holy water once, again on the third day, and again on the seventh day. On the seventh day the person would also wash their clothes and bodies. Only then were they clean. These preparations take a long time, so priests would need to be vigilant to prepare well enough in advance so that they could be ready to lead the people in sanctified worship when the time came.

For occasions requiring special purity, the Levites had to follow a three-fold purification ritual. First, the Levites had to purify the people, then they also needed to purify all the priests, then the Levites would also need to purify themselves. Such rituals reinforce the theological tenet of how far sinfulness divides us from God. The taint of sin effects all, even priests, even the Levites. Even those who help purify the people must be purified themselves. This cumbersome system is how the Jews interacted with God for hundreds of years. Thank God that He sent Jesus to be our perfect High Priest, who does not need to purify Himself of any sin and yet still welcomes us to be a part of Himself.

21 And the children of Israel, which were come again out of captivity, and all such as had separated themselves unto them from the filthiness of the heathen of the land, to seek the LORD God of Israel, did eat.

Those who had "separated themselves" refers to the proselytes who had embraced the Jewish religion during the time of their captivity in Babylon. The proselytes are proof that the Jewish captives had maintained the principles of their religion. The unbelievers saw it, and they converted to the religion of the one true God. These converts and those who were Jewish by birth joined together to eat the Passover meal.

22 And kept the feast of unleavened bread seven days with joy: for the LORD had made them joyful, and turned the heart of the king of Assyria unto them, to strengthen their hands in the work of the house of God, the God of Israel.

The Feast of Unleavened Bread was closely associated with the Passover. In fact, in preparation for the Passover the man of the house would search through the house for leaven (yeast) and remove it. For seven days after the Passover, Jewish families will continue to eat only unleavened bread. With each bite, they could renew their commitment to be free of sin before God. Passover is often a solemn affair when Jews humbly remember the mercy of God upon them. The Feast of Unleavened Bread afterwards, however, is a time of celebration. God had given the people both causes to rejoice and hearts to rejoice. God is the fountain from which all true joy flows.

The Persian king is here called the king of Assyria (two empires back) to emphatically stress the great power and goodness of God in turning the hearts of these present Persian monarchs, whose Assyrian predecessors had formerly been the chief persecutors and cruel oppressors of God's people.

Sources:
Henry, Matthew. *Matthew Henry's Commentary on the Whole Bible: New Modern Edition.* Vols. 1-6. Peabody, MA: Hendrickson Publishers, Inc., 2009.
Strong, James. *The New Strong's Exhaustive Concordance of the Bible.* Nashville, TN: Thomas Nelson, 2003.
Thayer, Joseph Henry. *A Greek-English Lexicon of the New Testament.* New York: American Book Company, 1889.

Say It Correctly

Artaxerxes. ar-tuh-ZURK-seez.
Adar. ah-DAR.
Iddo. EE-doe.
Persepolis. per-SHE-poe-liss.
Tishri. TEESH-ree.

Daily Bible Readings

MONDAY
Keep Holy Convocations
(Leviticus 23:4–8)

TUESDAY
God Institutes the Passover
(Exodus 12:1–14)

WEDNESDAY
Moses' Instructions about the Passover
(Exodus 12:21–28, 50–51)

THURSDAY
Praise the Name of the Lord
(Psalm 113)

FRIDAY
Christ Our Passover
(1 Corinthians 5:7–8; 10:1–4)

SATURDAY
Praise for God's Liberation from Egypt
(Psalm 114)

SUNDAY
Returned Exiles Keep the Passover
(Ezra 6:13–22)

Notes

_____

_____

_____

_____

Teaching Tips

Words You Should Know

A. Humble (Deuteronomy 8:2) *anah* (Heb.)—To afflict, weaken, humiliate

B. Prove (v. 2) *nasah* (Heb.)—To test, try, or tempt

Teacher Preparation

Unifying Principle—The Resolve to Remember. Humility can be thought of as a weakness in today's society. Why do people forget the road they traveled in life and who helped them in their accomplishments? Deuteronomy extols humility as liberating and explains its purpose.

A. Read the Bible Background and Devotional Reading.

B. Pray for your students and lesson clarity.

C. Read the lesson Scripture in multiple translations.

O—Open the Lesson

A. Begin the class with prayer.

B. Play a video of Frank Sinatra singing "My Way" from a video-sharing site. Help the class critique the attitude expressed in this popular song.

C. Have the students read the Aim for Change and the In Focus story.

D. Ask students how events like those in the story weigh on their hearts and how they can view these events from a faith perspective.

P—Present the Scriptures

A. Read the Focal Verses and discuss the Background and The People, Places, and Times sections.

B. Have the class share what Scriptures stand out for them and why, with particular emphasis on today's themes.

E—Explore the Meaning

A. Use In Depth or More Light on the Text to facilitate a deeper discussion of the lesson text.

B. Pose the questions in Search the Scriptures and Discuss the Meaning.

C. Discuss the Liberating Lesson and Application for Activation sections.

N—Next Steps for Application

A. Summarize the value of keeping the commands of God.

B. End class with a commitment to pray to turn to God alone for salvation and all blessings.

Worship Guide

For the Superintendent or Teacher
Theme: Lest We Forget
Song: "O God Our Help in Ages Past"

Humble yourself before the Lord, and he will lift you up.

Lest We Forget

Bible Background • DEUTERONOMY 8
Printed Text • DEUTERONOMY 8:1-11 | Devotional Reading • 1 CORINTHIANS 9:19-27

—————————— **Aim for Change** ——————————

By the end of this lesson, we will UNDERSTAND what humility is in the light of God's commandments, APPRECIATE God's blessings and our need for humility before the Lord, and PRACTICE living a life of humility.

—————————— **In Focus** —————————— *James 4:10*

After high school, Jimmy became a licensed barber. To gain experience he worked at a few shops. But each time it left a negative taste in his spirit. High booth rents, unprofessional management teams, and lack of respect from other barbers made him fed up with the industry. He decided to take a break.

Every week the customers he had gained over the years would hit him up to see when they could come to get a cut. Eventually, he gave in and slowly started back cutting hair. Soon every weekend Jimmy was booked up cutting hair in his basement. He fell back in love with cutting hair. Not only was he cutting hair, but also he was able to help his customers and give them advice whenever they needed it. That's what kept his customers coming back. Not many barbershops gave you a fresh cut and advice.

Barbering was his ministry, but soon weekends weren't enough to cut all of his customers. Finally, Jimmy decided to open up his own barbershop. He knew he wouldn't be able to open up his shop without the support of his customers, family, and friends. He dedicated his grand opening to everyone who helped him throughout the years.

"I just want to thank all of you for supporting me throughout the years," Jimmy said. "I've wanted to open my own shop since I was a teenager. Because of setbacks, I wasn't able to make it a reality until today. I fell out of love with cutting hair, and if it wasn't for you all supporting me, I wouldn't be here right now. So this is for you all!"

Whose prayers and support helped you get to the place you are right now? How have you thanked them for everything they've done?

—————————— **Keep in Mind** —————————— *Background sis Hill next*

"Beware that thou forget not the LORD thy God, in not keeping his commandments, and his judgments, and his statutes, which I command thee this day."
(Deuteronomy 8:11, KJV)

"But that is the time to be careful! Beware that in your plenty you do not forget the LORD your God and disobey his commands, regulations, and decrees that I am giving you today."
(Deuteronomy 8:11, NLT)

Focal Verses

KJV **Deuteronomy 8:1** All the commandments which I command thee this day shall ye observe to do, that ye may live, and multiply, and go in and possess the land which the LORD sware unto your fathers.

2 And thou shalt remember all the way which the LORD thy God led thee these forty years in the wilderness, to humble thee, and to prove thee, to know what was in thine heart, whether thou wouldest keep his commandments, or no.

3 And he humbled thee, and suffered thee to hunger, and fed thee with manna, which thou knewest not, neither did thy fathers know; that he might make thee know that man doth not live by bread only, but by every word that proceedeth out of the mouth of the LORD doth man live.

4 Thy raiment waxed not old upon thee, neither did thy foot swell, these forty years.

5 Thou shalt also consider in thine heart, that, as a man chasteneth his son, so the LORD thy God chasteneth thee.

6 Therefore thou shalt keep the commandments of the LORD thy God, to walk in his ways, and to fear him.

7 For the LORD thy God bringeth thee into a good land, a land of brooks of water, of fountains and depths that spring out of valleys and hills;

8 A land of wheat, and barley, and vines, and fig trees, and pomegranates; a land of oil olive, and honey;

9 A land wherein thou shalt eat bread without scarceness, thou shalt not lack any thing in it; a land whose stones are iron, and out of whose hills thou mayest dig brass.

10 When thou hast eaten and art full, then thou shalt bless the LORD thy God for the good land which he hath given thee.

11 Beware that thou forget not the LORD thy God, in not keeping his commandments, and his judgments, and his statutes, which I command thee this day.

NLT **Deuteronomy 8:1** "Be careful to obey all the commands I am giving you today. Then you will live and multiply, and you will enter and occupy the land the LORD swore to give your ancestors.

2 Remember how the LORD your God led you through the wilderness for these forty years, humbling you and testing you to prove your character, and to find out whether or not you would obey his commands.

3 Yes, he humbled you by letting you go hungry and then feeding you with manna, a food previously unknown to you and your ancestors. He did it to teach you that people do not live by bread alone; rather, we live by every word that comes from the mouth of the LORD.

4 For all these forty years your clothes didn't wear out, and your feet didn't blister or swell.

5 Think about it: Just as a parent disciplines a child, the LORD your God disciplines you for your own good.

6 So obey the commands of the LORD your God by walking in his ways and fearing him.

7 For the LORD your God is bringing you _Joyce_ into a good land of flowing streams and pools of water, with fountains and springs that gush out in the valleys and hills.

8 It is a land of wheat and barley; of grapevines, fig trees, and pomegranates; of olive oil and honey.

9 It is a land where food is plentiful and nothing is lacking. It is a land where iron is as common as stone, and copper is abundant in the hills.

10 When you have eaten your fill, be sure to praise the LORD your God for the good land he has given you.

11 But that is the time to be careful! Beware that in your plenty you do not forget the LORD your God and disobey his commands, regulations, and decrees that I am giving you today."

The People, Places, and Times

The Wilderness Wandering. When the Israelites left Egypt, there were more than 600,000 men, women, and children in the caravan. There was no way that the meager resources of the Sinai desert could support a multitude of that number, so the people were completely dependent on God for their survival.

God caused a sweetbread called "manna" to rain down from heaven to sustain them (Exodus 16:4, 31). When the people grew tired of the heavenly bread, God fed them with quail (vv. 13–14). When the people ran out of water, He miraculously provided them with water (Exodus 17:6; Numbers 20:11).

Ever since crossing the Red Sea, the people were quarrelsome and discontented. In spite of all that God had done for them, they could not find it in their hearts to trust Him. Whenever adversity struck, the people would complain rather than pray. God allowed the Israelites many different opportunities to trust Him when faced with hardship, but each time they failed.

Background

Deuteronomy is the second telling of God's Law to Moses and the Children of Israel. The people of Israel are about to enter the Promised Land after wandering in the wilderness for 40 years as a result of their disobedience. A new generation of Israelites is present to hear the Law who do not remember being delivered from slavery in Egypt or being called to worship God. Many of the people present do not remember being disobedient to the Lord and committing idolatry when they received the Covenant. Yet they have had their own experiences with temptation and sin as well as witnessing God's deliverance and provision.

Moses is retelling the Law and reminding the Israelites of the Covenant to encourage them to keep God's commandments and prepare them to begin their new lives in the Promised Land with the Lord. If the Israelites humble themselves and follow God's Law, they will prosper in the land God is giving them.

How can we pass down lessons we have learned to the generations that come after us?

At-A-Glance

1. A Promise Kept (Deuteronomy 8:1–2)
2. A Memory of Provision (vv. 3–6)
3. A Place of Plenty (vv. 7–11)

In Depth

1. A Promise Kept (Deuteronomy 8:1–2)

Moses is relaying the responsibilities of the Covenant the Lord made with the Children of Israel on Mount Horeb before they enter into the Promised Land. The Lord told the Children of Israel that they were to keep His commandments, including the Ten Commandments and many others found in Exodus and repeated in Deuteronomy. If the Israelites keep the commandments, then they will multiply and prosper in the Promised Land as a result of God's glorious presence.

Moses also notes that God is keeping His covenant with Abraham, Isaac, and Jacob by delivering the people into the Promised Land and allowing them to multiply and prosper there. But as a result of God's sovereign knowledge and the Israelites' disobedience when they received the covenant, the Lord tested them in the wilderness. They were shown the power and provision of God, as well as the result of their disobedience, for 40 years as they wandered.

Why do you think it is important that Moses reminds the Israelites about the promises God made to them and their ancestors?

2. A Memory of Provision (vv. 3–6)

Moses shares two examples of how the Lord miraculously provided for the Children of Israel during their time in the wilderness. The Lord supplied manna when they were hungry and preserved their clothes and shoes for decades. This was done not only to test their character, but to show the character of God. God is a provider, but also a parent to them. God will not leave them, but does want them to demonstrate obedience and faithfulness to Him. If they fear God—meaning they respect Him—they will obey Him. If they do not obey the Lord, they will face discipline through trials that are ultimately for their good and will develop them into the people of God they are called to be.

How is God like a parent in our lives? How is God different from an earthly parent?

3. A Place of Plenty (vv. 7–11)

Moses closes this portion of his address by describing the greatness of the Promised Land. The land God is giving the Children of Israel is plentiful. For the people of Israel who are living in a world of farmers, shepherds, and traders, this land will be paradise. The soil is fertile, there is natural fruit, there are abundant water sources, and there is mineral wealth for building and trading. God is giving this tiny soon-to-be nation all of the resources it needs to flourish.

Moses warns that the response to this abundance should be humility and thanksgiving. If the Israelites inherit all of these blessings and forget the Lord who gave it to them, they will face judgment. If they do not keep the commands, laws, decrees, and regulations of the Lord, they will not prosper as they are supposed to in the place of God's promise.

How *are the responsibilities the Lord gives the Israelites as they move from slavery to freedom similar to the responsibilities of a Christian moving from sin to freedom?*

Search the Scriptures

1. What were the Children of Israel told to do in order to prosper in the Promised Land (Exodus 8:11)?

2. How had God shown provision for the Children of Israel while they wandered in the desert (vv. 3–4)?

Discuss the Meaning

1. Moses reminded the Israelites of their past struggles as well as God's faithfulness through them. How can remembering what we have been through prepare us for our future?

2. Moses wanted the Israelites to remember to be humble as they walked into prosperity in the land of Canaan. How can we keep ourselves humble when we experience great blessings?

Liberating Lesson

Nationalism is on the rise all across the world as various leaders use the idea of their nation as the greatest nation to maintain power and polarize politics. There is increased pressure to fully support the government and all of its actions, or be labeled as unpatriotic or even a traitor. But this is not the way of Christ. No nation is perfect, and no nation should think it is above criticism. No person or group of people prospered because of their own work alone. It is the provision of God, the work of generations, and particular circumstances that allow for times of prosperity.

Today we are more interconnected than ever; every nation's policies and economy affect another. Events that are significant in one nation often impact a dozen others. We are called by God to be humble as believers, even as we recognize God calls us for promise. Israel was reminded before they entered the Promised Land to be humble as a nation. God had delivered them; they had not delivered themselves. It was only by their humility and obedience to God's command that they would prosper in the land. As believers we must remind ourselves to be humble, keep our leaders accountable, and resist the pride of nationalism. How have you seen pride in a particular group become destructive? How can you avoid that same pride in groups that you belong to whether church, ethnicity, government, or organization?

Application for Activation

We all need reminders of how far we have come in order to keep us from becoming prideful. Without them it is easy to believe that all of our success is because of how great we are. There is no one who has lived that is entirely "self-made." Success should not only be measured in material things and positions. Indeed even the great kings in Scripture, Solomon and David, were successes in some ways and failures in others, especially with their families. But God is able to deliver us as God delivered them. We must have people in our lives to keep us accountable, and also to remind ourselves of how God and others contributed to our success.

How do you keep yourself humble? This week take an opportunity to journal about your testimonies that keep you humble. It can be times you recognize you only made it by God's power, memories of lessons you've learned from past mistakes, or thinking about the people who paved the way for you to be where you are. Whatever reminds you to be humble, thank God for it, and also for His promise to be with you as you seek to do His will.

Follow the Spirit

What God wants me to do:

_____

_____

_____

Remember Your Thoughts

Special insights I have learned:

_____

_____

_____

_____

More Light on the Text
Deuteronomy 8:1–11

Moses has just reminded the Israelites of all the way they have come across the desert and 40 years in the wilderness. During this time God had protected them mightily and they had prospered. Moses reminds them of the basic tenets of following the Lord, the Ten Commandments and the Shema. He has reminded Israel that God has chosen them, but not because of any greatness of their own. Because God has chosen them, they should continually choose God over the gods of neighboring nations.

1 All the commandments which I command thee this day shall ye observe to do, that ye may live, and multiply, and go in and possess the land which the LORD sware unto your fathers.

Having established all this, Moses calls the people to observe all of the commandments of the Law. If they do so, God will prosper them. They will live and "multiply," words that recall God's original promise to Abraham to make him a great nation, with descendants as numerous as the stars and grains of sand. Indeed Moses continues to emphasize God's promises that they will not only multiply but also go in and possess the land "which the LORD sware unto your fathers." At long last, the Israelites are on the cusp of gaining the inheritance they have been waiting on for 685 years from Abraham's covenant through their time in Egypt plus their time in the wilderness.

2 And thou shalt remember all the way which the LORD thy God led thee these forty years in the wilderness, to humble thee, and to prove thee, to know what was in thine heart, whether thou wouldest keep his commandments, or no.

Moses sets up a kind of thesis statement describing his authoritative interpretation of God's actions over the past decades. God's purpose in the 40 years in the wilderness was (1) to humble them, (2) to test (KJV: "prove") them, and (3) to know what was in their heart. There is a sequence to these verbs. First God humbles them (Heb. '*anah*, aw-**NAW**), which means to afflict, weaken, or humiliate. God could have made the Israelites' wilderness wandering easier, but He chose to make it difficult for them. Why? In order to "prove" (Heb. *nasah*, naw-**SAW**) them. This means to test or try out. It is also translated as "tempt" (Deuteronomy 6:16). People cannot be truly tested when they go through something easy. Even though practice runs are designed to be easy enough to get through, the final test is designed to induce strain and requires the test-taker to remember and implement everything they have learned.

But why was it important for God to test the Israelites? In order to know (Heb. *yada'*, yaw-**DAH**) them fully. Were they going to continue following Him when the going got tough? Similar language is used to describe the narrative of God asking Abraham to sacrifice Isaac (Genesis 22). God sets out to test Abraham (same Hebrew word: *nasah*; v. 1) in order to "know" (again same word: *yada'*, v. 12) what Abraham would do.

God is omniscient and in some sense already knows what will happen, but He wants to witness it. The plot of history is not what drives God, but the relationships He delights in building. He wants to give us the chance to choose that future He has foreknown. He wants us to know—through our own observation—what we will do in difficult situations. Will we follow God, even when it means the seeming destruction of all we hold dear? Will we trust that He knows what is best, and will protect us and guide us to our Promised Land?

3 And he humbled thee, and suffered thee to hunger, and fed thee with manna, which thou knewest not, neither did thy fathers know; that he might make thee know that man doth not live by bread only, but by every word that proceedeth out of the mouth of the LORD doth man live.

In His plan to humble Israel, God allowed (KJV: "suffered") them to get hungry in the wilderness. The affliction He chose as His testing medium was hunger. He does not intend for the Israelites to starve, or simply to make their lives miserable. He has a plan to work a miracle. He gives them manna. Moses stresses that the Israelites did not even know what manna was, but God made it for them. Their parents also did not even know manna was an option, but God had been doing it every day for 40 years. Every day for 40 years, God had been providing bread for the Israelites that literally has the name "what's this stuff?"

As stated in Moses' first thesis statement (v. 2), this is done so that they would know to trust God. God didn't just give them bread; they knew about bread and how that worked. God gave them manna so that they would hang on His every word about how to use and collect it. Note the repetition of the word "know" in this verse. They did not "know" manna, nor did their parents "know" about it, but God gave it to them to "make them know" they could trust Him to provide for their every need.

347

"Man" here is 'adam (Heb. aw-**DOM**) with the definite article, which means a better translation would be "a human." Every human needs more than bread or food to survive. To fully live, we need God's instructions, and that is just what He always provides for us to miraculous extent, whether it be through prophets, or His Son, or the faithfully preserved word of Scripture.

This verse is widely known in Christian circles because Jesus quotes it when Satan tempts Him. During Satan's first test, he suggested Jesus turn stones into bread. Jesus perhaps selected this verse because Satan was tempting Him when He was hungry in the wilderness, just as the Israelites had been. Jesus responds with not just this verse, but with this entire passage in mind. He knows what it is to be in the wilderness, what it means for God to allow Him to become hungry. He knows that He need only wait for God and humbly trust Him that "man shall not live by bread alone…"

Jesus does not simply recite a random verse that happened to mention bread. He chose a verse that richly applied thematically to His situation. This can only be done with faithful study of the Word. We must read and reread the sacred texts so that they become a part of us. We must know their words, their contexts, their stories, and their themes. Those who know their Scriptures so well do not possess some special memorization skill. They do it by being in the Word daily. How would the church change if all Christians had such a deep and thorough knowledge of Scripture? Certainly when temptation comes, we would be ready, armed with the Sword of the Truth.

4 Thy raiment waxed not old upon thee, neither did thy foot swell, these forty years.

Moses reminds them of miracles they experienced during their wanderings. Their clothes did not grow (KJV: "wax") worn out, nor did their feet swell from so much walking through rough terrain. These are not as flashy as the miracle of Aaron's staff budding or calling water from a rock with the strike of a staff. Those miracles are certainly something to remember, but they only occurred once in the generational time-span the Israelites experienced. The big miracles are recorded in the Israelites' cultural texts, but the miracles Moses mentions here have a different significance.

This is a miracle that shows God providing for His children in the details of everyday life and physical needs that will help them survive. God cares not just about our eternal souls, but He cares about your life here and now too. He provides our daily bread, not only spiritual insight to help us grow more like Him, but physical bread to eat every day so that we can continue our bodily existence.

5 Thou shalt also consider in thine heart, that, as a man chasteneth his son, so the LORD thy God chasteneth thee. 6 Therefore thou shalt keep the commandments of the LORD thy God, to walk in his ways, and to fear him.

God has done all this for His people. It is exactly what a father does for his children. He provides food, clothes, and health. Even when the children have no idea how their parents will provide, they do. This illustration is also used in Hebrews, where it impresses that the hard discipline God uses on His people is for our benefit. Indeed, God through Moses explains here that the chastening God has forced them through in the Wilderness was to ensure that they would keep His commandments. When God "chasteneth" (Heb. yasar, yaw-**SAR**) this means He teaches and corrects. The word is sometimes used in the context of physical correction of a father of his children (1 Kings 12:14; Proverbs 29:19). It is also used of simple instruction (1 Chronicles 15:22; Isaiah 28:26).

Often in Deuteronomy, Moses states the same basic idea with three different words. This rhetorical device is often used in modern English too, known as the "Rule of Three." This technique is used primarily to aid the memory. God's chastening had the purpose of making sure the Israelites (1) keep the commandments (2) walk in His ways, and (3) fear Him. These all communicate the same idea. The way to walk in His way is to keep the commandments, which shows your fear of Him.

Throughout the Old Testament, many discuss the "fear of the LORD." This word (Heb. *yare'*, yaw-**RAY**) can refer to our common modern use of fear, as in to be afraid or terrified. This is not the best translation to understand the kind of relationship God desires with His children, however. The kind of fear God expects from His followers is a reverence for His power and glory. God is capable of changing our lives in a heartbeat. We only survive because of His mercy and forbearance. We know that He can and will dispense vengeance and judgment. If we are on the receiving end of this, truly, "It is a fearful thing to fall into the hands of the living God" (Hebrews 10:31). In His mercy, though, God has chosen not to destroy us for our sins, but to grow us through some measure of chastisement that would work to draw us closer to Him and to keeping His commandments.

7 For the LORD thy God bringeth thee into a good land, a land of brooks of water, of fountains and depths that spring out of valleys and hills; 8 A land of wheat, and barley, and vines, and fig trees, and pomegranates; a land of oil olive, and honey; 9 A land wherein thou shalt eat bread without scarceness, thou shalt not lack any thing in it; a land whose stones are iron, and out of whose hills thou mayest dig brass.

Expanding on the usual description of "flowing with milk and honey," Moses paints the Promised Land as a place of plenty. It has water sources, both streams and springs. It can grow food staples of wheat and barley, but it will also grow crops that show prosperity, like grapes, figs, and pomegranates. It will flow not only with olive oil to support their usual diet, but also honey as a special treat. This wide variety of crops will grow in abundance. There will be no scarcity of bread, nor any lack of any kind.

Having assured them of their basic needs, Moses moves on to other kinds of resources the Promised Land holds for them. They will possess valuable mineral deposits. The land will also provide for them strong, durable metals like iron and brass. Moses' time is right around the end of what is called the "Iron Age" and leading into the "Bronze Age." During this time, smiths improved their skill so that they could shape not only iron, but copper alloys as well. Brass is an alloy of copper and zinc, and bronze is copper alloyed with tin (with a few other metals sometimes added). The Hebrew word is *nekhosheth* (Heb. neh-**KHO**-shet), and is also translated copper, which is found in areas Israel would control during the early monarchy. The ancient Hebrew language does not distinguish between copper and its alloys, though by context we can usually infer if the text means the elemental material copper (like here), or the alloy bronze which was widely used in weapons and tools at the time (1 Samuel 17:5).

10 When thou hast eaten and art full, then thou shalt bless the LORD thy God for the good land which he hath given thee. 11 Beware that thou forget not the LORD thy God, in not keeping his commandments, and his judgments, and his statutes, which I command thee this day.

Moses encourages the Israelites that they should remember to bless God for all the abundance they will enjoy in the Promised Land and not forget Him. This illustrates another reason the parent/child illustration is accurate for God's relationship with His people. The example of manna shows this. After years and years of manna being there for them every morning, they got used to it. This is just like when someone's child does not realize how hard it is for their parents to put food in front of them every day. The child will eat without batting an eye, because that is how the parents have always provided for them. So too, we so often get used to miracles. That job you landed, that baby that survived a difficult pregnancy, that addiction you conquered. God did all those things, and we forget to keep thanking Him for them.

Moses closes this section of Scripture again with the rule of three to help the Israelites remember his words. Although commandments, judgments, and statues can have nuanced application in legal code, here they are used interchangeably. The repetition enforces Moses' insistence that God's people obey every single law God has given them.

Sources:
Henry, Matthew. *Matthew Henry's Commentary on the Whole Bible: New Modern Edition.* Vols. 1-6. Peabody, MA: Hendrickson Publishers, Inc., 2009.
Kaplan, Jacob. "Metals & Mining." Jewish Virtual Library, a Project of AICE. American-Israeli Cooperative Enterprise. https://www.jewishvirtuallibrary.org/metals-mining. 2008. Accessed 10/27/2020.
Strong, James. *The New Strong's Exhaustive Concordance of the Bible.* Nashville, TN: Thomas Nelson, 2003.
Thayer, Joseph Henry. *A Greek-English Lexicon of the New Testament.* New York: American Book Company, 1889.

Say It Correctly

Horeb. HOR-ebb.
Shema. shuh-MAW.

Daily Bible Readings

MONDAY
Remember God's Blessings
(Deuteronomy 8:12–20)

TUESDAY
Hear and Act
(James 1:19–27)

WEDNESDAY
Humble Yourselves and
Resist the Adversary
(1 Peter 5:5–9)

THURSDAY
Bless the Lord, O My Soul
(Psalm 103:1–10)

FRIDAY
God's Love Is Everlasting
(Psalm 103:11–22)

SATURDAY
Remember Christ and Endure
(2 Timothy 2:8–13)

SUNDAY
Keep the Lord's Commandments
(Deuteronomy 8:1–11)

Teaching Tips

Words You Should Know

A. Betray (Matthew 26:21) *paradidomi* (Gk.) —To surrender, yield or give up

B. Remission (v. 28) *aphesis* (Gk.)— Freedom, pardon, forgiveness

Teacher Preparation

Unifying Principle—The Unforgettable Leader. People need reminders of times of liberation in history. How do people deal with the burdens of daily life? In celebrating the Passover with His disciples, Jesus reminded them of the freedom He gave from fear and want.

A. Read the Bible Background and Devotional Reading.

B. Pray for your students and lesson clarity.

C. Read the lesson Scripture in multiple translations.

O—Open the Lesson

A. Begin the class with prayer.

B. Write the question from Exodus 12:26 on the board—"What do you mean by this observance?" Divide the class into two groups, having one answer the question about Passover, and the other about Communion.

C. Have the students read the Aim for Change and the In Focus story.

D. Ask students how events like those in the story weigh on their hearts and how they can view these events from a faith perspective.

P—Present the Scriptures

A. Read the Focal Verses and discuss the Background and The People, Places, and Times sections.

B. Have the class share what Scriptures stand out for them and why, with particular emphasis on today's themes.

E—Explore the Meaning

A. Use In Depth or More Light on the Text to facilitate a deeper discussion of the lesson text.

B. Pose the questions in Search the Scriptures and Discuss the Meaning.

C. Discuss the Liberating Lesson and Application for Activation sections.

N—Next Steps for Application

A. Summarize the value of Jesus willingly taking the role of the sacrificial Passover lamb.

B. End class with a commitment to intentionally look forward to their ultimate triumph in Christ at the end of this age.

Worship Guide

For the Superintendent or Teacher
Theme: The Passover with the Disciples
Song: "I Know It Was The Blood"

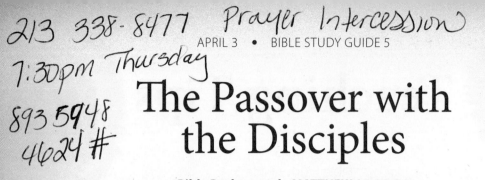

213 338-8477 Prayer Intercession
7:30pm Thursday
893 5948
4624 #

The Passover with the Disciples

Bible Background • MATTHEW 26:17–30
Printed Text • MATTHEW 26:17–30 | Devotional Reading • ZECHARIAH 9:9–12

Aim for Change

By the end of this lesson, we will UNDERSTAND the last meal Jesus shared with His disciples in light of the Jewish Passover, AFFIRM the new meaning Jesus gave to the bread and cup, and REJOICE in the freedom that comes through faith in Christ.

In Focus

Brittany grieved the recent loss of her mother. She had been the neighborhood "Nice Old Christian Lady," always inviting the kids to Sunday School and telling the teens to walk straight; she would be missed.

After the funeral Brittany had the role of taking care of her mother's estate. While cleaning out her mother's bedroom, she came across a Bible. She opened the Bible and found a beautiful cross, one her mother always wore on a beaded chain around her neck. The pain of seeing the cross was unbearable. She hid the Bible among the belongings in her basement.

One day a good friend invited Brittany to her church's revival. The pastor talked about the resurrected life of Christ and how the Cross represents new life for the Christian believer. Brittany remembered her mother's cross, but tried to see the Scriptures in the light of new Christian life, rather than through the lens of her own sorrow.

She began reading the Word of God and regularly attending Bible study. Her perspective of the Cross changed. The Cross no longer represented the memory of her mother's death but the resurrecting power of Christ. What had represented fear and pain became a symbol of joy and liberation.

In today's lesson we will examine how the Passover gives us freedom to rejoice. What Christian symbols remind you to rejoice?

Keep in Mind

"But I say unto you, I will not drink henceforth of this fruit of the vine, until that day when I drink it new with you in my Father's kingdom." (Matthew 26:29, KJV)

"Mark my words—I will not drink wine again until the day I drink it new with you in my Father's Kingdom." (Matthew 26:29, NLT)

Focal Verses

KJV **Matthew 26:17** Now the first day of the feast of unleavened bread the disciples came to Jesus, saying unto him, Where wilt thou that we prepare for thee to eat the passover?

18 And he said, Go into the city to such a man, and say unto him, The Master saith, My time is at hand; I will keep the passover at thy house with my disciples.

19 And the disciples did as Jesus had appointed them; and they made ready the passover.

20 Now when the even was come, he sat down with the twelve.

21 And as they did eat, he said, Verily I say unto you, that one of you shall betray me.

22 And they were exceeding sorrowful, and began every one of them to say unto him, Lord, is it I?

23 And he answered and said, He that dippeth his hand with me in the dish, the same shall betray me.

24 The Son of man goeth as it is written of him: but woe unto that man by whom the Son of man is betrayed! it had been good for that man if he had not been born.

25 Then Judas, which betrayed him, answered and said, Master, is it I? He said unto him, Thou hast said.

26 And as they were eating, Jesus took bread, and blessed it, and brake it, and gave it to the disciples, and said, Take, eat; this is my body.

27 And he took the cup, and gave thanks, and gave it to them, saying, Drink ye all of it;

28 For this is my blood of the new testament, which is shed for many for the remission of sins.

29 But I say unto you, I will not drink henceforth of this fruit of the vine, until that day when I drink it new with you in my Father's kingdom.

NLT **Matthew 26:17** On the first day of the Festival of Unleavened Bread, the disciples came to Jesus and asked, "Where do you want us to prepare the Passover meal for you?"

18 "As you go into the city," he told them, "you will see a certain man. Tell him, 'The Teacher says: My time has come, and I will eat the Passover meal with my disciples at your house.'"

19 So the disciples did as Jesus told them and prepared the Passover meal there.

20 When it was evening, Jesus sat down at the table with the Twelve.

21 While they were eating, he said, "I tell you the truth, one of you will betray me."

22 Greatly distressed, each one asked in turn, "Am I the one, Lord?"

23 He replied, "One of you who has just eaten from this bowl with me will betray me.

24 For the Son of Man must die, as the Scriptures declared long ago. But how terrible it will be for the one who betrays him. It would be far better for that man if he had never been born!"

25 Judas, the one who would betray him, also asked, "Rabbi, am I the one?" And Jesus told him, "You have said it."

26 As they were eating, Jesus took some bread and blessed it. Then he broke it in pieces and gave it to the disciples, saying, "Take this and eat it, for this is my body."

27 And he took a cup of wine and gave thanks to God for it. He gave it to them and said, "Each of you drink from it,

28 for this is my blood, which confirms the covenant between God and his people. It is poured out as a sacrifice to forgive the sins of many.

29 Mark my words—I will not drink wine again until the day I drink it new with you in my Father's Kingdom."

30 And when they had sung an hymn, they went out into the mount of Olives.

30 Then they sang a hymn and went out to the Mount of Olives.

Chronos —
Kairos —

The People, Places, and Times

Son of Man. A reference to a prophecy from Daniel (Daniel 7:13), "Son of Man" is a Messianic title Jesus used to express His heavenly origin, earthly mission, and glorious future coming. Jesus uses the term to refer to Himself throughout the Gospels about 80 times. As the Son of Man, Jesus is seated at the right hand of God (Matthew 26:64; Mark 14:62; Luke 22:69), and will return to earth from heaven in the glory of His Father with the angels (Matthew 16:27; Mark 8:38; Luke 9:26). Jesus' coming will restore righteousness in the world (Matthew 19:28; 25:46). In these passages Jesus' focus shifts from the provisional victory, passion, and resurrection to the final victory of the Son of Man at His second coming (Acts 17:31).

Judas. Surnamed Iscariot after his city of origin, Judas was one of the 12 disciples of Jesus during His public ministry. Judas managed the treasury of the group (John 13:29), from which he was known to pilfer money (John 12:4). As a betrayer, Judas contracted to turn Jesus over to the chief priests for 30 pieces of silver. He accomplished this act of treachery by singling out Jesus with a kiss in the Garden of Gethsemane (Matthew 26:14–47; Mark 14:10–46; Luke 22:3–48; John 18:2–5).

What do your nicknames say about you? Are they like "Iscariot," looking back to your origin, or like "Son of Man" looking forward to your purpose?

Background

The Passover held supreme theological and historical significance for the Israelites. The Passover represented one of the most significant acts of divine involvement and commenced their liberation from Egyptian oppression. The primary reason for removing all leaven from bread was paralleled to the fundamental practice of draining blood from animal flesh; the underlying belief is both leaven and blood had life-giving power. The first and seventh days of this period were marked by a holy assembly during which the only work permitted was the preparation of food (Exodus 12:16). By the New Testament times the festivals of Passover and Unleavened Bread were well-attended celebrations, as all practicing male Jews were supposed to gather at Jerusalem during this festival. The week was known as the "days of unleavened bread" (Luke 22:1; Acts 12:3).

What symbols are metaphors of life today? Blood? Yeast? Seeds?

At-A-Glance

1. The Preparation (Matthew 26:17–19)
2. The Betrayer (vv. 20–25)
3. The Partaking (vv. 26–27)
4. The Promise (vv. 28–30)

In Depth

1. The Preparation (Matthew 26:17–19)

According to biblical scholars, the disciples who were sent to make provisions for the Passover meal were Peter and John (Luke 22:8). The disciples prepared the Passover according to Moses' ancient instructions (Exodus 12:1–20). The Passover lambs were to be killed on the afternoon of the 14th of Nisan. The festival itself began with the ritual meal on the evening of the 15th of Nisan. The Festival of Unleavened Bread begins on the 15th and continues for seven days, during which no leaven should be found in the house.

Purchasing and preparing the food probably took the greater part of the day. Preparation for the Passover involved locating an appropriate place within the city walls of Jerusalem. The room had to be cleaned of all items containing leaven to include removing bread as well as bread crumbs. The lambs had to be ritually slaughtered by the priest in the Temple, then roasted and prepared with the additional items for the meal.

How do we prepare ourselves and our spaces for worship and remembrance?

2. The Betrayer (vv. 20–25)

When evening came, Jesus entered the prayer room (Luke 22:12) and partook of the Passover supper with the 12 disciples. Jesus takes the opportunity to state that someone within His inner circle (who had even eaten out of the same bowl as He did) would betray Him. Astonishingly no disciple pointed to another with an accusing finger, but each became very sad and asked if he would be the betrayer. Jesus mentioned that He would die just as it had been written by the prophets (Isaiah 53:4–8; Matthew 26:24, 56).

Jesus' interaction with Judas also lets us know God is not surprised by the betrayal that leads to the crucifixion. God's divine plan, expressed throughout the Scriptures, tells us that salvation would come to humankind through the shed blood of His beloved Son.

Do verses 22 and 25 signify that Judas truly did not believe his actions—accepting money to bring the priests to Jesus when He would be alone and pointing Him out for them—constituted betrayal?

3. The Partaking (vv. 26–27)

The taking of bread and drinking of the cup occurred during the course of the meal and not as a separate ceremony. This is the way the earliest Church celebrated the Lord's Supper until excesses at the common meal required the meal and the Eucharist (meaning service of thanksgiving) be separated (1 Corinthians 11:20–21). Today this sacrament is only a metaphorical supper, with just the bread and the cup. The bread symbolizes Jesus' total self which is given for humankind. The cup represents the life of Jesus, which is offered up to seal the New Covenant.

The Eucharist meal highlights the life of Jesus Christ and reveals His openness and acceptance of all people. The meal represents Jesus Christ, as a gift to all, unconstrained and undeserved. This meal exemplifies the love and selflessness of Jesus, the Holy One, who gave His life for the redemption of sin. The meal emphasizes the unspeakable joy Christians will experience during the Messianic banquet when God's Kingdom is finally revealed.

4. The Promise (vv. 28–30)

Jesus instituted a new meaning for the Eucharist by stating the cup of wine was His blood of the New Covenant and the bread was His body. This was done in keeping with the remission of sins promised in the New Covenant (Jeremiah 31:31–37; 32:37–40; Ezekiel 34:25–31; 36:26–28), a covenant that would replace the old Mosaic Covenant. Jesus' blood would be shed for sinners for the forgiveness of sins.

This ritual of the Passover Supper has been followed by Christians and is called the Lord's Supper or Communion. Jesus committed this ordinance to the Church to be followed as a continual reminder of His work in their salvation. It is to be remembered until He returns (1 Corinthians 11:23–26).

Celebrating the Eucharist had great importance for Jesus and the early Christian community. It represents a foretaste of the full fellowship to be experienced when the Kingdom of God has come and all God's people are gathered into one.

What reason for joy in the Eucharist does Jesus describe?

Search the Scriptures

1. How did the disciples respond to Jesus' statement, "I tell you the truth, one of you will betray me" (vv. 21–22)?

2. What warning did Jesus give His betrayer (v. 24)?

Discuss the Meaning

After reading this lesson, how can Communion give us cause for celebration? What are the important things we need to remember? Can we celebrate when we remember the cup represented Jesus' innocent spilled blood and the bread symbolized his beaten, battered, bruised, and crucified body? Is it possible to celebrate when we know God paid the ultimate sacrifice not for Himself but for our sake?

Liberating Lesson

Some Christian holidays are overly commercialized and have lost their spiritual importance. We go into debt and forget the true meaning of the season. In some Christian circles the ritual of taking communion has become underrated and has lost its spiritual significance. Some just go through the motions of drinking from the cup and taking the bread and forget what it really means spiritually. The ability to experience liberating power to deal with life's issues comes from Jesus Christ. And we must never forget this freedom comes with a hefty price, the death and resurrection of Jesus Christ.

Application for Activation

Many of us live in abundance. However, there are many people around us who have nothing to eat and no place to live. The Passover supper was not just drinking from the cup and breaking of bread; it was a time of fellowship. How many opportunities have we neglected to break bread and enjoy fellowship with those less fortunate than we are? Jesus was cordial and giving. He shared all that He had with others. Pray for God's guidance, wisdom, and opportunity. The next time you have a family dinner or get-together consider those around you in want. Commit to inviting someone from your church, work, or neighborhood to join you.

Follow the Spirit

What God wants me to do:

_____

_____

_____

_____

Remember Your Thoughts

Special insights I have learned:

_____

_____

_____

_____

More Light on the Text
Matthew 26:17–30

17 Now the first day of the feast of unleavened bread the disciples came to Jesus, saying unto him, Where wilt thou that we prepare for thee to eat the passover? 18 And he said, Go into the city to such a man, and say unto him, The Master saith, My time is at hand; I will keep the passover at thy house with my disciples. 19 And the disciples did as Jesus had appointed them; and they made ready the passover.

The exact location of Jesus' final Passover celebration is not designated in any of the Gospels; however, they do all agree it took place in Jerusalem (Matthew 26:1), more than likely in the home of one of Jesus' disciples; a follower of Christ, who not only freely opened his home, but also had knowledge of Jesus' messianic claims.

The Feast of Unleavened Bread is celebrated for an entire week and begins with a solemn assembly and day of rest. The evening meal on the first day of the Feast of Unleavened bread will be the Passover Sedar during which a lamb is slaughtered, roasted, and eaten completely in each household. After the Passover Sedar meal is observed, the Feast lasts six more days and involves eating bread only if it has been prepared with no leavening. Afterward, they hold another solemn assembly and observe another day of rest (Exodus 12; Leviticus 23; Numbers 28). These days of rest are not necessarily Sabbaths, though they might overlap some years. The Passover is celebrated on the 10th day of the Jewish month Nisan, no matter what day of the week the 10th lands on.

In Jesus' day, it was actually an honor for a renowned rabbi like Jesus to invite Himself over to someone's house for dinner. Jesus honored Zaccheaus in this way, and could expect hospitality in Jerusalem as well. This feast is one of the Pilgrimage Feasts, which means every Jewish male who was able was supposed to try to celebrate it in Jerusalem. Many people living in Jerusalem were likely used to sharing space with travelers for this feast.

20 Now when the even was come, he sat down with the twelve. 21 And as they did eat, he said, Verily I say unto you, that one of you shall betray me. 22 And they were exceeding sorrowful, and began every one of them to say unto him, Lord, is it I?

"Verily," translated from the Hebraic expression *amen* (Gk. *amen*, ah-MAIN) means "truly" and is a word that Jesus often uses to emphasize His words. He will use the word again, at this same meal, to insist that Peter will indeed deny Him. Jesus used it notably in the Sermon on the Mount (Matthew 6:2, 5, 16). Matthew records Jesus introducing His teachings with "verily" at least 30 times. While Matthew, Mark, and Luke record Jesus as often saying, "Verily," John records His sayings as starting with "Verily, verily." Jesus is the Way, the Truth, and the Life. We can trust that His word is always true, and should strive to follow His example in our own words.

The word "betray" gives the picture of handing over someone or something. It can be used in a good way, as Jesus Himself does in His parable of the talents (Matthew 25:20, 22), where it is translated as "deliver." However, when someone is handed over to their enemies, it is an act of betrayal.

Matthew has recorded three previous times Jesus told His disciples He would be betrayed. Each time Jesus reveals more information. First He simply says He'll be betrayed (Matthew 17:22), then He gives more details of the harsh treatment He will endure from His betrayal (20:18–19). Finally, He reveals it will occur that very Passover (26:2). Now He gives one more clue to narrow down this looming prophecy: one of them will betray Him.

The entire idea of Jesus being betrayed is alien to the faithful disciples. They cannot imagine how or why it would be done, so they have no idea which one of them would do it. Each one wonders if maybe he will be the one to somehow betray Jesus. The faithful disciples might have thought that they would accidentally betray Him. Each of the Twelve asks, "It isn't me, is it?" Each one calls Jesus "Lord." Not a single one of them jumps to conclusions and asks if it is another disciple, but each questions himself.

23 And he answered and said, He that dippeth his hand with me in the dish, the same shall betray me.

Jesus answers all 12 men by saying that the betrayer is one who has already begun eating with them. The tense of the participle "dippeth" in Greek indicates this action has already taken place. No doubt each disciple tried to recall the evening in great detail, wondering if their hand had been in the communal dish at the same time as Jesus' that night. This hint about Jesus' betrayal does not add any new information as the other hints had. Jesus had said one of them there that night would be the betrayer, and now only adds that they are eating the meal with Him. Betrayal at this point would certainly add insult to injury. Being false to someone with whom you had shared a meal was severely taboo in Jewish society.

24 The Son of man goeth as it is written of him: but woe unto that man by whom the Son of man is betrayed! it had been good for that man if he had not been born.

Later that night, Jesus would call Himself the "Son of Man" before the Sanhedrin. This is a reference to the prophet's vision in Daniel 7 in which "one like the son of man" appears bearing heavenly news. This messenger has divine attributes and is understood to be a reference to God. The Sanhedrin certainly takes it this way, as Jesus continues to identify Himself as the Son of Man, which the Jewish leaders of the Sanhedrin take as blasphemy. Interestingly, the phrase "son of man" in Aramaic was used to mean "anybody." Thus Jesus retained what is called the "messianic secret"; He does claim to be the Messiah, but He does so in such a way as to allow for ambiguity and doubt.

Jesus pronounces woe upon His betrayer. From Judas' point of view, it would have been better if he had not been born, rather than suffer the agony of crime, guilt, and condemnation that he did after he betrayed Jesus. From an eternal point of view, some poor soul was going to have to be the one to betray Jesus. Still, even though Jesus had to die to work out our salvation as had been planned since before time began, those who killed Him are responsible for their evil actions.

25 Then Judas, which betrayed him, answered and said, Master, is it I? He said unto him, Thou hast said.

Some believe Judas did not see himself as a betrayer. Rather, he might have thought he was forcing Jesus' hand to show His divine powers to all so that they would follow Him. Many awaited a messiah to overthrow the Roman government oppressing the Jews. Judas could have been planning to hand Jesus over to the Romans in hopes that He would raise up against their tyranny. Today, too, we often make excuses for our sinful behavior, convincing ourselves that what we are doing does not really betray our God whom we have sworn to as our Master. By God's grace, we can see ourselves in the light of all truth, as God Himself sees us. He will show us if our actions truly are sinful, but He will also show us our innate worth as His children.

Matthew first mentions Judas in his initial list of Jesus' 12 disciples (Matthew 10:4), and he does not reappear until this chapter when he makes his deal with the high priests (26:14). Similarly, in the other Gospels, Judas is named in the list of the Twelve and does nothing of note during Jesus' ministry until he agrees to betray his master (Mark 3:19; Luke 6:16; John 6:71). The only exception is John, who also mentions that Judas is the disciple who objects to Jesus' feet being anointed at Bethany (John 12:4). Each Gospel writer says that Judas will betray Jesus from their very first mention of him. No Gospel writer tries to keep their audience in suspense.

Some understand Judas' address of Jesus as "Master" to carry great significance. While the other disciples just called Him "Lord" (v. 22; Gk. *kurios*), Judas instead here calls Him "Master" (Gk. *rabbi*). The only other time Matthew uses the title Rabbi is in recording Jesus' admonishment that His disciples not desire to be called Rabbi (which is related to the Hebrew word for "great one"), and claiming the title solely for Himself (Matthew 23:7–8). In John, "Rabbi" is the common way His disciples address Him. "Master" is likewise common throughout Matthew and the other Gospels.

26 And as they were eating, Jesus took bread, and blessed it, and brake it, and gave it to the disciples, and said, Take, eat; this is my body. 27 And he took the cup, and gave thanks, and gave it to them, saying, Drink ye all of it; 28 For this is my blood of the new testament, which is shed for many for the remission of sins.

The bread eaten at this meal had to be prepared without yeast. This was to remember how when the Israelites left Egypt, they did so in such a hurry that they did not have time to wait for the bread to rise, but baked it without the leavening agent of yeast. Such unleavened bread was called the "bread of affliction" because it reminded them of their time as slaves in Egypt (Deuteronomy 16:3). As the Jews celebrated this feast year after year, yeast began to be a symbol for sin, as every bit of yeast was to be removed from the house before observing the holy celebration of Passover and the entire weeklong Feast of Unleavened Bread. Jesus reinforces this understanding with His warning against the "leaven of the Pharisees" (Matthew 16:6). In establishing a new covenant with His followers, Jesus identifies Himself with the unleavened bread, revealing Himself to be the sinless sacrifice for our sin.

The communal cup of wine that Jesus presents to His disciples is re-imagined not just as the normal beverage for a meal, but as a new covenant between God and His people. Jesus calls it a "new testament," translated with a word meaning "covenant," which is now only used in the phrase "last will and testament." This new promise between them is made with Jesus' blood to remit our sin. Without blood to symbolize the death of the sinful self, there is no way to atone for sin (Hebrews 9:22).

This meal is a reminder of the fulfillment of Christ's work in the kingdom of God. As we anticipate the joy of participating in God's heavenly banquet, we can remember Christ's life and the sacrifice He made for us. Every Eucharist is an assurance of the ultimate victory of God's Kingdom. The Eucharist represents a prophetic celebration of indisputable triumph.

Each participant who partakes of the Eucharist is invited to self-examination. As we read these Scriptures and examine the actions of Judas and the 12 disciples, we must also examine our own actions. We can ask God to take inventory of our own hearts. We can ask for forgiveness and know we have assurance of His divine grace and mercy.

The meal reminds us of the heavenly realm where the risen and exalted King is enthroned. The symbols of the body and blood of Jesus give us a glimpse of the unparalleled dominion of God. When we share in the taking of the Lord's Supper we know this ritual is celebrated beyond our own church; others are sharing along with us in our neighborhood, city, state, country, and around the world. It is a meal taken by a community of believers. The Eucharist is our testimony that reaches beyond the dimensions of our faith. It is a testimony to others, to those who know Christ and to those who have not yet been introduced to Him.

29 But I say unto you, I will not drink henceforth of this fruit of the vine, until that day when I drink it new with you in my Father's kingdom.

Jesus promised His disciples He would not eat this meal again with them until the institution of His Father's kingdom on earth. He drinks with them after the Resurrection. God's Kingdom is inaugurated in the Resurrection, even though its coming has not yet been fully consummated.

30 And when they had sung an hymn, they went out into the mount of Olives.

After the Passover meal, Jesus and the disciples sang a hymn, then left the disciple's home and went to the Mount of Olives. It was Jewish tradition then, and still is today, to sing the Hallel psalms (Psalms 113–118) during the Passover. These songs remember the Israelites' deliverance from Egypt and praise God joyously.

Mount of Olives was in an area east of Jerusalem, just on the next hill over. It is still producing olives to this day. Most recently, Matthew had mentioned the Mount of Olives as the location where the disciples asked Jesus to tell them more about the end times (Matthew 24); this teaching is even called the Olivet discourse. Luke records that one night in the last week of His life, Jesus avoided the large crowds of the Jerusalem Temple and slept the night in the Mount of Olives (Luke 21:37). He also records that it is the place where Jesus ascended into heaven (Acts 1:12). Knowing He will soon be arrested, Jesus chooses to go to this peaceful area and pray.

Sources:
Laymon, Charles M., *The Interpreter's One-Volume Commentary on the Bible*, Nashville, TN: Abingdon Press, 1971. 640-641.
Life Application Bible, New International Version: Grand Rapids, MI: Tyndale House Publishers, Inc., 1991. 1710-1711.
The New Interpreter's Bible, A Commentary in Twelve Volumes, Vol. VIII. Nashville, TN: Abingdon Press, 1995. 468-473.
Tyndale Bible Dictionary. Wheaton, IL: Tyndale House Publishers Inc., 2001. 1213-1214.
Walvoord, John F. and Zuck, Roy B., *The Bible Knowledge Commentary*. Colorado Springs, CO: Chariot Victor Publishing, 1983. 82-83.

Say It Correctly

Sedar. SAY-der.
Sanhedrin. san-HEE-drin.
Eucharist. YOU-kar-ist.
Hallel. hah-LELL.

Daily Bible Readings

MONDAY
God Is Gracious, Righteous, and Merciful
(Psalm 116:1–15)

TUESDAY
Keep the Festival Where God Chooses
(Deuteronomy 16:1–8, 15–17)

WEDNESDAY
Jesus Anointed and Betrayed
(Matthew 26:1–2, 6–16)

THURSDAY
Jesus Institutes the Lord's Supper
(1 Corinthians 11:23–26)

FRIDAY
Love One Another
(John 13:31–35)

SATURDAY
God's Steadfast Love Endures Forever
(Psalm 118:1–9)

SUNDAY
Jesus Shares Passover with His Disciples
(Matthew 26:17–30)

Teaching Tips

April 10
Bible Study Guide 6

Words You Should Know

A. Hosanna (Matthew 21:9) *hosanna* (Gk./Heb.)—"Save now," or "Save, we beseech Thee"

B. Blessed (v. 9) *makarios* (Gk.)—Fortunate, happy, spoken well of

Teacher Preparation

Unifying Principle—A Leader with Humility. People long for leaders who can liberate them from tyranny and be worthy of their praise. What does humility teach us about leadership? Matthew describes Jesus' humility and the crowd blessing Him.

A. Read the Bible Background and Devotional Reading.

B. Pray for your students and lesson clarity.

C. Read the lesson Scripture in multiple translations.

O—Open the Lesson

A. Begin the class with prayer.

B. Create a stack of index cards with the name of a type of transportation on each. Some examples would include: a private jet, an old VW microbus, a stretch limo, a hybrid car, a minivan, the Popemobile, a pickup truck with a rifle rack, a sports car, a black SUV, etc. Ask the class to describe the kind of person who might ride in each of these vehicles. Afterward, note that we made judgments about people based on their transportation. The transportation Jesus chose was also significant.

C. Have the students read the Aim for Change and the In Focus story.

D. Ask students how events like those in the story weigh on their hearts and how they can view these events from a faith perspective.

P—Present the Scriptures

A. Read the Focal Verses and discuss the Background and The People, Places, and Times sections.

B. Have the class share what Scriptures stand out for them and why, with particular emphasis on today's themes.

E—Explore the Meaning

A. Use In Depth or More Light on the Text to facilitate a deeper discussion of the lesson text.

B. Pose the questions in Search the Scriptures and Discuss the Meaning.

C. Discuss the Liberating Lesson and Application for Activation sections.

N—Next Steps for Application

A. Summarize the value of the Old Testament prophets' confirming Jesus' identity as the Messiah.

B. End class with a commitment to pray for courage to keep the faith regardless of public opinion.

Worship Guide

For the Superintendent or Teacher
Theme: Triumphal Entry into Jerusalem
Song: "All Glory, Laud, and Honor"

(handwritten: (213) 338-8477)

(handwritten: 893 5948 4624#)

Triumphal Entry into Jerusalem

(handwritten: Intercessory Prayer)

Bible Background • MATTHEW 21:1-11
Printed Text • MATTHEW 21:1-11 | Devotional Reading • 1 CORINTHIANS 11:27-32

—————— Aim for Change ——————

By the end of this lesson, we will STUDY the immediate response of the crowds to Jesus' arrival into Jerusalem, IDENTIFY reasons people today seek and follow new leadership, and ACCEPT Jesus as a leader who offers hope for the world in every age.

————— In Focus —————

The Hills family always attended church with Nana Rochelle on Easter Sunday before going to her house for dinner. When Nana died, none of her children felt they could be the host to continue this tradition. Nana's granddaughter Marie didn't like this, but she felt there was nothing she could do since she was fresh out of graduate school.

A few years later, Marie and her husband Gene bought a house. As she was shopping for decorations for their new home, the spring lilies, chicks, and bunnies made her remember Nana. When Marie got home, her husband's eyes grew wide when he saw all she had purchased. Marie, however, was grinning ear-to-ear as she hauled in more bags.

"Remember when Pastor Wayne talked about making new family traditions?" Marie asked. "This is an old tradition, but I'm bringing it back. We're going to host Easter dinner."

By the time Marie and Gene put the last of the dishes away, she realized the fun part was over. She had to get her family on board. Marie knew it wouldn't be easy to convince everyone, so she prayed God would soften their hearts in advance. She didn't want to come off too uppity, telling people they *had* to come over. Instead, she went to visit each family unit and encouraged them to keep Nana's legacy alive.

On Easter Sunday, Marie beamed when her family filled three whole pews. That evening, as the family gathered around the table for dinner, Marie gave thanks to Jesus. She was grateful that Nana Rochelle's legacy of love for God and family would live on.

What family traditions can you create or restart to remember Jesus' sacrifice for your salvation?

—————— Keep in Mind ——————

"Tell ye the daughter of Sion, Behold, thy King cometh unto thee, meek, and sitting upon an ass, and a colt the foal of an ass." (Matthew 21:5, KJV)

"Tell the people of Jerusalem, 'Look, your King is coming to you. He is humble, riding on a donkey— riding on a donkey's colt.'" (Matthew 21:5, NLT)

Focal Verses

KJV **Matthew 21:1** And when they drew nigh unto Jerusalem, and were come to Bethphage, unto the mount of Olives, then sent Jesus two disciples,

2 Saying unto them, Go into the village over against you, and straightway ye shall find an ass tied, and a colt with her: loose them, and bring them unto me.

3 And if any man say ought unto you, ye shall say, The Lord hath need of them; and straightway he will send them.

4 All this was done, that it might be fulfilled which was spoken by the prophet, saying,

5 Tell ye the daughter of Sion, Behold, thy King cometh unto thee, meek, and sitting upon an ass, and a colt the foal of an ass.

6 And the disciples went, and did as Jesus commanded them,

7 And brought the ass, and the colt, and put on them their clothes, and they set him thereon.

8 And a very great multitude spread their garments in the way; others cut down branches from the trees, and strawed them in the way.

9 And the multitudes that went before, and that followed, cried, saying, Hosanna to the son of David: Blessed is he that cometh in the name of the Lord; Hosanna in the highest.

10 And when he was come into Jerusalem, all the city was moved, saying, Who is this?

11 And the multitude said, This is Jesus the prophet of Nazareth of Galilee.

NLT **Matthew 21:1** As Jesus and the disciples approached Jerusalem, they came to the town of Bethphage on the Mount of Olives. Jesus sent two of them on ahead.

2 "Go into the village over there," he said. "As soon as you enter it, you will see a donkey tied there, with its colt beside it. Untie them and bring them to me.

3 If anyone asks what you are doing, just say, 'The Lord needs them,' and he will immediately let you take them."

4 This took place to fulfill the prophecy that said,

5 "Tell the people of Jerusalem, 'Look, your King is coming to you. He is humble, riding on a donkey— riding on a donkey's colt.'"

6 The two disciples did as Jesus commanded.

7 They brought the donkey and the colt to him and threw their garments over the colt, and he sat on it.

8 Most of the crowd spread their garments on the road ahead of him, and others cut branches from the trees and spread them on the road.

9 Jesus was in the center of the procession, and the people all around him were shouting, "Praise God for the Son of David! Blessings on the one who comes in the name of the LORD! Praise God in highest heaven!"

10 The entire city of Jerusalem was in an uproar as he entered. "Who is this?" they asked.

11 And the crowds replied, "It's Jesus, the prophet from Nazareth in Galilee."

The People, Places, and Times

Messiah. The word "anointed one" in Hebrew is the title *meshiach* or "Messiah," or in Greek *Christos* or "Christ." Since apostolic times, the name Christ has become the proper title of Jesus, whom Christians recognize as the God-given Redeemer of Israel and the Church's Lord. "Christ," or Messiah, is therefore a name admirably suited to express both the Church's link with Israel through the Old Testament and the faith that sees the worldwide scope of the salvation in Him. The Jewish Messiah was expected to be a warrior-prince who would expel the hated Romans from Israel and bring in a kingdom in which the Jews would be promoted to world dominion. However, some of the messianic prophecies showed Him as more of a priest. The alternation between a kingly Messiah and a priestly figure is characteristic of the two centuries of early Judaism prior to the coming of Jesus.

What symbols does being an anointed king or an anointed priest carry?

Background

The significance of Jesus' entry into Jerusalem was such that all four Gospel writers make records of it. As it was time for the Passover, over two million Jewish inhabitants of the land made the annual pilgrimage to Jerusalem for the feast and celebration. One could speculate this was the most excellent moment for the Messiah to make Himself known to so many of His people at one time. The symbolic focus of sacrifice was before them, and He would present Himself as the ultimate sacrifice.

Matthew's Gospel records includes 41 prophetic quotes from the Old Testament which confirm Jesus as the Messiah. The people had seen others who professed to be the messiah, the conqueror of the land, the warrior set to overthrow the ruling government. They were all too familiar with processions of great war-horses and armies entering cities. They did not, however, expect such a humble entrance of a King riding on an animal that was a symbol of quietness, humility, and goodwill.

Still, they knew this was the Messiah and gave Him a king's welcome, replete with an unridden colt, a carpet of garments off their backs, a pathway of palm leaves, and shouts of praise which rang out into the streets. Throngs of people, already gathering in the city, turned their attention to the King.

Jesus, ushered in as a King, knew this was the end of His earthly life and the beginning of His eternal reign. Jesus, regarded as an agitator,

faced the hostile religious leaders, knowing that before the festival was ended, His blood would be on their hands. Jesus entered the town of His trial assured of His triumph!

Why are the crowds of Jerusalem so enthusiastic about Jesus now, but eager for His death a week later?

At-A-Glance

1. Presence of the Prophet
(Matthew 21:1–7)
2. Procession of the People (vv. 8–11)

In Depth

1. Presence of the Prophet (Matthew 21:1–7)

Jesus sent two disciples to secure a donkey to ride into Jerusalem, in order to fulfill the prophecy of Zechariah. It is possible that Jesus made arrangements beforehand to have a donkey and her colt ready for His use, but it is also possible that only His reputation preceded Him. When the owner of the donkey and the colt learned that Jesus requested them, he gave them freely.

What is most significant is that Jesus chose a humble animal to ride into the city, not a mighty war-horse with sinewy muscles of great mass and strength leading a procession of highly trained warriors armed with breastplates of brass and plans for battle. Jesus rode on a colt, a symbol of humility, which made His entry and crucifixion forever memorable. But the presence of a King on a colt did not keep the people from praising Him. They perceived the prophet among them, and greeted Him as a King.

What do you do in your life to show humility?

2. Procession of the People (vv. 8–11)

As Jesus entered Jerusalem, the crowd threw down their coats and branches along the road, and shouted praises to Him. Their actions honored Him, and they greeted Jesus with shouts and songs of the hallel psalms (Psalm 118:26) that were customary greetings to people journeying to Jerusalem for the Passover. However, the people knew Jesus was much more than just another traveler. They were honoring Him for the miracles they had seen Him perform.

The throngs of people, the furor that the Messiah had come, and the deafening shouts of praise created a momentum in the city that could be seen, felt, and heard. Leading the procession were children, not soldiers, who sang His praises and shouted His glory. Jesus is proclaimed as the "Son of David," the rightful ruler of Israel and fulfillment of God's ancient covenant with David. They welcome Him as coming "in the name of the Lord," with the Lord God's full power and authority.

The people of Jerusalem were excited and asked about Jesus' identity. Most of Jesus' ministry had been done outside of Jerusalem to avoid agitating the Jewish leaders. But now these same people, to whom He had ministered, were leading the procession into the city, and the city dwellers wanted to know about this King who sat on a colt and not on a throne. The crowd replied that He was the prophet Jesus from Nazareth of Galilee. Even though Galilee was out of the way, and Nazareth was such a small town, the crowd did not mind making it known that such a great prophet came from obscurity.

As Jerusalem prepared for the solemn remembrance of Passover, Jesus' entrance whipped the people into a joyous frenzy. How do you respond to an unexpected leading of the Spirit during worship?

Search the Scriptures

1. What did the people say and do as Jesus entered Jerusalem? What was the significance of their words and actions (vv. 8–9)?

2. What was the difference between the people of Jerusalem and the multitude who went before and after Jesus (vv. 10–11)?

Discuss the Meaning

Jesus tried to instill in His disciples' minds the prospect that the road to His future glory was bound to the Cross, with its experience of rejection, suffering, and humiliation. Only after the Resurrection were the disciples in a position to see what true messiahship meant (see Luke 24:45-46). The national title Messiah then took on a broader connotation, involving a kingly role which was to embrace all peoples (Luke 24:46-47). One indication of this is the fact that the early followers of the Messiah called themselves "Christians," Christ's people (Acts 11:26; 1 Peter 4:16), as a sign of their universal faith in a sovereign Lord.

In fulfilling His mission, Jesus was careful to look and act differently from others professing to be the messiah. What were these characteristics, and which, if any, should Christians imitate?

Liberating Lesson

People today have heard stories of ridiculous or outrageous demands celebrities feel entitled to make. They have seen important people being honored with a parade. While the presence of an important person seems to automatically draw a big crowd, you may have tried to gather a group together for an important cause, but only had a handful of people show up. All these things make leaders seem distant and unapproachable.

Thankfully, Christians' leader is unlike any other. Jesus is both the King of all humanity and a humble servant leader. Jesus is far more important than any celebrity living today, tomorrow, or yesterday, and yet He does not let His prestige block us from approaching Him. As we follow His example, we do not need to first acquire all the shiny bling of fame to have the platform to get His message out. We are free to simply be ourselves and humbly serve one another.

Application for Activation

As a class devise a few short campaign slogans that communicate why Jesus is the ideal king for all people everywhere. This week use the humor and cheesiness of these slogans as a comedic entry point to explain the importance of Jesus' revelation of Himself on Palm Sunday to your friends, neighbors, and coworkers.

Follow the Spirit

What God wants me to do:

_____

_____

_____

_____

Remember Your Thoughts

Special insights I have learned:

_____

_____

_____

_____

More Light on the Text

Matthew 21:1–11

The Triumphal Entry is told in each of the Gospel accounts (Mark 11:1–10; Luke 19:29–38; John 12:12–19), but each includes different details and emphases. The Gospel of Matthew is plentifully endowed with the fulfillment of Old Testament prophecy. More prophets are quoted in Matthew than in Mark, Luke, and John combined. Matthew's writing style is also marked by his emphasis on the teaching ministry of Jesus.

To understand this text, consider the context. Immediately before entering Jerusalem, Jesus informs His disciples that He would be going to Jerusalem where the chief priest and scribes would mock, whip, and ultimately sentence Him to death. Jesus assures His disciples, however, that God would raise Him to life on the third day (Matthew 20:18-19). While Jesus is sharing this grave news, Salome, the wife of Zebedee and mother of two of the disciples, James and John, is so preoccupied with her sons' successes that she misses, or ignores, the gravity of the inhumane intent of Jesus' enemies. Though there is evidence (Matthew 20:17) that Jesus and company were in motion, talking and walking away from Judea and going to Jerusalem, Jesus hears, questions, and answers Salome. He settles the indignation of the 10 other disciples, a common reaction among the disciples toward women (Matthew 26:8) and children (Matthew 19:14). He also opened the eyes of two blind men sitting by the Jericho roadside.

From this context, today's text emerges. Jesus has expressed the purpose of their departure from Judea (Matthew 19:1). Their destination is Jerusalem and a place frequented by Jesus, the Mount of Olives (Matthew 21:1).

1 And when they drew nigh unto Jerusalem, and were come to Bethphage, unto the mount of Olives, then sent Jesus two disciples,

The Mount of Olives is the place where Jesus agonizes and is betrayed, the place where He ascended into heaven, and also the supposed place of His second advent (Acts 1:9–12). The Mount of Olives is mentioned often in each Gospel (Matthew 24:3; Mark 11:1; Luke 19:37; John 8:1), as Jesus and His disciples frequently passed by it. Heading east out from Jerusalem, one goes down into a valley, and up on the next hill over is called the Mount of Olives. An olive grove stands there to this day, with some of its trees being old enough to have been seen on that very day of the Triumphal Entry long ago.

Notice a common pattern in the number of disciples Jesus sent. In the Bible the number two is often given in an "either/or" way: two gates, two great lights, two eternal places, two masters, two debtors, two sons, etc. In these incidences, the Bible is teaching how to make choices by comparison. The number two is also given in a "both/and" way: Jesus sends two of His disciples to visit John the Baptist while he is imprisoned (Matthew 11:2); Jesus sends forth the disciples by two's and gives them power over unclean spirits (Mark 6:7); Jesus sends the 70 by twos into every city and place where Jesus would come (Luke 10:1) and Jesus walks with two on the Emmaus Road (Luke 24:13). In these references, as well as in the current text, Jesus alludes to camaraderie.

2 Saying unto them, Go into the village over against you, and straightway ye shall find an ass tied, and a colt with her: loose them, and bring them unto me. 3 And if any man say ought unto you, ye shall say, The Lord hath need of them; and straightway he will send them.

The village "over against" refers to a place on the opposite side of a valley from you. Since Jesus and the disciples are on the Mount of Olives, the city of Jerusalem and its suburbs are all "over against" them. They are told they will find these animals "straightway," just as soon as they reach the city.

If the two disciples are questioned about fulfilling His command, Jesus instructs the disciples to use words of urgency. Jesus takes no chances of offending the owner of the animals as He prepares for His triumphal entry into Jerusalem. Jesus is confident the owner will respond positively to His need.

The disciples are instructed to say, "The Lord has need of them." How much do we, as believers, trust God to supply our every need? Hopefully, we can answer confidently by quoting Philippians 4:19, "But my God shall supply all your need according to his riches in glory by Christ Jesus."

The grammar of Matthew's Gospel is not clear whether Jesus is assuring the disciples that "straightway" the owner of the animals will send them with the disciples, or if "straightway" Jesus will send the animals back to their owner. The Greek word *eutheos* (ew-**THEH**-oce) means at once. If it is the quick action of the owner, culturally speaking, in the words of Dr. Jeremiah A. Wright Jr., Jesus expects the owner to send the animals "rat now." If it is that the owner will get the animals back right away, it is another example of how God takes care of future consideration even before we can worry about it.

4 All this was done, that it might be fulfilled which was spoken by the prophet, saying, 5 Tell ye the daughter of Sion, Behold, thy King cometh unto thee, meek, and sitting upon an ass, and a colt the foal of an ass.

This is a frequent refrain throughout Matthew's Gospel. More than any other Gospel writer, Matthew is concerned with explaining how Jesus fulfilled all the messianic prophecies the Jews were expecting. Because of this, many scholars assume Matthew expects that his primary audience will be Jewish.

Behold (Gk. *idou*, ee-**DOO**) is a kind of interjection in Greek and draws attention to the subject "King" and the beginning of the long awaited day of liberation for God's people. The context of this prophecy originally spoken by Zechariah is that God is coming into Jerusalem to proclaim peace over the Israelites' perpetual enemies of the Philistines and Phoenicians (Zechariah 9:9). He further promises battle and victory against the Greeks. God as the returning King promises to break the bow and remove the chariot, because His people will need them no more. Prisoners will be freed from their dark dungeons. God's dominion will stretch from the Mediterranean to the Euphrates and down to the Red Sea, and to the ends of the world.

Though the King is arriving, He comes meekly. Historically, a king arrives with a legion of bodyguards, officers, property, housing, pomp, and circumstance. Instead of arriving on a beast of burden, kings approach their subjects in chariots carried by the palace entourage. Jesus, however, comes without a horde of attendants surrounding Him; He comes meekly and sitting on an ass, and a colt the foal of an ass, or beast of burden.

Matthew mentions both a donkey and her colt, even though the other Gospel writers only mention the donkey. Other Gospel writers simply record this particular happening. Matthew offers no explanation of why Jesus needed both animals, or of how He used both. Perhaps He only rode the donkey and the colt simply followed behind its mother. Perhaps He rode one for a section of the road, then switched to the other. Matthew mentions this detail likely to make sure his audience fully appreciates the fulfillment of Zechariah. The exact use of the colt, then, is not important. What is important is that Jesus is the fulfillment of prophecy.

6 And the disciples went, and did as Jesus commanded them, 7 And brought the ass, and the colt, and put on them their clothes, and they set him thereon.

It is not specified which two disciples went for the animals. Whoever the two disciples were, they acted to do as the Lord commanded. Obedience is an important characteristic in the life of God's children. Hopefully, God can count

on us to follow His instructions just as directly as these disciples did, even when we don't understand why such a task is needed.

Matthew describes the coming of the Christ in all meekness and mercy to effect salvation, not in His might and majesty. It was the opposite of envy, enterprise, and arrogance; Zion's King enters Jerusalem outwardly impoverished, representing the life of Zion's humble citizens. Indeed, Jesus' entrance into Jerusalem can be compared with His birth. His nursery was borrowed, humble, and meager. Likewise, His triumphant entrance was on a borrowed means of transportation, humble and meager.

Reading about the disciples putting their clothes on the animals is reminiscent of Jesus' earlier instruction to the disciples about sharing even the clothes off their backs (Matthew 5:40; Luke 6:29). There Jesus emphasized the importance of freely giving up your cloak should anyone sue you for your coat. Jesus downplays worrying about clothing, among other things (Matthew 6:28). Apparently the disciples have learned and accepted this lesson because they spread their clothes on the animals and set Jesus on it. The Greek word here (*himation*, hee-**MAH**-tee-on) refers to the words cloak, garment, clothes, raiment, robe, apparel, vesture, and coats interchangeably. Therefore, it is possible the disciples spread an array of clothing.

8 And a very great multitude spread their garments in the way; others cut down branches from the trees, and strawed them in the way.

This was the week of Passover. Jerusalem and surrounding regions were crowded with travelers from the diaspora. The law required this migration on a number of occasions. Again, note the connection with Christ's birth. Joseph and Mary were traveling to Bethlehem to register for the census. Bethlehem was so crowded that all of the lodging places were filled. "No room in the inn" was common during the festivals, also called feasts (particularly during the Feast of Passover, Pentecost, and the Day of Atonement).

During the Feast of Passover then, a "very great multitude" was available to spread their clothes and to cut down branches from the trees. The branches allowed a softer and gentler ride against the uneven, stony, dirt roadway for the King of the Jews. Mark does give us a hint to these leafy branches, which John specifically identifies as palm trees (John 12:13). The disciples and people of Jerusalem do not have an expensive red carpet to roll out for Jesus, but they provide the honor they can with their clothes and palms making a humble parade for a humble King.

9 And the multitudes that went before, and that followed, cried, saying, Hosanna to the son of David: Blessed is he that cometh in the name of the Lord; Hosanna in the highest.

For centuries, God's people awaited the fulfillment of the Old Testament promise of the perfect King who would reign over His people. He was coming to establish a kingdom with laws written on the heart, a kingdom of love, joy, and peace. Psalms 45 and 110 give the promise of a Messiah yet to come. Daniel verbalizes his vision of one who is given dominion, glory, and a kingdom in which all would serve (7:13–14). Matthew and Luke magnify the King in His earthly ministry. Remembering these prophecies, the crowd proclaims Jesus as King during His triumphal entry during the feast of Passover, later to be called Palm Sunday.

"Hosanna" is the greeting used by the gathered community of faith on the occasion of Jesus' triumphal entrance into Jerusalem. From Psalm 118:25–26, the Hebrew word for this greeting is most closely translated as the following prayer: "Save now," or "Save, we beseech Thee." It should be noted at this point that the annual festival, called Passover, commemorated the final plague on Egypt

when the firstborn of the Egyptians died, and the Israelites were spared because of the token of blood on the lintel and the two side posts at the door of the Israelites (Exodus 12:22). The thought of divine salvation is in the background of everyone's minds.

The crowd exclaims, "Hosanna to the Son of David" and "Hosanna in the highest." You cannot get any higher than highest. The highest is where God, angels, and the great cloud of witnesses dwell, and where heaven is. The phrase "Son of David," is presented several times throughout Scripture, referring to God's promise to David that there would always be a ruler in Israel of his bloodline. Because of the sin of David's biological children, God could not reward the Israelites with continued earthly reign from that line. What God provided instead was so much more: His own Son, also descended from the line of David through his adopted father, who would be King forever in heaven.

The word "Blessed" (Gk. *eulogeo*, ew-low-**GEH**-oh) means to speak well of. The Hebrew equivalent *barak* is used when the patriarchs were performing an act of adoration and a pronouncement of family prophecy and inheritance. Later in Matthew, Jesus blessed the gathered community with the Beatitudes during the Sermon on the Mount. In the context of the Beatitudes, *makarios* (maw-**KAW**-ree-oce) is the Greek word translated "blessed" and means fortunate and happy. The multitudes who witnessed Jesus' Triumphal Entry went before and behind Jesus speaking well of "he that cometh in the name of the Lord" (Matthew 21:9).

10 And when he was come into Jerusalem, all the city was moved, saying, Who is this?

Jesus' spiritual power stirs up the inhabitants of Jerusalem, and every fiber of their hearts is moved. The Greek here for "moved" (Gk. *seio*, **SAY**-oh) means to agitate or cause to tremble. Again we see parallels between Jesus' entrance into Jerusalem and His entrance into the world. Matthew's account of Jesus' birth also mentions the Magi's news that there was a new King of the Jews caused Herod to be "troubled, and all Jerusalem with him" (Matthew 2:3). In verse 10, the inquiring minds are among a group of trouble-making opponents with ill-intent toward Jesus. Some of them who are saying, "Hosanna" now would later say, "Crucify Him." Others would sing, "Pass me not, O gentle Savior."

11 And the multitude said, This is Jesus the prophet of Nazareth of Galilee.

Matthew presents Jerusalem in a very negative light. At the beginning of the Gospel, Jerusalem is where King Herod reigns and calls for Jesus and all the young boys of Bethlehem to be murdered. Later, Joseph moves his family from Bethlehem (near Jerusalem) to Nazareth because Herod's son Archelaus is king in Jerusalem (2:22). Early in Jesus' ministry, when Jerusalem politics land John the Baptist in jail, Jesus moves His ministry north to Galilee (4:12). Matthew does not record Jesus returning anywhere near Jerusalem until this point. This is perhaps why the people of Jerusalem do not know who Jesus is.

In answer to their question, Jesus' followers call Him a prophet. For the most part, the title "prophet" referred to an Old Testament character, and John the Baptist was a prophet quoting prophets and used prophetic words, "Prepare ye the way of the Lord." The New Testament is a book fulfilling the words spoken by prophets. Though Jesus is called Rabbi eight times throughout the Gospels, He is called prophet about a dozen times. Of course, Jesus also quoted Old Testament prophets. A prophet's role was to speak truth to power, and deliver God's word to the people. They might work miracles or warn of coming troubles. All of these Jesus does, so "prophet" is not an incorrect title for Him. It merely stops short of acknowledging His full title: Messiah.

Sources:
Martin, Ralph P. "Messiah." *Holman's Bible Dictionary for Windows.* Version 1.0. Parsons Technology, 1994.

Say It Correctly

Bethphage. BETH-fage.
Salome. SAH-low-may.
Ahijah. ah-HEE-juh.

Daily Bible Readings

MONDAY
Help Comes from the Lord
(Psalm 121)

TUESDAY
The First will be Last
(Matthew 20:1-16)

WEDNESDAY
The Greatest Must be a Servant
(Matthew 20:17-28)

THURSDAY
Faithful Commanded to
Appear before God
(Exodus 34:23-27)

FRIDAY
Jesus Weeps Over Jerusalem
(Luke 19:41-44)

SATURDAY
Trust in the Lord
(Psalm 125)

SUNDAY
Hosanna to the Song of David!
(Matthew 21:1-11)

Teaching Tips

April 17
Bible Study Guide 7

Words You Should Know

A. Sepulcher (Matthew 28:1) *mnema* (Gk.)—A memorial or tomb

B. Brethren (v. 10) *adelphos* (Gk.)—Male siblings, or close and dear associates

Teacher Preparation

Unifying Principle—The Eternal Hope. The world is full of sadness and despair. How can we find hope in the midst of our anguish? In Matthew, Jesus allays our fears and gives courage to face the future.

A. Read the Bible Background and Devotional Reading.

B. Pray for your students and lesson clarity.

C. Read the lesson Scripture in multiple translations.

O—Open the Lesson

A. Begin the class with prayer.

B. Search online for a survey used to measure stress (such as the Holmes-Rahe Stress Inventory). Make copies of the full survey or a shortened form of it. Point out the types of life changes on the inventory and their impact on a person's mental health. Lead into Bible study by noting that Jesus' disciples experienced a few significant factors on that list when Jesus was crucified.

C. Have the students read the Aim for Change and the In Focus story.

D. Ask students how events like those in the story weigh on their hearts and how they can view these events from a faith perspective.

P—Present the Scriptures

A. Read the Focal Verses and discuss the Background and The People, Places, and Times sections.

B. Have the class share what Scriptures stand out for them and why, with particular emphasis on today's themes.

E—Explore the Meaning

A. Use In Depth or More Light on the Text to facilitate a deeper discussion of the lesson text.

B. Pose the questions in Search the Scriptures and Discuss the Meaning.

C. Discuss the Liberating Lesson and Application for Activation sections.

N—Next Steps for Application

A. Summarize the value of a freedom not shared by those who fear death.

B. End class with a commitment to pray for courage to boldly proclaim Jesus' resurrection as the core tenet of their faith.

Worship Guide

For the Superintendent or Teacher
Theme: The Paschal Lamb Lives!
Song: "At the Lamb's High Feast We Sing"

---

(213) 338-8477
893 5948 4624 ## *7:30 pm THUR*

The Paschal Lamb Lives!

Bible Background • MATTHEW 27; 28:1-10
Printed Text • MATTHEW 28:1-10 | Devotional Reading • PSALM 136

an author

Aim for Change — SIS Hill

By the end of this lesson, we will UNDERSTAND Matthew's account of the Resurrection, EMBRACE the possibilities of liberation found in Jesus' resurrection, and LIVE courageously in the freedom that Jesus gives.

Sis Andrew

In Focus

Sheila tenderly held their son in her arms. His skin was so soft and warm. He smiled happily in his sleep. "How about Robert, Jr.?" she asked her husband softly through tears of joy. Robert gently hugged them both. They were speechless upon meeting the answer to their prayers for the blessing of a child.

The couple had been trying to have a baby since their Jamaican honeymoon 13 years ago. They were both young and healthy. But to their dismay, old-fashioned methods and modern medicine seemed to produce the same sad results, causing a deep-flowing discouragement in Sheila. Robert remained hopeful, though. He regularly requested prayer from their church's healing ministry. He knew God had a plan for their family, so in faith he remained patient.

Now, he couldn't believe how his sorrow had quickly turned to overwhelming, life-altering joy with God's promise finally fulfilled. "Actually, I was thinking Immanuel," he replied with a bright smile. He took his son and paced back and forth, retelling parts of the story—their story—to the sleeping baby.

Sometimes the sorrow of unanswered promises, unexpected circumstances, or death blinds us from seeing the future joy God is preparing for us through answered prayers and promises fulfilled. Which stories in your life that demonstrate God's glory have been too good to keep to yourself?

Keep in Mind

"Then said Jesus unto them, Be not afraid: go tell my brethren that they go into Galilee, and there shall they see me." (Matthew 28:10, KJV)

"Then Jesus said to them, 'Don't be afraid! Go tell my brothers to leave for Galilee, and they will see me there.'" (Matthew 28:10, NLT)

Focal Verses — *Liberation / Redemption*

Norma

KJV **Matthew 28:1** In the end of the sabbath, as it began to dawn toward the first day of the week, came Mary Magdalene and the other Mary to see the sepulchre.

2 And, behold, there was a great earthquake: for the angel of the Lord descended from heaven, and came and rolled back the stone from the door, and sat upon it.

3 His countenance was like lightning, and his raiment white as snow:

4 And for fear of him the keepers did shake, and became as dead men.

5 And the angel answered and said unto the women, Fear not ye: for I know that ye seek Jesus, which was crucified.

6 He is not here: for he is risen, as he said. Come, see the place where the Lord lay.

7 And go quickly, and tell his disciples that he is risen from the dead; and, behold, he goeth before you into Galilee; there shall ye see him: lo, I have told you.

8 And they departed quickly from the sepulchre with fear and great joy; and did run to bring his disciples word.

9 And as they went to tell his disciples, behold, Jesus met them, saying, All hail. And they came and held him by the feet, and worshipped him.

10 Then said Jesus unto them, Be not afraid: go tell my brethren that they go into Galilee, and there shall they see me.

NLT **Matthew 28:1** Early on Sunday morning, as the new day was dawning, Mary Magdalene and the other Mary went out to visit the tomb.

2 Suddenly there was a great earthquake! For an angel of the Lord came down from heaven, rolled aside the stone, and sat on it.

3 His face shone like lightning, and his clothing was as white as snow.

4 The guards shook with fear when they saw him, and they fell into a dead faint.

5 Then the angel spoke to the women. "Don't be afraid!" he said. "I know you are looking for Jesus, who was crucified. — *Andrea*

6 He isn't here! He is risen from the dead, just as he said would happen. Come, see where his body was lying. — *Felicia*

7 And now, go quickly and tell his disciples that he has risen from the dead, and he is going ahead of you to Galilee. You will see him there. Remember what I have told you."

8 The women ran quickly from the tomb. They were very frightened but also filled with great joy, and they rushed to give the disciples the angel's message.

9 And as they went, Jesus met them and greeted them. And they ran to him, grasped his feet, and worshiped him.

10 Then Jesus said to them, "Don't be afraid! Go tell my brothers to leave for Galilee, and they will see me there."

The People, Places, and Times

Women. Jesus paid attention to women, included them, and acknowledged their place in the Kingdom. At the risk of censure from a male-oriented society, Jesus talked to women, responded to their touch, healed them, received their emotional and financial support, and used them as main characters in His stories. Luke mentions a group of women who traveled with Jesus as He journeyed from town to town (Luke 8:1–3). Among them were Mary of Magdala, Joanna, and Susanna. These women provided financial support for Jesus and the 12 apostles. Women were the first at the tomb after the Resurrection. As such, they were the first to broadcast Jesus' victory over death (Luke

23:55–24:11). Matthew, Mark, Luke, and John all called attention to the loyal women who participated in Jesus' Galilean ministry and followed Him all the way to the Cross and the grave. The New Testament brings a distinct picture of women into focus. Jesus, and later Paul, elevated the social status of women since they are equally participants in the kingdom of God. They (as well as each man) are urged to use their responsibility, as well as their freedom, to find their place in the body of Christ. The spirit of freedom and love in Christ belongs to women as well as men.

What freedoms have historically been found for marginalized groups once they join the Church?

Background

SIS HILL

Women witnessed Jesus' crucifixion up close. Women, who had known His healing power, gathered at Jesus' feet in His finest and final hour. Motivated by gratitude, courage, and love, these women did not run away, hide, or deny Christ. In spite of His public humiliation and grotesque execution, these women wanted to be identified with the crucified Messiah. Although they could not trade places with Him or take Him down, these women were not watching out of helplessness or coincidence. They were witnesses to His crucifixion in preparation for their purpose of delivering the message of eternal faith that the Messiah had risen!

After Jesus died, His body was taken by the disciples and entombed. However, resonating among the religious leaders was Jesus' prophecy that He would be raised in three days. To ensure that the disciples did not come back to steal the body and then fabricate a story of resurrection, a large boulder was set before the tomb and soldiers were assigned to stand guard. They did not perceive, even then, His power.

At-A-Glance

1. Women at the Tomb
(Matthew 28:1–8)
2. Jesus Appears to the Women
(vv. 9–10)

In Depth

1. Women at the Tomb (Matthew 28:1–8)

As Mary Magdalene and the other Mary went to Jesus' tomb, the earth quaked, an angel opened the tomb, and the guards became like dead men. It stands to reason that because there are no specifics given on the Resurrection process, the most important point made is that the tomb was, and remains, empty. While the women were on their way to the tomb, laden with spices and hoping the guards would allow them to anoint Jesus' dead body in loving grief, an earthquake occurred. But the earthquake did not deter the women. The guards, on the other hand, upon seeing the angel, were so afraid they fainted into a deep sleep, an act that would become for them a convenient alibi and lie to explain the empty tomb. The women, instead of experiencing a teary-eyed, tragic scene at the sepulcher, were met by an angel.

The angel told the women that Jesus had been raised and instructed them to tell the disciples to meet Him in Galilee. Unlike the guards, the women's fear was not overwhelming or immobilizing, for they retained hope in the prophecies of a risen Messiah. They were frightened, but they were also filled with great joy. Their humanness made them afraid. Their hopefulness filled them with joy. Their fear was smothered by great joy as they listened to the angel, for their hope had been realized. The women were the first to know of the resurrected Messiah. Oh, what joy filled their souls! They were obedient and went to tell the disciples what they had seen (v. 8).

377

What hopes do the women have as they go to the tomb? How is that hope changed?

2. Jesus Appears to the Women (vv. 9–10)

Jesus first appeared to the women, not the 11 disciples. On their way to deliver the message, lest they be accused of relaying hearsay, the women were graced with the very presence of the Lord. As the women joyfully hurried to tell the disciples, Jesus met them and encouraged them to tell the disciples to go to Galilee where they would see Him. This was the Jesus they remembered, but He was now embodied in full divinity. They bowed to Jesus and grabbed His feet as a sign of ultimate reverence and submission.

Indeed, He was to be worshiped. He had fulfilled God's plan of salvation. Who could doubt that He was and is the Son of God? These women saw Him with their own eyes and believed. Even though the disciples had denied and deserted Him through His arrest and trial, Jesus forgave them. He sent the women to tell the brothers the Good News: Jesus was no longer dead (v. 10). Their relationship would now be even stronger than before. He would meet them in Galilee as He had previously told them (cf. Mark 14:28).

Sadly, the disciples were still afraid of the religious leaders and they were still hiding in Jerusalem (John 20:19). Therefore, Jesus met them first in Jerusalem (Luke 24:36), and later in Galilee (John 21).

How has fear stopped you from sharing the Gospel in the past? What can you do to overcome that fear?

Search the Scriptures

1. What four messages did the angel give the women (vv. 5–7)?

2. What emotions did the women express upon receiving the call to carry the Good News of the risen Lord (v. 8)?

Discuss the Meaning

1. What does Jesus' resurrection mean for believers everywhere? For sinners everywhere? For evil and death?

2. Why is it important for believers to share the Good News of Jesus' resurrection?

Liberating Lesson

When Jesus Christ rose from the dead, it was the most important, awesome, and unexpected event in history. It was so unexpected that the women who learned of it first, as well as the disciples, the guards who kept the tomb, and the religious leaders all reacted differently to the news. The Good News as we know it—Jesus Christ overcame sin, death, and the grave, and liberated us from the power and punishment for sin—was challenging news for those who held power.

As the Gospel was preached in the early church, people responded by accepting or rejecting it at the point of the Resurrection, because the wisdom of the world rejects it and tries to cover it up to maintain the status quo. As disciples of Jesus Christ who preach of a Savior who overcame death itself, we can expect opposition and denial from those who have something to lose by acknowledging the power of God over the principles and practices of the world. In what ways has your faith community faced opposition when trying to preach the truth of Jesus Christ's life in the face of a culture of death? How can we be bolder to share the Good News when people may question the power of God to challenge our expectations and transform our lives?

Application for Activation

Christ met unbelievers where they were. He realized what many Christians today still do not seem to understand. Cultivators have to get out in the field. According to one count, the Gospels record 132 contacts Jesus had with people. Six

Traded

were in the Temple, four in the synagogues, and 122 were out with people in the mainstream of life. When was the last time you told somebody about the crucified Christ and the risen Lord? Do you feel you lack opportunity? This week make a list of 10 people with whom you come into contact daily. Make it a point to ask them if they know Jesus, and share the tenets of salvation with them. As the women did, run and tell somebody that Jesus, the Christ, is risen!

Follow the Spirit

What God wants me to do:

_____

_____

_____

_____

Remember Your Thoughts

Special insights I have learned:

_____

_____

_____

_____

More Light on the Text

Matthew 28:1–10

1 In the end of the sabbath, as it began to dawn toward the first day of the week, came Mary Magdalene and the other Mary to see the sepulcher.

When the Sabbath was over, and it began to dawn on the first day of the week, Mary Magdalene and others went out to the grave. Counting days in the Jewish tradition challenges

the modern suggestion that Jesus was crucified on Thursday. It is worthwhile to recall that the Jewish day begins and ends at sundown rather than midnight. *6PM* He died and was buried before sunset on what we call Good Friday; that's day one. Saturday at sunset is the end of day two, and beginning of day three. Early on Sunday morning, day three, God raised Jesus from the dead.

Matthew highlights the roles of women in his Gospel. The first to carry the Word is Mary and the first to carry the Resurrection message are women. God chose a woman in the beginning of Matthew, and Christ sent women first, according to Matthew. Matthew records that Mary Magdalene and the other Mary had also been at the grave when Joseph of Arimathea wrapped the body and placed it inside (Matthew 27:61). It makes sense now that they are the same ones to return to the graveside, presumably to finish anointing the body as they were not able to do before the Sabbath.

2 And, behold, there was a great earthquake: for the angel of the Lord descended from heaven, and came and rolled back the stone from the door, and sat upon it.

The word "earthquake" in Greek is *seismos* (says-**MOCE**), which is where we get our English word "seismic." Earthquakes occur several places in the Bible, including at the cross when Jesus committed Himself into God's hands (Matthew 27:51), and on Mount Sinai when God gave Moses the Ten Commandments (Exodus 19:18). Notice the association of these two earthquakes with liberation. The Hebrews had been delivered from Pharaoh and Jesus had been delivered from death. It was certainly this phenomenal occurrence that brought the centurion to proclaim, "Truly this was the Son of God" (from Matthew 27:54). To their astonishment, the women found that a great earthquake had occurred that Sunday morning. At various places in our lives, God shakes our consciences to awareness and our sinful selves to repentance. The Resurrection should renew, revive, and refresh our hope in Jesus Christ.

The angel of the Lord then appears and rolls away the boulder so that the women can see that Jesus has risen. Jesus had already risen and with His Resurrection power and new heavenly body, He had no need of opening the door to His grave to come out. It was only necessary to open the grave to show His disciples He had already gone.

3 His countenance was like lightning, and his raiment white as snow:

The angel's appearance was as dazzling as lightning, and his clothes were snowy white. In some churches' baptismal candidates worship in white to symbolize purity. It is fitting for the angel of the Lord to wear a bright, white robe, symbolizing the fact that Jesus has come through a great tribulation and now advises His people to be of good cheer. Not only because He has overcome the world, but also because our resurrected bodies will also bear the garment of light (Revelation 7:9–15). The description of the angel of the Lord echoes aspects of Daniel's description of a heavenly messenger seen in one of his visions (Daniel 10:5–6).

4 And for fear of him the keepers did shake, and became as dead men.

The phrase "did shake" (Gk. *eseisthesan*, eh-**SAYS**-thay-sahn) denotes how the keepers of the tomb were shaking just as the earth had shaken. They were struck with terror and fell down as though dead. Of all the Gospel writers, only Matthew includes this detail. The appearance of the angel so terrified the guards posted at the tomb that they were rendered unconscious. The women were also in fear (vv. 5, 8; cf. Daniel 10:7–9; Revelation 1:17). According to the Gospel of Mark, the women were speechless (Mark 16:5). One can understand the women's fear in the light of the circumstances that surrounded the death of their Master.

5 And the angel answered and said unto the women, Fear not ye: for I know that ye seek Jesus, which was crucified.

The angel spoke to the women saying in his own way, "Don't be afraid. I know that you are looking for Jesus, the one who was killed on the Cross. There is reason, not for fear, but for joy, because Jesus who was crucified is risen from the dead." These women had no reason to be frightened. They were beloved by the Lord. The angel spoke to the women only. The reaction of the believing women is set in sharp contrast with the reaction of the pagan soldiers.

The angel reassured them that there was no need to be afraid. They came to anoint Jesus' body with oil and spices, but cannot since He is gone. In the book of Mark, they raised the question, "Who will roll the stone away?" In Luke, they found the stone rolled away and went in, but did not find Jesus. In John, Mary Magdalene sees the stone rolled away and runs to tell Peter that "they" have taken Jesus' body away. It is this panic that the angel addresses. Jesus is not stolen, lost, or taken away to some unknown place. He is risen!

Many times in Scripture, God as the Father or the Son tells His followers not to be afraid. When we serve an almighty and compassionate God who conquered even death itself, we have no reason to fear anything that this world can throw at us. Everything we suffer can only serve to point us more directly toward God. So often God's followers fear, and so often God calms the fears with simple words: Fear not.

6 He is not here: for he is risen, as he said. Come, see the place where the Lord lay.

In both Matthew and Mark, the angel invites the women to enter the tomb and examine the place where Jesus was laid to rest. In John, the women are asked, "Why do you seek the living among the dead?" The angel graciously extends an invitation to these women to believe God's Word. Jesus was raised to life from the dead just as He said He would be.

Understandably, the women had been through a lot and had cause to be concerned about the body of Jesus. They had witnessed the government's abusive treatment of Jesus and watched in horror as He was beaten, tortured, and forced to carry the old rugged cross. They were at Golgotha and heard the cruel accusations hurled at Jesus.

The angel is assuring these women that it was God—not the government, the culture, or the opinions of man—who had the last word and that "He is risen." The words of the angel echo throughout the Scriptures (see Matthew 28:10; Luke 2:10). They are meant to cheer the hearts of Christians in every age in the expectation of the Resurrection. They remind us that Christians have no cause for alarm, whatever may happen in the world. God does not want His servants to dwell in fear.

7 And go quickly, and tell his disciples that he is risen from the dead; and, behold, he goeth before you into Galilee; there shall ye see him: lo, I have told you.

The Greek word *tachu* (ta-**KHOO**), which means "quickly," is used here in conjunction with a past participle that means "having gone" to come together to mean "when you have gone quickly." The women were to run to tell the disciples of Jesus' resurrection. The command is not to go, but to tell. The angel already assumes they will be on their way.

There is no time for delay, apathy, or doubt. Jesus is not only risen, but also en route to the place where He devoted most of His earthly ministry, Galilee. It is also a major center of Judaism during the life of Jesus. There the women, the disciples, and others will see the man from Galilee, their friend and resurrected Lord.

8 And they departed quickly from the sepulchre with fear and great joy; and did run to bring his disciples word.

Obeying the angel's message, the women did in fact leave "quickly" and "did run" to tell the Good News, doing so with both fear and joy. The "fear" Matthew refers to here is from the Greek word *phobos* (**FOE**-boce), which includes respectful, reverence, and a sense of awe in its definition. Since it is used in tandem with Matthew's reference to "great joy," it can be concluded this fear is not the same as being afraid. The fear of the women did not disappear completely, but it was overpowered with a "great joy" because of the reality of the Resurrection. Matthew rarely speaks of "joy" in his Gospel, but the one other place he mentions "great joy" is surrounding Jesus' birth (Matthew 2:10; cf. Luke 2:10). Now again, those seeking Jesus in an unexpected place are filled with "great joy."

Mark's account specifically directs the women to "go tell His disciples and Peter." Luke reads more casually, "And returning from the tomb they told all this to the eleven and to all the rest." There is not the same intensity in Luke as there is in Matthew's and Mark's narrations. John highlights the importance of the Gospel writer's message to Christ's disciples and Peter.

You may remember that John, identified as the disciple whom Jesus loved, outran the others to the tomb upon hearing Mary Magdalene say, "They have taken away the LORD out of the sepulchre, and we know not where they have laid him" (from John 20:2). Only John writes of the Jewish burial linen wrappings and their neatness, implying that Jesus experienced no particular anxiety or struggle in getting out of them. And such is the case with eternal things. They shall come to pass in God's time and in God's way. The message of the Resurrection is one of trusting in God. It also indicates His body had not been stolen.

9 And as they went to tell his disciples, behold, Jesus met them, saying, All hail. And they came and held him by the feet, and worshipped him.

As the women obeyed the angel's instructions, Jesus appears and greets them with the common greeting of the time. At this simple greeting, the women fall at His feet and worship. The person who meets the risen Lord lives in the joy of His presence. There is no indication the women ever doubted Him.

These who believed touched His feet. There are times when kneeling at the feet of Him, who was, is, and is to come, is the most appropriate posture to take. By this action they are showing their submission to Jesus, as practiced in their culture when a subject rendered obeisance to a sovereign prince. They prostrate themselves in adoration. This gesture is viewed as a sign of a living faith where the touch and the bended knee welcomes the Christ. It has been said the condition of the heart is more important than the position of the body while praying. Conversely, the position of the body often determines the condition of the heart. His presence will surely call forth some form of worship.

10 Then said Jesus unto them, Be not afraid: go tell my brethren that they go into Galilee, and there shall they see me.

Jesus calls the women to believe in the promise of God, share the Good News, rejoice at His appearing, and not be afraid of others' disbelief. The disciples labeled these women foolish (Luke 24:11) and refused to believe

them. They were preoccupied with the sad turn of events: Peter's denial, Judas's betrayal and suicide, Jesus' presumed abandonment and death. And yet, they have nothing to lose by going to the place where they first met the Lord.

Jesus uses the word "brethren" (Gk. *adelphos*, ah-dell-**FOS**) to refer to His disciples (John 20:17). Matthew records that Jesus had used the word "brethren" more generally and symbolically (Matthew 12:50; 25:40). Jesus also used the more familiar term "friend" before (John 15:15). If we think of their recent infidelity and cowardliness shown at the time of Jesus' suffering, to call the disciples brothers is surprising. By calling them "brethren," Jesus is not only showing them His love, He is also underlining their privileged position as co-heirs of His inheritance (Romans 8:17).

Most adults know what it is to mourn the death of a loved one. Fear of our own death can shape many of our actions. But believers can find courage to face the future. Christ has died, but He has risen in glory, and when we abide in Him, we share in that glory. Jesus' resurrection offers abundant liberation. While the world worries and sorrows, Christians enjoy the freedom of being unafraid of death, for we know that Jesus has overcome death itself. Death and sin have been conquered, so we are captive to them no more. Those who follow Jesus can rejoice in a fresh start and a new life in Christ. Believers will live courageously in the freedom the Resurrection gives.

Sources:
Henry, Matthew. *Matthew Henry's Commentary on the Whole Bible: New Modern Edition*. Vols. 1-6. Peabody, MA: Hendrickson Publishers, Inc., 2009.
Holman's Bible Dictionary for Windows, Version 1.0, Parsons Technology, 1994.
Strong, James. *The New Strong's Exhaustive Concordance of the Bible*. Nashville, TN: Thomas Nelson, 2003.
Thayer, Joseph Henry. *A Greek-English Lexicon of the New Testament*. New York: American Book Company, 1889.

Say It Correctly

Magdala. MAG-dah-lah.
Arimethea. AIR-ih-meh-THEE-ah.

Daily Bible Readings

MONDAY
John Proclaims the Lamb of God
(John 1:29–36)

TUESDAY
Jesus Prays in Gethsemane
(Matthew 26:36–46)

WEDNESDAY
Jesus Is Arrested
(Matthew 26:47–56)

THURSDAY
Jesus Is Crucified
(Matthew 27:35–43, 45–50)

FRIDAY
Why Have You Forsaken Me?
(Psalm 22:1–9, 14–19)

SATURDAY
God Is My Strength and Might
(Psalm 118:14–17, 19–29)

SUNDAY
Jesus Is Risen!
(Matthew 28:1-10)

Notes

_____

_____

_____

_____

Teaching Tips

April 24
Bible Study Guide 8

Words You Should Know

A. Continue (John 8:31) *meno* (Gk.)—To abide or remain

B. Indeed (v. 32) *alethos* (Gk.)—Truly, in truth

Teacher Preparation

Unifying Principle—Experiencing Liberation. Many people are bound by bad habits and vices. How can one experience deliverance? Jesus is the truth that sets us free and enables us to be His disciples.

A. Read the Bible Background and Devotional Reading.

B. Pray for your students and lesson clarity.

C. Read the lesson Scripture in multiple translations.

O—Open the Lesson

A. Begin the class with prayer.

B. Work together as a class to create a word cloud of synonyms of the word "free."

C. Have the students read the Aim for Change and the In Focus story.

D. Ask students how events like those in the story weigh on their hearts and how they can view these events from a faith perspective.

P—Present the Scriptures

A. Read the Focal Verses and discuss the Background and The People, Places, and Times sections.

B. Have the class share what Scriptures stand out for them and why, with particular emphasis on today's themes.

E—Explore the Meaning

A. Use In Depth or More Light on the Text to facilitate a deeper discussion of the lesson text.

B. Pose the questions in Search the Scriptures and Discuss the Meaning.

C. Discuss the Liberating Lesson and Application for Activation sections.

N—Next Steps for Application

A. Summarize the value of seeking truth, even when it hurts.

B. End class with a commitment to pray for freedom, both for ourselves and others.

Worship Guide

For the Superintendent or Teacher
Theme: Freedom in Christ Jesus
Song: "For Freedom Christ
Has Set Us Free"

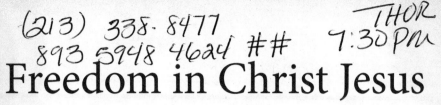

(handwritten) (213) 338·8477
893 5948 4624 ## 7:30 PM THOR

Freedom in Christ Jesus

Bible Background • JOHN 8:31-38
Printed Text • JOHN 8:31-38 | Devotional Reading • 1 JOHN 1:1-4

—— Aim for Change ——

By the end of this lesson, we will CONSIDER the double meaning of slavery and freedom in Jesus' conversation with believing Jews, PONDER the many ways people are enslaved in current society, and LIVE in the freedom that Jesus gives to those who follow Him.

—— In Focus ——

Earl had heard many stories about his absentee father Carl over the years. As a boy, Earl had resented his father for leaving him without even saying good-bye. Earl's mother had long since remarried but still had nothing but negative things to say about her former husband.

Many people had told Earl things about his father, some were good things but some were not. Mainly what he heard was a lot of conflicting stories about his dad. Old Ms Morgan spoke about how Carl would do odd jobs for her around the house, rake her leaves and such. Earl's Aunt Ruby, however, only ever talked about how Carl would loaf around the house, not lifting a finger to help Earl's mother with their new baby. Earl just wanted to know the truth!

He often felt like a big piece of his life was missing because he didn't know the truth about his father. Now a father himself, Earl thought perhaps he could even understand his father's struggles and problems if given the chance.

Without telling anyone, Earl hired a detective agency to investigate whether his father was still alive. A few weeks later, the agency reported back to Earl that his father was alive and well, living only about 2 hours' drive away.

"That's it!" Earl said, "I'm just going to see him and ask him why he left us." Earl sighed and thought, *Now I will find out the truth!*

How often do you go out of your way to seek the truth?

—— Keep in Mind ——

"If the Son therefore shall make you free, ye shall be free indeed." (John 8:36, KJV)

"So if the Son sets you free, you are truly free." (John 8:36, NLT)

Focal Verses

KJV **John 8:31** Then said Jesus to those Jews which believed on him, If ye continue in my word, then are ye my disciples indeed;

32 And ye shall know the truth, and the truth shall make you free.

33 They answered him, We be Abraham's seed, and were never in bondage to any man: how sayest thou, Ye shall be made free?

34 Jesus answered them, Verily, verily, I say unto you, Whosoever committeth sin is the servant of sin.

35 And the servant abideth not in the house for ever: but the Son abideth ever.

36 If the Son therefore shall make you free, ye shall be free indeed.

37 I know that ye are Abraham's seed; but ye seek to kill me, because my word hath no place in you.

38 I speak that which I have seen with my Father: and ye do that which ye have seen with your father.

NLT **John 8:31** Jesus said to the people who believed in him, "You are truly my disciples if you remain faithful to my teachings.

32 And you will know the truth, and the truth will set you free."

33 "But we are descendants of Abraham," they said. "We have never been slaves to anyone. What do you mean, 'You will be set free'?"

34 Jesus replied, "I tell you the truth, everyone who sins is a slave of sin.

35 A slave is not a permanent member of the family, but a son is part of the family forever.

36 So if the Son sets you free, you are truly free.

37 Yes, I realize that you are descendants of Abraham. And yet some of you are trying to kill me because there's no room in your hearts for my message.

38 I am telling you what I saw when I was with my Father. But you are following the advice of your father."

The People, Places, and Times

The Feast of Tabernacles. The dialogue in John 7 and 8 (excluding 7:53–8:11) occurs in the Jerusalem Temple during the Feast of Tabernacles (7:2, 37; 8:12). Often referred to simply as "the feast," the Feast of Tabernacles was a seven-day observance that included celebrating the Lord's protection and providence (Leviticus 23:41; Deuteronomy 16:14). This festival was celebrated at the time of the barley harvest. Many fruits are also ripening when this autumnal memorial occurs, and feasting is a major part of how it is observed. The booths, or "tabernacles," the feast is named for refer to the tents the Jews construct to live in for the weeklong festival. These tents remind them of their time wandering in the wilderness before coming to the Promised Land. Both the tents and the harvest fruits remind God's people of how He provided for them in the past and continues to provide for them now.

Background

The tone of the discussion in John 7-8 is somewhat argumentative. Jesus preaches in the Temple area, telling His listeners many abstract theological concepts about Himself and His relation to the Father. The crowd always questions Him, answering Him with confusion or with contradiction. John makes a point of gathering these theological discussions, as Christ explains many concepts to His followers: the glory of God, following Sabbath laws, knowledge of God, the living water of the Spirit,

His coming death, true light for the world, standards for judgment, and truth.

In the Bible, the essence of truth is not adherence to an external set of rules, laws, and regulations. Truth is more than accuracy. Central to the biblical concept of truth is faithfulness or reliability. God is the standard for truth. God's truth is that by which all other truth is measured. God's truth can be measured according to His unbroken promises and covenants and His unfaltering love for His people. God's truth is not just reflected in His commandments. God's truth is to be reflected in the way we as human beings live our lives.

At-A-Glance

1. Set Free (John 8:31–32)
2. Truly Free (vv. 33–36)
3. Free to Follow (vv. 37–38)

In Depth

1. Set Free (John 8:31–32)

Those who believe in Christ, who have faith in Him, follow a certain condition. Believers would "indeed be" His disciples only if they "continue in [His] word." Jesus obviously saw the possibility of disciples being only partially committed in their faith. He was clear that partial faith is insufficient. A disciple who is not totally committed cannot be relied upon to follow and obey His commands. Weak, uncommitted faith keeps us in bondage to sin.

Jesus offered His disciples absolute freedom from the bondage of sin. Those who "abideth" in the teachings of Jesus would know God's truth. In Christ Jesus lies the power to set people free.

His words, "the truth shall make you free" (v. 32), are not a reference to an academically learned truth. It is not education or knowledge that frees us from spiritual bondage. Rather, we are freed by our spirit awakening through the power of Christ.

What has the power of Jesus' truth freed you from?

2. Truly Free (vv. 33–36)

Even the Jews who believed in Him did not understand the kind of bondage Jesus was referring to. Any talk of bondage made them recall the experience of their enslaved ancestors. When Jesus spoke of them being in bondage, they hotly informed Him that, as descendants of Abraham, they had never been a slave to anyone. The only form of slavery they understood, however, was physical bondage. They were blind to the fact that sin kept them in spiritual bondage.

Many preachers have been heard to say from the pulpit, "Sin costs more than you want to pay and keeps you longer than you want to stay." The power in sin lies in its ability to deceive. A person trapped in the bondage of sin probably never envisioned that he or she could be so enslaved.

Apart from Christ, no man or woman can boast of being free. According to the Master, anyone who has committed sin is a slave to sin (v. 34). But the power that lies within Him sets us free. Jesus' mission was to give eternal truth to all people. If we love truth, we love Jesus, the Son of the living God. If we love the Son, we love His Father's truth. When we accept Him, truth finds a dwelling place in our hearts.

How does the permanence of Christ's freedom show itself in your life?

3. Free to Follow (vv. 37–38)

The freedom Christ offers releases us from sin's hold over our actions, but this does not mean we are completely free from all control. We are freed to serve God instead. When we are free from sin and hold God's message in our hearts, we are compelled to speak of it. If we are still slaves to sin, we are still compelled to speak. But then we speak from the poor understanding offered by the world and the Enemy.

Jesus already held God's truth in His heart. Because He knew the truth He was free, certainly free from sin but also free to speak boldly in the face of fierce and mounting opposition. Contemporary Christians should decide how they will follow in His steps.

Are we willing to speak His truth, even when it is opposed by others? Are we willing to embrace the freedom He has provided for us?

Search the Scriptures

1. Why did the Jews take offense to Jesus' assertion that they were in bondage (v. 33)?

2. Who is a servant of sin (v. 34)?

Discuss the Meaning

Explain how a person becomes enslaved by sin. Discuss the bondage of sin as it manifests itself in substance abuse, promiscuity and marital infidelity, dishonesty, hatred, racism, sexism, classism, and false piety. Why do people often remain in bondage when Christ has offered to set us free?

Spend some time talking about how often the sins that hold us in bondage seem so pleasurable and relatively harmless in the beginning. By the time we see the ugliness of our condition, we are already in bondage.

Liberating Lesson

Coming from a history of enslavement, both legal and socioeconomic freedom are especially important concepts to African Americans. Sadly, many of our people are still enslaved to a life of incarceration, addiction, violence, self-hatred, and poverty. Jesus said that those whom the Son sets free are truly free. In what ways can the freedom that comes through Christ manifest itself and break loose the chains that

hold so many African Americans in spiritual bondage? How might the church actually perpetuate that bondage by causing people to feel they cannot enter God's house because of their present circumstances? What are you and your church doing to help others know the truth so they might be set free?

Application for Activation

Examine your own life for ways in which you are still in bondage to sin. List at least one condition from which you wish to be set free. Pray sincerely for God to give you the desire to be led out of bondage from that issue. As you grapple with your own issues of bondage, you will be molded into a grateful, compassionate, and understanding witness for Christ.

Follow the Spirit

What God wants me to do:

_____

_____

_____

_____

_____

Remember Your Thoughts

Special insights I have learned:

_____

_____

_____

_____

_____

More Light on the Text

John 8:31–38

31 Then said Jesus to those Jews which believed on him, If ye continue in my word, then are ye my disciples indeed.

As Jesus teaches at the Temple during the Feast of Tabernacles, He tells many about His mission on earth. He assures them that everything He does and says is from the Father, and that when He dies, they will know for certain that He is the Messiah. Many come to believe Jesus because of this sermon (vv. 28–30).

He continued and addressed these words to those in Jerusalem who believed on Him. Sometimes among non-Jewish Christians there is a tendency to believe that all Jews were against Jesus and disagreed with Him. But it should be remembered that in every community there are disagreements, and sometimes these disagreements are nasty. Here in this passage we find clear evidence that many Jews believed in the message of Jesus. To believe (v. 31) means to have faith; by implication it means to entrust (especially one's spiritual well-being to Christ).

These believers needed to be encouraged by Jesus. So Jesus tells them to "continue" in His "word" (v. 31). In other words, it is the Word that leads to true discipleship. In the Samaritan woman episode, her testimony to her own social group led them to believe, and they decided to "remain beside" Him. The word to "continue" (Gk. *meno*, **MEH**-no) in Christ is the same as for "abiding" in Him. His disciples are to remain in Jesus' Word, to continue to live there. "Continuing" in Him strengthens the believers' faith. It deepens their commitment to Jesus as they learn to know Him better as "the Savior of the world" (4:39–42). Those who believed in Jesus would "remain" with Him, and their faith would deepen its roots so that those who were opposed to Jesus would not be able to move them. Jesus' disciples must always continue in His Word; determining to be His disciple is a lifetime commitment.

Jesus' audience has just decided to trust Jesus and now needs to know how to go about being His disciples. Jesus has also cautioned that not everyone who claimed to be His disciple would actually enter into His Kingdom, since they were not truly His disciples. Jesus tells them that remaining in Jesus and His Word is the best way to act as His disciples. Jesus later lays this out clearly for the Twelve at their final Passover meal together: "If you love me, you will obey my commands." You cannot truthfully claim to follow Jesus and then not actually follow His lead as revealed to us in His Word. To be a "disciple" (Gk. *mathetes*, mah-thay-**TAYS**) literally means to learn from someone, so we must pay attention to Jesus' words and actions and learn from them to be His disciples.

32 And ye shall know the truth, and the truth shall make you free.

Living in Jesus' Word would make them disciples "indeed" (Gk. *alethos*, ah-lay-**THOCE**), which is also translated "truly" or "in truth." Speaking of the truth, Jesus assures His new believers that they will know and be set free by the truth of His Word. The Word would lead them to the truth, and the truth would make them free. Setting the captive free was one of the key goals of God's Suffering Servant, which Jesus identified as Himself. Paul adopts this language of freedom in Christ versus slavery to sin in his letter to the Galatians. The young Galatian church must accept the doctrine that they are freed from slavery to sin, and freed from bondage to the Law, and are instead free to walk in the Spirit.

Truth and freedom are ideals that many seek, and which are only found in Christ. One great promise for Christians is to know the mind of Christ, and to know as we are known. Other religions might secret away their supposed religious insights, only revealing them at increasingly difficult stages of initiation. Christianity, however, freely provides truth for all who believe and seek it. From your first day as a Christian, you are privy to the full revelation of God in the person of Christ, as recorded in the Scriptures.

Today, many are held in bondage to the many lies Satan whispers into our hearts. Perhaps you hear the lie that you are not enough, or that you are unlovable. He spreads lies that we would be better on our own, apart from the faith community, and that we cannot survive without our vices that make us live in shame. He tries to convince you that some groups are inherently better than others, and that you must make sure no lesser person tries to horn in on your turf.

Jesus offers us the truth. Sometimes that truth is hard to hear and even harder to accept. Sometimes we will accept the truth, but then forget and live our lives in the habits we had developed before we knew better. No matter how far you had fallen into Satan's lies, if you have believed in Christ, you are delivered from that sinful lifestyle and have the power to live henceforth and forever more free.

33 They answered him, We be Abraham's seed, and were never in bondage to any man: how sayest thou, Ye shall be made free? 34 Jesus answered them, Verily, verily, I say unto you, Whosoever committeth sin is the servant of sin.

Showing immediately how hard the truth of our imprisonment is, Jesus' new followers deny being in bondage at all. The skeptics want to affirm their heritage and their privileged status as members of the Chosen People first. It is odd that they bristle so quickly at the implication of their servitude, and think that claiming Abraham as their father must mean they are free. Abraham's descendants were, after

all, slaves for generations in Egypt, a cultural heritage that is enshrined multiple times in their law. As Jews of Jesus' day, they were not likely to be classified by their Roman governors as "slaves" or even "freedmen." However, all Jews felt the limitations of Roman rule, as they were almost never considered full citizens and mistrusted Roman governance because of it.

Even though their objection is false, irrelevant, and made in fear, Jesus answers them honestly. He begins His statement with the affirmation "Verily, verily." This word means "truly." In John's Gospel, Jesus usually says it twice, doubly promising that His Words are Truth.

Jesus truly encourages them to give up their inherited pride. It is like the Samaritan woman (ch. 4) who was told that true worship took place in neither Samaria nor a Judean "holy mountain." No cultural inheritance saves from sin. It is the challenge that every believer must face. Loyalty to our fathers and to heritage of the dominant group does not count when it comes to salvation. Even if you grow up in the church and your father is the pastor, this does not mean that you are automatically saved. Jesus is not interested in a person's relationship to other people; He is interested in building a relationship with each individual. The actions of the ancestors do not determine, for good or ill, the fate of the descendants. Each is responsible for their own actions.

Jesus explains He is not speaking of slavery in terms of servitude to another person. He is speaking of slavery to sin, of which no human being can claim freedom (v. 34). It is sin that stirred their pride as to their heritage. They discriminate against the Samaritans, their Temple cult is corrupt, they oppress the poor because of greed based on their interpretation of the Torah, and finally they plot to kill Jesus. Jesus reminds His hearers that no one can escape from slavery to sin. We might think that by breaking God's law we are freeing ourselves from stodgy, old-fashioned rules designed to keep people from having fun. When we commit those sins, however, we realize that one sin will lead to another and that we will be forever indebted, unable to repay our debt to society. It is not freedom to step away from God's Law, but slavery. They might think that by following the Law they could earn their own freedom from sin, but this too reveals that they can never pay enough to buy their own freedom.

35 And the servant abideth not in the house for ever: but the Son abideth ever. 36 If the Son therefore shall make you free, ye shall be free indeed.

Jesus seems to mix His metaphor in this verse. He has already identified Himself as the Son (v. 28), but He has just identified His audience as slaves. But they are not the Son's slaves, for Jesus certainly is not the son of the sin that enslaves the Jews, but the Son of God. This is reading too much into the metaphor, though, and would be a bad-faith reading of the text. Jesus only means to label the Jews' position as servitude and His position as heir.

In verse 35 Jesus reminds them that a slave is a functional element of the household. They are bound to dismissal when their services are no longer needed. They are not a permanent part of the household, and therefore cannot make any lasting decisions for the house. On the other hand, the son is a blood member of the family. By virtue of being a full member of the household, he is bound to remain in the house forever. If one identifies with the Son, they have security and permanence. Identifying with the servant, however, means living in constant fear of being forced from the shelter of the house.

Reading the passage another way, Jesus is giving them hope amid His message of the bondage of sin. Even though Jesus' audience is enslaved to sin, slaves are not bound to their masters forever. They may be freed by the word of the son. In other words, the status of the Judeans as children of Abraham does not make them children of God so long as they are enslaved to sin. Freedom from sin can be attained only through Jesus. Members of Jesus' or God's household are only those who have decided to remain in Jesus' word. It is Jesus' word that sets people free.

Jesus' freedom is multi-faceted, depending on what freedom His believer needs. He is able to free from service to sin. He is able to free from service to the Law. He is even able to free from citizenship of an earthly kingdom and grant heavenly citizenship. This freedom is freedom "indeed," which translates a different word than it translated previously (v. 31). There the word *alethos* was related to the word for truth. Here the word (Gk. *ontos*, **ON**-toce) is based on the word "to be." Those whom the Son sets free are freed in their very beings. They are freed in the reality of all things that are.

37 I know that ye are Abraham's seed; but ye seek to kill me, because my word hath no place in you. 38 I speak that which I have seen with my Father: and ye do that which ye have seen with your father.

Jesus affirms that the Jews listening to Him are indeed flesh-and-blood descendants of Abraham. Sadly, though, they are not acting the way proper children of Abraham should act. Jesus will soon tell them they are actually children of the devil (v. 44). Jesus speaks axiomatically in verse 38, saying that child will imitate the actions of their fathers. Just as one can tell what kind of tree it is by its fruit, one can also examine fruit to tell what kind of tree it came from. Jesus imitates His Father by speaking everything He has shown Him and instructed Him to say. The Jews, in turn, are following their father (the Father of Lies) by seeking to kill Jesus. Even though earlier in this sermon, the Jews scoffed at the idea of Jesus dying (v. 22), by the end of this very discourse, they will pick up stones to throw at Jesus to kill Him (v. 59).

In his letter to the Ephesian church, Paul will pick up on this imagery and encourage the believers to "be imitators of God, as beloved children" (Ephesians 5:1). We see this still today as little toddlers will stand by their fathers while he is shaving in the bathroom and want to shave their own chins, or how teens will consider following in their mother's profession as they think about their future. When we are God's children, we must make room in our hearts for His words. We cannot crowd Him out with feel-good affirmations or with shameful lusts. We must clear such things away so that only God's truth remains.

Sources:

Butler, Trent. *Holman Bible Dictionary*. Nashville, TN: Broadman & Holman Publishers, 1991. 1374-1375.

Henry, Matthew. *Matthew Henry's Commentary on the Whole Bible: New Modern Edition*. Vols. 1-6. Peabody, MA: Hendrickson Publishers, Inc., 2009.

Strong, James. *The New Strong's Exhaustive Concordance of the Bible*. Nashville, TN: Thomas Nelson, 2003.

Thayer, Joseph Henry. *A Greek-English Lexicon of the New Testament*. New York: American Book Company, 1889.

Say It Correctly

Torah. TORE-ah.

Daily Bible Readings

MONDAY
Remember You Once Were Slaves
(Deuteronomy 15:12–15)

TUESDAY
Children of the Free Woman
(Galatians 4:21–31)

WEDNESDAY
Anointed to Proclaim Liberty
(Isaiah 61:1–3)

THURSDAY
The Light of the World
(John 8:12–20)

FRIDAY
Jesus Is from Above
(John 8:21–30)

SATURDAY
I Shall Walk at Liberty
(Psalm 119:41–56)

SUNDAY
Jesus Brings True Freedom
(John 8:31–38)

Notes

_____

_____

_____

_____

Teaching Tips

Words You Should Know

A. Resurrection (Romans 6:5) *anastasis* (Gk.)—Standing up again

B. Dominion (v. 14) *kurieuo* (Gk.)—To rule or lord over

Teacher Preparation

Unifying Principle—Freed from the Past. In life, we are constantly struggling to do what is morally right. How can we overcome temptations? Through Jesus' death and resurrection, we become dead to sin and instruments of righteousness.

A. Read the Bible Background and Devotional Reading.

B. Pray for your students and lesson clarity.

C. Read the lesson Scripture in multiple translations.

O—Open the Lesson

A. Begin the class with prayer.

B. Perform an Internet search for the phrase "declared dead by mistake." Tell some of the stories of people who were declared dead in the eyes of the law but were alive. What were some ramifications of this mistake?

C. Have the students read the Aim for Change and the In Focus story.

D. Ask students how events like those in the story weigh on their hearts and how they can view these events from a faith perspective.

P—Present the Scriptures

A. Read the Focal Verses and discuss the Background and The People, Places, and Times sections.

B. Have the class share what Scriptures stand out for them and why, with particular emphasis on today's themes.

E—Explore the Meaning

A. Use In Depth or More Light on the Text to facilitate a deeper discussion of the lesson text.

B. Pose the questions in Search the Scriptures and Discuss the Meaning.

C. Discuss the Liberating Lesson and Application for Activation sections.

N—Next Steps for Application

A. Summarize the value of distinguishing between liberty and license.

B. End class with a commitment to pray to live courageously as those who are not threatened by death.

Worship Guide

For the Superintendent or Teacher
Theme: Freedom from Sin
Song: "Jesus Lives"

(handwritten: (213) 338-8477)
(handwritten: 893 5948 4624 ##)
(handwritten: 7:30 pm THUR)

Freedom from Sin

Bible Background • ROMANS 6:1–14
Printed Text • ROMANS 6:1–14 | Devotional Reading • 1 PETER 4:7-11

(handwritten: Paul author) ___ **Aim for Change** ___ *(handwritten: Saul)*

(handwritten: Discover/ adventure)

By the end of this lesson, we will EXPLORE what it means to live by grace rather than living under the law, DISCERN how following Jesus can impact the way they handle these temptations and sins, and CHOOSE to live in the power of Jesus' life and resurrection.

(handwritten: pick out) ___ **In Focus** *(handwritten: detect recognize)*

Reverend Monica Jackson was recently ordained and senior pastor Rev. Clay Gosberry wasted no time putting her to work. One of the assignments she was given was Baptism Ministry Leader. She thought she would be excited to do it but on baptism day her mood was more reflective. There were 12 people who were going to be baptized including her cousin Raven whom she once ran the streets with.

As Rev. Jackson filled the pool with water, she thought about how God delivered her from recruiting young girls like Raven to be in her gang, to evangelizing on the street and winning souls for Christ. As Monica put on her robe she thought about the time, on a dare, she went into a church drunk and received life-changing prayer at the altar. Once the baptisms began, she and Minister Paul Diaz took Raven's hand as she stepped into the pool. As Raven shared her testimony, Rev. Jackson remembered how God gave her the courage to sever ties with the married man she thought she couldn't live without.

"Based upon your profession of faith in the Lord Jesus Christ, I now baptize you in the name of the Father, Son, and Holy Ghost," said Rev. Gosberry as Rev. Jackson and Minister Diaz baptized Raven and the other candidates.

Once all 12 candidates were baptized, Rev. Jackson asked Rev. Gosberry if she could lead the new believer's class. "I'd like to continue to remind myself and others that God has set us free and we never have to turn back," said Rev. Jackson.

What has God delivered you from? When you are tempted to turn back to your old ways, how do you fight against it?

Keep in Mind *(handwritten: New creature in christ)*

"For if we have been planted together in the likeness of his death, we shall be also in the likeness of his resurrection." (Romans 6:5, KJV)

"Since we have been united with him in his death, we will also be raised to life as he was."
(Romans 6:5, NLT)

Focal Verses

KJV **Romans 6:1** What shall we say then? Shall we continue in sin, that grace may abound?

2 God forbid. How shall we, that are dead to sin, live any longer therein?

3 Know ye not, that so many of us as were baptized into Jesus Christ were baptized into his death?

4 Therefore we are buried with him by baptism into death: that like as Christ was raised up from the dead by the glory of the Father, even so we also should walk in newness of life.

5 For if we have been planted together in the likeness of his death, we shall be also in the likeness of his resurrection:

6 Knowing this, that our old man is crucified with him, that the body of sin might be destroyed, that henceforth we should not serve sin.

7 For he that is dead is freed from sin.

8 Now if we be dead with Christ, we believe that we shall also live with him:

9 Knowing that Christ being raised from the dead dieth no more; death hath no more dominion over him.

10 For in that he died, he died unto sin once: but in that he liveth, he liveth unto God.

11 Likewise reckon ye also yourselves to be dead indeed unto sin, but alive unto God through Jesus Christ our Lord.

12 Let not sin therefore reign in your mortal body, that ye should obey it in the lusts thereof.

13 Neither yield ye your members as instruments of unrighteousness unto sin: but yield yourselves unto God, as those that are alive from the dead, and your members as instruments of righteousness unto God.

14 For sin shall not have dominion over you: for ye are not under the law, but under grace.

NLT **Romans 6:1** Well then, should we keep on sinning so that God can show us more and more of his wonderful grace?

2 Of course not! Since we have died to sin, how can we continue to live in it?

3 Or have you forgotten that when we were joined with Christ Jesus in baptism, we joined him in his death?

4 For we died and were buried with Christ by baptism. And just as Christ was raised from the dead by the glorious power of the Father, now we also may live new lives.

5 Since we have been united with him in his death, we will also be raised to life as he was.

6 We know that our old sinful selves were crucified with Christ so that sin might lose its power in our lives. We are no longer slaves to sin.

7 For when we died with Christ we were set free from the power of sin.

8 And since we died with Christ, we know we will also live with him.

9 We are sure of this because Christ was raised from the dead, and he will never die again. Death no longer has any power over him.

10 When he died, he died once to break the power of sin. But now that he lives, he lives for the glory of God.

11 So you also should consider yourselves to be dead to the power of sin and alive to God through Christ Jesus.

12 Do not let sin control the way you live; do not give in to sinful desires.

13 Do not let any part of your body become an instrument of evil to serve sin. Instead, give yourselves completely to God, for you were dead, but now you have new life. So use your whole body as an instrument to do what is right for the glory of God.

14 Sin is no longer your master, for you no longer live under the requirements of the law. Instead, you live under the freedom of God's grace.

The People, Places, and Times

Grace. The concept of grace is defined as God's undeserved love and favor toward sinful humankind. As Christians, grace is given to us through our faith and relationship with the Lord Jesus Christ. In the Bible, the essential meaning of grace refers to God's character to exercise goodwill toward His creation. This favorable disposition of God finds its supreme expression in Jesus Christ. This grace is rendered fully accessible to all humans with no other precondition than a desire to receive it (Titus 2:11–12). As a result, the human condition of separation from God becomes replaced with access to the otherwise unapproachable majesty of the Lord (Hebrews 4:16).

The Law. In the New Testament, this term referred to the Mosaic legislation. "The law and the prophets" refers to all the Scriptures of the Old Testament. The legal body of the Old Testament is not given in one book; moreover, the laws reflect the development from the desert context (Exodus) to the context of the Promised Land (Deuteronomy). The Old Testament's legal material is found throughout Exodus, Leviticus, Numbers, and Deuteronomy. The purpose of the law is to transform regenerated believers into maturity. Spiritual maturity is not a privilege that was reserved for believers after Christ. Old Testament saints also walked with God (Enoch, Genesis 5:22–24; Noah, 6:9; Abraham 17:1) and lived with integrity in the presence of God (Genesis 17:1; Deuteronomy 18:13; Proverbs 11:5).

Background

God's provided righteousness involves more than declaring believers righteous on the basis of faith. In Romans the first clue to this fact is in Romans 5:5, "God has poured out his love into our hearts by the Holy Spirit whom he has given us." The presence of the Holy Spirit within believers speaks of a new nature. This new nature is created by the sanctifying ministry of the Holy Spirit, which Paul discusses at length in Romans 6–8. Christians are sure of salvation, but they have to develop in moral stature. Grace does not mean a license to sin (6:1, 14) but moral power (v. 11). Moral obligation continues and should be gladly faced in the newness of life (v. 4) on which the Christian embarks.

At-A-Glance

1. Baptized with Christ (Romans 6:1–4)
2. Crucified with Christ (vv. 5–11)
3. New Life with Christ (vv. 12–14)

In Depth

1. Baptized with Christ (Romans 6:1–4)

Paul's questions command our attention. The teaching on God's justification of sinful people (Romans 3:21–5:21) and the declaration that the Law was made to make sin abound, so that grace could abound more (5:20) might lead some to believe what Paul expressed: shall we go on sinning so that grace may increase? Some may have reasoned that since grace increases all the more when sin abounds, then believers ought to sin more so they could experience more grace! The Apostle Paul penned this idea only to reject it fervently: by no means! In no way is the abundance of God's grace designed to encourage sin.

Paul explains why this thinking is erroneous. Believers died to sin. Being dead to sin means being "set free from sin" (vv. 18, 22). With that said, Paul asks, if believers have died to sin how can they live in sin anymore? All of us who were baptized into Christ Jesus were baptized into His death.

Christ's sacrificial death involved taking on all the world's sin in His body and killing them on the Cross. Christians' "burial" with Christ affirms we too have died to our former sinful ways of living. Our identification with Christ in His death means that just as Christ was raised from the dead to the glory of the Father, we too may live a new life. The resurrection of Jesus was not just resuscitation; it was a new form of life. In the same way the spiritual lives of believers in Jesus have a new, fresh quality. In the process of sanctification, the Holy Spirit works by separating the believer from the power of sin and restoring a new quality of life.

How does Paul say baptism is like a burial?

2. Crucified with Christ (vv. 5-11)

A believer's "old sinful self" or "old man" is the person they were spiritually before they trusted Christ. The "old man" was under the influence of sin: powerless, ungodly, and an enemy of God. The former self was then "crucified" with Christ so that the body of sin might be rendered powerless. The phrase "the body of sin" does not mean that a human body is sinful in itself. It means that one's physical body is controlled or ruled by sin. This was the condition of each believer before conversion. But now at salvation, the power of controlling sin is broken. Before salvation, a believer was enslaved to sin. Since we have "died" with Christ who has set us free, sin no longer has the legal right to force its mastery and control over us.

In resurrection Jesus Christ was victorious over death. Resurrection life is eternal in quality and everlasting in duration. What is true for Jesus Christ is true for us! We ought to count ourselves dead to sin and alive to God. Since we are dead to sin's power, we should recognize this fact and not continue to sin. Instead, let us acknowledge and rejoice in our new resurrected life in Christ! (Ephesians 2:5–6; Colossians 2:12–13).

In what ways is our freedom from sin a once-and-for-all gift, and in what ways is it a daily choice?

3. New Life with Christ (vv. 12-14)

In our new life, sin should not reign as it did before salvation. When sin reigns in a person's life, they obey its evil desires manifested through their words and actions. As Christians we should not be used as instruments of unrighteousness or wickedness. We ought to present our minds, hearts, and bodies over to God to be used as instruments of righteousness. In Christ we are new creations, alive in Him; so let us live for God! It is God's design that sin not be our master. It is by God's strategy that we no longer live under the law but under grace. If believers were still under the law, it would be impossible to keep sin from exercising mastery. But since believers are under grace, it is possible to live this new life victoriously by having faith in our Lord and Savior, Jesus Christ.

Search the Scriptures

1. What does the Scripture say about our old sinful self (Romans 6:6)?

2. When we died with Christ what were we set free from (v. 7)?

3. Since we no longer live under the law, what do we live under now (v. 14)?

Discuss the Meaning

When we are "dead" to our old self and no longer mastered by sin, how does this knowledge change our attitudes about daily living? How might it appear in our actions toward our family, work, and church? How does it motivate our choices in life?

Liberating Lesson

Evil is rampant in our society. We see evidence of its devastation on the evening news and in social media. Stories of violence, mayhem, abuse, and affliction can make us feel helpless. When we are a victim of one of these senseless acts, we might decide to retaliate and become instruments of unrighteousness.

Despite all the wickedness going on in the world, we are not without hope. We do not have to respond to life's tragedies out of sinful desires or become instruments of unrighteousness. We can live a life dead to sin by trusting and relying on God's grace manifested in our Lord Jesus Christ.

Application for Activation

When we think about our past, before conversion, we can honestly admit that some of the things we did were not motivated by godly intentions. We understand now that our God-given skills and talents should be used to glorify God. Are you a gifted storyteller? An excellent organizer, a painter, or an exceptional orator? Whatever skills you possess, ask the Lord where best to use them and volunteer your time! We are growing in grace and becoming more like the righteous instrument God created us to be!

Follow the Spirit

What God wants me to do:

_____

_____

_____

_____

Remember Your Thoughts

Special insights I have learned:

_____

_____

_____

_____

More Light on the Text
Romans 6:1–14

The apostle Paul begins the chapter with a series of questions to ascertain, in a sense, "how should we respond to the aforementioned dilemma?" (cf. Romans 5:18ff). He contends that the condemnation of Christ and His subsequent exaltation, should prompt men and women to part ways with sin so that the atonement is not cheapened. The result of Christ's sacrifice should lead us to lives of greater freedom. Christ's death, burial, and resurrection has created new lenses to view through. Within these verses, if studied carefully, one can witness the inferences to Adam and how Paul contrasts life in him with life in Christ.

1 What shall we say then? Shall we continue in sin, that grace may abound?

Paul begins by using a rhetorical question to anticipate an appropriate response from the audience. This is accomplished by use of the subjunctive (a mood of probability) to query, "Should we just keep on sinning?" Paul phrases the question in such a way as to expect a negative response. Sin particularly in an uninterrupted state represents an inappropriate response to Paul's argument. In the previous section he says "so one man's act of righteousness leads to acquittal and life for all men" (5:18), which means that sin's power to hold onto the believer has been broken. We should be ever mindful not to cheapen the grace of God by seeing the death of Jesus as a singular event without implications for here and now. His death resonates for all eternity for the believer and should compel us to respond as such.

2 God forbid. How shall we, that are dead to sin, live any longer therein?

The death of Christ appeases the judicial requirements of sin. His death paid a debt that we owed. As a means to argue his case, Paul engages in a hypothetical scenario. His logic suggests, "If we have received salvation without personal merit, why not go ahead and sin like there's no tomorrow?" What harm would come to us? In fact, would not grace increase in a moment like this? These rhetorical questions serve to make Paul's argument penetrate deeper. The answer comes to us in one of the strongest negations in the Greek language (*me genoito,* **MAY GEH**-noy-tow), "no way!" The Christian life provides freedom to the adherent such that craven impulses to appease the flesh should gradually diminish. Paul therefore asks, "How could Christians who are dead to sin keep on living in sin?" Though forgiven, the believer will constantly need to evaluate their behavior and impulses to ensure that they keep short accounts in the event that they do sin. We cannot return to life as usual after identifying with Christ, and Paul wants to make this clear.

3 Know ye not, that so many of us as were baptized into Jesus Christ were baptized into his death?

As the third interrogative in this section, Paul appeals to the early creedal understanding of baptism and its act as a type of initiation into the Christian community. Such an appeal interrogates the recipients' understanding of Jesus' sacrifice once again. Worded differently, Paul would be saying, "Don't you know what Jesus' death means for you?" The outcomes of Jesus' successful mission were the early sources for grassroots efforts in the early Christian community. Hence, solidarity within this community was evident by the strong bonds that were signaled in the act of baptism as the participant now identifies with this community of Christ followers. By posing this question, Paul furthermore appeals to the group association that was similarly communicated in his letter to Colosse, "you were buried with him in baptism, in which you were also raised with

him through faith in the working of God, who raised him from the dead" (Colossians 2:12). Consequently, we cannot return to any form of life as usual because we are dead and buried.

4 Therefore we are buried with him by baptism into death: that like as Christ was raised up from the dead by the glory of the Father, even so we also should walk in newness of life.

The results of Christ's atonement yield a corollary that early Christian teaching affirms. Christ's Cross work substituted His righteousness for our sinfulness, but it did more than that too. Those who are in Christ have been ushered from the "old humanity" into a new, richer, and more fulfilling "messianic humanity." The metaphor of baptism in these verses suggests that the dramatic outworking of Christ's three-day interment was not only symbolic, it was also inclusive of those who would believe on Him for all time. The outworking of our solidarity with Jesus amounts to a new way of living our lives that is as distinct from our old lives as Christ's resurrected body and life was different from His prior life.

5 For if we have been planted together in the likeness of his death, we shall be also in the likeness of his resurrection:

As the apostle Paul continues his argument through a series of conditional statements in this verse, he proposes a complete embrace of the implications of Christ's successful mission (cf. 2 Corinthians 5:17; Philippians 3:10). The "if… then" construction serves as a powerful literary device to illustrate the profundity of our union with Christ. This phrase "if we have been planted (Gk. *sumphutoi* , **SOOM**-foo-toy, literally united, born together with) together" suggests that there is symmetry between our existence and our new corporate identity in Christ. Such a partnership and gathering will be heightened as the subsequent clause suggests, "we shall be also in the *likeness* (Gk. *homoiomati,* hoe-moy-**OH**-mah-tee; figure, resemblance such as amounts almost to equality or identity) of his resurrection." Such a promise is contingent upon our appraisal of Christ's death in order that we might be animated by His resurrection (cf. 1 John 3:2–3). It is evident that through this discourse, Paul has sought to demonstrate a rhetorical symmetry between the acts of Christ and the inclusion of the audience as participants.

6 Knowing this, that our old man is crucified with him, that the body of sin might be destroyed, that henceforth we should not serve sin.

The knowledge that Paul appeals to in this verse at the time of writing was in its earliest stage of development. The meaning of the crucifixion was what occupied Paul's writings during the decades following the Christ event. However, even here, Paul elaborates upon the effect of Jesus' sacrifice so that the early church community could understand what an ideal response should resemble. Therefore, in providing a type of editorial summary of the verses above, Paul provides us with insight to one of his major contentions: the *old* versus the *new* man in Christ. Are believers still corporately tethered to Adam? Or have they been led out of the old humanity into a new mode of existence in Christ? Of course the latter is Paul's conclusion. In order for us to appreciate the new existence that Christ has called us to, we must see our old Adamic nature as dead, inoperative, and no longer "calling the shots" in our lives. Such a posture not only aids one's ability to comprehend their union with Christ, but also helps to live a life of freedom that is being offered here.

When the Scriptures are read in unison with each other, one can gather the broad themes and theological import that cause them to speak with one voice. In this verse, Paul captures the theological outworking of a right way to view the crucifixion. It should prompt us to leave the bondage of sin behind.

7 For he that is dead is freed from sin.

Paul signals that the slaves in bondage to sin have been emancipated! Death in this sense is tied to the aforementioned crucifixion of Christ and further defined as the meaning behind baptism. Therefore, the means of their manumission was not physical currency, but the blood of Jesus Christ. Hence, now that freedom is theirs, all Christ followers must learn to live according to this reality (cf. Acts 13:39; 1 Peter 4:1).

A radical shift like this must be placed into context. While it is appropriate to consider new life in Christ as an exodus from a life of sin and self-centeredness, it does not completely prevent the believer from engaging in sin from time to time. It simply means that sin no longer serves as their master. The term "freed" (Gk. *dikaioo,* dee-kie-**OH**-oh, to declare, pronounce, exhibit, evince, righteousness) underscores a judicial standing for the believer—one that renders a verdict of guiltlessness and provides proof that freedom represents a more robust idea than a simple "lack of confinement." It speaks to the pronouncement God makes over those whose lives are lived in Christ.

8 Now if we be dead with Christ, we believe that we shall also live with him:

Paul returns to his trusted literary device in this section by building off of another conditional clause. "If we be dead with Christ" functions as the protasis, (the clause expressing the condition in a conditional sentence) and is resolved by the apodosis "[then] we believe that we shall also live with him." Much can be said about the implications of this verse. First, this text assumes that the apostle Paul has clearly communicated the scope of the atonement here and in his other texts (cf. 1 Thessalonians 4:17; 2 Timothy 2:11) namely that the death of Christ provides entry into an eternal existence with Him. Second, Paul makes it unequivocally clear that belief (Gk. *pisteuo*, peese-**TEW**-oh) is absolutely necessary for entry into this life with Christ. Taken together, both aspects are at work in this verse creating another way of elaborating upon life in the Messiah.

9 Knowing that Christ being raised from the dead dieth no more; death hath no more dominion over him.

Verse 9 begins with a participle rather than its own subject and verb, anchoring this verse to the previous one. If we rightly evaluate our life as "dead with Christ," and the quality of our subsequent life that we can experience in Him, then we should also know that death itself has been rendered powerless by Christ and He cannot be subject to its influence any more. Jesus has overcome death by means of the Resurrection (1 Corinthians 15:54–55). This knowledge should compel the believer to enjoy a type of freedom that removes the fear of death.

10 For in that he died, he died unto sin once: but in that he liveth, he liveth unto God.

By dying, Jesus had a cleansing effect upon the world. He fought the dark world of the dead, and overcame it. This was a one-time event (1 Peter 3:18) with everyday implications. We know that His post-resurrection life continues in the church and the community of faith. The post-death life that Jesus now enjoys is uniquely equipped, physically and spiritually, to lead others to God. Believers benefit from the life that Christ lives unto God not only in an ultimate sense—bringing believers to heaven—but also in an immediate sense (cf.

Galatians 2:19) providing us with assurance and wisdom. Finally, in being united with Christ, His followers also have the means to throw off the old nature of sin and live into their new existence in Christ.

11 Likewise reckon ye also yourselves to be dead indeed unto sin, but alive unto God through Jesus Christ our Lord.

The term reckon (Gk. *logizomai*, low-**GEED**-zo-my) suggests the idea of appraisal. Appraise your life in light of your death to sin. To do so further embeds our ability to identify as Christ followers in the complete sense. Dying to sin means that it no longer maintains its grip upon the believer, enabling them to live their lives with a renewed sense of vigor. This is made possible by the animating power of God as alluded to in the second clause. We are to simultaneously see ourselves as unresponsive to sin while actively living to please God.

Another key aspect introduced in this verse is the idea of being "in Christ." To be in Christ is to be in union with Him. This important theme for Paul is at the heart of biblical soteriology (the doctrine of salvation). It is necessary to see both actions (dying to sin and living unto God) as part of the appraisal process for believers to live the normal Christian life.

12 Let not sin therefore reign in your mortal body, that ye should obey it in the lusts thereof.

The entreaty of this verse ("Let not sin reign") purports that sin is not just an individual issue, but a corporate one. The "your" and "ye" are plural in Greek. Paul appeals to the entire group to heed his advice about it. Not only must one keep short accounts with sin, we must do all that we can to eradicate it from our lives. To do so marks a radical departure from our old nature. If, as this discourse has suggested, the apostle Paul is advocating that we depart from life according to Adam and embrace a new manner of existence in Christ, then such a shift must be evident in our lives. Being in union with Christ is to adopt a new way of living. It is a life wherein our normal lusts are not entertained, acted upon, or obeyed. They are jettisoned with the aid of the Holy Spirit. This section has combined two beliefs together (don't let sin reign... don't obey its offspring lusts) to illustrate that the meaning of Christ's atonement immediately incites a new mode of existence.

13 Neither yield ye your members as instruments of unrighteousness unto sin: but yield yourselves unto God, as those that are alive from the dead, and your members as instruments of righteousness unto God.

In tandem with a refusal to give in to lust, Paul recommends that we keep the members of our bodies in check. Elsewhere (Colossians 3:5-7), Paul has suggested that body parts can be complicit in carrying out sinful acts and are in need of reigning in. This concept seems to allude to a type of fragmentation of the body, yet in the apostle's theological imagination he merely posits that enticement can affect us in various ways. It stands to reason that believers should be vigilant in yielding their lives to God not only at conversion but every subsequent day. Members of our body should not be enticed to do their own thing; they must function within the economy of the whole self. An active submission as an instrument of righteousness allows others to see Christ within. If believers willingly submit their bodies to the leading of God, they can rest assured that He has tailor-made purposes in mind for each of us.

14 For sin shall not have dominion over you: for ye are not under the law, but under grace.

The discourse concludes with an affirmation that sin and its effects are rendered void in the life of the believer. Within this brief section, the apostle Paul has argued that a transference of power has officially shifted. No longer are believers bound to obey sin and its cruel demands; instead, they have opted to be governed by grace and its effects. Christ has freed believers from bondage. We have new marching orders from a benevolent God.

Perhaps more than any other group, African Americans understand Paul's concept of manumission at work here. It resonates deeper within the audience. If you listen closely, the words to James Weldon Johnson's "Lift Every Voice and Sing" can be heard as the songwriter shares how God has walked side by side with the men and women of color in recent history. This song mimics the notes of freedom that Paul lays bare here. Freedom is always the outcome for believers in Christ and as such communicates just how far-reaching it can impact, touching both the community and the individual.

Sources:

Hoyt, Thomas L, Jr., "Romans," in *True To our Native Land*. Eds. Brian K. Blount, Cain Hope Felder, Clarice J. Martin, and Emerson B. Powery. Minneapolis, MN: Fortress Press, 2007. 249-275.

Latham, Robert. *Systematic Theology*. Wheaton, IL: Crossway, 2019.

Laymon, Charles M., *The Interpreter's One-Volume Commentary on the Bible*, Nashville, TN: Abingdon Press, 1971. 779-780.

Life Application Bible, New International Version: Grand Rapids, MI: Tyndale House Publishers, Inc., 1991. 2037-2038.

The New Interpreter's Bible, A Commentary in Twelve Volumes, Vol. X. Nashville, TN: Abingdon Press, 1995.536-542.

Tyndale Bible Dictionary. Wheaton, IL: Tyndale House Publishers Inc., 2001. 550-551, 804.

Walvoord, John F. and Roy B. Zuck. *The Bible Knowledge Commentary*. Colorado Springs, CO: Chariot Victor Publishing, 1983. 460-464.

Say It Correctly

Mosaic. moe-ZAY-ik.
Soteriology. sow-teir-ee-AW-low-gee.

Daily Bible Readings

MONDAY
Out of the Depths I Cry
(Psalm 130)

TUESDAY
Go and Sin No More
(John 7:52–8:11)

WEDNESDAY
God's Righteousness Disclosed in Christ
(Romans 3:19–31)

THURSDAY
The Justified Have Peace with God
(Romans 5:1–11)

FRIDAY
God's Free Gift Brings Justification
(Romans 5:12–21)

SATURDAY
Seek the Lord and Repent
(Isaiah 55:6–13)

SUNDAY
Baptized into Christ's Death
(Romans 6:1–14)

Notes

_____

_____

_____

_____

Teaching Tips

Words You Should Know

A. Suffering (Romans 8:18) *pathos* (Gk.)—To experience agony, intense pain, distress, or sorrow

B. Vanity (v. 20) *mutaiotes* (Gk.)—Depravity, changeability

Teacher Preparation

Unifying Principle—Hope for the Future. Living in the world we sometimes suffer because of evildoers. Where can one find inspiration and hope for the future? God promises to bring good out of our suffering and give us a blessed future.

A. Read the Bible Background and Devotional Reading.

B. Pray for your students and lesson clarity.

C. Read the lesson Scripture in multiple translations.

O—Open the Lesson

A. Begin the class with prayer.

B. Use a large strip of newsprint or shelf paper to create a timeline for the Christian life. The timeline should include foreknowledge, predestination, calling, justification, and glorification. Discuss the meaning and examples of each.

C. Have the students read the Aim for Change and the In Focus story.

D. Ask students how events like those in the story weigh on their hearts and how they can view these events from a faith perspective.

P—Present the Scriptures

A. Read the Focal Verses and discuss the Background and The People, Places, and Times sections.

B. Have the class share what Scriptures stand out for them and why, with particular emphasis on today's themes.

E—Explore the Meaning

A. Use In Depth or More Light on the Text to facilitate a deeper discussion of the lesson text.

B. Pose the questions in Search the Scriptures and Discuss the Meaning.

C. Discuss the Liberating Lesson and Application for Activation sections.

N—Next Steps for Application

A. Summarize the value of trusting God has a plan for your life.

B. End class with a commitment to pray for accepting the promise of the Holy Spirit to give strength, direction, and advocacy.

Worship Guide

For the Superintendent or Teacher
Theme: Freedom for the Future
Song: "And Can It Be"

Freedom for the Future

Bible Background • ROMANS 8:18-30
Printed Text • ROMANS 8:18-30 | Devotional Reading • 1 PETER 5:1-4

—————— Aim for Change ——————

By the end of this lesson, we will UNDERSTAND the role of the Holy Spirit in our relationships with God and Jesus; FEEL empowered by the Holy Spirit even in the midst of suffering, weakness, or loss of direction; and LIVE with hope as we seek God's purpose and calling.

————————— In Focus —————————

Thomas would always arrive 20 minutes late for work. His attitude was "I can always stay late and finish what I need to do." He would lie and tell his boss he had car trouble. The truth of the matter was Thomas had trouble getting out of bed in the morning. The thought of facing the multitude of tasks on his to do lists gave him real mental stress, so much so that he delayed going to bed and tossed and turned through the night, making his morning alarm even harder to obey. He was even considering talking to his doctor about the problem. In the meantime, he felt 20 minutes should not matter as long as he got his work done before he left the office.

One day in the cafeteria he overheard a coworker telling someone how his lateness hinders others in the office from meeting their deadlines because they are waiting on him to do his part. Thomas realized his actions had a negative impact on those who depended on him. His behavior had to change, but he didn't think he had the strength.

That night he forced himself into bed a full eight hours before his morning alarm. He didn't have an entire plan, didn't even know what the root of the problem was. He just knew he should pray about it. God would understand what he meant. God would grant him the miracle he needed.

God helps us in our struggles to do what is right and empowers us to overcome sin through our faith in Jesus Christ. How has the Spirit helped you to pray and helped in your struggles?

—————— Keep in Mind ——————

"For I reckon that the sufferings of this present time are not worthy to be compared with the glory which shall be revealed in us." (Romans 8:18, KJV)

"Yet what we suffer now is nothing compared to the glory he will reveal to us later."
(Romans 8:18, NLT)

Focal Verses

KJV **Romans 8:18** For I reckon that the sufferings of this present time are not worthy to be compared with the glory which shall be revealed in us.

19 For the earnest expectation of the creature waiteth for the manifestation of the sons of God.

20 For the creature was made subject to vanity, not willingly, but by reason of him who hath subjected the same in hope,

21 Because the creature itself also shall be delivered from the bondage of corruption into the glorious liberty of the children of God.

22 For we know that the whole creation groaneth and travaileth in pain together until now.

23 And not only they, but ourselves also, which have the firstfruits of the Spirit, even we ourselves groan within ourselves, waiting for the adoption, to wit, the redemption of our body.

24 For we are saved by hope: but hope that is seen is not hope: for what a man seeth, why doth he yet hope for?

25 But if we hope for that we see not, then do we with patience wait for it.

26 Likewise the Spirit also helpeth our infirmities: for we know not what we should pray for as we ought: but the Spirit itself maketh intercession for us with groanings which cannot be uttered.

27 And he that searcheth the hearts knoweth what is the mind of the Spirit, because he maketh intercession for the saints according to the will of God.

28 And we know that all things work together for good to them that love God, to them who are the called according to his purpose.

29 For whom he did foreknow, he also did predestinate to be conformed to the image of his Son, that he might be the firstborn among many brethren.

NLT **Romans 8:18** Yet what we suffer now is nothing compared to the glory he will reveal to us later.

19 For all creation is waiting eagerly for that future day when God will reveal who his children really are.

20 Against its will, all creation was subjected to God's curse. But with eager hope,

21 the creation looks forward to the day when it will join God's children in glorious freedom from death and decay.

22 For we know that all creation has been groaning as in the pains of childbirth right up to the present time.

23 And we believers also groan, even though we have the Holy Spirit within us as a foretaste of future glory, for we long for our bodies to be released from sin and suffering. We, too, wait with eager hope for the day when God will give us our full rights as his adopted children, including the new bodies he has promised us.

24 We were given this hope when we were saved. (If we already have something, we don't need to hope for it.

25 But if we look forward to something we don't yet have, we must wait patiently and confidently.)

26 And the Holy Spirit helps us in our weakness. For example, we don't know what God wants us to pray for. But the Holy Spirit prays for us with groanings that cannot be expressed in words.

27 And the Father who knows all hearts knows what the Spirit is saying, for the Spirit pleads for us believers in harmony with God's own will.

28 And we know that God causes everything to work together for the good of those who love God and are called according to his purpose for them.

29 For God knew his people in advance, and he chose them to become like his Son, so that

30 Moreover whom he did predestinate, them he also called: and whom he called, them he also justified: and whom he justified, them he also glorified.

his Son would be the firstborn among many brothers and sisters.

30 And having chosen them, he called them to come to him. And having called them, he gave them right standing with himself. And having given them right standing, he gave them his glory.

The People, Places, and Times

The Suffering of the Righteous. The Bible provides numerous examples of godly people who experienced a significant amount of suffering for various reasons—Joseph, David, Job, Jeremiah, and Paul, to name a few. Historically, many of African descent suffered for the sake of the Gospel.

The Bible gives various reasons believers suffer, including: (1) an ongoing consequence of the Fall. When sin entered the world, pain, sorrow, conflict, and eventual death invaded the lives of all human beings (see Genesis 3:16–19). In fact, the entire created universe groans under the effects of sin and yearns for the time of the new heaven and new earth when God will abolish the curse (see Romans 8:20–23; 2 Peter 3:10–13); (2) the same reason that unbelievers suffer—as a consequence for their own actions (see Galatians 6:7); (3) because we live in a sinful and corrupt world. All around us are the effects of sin, and we experience distress and anguish as we see the power that evil holds over so many people's lives (see Ezekiel 9:4; Acts 17:16); and (4) the devil has been given power to afflict us in a variety of ways (1 Peter 5:8–9). The story of Job is an example of this kind of suffering (see Job 1–2).

Background

In Romans 7, Paul writes about the grace of Christ. He shows us that without grace, a believer would live a defeated and miserable life, in bondage to their sinful nature. However, in Romans 8, Paul changes his focus and begins sharing about the supernatural life that has been made available to all believers in Jesus Christ.

Through our union with Christ by the indwelling presence of the Holy Spirit, believers are now able to live a life free from condemnation, and they no longer have to be enslaved by sin. The Spirit gives believers victory over sin and allows them to experience true fellowship with God. Paul lets us know that the only way we can be delivered from the power of sin is by receiving—and being controlled by—the Spirit. In other words, the Spirit, working in the life of a believer, will lead them to victory.

The apostle affirms there are two kinds of people: those who live according to the flesh, and those who live according to the Spirit. People who choose to live "after the flesh" take pleasure in the corrupt desires of sinful human nature, including fornication, adultery, strife, and uncleanness (see Galatians 5:19–21). Those who live by the Holy Spirit will submit to His leading and exhibit love, peace, goodness, and self-control (see Galatians 5:22–23).

Every true believer receives the indwelling presence of the Holy Spirit the moment they accept Jesus Christ. Thus, it is only through the Spirit that we are able to put to death the deeds of the body (Romans 8:13). The mark of a true believer is the ability to be led by the Spirit.

Paul also reminds us that living in the Spirit and being victorious are not always easy. We are to prepare ourselves through the Spirit to suffer even as Jesus suffered. We identify with Christ through our suffering with Him that we may be also glorified together.

If we have been glorified with Christ, why must the Christian still suffer?

In Depth

1. Freedom for Creature and Creation (Romans 8:18–25)

All the sufferings, injustices, hurt, pain, disappointment, rejection, financial woes, health problems, heartaches, and other trials that a believer may now experience will seem so insignificant when God's glory is revealed in us in the age to come. Believers have a future hope—the manifestation of God's glory will be fully revealed in us one day.

Ever since Adam and Eve chose to disobey God, creation has also been subjected to suffering, catastrophes, groanings, and travailings. Not only will faithful believers be glorified in the new age, but nature itself will be recreated. There will be a restoration of all things, including a new heaven and earth.

Believers desire full redemption, even though we possess the Spirit and experience God's blessings today. Believers groan for the full manifestation of God's glory to be revealed and for the honor and privileges of full adoption (see 2 Corinthians 5:4), which includes the redemption of our body (Romans 8:23). That resurrection body will be our heavenly house (see 2 Corinthians 5:2), not subject to the harshness of this present world. The Christian's faith in Jesus Christ, His Word, and the Spirit enables us to patiently wait for the fulfillment of God's manifested glory.

In what ways have you seen creation itself suffering from the effects of sin?

2. The Spirit's Freeing Intercession (vv. 26–27)

Paul says that the Spirit also helps our infirmities (v. 26)—our weakness in praying effectively. Paul affirms that God will not listen to prayers based on our selfish desires (v. 26). Often we pray based on the right now instead of basing our prayers on God's eternal purpose for our lives and our family and friends. Either we pray our own will or we pray amiss (James 4:3). As a result, many of our prayers go unanswered. The Holy Spirit helps us pray prayers that will glorify the Father.

Paul reminds us that God searches our hearts. He knows our motives, and the reason for our prayers. Thus, the Holy Spirit's ministry is to make intercession for the saints according to the will of God. The Holy Spirit working effectively in the life of a believer will line up the believer's will with the Lord's and will cause us to pray prayers that will glorify God. It is encouraging to know that we have two divine intercessors assisting us in our walk with the Lord: the Holy Spirit (vv. 26–27) and Jesus Christ (v. 34).

What does the Spirit do when our prayers do not align with God's will? Does the Spirit still intercess for us then?

3. Free to Hope (vv. 28–30)

Despite all the trials we will face in this life, with the help of the Spirit interceding for us, we can have the confident hope that it will all work together for good. Not that everything will be good for everyone. This promise is for "those who love God and are called" to His purpose. Those devoted to God, who are doing His work, will see that the overall arch of history is working toward the good will of the Lord.

Many theologians have long debated the tension between predestination and free will. When interacting with these verses, however, it is enough to know that the omniscient God has always known who would be His. He calls these people, provided Jesus for their justification, and provides the Spirit as the seal for a promised glorification.

How has God called you throughout your life?

Search the Scriptures

1. Why should the sufferings of this present age be considered insignificant (Romans 8:18)?

2. Why does the Spirit make intercession for the believer (vv. 26–27)?

3. What does the Christian ultimately hope for (vv. 23, 30)?

Discuss the Meaning

1. Is it necessary for a believer to suffer? Why or why not?

2. What is the Holy Spirit's main responsibility? Why do we need the Holy Spirit?

3. If the Spirit is our intercessor, does that mean we can live any way we want and just ask Him to go to God on our behalf? Why or why not?

Liberating Lesson

To tell new believers (and sinners) that they will never experience pain, sorrow, or sufferings once they have come to Christ contradicts biblical texts such as Philippians 2:26, 27; John 16:33; Romans 8:18. This unfounded teaching has caused many new converts to fall away from the church, or become hostile and indifferent to the Gospel. Similarly, some people believe and teach that suffering is a sign of God's disfavor because of sin. However, Scripture declares that people who desire to live godly

lives will suffer persecution (2 Timothy 3:12). When people choose godly lives, persecution and suffering are inevitable. A believer who refuses to compromise their faith to conform to the world will often be rejected, mistreated, and ridiculed. A lack of suffering could be a sign that the believer has not taken a stand for righteousness. How does this knowledge reflect on your life today?

Application for Activation

Create a song or poem to praise and thank God for the hope He gives in times of trouble. Review it daily this week and look for how you feel the Holy Spirit working in you. Maybe you can add another stanza to your piece based on the week's experiences with the Spirit.

Follow the Spirit

What God wants me to do:

_____

_____

_____

_____

_____

Remember Your Thoughts

Special insights I have learned:

_____

_____

_____

_____

_____

More Light on the Text
Romans 8:18–30

8:18 For I reckon that the sufferings of this present time are not worthy to be compared with the glory which shall be revealed in us.

Paul weighed suffering against the future revelation of glory and found suffering to be not worthy of comparison to the glory in store for the Christian. Suffering (Gk. *pathos*, **PAY**-thoce, agony, intense pain, distress, or sorrow) has been part and parcel of the human condition since the fall of humankind (see Genesis 3). Old Testament examples of suffering are present in many of the psalms (compare Psalms 22; 38; 64; 77; 79). Job uses suffering as a dominant theme as well. Paul's reference to suffering as being for "this present time" (Gk. *kairos*, **KIE**-roce, a short while or season) seems to indicate that suffering is limited in duration, while the future glory is timeless.

Suffering may refine and fashion lives (1 Peter 1:6-7; 5:10) or transform lives. Jesus learned obedience and was perfected through suffering (Hebrews 5:8–9) which also demonstrated God's power. Suffering helps us show more sympathy for others who suffer (2 Corinthians 1:3-6; 12:7). Believers increasingly identify with Christ as they suffer for Him (Philippians 3:10). The suffering makes us more like Christ.

Glory (Gk. *doxa*, **DOKE**-sah) refers to the beauty, power, and honor of God and symbolizes God's power and authority. The word "glory" may be used to denote three different aspects of God: morality, beauty, and divine perfection. These divine qualities are beyond what the human brain can understand (Psalm 113:4). God's glory is manifested in Christ (Luke 29–32) and the members of the Church with whom Christ's glory is shared (John 17:5–6). Through this sharing, Christians will be completely transformed in the last days, when the glory of God will be revealed to all of creation (Revelation 21:23). A third meaning of the glory of God is the praise and honor which the people of God give to Him (Psalm 115:1; Revelation 5:12–13).

When Paul compares these two, the goodness of the glory far exceeds the badness of the sufferings. There is really no contest between the two. The glory that God promises wins an overwhelming victory. On this side of eternity it might seem like the trials are terrible. From the viewpoint of eternity, however, those same trials are not even worth mentioning.

19 For the earnest expectation of the creature waiteth for the manifestation of the sons of God.

The word translated "creature" here and "creation" in verse 22 is the same (Gk. *ktisis*, kuh-**TEE**-seese). It can refer to a single created being (i.e., a creature) or to all of creation. Context here makes "creation" the preferred reading, referring to all of nature, but usually understood as excluding humankind because of our special place among God's creatures. Creation will be set free from its bondage to decay when the children of God enter their glory. Paul personifies creation, giving it human qualities (it waits with earnest anticipation). The phrase "earnest expectation" (Gk. *apokaradokia*, ah-po-kah-rah-doe-**KEE**-ah) refers to the manner in which creation waits for the glory to be revealed. Creation waits as we might say "with baited breath." The word "waiteth" (Gk. *apekdechomai*, op-eck-**DEH**-kho-my) means to expect fully, to look out, or wait for. "Manifestation" (Gk. *apokalupsis*, ah-poe-**KAH**-loop-seese) means disclosure, or revelation. Paul is likely intending a bit of alliteration here in the words *apokaradokia*, *apekdechomai*, and *apokalupsis*, as they all begin with the same prefix *ap(o)-* and then a *k* at the beginning of the root verb. This repetition of sounds emphasizes and helps the hearer remember the point.

The "sons" of God (Gk. *huios*, hoo-ee-**OCE**) means those having kinship to God. When used in the plural, as here, the word can be gender neutral, and is better translated "children." Paul puts forth our relationship to God through Christ as "heirs of God and joint heirs with Christ" (8:17). Paul posits that we are children of God if we are "led by the Spirit" (v. 14). This parent/child relationship goes both ways. While we have the responsibility to obey God's law, we also have the privileges of His heir. In fact, we have a "spirit of adoption" which is witnessed to by the Spirit (v. 5). As joint heirs with Christ, we suffer His trials, but also enjoy His glory.

20 For the creature was made subject to vanity, not willingly, but by reason of him who hath subjected the same in hope, 21 Because the creature itself also shall be delivered from the bondage of corruption into the glorious liberty of the children of God.

Paul here takes us back to the creation and fall. The implied idea here is that the world which God created waited for the manifestation of human beings for its fulfillment. Humanity is the crown of creation. However, when humanity fell, creation lost its glory. Just as it waited for the manifestation of God's son Adam, now through the death and resurrection of Jesus, it awaits the completion of the new creation when the redeemed are restored to their rightful place. But this expectation is not passive, it is a dynamic hope in divine desire for human restoration to God's primary intention.

Creation will be set free from its forced bondage to decay when the children of God enter their glory. Creation did not cause its own subjection, as humankind did, but rather was made subject to decay by God. The Greek phrase "in hope" is placed so that it is unclear who is hoping, whether God (KJV) or creation (NLT). Either God placed creation under the pain of corruption "in hope" that humanity

would soon repent and be glorified; or creation waits "in hope" to be delivered. Paul has already stated that creation is waiting with eagerness (v. 19), which leads many to translate the phrase differently from the KJV. Either way, all of creation is "subjected" (Gk. *hupotasso*, hoo-poe-**TAS**-so; put under obedience) to "vanity" and the "bondage" (Gk. *douleia*, doo-**LAY**-ah, slavery) of "corruption" (Gk. *phtora*, fuh-thor-**AH**). It hopes for deliverance from bondage to "glorious liberty." The KJV usage of "vanity" is not the same as today's meaning, which is limited to selfish self-centeredness, but refers to anything that, like physical beauty, is fleeting or flimsy. Creation suffers from transience, always on the brink of total chaos, always restlessly changing. It is also bound as a slave to "corruption," which refers to death and decay. Paul here implies that the perfect world God created in Eden was not made to be fleeting or to be forced to die and decay. It was made to last.

Vanity and corruption are described as a kind of bondage. This bondage is contrasted with God's liberty. To the Corinthian church, Paul writes of God's liberty from the veiled and misunderstood Law, freeing God's people to be transformed into ever increasingly glorious creatures of God's likeness (2 Corinthians 3:17-18). Liberty from the Law allows the Spirit to move us closer and closer to God. Here, Paul explains that not only will God's children enjoy this glorification, but all of creation itself too.

22 For we know that the whole creation groaneth and travaileth in pain together until now. 23 And not only they, but ourselves also, which have the firstfruits of the Spirit, even we ourselves groan within ourselves, waiting for the adoption, to wit, the redemption of our body.

Those who possess the Holy Spirit long for the redemption of their bodies. Paul is suggesting a relationship between creation and humankind, as they "groaneth and travaileth" and await the adoption and the redemption of their bodies. The phrase "travaileth in pain together" (Gk. *sunodino*, soon-oh-**DEE**-no) means to sympathize in expectation of relief from suffering. Paul's use of this birth metaphor suggests that the appearance of a new age, just as an actual birth, results in the appearance of a new person. Groanings do in fact accompany the process of birth, and it is also joined with the expectation of something new. Continuing the birth metaphor, Paul speaks of "adoption" (Gk. *huiothesia*, hoo-ee-oh-theh-**SEE**-ah), which literally means the process of becoming a son. When the process of producing a son is done naturally, it involves much pain, and so it is with our spiritual births. Roman adoption laws gave the adopted child all the rights of a natural-born child, rights that could never be revoked. Our adoption into God's family provides us with many benefits, but the one Paul highlights in this particular verse is "the redemption of our body." "Redemption" (Gk. *apolutrosis*, ah-poe-**LOO**-troh-seese) means ransom in full or salvation, as the body is redeemed and the glory is revealed (vv. 17, 23). No longer will we have to suffer the physical pains of a corporeal life. No longer will any created thing have to suffer to survive. All will be healed when full glorification comes.

24 For we are saved by hope: but hope that is seen is not hope: for what a man seeth, why doth he yet hope for? 25 But if we hope for that we see not, then do we with patience wait for it.

In verses 24 and 25, Paul lifts up hope as the means to salvation. By hope (Gk. *elpis*, ell-**PEESE**), we are saved. The invisibility of what is hoped for keeps us anticipating, waiting in earnest. If what was "hoped for" were visible, the need to either wait or develop patience would not exist (v. 25).

26 Likewise the Spirit also helpeth our infirmities: for we know not what we should pray for as we ought: but the Spirit itself maketh intercession for us with groanings which cannot be uttered. 27 And he that searcheth the hearts knoweth what is the mind of the Spirit, because he maketh intercession for the saints according to the will of God.

The Spirit searches the hearts of believers and intercedes for them when they cannot express their needs. Paul notes the relationship between humankind and the Spirit. In addition to witnessing our adoption and being joint heirs with us, the Spirit intercedes for us with groanings which cannot be uttered. The Spirit helps us when we are unable to express our desires in prayer. The Spirit uses "unutterable groanings" to interpret our wishes to God.

Additionally, the Spirit "maketh intercession" for the children of God "according to the will of God." When making intercession for us, the Spirit confers with God on our behalf or comes to our defense. The phrase "maketh intercession" (Gk. *huperentungchano*) means "to confer" with God. The Spirit intercedes "according to the will of God" (v. 27).

Paul also affirms that the Spirit of God is suffering within the believer as He awaits the manifestation of the final days of redemption (vv. 23–25). This groaning of the Holy Spirit occurs in the hearts of believers (v. 26).

One of Holy Spirit's ministries is to help believers in prayer. When we face trying circumstances, it is encouraging to know that the Holy Spirit can assist us when we pray. Many of the attacks we encounter are spiritual (Ephesians 6:12). The Spirit gives us the power and assistance we need in order to fight.

For example, when James and John's mother approached Jesus, her desire was for her sons to sit on the left and right hand of the Savior in the Kingdom (Matthew 20:20–23). Jesus knew that this mother had no idea what she was asking for and neither did James and John realize the implication of the request. Little did they realize that one of them would die an unnatural death (Acts 12:2), while the other one would suffer imprisonment (Revelation 1:9). Many believers do not realize the consequences or the price we may have to pay when we offer up selfish prayers. That's why we need the Holy Spirit's intercession for us (or through us) according to the will and eternal purpose of the Father.

28 And we know that all things work together for good to them that love God, to them who are the called according to his purpose.

As a Christian, we are promised a happy ending. Those who love God, whom He has called, who work toward His purpose, are promised to have "all things work together for good." What an amazing promise!

This promise does not mean, however, that everything in everyone's lives will be pleasant. We cannot look at individual events, but at "all things." We cannot expect instant results, but wait for them to "work together." We also might see disaster in the life of someone we love and want to assure them that it will all work out, but if they are not a God follower, then we cannot make that promise.

This promise also does not free us from responsibility to work toward the purpose God has given us. Some might think that since everything will work out for good, then they do not have to worry about doing their part. However, there is great reward and honor in being the one to help bring about God's purpose. One way we show God that we love Him is by holding true to our calling.

29 For whom he did foreknow, he also did predestinate to be conformed to the image of

his Son, that he might be the firstborn among many brethren. 30 Moreover whom he did predestinate, them he also called: and whom he called, them he also justified: and whom he justified, them he also glorified.

Paul shows that one reason we can trust that all will work together for good for those called by God is this list that builds upon itself all the way into heaven. In this list, Paul shows that the reason those called by God can trust all will be well is that God already justifies and even glorifies those He has called. Even though on the human side of salvation, it might seem like a simple one-step process of saying the "Sinner's Prayer," Paul tells the Romans that God has fulfilled all the other steps of salvation on our behalf already. In addition to saving us, God also foreknew us, predestined us, called us, justified us, and gloried us.

There is much biblical evidence for God's foreknowledge of His people. David speaks of God knowing him in his mother's womb. Jeremiah speaks of receiving his call to ministry also in the womb, which is also when Samson was set aside for protecting Israel. Jesus tells Nathan that He saw him "under the fig tree," which some scholars understand as meaning "as an infant," as mothers would let their babies play in the shade of a fig tree. The omniscient God who exists outside of time knows everything that was, is, and will be.

Many scholars have pondered and discussed the full implications of Paul's reference to predestation and its relationship to human free will, and many more will continue to do so. For understanding this particular passage, it is enough to know that God has decided that His followers will all conform to the image of Christ. This will make Jesus the first among many siblings, because God has always wanted a huge family. To conform to Christ's image is to identify with Him and make ourselves more and more like Him. As Paul says to the

Philippian church, we become like Christ in His suffering and even death, so that we can be like Him also in His glorification.

Those who are going to conform to Jesus' example are also called. The call of the Spirit to repentance and freedom from sin is persistent, and becomes increasingly difficult to ignore. The language of being "called" recalls for the Jews in Paul's audience the common name for the Jewish community of faith of the "called out ones," the *ekklesia* in Greek. These are those who have been called out from their tents to gather at the sanctuary for worship, but also those who have been called out from the world to be separate and holy for God.

When we accept God's calling, we are instantly and completely justified or made righteous in God's eyes. Having accepted the call and identified ourselves with Christ, we can stand before God as though we had never sinned because Christ's death paid for the sins already. This is the step that we most often think of when we think of salvation. Salvation does not end here, though, because God has something even better in store for His children.

The justified are also glorified! This is why we can trust that everything will work for good if we are called: because we know the called will be glorified, and indeed are already glorified. Paul speaks of these steps of salvation all in the aorist tense. This Greek verb tense marks an action completed in the past that has an effect on the present. Truly, all of it was finished at the Cross. Let us not focus on the temporary pains this world brings, but fix our eyes on the fact that God has already glorified His chosen people.

Sources:

Henry, Matthew. *Matthew Henry's Commentary on the Whole Bible: New Modern Edition.* Vols. 1-6. Peabody, MA: Hendrickson Publishers, Inc., 2009.

Strong, James. *The New Strong's Exhaustive Concordance of the Bible.* Nashville, TN: Thomas Nelson, 2003.

Thayer, Joseph Henry. *A Greek-English Lexicon of the New Testament.* New York: American Book Company, 1889.

Say It Correctly

Travaileth. tra-VALE-eth.

Daily Bible Readings

MONDAY
No Longer Slave of Sin
(Romans 6:15–23)

TUESDAY
God Bestows the Spirit
(Ezekiel 36:25–30)

WEDNESDAY
We Have Died to the Law
(Romans 7:1–13)

THURSDAY
An Inner Struggle to Obey
(Romans 7:14–25)

FRIDAY
No Condemnation for Heirs with Christ
(Romans 8:1–4, 10–17)

SATURDAY
Receive the Holy Spirit
(John 20:19–23)

SUNDAY
All Things Work Together for Good
(Romans 8:18–30)

Teaching Tips

[handwritten marginalia: Mosic Law, Isaelites, Jesus Christ, all who believe]

Words You Should Know

A. Transgressions (Galatians 3:19) *parabasis* (Gk.)—A breach of an existing law

B. Mediator (vv. 19-20) *mesites* (Gk.)—One who links two parties

Teacher Preparation

Unifying Principle—Receiving a Good Inheritance. Laws are provided to govern and ensure a functioning society. If there were no laws, what would guide human behavior? Paul taught that God's Law served a purpose, but when Christ came grace made it possible for all people to become children of God and heirs of God's promises.

A. Read the Bible Background and Devotional Reading.

B. Pray for your students and lesson clarity.

C. Read the lesson Scripture in multiple translations.

O—Open the Lesson

A. Begin the class with prayer.

B. Invite an adult who was adopted to speak about what helped him or her feel a part of his or her new family. Compare and contrast these things with what your church does to assimilate new members.

C. Have the students read the Aim for Change and the In Focus story.

D. Ask students how events like those in the story weigh on their hearts and how they can view these events from a faith perspective.

P—Present the Scriptures

A. Read the Focal Verses and discuss the Background and The People, Places, and Times sections.

B. Have the class share what Scriptures stand out for them and why, with particular emphasis on today's themes.

E—Explore the Meaning

A. Use In Depth or More Light on the Text to facilitate a deeper discussion of the lesson text.

B. Pose the questions in Search the Scriptures and Discuss the Meaning.

C. Discuss the Liberating Lesson and Application for Activation sections.

N—Next Steps for Application

A. Summarize the value of accepting the privilege and responsibility of being God's adopted children.

B. End class with a commitment to praise God that divine blessings are available to all nations.

Worship Guide

For the Superintendent or Teacher
Theme: Freedom and the Law
Song: "I'm a Child of the King"

Freedom and the Law

Bible Background • GALATIANS 3
Printed Text • GALATIANS 3:18-29 | Devotional Reading • 2 THESSALONIANS 2:13-17

Aim for Change

By the end of this lesson, we will EXPLORE the difference between living according to God's law and living by faith in Christ Jesus, CELEBRATE the freedom God's promise gives to all who believe in Christ, and PRACTICE ways they can embrace this liberation and oneness in Christ.

In Focus

Hilton wanted to be a teacher as long as he could remember. He always admired and respected the teachers he had over the years, and believed that teaching would be a way to give back to the community. He had spent the past year in a special program designed to recruit teachers to urban and rural schools. The program paired Hilton and other student teachers with a more experienced master teacher, who observed them in the classroom and helped out when necessary. It also provided Hilton with professional development training that teachers needed to advance in their profession.

Hilton tried his best over the months to be the best teacher he could be. However, the students were aware that Hilton was not the "real" teacher, and caused disciplinary problems for him. The master teachers' treatment of their protégés also sometimes contributed to a feeling of inferiority, but that was about to change.

Hilton was completing the program in one month and had already received a job offer. Once Hilton was hired, he would earn a salary commensurate with other teachers with his experience; but more importantly, Hilton would be accorded equal status with the other teachers. He would no longer be a student teacher, but would receive the same benefits and privileges as the other teachers. Hilton could not wait to sign the contract.

How did Hilton's time as a student teacher train him to be a better teacher? How do similar in-between times train us in our own lives?

Keep in Mind

"And if ye be Christ's, then are ye Abraham's seed, and heirs according to the promise."
(Galatians 3:29, KJV)

"And now that you belong to Christ, you are the true children of Abraham. You are his heirs, and God's promise to Abraham belongs to you." (Galatians 3:29, NLT)

Focal Verses ——————— Gen: 15 20b

KJV **Galatians 3:18** For if the inheritance be of the law, it is no more of promise: but God gave it to Abraham by promise.

19 Wherefore then serveth the law? It was added because of transgressions, till the seed should come to whom the promise was made; and it was ordained by angels in the hand of a mediator.

20 Now a mediator is not a mediator of one, but God is one.

21 Is the law then against the promises of God? God forbid: for if there had been a law given which could have given life, verily righteousness should have been by the law.

22 But the scripture hath concluded all under sin, that the promise by faith of Jesus Christ might be given to them that believe.

23 But before faith came, we were kept under the law, shut up unto the faith which should afterwards be revealed.

24 Wherefore the law was our schoolmaster to bring us unto Christ, that we might be justified by faith.

25 But after that faith is come, we are no longer under a schoolmaster.

26 For ye are all the children of God by faith in Christ Jesus.

27 For as many of you as have been baptized into Christ have put on Christ.

28 There is neither Jew nor Greek, there is neither bond nor free, there is neither male nor female: for ye are all one in Christ Jesus.

29 And if ye be Christ's, then are ye Abraham's seed, and heirs according to the promise.

NLT **Galatians 3:18** For if the inheritance could be received by keeping the law, then it would not be the result of accepting God's promise. But God graciously gave it to Abraham as a promise. *Andrea*

19 Why, then, was the law given? It was given alongside the promise to show people their sins. But the law was designed to last only until the coming of the child who was promised. God gave his law through angels to Moses, who was the mediator between God and the people.

20 Now a mediator is helpful if more than one party must reach an agreement. But God, *Jill* who is one, did not use a mediator when he gave his promise to Abraham.

21 Is there a conflict, then, between God's law and God's promises? Absolutely not! If the law could give us new life, we could be made right with God by obeying it.

22 But the Scriptures declare that we are all prisoners of sin, so we receive God's promise of freedom only by believing in Jesus Christ. *Loretta*

23 Before the way of faith in Christ was available to us, we were placed under guard by the law. We were kept in protective custody, so to speak, until the way of faith was revealed.

24 Let me put it another way. The law was our guardian until Christ came; it protected *Ann* us until we could be made right with God through faith.

25 And now that the way of faith has come, we no longer need the law as our guardian.

26 For you are all children of God through faith in Christ Jesus.

27 And all who have been united with Christ *Felicia* in baptism have put on Christ, like putting on new clothes.

28 There is no longer Jew or Gentile, slave or free, male and female. For you are all one in Christ Jesus. 29

Norma

29 And now that you belong to Christ, you are the true children of Abraham. You are his heirs, and God's promise to Abraham belongs to you.

Loretta

The People, Places, and Times

Promise. The Bible contains many promises from God to His people. Significant among God's promises is His promise to bless Abraham with a son, who would become a great nation, and that all the nations of the earth would be blessed in Abraham. God also promised Abraham that his descendants would be too many to count. God's promise to Abraham was in the background as God delivered the Children of Israel from Egyptian slavery and made a covenant with them. Israel descended from Abraham through Isaac. God's presence was continually with the Israelites, who trusted in God's future salvation because of His promise to Abraham.

Slavery. Slavery was an integral part of Greco-Roman civilization. Slaves accounted for one-fifth of the population. People became slaves through various circumstances, including wars, piracy, debt, and birth to a slave mother. Slaves were the property of their owners and had no legal rights, but could be freed and suffer few legal limitations as a freedman. Slaves functioned broadly within the society from civil service to hard labor. Household slaves were entrusted with the care of the home and child rearing. School-age children were under the moral guidance of "pedagogues," or custodians, who were slaves who looked after the children's general well-being, but were not the children's teachers. A benevolent master might grant a slave freedom in his will, freeing the slave upon the death of the master. A friend, relative, or other benefactor might also purchase a slave's freedom. "Redemption" means "to buy back," as in to purchase from slavery.

Background

At this time in his letter to the Galatians, Paul had introduced God's promise to Abraham and his "seed" (descendants) into his defense of his Gospel to the Gentiles. For Paul, God's promised blessing extended to all Abraham's heirs, both Jews as well as the Gentiles who shared Abraham's faith. Some Jews did not accept this teaching, believing that new believers must become Jewish in order to follow Jesus. Paul countered that anyone who lives by faith in Jesus Christ, the "Seed" of Abraham, are the sons of Abraham and recipients of the promise.

How do modern Christians add unnecessary requirements to following God?

At-A-Glance

1. Purpose of the Law (Galatians 3:18–22)
2. The Coming of Faith (vv. 23–29)

In Depth

1. Purpose of the Law (Galatians 3:18–22)

Paul argues throughout his letter to the Galatians that observance of the Jewish law was not a requirement for them to be accepted into the Christian community. Paul shifts to legal language to provide further evidence of why they were justified by faith, not by the works of the law. First off, he establishes that one does not come into the promised inheritance by keeping the law. The reason behind this is simple: the inheritance is part of the Abrahamic covenant, not the Mosaic Law.

He explains that God gave the law to Israel as a supplement to the promise to help them see that sin is contrary to His will. The law, Paul insisted, was a temporary system until the arrival of the promised offspring ("Seed"). Furthermore, the law was compromised because Moses received it through a mediator, a go-between, in the form of an angel. Abraham, on the other hand, received the promise directly from God. (The notion that God gave the law through angels is most clearly seen in the Greek language version of the Old Testament translated by Jewish scholars for the Greek-speaking Jewish community.)

Paul maintained that the law did not oppose God's promise. Rather, the law could not save the people from death because it could not prevent people from sinning. The Scripture, according to Paul, concluded that the law had imprisoned the people under the power of sin. The only way to be released from under the power of sin is through faith in Jesus Christ.

Why did God choose to give His people the Law instead of immediately providing the Savior?

2. The Coming of Faith (vv. 23–29)

Paul contended that before faith came, the law was like a "pedagogue" (custodian or guardian) over the Jewish people, who were as children in need of moral supervision and discipline. Now that faith had come, the people were no longer charges of the law, but had matured to the point when they were no longer in need of a custodian. They were now children of God through faith in Jesus Christ, and full heirs of the promise, not by birth, but by faith expressed through baptism. Baptism into Christ clothed the Gentile with Christ, and afforded him or her the status of Abraham's offspring (3:27). Baptism, unlike circumcision, was a sign of inclusion into God's covenant family for women, as well as men. Social, economic, racial, and gender discrimination was erased as

a part of acceptance into God's family. Native born versus non-native born was no longer an issue. They were all one in Christ Jesus, and if they were in Christ, they were Abraham's offspring and heirs to the promise.

In what ways are our social, economic, racial, and gender differences significant to the Church? In what ways are they not?

Search the Scriptures

1. Paul says the law was added for what purpose (Galatians 3:19)?

2. Who does Paul say is the seed of Abraham and heirs of the promise (v. 29)?

Discuss the Meaning

1. The pedagogue functioned as a custodian of minor children until they came of age. What does it mean to no longer be under a "schoolmaster" (Galatians 3:24–25)?

2. What does Paul mean when he said, "There is neither Jew nor Greek, there is neither bond nor free, there is neither male nor female: for ye are all one in Christ Jesus" (v. 28)?

3. Compare and contrast what it means to be naturally born or adopted into the family of God.

Liberating Lesson

As families blend, some people will distinguish between their half-brothers, or step-sisters, or adopted cousins, and their "real" relatives. These demarcations are based on someone not being biologically related, but instead being related by marriage or adoption. Learning these nuances of relation should not change our relationships, or how much love is shared among family members. Some, however, are guilty of treating their half-siblings or step-cousins as some of the Jewish Christians treated the Gentiles. The Gentiles were treated as inferior because they were not natural-born Jews, and therefore were not considered the seed of Abraham. However,

Paul assures us that in Christ Jesus, we are all children of God, through baptism, and that God does not make distinctions between Jews and Gentiles, slaves and free persons, or men and women.

Application for Activation

How does it make you feel to know that no matter what the circumstances were surrounding your birth, that through Christ Jesus, you have been adopted into God's family, and made one with Christ by baptism? All your debts are paid, and you now have all the rights of a natural-born child. You share an equal inheritance with all God's children. That is good news! Create a "certificate of adoption" for yourself as an adoptive child of God.

Follow the Spirit

What God wants me to do:

_____

_____

_____

_____

_____

Remember Your Thoughts

Special insights I have learned:

_____

_____

_____

_____

_____

More Light on the Text

Galatians 3:18–29

18 For if the inheritance be of the law, it is no more of promise: but God gave it to Abraham by promise.

The Galatian church was plagued by false teachers confusing the nascent believers about what God required. Did they still have to abide by the Mosaic Law? Did they have to become Jews in order to become Christians? Paul argues that God gave Abraham a promise 430 years before giving the Law. That is the promise to which the Gentiles cling as they follow God. In order to inherit Abraham's promise of blessing, Paul argues, one must simply follow Abraham's method of attaining righteousness: belief. If a person believes and is faithful to God, they will be made righteous. If they expect to inherit righteousness by obeying the Law, then they have forgotten that God's family of faith began not at Sinai with the Law, but in Haran with a promise.

19 Wherefore then serveth the law? It was added because of transgressions, till the seed should come to whom the promise was made; and it was ordained by the angels in the hand of a mediator.

The thrust of Paul's argument is to show how the law functions to reveal sin in human nature for what it is. As they infringed on the law, they were reminded of their sinfulness despite their covenant relationship to God. Violating the law did not make the Israelite a sinner; instead, the Israelite violated the law *because* he or she was a sinner. The Greek word translated as "transgressions" is *parabasis* (pah-**RAH**-bah-seese) and denotes a breach of an existing law. Before the law, it was easy for the Israelite to gloss over sin as a subjective thing; but the law shows sin to be an objective reality, a violation of God's standards (cf. Romans 7:13).

The law also stimulates faith in the promised Seed, whose coming was to fulfill the law. This phrase refers back to an earlier part of Paul's reasoning that showed Jesus is the true heir of Abraham (v. 16). Paul reads the Abrahamic covenant as being made to Abraham "and his seed." Since it says "seed" instead of "seeds," Paul interprets Jesus as the true heir to Abraham's promise. As the Israelites come to terms with the reality of sin through the law, they were pointed to the coming Messiah who will deal decisively with it. The law was interim, pending the coming of the Seed who fulfilled the promise.

The law was inferior because it was given through angels and the mediatorial role of Moses. "Mediator" (Gk. *mesites*, meh-**SEE**-tace) suggests one who liaises between two parties. It has been rightly observed that the involvement of a mediator points to the contractual nature of the Law and implies obligations for both parties. In a land contract, for example, a mediator may be needed to facilitate the deal between the buyer and the seller and both parties assuming certain responsibilities. With their final agreement witnessed by the mediator, the Israelites were contractually obligated to follow the Law.

20 Now a mediator is not a mediator of one, but God is one.

In contrast to the two-party contract of the Law, God's promise to Abraham is only one-sided. Here, Paul contrasts the promise with the Law by showing that the promise was solely a divine affair. God told Abraham to set up the sacrifices to formalize their covenant. The sacrificed animals were cut in two and laid out with a path between. The two parties of the covenant were supposed to walk together between the carcasses and vow that such a brutal fate would await them if they violated the agreement. But God caused Abraham to fall asleep and as Abraham slept, God Himself moved between the sacrifices alone, validating the promise Himself (Genesis 15). Abraham was not obligated to do anything to validate the promise. Therefore, no mediator was needed. This again shows that the promise was superior to the Law because its fulfillment does not depend on Israel.

How comforting to know that the believer's status as an heir of salvation does not depend on the believer's efforts but rests solely on God's grace through Christ. It is like our relationship with our loving parents. You did absolutely nothing to merit being your mother's child, but in deciding to be your mother, she bound herself to certain promises of love and protection that do not depend in any way on what you do or fail to do.

21 Is the law then against the promises of God? God forbid: for if there had been a law given which could have given life, verily righteousness should have been by the law.

A Jewish Christian might think the law negates the promises of God. Paul very strongly rejects this notion. The expression translated as "God forbid" in the Greek literally means "May it not be" (Gk. *me genoito*, **MAY GEH**-noy-toe). The purpose of the promise was to impart life. In order for the law to replace the promise, it would have to be able to impart life too. God did not reveal His law to us so that we would be confused, fail at His regulations, and lose hope for salvation. God certainly would have provided a set of laws that could give life and righteousness if such a set of laws could have been devised. The Law, then, must have had a different purpose than actually working out the salvation of those who followed it.

22 But the scripture hath concluded all under sin, that the promise by faith of Jesus Christ might be given to them that believe.

23 But before faith came, we were kept under the law, shut up unto the faith which should afterwards be revealed.

Paul does not completely discount the Law, but respectfully calls it "scripture," (Gk. *graphe*, grah-**FEY**) literally "the writing." Instead of imparting life, the law of Moses condemns all humanity under sin. The word the KJV translates as "concluded" is the Greek word *sugkleio* (soong-**KLEE**-oh), meaning to shut or enclose. Paul is personifying Scripture (the law) as a jailer who keeps the condemned secure in prison. Interestingly, this Greek word is also used of enclosing a catch of fish in a net (Luke 5:6). The law wraps around, ensnares, and limits those that follow it. Before long, it convicts all humanity as being guilty of sin. Therefore, those under the Law will appreciate the fact that eternal life is dependent on faith in Christ and is therefore open to all who believe.

Paul continues his personification, but this time he changes from "scripture" (v. 22) to the "law," suggesting that both terms are used interchangeably. The verb "kept" (Gk. *phroureo*, froo-**REH**-oh) is a military term meaning to guard a place in order to prevent an escape from inside or an invasion from outside. The law functioned like a siege, keeping those under it from escaping from the reality of their sin until Christ comes. Someone has compared the law in this connection to the natural law of gravity which pulls down anyone who tries to defy it without depending on a device.

These images of the Law could make someone think God is harsh and cruel. In truth, however, God's Law encloses His people to keep them safe. If they were free from the restrictions of the Law, they would be lost wandering about in the wide world without any direction from God. The Law reminds them of the guilt of their sin, but it also keeps them close to God so that when faith comes and is revealed, they can partake of it. God ensnared His people in the Law so that they could all be gathered together to receive the gift of Jesus all at once.

24 Wherefore the law was our schoolmaster to bring us unto Christ, that we might be justified by faith. 25 But after that faith is come, we are no longer under a schoolmaster.

Again Paul personifies the Law; this time as a "schoolmaster" (Gk. *paidagogos*, pie-dah-go-**GOCE**). This servant would escort the family's children as they journey to and from school. They were to serve as a guide, mentor, and protector. Even though a trusted and wise servant would be chosen for this role in bringing up the children, it is no substitute for the teacher who has trained and practiced in providing higher education. Just as a modern school bus driver takes the children to school to be taught by the teacher, so the law served to guide those under it to Christ for their justification by faith. The Law is wise and useful, but it is not the end goal. It was always designed to lead followers to Christ.

Since Christ had come and fulfilled the promise, the law was no longer needed. Just as the child does not need the school bus driver any longer once they have arrived at school, God's followers are no longer under the law now that Christ is here to teach us.

26 For ye are all the children of God by faith in Christ Jesus.

Special emphasis is placed on the word "all," which here includes both Jews and Gentiles. Through faith in Christ, both Jews and Gentiles have equal privileges before God as His children. Faith in Christ, and not obedience to the law, confers the privileges of a child of God. Christians are not called children of Moses because they follow the Law. They are not called Children of Israel because they have the right bloodlines. They are not even called children of Abraham, hoping for a promise of land and blessing. Christians are children of God Himself, because we identify ourselves with Christ Himself, God's only Son. By faith, we trust that Christ is the fulfillment of all God's promises to save His people. By faith, we see Him as the one true Seed of Abraham, the true and faithful Israel, and the Prophet greater than Moses. By faith then, we follow Christ's example and identify ourselves with Him, becoming God's child just as much as Christ is Himself.

27 For as many of you as have been baptized into Christ have put on Christ.

Just as circumcision was the sign of entering into the covenant of Abraham, baptism is the sign of entering the covenant of Christ. This is the spiritual baptism by which new believers are incorporated into the body of Christ (see 1 Corinthians 12:13). Only faith in Christ is required to be joined to Him. The Law is not needed, nor any part of the Law. Even baptism itself is an outward sign of an inward change.

This unity with Christ is tantamount to putting Christ on figuratively as a garment. The Greek verb *enduo* (en-**DOO**-oh) is normally used with reference to putting on a garment. Paul uses this same metaphor with the Corinthian church, speaking of Christians putting on our eternal, heavenly bodies and no longer suffering here on earth (1 Corinthians 15:54; 2 Corinthians 5:3). Here, however, Paul is not looking to the end times, but to the moment of salvation. He highlights the need to make visible our spiritual union with Christ here and now. In Paul's society, clothes really did "make the man," so once the new Christian has "put on Christ," that Christian becomes Christ. Everyone who sees someone who has put on Christ will only see the Savior. This is why God can accept us even though we are sinful. When we put on Christ, God looks at us and sees His sinless Son, who completely covers and pays for our sin.

28 There is neither Jew nor Greek, there is neither bond nor free, there is neither male nor female: for ye are all one in Christ Jesus.

Paul is not denying that differences between nationalities or sexes exist after one becomes a believer. Paul's point is that the merits of these distinctions do not give one an edge over others as God's child. For the purpose of pursuing salvation, it does not matter who you are. Jews are no closer to reaching Jesus than Greeks are. Slaves do not have to settle their earthly affairs and become free before they can pursue God. Men do not gain any preferential treatment over women in the process of salvation. All are equally sinners in need of a Savior. In Christ, we are all one, i.e., we are the same.

29 And if ye be Christ's, then are ye Abraham's seed, and heirs according to the promise.

Paul has already set up that Christ is Abraham's only real seed (v. 17). Therefore, if the believer puts on Christ, in essence becoming Christ, that person also becomes the real seed of Abraham and the true heir of God's promise to Abraham. The contrast is clear, faith in Christ rather than obedience to the law is the way to inherit God's promise. Abraham's promise was inherited by his Seed; not seeds plural as in his descendants, but Christ who perfected Abraham's example of faith which would be credited as righteousness. Christ fulfilled the promise of Abraham by His complete faith in God (making Him righteous), plus He also fulfilled the Law (keeping Him pure), which no one else had ever or would ever be able to do. He completed the Law and shows us the example of faith. When we hide ourselves in Him, we too enjoy the fruit of God's promise to Abraham of blessing, protection, and prosperity.

Sources:
Buttrick, George A., ed. "Promise." *The Interpreters' Dictionary of the Bible*. Nashville, TN: Abingdon Press, 1962. vol. 3, 893-94.
Ferguson, Everett. *Backgrounds of Early Christianity*. Grand Rapids, MI: Eerdmans, 1987. 46-47, 84.

Say It Correctly

Pedagogue. PEH-dah-gog.
Mediatorial. mee-dee-ah-TOR-ee-al.

Daily Bible Readings

MONDAY
Receiving the Spirit through Faith
(Galatians 3:1-5)

TUESDAY
Abraham's Blessing
Comes through Christ
(Galatians 3:6-17)

WEDNESDAY
God's Power Grants Life and Godliness
(2 Peter 1:2-4)

THURSDAY
A Faithful and Just People
(Hosea 2:16-23)

FRIDAY
A Wise and Faithful Builder
(Luke 6:45-49)

SATURDAY
Walk Blameless before God
(Genesis 17:1-8)

SUNDAY
No Longer Subject to the Law
(Galatians 3:18-29)

Notes

_____

_____

_____

_____

Teaching Tips

Words You Should Know

A. Liberty (Galatians 5:1, 13) *eleutheria* (Gk.)—Freedom, especially from bondage

B. Flesh (v. 13) *sarx* (Gk.)—Animal or human skin; the physical body; the mortal part of existence

Teacher Preparation

Unifying Principle—Freed to Love. Sometimes people feel bound by laws and desire that keep them in chains. Where can we find freedom to experience life in transforming ways? According to Galatians, God calls us to a freedom that is guided by love for others.

A. Read the Bible Background and Devotional Reading.

B. Pray for your students and lesson clarity.

C. Read the lesson Scripture in multiple translations.

O—Open the Lesson

A. Begin the class with prayer.

B. Display a collection of popular self-help books. Why is it so attractive to believe that there is a simple set of actions one can follow to have a successful life? How does that differ from the freedom offered through Jesus?

C. Have the students read the Aim for Change and the In Focus story.

D. Ask students how events like those in the story weigh on their hearts and how they can view these events from a faith perspective.

P—Present the Scriptures

A. Read the Focal Verses and discuss the Background and The People, Places, and Times sections.

B. Have the class share what Scriptures stand out for them and why, with particular emphasis on today's themes.

E—Explore the Meaning

A. Use In Depth or More Light on the Text to facilitate a deeper discussion of the lesson text.

B. Pose the questions in Search the Scriptures and Discuss the Meaning.

C. Discuss the Liberating Lesson and Application for Activation sections.

N—Next Steps for Application

A. Summarize the value of understanding faith as maintaining a relationship with God rather than just keeping rules.

B. End class with a commitment to pray to express love in terms of concrete action rather than empty promises.

Worship Guide

For the Superintendent or Teacher
Theme: The Nature of Christian Freedom
Song: "Free At Last"

The Nature of Christian Freedom

Bible Background • GALATIANS 5:1-15
Printed Text • GALATIANS 5:1-15 | Devotional Reading • 1 THESSALONIANS 4:9-12

[handwritten: (213) 338-8477]
[handwritten: 893 5948 4624]
[handwritten: 7:30 PM I.P. THUR]
[handwritten: allegory · metaphor]
[handwritten: Gal]

Aim for Change

By the end of this lesson, we will <u>DISCERN</u> the differences between legalism and freedom that comes with responsibility, EXPERIENCE freedom as trusting in the work of Christ rather than our own efforts for salvation, and CHOOSE a life of freedom in Christ that is guided by serving and loving others with humility.

In Focus

"What's wrong with you, Elijah?" Ben asked as his roommate came in and slumped down on the couch.

"I'm tired. Between soup kitchen duty and my usher board meeting, I was helping the night ministry collect clothes for the homeless. It's exhausting serving God's people."

"I suppose," replied Ben. "You have to pace yourself."

Elijah went on like he hadn't heard Ben. "I think I'm joining the sick-and-shut-in committee next. That would be good, right?"

"Sounds like you have too much on your plate already. You might want to slow down."

"Nah, we're supposed to serve one another, right?" asked Elijah. "How else am I going to stay on God's good side?"

"Elijah, we should serve as an outpouring of God's love for us, not to gain points with Him."

"Ouch! Am I that calculating?"

"Hey, I know your intentions are good," Ben reassured Elijah. "Just understand that God has freely given us His grace, and because of that, we have His favor. So we don't have to figure out what to do when we can seek the Holy Spirit to guide our lives."

Why is it so easy for believers to get caught up in the extremes of legalism or catering to their fleshly desires?

Keep in Mind

"For all the law is fulfilled in one word, even in this; Thou shalt love thy neighbour as thyself." (Galatians 5:14, KJV)

"For the whole law can be summed up in this one command: 'Love your neighbor as yourself.'" (Galatians 5:14, NLT)

Focal Verses

KJV **Galatians 5:1** Stand fast therefore in the liberty wherewith Christ hath made us free, and be not entangled again with the yoke of bondage.

2 Behold, I Paul say unto you, that if ye be circumcised, Christ shall profit you nothing.

3 For I testify again to every man that is circumcised, that he is a debtor to do the whole law.

4 Christ is become of no effect unto you, whosoever of you are justified by the law; ye are fallen from grace.

5 For we through the Spirit wait for the hope of righteousness by faith.

6 For in Jesus Christ neither circumcision availeth any thing, nor uncircumcision; but faith which worketh by love.

7 Ye did run well; who did hinder you that ye should not obey the truth?

8 This persuasion cometh not of him that calleth you.

9 A little leaven leaveneth the whole lump.

10 I have confidence in you through the Lord, that ye will be none otherwise minded: but he that troubleth you shall bear his judgment, whosoever he be.

11 And I, brethren, if I yet preach circumcision, why do I yet suffer persecution? then is the offence of the cross ceased.

12 I would they were even cut off which trouble you.

13 For, brethren, ye have been called unto liberty; only use not liberty for an occasion to the flesh, but by love serve one another.

14 For all the law is fulfilled in one word, even in this; Thou shalt love thy neighbour as thyself.

15 But if ye bite and devour one another, take heed that ye be not consumed one of another.

NLT **Galatians 5:1** So Christ has truly set us free. Now make sure that you stay free, and don't get tied up again in slavery to the law.

2 Listen! I, Paul, tell you this: If you are counting on circumcision to make you right with God, then Christ will be of no benefit to you.

3 I'll say it again. If you are trying to find favor with God by being circumcised, you must obey every regulation in the whole law of Moses.

4 For if you are trying to make yourselves right with God by keeping the law, you have been cut off from Christ! You have fallen away from God's grace.

5 But we who live by the Spirit eagerly wait to receive by faith the righteousness God has promised to us. 6 For when we place our faith in Christ Jesus, there is no benefit in being circumcised or being uncircumcised. What is important is faith expressing itself in love.

7 You were running the race so well. Who has held you back from following the truth?

8 It certainly isn't God, for he is the one who called you to freedom.

9 This false teaching is like a little yeast that spreads through the whole batch of dough!

10 I am trusting the Lord to keep you from believing false teachings. God will judge that person, whoever he is, who has been confusing you.

11 Dear brothers and sisters, if I were still preaching that you must be circumcised—as some say I do—why am I still being persecuted? If I were no longer preaching salvation through the cross of Christ, no one would be offended.

12 I just wish that those troublemakers who want to mutilate you by circumcision would mutilate themselves.

13 For you have been called to live in freedom, my brothers and sisters. But don't

432

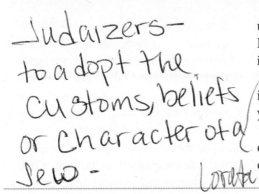

Judaizers—
to adopt the
customs, beliefs
or character of a
Jew — Lorata

use your freedom to satisfy your sinful nature. Instead, use your freedom to serve one another in love.

14 For the whole law can be summed up in this one command: "Love your neighbor as yourself."

15 But if you are always biting and devouring one another, watch out! Beware of destroying one another.

The People, Places, and Times

Galatia. The Galatia of the New Testament was an area in what is now north central Turkey, where people of many different cultural backgrounds lived together. The Gauls, a Celtic people, had invaded the Asia Minor peninsula by invitation of the king of Bithynia, who enlisted their help in fighting civil wars. They eventually settled in parts of the region formerly known as Cappadocia and Phrygia. The area became a Roman province in 25 BC. Because of Rome's tendency to rezone its provinces, the Galatians Paul addressed in his letter would not have only been inhabitants of Galatia proper, but also citizens of other nearby regions.

Circumcision. Every male among Abraham's household (blood relatives and servants) was to be circumcised as a symbol of God's covenant (Genesis 17). Adult male circumcision was common in some ancient societies, symbolizing a young man's full acceptance into society with all its responsibilities and privileges. The Abrahamic covenant's circumcision was unique in that, after the initial group of men was circumcised, the ritual was from then on practiced on 8-day-old infant boys. This showed that no special deed of the person was needed to enter into the covenant with God. Simply living made a boy part of the community of faith. When circumcision was written down as part of the Law (Leviticus 12:3), Moses shared the procedure's spiritual understanding

by "instructing the Israelites to circumcise their hearts" (Deuteronomy 10:16), which meant that in addition to the physical sign, they were also under God's covenant and had to follow His instructions. As Judaism grew, circumcision also became a symbol of Jewish identity, especially in the Greco-Roman Empire, where the dominant culture did not circumcise their males.

Background

At the time Paul wrote this letter to the Galatians, a group of Jewish Christians known as Judaizers was teaching that Gentile converts needed to be circumcised both as a sign of their covenant with God and a means of justification or being made right with Him. They also insisted the Gentile Christians also observe other parts of Mosaic Law. Paul and others of like mind found the demand for circumcision was in contradiction to salvation by the grace of Jesus Christ. The debate about circumcision and the Law in the growing Christian community had created such division among believers that it threatened to implode Christianity.

In chapter 4, Paul reminds the Galatians that before they knew God, they had been slaves to pagan gods, and he asks them why they would want to be slaves once again now that God knows them (Galatians 4:8–9). Paul tells them they are not the children of bondage, but of freedom (4:31).

emotionally at least
burst inward

433

At-A-Glance

1. Be Not Entangled (Galatians 5:1–6)
2. Stay on the Right Course (vv. 7–12)
3. Called to Be Free (vv. 13–15)

In Depth

1. Be Not Entangled (Galatians 5:1–6)

Today's text begins in the middle of Paul's efforts to persuade the Galatians to stop following false teachers who want them to be subject to Mosaic Law. Paul urges the Galatians to stand firm in the freedom Christ has set before them. The yoke of bondage, a metaphor for the Law, is meant to illustrate that the Law stands in contrast to the yoke of Christ, which is easy and light (Matthew 11:29–30).

Anyone who accepts circumcision must observe the entire Law, "for whosoever shall keep the whole law, and yet offend in one point, he is guilty of all" (James 2:10). In this regard, those under the Law are in constant debt, because keeping all the statutes without fail is impossible. Paul writes that anyone seeking to be right with God through observing the Law has in fact "fallen from grace" (Galatians 5:4). In essence, for those intending to follow the Law, the grace of Jesus Christ is useless to them because they have forsaken the advantages of His gift of grace. To persuade the Galatians to not be entangled by the Law, Paul explains that the Holy Spirit and faith, not the Law, make their relationships with God right (v. 5). He adds that in Christ, it is of no consequence whether one is circumcised, because what matters is faith manifested in love.

When Paul talks about those who have "fallen from grace," does he mean they have forfeited their salvation?

2. Stay on the Right Course (vv. 7–12)

In verse 7, Paul reminds the Galatians that when they were new believers, they were striving in the faith. However, false teachers wanted to divert them from truth. These people's plans are not the work of God, and their teachings do not reflect the foundation of Christianity. To illustrate the harm these false teachings could cause, Paul compares them to yeast, a fungus which, when a small amount is used, can spread throughout an entire loaf of dough. If these teachers' tongues were left unfettered, they could infect the whole church. However, Paul is confident God will keep the Galatians from believing their erroneous claims. Those trying to confuse them will have to contend with God's judgment for their behavior. ✗ /0

The false teachers were lying by telling the people that Paul had preached that circumcision was necessary to salvation (v. 11). Paul asks why he is still persecuted by Pharisees at the synagogues (2 Corinthians 11:24) and Jewish Christians who had once been Pharisees (Acts 15), if he had changed his teachings. If he had agreed with them, then the Cross of Christ would no longer be an obstacle for them (1 Corinthians 1:18–25). Out of his exasperation, Paul wishes that those insisting upon circumcision would fully castrate themselves. (Such a mutilation would bar them from Temple worship according to the full Law.)

What systems does your church have in place to remove false teaching and teachers before they can cause too much damage?

3. Called to Be Free (vv. 13–15)

Today's text ends with Paul again reminding the Galatians that they were called to be free and should not use their freedom as an opportunity to sin, but instead they should serve each other in love. For those still concerned with the Law, Paul writes that the whole Law is summed up in the command "Thou shalt love thy neighbor as thyself" (Leviticus 19:18). Engaging in conflict would only destroy their community. Paul beseeches the Galatians to live lives led by the Holy Spirit so they will not give in to their sinful nature. He explains that the desires of the flesh and the Spirit are constantly warring within believers, preventing us from doing what is right (cf. Romans 7:15–24).

How do you tell if you are succeeding at living by the Spirit?

Search the Scriptures

1. Why is Paul against the practice of circumcision for believers (Galatians 5:2–4, 6)?

2. How should believers use their liberty (v. 13)?

Discuss the Meaning

This world believes that to get anything, you must work. It's hard to accept that salvation is free with no task required.

1. What are some ways we try to work for salvation?

2. How can you discern whether you are working for salvation or walking in the Spirit?

Liberating Lesson

Our society is merit-based, meaning we perform to get rewards. We perform certain duties at work to get a raise. We must meet certain requirements to get As in school. Some even make grand gestures to win the heart of someone they love. We are enslaved by our own actions. It's a foreign concept that salvation is given by grace, not acts, but this is the gift of Christ. Allow this joyous news to shape how you interact with your faith and with every aspect of your life.

Application for Activation

It's a blessing to have the Holy Spirit guide us in the right direction. In your daily devotion, before sharing your petitions, ask God to help

you be sensitive to the Holy Spirit's leading. Study scriptural accounts of those who were Spirit-led to understand the ways He speaks to us (Acts 8:26–40; 15:5–29; 16:1–15). As you learn to recognize the urging of the Spirit, commit to following His guidance, even if it means you will be traveling outside of your comfort zone. It will be worth it.

Follow the Spirit

What God wants me to do:

_____

_____

_____

_____

Remember Your Thoughts

Special insights I have learned:

_____

_____

_____

_____

More Light on the Text

Galatians 5:1–15

1 Stand fast therefore in the liberty wherewith Christ hath made us free, and be not entangled again with the yoke of bondage.

This is a connecting verse; it summarizes all that has been said and anticipates what will be said. There is greater clarity of thought when this verse is read as two separate statements. First is a statement emphasizing the method of God's saving act in Christ: "the liberty wherewith Christ hath made us free." Second is a statement of entreaty, a plea or an appeal, based upon the purpose of God's saving activity: "Stand firm, therefore, and do not let yourselves be burdened again by a yoke of slavery."

The "yoke of slavery" was more than the "yoke" of the Jewish Law. The Gentile Christians were never under the "yoke" of the Jewish Law, but under paganism. Therefore, Paul uses the phrase "yoke of slavery" to mean "the elements of the world" (4:3) that he calls "weak and beggarly" (4:9). Both the Jewish Law and paganism were included in "the elements of the world" that rob people of their freedom in Christ. Another word to examine is "entangled" (Gk. *enecho*, en-**EH**-koh), meaning to be subject to or loaded down with. Paul says to not be loaded down or subjected again to the yoke of bondage.

2 Behold, I Paul say unto you, that if ye be circumcised, Christ shall profit you nothing. 3 For I testify again to every man that is circumcised, that he is a debtor to do the whole law.

The worldly entanglement Paul is most worried about in this letter is the Galatians' understanding of the place of circumcision in the Church. Since Christianity largely spread as an offshoot of Judaism, many thought one had to become a Jew in order to become a Christian. For men, this would involve undergoing circumcision. Ever since the time of Abraham, Jewish males had been circumcised in infancy to mark them as part of the covenant community. It became such an important sign, however, that many thought one could not be justified before God without being circumcised. However, they did not take this reasoning to the next step.

Paul shows that if they assume circumcision justifies them and puts them in right standing before God, then "Christ shall profit you

nothing." The inference is that the Gentile Christians had not yet been circumcised, but were seriously considering doing so. Paul's aim is to correct their thinking that circumcision justifies without offending the Jews for having been circumcised. It is helpful to read this verse in conjunction with some of Paul's other comments, where Paul shows that circumcision is not the issue (Romans 7:17–20). The issue lies in the mistaken notion that circumcision has value in salvation. The Greek word for "profit" is *opheleo* (oh-feh-**LEH**-oh), which means benefit, help, use, or aid. Paul states that if we rely on works and fulfillment of the Law for salvation, then we benefit nothing from Christ. The benefits we have in Him become void, and we find ourselves back under the entire Law.

Paul has already stated that to consent to circumcision is a confession that Christ's death has no saving value or power for Christian living. Now, he adds that to allow oneself to be circumcised is to make oneself a "debtor" obligated to perform the duty of "the whole law." James similarly states that breaking one law is the same as breaking the entire law (James 2:10). One cannot perform just part of the Law, because the entire body was written as a covenant between God and His people. Circumcision is only important as a sign of partaking in God's covenants with Abraham and Moses. But Jesus came to save everyone, not just those who identify themselves with Abraham.

4 Christ is become of no effect unto you, whosoever of you are justified by the law; ye are fallen from grace.

Paul has said that to put your trust in the Law means Christ has no benefit for you (v. 2). In this verse, Paul uses a different Greek word, *katargeo* (kah-tar-**GEH**-oh), meaning to make void or powerless or to nullify. He states that if one tries to practice both faith and the Law, they have nullified what Christ has done. To think that obeying the Law justifies us before God is to separate oneself from Christ, tantamount to falling from the grace of God. The choice is mutually exclusive: either give up legalism, choose grace, and live in the power of His might; or choose legalism, forfeit grace, and live life on your own. Definite and inevitable consequences follow each choice. Although many of the laws are generally beneficial to running a healthy society and faith community, Jesus fulfilled all the parts of the Law that provided for righteousness before God. Those who follow Jesus need not follow the Law because Jesus has already finished that part for us.

5 For we through the Spirit wait for the hope of righteousness by faith.

Paul identifies with the faithful in Galatia, including himself by saying "we" here. A paraphrase of Paul's words would be, "We wait for the full realization of our salvation in the faith that we already have it." This is implied by Paul's use of the word "hope" from *elpis* (Gk. el-**PEECE**), which means an expectation for what has not happened yet. Another image helps to understand the full meaning of verse 5. The word "wait" is translated from *apekdechomai* (Gk. op-ek-**DEH**-kho-my) and refers to awaiting eagerly. This kind of waiting does not suggest sitting around with arms folded doing nothing. Rather, it conjures the image of a waiter in a restaurant, who is patiently and attentively serving, discharging the expectations of the job.

It is also important to note that this waiting is "through the Spirit"; we continue to be on the job, empowered by the Spirit, patiently serving our Lord with pleasure—in anticipation of the day when God "will render to every man according to his deeds" (Romans 2:6). At that time, true followers of Christ will be declared righteous by their faith, fulfilling their hope.

6 For in Jesus Christ neither circumcision availeth any thing, nor uncircumcision; but faith which worketh by love.

Under the Law, circumcision mattered, but under the freedom that comes through faith in Christ, neither circumcision nor uncircumcision matters. The circumcised Jew and the uncircumcised Gentile share equal footing in the fellowship of those who are "in Jesus Christ" expressing the "faith which worketh by love." Neither circumcision nor uncircumcision "availeth" anything, or has any capability (Gk. *ischuo*, is-**CUE**-oh; to have power or ability) with Christ. Instead, faith works through love. Love is the way that faith accomplishes God's will. As we are told by James, "faith without works is dead" (James 2:26). All that matters in salvation is human sinfulness and divine grace.

7 Ye did run well; who did hinder you that ye should not obey the truth?

Having stated his case, Paul now strings together a series of comments and questions in anticipation of a closing exhortation.

The sense of the Greek here is "You were running well; who cut in on you to keep you from obeying the truth." "Obey" here is from the verb *peitho* (Gk. **PAY**-tho), which can also mean to be persuaded, comply with, believe, and rely on. Paul is not simply asking, "Who hindered you from obeying?" but rather, "Who hindered you from obeying and relying on the truth of which you have already been persuaded?" The question of "who" is obviously rhetorical in nature; Paul knows it was the Judaizers. They were guilty of "cutting in," a phrase translating the Greek word *anakopto* (ah-nah-**COP**-toe). This word is used to refer to runners who come across their prescribed course and throw other participants off the track, too. It was also a military term used to refer to breaking up a road or erecting an obstacle to hinder or prevent the opposing army's progress. The Galatians were familiar with these images and therefore understood Paul's question. Paul anticipates and affirms their answer in the following verse.

8 This persuasion cometh not of him that calleth you. 9 A little leaven leaveneth the whole lump.

Paul reminds the Galatians that God calls them and is not the author of their confusion. It is interesting that Paul does not blame Satan for the Galatians' confusion. It appears that Paul wants to keep the focus upon the false brethren who cut in and broke up the road that the Galatians were successfully traveling on.

Paul next uses a proverbial saying as a literary technique to call further attention to the corruptive influence of the Judaizers' message. Jesus uses the image of "leaven" or yeast both positively and negatively. Once, it is a metaphor for the Kingdom of God, in that this small, invisible thing permeates something much larger than itself (Matthew 13:33; Luke 13:21). He also uses the metaphor that Paul hints at here, disparaging the "leaven" of the Pharisees' hypocritical doctrine (Matthew 16:12; Luke 12:1). Even if there are only a few of these Judaizers in Galatia, they can spoil the whole congregation. It is similar to the modern saying "One bad apple spoils the barrel." Even though a single apple is small, it can affect an entire barrel's worth of apples. The bad apple must be removed from the rest in order to keep them from spoiling too.

10 I have confidence in you through the Lord, that ye will be none otherwise minded: but he that troubleth you shall bear his judgment, whosoever he be.

Paul speaks now confidently that although the Gentile converts might be considering circumcision, his Galatian letter will hopefully cause them to recommit to faith in Christ alone. Paul's confidence in them is "through the Lord"; he is confident of the Lord's rule and reign in the lives of him and the Galatians. Paul calls out the man "that troubleth you." The Greek word for "troubleth" is *tarasso* (tah-**RAS**-so), meaning to stir up, disturb, or throw into confusion. Paul is not just talking about someone being a pain, but about someone intentionally causing havoc. Probably feeling that his letter will not change his opponents, he leaves their fate to the divine judgment that their false message will inevitably incur.

11 And I, brethren, if I yet preach circumcision, why do I yet suffer persecution? Then is the offence of the cross ceased. 12 I would they were even cut off which trouble you.

Paul again affirms that he does not preach the value of circumcision, responding to a specific charge from his opponents. The Judaizers could have tried to claim Paul was on their side, pointing out Paul's association with Timothy's circumcision (Acts 16:3). They could also reference Paul's being circumcised (Philippians 3:5). However, Paul refutes the suggestion that he now preaches circumcision. He implies that doing so would make his life a lot easier, because then the Cross of Christ would cease to offend so many and Paul would not suffer some of the persecution that followed him wherever he preached the Gospel.

The tone of Paul's Greek is harsh. What Paul says is a terrible thing to wish on anyone: that instead of just circumcising themselves, they should castrate themselves fully. For a Jew to be castrated, however, would undo all the benefit circumcision was supposed to offer. In Mosaic Law, those with a severed or wounded penis would be barred from the congregation of the Lord (Deuteronomy 23:1). If we assume that the Galatians were familiar with this Scripture, we can also assume that they would have heard Paul's harsh comment as a wish that the Judaizers remove or sever themselves from the Christian community. The harshness of Paul's language helps us understand the depth of his disagreement with the Judaizers' message.

13 For, brethren, ye have been called unto liberty; only use not liberty for an occasion to the flesh, but by love serve one another. 14 For all the law is fulfilled in one word, even in this; Thou shalt love thy neighbor as thyself.

Whereas Paul has been concerned about the threat of the Judaizers, here he shifts focus to the threat of the flesh or the Galatians' misuse of their Christian freedom. Paul frames his concern by saying two things about the Galatian Christians: first, that they "have been called," and second, that that calling is "unto liberty." Previously, Paul has spoken about the Galatians' "call" with the emphasis on the "call of God" (Galatians 1:6; 5:8). The liberty the Galatians have been called to is Christian freedom. In other words, God has called the Galatians to be free from the elements of the world so as to be free to live for Him. This call by God is the essence of Christian freedom and therefore has ethical implications. In other words, Christian freedom, more than being a good end, is really a means for fulfilling God's will and lovingly serving one's neighbor. Christian freedom provides both the opportunity and possibility to serve ethical ends.

The balance of verse 13 gives focus to the ethical implications. As the Galatians are warned not to use their Christian freedom to serve their selfish, corrupt, sinful desires (i.e., the flesh, Gk. *sarx*, **SARKS**), but rather they are to serve the will of God by lovingly serving one another and thus—in the spirit of Jesus—fulfill the Law. Paul seems to make a distinction between doing the Law as required by those "under the law" and fulfilling the Law which

is the result of living "in Christ." Those who live in the realm of Christian freedom obey not because the Law commands, but because of their love of Christ who set an example for us. Therefore a Christian obeys the Law, but not simply because it is the law, but because it will please God.

Paul tries to calm fears about which parts or how much of the Law is required of Christians by explaining what had long been known in the Jewish community and what Jesus Himself had said: that the entire Law really boils down to "love thy neighbor as thyself." As the parable of the Good Samaritan (Luke 10:25–37) teaches, "thy neighbor" is anyone a Christian comes in contact with, anyone on whom you can show mercy—including the person who lives next door.

15 But if ye bite and devour one another, take heed that ye be not consumed one of another.

Here Paul highlights the consequences of failure to make doing God's will and loving others the aim of Christian living. Paul uses a conditional clause, saying that if you do such and such, this might happen. He warns the church not to bite and devour one another. The Greek word for bite here is generally used for snakes. The word for devour is *katesthio* (Gk. kah-tess-**THEE**-oh), meaning to eat up, consume, or tear to pieces; this word is often used for beasts. In other words, Paul is warning them that they were fighting like wild animals, and if they did not stop, they would all be consumed—thus the preceding admonition to love one another, fulfilling the Law (v. 14).

Sources:

Henry, Matthew. *Matthew Henry's Commentary on the Whole Bible: New Modern Edition.* Vols. 1-6. Peabody, MA: Hendrickson Publishers, Inc., 2009.

Strong, James. *The New Strong's Exhaustive Concordance of the Bible.* Nashville, TN: Thomas Nelson, 2003.

Thayer, Joseph Henry. *A Greek-English Lexicon of the New Testament.* New York: American Book Company, 1889.

Say It Correctly

Bithynia. bih-THIN-ee-ah.
Cappadocia. cap-poe-DOE-shaw.
Phrygia. FRIDGE-ee-ah.
Judaizer. JEW-dee-ize-er.

Daily Bible Readings

MONDAY
Children and Heirs through God
(Galatians 4:1–7)

TUESDAY
Authentic Circumcision
(Philippians 3:1–8)

WEDNESDAY
Press toward the Goal
(Philippians 3:8–14)

THURSDAY
Let Us Love One Another
(1 John 4:7–13)

FRIDAY
Love and Pray for Your Enemies
(Matthew 5:43–48)

SATURDAY
Avoid Strife; Love Always
(Proverbs 17:13–17)

SUNDAY
Faith Working through Love
(Galatians 5:1–15)

Notes

_____

_____

_____

_____

Teaching Tips

Words You Should Know

A. Drunkenness (Galatians 5:21) *methe* (Gk.)—Intoxication

B. Revellings (v. 21) *komos* (Gk.)—Drunken behavior

Teacher Preparation

Unifying Principle—Choosing Well. In the world many opposing forces influence our lives. When we feel conflicted, what can we do? Paul reminds us that choosing to be guided by the Spirit will result in good fruit.

A. Read the Bible Background and Devotional Reading.

B. Pray for your students and lesson clarity.

C. Read the lesson Scripture in multiple translations.

O—Open the Lesson

A. Begin the class with prayer.

B. Place a fresh-cut flower in a vase and invite early arriving participants to try to draw a picture of it. To begin class, ask: Which is more beautiful—the flower or the drawing? Which took more human effort to create? Note that Paul will make a similar observation about the beauty God's Spirit grows in us and the beauty we create by our own efforts.

C. Have the students read the Aim for Change and the In Focus story.

D. Ask students how events like those in the story weigh on their hearts and how they can view these events from a faith perspective.

P—Present the Scriptures

A. Read the Focal Verses and discuss the Background and The People, Places, and Times sections.

B. Have the class share what Scriptures stand out for them and why, with particular emphasis on today's themes.

E—Explore the Meaning

A. Use In Depth or More Light on the Text to facilitate a deeper discussion of the lesson text.

B. Pose the questions in Search the Scriptures and Discuss the Meaning.

C. Discuss the Liberating Lesson and Application for Activation sections.

N—Next Steps for Application

A. Summarize the value of submitting one's will to God's will.

B. End class with a commitment to pray to yield to the Spirit's control and, by doing so, build healthy relationships.

Worship Guide

For the Superintendent or Teacher
Theme: The Spiritual Fruit of Freedom
Song: "The Bond of Love"

[Handwritten notes in margin: "Explore = search, investigate", "Desire = want, yearning", "Support = help, hold up, assist"]

The Spiritual Fruit of Freedom

Bible Background • GALATIANS 5:16-26
Printed Text • GALATIANS 5:16-26 | Devotional Reading • ISAIAH 32:1-8

Aim for Change

By the end of this lesson, we will EXPLORE the freedoms gained when "walking by the Spirit," DESIRE the personal and relational qualities of a Spirit-led life, and SUPPORT one another in living a life centered on Jesus Christ.

[Handwritten note: "requires sharing thoughts/needs"]

In Focus

Since the day they met in high school, Cassandra and Lisa had been best friends. At proms, birthdays, and college, they were inseparable. As adults, they started going to church together and became Christians at the same time. Lisa, who had always been more outgoing, immediately started serving in church auxiliaries while Cassandra shied away from getting to know their new church family. Although Lisa was making new friends, she and Cassandra had become even closer because they now shared a deep love for Christ.

When Lisa got married and moved away, Cassandra felt so alone and started to isolate herself. She began to feel like God had abandoned her. Lisa could hear the sadness in Cassandra's voice whenever they'd talk on the phone.

Cassandra said, "I wish I could be more extroverted like you. It's not that I don't like people. I just wish I knew where my talents could fit."

"You've already shown a lot of patience, Cassandra," Lisa said. "God always knows how to use His people. I've got an idea to help, if you don't mind."

She called her friend Betty at the church and asked her to pray for Cassandra.

Betty and a few other women from the church prayed. Then she and the others stopped by Cassandra's home to let her know they'd been thinking about her. To this day, Cassandra, Betty, and the other women still meet weekly for prayer and support. Cassandra's Christian walk is stronger than ever because her fellow believers reached out to her in love.

How can you discern the fruit of the Spirit in your own life?

[Handwritten note: "see, recognize"]

Keep in Mind

"If we live in the Spirit, let us also walk in the Spirit." (Galatians 5:25, KJV)

(213) 338-8477
893 5948 4624
THUR 7:30 PM.   I.P.
Fruit of spirits
Gal 5:22-23

love, joy, peace
long suffering
temperance; =restraint
gentleness, goodness
faith

"Since we are living by the Spirit, let us follow the Spirit's leading in every part of our lives."
(Galatians 5:25, NLT)

Focal Verses

KJV **Galatians 5:16** This I say then, Walk in the Spirit, and ye shall not fulfil the lust of the flesh.

17 For the flesh lusteth against the Spirit, and the Spirit against the flesh: and these are contrary the one to the other: so that ye cannot do the things that ye would.

18 But if ye be led of the Spirit, ye are not under the law.

19 Now the works of the flesh are manifest, which are these; Adultery, fornication, uncleanness, lasciviousness,

20 Idolatry, witchcraft, hatred, variance, emulations, wrath, strife, seditions, heresies,

21 Envyings, murders, drunkenness, revellings, and such like: of the which I tell you before, as I have also told you in time past, that they which do such things shall not inherit the kingdom of God.

22 But the fruit of the Spirit is love, joy, peace, longsuffering, gentleness, goodness, faith,

23 Meekness, temperance: against such there is no law.

24 And they that are Christ's have crucified the flesh with the affections and lusts.

25 If we live in the Spirit, let us also walk in the Spirit.

26 Let us not be desirous of vain glory, provoking one another, envying one another.

NLT **Galatians 5:16** So I say, let the Holy Spirit guide your lives. Then you won't be doing what your sinful nature craves.

17 The sinful nature wants to do evil, which is just the opposite of what the Spirit wants. And the Spirit gives us desires that are the opposite of what the sinful nature desires. These two forces are constantly fighting each other, so you are not free to carry out your good intentions.

18 But when you are directed by the Spirit, you are not under obligation to the law of Moses.

19 When you follow the desires of your sinful nature, the results are very clear: sexual immorality, impurity, lustful pleasures,

20 idolatry, sorcery, hostility, quarreling, jealousy, outbursts of anger, selfish ambition, dissension, division,

21 envy, drunkenness, wild parties, and other sins like these. Let me tell you again, as I have before, that anyone living that sort of life will not inherit the Kingdom of God.

22 But the Holy Spirit produces this kind of fruit in our lives: love, joy, peace, patience, kindness, goodness, faithfulness,

23 gentleness, and self-control. There is no law against these things!

24 Those who belong to Christ Jesus have nailed the passions and desires of their sinful nature to his cross and crucified them there.

25 Since we are living by the Spirit, let us follow the Spirit's leading in every part of our lives.

26 Let us not become conceited, or provoke one another, or be jealous of one another.

444

The People, Places, and Times

Fruit. Most of the time, we cannot recognize a fruit from only its seed. Only after seeds are planted in the ground and start sprouting do we know what type of fruit has been planted. Fruit is used metaphorically in Scripture to illustrate this fact. We do not know the power at work in people's lives until we see the fruit that power produces. In Scripture, fruit (works or deeds) is the sign of God's power moving within a person. Sin produces fruit (works) of the flesh, but the Holy Spirit produces the fruit of the Spirit in the lives of believers.

Early Church Identity. The Roman government viewed first-century Christianity as merely a sect of Judaism because the church was still searching for its identity, and many in the first-century churches identified as Jews (according to their ancestry). Many Christians in fact still worshiped in the Jewish synagogues. The first believers did not even call themselves Christians, but "followers of the Way." Antioch was where the term "Christian" was first used (Acts 11:26). As increasing numbers of Gentiles became believers, due largely to Paul's endeavors, the necessity of observing the Mosaic Law came into question.

Paul reflected that our righteousness being based on Christ's righteousness and received as a gift was the foundation of the Christian faith. This marked the separation of Christianity from Judaism. In Paul's letter to the Galatians, he consistently emphasizes the difference between being enslaved by the Law and being free in the Holy Spirit as a means to teach the true Gospel and solidify the church's identity.

Background

The apostle Paul challenged the believers of his day to learn what every believer today would do well to remember: the key to making progress in the realm of Christian freedom is to keep walking in the Spirit.

Paul is very much aware of the Galatians' need for a power that the law could not give. He realized from personal experience (see Romans 7), that there are some things the law cannot do (8:3). Rules and regulations can command, but they cannot empower one to do what is commanded. Rules and regulations serve as a guide or a road map, but they cannot motivate and enable one to follow the direction and guidance given.

If the Galatians were to live free from sin's power to control their lives, if they were to fulfill the law, it would be because they surrendered themselves to the enabling power of the Holy Spirit. Only those who have surrendered and who keep on surrendering themselves to the complete control of the Spirit are empowered to walk according to the Spirit's orders.

Paul was convinced of the Spirit's sufficiency to guide and strengthen believers to live righteously. Moreover, he was convinced that the Spirit is always present to guide and strengthen believers in their warfare against the desires of the flesh. Paul's message to Galatians called them to be careful to follow the marching orders of the Spirit. Those who march by the Spirit's orders will not—and indeed cannot—fulfill the desires of the flesh. "This I say then," wrote Paul, "Walk in the Spirit, and ye shall not fulfil the lust of the flesh" (Galatians 5:16).

At-A-Glance

1. Works of the Flesh (Galatians 5:16–21)
2. The Fruit of the Spirit (vv. 22–26)

In Depth

1. Works of the Flesh (Galatians 5:16–21)

Today's lesson begins in the midst of Paul's attempt to convince the Galatians to not become enslaved by the Law, which—unlike the Holy Spirit—was not intended to save, but rather to shed light on sin (Romans 3:20). Paul informs the Galatians that those led by the Spirit (i.e., those under the continual guidance of and in abiding relationship with the Spirit) are no longer subject to the Law, nor can be condemned by it (Romans 8:1).

The question would follow then, "How does one go about following the Spirit, but not the Law and not the world?" Those listening to Paul had been used to thinking of the world in two groups: those who sinned and those who followed the Law. Now that Paul has told them not to follow the Law, he must explain that they aren't supposed to follow the world either. Instead, the Spirit is unique from both the world and the Law (vv. 17–18).

It turns out, Paul tells the Galatians, that following the Spirit will end up looking a lot like following the Law. The things God already told His people not to do, they still should not do. Paul uses a vice list (a convention of Greco-Roman moral rhetoric) to emphasize that those who continually practice these sins will not inherit the kingdom of God. On this list we see items that we might consider "big sins" like idolatry, heresy, and murder. But we also see sins that you and I might commit on a regular basis: hatred, strife, or drunkenness. All sins are equal before God, for any sin means that we have decided to set ourselves against God's protective Law, thinking we know better.

What are some other sins that we might not think to put on a list alongside murder and idolatry?

2. The Fruit of the Spirit (vv. 22–26)

The works of the flesh contrast the fruit of the Spirit. The word "fruit" denotes an organic growth that stems from the believer's relationship with Christ. The first fruit listed is love. It is also the virtue upon which all the other fruit are based (1 Corinthians 13:1–3). In essence, the operation of the Holy Spirit is love manifested in believers' lives; there is no law against love.

Followers of Christ still struggle with sinful human desires, but strive to do good. Instead of following the Law and covering their sin with an animal sacrifice, Paul uses the image of believers nailing their sins to Christ's Cross. Instead of trusting the Law to cover up their faults, they trust in the Cross to pay them off once and for all.

Paul adds that if believers live by the Spirit, they should walk in the Spirit. In other words, believers should be in one accord in following the Spirit instead of giving in to competition or jealousy. So much trouble comes when we compare our Christian lives to that of others. Our insecurities lead us to think it's not fair for someone to be higher than we are, so we envy them or we try to bring them down. We might also lord our seeming height over another, provoking them to jealousy or spiteful action. Such things are also of the world just as much as witchcraft, heresy, and murder are.

How do you remind yourself that your sinfulness was nailed to the Cross?

Search the Scriptures

1. Why does Paul compare and contrast the works of the flesh with the fruit of the Spirit (Galatians 5:19–26)?

2. What significance do you see in the order in which Paul lists the Spirit's fruit (vv. 22–23)?

Discuss the Meaning

We often think holy living is only a personal endeavor. However, God wants us to live in the Spirit as a community.

1. How do the works of the flesh undermine the Christian community?

2. How does the fruit of the Spirit unify us?

Liberating Lesson

From the moment we're born, laws govern our lives. Babies must have birth certificates. Children must go to school. Drive on green. Stop on red. Most people try to follow the law to the letter. It's easy for us to look at the fruit of the Spirit as more laws to follow. The Lord desires that our lives reflect the fruit, but not in legalistic ways. Our lives should be an outpouring of our love for Christ and our desire to serve one another.

Application for Activation

We have many opportunities to do good in this world. The question is, what should we do? Create a plan to exhibit at least one fruit of the Spirit each day of the week. Come back and report to the class the challenges and rewards.

Follow the Spirit

What God wants me to do:

_____

_____

_____

_____

_____

Remember Your Thoughts

Special insights I have learned:

_____

_____

_____

_____

_____

More Light on the Text
Galatians 5:16–26

This passage provides a frank and insightful look at how virtue and vice lists function within the New Testament broadly. The chapter began by signaling the types of moral behaviors that inform Christian freedom. Paul purports that the acts of circumcision and law keeping could potentially distance the believer from actually experiencing Christian freedom and consequentially alienate themselves from Christ. The paradox of enjoying freedom from the law was potentially causing friction within the community by encouraging adherents to untangle themselves from the law while being entangled to the welfare of their fellow citizens. As our discourse opens, the stark polemics of the works of the flesh versus the fruit of the Spirit are on full display.

16 This I say then, Walk in the Spirit, and ye shall not fulfil the lust of the flesh.

A significant break here signals that the author has now shifted into his normal didactic rhetorical mode by instructing the recipients to walk in the Spirit. To do so will enable one to not carry out the lusts of the flesh. The stark polarity between the Spirit and the flesh is unavoidable and a common tactic by Paul to juxtapose contradictory lifestyles for emphasis. In choosing to walk by the Spirit, the Galatians are given both a sufficient guide for orienting their moral lives and the power to avoid the pitfalls of the flesh. The two options that are laid bare demand a choice upon believers, it is necessary to choose wisely.

17 For the flesh lusteth against the Spirit, and the Spirit against the flesh: and these are contrary the one to the other: so that ye cannot do the things that ye would.

The verse begins with a conjunction to further develop the way that this Pauline juxtaposition (flesh versus spirit) unfolds. Paul says, "the flesh lusteth against the Spirit." In other words the two are diametrically opposed to one another. This ongoing contest occurs internally (cf. Romans 7:15–20) and has the potential to lead one into wholesale abdication of the leading of the Spirit. Of course to do so would signal disaster for the believer, which is precisely what the apostle will articulate in the next few verses, yet could also render their ability to respond to the Spirit null and void (cf. Romans 4:14; 7:23).

18 But if ye be led of the Spirit, ye are not under the law.

While yielding to the flesh is dangerous, a Spirit-inspired life emancipates the believer from the law's requirements. This statement does not mean that laws are to be disobeyed and overlooked—a notion likewise unsupported in the rest of the New Testament—however it does contend that the law has lost its parental role in the life of the Christ follower. Paul connects life in the spirit with the theological concept of adoption, suggesting, "all who are led by the Spirit are sons of God" (Romans 8:14). The polarities stated in vv. 16–18 prepare the framework for the upcoming vice list within vv. 19–21 and help to distinguish them from the fruit of the Spirit.

19 Now the works of the flesh are manifest, which are these; Adultery, fornication, uncleanness, lasciviousness,

This list is composed of vices that are anchored to self-centeredness and destroy life within community. Sixteen behaviors in total are named, each of them grouped according to the semantic domains they emerge from. Within the first clause, Paul argues that these manifestations of the flesh are its "works" (Gk. *erga*, **AIR**-gah), suggesting that they are actively producing outcomes. The first

subset are sexual sins that were to some extent acceptable within pagan circles, but completely disparaged by Christ followers. The first subset of terms—adultery, fornication, uncleanness, and lasciviousness—share the sense of lustful actions carried out with one's body. While "uncleanness" (Gk. *akatharsia*, ah-kah-thar-**SEE**-ah) can mean any ritual impurity, Paul usually uses the word in the context of other sexual sins (Romans 1:24; 2 Corinthians 12:21; Colossians 3:5). Lasciviousness (Gk. *aselgeia*, ah-**SEL**-gay-ah) is also translated wantonness (Romans 13:13) and filthy (2 Peter 2:7). Today one might think that these actions are excusable, since they take place between consenting adults or only in one person's thoughts. Make no mistake about it: these actions work much harm into the life of those who participate in them. Breaking promises also breaks hearts. Images and thoughts that we think are just in our own minds effect how we interact with people. These are indeed sins of the flesh.

20 Idolatry, witchcraft, hatred, variance, emulations, wrath, strife, seditions, heresies,

A second subset of vices related to social structures emerges. Idolatry (Gk. *eidololatreia*, eye-dow-low-la-**TRAY**-ah, the worship of false gods), witchcraft (Gk. *pharmakeia*, far-mah-**KAY**-ah, sorcery, magical arts), hatred (Gk. *echtra*, **EKH**-trah, holding someone as your personal enemy), exclusion (KJV: variance; Gk. *eris*, **AIR**-iss, strife or contention), rivalry (KJV: emulations; Gk. *zelos*, **ZEH**-loce, zeal), and wrath (Gk. *thumoi*, **THOO**-moy, passion) are sins committed by individuals in a community. In a fierce way, they exacerbate division in societies. Identifying these vices represents Paul's way of attempting to call them out and lessen their hold upon the community.

The third subset—strife (Gk. *eritheia*, eh-ree-**THAY**-ah, partisan infighting), seditions (Gk. *dichostasia*, die-kho-**STAH**-see-ah, division) and heresies (Gk. *hairesis*, hi-**REH**-seese, dissensions)—relates to the structural fabric of the community. The apostle Paul uses this space to name the individual vices that are at work in his community to heighten the community's social injustices, which is something no church wants to see.

21 Envyings, murders, drunkenness, revellings, and such like: of the which I tell you before, as I have also told you in time past, that they which do such things shall not inherit the kingdom of God.

The final subset of vices emerges from individual greed and covetousness. The New Testament contains a bevy of texts that assert how lust for unattainable items has the potential to "devour." Envyings (Gk. *phthonos*, **FTHO**-noce, envy, jealousy) appears next to murders to communicate the impulse that has perhaps motivated a host of evil behaviors up to and including murder. Drunkenness (Gk. *methe*, **MEE**-thee, intoxication) and revellings (Gk. *komos*, **KOH**-moce, drunken behavior) portend a possible connection to the Dionysian cult of the first century in which Bacchus or a similar deity was worshiped by throwing drinking parties. Paul concludes this verse with an editorial statement. He wants to be crystal clear that a firm cease and desist must be applied to all former pagan practices for those who now identify as Christians. Those who commit actions like these are following after the flesh, and not the Spirit, which guides all Christians.

22 But the fruit of the Spirit is love, joy, peace, longsuffering, gentleness, goodness, faith,

Contrasting the vices, Paul now shares the virtues that promote holiness and wholeness within the community of faith. The nine virtues listed here can be explained in triads in the order that they appear. Love, joy, and peace all function as virtues that are displayed within the individual. They grow internally like roots, below the surface, deeply rooted in the life of the believer. These are inner-oriented virtues that foster a type of wholeness by showing concrete expression in the face of adversity. The second triad, longsuffering, gentleness, and goodness, represent fruit of an outward-orientation, or how we interact with others. These virtues allow the Christian to hold up under cruel pressure, to act with calm respect toward others, and generally display the wholesomeness acquired by the first triad of virtues.

23 Meekness, temperance: against such there is no law.

This final triad—faith, meekness, and temperance—represents the fruit of self-mastery. Each one demonstrates the loyal responsibility of the Christian to act in accordance to the Spirit of God. What benefit do these virtues add to the believer's life? To begin, faith represents the act or attitude of believing, and underscores an idea of God's trustworthiness. God has proven His trustworthy character to believers throughout all time, so it should not surprise readers to find this virtue affirmed here. Meekness, or gentleness, produces great benefits for the believer in Christ Jesus (cf. 1 Timothy 6:11) particularly in the realm of undeserved criticism (i.e., Moses, cf. Numbers 12:3) and also demonstrates itself in the realm of anger as one who possesses meekness tends to rein in their anger even in situations when it would be an appropriate response. Self-control (KJV: temperance) is a characteristic of those guided by the Spirit rather than the impulsiveness of the flesh. Even though Paul does not often explicitly use this word, he places it here among the highest virtues, because when all the theology and guidelines Paul explains at length in his letters are enacted, they often look like simple self-control.

The possessor of these virtues cannot be indicted. These nine virtues will not impugn the law. In other words, we can't be at fault for having joy, though many may seek to rob us of joy. We can't be arrested for having peace, though sometimes being peaceable may cost us. No laws exist against forbearance, kindness, being gentle, faithful, or austere. This is precisely the point Paul makes in the final clause. He's saying "if you have these fruit, there are no laws against living them out."

Paul assures his audience that following the Spirit will look a lot like obeying the Law of Moses. The freedom that Christ offers from the heavy weight of the Law does not mean Christians will go around breaking those Jewish laws. Christ is the same God who gave those rules on Mt. Sinai, so those being guided by His indwelling Spirit will end up adhering to the moral guidelines of Judaism. However, the Christian will know that it is not their own efforts or animal sacrifices that make them follow these rules, but the power of the Spirit within them.

24 And they that are Christ's have crucified the flesh with the affections and lusts.

Paul had admitted to the Galatians that he had been "crucified with Christ. It is no longer I who live, but Christ who lives in me" (2:19–20). Here, this confession corresponds to the now corporate mode of existence for the believers and enables them to live liberated lives. No longer are they captive to their worst impulses and craven urges. Paul says that the flesh has been nailed to the cross with Christ. This process is necessary for the cultivation of the fruit of the Spirit to ensure the new life that Christianity entails.

25 If we live in the Spirit, let us also walk in the Spirit.

The conditional statement "if we live in the Spirit" is contingent upon our constant yielding to His leading. The spirit-filled life is not a complicated formula measured by legalistic to-do lists. It is a lifestyle informed by Scripture and empowered by a willing submission to the Holy Spirit's leading. The ability to pursue a life pleasing to God is contingent upon a complete abandonment of our lives prior to conversion. If one is skilled in yielding their life to the leading of the Spirit, that person will also live a lifestyle that reflects this reality.

26 Let us not be desirous of vain glory, provoking one another, envying one another.

The entreaty of this final verse makes an appeal for the audience to avoid vain glory (Gk. *kenodoxos*, keh-no-**DOXE**-oce, glory without reason), provocation (Gk. *prokaleomai*, pro-kah-**LEH**-oh-my, irritating), and envy (Gk. *phthoneo*, fthow-**NEH**-oh, bearing ill will or jealousy) so that neighborly love could continue unabated. To combat the way the fleshly vices take root, Paul sought to head them off before they became problematic within the community. It is easier to focus upon these vices when they're small and remove them as one would remove an invasive species of weed, to ensure that the fruit of the Spirit have the chance to thrive in the life of the individual and expand into the community as a whole. We know that in our Christian lives the invisible battle between good and evil is also waged at the level of the individual. This text can steel our souls to live lives in the victory that Jesus' atonement has secured. We are informed by the Scriptures and empowered by the Holy Spirit to walk in lockstep with Him. This invitation will help us live the life Paul promises us in these verses and enable us to be fruitful in our efforts.

Sources:

Braxton, Brad. "Galatians" in *True To Our Native Land*, eds. Brian K. Blount, Cain Hope Felder, Clarice J. Martin, and Emerson B. Powery. Minneapolis, MN: Fortress Press, 2007. 333-347.

Schriener, Tom. *Galatians: ZEGCNT*. Grand Rapids, MI: Zondervan, 2010.

Wright, N. T. "Faith, Virtue, Justification and the Journey to Freedom." *The Word Leaps the Gap: Essays on Scripture and Theology Sparked in Honor of Richard B. Hays*. Grand Rapids, MI: Eerdmans, 2008. 472–497.

Say It Correctly

Lasciviousness. lah-SI-vee-us-nes.
Variance. VA-ree-ens.
Emulations. em-yoo-LAY-shuns.

Daily Bible Readings

MONDAY
The Righteous Yield Their Fruit
(Psalm 1)

TUESDAY
Abide in Christ and Bear Fruit
(John 15:1–8)

WEDNESDAY
Wisdom's Harvest of Righteousness
(James 3:13–18)

THURSDAY
The Spirit Produces a Fruitful Field
(Isaiah 32:9–20)

FRIDAY
Known by Their Fruits
(Matthew 7:15–20)

SATURDAY
God's Presence Brings
Forth Healing Fruit
(Ezekiel 47:1–7, 12)

SUNDAY
Live by the Spirit
(Galatians 5:16–26)

Notes

Partners in a New Creation

Members of Christ's body have the grand opportunity to be co-laborers with the ever-abiding Spirit of God in reconciling, re-creating, and rightly restoring all things in the eternal reign of God. This summer quarter considers ways in which believers are partners with God in creation.

UNIT 1 • God Delivers and Restores

This unit has four lessons. Using three chapters of Isaiah, this study explores God's predictions of the future destruction of Babylon and deliverance for Israel. These events were evidence of God's power at work to grant mercy and redemption to the penitent and to restore God's people to a state of peace and prosperity.

humble, sorry.

Lesson 1: June 5, 2022
God Foretells Destruction
Isaiah 47:10–15

Humans trust in their own abilities and the systems they develop to control their lives and the lives of others. How does this confidence shape us? Isaiah affirms that God, the Creator of all, humbles the proud and the powerful.

Lesson 2: June 12, 2022
God Foretells Redemption
Isaiah 49:1–11

Individuals and nations aspire to accomplish great things even in the midst of great challenges. How can we make a difference? Creator God covenants with us to redeem us—even when we don't realize it—for a higher purpose and important mission.

Lesson 3: June 19, 2022
God's Restored People Shall Prosper
Isaiah 49:18–23

When freedom from oppression is realized, it is hard to believe. From where do freedom and blessings come? Creator God will restore relationships between God's people, nations, the land, and the next generation in ways that confirm God's Lordship.

Lesson 4: June 26, 2022
God Offers Deliverance
Isaiah 51:1–8

People of integrity find it difficult to ignore criticism. Where do they find affirmation in the face of adversity? God delivers the righteous from the judgment of others when they are faithful to God's teachings.

UNIT 2 • The Word: The Agent of Creation

This unit has five lessons taken from John's Gospel. The lessons stress how the Creating Word, at work in and with humanity, became flesh, healed the sick, saved the lost, resurrected the dead and granted—through the Holy Spirit—peace.

Lesson 5: July 3, 2022
The Creating Word Becomes Flesh
John 1:1–14

People are often curious about how things began. How do we understand the origins of life? John begins by explaining that Jesus, the Word, was God's creating and redeeming agent in the world.

Lesson 6: July 10, 2022
The Word Heals
John 4:46–54

When we or our loved ones are sick, we seek restoration and healing. When all efforts fail, what can we do? Jesus invites our active, faith-filled participation with his power to create new life through healing—even at a distance.

Lesson 7: July 17, 2022
The Word Resurrects the Dead
John 11:17–27, 38–44

When people experience tragic situations, they long for comfort. Where can we find hope and strength for the future? Our faith in Jesus releases the power of God to bring resurrection and new life.

Lesson 8: July 24, 2022
The Word Saves
John 12:44–50

Most people acknowledge a sense of a higher, spiritual power that exceeds our human capabilities. How do we understand the mysteries of the universe, the world, and our lives? Jesus' mission is to save the world so that the world can live in an eternal relationship with His Father, God the Creator.

Lesson 9: July 31, 2022
The Word Gives Peace
John 14:15–29

People seek trustworthy guidance for their lives. How can we find guidance? Our love for Jesus, shown through our obedience to his words and the Holy Spirit's teachings, creates an incredible peace.

UNIT 3 • The Great Hope of the Saints

In this unit, a four-lesson study draws from Revelation to help learners envision the new home and city God has prepared for the redeemed. In this new heavenly environment, the saints will enjoy the new water of eternal life.

Lesson 10: August 7, 2022
A New Home
Revelation 21:1–8

People long for a place and time when life's stresses and death will not exist. Where can we find such a peaceful existence? The vision in Revelation 21 foretells that God will create a new heaven and earth where life's challenges will be banished forever.

Lesson 11: August 14, 2022
A New City
Revelation 21:9–21

It is difficult for people to imagine living in a place that is totally different from the one in which they presently live. What will the new place be like? Revelation 21 uses figurative language to describe the brilliant new city God will create.

Lesson 12: August 21, 2022
The River of Life
Revelation 22:1–7

Rivers give life and nourishment to the things that exist around them. How do rivers nourish our lives? In God's new creation, God's power will be in the river, nourishing and healing people and nations in the New Jerusalem.

Lesson 13: August 28, 2022
Come and Enjoy
Revelation 22:10–21

Everything has a beginning and an end. What is the source and ultimate purpose of human life? Revelation affirms that God, who is the Alpha and Omega, creates and controls all things.

"I Do, Lord! I Will!": God Calls His Bride!

by Evangeline Carey, *posthumous*

Wow! It was a splendid day for a wedding! Nature smiled on us with exceptional weather, and the church, which was arrayed in rich burgundy and white flowers adorning each pew, communicated elegance. A huge arch covered with matching flowers had been strategically situated at the front of the church. All attendees were seated, anxiously waiting for the commencing of the blessed event—this time of celebration of love and commitment. After the appropriate songs and prayer, the wedding party entered. The musician played "Here Comes the Bride," the minister asked the congregants to stand, and the bride joined her groom before the clergy.

She wore a white, flowing gown that complemented her beauty in every way. Following tradition, her face was hidden beneath her white veil. As the minister read the list of promises (the covenant agreement), both answered "I do! I will!" The bride and groom voiced their marriage commitment loudly and clearly before God and humanity. They pledged to be loyal to each other both in sickness and in health. They pledged never to violate their marriage vows.

The church—the new community—means "a called-out group." The term may refer to a local church (1 Thessalonians 1:1) or the universal church all across the world who have believed on the Lord Jesus Christ as their Lord and Savior (John 3:16). Also, the Old Testament

believers—Abraham, Samuel, Moses, Elijah—are also a part of God's universal church. Genesis 15:6 says, "And he [Abraham] believed in the LORD; and he counted it to him for righteousness." Therefore, they are still a part of the triumphant church.

The universal church is also called Christ's Body (Ephesians 1:22–23). God's Word metaphorically describes the church as "the bride" of Christ. Revelation 21:2 declares, "And I John saw the holy city, new Jerusalem, coming down from God out of heaven, prepared as a bride adorned for her husband." The New Jerusalem is where a holy God lives among His people, who have been made holy by the shed blood of the Lamb, Jesus Christ. While John was exiled on the island of Patmos off the coast of Asia, God gave him a vision of the bride (the church—the new community) and her husband, the Lamb (Jesus Christ).

When believers accept Jesus Christ as Lord and Savior, they are saved (John 3:16). They become a part of the church community. Symbolically, they are included with the "bride" and are invited (called) to the "wedding of the Lamb" (Revelation 19:6–9). Here Christ refers to the coming of His kingdom as a wedding. Jesus Christ (the husband) did much to secure His bride's salvation—to bridge her broken, shattered relationship with God. In fact, He gave His all; He gave His life to pay her sin penalty in full. When believers accept Him as Lord and Savior, He expects total commitment from His bride to Him and His cause—building His kingdom. Believers, then, must declare their faithfulness and commitment to a holy God by choosing daily to let Him be their God—their only God. They must also answer His call upon their lives to be witnesses for Him.

As a husband and wife should expect faithfulness in their marriage, Jesus Christ expects no less from believers. Therefore, God's church—His bride—is called to be faithful! In fact, Exodus 20:1–3, the beginning of the Ten Commandments, gives us this edict: "I am the LORD thy God, which have brought thee out of the land of Egypt, out of the house of bondage. Thou shalt have no other gods before me." It is the Lord our God who has brought us out of our Egypt of sin and bondage. He brought us out of sin by covering our sins with His own precious blood.

The Israelites

After choosing Israel to be His chosen people, God entered into a covenant relationship or commitment with them—a marriage (Genesis 12:1–25:18). He would be their God, and they were called to be His people. They were called to worship only Him as their God and not serve other, lesser gods. God was faithful to this marriage or covenant; however, the Israelites broke their vows again and again. They committed spiritual adultery. They were a hardheaded, stiff-necked, rebellious people.

The book of Hosea depicts Israel's willful whoring after other gods and her unfaithfulness to the one true God. Hosea represents God and Gomer, his wandering, wayward, whorish wife, represents Israel. God told the prophet Hosea to marry Gomer (Hosea 1:2). In other words, a holy God commanded His prophet, Hosea, to marry a woman who would be unfaithful to him to illustrate the Israelites' unfaithfulness in their commitment to God. As Gomer broke her marriage vows to Hosea time and time again,

Israel did the same to a faithful, loving, and merciful God.

Being obedient to God's instructions—being obedient to God's call—Hosea constantly went after his unfaithful wife. God also constantly went after unfaithful Israel, who compounded their sin by worshiping both Baal and God. He called judges, prophets, and priests to warn His chosen people of their breach of the marriage contract. Of course with God it is either/or. He will share His glory and His position in our lives with no one or nothing else.

The Rolls of the Faithful

(Those Who Answered God's Call)

The Bible tells us that Mary, Joseph, Elisabeth, and Zechariah answered God's call upon their lives. They committed themselves to the Messiah, Jesus Christ. They kept their marriage covenant to a holy God. In fact, they took God at His Word, believed His promises, and saw them come to fruition when John the Baptist (the one who came to prepare the way for Jesus' coming) and Jesus Himself were born. The long-awaited Messiah indeed came to fulfill God's promise of a Savior to save humanity from their sins (Romans 5:15, 17; 1 Corinthians 15:21). He was 100 percent God and 100 percent man—the God/man, who was without sin. Yet, He took on the sins of humanity and paid our death penalty in full.

Because of Jesus Christ, we can join the rolls of sold-out believers to God, those who obeyed God's call upon their lives. These rolls include the midwives, Shiphrah and Puah, who were so devoted to God that when Pharaoh decreed that all the Hebrew boy babies should be killed at birth, they saved baby Moses (Exodus 1:15–21). Moses grew up and later led God's people, the Israelites, out of Egypt—after more than 400 years of slavery.

Add to these rolls the prostitute, Rahab, who was committed to helping God's people spy out Jericho before they went to war and took the land.

Because of her dedication—because she faithfully answered God's call—she saved herself and her household and became a part of the Messiah's lineage (Joshua 2:1–4, 12–14; 6:22–25).

We can also join the rolls with Joshua, who obeyed God's call upon His life, and after the death of Moses led God's chosen people to the Promised Land, Canaan (Joshua 3:1–13). Then there was Samson's mother, who prepared for Samson's birth. Of course, Samson was one of the great judges that God used to deliver His people out of bondage—the hands of the Philistines, after the Israelites had sinned against the living God yet again (Judges 13:1–13, 24).

We can join the rolls of the faithful with the barren Shunammite woman, who faithfully helped the man of God, Elisha, by preparing a room for him whenever he was in town. Even though she expected nothing in return for her services, Elisha prophesied that she would have the child she so desperately wanted (2 Kings 4:8–17).

We can join with the prophet Nathan, who answered God's call upon his life and did not recoil from confronting King David about King David's adulterous affair with Bathsheba. Nathan helped David see his sin in taking Uriah's wife, impregnating her, and having her husband killed (2 Samuel 12:1–7, 13–15).

We can also join with Queen Esther, who faced an edict designed to destroy her people. The letter decreed that all Jews, young and old, including women and children, must be killed, slaughtered, annihilated on a single day (Esther 3:13). Even though she could have been killed, she committed to go before King Xerxes with her plea for them. Because of her commitment—because she faithfully answered God's call—her people were saved from extermination (Esther 8:5–7).

Finally, we can join the rolls of the faithful with the prophet Isaiah, who had an active ministry for 60 long years. He answered God's call to be a spokesman for Him, warning, condemning, and encouraging God's disobedient children to recommit to God (Isaiah 6:1–8). Even though the Israelites would not hear His message, Isaiah still obeyed God's call upon his life. Even though he suffered much in carrying out his ministry, he was still faithful to God.

Our Call to Commitment

Today, God wants our complete loyalty. He wants us, too, to answer His call to faithfulness and sincerity, to be His bride, to be a part of His church. He wants us to acknowledge Him for who He is—the living God—Creator of all that is. He wants us to love Him with all our heart, soul, and strength (Deuteronomy 6:5). He wants us to avoid hypocrisy, apathy, and careless living—to avoid having lesser gods in our lives. Sometimes we make gods out of bank accounts, cars, education, family, power, pleasure, and other things.

Be reminded that upon accepting Jesus Christ as our personal Savior, we enter into a covenant commitment (a marriage) with God. In essence, we are standing before Him and promising to be faithful and loyal. We are saying, "I do! I will! I pledge to keep my vows to love, honor, respect, and fear You because of who You are—Almighty God. You will be my only God!"

God wants us to honor our covenant commitment to Him and His call upon our lives. He wants us to set or reset our spiritual compasses to obey and follow Him. He is true to His vows to you. Are you true to your vows to Him?

Evangeline Carey was a staff writer for UMI. Evangeline had also been an adult Sunday School teacher for more than 25 years.

Sources:
Enns, Paul. *The Moody Handbook of Theology*. Chicago, IL: Moody Press, 1989.
Life Application Study Bible (New Living Translation). Wheaton, IL: Tyndale House Publishers, 1996.

Motivating Christ-Like Behavior

Image is everything—so a once popular advertising slogan used to tell us. We were encouraged through this advertisement to emulate the people we saw on television, imitate them, and mold our lives similar to theirs. We do need to be modeling our lives after someone who is worthy of imitating. We can't, however, look to the television or pop culture for that person. The only One whose image we should model our lives after is Christ Jesus.

When we explore the records of Jesus' life, we will see Jesus as teacher, healer, leader, intercessor, and the only way to salvation. But we will also see Jesus as servant. We will see a humble Jesus serving His disciples—showing by example how to live out the Word. We take from these lessons the knowledge of who Jesus is and what it means to live out the Word.

We may already know a lot about Jesus' life and His instructions to us. Do we act on what we know? Do we integrate our biblical knowledge into our day-to-day lives? Do we recall the familiar biblical commands—love one another, be kind to one another, or seek first the kingdom of God—and live them out each day? Do we encourage our students to do the same? As Christian educators, how can we motivate students into transforming what they learn into what they do?

Motivation is something that energizes, directs, and sustains behavior. It gets students moving, points them in a particular direction, and keeps them going. Students are not all motivated by the same things. Some students are motivated by extrinsic factors, such as earning high grades, being rewarded with special privileges, or receiving the praise of others. Even in some Sunday School and Bible study classes, students memorize a Scripture or answer questions because they are rewarded with a tangible gift or teacher approval. External motivators have their place and can be effective if used cautiously, especially when working with younger students. The problem with external motivators, however, is that once they are taken away, oftentimes the desired behavior leaves as well. Christians' motivation to live out the Word should be intrinsic—it should come from within, from the heart. It should be rooted in faith and love (John 14:15). It should come from the fact that we are born again—new creations in Christ (2 Corinthians 5:17) with a heart and mind to serve Him. He should be our focus each day.

We must realize that the students we encounter have varying levels of spiritual maturity and faith and various reasons for being in class. Although the motivation to be Christ-like should be intrinsic and heartfelt, it may not initially be in some cases. Educational psychologists have suggested, however, that students can come to adopt the values and priorities of those around them as their own—internalized motivation—and that several educational strategies can affect a student's level of motivation. So, Christian educators can do certain things in a learning environment to foster intrinsic motivation in their students and encourage them to live as the Bible instructs.

Encourage students to relate lessons to their personal lives. People tend to value things more and act more quickly and genuinely when they are personally vested in something or can relate it to their own lives. As you discuss a biblical topic, encourage the students to stop and examine how the topic directly affects them. For example, James 2:1–13 instructs Christians to be impartial in our treatment of others. Allow students to think about times when they may have been mistreated or have experienced someone receiving preferential treatment over them. How did they feel? How would they have liked to have been treated instead? Would they want to make someone else feel that way? Now ask them, "What can they do to ensure that they treat people impartially?" You may suggest that students keep an application journal that helps them relate lessons to their own lives. Challenge students to set goals. Goals drive what people do, state an intention, and direct activities. Goals must be personally meaningful to a student. Students are more likely to meet a goal when they help to set it, and when they believe the goal is reasonable, achievable, and can be broken down into manageable tasks.

When it comes to integrating our biblical knowledge into our day-to-day lives, James has stated the long-term goal for us: "Be ye doers of the word" (James 1:22). In order to live lives that reflect images of Christ in us, we must do what the Bible instructs us to do. This is not an unreasonable goal, nor is it an unachievable goal. In fact, quite the opposite is true. We can become doers of the Word by yielding to God's will and authority, by resisting Satan and by humbling ourselves (James 4:7, 10). We can allow the power of God to transform us (Romans 8:5). While James has provided the long-term goal, your students can self-direct how they can achieve the goal. They can decide how to break the goal into smaller tasks: to love their neighbor as themselves (James 2:8); to be thoughtful and discipline their speech (James 3:5– 12); to recognize that fighting, greed, and other sins come from a lack of submission to God, and thus, they need to submit to Him (James 4:1–12); to meditate on God's Word through daily Bible study; and to pray (James 5:16).

Model a Christ-like way of living. Social learning theorists believe that people often learn from one another by observing each other and through techniques such as imitation and modeling. A popular example of modeling is a child watching a parent read a book. If over time children observe parents, say, turning off a television and enjoying silent reading, they will imitate what they see and learn reading as an appropriate behavior.

Actually, this concept is not new—it's biblical. When it comes to modeling a Christ-like way of living we should point students toward Jesus— the perfect example. But, we, too, are to live our Christian lives as examples to others (1 Peter 5:3). We have to let students see Christ in our actions and conduct, and hear Him in our speech, so we can urge them to imitate us, as Paul did (2 Thessalonians 3:9). It's quite easy to study the Bible and tell others what they are supposed to do, but quite another— and more effective—to teach by example.

Encourage your students to find their strength in Christ. Lack of motivation is sometimes caused by low self-efficacy. Self-efficacy is people's belief that they have the ability to successfully do something. When people have low self-efficacy, they don't believe that they can accomplish a task and will do things such as give up, not make any genuine attempts to perform the task, or refuse to do the task. When it comes to living out the Word, people dismiss their lack of effort or motivation to try by saying, "I'm not perfect; I'll never be perfect." Counter this with two important points: First, God knows that we are not perfect, and second, help is available. God's Word and the Holy Spirit can lead and guide us.

Bible study is ineffective if the knowledge gained is not put into action. To truly believe what the Bible teaches is to live out what it says. Like the apostle Paul, like James, Christian educators must be diligent in motivating others to action.

Source:
Ormrod, J. *Educational Psychology: Developing Learners.* Upper Saddle, NJ: Pearson Education, 2006.

DOROTHY WEST

(1907-1998)
Novelist, Publisher

Dorothy West's pioneering writing and publishing accomplishments have inspired writers throughout several generations. She was a novelist, short story writer, editor, publisher, and journalist, who masterfully explored issues of race, class, and color in the African-American community. Until her death at the age of 91, West was hailed as the last living figure of the Harlem Renaissance movement, where literature by Black writers flourished.

West was the only child of a former slave who became a successful businessman, Isaac Christopher West, and his wife, Rachel Pease Benson. Born and raised in Boston, West penned her first story when she was only 7 years old. The young West continued to write and by the time she was 14, she had received several writing awards. In 1926, West's story "The Typewriter" tied for second place with another Harlem Renaissance writer Zora Neale Hurston in a competition sponsored by the National Urban League's journal *Opportunity*.

West continued to cultivate her writing skills at Boston University and the Columbia University School of Journalism in New York. When West moved to Harlem, she made contact with Hurston and other greats of this time, including Countee Cullen, Wallace Thurman, and Langston Hughes. The gifted writer also traveled with several literary artists to London and the Soviet Union as a cast member of two drama productions.

West made a significant contribution to the Harlem Renaissance when she published the magazine *Challenge* in 1934. She, along with esteemed writer Richard Wright, founded the magazine with $40 West had in her savings. The magazine was the first to give Black writers of the Harlem Renaissance a forum to present their writings, which had realistic portrayals of Blacks.

Later, West moved to Martha's Vineyard, an island off the coast of Massachusetts, where she cared for a sick aunt. While there, she wrote for the island's newspaper and penned her first novel, *The Living Is Easy*, which was published in 1948 and later reprinted in 1982.

West's second novel, *The Wedding*, was not published until 1995 although she had began working on it many years earlier. Because of the success of *The Wedding*, the publishing company soon bought West's collection of short stories, "The Richer, The Poorer." *The Wedding* was made into a TV miniseries by Oprah Winfrey's production company.

The talented writer lectured on the Harlem Renaissance until her death in 1998.

Source:
Sedwick, Judith, photographer. Photograph used by permission from Schlesinger Library, Radcliffe Institute, Harvard University.

Teaching Tips

June 5
Bible Study Guide 1

Words You Should Know
A. Perverted (Isaiah 47:10) *shub* (Heb.)—To turn back, apostatize

B. Prognosticators (v. 13) *yada'* (Heb.)—Those who show, teach, or make known their observations

Teacher Preparation
Unifying Principle—Nowhere to Run. Humans trust in their own abilities and the systems they develop to control their lives and the lives of others. How does this confidence shape us? Isaiah affirms that God, the Creator of all, humbles the proud and the powerful.

A. Read the Bible Background and Devotional Reading.

B. Pray for your students and lesson clarity.

C. Read the lesson Scripture in multiple translations.

O—Open the Lesson
A. Begin the class with prayer.

B. Write a few phrases on the board that relate to being humbled (e.g. taken down a peg, eat crow, put in one's place). Ask what the phrases have in common. Discuss situations in which a person needs to be humbled. How does God humble someone who defies divine authority?

C. Have the students read the Aim for Change and the In Focus story.

D. Ask students how events like those in the story weigh on their hearts and how they can view these events from a faith perspective.

P—Present the Scriptures
A. Read the Focal Verses and discuss the Background and The People, Places, and Times sections.

B. Have the class share what Scriptures stand out for them and why, with particular emphasis on today's themes.

E—Explore the Meaning
A. Use In Depth or More Light on the Text to facilitate a deeper discussion of the lesson text.

B. Pose the questions in Search the Scriptures and Discuss the Meaning.

C. Discuss the Liberating Lesson and Application for Activation sections.

N—Next Steps for Application
A. Summarize the value of welcoming God's presence everywhere.

B. End class with a commitment to pray to avoid arrogance and godlessness that result in God's judgment.

Worship Guide

For the Superintendent or Teacher
Theme: God Foretells Destruction
Song: "You Are God Alone"
by William McDowell

THUR 7:30pm
I.P
(213) 338-8477 - 893 5948 4624 ##

God Foretells Destruction

Bible Background • ISAIAH 47
Printed Text • ISAIAH 47:10–15 | Devotional Reading • PSALM 137

Aim for Change

By the end of this lesson, we will UNDERSTAND why God would destroy Babylon; GRAPPLE with the destructiveness of delighting in power and pleasure; and REPENT from thoughts, actions, and feelings that separate us from God.

In Focus

CODE# 8487460 2468

Jeremy's life turned around when he earned a free ride scholarship to Yale. When he graduated, he went into investment banking. His salary was more than anything his family had imagined. He could afford the finer things in life, and he wasn't ashamed to flaunt it.

Time passed and Jeremy got married and had kids of his own. He rose up in the ranks at his company and even became vice president. Soon Jeremy abandoned going to church, claiming he was too busy and that the preacher only wanted money. He also rarely visited home and often talked down about the neighborhood where he came from.

One day his wife Judy said, "Your mom called earlier. Wanted to see if we could come over for dinner on Friday."

"We'll see her on the Fourth," Jeremy said. "Isn't that soon enough?"

"Maybe she just wants to see her son," Judy said.

Jeremy doubted it. "Or maybe Aunt Pearl wants to ask me again if I'll cover her rent."

"Times have been hard for people in your old neighborhood."

"They were hard for me too, but I got out of it. Why can't they? They're poor because they're just lazy and wouldn't take advantage of the opportunities they have like I did."

One day everything Jeremy trusted in came crashing down. His doctor told him he had a brain tumor. Now he wished he had a stronger relationship with God, and in the corner of his office, he knelt down to ask God to forgive him for his pride.

Has your pride ever separated you from God?

Keep in Mind

"Thus shall they be unto thee with whom thou hast laboured, even thy merchants, from thy youth: they shall wander every one to his quarter; none shall save thee." (Isaiah 47:15, KJV)

"And all your friends, those with whom you've done business since childhood, will go their own ways, turning a deaf ear to your cries." (Isaiah 47:15, NLT)

Focal Verses

KJV Isaiah 47:10 For thou hast trusted in thy wickedness: thou hast said, None seeth me. Thy wisdom and thy knowledge, it hath perverted thee; and thou hast said in thine heart, I am, and none else beside me.

11 Therefore shall evil come upon thee; thou shalt not know from whence it riseth: and mischief shall fall upon thee; thou shalt not be able to put it off: and desolation shall come upon thee suddenly, which thou shalt not know.

12 Stand now with thine enchantments, and with the multitude of thy sorceries, wherein thou hast laboured from thy youth; if so be thou shalt be able to profit, if so be thou mayest prevail.

13 Thou art wearied in the multitude of thy counsels. Let now the astrologers, the stargazers, the monthly prognosticators, stand up, and save thee from these things that shall come upon thee.

14 Behold, they shall be as stubble; the fire shall burn them; they shall not deliver themselves from the power of the flame: there shall not be a coal to warm at, nor fire to sit before it.

15 Thus shall they be unto thee with whom thou hast laboured, even thy merchants, from thy youth: they shall wander every one to his quarter; none shall save thee.

NLT Isaiah 47:10 You felt secure in your wickedness. "No one sees me," you said. But your "wisdom" and "knowledge" have led you astray, and you said, "I am the only one, and there is no other."

11 So disaster will overtake you, and you won't be able to charm it away. Calamity will fall upon you, and you won't be able to buy your way out. A catastrophe will strike you suddenly, one for which you are not prepared.

12 Now use your magical charms! Use the spells you have worked at all these years! Maybe they will do you some good. Maybe they can make someone afraid of you.

13 All the advice you receive has made you tired. Where are all your astrologers, those stargazers who make predictions each month? Let them stand up and save you from what the future holds.

14 But they are like straw burning in a fire; they cannot save themselves from the flame. You will get no help from them at all; their hearth is no place to sit for warmth.

15 And all your friends, those with whom you've done business since childhood, will go their own ways, turning a deaf ear to your cries.

The People, Places, and Times

Isaiah. Isaiah was a prophet during the eighth century. His prophetic ministry spanned the reigns of Jotham, Ahaz, and Manasseh. Scholars have argued that Isaiah was more than likely connected to the king's court in some way based on his call narrative. Throughout his ministry, Isaiah's prophecies are directed at Judah and its idolatry and oppression. Isaiah's prophetic ministry can be summarized as judgment, renewal, and hope as he foretold Judah's Babylonian captivity as well as its return from exile and the coming of the Messiah.

Tradition tells us Isaiah was eventually sawn in half during the reign of Manasseh.

Babylon. Babylon is an ancient city, and the name Babylon can be translated as "the gate of gods." It is mentioned in the Bible, along with Egypt, as the antithesis to God's people. When Israel sinned against God through idolatry and injustice, God allowed the Babylonians to punish Israel by sending Nebuchadnezzar to conquer Judah and send the Jews into exile. Babylon remained a superpower until the Medes and Persians conquered Babylonia in 539 BC.

Background

Isaiah prophesies the demise of Babylon (Isaiah 45). Isaiah announces the conquest of Babylon by King Cyrus of the Medo-Persian Empire. This prophecy is linked to the salvation and restoration of Israel as they return from exile under Cyrus' reign. Babylon is condemned for its idolatry (Isaiah 46). The idols of Babylon are deemed powerless. They are made from created things and cannot save their worshipers. The reign of Babylon is over, and its gods cannot protect its people.

God calls the Babylonian sorcerers and astrologers to account (Isaiah 47). Their knowledge is world renowned, but it is powerless against the sovereign judgment of the Lord. None of their astrological understanding or spells of witchcraft can prevent the disaster coming upon them. The once proud city will be humbled through the divine arrangement of its conquest by a foreign power.

What is bad news for the Babylonians is good news for the Jews. Because of Babylon's conquest, they will gain an ally in Cyrus who will give them freedom to return to their homeland and rebuild their capital Jerusalem as well as their Temple. God assures them no idol could have foretold these things and establishes His superiority over the gods and idols of other nations (Isaiah 48). He is God and He is in control of the destiny of not only Israel but all the nations of the globe.

At-A-Glance

1. The Pride of Babylon and Its
Consequences (Isaiah 47:10–11)
2. False Trust in Babylon's Expertise
(vv. 12–13)
3. The Ultimate Demise of Babylon
(vv. 14–15)

In Depth

1. The Pride of Babylon and Its Consequences (Isaiah 47:10–11)

God through Isaiah calls out Babylon's prideful attitude. They have committed wickedness brazenly as if they were accountable to no one. The Babylonians were renowned for their knowledge, and this knowledge was the source of Babylon's pride. Because of this they put themselves in the place of God by saying, "I am, and none else beside me" (v. 10). These are proud, blasphemous words which display the inward attitude of the heart.

God would not allow Babylon to remain unpunished for this sin of pride. Calamity and disaster would come upon the city in the form of the Medo-Persian Empire and King Cyrus. None of Babylon's sorcery and knowledge could conjure an escape from the Medes and Persians. Their kingdom would be taken over, and they could do nothing about it. As believers we have no reason to despair when proud and wicked rulers or leaders are in power. Eventually all of us will come before the judgment seat of God. There, none of our knowledge, wealth, or social standing will be of any use—only whether we were righteous and humble before Him.

What is your response when you see wicked and proud people in power?

2. False Trust in Babylon's Expertise (vv. 12–13)

Isaiah mocks the knowledge and abilities of Babylon's sorcerers and astrologers. No matter what they do, they could not stop the judgment of God. Isaiah taunts them by pointing out that although they are experienced in enchantments and sorceries, they still will not withstand God's disaster. Astrology and sorcery were ways to control destiny. Babylon would soon face the truth that it was not in control of its destiny.

With all of their counselors, they weary themselves. They cannot figure a way out of their situation. Their astrologers try to predict an overturning of their fate, but it will not make a difference. Babylon's wisdom and knowledge will not be able to help it. Nothing they take pride in will pull them out of the ditch they dug for themselves through blasphemous pride and wickedness.

This same understanding of reality needs to be imprinted on our own hearts and minds. We are not in control, and any attempt to control our destiny is empty and vain. God is sovereign over our lives, and we need to look to Him for help. He controls our future and our destiny.

How do you respond to the fact that God controls your future and your destiny?

3. The Ultimate Demise of Babylon (vv. 14–15)

The astrologers and sorcerers of Babylon are compared to straw or stubble burning in the fire. They will not be able to save Babylon. Their fate was with the city and its empire. Looking to them for help would be fruitless. Sitting by their fire would bring no warmth. They can't save Babylon because they can't save themselves.

The nations who have dealt with Babylon since its origin will turn their backs on it. They will not help Babylon when calamity strikes. The pride of Babylon will be broken by the sovereign will of God. Babylon will have no way to escape it, no one to turn to, and no resources to meet this disaster.

Where do you turn when you are facing an impossible situation?

Search the Scriptures

1. What is Babylon's declaration of pride (Isaiah 49:10)?

2. What did Babylon rely on in times of disaster (vv. 12–13)?

Discuss the Meaning

1. What are the modern equivalents in our country to Babylon's knowledge and witchcraft? What do we trust in as a nation?

2. Why do people turn to things like astrology and witchcraft?

Liberating Lesson

We may be tempted to despair as we see the world and its leaders walk in pride and wickedness. When it comes to our own nation, hyper-patriotism and blind allegiance has puffed up many with misplaced pride. They believe we as a nation are superior to others and continually progressing toward increasing splendor. Our Scriptures tell us God is in control of the nations. He lifts up some and casts down others. Loyalty to your country is a good thing but blind loyalty and pride absent of dependence on God is a path to ruin. We may despair at the injustice we see in the world, but God will call the nations to account for their pride and wickedness. Oppressive regimes and unjust laws are a result of human pride. But human pride will always be brought low under the sovereignty of God.

Application for Activation

No nation is beyond the pride we read about in Isaiah's description of Babylon. As individuals we are equally in danger of exhibiting this kind of pride. In the coming week take some time to pray for our nation and its leaders. Also make a plan to serve others. This is a surefire way to root out pride in your life.

Follow the Spirit

What God wants me to do:

_____

_____

_____

Remember Your Thoughts

Special insights I have learned:

_____

_____

_____

_____

More Light on the Text
Isaiah 47:10–15

In Isaiah 46, the prophet begins to focus on the nation of Babylon. First, he attacks the so-called gods of Babylon for being powerless and pathetic (see 46:1–7). Now, in Isaiah 47 he turns to pronounce judgment on Babylon itself. For centuries the Southern Kingdom of Judah had rebelled against God and been unfaithful to the covenant He had made with them. The time for their judgment had come, and God had chosen Babylon as His instrument of judgment against His own people. God now reminds Babylon that it was He who had "given" Judah into their hand (v. 6). Historically, this took place in 586 BC, when Babylon destroyed Jerusalem and the Temple, and carried many of the people into exile. However, Babylon had overstepped their bounds and showed them no mercy (see v. 6). For this and other crimes, Babylon is now just as deserving of God's judgment as Judah (see also Isaiah 13).

10 For thou hast trusted in thy wickedness: thou hast said, None seeth me. Thy wisdom and thy knowledge, it hath perverted thee; and thou hast said in thine heart, I am, and none else beside me.

The Hebrew word for "wickedness" is *ra'ah* (ra-**AH**), the most common word used to refer to moral evil in the Old Testament. Babylon's wickedness includes idol worship

(46:1–2, 5–7), pride (vv. 5, 7–8), love of luxury and "pleasures" (v. 8), and sorcery and enchantment (v. 9). All of these sins may be in mind in verse 10, but perhaps sorcery above all since it was just mentioned and will be the main focus of the following verses. Babylon feels perfectly secure in their evil because they are the current world superpower, and no one on earth can hold them accountable for their actions. They boast in their "wisdom" and "knowledge." This is a worldly kind of wisdom, polluted by sin and based on the magical arts of false religion. This is quite different from true wisdom that comes from God alone (see Proverbs 1:7). In their pride and arrogance, they conclude, "I am, and none else [are] beside me," an attitude also stated previously (v. 8). Babylon believes that they are supreme, independent, and cannot be defeated. They can do whatever they please.

But God has made this very same claim to be alone and unique in greatness and supremacy (see 45:18, 21; 46:9). Also, Babylon's simple statement, "I am" echoes God's words of self-identification (Exodus 3:14). In reality, though, Isaiah's description of God's incredible power (Isaiah 40) makes it quite clear that the arrogant claims of Babylon and all other earthly powers are simply laughable: all people are "as grasshoppers" (v. 22); the world's rulers are as "nothing" (v. 23); God can merely "blow upon them, and they shall wither" (v. 24). When Babylon's power confronts God's, there is simply no contest.

We may often treat pride as one of the so-called "acceptable sins." In other words, we acknowledge that pride is wrong, but don't take it seriously when we see it in ourselves or in others. But the Bible teaches that God "resisteth the proud" (James 4:6). One of the sins the prophets most often emphasize that leads to God's judgment on various nations is the sin of pride (e.g., Isaiah 10:5–19). Pride is also at the root of the first sin committed by Adam and Eve (Genesis 3). They were created to submit to God's good rule, but instead they wanted to make their own rules and determine good and evil for themselves. When they sinned, then, they were arrogantly trying to elevate themselves to the place of God. Anyone, even those who are poor and of lower social status, can develop a prideful heart and must humble themselves before the Lord. However, as in Isaiah's day, it is usually the most powerful and wealthy individuals and nations of the world who are most likely to echo the prideful words of Babylon: "I am, and none else [are] beside me." Around the world, there remain many "Big Men" who engage in corruption, live as though they are above the law, and feel secure in their wickedness. But God will ensure that justice is done.

11 Therefore shall evil come upon thee; thou shalt not know from whence it riseth: and mischief shall fall upon thee; thou shalt not be able to put it off: and desolation shall come upon thee suddenly, which thou shalt not know.

Verse 11 shifts from the sins of Babylon to the judgments that God will bring against the nation as a result of their sin. This verse includes three statements, and all three make the same point: Judgment is coming, and they won't be able to do anything about it.

Isaiah warns that "evil," "mischief," and "desolation" will come upon them. The first word is once again the Hebrew word *ra'ah* (ra-**AH**). Because Babylon had committed *ra'ah* against God (verse 10), they will now receive *ra'ah* from God. Here, though, the word is best translated as "disaster" or "trouble" in English since when *ra'ah* comes from God it indicates the judgment people deserve for sin rather than moral evil. These three terms are probably not three separate kinds of judgment, but three

ways of describing the one general idea of God's coming punishment.

When it comes, they won't be able to charm it away or buy their way out. The first expression is from a rare verb *shachar* (sha-**HAR**), which occurs only here and in verse 15 in the entire Old Testament, and thus its meaning is somewhat uncertain. The KJV translates this "thou shalt not know from whence it riseth," but most scholars today suggest that it means "you will not be able to cause it to disappear by magic." This would mean their well-known attempts to use magic and sorcery to change the future are powerless against God's judgment. It does not matter how much wealth Babylon possesses. It does not matter how powerful they are or that they have conquered much of the known world. It doesn't matter how skilled they believe they are in controlling the spiritual world. None of it will do any good. God cannot be controlled or manipulated. This judgment is unavoidable.

While such words of judgment are meant to warn and terrorize the powerful wicked, these same words are meant to comfort and encourage those who suffer at the hands of oppressors. In recent centuries, those of African descent have been especially abused and oppressed by others who possess greater power and wealth. In many cases, justice seems unattainable. Yet the oppressed can be assured that God does not let the guilty go unpunished (Exodus 34:7). This justice may come in the present, as it did for Babylon when Medo-Persia conquered them. It may come in the more distant future. In many cases, wicked individuals live out their days on earth in comfort, but will receive justice when Jesus Christ returns one day. Ultimately, God will make sure that justice is done. It is in His character to raise up the weak and bring down the proud (1 Samuel 2:2–8).

Predictions of judgment in the prophets should also be a constant reminder of the need of all people for the Gospel of Jesus Christ.

Judgments like those that God brought against Babylon in history are a small taste and warning of the greater, eternal judgment that will fall upon all those who persist in prideful sin and refuse to repent and turn to Christ in faith. Yet for those who do humble themselves and cling to Christ alone for the forgiveness of sins, God's judgment upon sin has been absorbed by Jesus' taking their place at the Cross (see Romans 5:6–11).

12 Stand now with thine enchantments, and with the multitude of thy sorceries, wherein thou hast laboured from thy youth; if so be thou shalt be able to profit, if so be thou mayest prevail. 13 Thou art wearied in the multitude of thy counsels. Let now the astrologers, the stargazers, the monthly prognosticators, stand up, and save thee from these things that shall come upon thee.

Isaiah has already stated in verse 11 that this judgment cannot be avoided, especially not through their magical religious practices. But now, with a tone of sarcasm or mockery, he invites the Babylonians to give it their best try anyway! If ever there is a time to use their religious powers, this is it! The prophet, then, is addressing Babylon in the same way that Elijah addressed the prophets at Baal of Mount Carmel (see 1 Kings 18:27). He encourages them to put their faith to the test so that the worthlessness of false religion might be exposed.

The Babylonians were well-known in the ancient world for their rituals that were designed to influence the present and the future through magic (see Daniel 1–5). Some spells, for example, were meant to bring immediate health or prosperity, while others were designed to bind harmful spiritual powers and avoid future trouble. This is the false religion that emerges out of cultures that do not know or have rejected the true God. The terms "enchantments" and "sorceries" are the same Hebrew words used in v. 9, where these techniques were already said to be powerless to stop judgment. But since this is the normal strategy of the Babylonians to avoid trouble, they might as well try it: "maybe they will do you some good" (v. 12, NLT)!

Verse 13 refers specifically to the astrologers who attempted to understand the future by interpreting patterns in the sky. It was the ancient Babylonians who created what we now know as the horoscope. The term for "astrologers" is literally "those who divide the heavens," based on the rare verb *havar* (ha-**VAR**), which appears only here in the Old Testament. They too are useless, so Isaiah mocks them as well: Let them "save thee from these things that shall come upon thee"!

All of these practices are illegal under Israel's law and bring harsh penalties (Deuteronomy 18:9–14). Witchcraft was one of the practices of the evil queen Jezebel (2 Kings 9:22). Magical rituals involve evil powers, and they are attempts to control God and His world. Instead, Israel is called to submit to God's good and wise control. Of course, Babylon did not follow the laws of Israel, but they are still accountable before the Lord for these worthless evils.

Isaiah and the other prophets consistently teach that there is only one way to avoid judgment, one response that God is looking for: repentance. This repentance means turning from their sins against God and others, and turning toward God in worship and toward others in love (cf. Isaiah 1:16–20). This is the same response demanded of those who would follow Christ today: turning from sin in repentance and toward Christ in faith. But in this case the prophet does not even call them to repentance, perhaps because he knows they will not listen, or perhaps because they are beyond the point of avoiding punishment. Instead, he encourages them to march further down the path to destruction.

Similar magical practices can be found in today's world. Some in modern Africa attempt to combine Christianity with magic, consulting the pastor on Sunday and the witch doctor or medicine man on Monday. These aspects of African traditional religions are attractive because they claim to give one control over the spirit world, which enables them to control their own present and future. Some aspects of the so-called "prosperity gospel," which originated in the United States and has been influential in Africa, are attractive for the same reasons. Many preachers are telling Christians to "sow seed" by giving money to the church with the guarantee that they will receive back 10 times the money they give. They are encouraged to purchase "anointed" oils, handkerchiefs, and water that will ward off evil and bring prosperity. Some sleep with a Bible under their pillow for spiritual protection. These are some examples of a Christianized form of magic or sorcery that has more in common with evil Babylonian magic than with the Christian faith. As in Babylon, these are attempts to control God and one's life. Instead, God's people should bring their concerns to the Lord in prayer and trust that He hears and responds as a loving Father in ways that are for our good.

14 Behold, they shall be as stubble; the fire shall burn them; they shall not deliver themselves from the power of the flame: there shall not be a coal to warm at, nor fire to sit before it.

Here the prophet further emphasizes the uselessness of the astrologers and other so-called religious experts. Fire is a common image for destructive judgment, and in this case these men who supposedly possess great power are no better than "stubble," or straw, thrown into the fire. Clearly, God's power, represented by the flame, is far greater. They will be quickly consumed, and cannot even save themselves.

If this is true, how foolish to think that they can save anyone else? The second half of the verse warns that this is not a welcome fire; it is not a fire to keep one warm. This is purely destructive.

15 Thus shall they be unto thee with whom thou hast laboured, even thy merchants, from thy youth: they shall wander every one to his quarter; none shall save thee.

It is possible that the "merchants" are a new group introduced at the end of Isaiah's message to Babylon. But it is more likely that the astrologers and sorcerers are still the focus, but are referred to more figuratively as "business men." This is because the religious specialists were making a great deal of money from their fraudulent services to the people. But when God's judgment comes, they will be no help at all and will suddenly disappear. It will now be "every man for himself." The last statement in the chapter summarizes the main point of verses 10–15: judgment is coming, and "none shall save thee." Not their gods, not their wisdom, and not their religious experts.

The last word in the chapter in Hebrew is literally "savior," based on the Hebrew verb *yasha* (ya-**SHAH**). This verb is the basis for the Hebrew name Joshua, and for the Greek name Jesus (Matthew 1:21). Babylon had no savior from their physical judgment in this world, but today there is a Savior who rescues from the greater final judgment that is coming upon all people for their wickedness. Other gods cannot save us (Isaiah 46:7). We cannot save ourselves (vv. 11–14). Others cannot save us (v. 15). Only God Himself can rescue us, and He has done so by sending His Son to suffer God's judgment in our place out of love (see John 3:16). Indeed, there is no other Savior but Jesus (see Acts 4:12; Isaiah 46:4).

Sources:

Childs, Brevard S. *Isaiah*. Old Testament Library. Louisville: Westminster/John Knox, 2001.

Goldingay, John *Isaiah: New International Biblical Commentary*. Peabody, MA: Hendrickson, 2001.

Köhler, L., W. Baumgartner, and J. Stamm. *The Hebrew and Aramaic Lexicon of the Old Testament*. Study Edition. 2 vols. Translated and edited by M. E. J. Richardson. Boston: Brill, 2001.

Life Application Study Bible, King James Version. Wheaton, IL: Tyndale House Publishers, Inc., 1997. 2154-2155, 2170-2172.

Motyer, J. Alec. *Isaiah*. Tyndale Old Testament Commentaries. Downers Grove: InterVarsity, 1999.

Nsiku, Edouard Kitoko. "Isaiah." Pages 809–52 in *Africa Bible Commentary*. Tokunboh Adeyemo, Ed. Nairobi: Word Alive, 2006.

Oswalt, John N. *The Book of Isaiah: Chapters 40–66*. New International Commentary on the Old Testament. Grand Rapids: Eerdmans, 1998.

Tenney, Merrill C., ed. *Pictorial Encyclopedia of the Bible Volume 1: A-C*. Grand Rapids, MI: Zondervan, 1975. 439-448.

Walton, John H., Victor H. Matthews, and Mark W. Chavalas. *The IVP Bible Background Commentary: Old Testament*. Downers Grove: InterVarsity, 2000.

Say It Correctly

Jotham. JAW-thum.
Ahaz. AYE-hazz.
Manasseh. Mah-NAH-suh.
Antithesis. an-TIH-thuh-siss.

Daily Bible Readings

MONDAY
Babylon's Days Are Numbered
(Jeremiah 29:8–14)

TUESDAY
Let Your Compassion Come Speedily
(Psalm 79)

WEDNESDAY
Persecution Foretold
(Mark 13:1–13)

THURSDAY
Keep Awake!
(Mark 13:28–37)

FRIDAY
Rise Up, O God!
(Psalm 74:10–23)

SATURDAY
The Humiliation of Babylon
(Isaiah 47:1–9)

SUNDAY
No Security in Wickedness
(Isaiah 47:10–15)

Notes

Teaching Tips

Words You Should Know

A. Gentiles (Isaiah 49:6) *goyim* (Heb.)—Various people groups of the world apart from the Jews

B. People (v. 8) *'am* (Heb.)—The Jews, as opposed to the Gentiles

Teacher Preparation

Unifying Principle—A Mission to Save. Individuals and nations aspire to accomplish great things even in the midst of great challenges. How can we make a difference? Creator God covenanted with us to redeem us—even when we didn't realize it—for a higher purpose and important missions.

A. Read the Bible Background and Devotional Reading.

B. Pray for your students and lesson clarity.

C. Read the lesson Scripture in multiple translations.

O—Open the Lesson

A. Begin the class with prayer.

B. Begin class by writing a list of words on the board. These can be any part of speech, but try to list words that have clear opposites. Ask for volunteers to choose one word and give its opposite. Continue until all words are used. Then ask for the opposite of "servant" (a common response might be "ruler").

C. Have the students read the Aim for Change and the In Focus story.

D. Ask students how events like those in the story weigh on their hearts and how they can view these events from a faith perspective.

P—Present the Scriptures

A. Read the Focal Verses and discuss the Background and The People, Places, and Times sections.

B. Have the class share what Scriptures stand out for them and why, with particular emphasis on today's themes.

E—Explore the Meaning

A. Use In Depth or More Light on the Text to facilitate a deeper discussion of the lesson text.

B. Pose the questions in Search the Scriptures and Discuss the Meaning.

C. Discuss the Liberating Lesson and Application for Activation sections.

N—Next Steps for Application

A. Summarize the value of reflecting the light of Jesus.

B. End class with a commitment to pray to seek the same servant heart when ministering to the world around them.

Worship Guide

For the Superintendent or Teacher
Theme: God Foretells Redemption
Song: "Make Me a Servant"

God Foretells Redemption

Bible Background • ISAIAH 49:1-17
Printed Text • ISAIAH 49:1–11 | Devotional Reading • PSALM 111:9–10

———————— **Aim for Change** ————————

By the end of this lesson, we will UNDERSTAND that God's mission for the people of Israel is to show all people the way to God, CELEBRATE that all people who serve God are included in God's promises, and TELL others about God's never-ending love and salvation for all people.

———————— **In Focus** ————————

For two centuries, African Americans were slaves with seemingly no hope of deliverance. As they toiled in wretched conditions they sang songs and prayed prayers, hoping for relief. God heard their cries, and He allowed someone to rise among them. Her name was Harriet Tubman, and she was known as the "Moses" of her people.

Tubman was born in slavery and experienced many hardships. Unlike some who had accepted their lot, she longed for freedom. God did indeed allow her to escape the bonds of slavery. She enjoyed her freedom, but she couldn't forget her brothers and sisters who were still in bondage. She returned to the South many times and led her people to freedom, just as Moses had done in Egypt for his people.

The slaves were clever. They included coded escape signals in their songs. After dark, "Steal Away" was the song used to signal slaves to move to a meeting place from which to escape to the North via the Underground Railroad. Harriet Tubman helped more than 300 slaves escape to freedom this way. And though she only delivered a relatively few from the bonds of slavery, her heroic deeds focused attention on the need for emancipation. Moses, Harriet Tubman, Martin Luther King Jr., and others were powerful leaders led by God. Each came to lead a particular people at a particular time. However, Jesus came for ALL people and His great work has and will be felt through all eternity.

How have you helped spread the Word of God's deliverance to all people?

———————— **Keep in Mind** ————————

"Thus saith the LORD, In an acceptable time have I heard thee, and in a day of salvation have I helped thee: and I will preserve thee, and give thee for a covenant of the people, to establish the earth, to cause to inherit the desolate heritages." (Isaiah 49:8, KJV)

"This is what the LORD says: 'At just the right time, I will respond to you. On the day of salvation I will help you. I will protect you and give you to the people as my covenant with them. Through you I will reestablish the land of Israel and assign it to its own people again.'"
(Isaiah 49:8, NLT)

Focal Verses

KJV Isaiah 49:1 Listen, O isles, unto me; and hearken, ye people, from far; The LORD hath called me from the womb; from the bowels of my mother hath he made mention of my name.

2 And he hath made my mouth like a sharp sword; in the shadow of his hand hath he hid me, and made me a polished shaft; in his quiver hath he hid me;

3 And said unto me, Thou art my servant, O Israel, in whom I will be glorified.

4 Then I said, I have laboured in vain, I have spent my strength for nought, and in vain: yet surely my judgment is with the LORD, and my work with my God.

5 And now, saith the LORD that formed me from the womb to be his servant, to bring Jacob again to him, Though Israel be not gathered, yet shall I be glorious in the eyes of the LORD, and my God shall be my strength.

6 And he said, It is a light thing that thou shouldest be my servant to raise up the tribes of Jacob, and to restore the preserved of Israel: I will also give thee for a light to the Gentiles, that thou mayest be my salvation unto the end of the earth.

7 Thus saith the LORD, the Redeemer of Israel, and his Holy One, to him whom man despiseth, to him whom the nation abhorreth, to a servant of rulers, Kings shall see and arise, princes also shall worship, because of the LORD that is faithful, and the Holy One of Israel, and he shall choose thee.

8 Thus saith the LORD, In an acceptable time have I heard thee, and in a day of salvation have I helped thee: and I will preserve thee, and give thee for a covenant of the people, to establish the earth, to cause to inherit the desolate heritages;

9 That thou mayest say to the prisoners, Go forth; to them that are in darkness, Shew

NLT Isaiah 49:1 Listen to me, all you in distant lands! Pay attention, you who are far away! The LORD called me before my birth; from within the womb he called me by name.

2 He made my words of judgment as sharp as a sword. He has hidden me in the shadow of his hand. I am like a sharp arrow in his quiver.

3 He said to me, "You are my servant, Israel, and you will bring me glory."

4 I replied, "But my work seems so useless! I have spent my strength for nothing and to no purpose. Yet I leave it all in the LORD's hand; I will trust God for my reward."

5 And now the LORD speaks—the one who formed me in my mother's womb to be his servant, who commissioned me to bring Israel back to him. The LORD has honored me, and my God has given me strength.

6 He says, "You will do more than restore the people of Israel to me. I will make you a light to the Gentiles, and you will bring my salvation to the ends of the earth."

7 The LORD, the Redeemer and Holy One of Israel, says to the one who is despised and rejected by the nations, to the one who is the servant of rulers: "Kings will stand at attention when you pass by. Princes will also bow low because of the LORD, the faithful one, the Holy One of Israel, who has chosen you."

8 This is what the LORD says: "At just the right time, I will respond to you. On the day of salvation I will help you. I will protect you and give you to the people as my covenant with them. Through you I will reestablish the land of Israel and assign it to its own people again.

9 I will say to the prisoners, 'Come out in freedom,' and to those in darkness, 'Come into the light.' They will be my sheep, grazing in green pastures and on hills that were previously bare.

yourselves. They shall feed in the ways, and their pastures shall be in all high places.

10 They shall not hunger nor thirst; neither shall the heat nor sun smite them: for he that hath mercy on them shall lead them, even by the springs of water shall he guide them.

11 And I will make all my mountains a way, and my highways shall be exalted.

10 They will neither hunger nor thirst. The searing sun will not reach them anymore. For the LORD in his mercy will lead them; he will lead them beside cool waters.

11 And I will make my mountains into level paths for them. The highways will be raised above the valleys.

The People, Places, and Times

The Suffering Servant. Arising out of the complex prophecies of Isaiah, this enigmatic figure serves God and will suffer for others (see Isaiah 42:1–4; 49:1–7; 50:4–11; 52:13–53:12). In their original context, these passages attempt to explain the harsh suffering the Israelites would pass through during their exile.

One song explicitly identifies the servant and Israel (Isaiah 49:3). But the servant was also said to be God's perfect Servant, which can only be Jesus. This paradigm makes sense of the most difficult aspect of the Jesus tradition—His suffering. Equally important, it pointed to the Gentiles as the object of God's healing and forgiveness alongside the Jews.

Background

God instructed His prophet, Isaiah, to write concerning Israel's captivity in Babylon. For seventy years, the nation suffered under this oppression. Then the Lord allowed them to return to Jerusalem. He gave them the resources to rebuild the Temple and establish themselves once again as God's representative.

But the Israelites got comfortable in Babylon. They became accustomed to the Babylonian ways and their gods. Most of the Israelites refused to move. Only a small remnant traveled back to Judah.

God speaks through Isaiah about these upcoming problems (Isaiah 48). In the first part of the chapter, he rebukes their negative attitudes and behaviors. However, God changes His tone in the last half of the chapter. In several of the later chapters of Isaiah, the Lord offers hope and help with the promise of the Messiah's coming. Like a loving mother attempting to get her cranky toddler to take a nap, the Father begins to speak softly. He highlighted promises about a coming Savior, Jesus, to save Israel and the entire world.

Are you willing to move forward on God's promises? Or are you staying behind, enjoying Babylonian, worldly comforts?

At-A-Glance

1. The Servant's Call and Mission
(Isaiah 49:1–7)
2. The Servant Saves and Restores
(vv. 8–11)

In Depth

1. The Servant's Call and Mission (Isaiah 49:1–7)

In the book of Isaiah, four passages are called "the Servant Songs" (Isaiah 42–50). The second song found here outlines the coming Messiah's mission on earth. Jesus, God's redeemer, brings light, healing, and restoration. He offers His salvation promises to the Jewish people and the entire world.

God speaks through the Messiah in the first person. He asks for listening ears. His calling started in the womb of His mother. Before the Holy Spirit placed Jesus' embryo in Mary's body, the angel said, His name is Jesus, the Savior of all humanity (Luke 1:31).

Isaiah compared Jesus' mouth, His words, to instruments of war. The well-polished sword and the shaft pierces the intended target. God kept Jesus out of the main limelight until a particular time in history. At the appointed time, He introduced the Savior and His penetrating message (Galatians 4:4–5).

Isaiah calls the Servant, whom we now understand to be the Messiah, by the name Israel. This nation originally carried God's salvation message. When the Jewish people rebelled, the Messiah picked up the baton, committed to completing God's assignment.

God called Jesus to draw back the Israelites to Jehovah. God raised Him and gave Him the might and power to carry out the task. The first Christian missionary and the authors of the Bible were Jewish people. God's instruments to introduce salvation to the world. The Servant fulfilled the covenant God made with the Israelites, and He is the actual covenant. Some of the Jewish people pushed Jesus aside, denying His claim as Messiah. They looked down upon Him, calling Him unclean, a liar. However, God viewed Him as valuable and deemed worthy of praise (1 Peter 2:4).

Jesus respected those in positions of authority in the secular government and within the Jewish religion. But both plotted against Him. When Jesus returns to the earth for the second time, He will be honored and worshiped. Rulers and every human being will prostrate before Him (Philippians 2:10–11).

How did Jesus complete the work that Israel was supposed to do?

2. The Servant Saves and Restores (vv. 8–11)

Jehovah heard the prayer of the Servant and helped Him fulfill a fruitful ministry. God is committed to lifting this universe out of its critical condition, placing His Spirit in desolate, godless places. His desire is for the entire human race to know the truth through His Son Jesus.

God frees captives. God freed the captives in Babylon, and He offers freedom to all humanity bound in sin. It is now possible to bask in the presence of a Holy God—no sin hinders or divides (Isaiah 61:1).

Messiah bids everyone come openly to the light. Christ found the Jews enslaved to the law, covered in the darkness, and separated from God. Christ lifted their burdens. The Compassionate Shepherd is always leading to greener pastures. Jesus keeps His sheep away from the scorching sun, leads them to lush feeding grounds and fresh water. Even in places that are downtrodden and barren—God provides for His sheep.

These promises are not only for the Jewish nation or people in biblical days. Jesus still saves and restores anyone willing to come to Him.

In a letter to the Corinthians, Paul references these verses and explains that "today is the day of salvation" (2 Corinthians 6:2). How does this affect our reading of Isaiah?

Search the Scriptures

1. Use the Scripture verses in Isaiah 49:1–11 to describe the characteristics and mission of the Lord's servant. (Example characteristics, v. 1 called before birth, v. 2 words of judgment are sharp, v. 3 a Servant; Example mission points: v. 1 wants people in distant and faraway lands to listen, v. 4 work seems useless)

2. In verse 1, Isaiah addresses the "isles," meaning a place far, far away from him. What expression would we use today to confer this understanding?

Discuss the Meaning

The Scriptures clearly state Jesus' job description. He came to seek and save humanity. His death on the Cross allowed freedom from the bondage of sin. This lesson reminds Christians that the Savior is light out of darkens, He restores, and our Shepherd to lead us into His beautiful pastures. Think about the past couple weeks. How have you seen Jesus do this in your life? What kinds of people or things have you or others turned to instead of Christ to foster a better life?

Liberating Lesson

The word "servant" does not always sit well with African Americans. It rakes up pictures in our minds of Black people as slaves or only getting a job as a maid, driver, or butler. Yet, when the word "servant" is used in the Bible, God desires for Christians to have a different picture. Jesus came to serve all humanity. He, too, was mistreated and unappreciated. But He kept placing itself in God's protective hands, being assured of God's watchful eye.

Get alone with God and express any anger or hostility you may feel about the mistreatment of people of color. Ask God to begin a transformation in your heart about how to be a true servant.

Application for Activation

Many individuals today continuously wonder, "What about me? What about me?" God saw the need for salvation. He sent Jesus to meet that need in our world, and Jesus completed God's assignment. As Christians, we are to answer the same call. Pray for more sensitivity to the Holy Spirit as we go through our daily activities. How can I help those around me foster the same attitude and be less selfish and self-centered?

Follow the Spirit

What God wants me to do:

_____

_____

_____

_____

Remember Your Thoughts

Special insights I have learned:

_____

_____

_____

_____

More Light on the Text

Isaiah 49:1–11

1 Listen, O isles, unto me; and hearken, ye people, from far; The LORD hath called me from the womb; from the bowels of my mother hath he made mention of my name.

Scholars often identify Isaiah 49:1–13 as the second of four "Servant Songs" that focus on an individual that we can now identify as the Messiah, Jesus Christ. (The others are found in Isaiah 42:1–9; 50:4–11; and 52:13–53:12.)

It is clear that this is a message that needs to be heard by all nations since even the "isles" are addressed. This remains true even today: the following message is relevant for all nations and all peoples, including African nations and those of African descent.

The speaker emphasizes that God had a special purpose for him even before he was born. God had chosen and "called" him even while in his mother's womb. This was certainly true of Jesus (Matthew 1:18–25). Every human being is placed on earth by God Himself, born in His image with great dignity, and with a purpose to bring God glory. So in a sense all people are named by God from birth. But in this case the speaker has received a unique calling that applies only to Jesus.

2 And he hath made my mouth like a sharp sword; in the shadow of his hand hath he hid me, and made me a polished shaft; in his quiver hath he hid me;

The speaker now describes how God has used him, based on his special calling. He is compared to a "sharp sword" and a "polished [arrow] shaft," images that likely mean that he will be used as an agent of God's judgment. But he will accomplish this task not through actions but through his mouth, through his words. He is described here as a prophet, since the prophets served as God's spokesmen, declaring God's judgment (see Jeremiah 23:29). The speaker also emphasizes that God "hid" him. God has protected him and kept him so that he will be available for God to use at the right time.

During Jesus' ministry on earth, teaching about the kingdom of God was His highest priority (see Mark 1:14–15). Through His words He called sinners to repent and rebuked religious leaders and others with prideful and hard hearts. Though His ultimate purpose was to bring salvation, He also proclaimed judgment and warned of the eternal wrath of God upon those who do not turn to Christ. This is a warning that all must hear in every time and place.

3 And said unto me, Thou art my servant, O Israel, in whom I will be glorified.

God now speaks to this man He has chosen from birth. His first words summarize his identity and purpose. We might call this his commission. First, He refers to him as "my servant." The Hebrew word for "servant," *ebed*

(**EH**-ved), appears many times throughout Isaiah 40–66 as a theme of this part of the book. In general, those God refers to as servants are those He has claimed for Himself and called for a special purpose in His plans. The nation of Israel is described as God's "servant" (Isaiah 41:8–10; 43:8–10), but they are blind and deaf, and have failed in their mission to the nations (42:18–20). So God now raises up an individual "servant," whose mission is about to be defined in verses 5–6.

God addresses this servant as "Israel." Because of this, one might be tempted to think that God is speaking to the whole nation here, but it is clear that this servant has a mission *to* Israel (vv. 5–6), so cannot at the same time *be* the whole nation. Most Christian scholars suggest that this does indeed refer to an individual, but God calls him "Israel" because he is now going to take on the role God had given the nation—and he will succeed where they have failed. The nation is no longer worthy of the name God had given to it (48:1–2), so this one servant will now represent the nation and carry out its task.

God's goal in using this servant is that He might be glorified. The word translated "be glorified" is *pa'ar* (pa-**AR**). This is a rare word that expresses God's desire to receive the honor and praise that He deserves. He will mainly achieve this through the salvation He brings to the nations through this servant (49:5–6).

All followers of Christ today are among the foreign "servants" Isaiah speaks of later in the book (Isaiah 56:6). We as believers have benefited from the work of the servant, who has died for our sins that we might be forgiven (Isaiah 53). Our ultimate goal is similarly to bring glory to God. We do not do this as Jesus did by dying on the Cross, but we do spread this message of salvation through evangelism. We also bring glory to God in many other ways through living as Christ did, including pursuing love and justice.

4 Then I said, I have laboured in vain, I have spent my strength for nought, and in vain: yet surely my judgment is with the LORD, and my work with my God.

Despite this high calling, the servant replies to God with discouragement. The work has not been easy, he has faced much resistance, and he feels as though it has all been "in vain" and useless. This servant will not minister in power but in weakness and suffering, which will be especially clear in later Servant Songs (Isaiah 53:3–12). But the servant expresses not only discouragement but also confidence in God. He leaves the outcome of his work to God's judgment and in God's hands. Jesus faced exhaustion in His ministry at times, and was discouraged even with His own disciples in their inability to understand His teachings and have faith in Him (Mark 4:35–41). Still, He strove to do the Father's will and in the last, commended His spirit to the Father.

Many will find it easy to identify with the feelings of the servant here, especially those who have been neglected and forgotten. Many may work faithfully unto the Lord, but see little of the fruit or results of their labors. Many remain unrecognized and unappreciated. Nevertheless, the follower of Christ must place their ultimate confidence in God, knowing that He alone remains the judge of our work on earth. We must, then, seek to use our time and efforts to bring glory to Christ and advance His kingdom, and trust that we will one day be rewarded despite the hardships involved now.

5 And now, saith the LORD that formed me from the womb to be his servant, to bring Jacob again to him, Though Israel be not gathered, yet shall I be glorious in the eyes of the LORD, and my God shall be my strength.

The focus now shifts back to the Lord and His announcement of the servant's mission. God connects the servant's calling from birth (from verse 1) to his role as God's servant (from verse 3). He then reveals "part one" of his mission: to bring the nation of Israel back to God. This does not refer to Israel's physical return to the land of Canaan (as in 48:20–21), but their spiritual return to God Himself. Throughout Israel's history they have been rebellious, worshiping other gods and disregarding the God who had delivered them from Egypt. Yet God will use this servant to finally restore Israel to fellowship with God, repairing the broken relationship.

The servant further explains his relationship with God in the second part of the verse. He is fully dependent on the Lord, looking to Him for strength to accomplish his mission. And because of his obedience and success, God Himself makes him "glorious."

6 And he said, It is a light thing that thou shouldest be my servant to raise up the tribes of Jacob, and to restore the preserved of Israel: I will also give thee for a light to the Gentiles, that thou mayest be my salvation unto the end of the earth.

This is the central verse in the text, where God clearly describes the mission of this servant: he will restore the "preserved" of Israel. This indicates that it is not necessarily the case that every ethnic Israelite will be redeemed, but only that portion of the nation that turns back to God (a remnant). But then God says that restoring Israel is not enough! This is only "part one" of his mission! This statement comes as some surprise because restoring Israel is not a small or "light" (KJV) matter at all. This has been a major focus of the Old Testament, something God's faithful people have awaited for centuries. Yet God has even bigger plans in mind.

"Part two" of his mission is to be "a light to the Gentiles, that thou mayest be my salvation unto the end of the earth" (see also Isaiah 42:6). The Hebrew word translated "Gentiles," *goyim* (go-**YIM**), typically refers to the various people groups of the world apart from the nation of Israel. God's plan, then, is for salvation to reach all peoples, even to "the end of the earth." This has always been true. From the time God first called Abraham and blessed him, He did so not simply so that Israel could enjoy being blessed, but so that they might be a channel of blessing to all peoples (see Genesis 12:3). Israel had failed to be this blessing. But the individual servant, the new "Israel," will now succeed.

Jesus is this servant. He calls Himself the "light of the world" (John 8:12; see also John 1:9). The name Jesus is based on the Hebrew word for "salvation," *yeshuah* (ye-shu-**AH**), because "he will save his people from their sins" (Matthew 1:21). He accomplishes this when He takes the deserved punishment for sins upon Himself at the Cross (see Isaiah 53:4–6), and then defeats death through His resurrection. Because this salvation is not only for the Jew but the Gentile as well, He commissions His followers to "teach all nations" (Matthew 28:19).

We are living in a time when we can see that God's salvation in Jesus Christ truly has reached to the ends of the earth and covered the globe. From the very beginning, it was God's design to incorporate African peoples into His Church, and today there are more professing Christians in Africa than on any other continent. In response, God's people should worship, praise, and give thanks to God for His grace and mercy toward undeserving sinners, and continue to spread this good news among those who have not yet experienced this salvation.

We now see the response of the people to the servant. After the joyful tone of verse 6, it is surprising to discover that this man who has brought salvation to all nations will be despised and abhorred. He is also described here as "servant of rulers." Although "servant" has been used in a positive sense throughout the passage so far, in this case it is negative, and probably better translated "slave." This may refer to Jesus' experience of being dominated and abused by Jewish and Roman rulers as He was sentenced to crucifixion.

But God's message for His servant is that this is not the end of the story. Though rejected initially, kings and princes will eventually give him the respect and honor that he deserves. He will be acknowledged as King of kings and Lord of lords. This dramatic change from rejection to honor, and the exaltation is entirely the Lord's doing. He is faithful to His chosen servant. Verse 7 summarizes and anticipates the final "Servant Song" (Isaiah 52:13–53:12). There, his rejection is described in greater detail, but the story again ends in triumph and the submission of kings (see 52:13–15; 53:12), all brought about by the Lord.

Many of African descent have similarly experienced being despised and rejected. But they too will experience God's faithful vindication, as Christ did, if they are united to Christ by faith. The book of Revelation envisions that one day, when Christ returns, all of His people will reign over the world with Him as kings and queens (see Revelation 5:10; 22:5). But this is only true of those who have received the forgiveness of sins through faith in Christ.

7 Thus saith the LORD, the Redeemer of Israel, and his Holy One, to him whom man despiseth, to him whom the nation abhorreth, to a servant of rulers, Kings shall see and arise, princes also shall worship, because of the LORD that is faithful, and the Holy One of Israel, and he shall choose thee.

8 Thus saith the LORD, In an acceptable time have I heard thee, and in a day of salvation have I helped thee: and I will preserve thee, and give thee for a covenant of the people, to establish the earth, to cause to inherit the desolate heritages;

God assures His Servant that He will be with him to help in his greatest need, which probably refers to the road to the Cross. God again describes His purpose for the servant, but says it in a different way: "I will…give thee for a covenant of the people." Jesus is the mediator of the new covenant described in the prophets (Jeremiah 31:31–34). His death for the sin of the people is the basis for the new covenant. The blessings of the new covenant in the Church today are only experienced "in Christ" (see Ephesians 1:3–14). Since Jesus is at the center of this new covenant relationship between God and His people, it is appropriate to identify the servant Jesus with the covenant itself.

Who the "people" are in this covenant is not entirely clear. On one hand, the term here for people, *am* (**AHM**), is usually used to refer to the nation of Israel, to be distinguished from the *goyim* (go-**YIM**) mentioned in verse 6. On the other hand, verse 6 just emphasized that salvation will be for all peoples. Also, in the chapters to come Israel is redefined so that foreigners who worship the Lord are fully included in the new people of God. So the "people" could include all of the "servants" who follow Jesus, regardless of their ethnicity.

9 That thou mayest say to the prisoners, Go forth; to them that are in darkness, Shew yourselves. They shall feed in the ways, and their pastures shall be in all high places. 10 They shall not hunger nor thirst; neither shall the heat nor sun smite them: for he that hath mercy on them shall lead them, even by the springs of water shall he guide them.

In the ancient world a just and good king would provide for his people, bring prosperity, and free prisoners. This is what this servant King does as well. He proclaims that those imprisoned are free and brings those living in oppressive darkness into the light. Although God is surely concerned with unjust physical bondage, as seen in the Exodus, his greater concern is with spiritual bondage to sin and the powers of darkness, which is likely the focus here (Colossians 1:13–14).

It is tempting to rely on our own efforts, others, or even the government for protection, provision, and freedom. But ultimately as God's people we must look to Christ for these things as our Good Shepherd. We look to God to provide for our needs while on earth when we seek first His kingdom (Matthew 6:33). And we endure hardships, knowing that they are just a light momentary affliction compared to the eternal rest we will experience with Christ when He returns one day (see 2 Corinthians 4:16–18).

11 And I will make all my mountains a way, and my highways shall be exalted.

In the ancient world without cars and airplanes, natural features such as mountains, valleys, and bodies of water were significant obstacles for travel. So one of the common images of return to the Promised Land is that God will make the journey as easy as possible. He will flatten the mountains. He will lift up a broad highway above the valleys so that the path is visible, straight, and smooth. Nothing will get in the way of this grand gathering of peoples to God. Even if these verses have a physical return to land in mind, this is clearly figurative language. The point is not really that God will cut down mountains but that He will enable a smooth return at every step along the way. As explained above, though, it is likely that these images from the exodus from Egypt and the return from Babylon are being used to describe a greater, more important exodus: a return to a right relationship with God through the forgiveness of sins, brought about through the work of the servant.

Sources:

Barr, David L. *The New Testament Story: An Introduction*. Belmont, Calif.: Wadsworth Publishing Company, 1987, 27.

Childs, Brevard S. *Isaiah*. Old Testament Library. Louisville: Westminster/John Knox, 2001.

Motyer, J. Alec. *Isaiah*. Tyndale Old Testament Commentaries. Downers Grove: InterVarsity, 1999.

Oswalt, John N. *The Book of Isaiah: Chapters 40–66*. New International Commentary on the Old Testament. Grand Rapids: Eerdmans, 1998.

Walton, John H., Victor H. Matthews, and Mark W. Chavalas. *The IVP Bible Background Commentary: Old Testament*. Downers Grove: InterVarsity, 2000.

Say It Correctly

Enigmatic. eh-nig-MAH-tik.
Eunuch. YOU-nik.

Daily Bible Readings

MONDAY
God's Redemption Defies
Human Wisdom
(1 Corinthians 1:18–25)

TUESDAY
Righteousness, Sanctification,
and Redemption
(1 Corinthians 1:26–31)

WEDNESDAY
God Sent Redemption to God's People
(Psalm 111)

THURSDAY
Christ Brings Eternal Redemption
(Hebrews 9:11–14)

FRIDAY
Pardon My Guilt, O Lord
(Psalm 25:1–11)

SATURDAY
Redeem Israel, O God
(Psalm 25:12–22)

SUNDAY
The Lord Will Have Compassion
(Isaiah 49:1–11)

Notes

_____

_____

_____

_____

Teaching Tips

Words You Should Know

A. Standard (Isaiah 49:22) *nasas* (Heb.)—Sort, kind

B. Nursing (v. 23) *yanaq* (Heb.)—Tending, nourishing at the breast, education, maintaining

Teacher Preparation

Unifying Principle—All Things Put Right. When freedom from oppression is realized, it is hard to believe. From where do freedom and blessings come? Creator God will restore relationship between God's people, nations, the land, and the next generation in ways that confirm God's Lordship.

A. Read the Bible Background and Devotional Reading.

B. Pray for your students and lesson clarity.

C. Read the lesson Scripture in multiple translations.

O—Open the Lesson

A. Begin the class with prayer.

B. Play a trailer for a popular dystopian movie (*1984*, *Fahrenheit 451*, *Minority Report*, *Metropolis*, etc.). Discuss why we fear that the world will get worse and worse. The Bible tells us the only way the world will become better.

C. Have the students read the Aim for Change and the In Focus story.

D. Ask students how events like those in the story weigh on their hearts and how they can view these events from a faith perspective.

P—Present the Scriptures

A. Read the Focal Verses and discuss the Background and The People, Places, and Times sections.

B. Have the class share what Scriptures stand out for them and why, with particular emphasis on today's themes.

E—Explore the Meaning

A. Use In Depth or More Light on the Text to facilitate a deeper discussion of the lesson text.

B. Pose the questions in Search the Scriptures and Discuss the Meaning.

C. Discuss the Liberating Lesson and Application for Activation sections.

N—Next Steps for Application

A. Summarize the value of strengthening a transparent and intimate relationship with God.

B. End class with a commitment to pray to trust that God works in their best interest, even when they fail God.

Worship Guide

For the Superintendent or Teacher
Theme: God's Restored People
Shall Prosper
Song: "There Shall be Showers of Blessing"

God's Restored People Shall Prosper

Bible Background • ISAIAH 49:18–26
Printed Text • ISAIAH 49:18–23 | Devotional Reading • PROVERBS 25:21–26

—————— Aim for Change ——————

By the end of this lesson, we will IDENTIFY relationships in which individuals or congregations have experienced God's restoration, FIND comfort in the plans God has for their lives, and PROCLAIM God's justice and mercy for His people.

———————— In Focus ————————

Jakiesha, an accountant, was going through a difficult time in her life. She was angry with God and the church. No one was doing things the way they should, so she thought. She became so angry she refused to pray anymore. She even made the decision to no longer attend church. Lastly, she gave Pastor Fred a piece of her mind.

Concerned, Jakiesha's Gran-gran, persuaded her to come over for dinner one evening. They talked about all God had provided in Jakiesha's life: her safe home, her scholarship to an HBCU, her first job. "What are you even mad about, baby?" Gran-gran asked.

Jakiesha felt ashamed now even mentioning it to her grandmother. "There's just a certain way I know they can be done. The church doesn't want to take the shortcuts I show them, even though—trust me—EVERYONE else saves themselves money that way."

"Baby," Gran-gran said, "I love you, but that sounds like some shady dealings in my book."

Jakiesha couldn't keep up her excuses to her grandmother. God changed her heart. She and her grandmother prayed for forgiveness.

After prayer, Jakiesha told her grandmother, "God has forgiven me and restored me in right relationship with Him. He is a God of justice and mercy and I am a recipient. I'm going to apologize to Pastor Fred and to the entire congregation."

After speaking with Pastor Fred, he told her, "We thank God for answering our prayers. Now that we know you have repented, Jakiesha, we do need an accountant again."

After experiencing difficult challenges, being restored back to God, are you a witness to God's indescribable faithfulness?

—————— Keep in Mind ——————

"And kings shall be thy nursing fathers, and their queens thy nursing mothers: they shall bow down to thee with their face toward the earth, and lick up the dust of thy feet; and thou shalt know that I am the LORD: for they shall not be ashamed that wait for me."
(Isaiah 49:23, KJV)

"Kings and queens will serve you and care for all your needs. They will bow to the earth before you and lick the dust from your feet. Then you will know that I am the LORD. Those who trust in me will never be put to shame." (Isaiah 49:23, NLT)

Focal Verses

KJV Isaiah 49:18 Lift up thine eyes round about, and behold: all these gather themselves together, and come to thee. As I live, saith the LORD, thou shalt surely clothe thee with them all, as with an ornament, and bind them on thee, as a bride doeth.

19 For thy waste and thy desolate places, and the land of thy destruction, shall even now be too narrow by reason of the inhabitants, and they that swallowed thee up shall be far away.

20 The children which thou shalt have, after thou hast lost the other, shall say again in thine ears, The place is too strait for me: give place to me that I may dwell.

21 Then shalt thou say in thine heart, Who hath begotten me these, seeing I have lost my children, and am desolate, a captive, and removing to and fro? and who hath brought up these? Behold, I was left alone; these, where had they been?

22 Thus saith the Lord GOD, Behold, I will lift up mine hand to the Gentiles, and set up my standard to the people: and they shall bring thy sons in their arms, and thy daughters shall be carried upon their shoulders.

23 And kings shall be thy nursing fathers, and their queens thy nursing mothers: they shall bow down to thee with their face toward the earth, and lick up the dust of thy feet; and thou shalt know that I am the LORD: for they shall not be ashamed that wait for me.

NLT Isaiah 49:18 "Look around you and see, for all your children will come back to you. As surely as I live," says the LORD, "they will be like jewels or bridal ornaments for you to display.

19 Even the most desolate parts of your abandoned land will soon be crowded with your people. Your enemies who enslaved you will be far away.

20 The generations born in exile will return and say, 'We need more room! It's crowded here!'

21 Then you will think to yourself, 'Who has given me all these descendants? For most of my children were killed, and the rest were carried away into exile. I was left here all alone. Where did all these people come from? Who bore these children? Who raised them for me?'"

22 This is what the Sovereign LORD says: "See, I will give a signal to the godless nations. They will carry your little sons back to you in their arms; they will bring your daughters on their shoulders.

23 Kings and queens will serve you and care for all your needs. They will bow to the earth before you and lick the dust from your feet. Then you will know that I am the LORD. Those who trust in me will never be put to shame."

The People, Places, and Times

The Progeny Blessing. Having children as heirs to continue the covenant people of God has always been a major theme of God's story with humanity. Scholars call this aspect of God's promise to His people the "progeny blessing." When Abram first arrived in Canaan, God promised to give the land to his descendants, even though at the time, he was 75 years old and had no heir. Later, God again promises Abram an heir of his own flesh and blood, and as many descendants as stars in the sky (Genesis 15:4–5). By the time Abram is 99 years old, he has fathered a son who will indeed become a great nation, but God makes a further promise. Abram will be the father of many nations, and is renamed Abraham. Sarai is renamed Sarah, and named as the one who will mother the child of God's covenant with Abraham. Isaac fulfills this promise. Isaac and Rebekah struggle for many years to have children before God blesses them with twins. The elder son, Esau, fathers his own nation, and the younger son, Jacob, ends up with four wives. For a time, the favored wife Rachel is concerned that she will not bear, and though she does give birth to two sons, she dies in bearing the second. This gives Jacob a total of 12 sons, who each have multiple children themselves. The nation of Israel blossoms from this point.

The rollercoaster drama of the difficulty of conceiving, bearing, and raising one (let alone many) children is a constant narrative thread from Genesis 12 through chapter 30. It continues to play a large role in later sacred stories of Samson's family, Hannah, Bathsheba, and others. Even in less drastic stories, children are always seen as a blessing from God. Throughout Scripture, Israel can judge if it is being blessed or not by how many children they are having.

In the pre-industrial age, more children meant more workers to help bring in food or trade to help the family survive. Children were their parents' only financial safety net in old age. In an economic system like this, losing one's children was financially devastating, in addition to being heartbreaking. This is why it is a major theme in the prophecies of returning from exile that they will have many children.

Background

God's people were in captivity because they were obstinate and stubborn (Isaiah 48:4). He told Israel if they disobeyed, He would scatter them. Then He would restore them back (Deuteronomy 30:1–3). God placed His people in a place of affliction (Isaiah 48:10). Through Isaiah, God is speaking to His people

with comfort and mercy (Isaiah 48:20; 49:13). He says, "All things begin and end with me" (Isaiah 48:12).

God declares to His people they should flee from the Chaldeans (Isaiah 48:20). This was similar to the charge given their ancestors who had fled from Egypt while depending on God to sustain them (Isaiah 48:21). God's people are given the promise to be released, restored, and prosperous once again. God's people are promised a temporary freedom from their earthly captivity and a permanent freedom through Jesus Christ from captivity of sin. Restoration will be given on the day of salvation. This is in reference to Christ's kingdom when God's people will be restored and prosper (Isaiah 48:8-9).

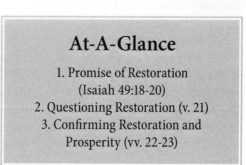

At-A-Glance

1. Promise of Restoration
(Isaiah 49:18-20)
2. Questioning Restoration (v. 21)
3. Confirming Restoration and
Prosperity (vv. 22-23)

In Depth

1. Promise of Restoration (Isaiah 49:18–20)

Look all around and see all the people gathering back to the Lord. They are the children of the people of captivity. Coming from many different places to meet in one place, they will make one body and join themselves to glorify God. These words spoken during the exile were intended to encourage God's people. He implies that the land of Judea was lying in waste during the Babylonian captivity. "Thy land of destruction" contrasts with what was to come.

The increase of people will be so great in number. This will come after many have been killed in wars and died in captivity in a faraway land. There will be a great increase as if these children had been given to a widowed mother.

The added people would be a blessing and strength as an ornament to God's people. The Lord wanted to assure them of His commitment to what He was saying. "As I live, saith the LORD" was a solemn promise between God and His people. The bride, wearing fancy jewelry, indicated these children will portray beauty and glorify the Lord.

Likewise, when the people of God were in a wasted, desolate, and unproductive state, there manifested the Savior of the world, the introduction of the Gospel, and the transformation of the Gentiles.

How do we see God fulfilling this kind of restoration throughout salvation history?

2. Questioning Restoration (v. 21)

This describes the great increase of the true people of God. The image given is of a mother who had been robbed of her children and made a widow. She had seen the devastation of ruin that was spread all around her. She felt alone. Then all of sudden the mother sees herself completely surrounded with more children than she lost. She is home and blessed by the happy family that surrounds her. Then the mother asks, "Who hath begotten me these?" She wants to know where they had been. God's restoration would be beyond what we could hope for.

Why does God choose the image of children to illustrate the overflowing blessing of restoration He has in store?

3. Confirming Restoration and Prosperity (vv. 22–23)

God will call His people to Himself, like a general calling the troops together. He will set the standard for His people. Those that God has adopted as His own and those that claim Him for

their Father will be in His arms. Those He adopts will be given great care, devotion, and loving-kindness, as a nurse would care for babies. The daughters will be carried as a sick and weak person might be carried. Nonbelievers will give to the increase, protection, and maintenance of these children. Even those in high positions such as kings and queens will have a heartfelt love and caring concern toward God's people.

How does God use non-Christians to aid His Church today?

Search the Scriptures

1. What shall cause the desolate places to become too small (Isaiah 49:19)?

2. Who can ask for another place to dwell (v. 20)?

3. When kings and queens become nursing fathers and mothers to God's people, what shall they know (v. 23)?

Discuss the Meaning

1. God restores and prospers His people. Should His people do anything to help secure their prosperity?

2. When God grants restoration, what is our responsibility? How do we show our gratitude? How do we maintain our blessings?

Liberating Lesson

Today, there are many people who need to be restored to God because of sin. Who can restore us? Jesus will lift us up when we feel neglected, abandoned, and bereaved. God restored Israel; He will also restore us. He will give us freedom when we're enslaved by our own choices and disobedience. Jesus is waiting to restore us so that we can have a relationship with God. We must repent, pray, and wait on the restoration of the Lord! We must depend on God's promises to bring the Gentiles and His people together into one people of God through Jesus Christ.

Application for Activation

This week think of how you can overcome discouragement from the enemy who creeps into your peace. Ask God to restore you to Himself when you have allowed the enemy to take your joy. Remember that Jesus Christ has come to redeem you and wants you to have the right relationship with Him and others. He's coming back!

Think of what you can do to restore a broken friendship with a family member or a friend who you consider to be your enemy. Ask yourself, "Am I the enemy?" What should you do to become a better Christian?

Follow the Spirit

What God wants me to do:

_____

_____

_____

_____

Remember Your Thoughts

Special insights I have learned:

_____

_____

_____

_____

More Light on the Text
Isaiah 49:18–23

Reading the prior lesson is necessary to fully grasp the beauty of what the Lord is expressing in this week's verses. Let us begin with an overall picture for context: this lesson is ultimately about God's deliverance and grace as He liberates His people—the people who were once the ancient kingdom of Judah—who have been both held in captivity and exiled from Jerusalem by the Babylonians after Nebuchadnezzar prevailed against the King Zedekiah and the Judeans. After King Zedekiah, the last wicked king was defeated, the Babylonians destroyed Solomon's Temple. In our lesson, the Lord not only vows to liberate them, but He promises to restore what they have lost in terms of the Temple and community. Not only will God restore what they have lost, but He will give them more than they ever asked for. This restoration will also include enlisting new people into the family of God. Even Gentiles will come to know God and worship Him unashamedly.

18 Lift up thine eyes round about, and behold: all these gather themselves together, and come to thee. As I live, saith the LORD, thou shalt surely clothe thee with them all, as with an ornament, and bind them on thee, as a bride doeth.

Zion (also known as Jerusalem)—personified as a woman, as the restored bride of God—is coping with her feelings of loss, desertion, and abandonment. Zion recognizes that her position of captivity was the result of her own choices but still bemoans the pain of not being in the presence of the Lord any longer. We imagine that she is filled with regret, coping with the guilt of knowing that she broke God's heart with her unfaithfulness. Picture her crying every day while reflecting about her previous life with God. Her tears are dried, however, when she learns that the Lord has not left her permanently. Through the Lord's grace and forgiveness, He plans on restoring all that was taken from her and destroyed. Zion, in shock and glee, is comforted by not only the Lord's presence but the Lord's explicit declaration of commitment to His covenant in spite of what she has done historically by breaking her vows to Him.

In verse 18, the Lord says to Zion, to the broken-hearted exiles, look around, look up, open your eyes and behold the process of your own restoration. When the text says "As I live, saith the LORD," the Lord is in many ways renewing the vows, breathing fresh air into the ancient Abrahamic covenant and declares once again that Zion is His bride—in spite of what she has done—and she will be adorned with the children who are returning to her. John alludes to this text when he describes the New Jerusalem "as a bride adorned for her husband" (Revelation 21:2). In the New Testament, the church of Jesus Christ is the extension of the Lord's covenant with the kingdom of Judah. Isn't it wonderful to be bound with God in the name of Jesus? The Hebrew word for "bind" in this text is *qashar* (kaw-**SHAR**), which means to "league together" or "conspire." It means to politically form a group or plot together. This means the Lord and His children will conspire together and be freed from the oppressors that God used to punish them. This is the beginning of the Lord renewing the relationship between Himself and Zion, and restoring them with more children and more blessings than they lost.

19 For thy waste and thy desolate places, and the land of thy destruction, shall even now be too narrow by reason of the inhabitants, and they that swallowed thee up shall be far away.

After stating God will regroup the people who were lost and separated because of the Babylonians, God then says through Isaiah that He will restore the land with people to the point where it will be overpopulated. In spite of the fact that Zion is at this moment wasted and desolated, it can be restored. The Hebrew word for "desolate" in this text is *shamem*

(shaw-**MEM**), and it is used repeatedly in Jeremiah's writings when referring to the Exile (Jeremiah 10:25; 33:10; Lamentations 1:4; 5:18). *Shamem* simply means to be either desolated or appalled. Both words carry the logic and reason for the destruction of the Temple and the subsequent captivity of the people of Judea. Because of Judea's unfaithfulness to the Lord, because they were enamored with other gods and rituals that were not their own, the Lord allowed the destruction and enslavement of the Babylonians.

But the Lord recovers what was once lost; the Lord repairs that which was once broken; and the Lord restores whatever was once damaged. Through the Lord's redemption, Zion will be restored and even though she lost soldiers in battle, even though she lost children in captivity, the new inhabitants who will benefit from the Lord's redemption will grow in number exponentially, and the people will once again be free and far from the enemies who seek to destroy them and keep them captive. This highlights that even in God's anger, He has an irrevocable love for His people. God's anger does not last once there is repentance. God forgives.

God forgives so much that the blessings that Israel imagines will make them happy is too narrow to God. Have you ever asked God for something and He not only provides you with it but He adds additional blessings? Have you experienced God's love in ways that exceeded even your own expectations and desires? Isn't it a blessing that the Lord's goodness exceeds our own imaginations of goodness? What God wants for us as His people is better and more than anything we can imagine for ourselves. Since we are God's bride, bound to God in the name of Jesus, God delights in giving blessings. God loves His people and wants nothing more than to maintain the relationships He has with those who seek to sustain a mutual relationship with Him.

20 The children which thou shalt have, after thou hast lost the other, shall say again in thine ears, The place is too strait for me: give place to me that I may dwell.

After the Lord promises to restore Zion and fill the land with people, the Lord then says that the number of people will have grown to the point that Zion declares she is out of room. What was once deserted and abandoned will eventually become overcrowded. This change will once again display God's ability to deliver and restore.

"Give place" is technically a rough translation of the Hebrew. The Hebrew word for "give place" is *nagash* (naw-**GOSH**) and means "to draw near" or "approach." In other words, it can also mean to come close or stand near. Therefore, the children born during bereavement and grief will say that it is crowded here, but provide me with space that is near you, that is not too far from you, that is close to you at all times. Zion will be filled with people once again, but the people will not want to be out of proximity from what they lost. They will remember what happened and cherish being in the land of their ancestors and their God.

21 Then shalt thou say in thine heart, Who hath begotten me these, seeing I have lost my children, and am desolate, a captive, and removing to and fro? and who hath brought up these? Behold, I was left alone; these, where had they been?

There will be so many people in Zion that the bereaved mother and bride will wonder where these people came from. How could they be her children if so many of her sons were lost in captivity? Zion will be astonished at the restoration happening in front of her eyes. This astonishment is also connected to imagery of the mothers of the Jewish people who were once incapable of conceiving children (Genesis 16:1; 30:1) and found themselves astonished at

what the Lord did for them. Zion, like Sarah and Rachel, were at one point despondent about their condition until the Lord surprised them with a blessing they considered unfathomable. Isaiah invokes the mothers in Genesis to highlight what the Lord has done in the past in order to show what God is capable of doing in the present and future.

The blessings of restoration and redemption will also overwhelm Zion. Jerusalem will return and be plentiful. This blessing will overwhelm Judea to the point where she will ask questions in her heart that reveal the embarrassing abundance of God's blessings. As already stated, she has lost children in captivity, but the growth in new children arriving during bereavement will compel her to ask how this restoration is possible. While the land was emptied by the Babylonian Exile, Yahweh—through His servant—will not only restore the population but fill the land to overflowing with returning people. The fourth servant song is immediately followed with the command to a redeemed Israel to "enlarge the site of your tent" and to "spread out to the right and to the left" to "settle the desolate towns" (Isaiah 54:2–3).

As we read this passage as New Testament believers, we also see that even as much as God fulfilled the promise to the Israelites when they returned to the Promised Land from exile, He also brought another kind of fulfillment after Christ's resurrection. He again brought in a flood of believers to join the faithful by welcoming Gentiles into the family. Then again, we look forward to seeing the ultimate fulfillment of this promise in heaven as every nation, tribe, and tongue glorify God.

The church can also understand it has a part to play in bringing about this influx of people. God commanded Adam and Eve to be fruitful and multiply. In a way, Jesus' Great Commission is a similar command that when we go out into the world, we are to grow the number of faithful.

22 Thus saith the Lord GOD, Behold, I will lift up mine hand to the Gentiles, and set up my standard to the people: and they shall bring thy sons in their arms, and thy daughters shall be carried upon their shoulders.

Not only will the Lord bless the chosen people, but the Lord will also invite Gentiles to recognize the truth of God's existence. These Gentiles will then turn from worshiping false gods and start worshiping Yahweh in spirit and in truth. When God says, "Behold, I will lift up mine hand," it is meant to bring the imagery of a sworn oath as in the military.

What Isaiah is saying here is that God will do two things. First, God will enlist other peoples to help free the captives. Secondly, God will also invite and accept them into His care and concern. In other words, in the process of delivering the captives from their oppressors, that deliverance will function as a type of witnessing. Non-Jewish people will see the glory of the Lord in the event of Zion's redemption. Historically, this shows that God has the power to not only use Cyrus and the Persians to free the people from captivity in Babylon, but also that God has the power to convince the world that He can do the same for them. The Gentiles across the world will be able to recognize God's grace and compassion and will ultimately want to serve Him, too.

After using military imagery, Isaiah then uses the imagery of children. The imagery of sons who are brought in arms and daughters carried on shoulders creates an imagery of God using Gentiles to carry the people of Zion back to their land. The event described by Isaiah is reminiscent of the Exodus. Just like children were carried out of Egypt, out of slavery, children will again be carried out of Babylonian bondage. The same God who freed the people once can free them again. What God has done and accomplished in the past is not frozen in history, but proof of what God can always do in a moment of His choosing.

23 And kings shall be thy nursing fathers, and their queens thy nursing mothers: they shall bow down to thee with their face toward the earth, and lick up the dust of thy feet; and thou shalt know that I am the LORD: for they shall not be ashamed that wait for me.

When Isaiah says "kings shall be thy nursing fathers" the text uses the word *aman* (Heb. aw-**MON**) or guardian. God will use Gentiles to free Israel, protect them, and provide for them. For sure, it is easy to misinterpret the text here; but we must remember the socio-politics of the relationship between Zion, the bride of God, and God in general. We must also remember the allegorical nature of the text. When the text says kings and queens will nurse them, he is saying that the Gentiles will also be a source of sustenance for them. Moreover, the Lord is also saying that the kings and queens will also bow to them, what Isaiah is saying is that they will bow to Zion as a way of bowing directly to God. Zion, as the bride of God, is the representative of God. God exists in and through Zion. Thus, when the kings and queens of other people "lick up the dust of [Zion's] feet," they are acknowledging the supreme power and grandeur of Yahweh. God's enlisting of Gentiles, and subsequent invitation into the true religion of Yahweh, will also mean that God will welcome these non-Jewish people into the family. They will not only worship the Lord, but they will do so unashamedly.

This lesson sheds light on God's ability to restore what was lost. He renews His vows with the chosen people, exhibits unfathomable grace and forgiveness and then promises to restore them to the point that will run out of room. This oncoming event will be so glorious that Gentiles will eventually make Yahweh their God and worship Him in spirit and in truth. This lesson highlights the notion that God will never abandon you, and even when it seems like it, take heart and know that God is faithful and committed. God will never leave you nor forsake you.

Sources:
Blenkinsopp, J. *Isaiah 40-55*. New York: Doubleday. 2002.
Kissane, E. *The Book Of Isaiah*. Dublin: Browne and Nolan, 1960
Knight, G. *Servant Theology*. Edinburgh: Handsel Press, 1984.
Roberts, J. and Machinist, P. *First Isaiah*. Baltimore, MD: Fortress Press, 2016.

Say It Correctly

Nebuchadnezzar. neh-buh-kad-NEZZ-zer.
Zedekiah. zeh-deh-KIE-uh.

Daily Bible Readings

MONDAY
God Puts Down and Lifts Up
(Psalm 75)

TUESDAY
God Protects a Restored, Holy People
(Leviticus 26:3–13)

WEDNESDAY
Blessings upon God's People
(Luke 6:20–26)

THURSDAY
God Has Turned Mourning into Dancing
(Psalm 30)

FRIDAY
God Gives Good Gifts
(James 1:13–18)

SATURDAY
Blessings for Obedience
(Deuteronomy 28:9–14)

SUNDAY
Wait for the Lord
(Isaiah 49:18–23)

Notes

_____

_____

_____

_____

Teaching Tips

June 26
Bible Study Guide 4

Words You Should Know

A. Hearken (Isaiah 51:1) *qashab* (Heb.)—To prick up the ears, to cause to hear, give heed

B. Hewn (v. 1) *gazith* (Heb.)—To cut or carve, to split or divide

Teacher Preparation

Unifying Principle—Back to Basics. People of integrity find it difficult to ignore criticism. Where do they find affirmation in the face of adversity? God delivers the righteous from the judgment of others when they are faithful to God's teachings.

A. Read the Bible Background and Devotional Reading.

B. Pray for your students and lesson clarity.

C. Read the lesson Scripture in multiple translations.

O—Open the Lesson

A. Begin the class with prayer.

B. Begin class by asking volunteers to respond to some questions about their families. For example: Whose family immigrated to this country in the past three generations? Who can tell us the meaning of their family name? Who knows that they are distantly related to someone famous? Has any member of your family ever started a family business? After allowing a few volunteers to share, lead into Bible study by saying Isaiah encouraged Israel to be encouraged by looking back at their family history.

C. Have the students read the Aim for Change and the In Focus story.

D. Ask students how events like those in the story weigh on their hearts and how they can view these events from a faith perspective.

P—Present the Scriptures

A. Read the Focal Verses and discuss the Background and The People, Places, and Times sections.

B. Have the class share what Scriptures stand out for them and why, with particular emphasis on today's themes.

E—Explore the Meaning

A. Use In Depth or More Light on the Text to facilitate a deeper discussion of the lesson text.

B. Pose the questions in Search the Scriptures and Discuss the Meaning.

C. Discuss the Liberating Lesson and Application for Activation sections.

N—Next Steps for Application

A. Summarize the value of rejecting charges that their hopes lay in feelings or fairy tales and pointing to historical accounts of God's work.

B. End class with a commitment to praising God that the best days are yet to come, when He restores them for eternity.

THUR 7:30pm
I. P.

(213) 338- 8477

God Offers Deliverance

893 5948 4624 ##

Bible Background • ISAIAH 51
Printed Text • ISAIAH 51:1-8 | Devotional Reading • 2 THESSALONIANS 3:1-4

— Aim for Change —

By the end of this lesson, we will EXAMINE Isaiah's example of God's rich faithfulness in Israel's spiritual history, TRUST God even when others speak disparagingly about our faith, and SHARE the goodness and deliverance of God with others.

— In Focus —

Kaylynn had been incarcerated for a crime he did not commit. He believed the day would come when God would clear his name and he would be delivered from his bondage. He had held close to the words found in Isaiah, "The Sovereign Lord helps me, I will not be put to shame, He who vindicates me is near. Who then will bring charges against me? It is the Sovereign Lord who helps me!" (Isaiah 50:7–9).

He trusted God. He had gotten into some situations in the past, being accused falsely and misjudged, and God delivered him out every time.

But, this time, the setup led to his imprisonment. His friends and associates felt sorry for him. But they didn't believe Kaylynn would get out of this one easily and they told him to plead guilty and he would get a lesser charge. Kaylynn stood his ground and said, "How can I confess to what I have not done? God has never failed me and neither will He this time."

Kaylynn was given the maximum sentence of 20 years without a chance of parole.

That was two years ago. Today he was preparing to leave prison. All charges had been dropped. He was exonerated. As he was singing and praising God, Paul and Silas's jail experience came to mind. After their release they told the brethren all about it. Kaylynn could hardly wait to meet up with his former friends and associates to share with them how God delivered him out of prison.

When we are in a jam and things don't look good, do we still keep the faith? Do we still believe and hope in God to deliver us?

— Keep in Mind —

"Hearken to me, ye that follow after righteousness, ye that seek the LORD: look unto the rock whence ye are hewn, and to the hole of the pit whence ye are digged."
(Isaiah 51:1, KJV)

"Listen to me, all who hope for deliverance—all who seek the LORD! Consider the rock from which you were cut, the quarry from which you were mined." (Isaiah 51:1, NLT)

Focal Verses

KJV **Isaiah 51:1** Hearken to me, ye that follow after righteousness, ye that seek the LORD: look unto the rock whence ye are hewn, and to the hole of the pit whence ye are digged.

2 Look unto Abraham your father, and unto Sarah that bare you: for I called him alone, and blessed him, and increased him.

3 For the LORD shall comfort Zion: he will comfort all her waste places; and he will make her wilderness like Eden, and her desert like the garden of the LORD; joy and gladness shall be found therein, thanksgiving, and the voice of melody.

4 Hearken unto me, my people; and give ear unto me, O my nation: for a law shall proceed from me, and I will make my judgment to rest for a light of the people.

5 My righteousness is near; my salvation is gone forth, and mine arms shall judge the people; the isles shall wait upon me, and on mine arm shall they trust.

6 Lift up your eyes to the heavens, and look upon the earth beneath: for the heavens shall vanish away like smoke, and the earth shall wax old like a garment, and they that dwell therein shall die in like manner: but my salvation shall be for ever, and my righteousness shall not be abolished.

7 Hearken unto me, ye that know righteousness, the people in whose heart is my law; fear ye not the reproach of men, neither be ye afraid of their revilings.

8 For the moth shall eat them up like a garment, and the worm shall eat them like wool: but my righteousness shall be for ever, and my salvation from generation to generation.

NLT **Isaiah 51:1** "Listen to me, all who hope for deliverance—all who seek the LORD! Consider the rock from which you were cut, the quarry from which you were mined.

2 Yes, think about Abraham, your ancestor, and Sarah, who gave birth to your nation. Abraham was only one man when I called him. But when I blessed him, he became a great nation."

3 The LORD will comfort Israel again and have pity on her ruins. Her desert will blossom like Eden, her barren wilderness like the garden of the LORD. Joy and gladness will be found there. Songs of thanksgiving will fill the air.

4 "Listen to me, my people. Hear me, Israel, for my law will be proclaimed, and my justice will become a light to the nations.

5 My mercy and justice are coming soon. My salvation is on the way. My strong arm will bring justice to the nations. All distant lands will look to me and wait in hope for my powerful arm.

6 Look up to the skies above, and gaze down on the earth below. For the skies will disappear like smoke, and the earth will wear out like a piece of clothing. The people of the earth will die like flies, but my salvation lasts forever. My righteous rule will never end!

7 Listen to me, you who know right from wrong, you who cherish my law in your hearts. Do not be afraid of people's scorn, nor fear their insults.

8 For the moth will devour them as it devours clothing. The worm will eat at them as it eats wool. But my righteousness will last forever. My salvation will continue from generation to generation."

The People, Places, and Times

Abraham and Sarah. Abraham did not always follow God's plan as God had intended. On occasion, he and Sarah both seemed to have an urge to give God a helping hand. At other times, the two acted out of cowardice, not out of faith in the God who called them.

From the time of his call, Abraham had no knowledge of where he would be going. He stepped out on the word of God. He never stopped believing in God's purpose, even when it seemed that everything was working against him.

Eden. The name Eden is derived either from the Hebrew root word meaning "to be fruitful, plentiful" or from a Sumerian word meaning "steppe, flatland." After creating the entire universe, God consecrated the particular garden called Eden as a place of paradise and worship. He placed His newly created human beings to care for it, and communed with them there. There was still work to do to care for Eden, but no weeds or thorns to make the work especially hard. Many prophecies of the end times pull on images of Eden to indicate that God will heal the world so completely as to restore the paradise we knew before the Fall.

Background

Even though the Israelites are worried that foreign countries will conquer them, God reassures His people He is willing, able, and capable of providing for their release from their captives. In Isaiah 50, the one who is responsible for delivering this message of hope shows he has been commissioned by God and he is ready to carry out his mission, God's message, out to the fullest (Isaiah 50:4–5).

Jesus also fulfilled this prophecy when He was commissioned by God and carried out His duties in securing salvation for mankind to the fullest. Some Jews rejected Jesus as Christ on their own accord. We make a choice to accept what God offers. In Isaiah's message, the people of God are encouraged to trust in Him, while sinners are discouraged not to trust in themselves (Isaiah 50:11).

At-A-Glance

1. The Offer of Deliverance
(Isaiah 51:1–3)
2. The Way to Deliverance (vv. 4–6)
3. An Everlasting Deliverance (vv. 7–8)

In Depth

1. The Offer of Deliverance (Isaiah 51:1–3)

This conversation is to those who follow after righteousness, seriously yearning to practically obey God's law. They are told, "Listen to Me!" God is making them an offer of deliverance. God's people are seeking Him because they want His favor brought back to them.

They are told to look back to Abraham and Sarah. You are Sarah's daughters, if you strive for righteousness. To encourage the captives in Babylon, God calls them to remember when He called Abraham and how by His Word He blessed and increased him. They, too, were very small in number, but the Lord has promised to increase them also (Isaiah 49:19).

The Lord shall comfort Zion: God will restore it from despair. He will make them happy—giving them hearts that are glad. Their gladness will lead to their satisfaction making them thankful to God. They will sing from their hearts songs of joy and thanksgiving unto their God.

What role models of righteousness do you identify in your life?

2. The Way to Deliverance (vv. 4–6)

God is speaking to a specific group, His people. This isn't for everyone. This is for the people of God. The ones who have the law of

God within them. In addition to knowing what is right, God's people do what is right. God wants His people to listen and be attentive. He wants His people to adhere to what He is saying and take notes on their hearts.

God's righteousness is near; He will soon come to their rescue. Those that He has made promises to will see the fulfillment of those promises. God's arms will judge the people, because He has the power to judge all. He has the ability to draw them together, and He has the ability to scatter them. They should put their trust in Him.

Heaven and earth are going to pass away (Matthew 24:35). The description here is the heavens will disappear like a vapor, or smoke, into thin air. The earth will fall off like an old piece of clothing no one wants to wear. Just as the earth and the heavens will no longer exist, this will be true of people. In contrast, the way to deliverance, salvation and righteousness will remain.

How do you remind yourself to chase after eternal things, rather than passing earthly things?

3. An Everlasting Deliverance (vv. 7–8)

Isaiah is requesting the attention of the righteous, God's people, the keepers of the Law. God's people are told to not fear the rebuke and criticism of men. We have the assurance of God's promises. Others might say anything to attempt to destroy our faith in God, but God has given His promise. He will not turn back on His Word. God is faithful.

People will become food for the insects and animals when they die. As time goes on, those same people won't be around to express disapproval. In contrast, the salvation and righteous of God will always be. Salvation and righteousness will continue to exist, from generation to generation, forever.

What would you be able to do for God if you weren't afraid of others' scorn?

Search the Scriptures

1. Is God offering deliverance to all (Isaiah 51:1)?

2. Who shall comfort the people of Zion (v. 3)?

3. Who are they that know righteousness (v. 6)?

Discuss the Meaning

1. God shows He is willing and able to deliver us from our captivity, which is sin. But He does not force us to accept His offer. Should He or should He not? Why?

2. God tells His people, "hearken unto me" three times. When something is told to us repeatedly should we consider it? Should we pay more attention to what's being said or should we find the person to be a nuisance trying to force us to accept what they are saying?

Liberating Lesson

In spite of what we see, we must remember God is faithful and He will deliver us, just as He did the remnant of Israel. He encourages us to listen to Him and to look back at what He did for Abraham and Sarah. Abraham believed God and became a great nation, we too must believe God and trust Him. God comforts and consoles us as we fear Him. If we are faithful, God will deliver us. We must be willing to tell others that God's Word will last forever. We should encourage others to trust Jesus for deliverance and salvation.

Application for Activation

This week, pray and trust God daily to deliver you from any situation that will cause you not to demonstrate your faith in God. Do not let anyone discourage you from believing that God can deliver you from those that speak negatively. You can ask God to speak to your heart so the Holy Spirit will remind you that God is faithful and He will deliver you.

Ask God to help you encourage others because Jesus loves you and wants everyone to be saved. Tell others that those who reject the Lord will be judged by God, not man.

Follow the Spirit

What God wants me to do:

_____

_____

_____

_____

Remember Your Thoughts

Special insights I have learned:

_____

_____

_____

_____

More Light on the Text
Isaiah 51:1–8

Isaiah 51 seems to be addressed to the people of Israel who lived more than a century after the time of Isaiah—the nation suffering through the Babylonian Exile. Much of Isaiah 40–66 looks beyond the time of the prophet to the Exile and the returning exiles. The background of this passage is that the people are exiled away from Judea and are being held captive by the Babylonians. They are desperate. They are heart-broken and struggling to make sense of their predicament. Yet they still remember Yahweh. But does Yahweh remember them?

He does. The Lord calls upon the people to trust and believe in Him once again like their ancestor Abraham. The Lord employs the Abrahamic story in Genesis—a story they never forgot about—to remind the Jews what He is capable of. The Lord tells them that He is about to move. He is about to bring salvation once again for those who are pursuing His righteousness and glory. Cyrus, the king of the Persians, defeated the Babylonians in 539 BC and subsequently freed the Israelites from bondage. This passage tells the story of God revealing His plans to them.

1 Hearken to me, ye that follow after righteousness, ye that seek the LORD: look unto the rock whence ye are hewn, and to the hole of the pit whence ye are digged.

In verse 1 the Lord bids the people exiled out of Jerusalem to listen and listen closely to what He has to say. He is preparing to share important news. Note that those who listen to the Lord are also the same people who "follow after righteousness." A person cannot do one without the other. The Hebrew word for righteousness in this text is *tsedeq* (**TSEH**-dek), which means ethical fairness or governmental justice. Many people turned from God before the Babylonian captivity and many others turned from God because of Babylonian captivity. Those who turned during captivity may have felt that God was unjust. They may have felt that God was unfair. Those who still had faith in the Lord are the ones the Lord was speaking to particularly. Listening to and seeking the Lord are the preconditions for following after righteousness. One cannot follow after righteousness without listening to and seeking the Lord in spite of their predicament in life. Moreover, following after God does not necessarily mean following behind Him in the sense of committing to religious rituals without much dedication. It means pursuing Him. It means chasing after His ways. It means actively trying to please Him according to His desires.

When those who are both exiled and still pursuing God hear God's voice in spirit, Isaiah says to "look unto the rock whence ye are hewn." When Isaiah says "look" the Hebrew word is *nabat* (naw-**BOT**) which means to look in more than just a literal fashion. It means to behold or to look in high regard. Isaiah is saying to look at the rock (Heb. *tsur*, **TSOOR**) from which you were hewn (Heb. *chatsab*, khaw-**TSOB**). In proper context, the Lord is saying to behold the tradition upon which your people have historically relied or stood. The Lord is saying to honor the tradition, hold it in high regard. It is as solid as a rock. The Lord beckons the people to remember their culture, their past, their tradition. Look backwards and remember what God has done is important because it is a sheer reminder of what God is fully capable of. In other words, that which God was capable of in the past is what God is still capable of in the present.

2 Look unto Abraham your father, and unto Sarah that bare you: for I called him alone, and blessed him, and increased him.

When the people look at their tradition and remember their culture, they will remember the patriarch Abraham who is the father of their faith. The Lord directed Abraham's path by telling him to depart from his country and people to a land that God selected (Genesis 12:1). In this history, Abraham was alone with his wife Sarah who could not conceive children, and the Lord blessed them more than they could ever have imagined. The blessing of Abraham did not cease with Abraham but extended to Isaac and Jacob and all his sons. The Lord's covenant with Abraham did not stop with Abraham but continued regardless of circumstance or situation through all of his descendants who continued to have faith in the Lord. This great story of Abraham in the Torah that the people knew so well says to them that

if the Lord can take one man, Abraham, and separate him from his people, and still make a great nation out of his descendants, then the Lord can do it again.

These words were encouraging for those who struggled with wondering not if God was willing to deliver them but if the Lord was capable of doing it. These people had experienced military defeat at the hands of countless enemies. They knew in their heart of hearts that they were guilty of not keeping the covenant. They remembered the times that they worshiped other gods and didn't care for the God who freed them from Egypt and protected their ancestors. Some even scoffed at their tradition. Some ignored their heritage. So, they thought, why would God save us? Why would God return to us? Why would God rescue us in light of everything we have done against Him? It is a wonderful blessing to know that God is a forgiving God. And not only is He forgiving, He is able to forgive and restore when He pleases.

3 For the LORD shall comfort Zion: he will comfort all her waste places; and he will make her wilderness like Eden, and her desert like the garden of the LORD; joy and gladness shall be found therein, thanksgiving, and the voice of melody.

After mentioning what was done for Abraham, the Lord invokes Zion (Jerusalem), the conquered land. Although, at the moment, Jerusalem as they understand it is no more, God promises to comfort her and recreate her once again. God promises with figurative hyperbole to turn their wilderness, their deserted wasteland, into something as beautiful and plentiful as the historic Garden of Eden. All the corners of their former land that have been ruined and desecrated will be comforted and taken care of once more. The Garden of Eden represents a paradise filled with delightful resources, splendor, food, and a host of unimaginable goods. By using the Garden in this context, Isaiah invokes the image of not just Israel returning to Canaan, but of all humanity returning to a Garden modeled on the first Eden, but even more glorious. Isaiah is implying that the Lord will redeem all of humanity through His power. That is to say, God has the power to take what has been destroyed and renew it into something wonderful.

The Lord will take their desert *arabah* (aw-raw-**BAW**), a steep or desert plain of uninhabited land, and make it like the garden of the Lord. The Lord also says that this garden will be filled with joy and music. There will be thanksgiving, gratitude as opposed to shame and defeat. There will be melody as opposed to wails.

4 Hearken unto me, my people; and give ear unto me, O my nation: for a law shall proceed from me, and I will make my judgment to rest for a light of the people.

Again, the Lord bids His people to listen to Him closely. His people, either Gentiles from other parts of the land or the Jews who have known him since Abraham, heed His words carefully and recognize Him as their God. Here the Lord is saying that He will make His judgment—His law—a light for the people who recognize Him as their Lord and seek to follow Him in the ways of righteousness. When God delivers them, it will include non-Jewish people who see His works in their redemption and can recognize His power and awesomeness. The Lord will make judgment to rest (Heb. *raga*, **RAW-GAH**), or to dwell in peace and quiet. In this latter portion of Isaiah, the prophet repeatedly states the promise that Yahweh's covenant and teaching that Israel itself will illuminate the entire world (Isaiah 42:6; 49:6; 51:4; 60:3). The apostle John sees these promises reach their ultimate fulfillment in the New Jerusalem (Revelation 21:24).

5 My righteousness is near; my salvation is gone forth, and mine arms shall judge the people; the isles shall wait upon me, and on mine arm shall they trust.

The Lord means a few things when He says His righteousness is near. On one hand, the Lord is saying that His righteousness is close in the sense that it is not far from people who once assumed it was distant and too far for them to grasp, because they were not members of the chosen people. Here the Lord is explicit as to the proximity to His glory, even for those living as far-flung as "the isles." His salvation has gone forth, and it is there for any who desire to pursue it. The Lord is the Lord of all peoples. And He welcomes all peoples. What was once limited is now open; a covenant that was once particular is now open for anyone who is willing to accept and embrace.

On the other hand, however, when the Lord says His righteousness is near, He is also saying that Cyrus, king of the Persians, is on his way to battle the Babylonians. When the Persians and the Babylonians engage in war, the Lord has set it up for Cyrus and the Persians to emerge victorious. After Cyrus defeats the Babylonians, he will then free the people of Judea who were held in Babylonian bondage. This defeat and subsequent liberation will be in the name of the Lord for the world to see. Those who will be delivered will rest in God's arms in whom they trust because they will know that only the Lord could have kept such a promise of commitment.

6 Lift up your eyes to the heavens, and look upon the earth beneath: for the heavens shall vanish away like smoke, and the earth shall wax old like a garment, and they that dwell therein shall die in like manner: but my salvation shall be forever, and my righteousness shall not be abolished.

God, through the words of Isaiah, says to look: look up and see heaven, look around and see the soil beneath our feet and know that the cosmos that all living creatures inhabit is impermanent. The world, the universe, all that is visible to our sight—from the vast, innumerable star, to the deep stones supporting our homes—are, in fact, temporary. One day it will all be gone. The Lord also says that the earth ages, it is an object that exists within the space-time continuum, which means it is not eternal. It will not last forever. It will grow (KJV: "wax") old as clothing does, fraying and thinning until it is of no further use.

Yet what does last forever is God and His salvation. God's Word, salvation, and righteousness are eternal. They exist outside of the temporal motion of time. They last because they have always existed and will continue to exist even after everything else vanishes away.

7 Hearken unto me, ye that know righteousness, the people in whose heart is my law; fear ye not the reproach of men, neither be ye afraid of their revilings.

Again, the Lord calls to the people to listen to Him. And those people are people that know and recognize God's righteousness and not the righteousness of humanity. The Lord is speaking to the people who not only know the Torah and remember the covenant, but to the people who have inscribed God's righteousness in their hearts. He says to them to not fear men or *enosh* (**EN-NOASH**) which means "mere men" or "mere mortals." Do not fear people in power. Do not fear the Babylonians. Do not fear the Persians. Do not be afraid of what they have the power to do to you. You belong to the Lord.

8 For the moth hall eat them up like a garment, and the worm shall eat them like wool: but my righteousness shall be for ever, and my salvation from generation to generation.

One should not be concerned about mere mortals or the power of human beings because evil will always lose in the end. Evil will eventually devour itself and destroy the world it infests. God's righteousness, that lasts for all time, will do away with it in the end. Isaiah is saying that no matter who emerges as an enemy of God and God's people, they will eventually fall. Connected to the Lord's salvation is the Lord's consistent and promised deliverance from His enemies. The Jewish idea of salvation is centered on physical protection and deliverance from one's enemies. Jesus, a Jew himself, re-imagines this understanding and expands the definition to include God's eternal protection and deliverance from Hell and evil. Remember that God restores, no matter what was lost, destroyed, or taken. The Lord has the power to redeem and deliver like He has done in the past. Always look to God's faithfulness in the past as assurance that God will continue to work on your behalf. God reminds His people that just as He did the unimaginable with Abraham, He can continue to do so with His people through the ages.

Sources:
Benson, Joseph. *Commentary of the Old Testament and New Testament*. New York: T. Carlton & J. Porter, 1857.
Blenkinsopp, J. *Isaiah 40-55*. New York: Doubleday, 2002.
Harrison, R. K. Editor. *The New Unger's Bible Dictionary*. Chicago: Moody Press, 1988. 1382-1383
Kissane, E. *The Book of Isaiah*. Dublin: Browne and Nolan, 1960.
Knight, G. *Servant Theology*. Edinburgh: Handsel Press, 1984.
Life Application Study Bible, King James Version. Wheaton, IL: Tyndale House Publishers, Inc., 1997. 2154-2155, 2170-2172.
Peterson, Eugene H. *The Message: The Bible in Contemporary Language*. Colorado Springs, CO: NavPress Publishing Group 2002. 1755
Roberts, J. and Machinist, P. *First Isaiah*. Baltimore, MD: Fortress Press, 2016.
Walvoord, John F. And Roy B. Zuck. *The Bible Knowledge Commentary: An Exposition of the Scriptures*. Old Testament. Wheaton, IL: Victor Books, 1983.

Say It Correctly

Hearken. HAR-ken.

Daily Bible Readings

MONDAY
God Will Vindicate His Servant
(Isaiah 50:4–9)

TUESDAY
Remember God's Mighty Deeds
(Isaiah 51:9–16)

WEDNESDAY
God Defends Israel's Cause
(Isaiah 51:17–23)

THURSDAY
God Rescues Us from Peril
(2 Corinthians 1:7–14)

FRIDAY
Jesus Rescues Us from Wrath
(1 Thessalonians 1:6–10)

SATURDAY
Deliverance Belongs to the Lord
(Psalm 3)

SUNDAY
God's Deliverance Is Coming
(Isaiah 51:1–8)

Notes

Teaching Tips

Words You Should Know

A. Power (John 1:12) *exousia* (Gk.)—Authority, influence, capability

B. Dwell (v. 14) *skenoo* (Gk.)—To abide or live, specifically in a tent or tabernacle

Teacher Preparation

Unifying Principle—The Reason for It All. People are often curious about how things began. How do we understand the origins of life? John begins by explaining that Jesus, the Word, was God's creation and redeeming agent in the world.

A. Read the Bible Background and Devotional Reading.

B. Pray for your students and lesson clarity.

C. Read the lesson Scripture in multiple translations.

O—Open the Lesson

A. Begin the class with prayer.

B. Create a quiz in which participants should match a fictional superhero with that hero's backstory—how the hero gained superpowers. Lead into the Bible story explaining that John offers a true origin story of the world's greatest hero.

C. Have the students read the Aim for Change and the In Focus story.

D. Ask students how events like those in the story weigh on their hearts and how they can view these events from a faith perspective.

P—Present the Scriptures

A. Read the Focal Verses and discuss the Background and The People, Places, and Times sections.

B. Have the class share what Scriptures stand out for them and why, with particular emphasis on today's themes.

E—Explore the Meaning

A. Use In Depth or More Light on the Text to facilitate a deeper discussion of the lesson text.

B. Pose the questions in Search the Scriptures and Discuss the Meaning.

C. Discuss the Liberating Lesson and Application for Activation sections.

N—Next Steps for Application

A. Summarize the value of testimony of Scripture.

B. End class with a commitment to pray that Christ will change lives and make people different.

Worship Guide

For the Superintendent or Teacher
Theme: The Creating Word Becomes Flesh
Song: "Shine, Jesus, Shine"

The Creating Word Becomes Flesh

Bible Background • JOHN 1:1–14
Printed Text • JOHN 1:1–14 | Devotional Reading • GENESIS 2:1–3

———— Aim for Change ————

By the end of this lesson, we will EXPLORE the meaning of the Word for the world, FIND true inspiration for life in Jesus, and LIVE in relationship with Creator God because of the "light" (grace and truth) that Jesus gives.

———— In Focus ————

Sister Nancy is a gifted Christian who serves on her church's Board of Trustees. However, this was not always the case. She is a recovering alcoholic who used to verbally abuse her husband and children. After years of tolerating Nancy's behavior, her husband had finally had enough. One weekend Nancy arrived home drunk as usual and found her husband, children, and all their possessions gone.

Nancy had been miserable without her family. One of her coworkers, Mitch, noticed her downward spiral and invited her to come to church with his family next Sunday. After service, they all went out for lunch together. Mitch's wife, Bea, asked Nancy what she thought about coming to church with them more often. Nancy said she probably wouldn't be able to make it. Mitch and Bea pressed her, and Nancy confessed she didn't feel comfortable going to church when her life was so messed up.

Her co-worker, Mitch, told her about the life-changing relationship he had with Jesus. Jesus was Mitch's light and life, and from what Nancy could see, it was a glorious light and life. Then Bea asked Nancy if she would like to become a new person in Christ. Right there in the restaurant, Sister Nancy gave her life to Christ. She no longer drinks; she and her family are reunited and happy.

Sister Nancy did not just turn over a "new leaf." She actually became a new person in Christ.

How would your life have been different if you didn't have new life in Christ?

———— Keep in Mind ————

"All things were made by him; and without him was not any thing made that was made."
(John 1:3, KJV)

"God created everything through him, and nothing was created except through him."
(John 1:3, NLT)

Focal Verses

KJV **John 1:1** In the beginning was the Word, and the Word was with God, and the Word was God.

2 The same was in the beginning with God.

3 All things were made by him; and without him was not any thing made that was made.

4 In him was life; and the life was the light of men.

5 And the light shineth in darkness; and the darkness comprehended it not.

6 There was a man sent from God, whose name was John.

7 The same came for a witness, to bear witness of the Light, that all men through him might believe.

8 He was not that Light, but was sent to bear witness of that Light.

9 That was the true Light, which lighteth every man that cometh into the world.

10 He was in the world, and the world was made by him, and the world knew him not.

11 He came unto his own, and his own received him not.

12 But as many as received him, to them gave he power to become the sons of God, even to them that believe on his name:

13 Which were born, not of blood, nor of the will of the flesh, nor of the will of man, but of God.

14 And the Word was made flesh, and dwelt among us, (and we beheld his glory, the glory as of the only begotten of the Father,) full of grace and truth.

NLT **John 1:1** In the beginning the Word already existed. The Word was with God, and the Word was God.

2 He existed in the beginning with God.

3 God created everything through him, and nothing was created except through him.

4 The Word gave life to everything that was created, and his life brought light to everyone.

5 The light shines in the darkness, and the darkness can never extinguish it.

6 God sent a man, John the Baptist,

7 to tell about the light so that everyone might believe because of his testimony.

8 John himself was not the light; he was simply a witness to tell about the light.

9 The one who is the true light, who gives light to everyone, was coming into the world.

10 He came into the very world he created, but the world didn't recognize him.

11 He came to his own people, and even they rejected him.

12 But to all who believed him and accepted him, he gave the right to become children of God.

13 They are reborn—not with a physical birth resulting from human passion or plan, but a birth that comes from God.

14 So the Word became human and made his home among us. He was full of unfailing love and faithfulness. And we have seen his glory, the glory of the Father's one and only Son.

The People, Places, and Times

Gnosticism. Many of the early Gentile believers had been exposed to varying strains of Gnosticism (an early heresy) and did not believe in the humanity of Jesus. As people from diverse backgrounds became part of the church, it became necessary for the apostles to correct errors in doctrine as well as encourage the existing believers. In the Gospel of John, the writer seems to be addressing a mixed audience of believers and unbelievers, Jews, and Greeks. The other Gospels had already been written and circulated. John used his writing not to simply tell stories about Jesus, but to explain Christian theology, especially the place of Christ Jesus.

Background

The author of the book of John identifies himself as "the disciple whom Jesus loved" (John 13:23; 19:26; 21:7, 20). Most scholars agree that the apostle John is the author of this book. John was well-known in the early church and was intimately familiar with Jewish life. He would have been an eyewitness to many of the events recorded in the Gospel of John.

Dating of the Gospel of John is a matter of debate, with dates ranging from AD 50 to 95 or later. However, most scholars accept the later date of AD 95. Although we may not know the exact date of the writing, we do know that the first-century church was thriving. Even amid the threats of persecution and heresy, the church continued to grow.

John wrote to encourage the believers, most of whom were Jewish. He affirms their Jewishness as well as their faith in Jesus Christ, contrasting them with the Pharisees, who claimed to be the true or real Jews. The first 14 verses of the book of John summarize the whole Gospel. In these verses, we are introduced to Jesus—who He is, what He does, and the role He plays in the eternal plan of God for the world.

At-A-Glance

1. Jesus Is the Word (John 1:1–3)
2. Jesus Is the Light (vv. 4–9)
3. Jesus Reveals God's Character (vv. 10–14)

In Depth

1. Jesus Is the Word (John 1:1–3)

John introduces Jesus as the "Word." The word used here is *logos*. The Greeks understood *logos* to mean not only the written or spoken word, but also the thought or reasoning in the mind. Jewish believers also used the word *logos* to refer to God and would have connected this concept to the wisdom personified in the Old Testament (see Proverbs 8). In tandem with wisdom was ability; in this case, God's wisdom was used to create the universe. Jesus is that wisdom personified. Through Jesus, all things were created. To understand the creation, we must know the Creator. All of these concepts are bound up in the word *logos*.

As believers today, we may not realize all the nuances that the author intended. But what we must learn is clear: Jesus was, is, and always will be. He is God. He is the Creator and the Source of all life. The entirety of our Christian faith rests upon accepting these truths.

How have you seen loaded words used or abused in your life?

2. Jesus Is the Light (vv. 4–9)

John speaks of Jesus as "the light." Jesus is Life itself, and that Life is our Light (v. 4). When we receive this life Jesus offers, His light replaces our spiritual darkness, and we become more like our Creator. However, many people live in deep darkness, which often connotes sin *indicate* in the Bible. Even though Jesus is the light to dispel darkness, many people refuse to accept the light of salvation. It's the same today. People are so thoroughly entrenched in their sin and ignorance that they are blind to the light.

God can use anyone to pierce through the darkness. In Jesus' time, God sent John the Baptist to bear witness to Jesus (vv. 6–7). John the Baptist did not want people to believe in him; he pointed the way to Jesus. Today, God uses His written Word and the power of the Holy Spirit to testify to the Light. He also uses believers. Every believer should view himself or herself as a testimony to the truth of salvation through Jesus Christ.

What has the Light of Christ made clear to you?

3. Jesus Reveals God's Character (vv. 10–14)

Although Jesus created the world (Colossians 1:16), the world did not recognize Him as Savior (John 1:10). Jesus came to the Jews first, but most of them rejected Him as their Messiah. His gift of salvation is offered freely to all. When we do receive Jesus, God gives us the right to become His children (v. 12), not physically, but spiritually. We are considered His heirs (Galatians 3:29), eligible to receive all of His promised blessings.

We cannot become God's children by any means other than through salvation in Jesus Christ whom God sent to the earth to take on human flesh. He came to live with us, to feel our pain, to experience our joy, and to know our sorrow.

John's Jewish readers would have understood the word "dwelt" to be connected to the word for "tabernacle," where God's presence dwelt. As modern-day believers, we can't physically touch Jesus, yet we can see His glory. We can testify to the miracles He has worked in our lives and the lives of others. We can bear witness to the power of salvation.

Why did Jesus need to become a human to understand humanity?

Search the Scriptures

1. Who is the "Word" (John 1:1)?
2. What is the "light of men" (v. 4)?

Discuss the Meaning

Jesus came to give meaningful, real life to all who will receive Him. He is the living revelation of God, who expressed God's truth in a way we can understand. It is our task to share this light with others. What are effective ways to be witnesses to Jesus' light today?

Liberating Lesson

Jesus came into this world in the form of human flesh, yet those around Him did not acknowledge Him for who He is: God. They chose to continue living in darkness rather than receiving the Light. Things aren't so different in our world today. In modern society, many people have become accustomed to a fast-paced, hectic lifestyle. They are easily distracted, often bored, or generally dissatisfied with life.

Jesus came to free us from the rat race. His light reveals that we are in fact human beings, made in the glorious image of God. Jesus' light burns away our ignorance and reveals our worth. It is then up to us to embrace that worth instead of taking the darker, but easier, path.

Application for Activation

This week, ask God to reveal Himself to you in a new way. Spend time praying, reading the Word, and meditating on what you have read. Let God's Word permeate your spirit so that you might know God more deeply. Rejoice in the fact that God has revealed Himself to you through Jesus, the Word made flesh, and that He will continue to do so.

Follow the Spirit

What God wants me to do:

Remember whenever you're in a position to help someone.

Remember Your Thoughts

Special insights I have learned:

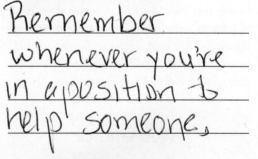

be glad and always do it because that's God's answering someone else's prayers through you

More Light on the Text
John 1:1–14

1 In the beginning was the Word, and the Word was with God, and the Word was God.

John begins his Gospel with a clear reference to Genesis 1:1. The book of Genesis opens with an affirmation of the nature and character of God, the Creator and Sustainer of the universe. The purpose of the statement in Genesis is threefold: (1) to identify the Creator, (2) to explain the origin of the world, and (3) to tie the work of God in the past to the work of God in the future. Likewise, John is clearly identifying Jesus, the Living Word made flesh, as God the Creator (John 1:3) and affirming Him as the only source of life and redemption. This Gospel from its very start is heralding the deity of Jesus Christ. John is not referring here to a particular time in the past; rather, he is affirming the preexistence of Jesus.

"Word" here is expressed using the Greek word *logos* (**LOW**-goce), which has several meanings. Ordinarily, *logos* refers to a spoken word, with an emphasis on the meaning conveyed, not just the sounds produced. But here, *logos* is used as an expression of communication with God. It is more than everyday speech; it is the creative power of God (see Psalm 33:6). John's Greek readers would have understood the nuances of *logos*, realizing that John was presenting Jesus as the power that controlled all things. John is clearly asserting that the divine Word is the source of creation and of all that is visible and invisible in the world. John leaves no question as to the nature, character, and glory of the Word—the "Word was God" (John 1:1). John is saying that the Word is deity—one with God in nature, character, and glory.

2 The same was in the beginning with God. 3 All things were made by him; and without him was not any thing made that was made.

John begins the second verse by reiterating the divine, preexistent nature of the Word. He proceeds to explain the role of the Word in the beginning. The word "made" (Gk. *ginomai*, **GHI**-no-my) means "came into being, happened, or became." John is communicating the idea that this creative work happened out of nothing, that the Word did not rely on preexisting material to create the universe (Colossians 1:16; Hebrews 1:2).

John also begins to give us a hint as to the identity of the Word by referring to the Word as "him." The Word is more than just an expression of the personality of God; it is the person of Jesus Christ. So John is saying that the Word, which was preexistent with God, was in complete fellowship with God, possessed all the divine nature and characteristics of deity, and created everything.

4 In him was life; and the life was the light of men. 5 And the light shineth in darkness; and the darkness comprehended it not.

"Life" in Greek is *zoe* (dzo-**AY**) and is used throughout the Bible to refer to both physical and spiritual life. It is frequently qualified with the word "eternal." Jesus was the embodiment of the fullness and quality of life that God offers to those who believe (John 14:6). The life that Jesus was to offer would be the light of all humanity.

Here, John uses the metaphors of "light" (Gk. *phos*, foce, "to manifest") and "darkness" (Gk. *skotia*, sko-**TEE**-ah, "dimness" or "obscurity") to illustrate the differences between a life of grace, mercy, and forgiveness and a life of sin and death. The word "comprehended" (Gk. *katalambano*, kat-al-am-**BAN**-o) has two possible meanings. One meaning is "understood, perceived, or learned" and communicates the fact that those who live in the darkness do not receive the light because of a lack of understanding—they don't get it. Another meaning is the idea "laid hold of or seized" and communicates the fact that the darkness (perhaps Satan or more generally sinful humanity) will never have the ultimate victory over the light of Jesus.

John is saying that some who see the light will be unable to understand and receive it because Satan has blinded them (2 Corinthians 4:4). But John says that no matter how dark the darkness of evil seems in the world, no matter how the global circumstances seem to indicate that evil is winning, darkness cannot overcome the light that comes from the life of Christ.

6 There was a man sent from God, whose name was John. 7 The same came for a witness, to bear witness of the Light, that all men through him might believe.

The apostle John goes on to talk about John the Baptist. The ministry of John the Baptist is prominent in the Gospel of John. Here, the apostle John is affirming the prophetic ministry of John the Baptist. Jesus echoed this assertion when He said that John the Baptist was the last of the great Old Testament prophets, who came in the spirit of Elijah (Matthew 11:9–10; Mark 9:13). John the Baptist had a unique call and ministry to be a witness of Jesus, the Light (Matthew 4:4; John 1:4).

In verse 7, the word "witness" (Gk. *marturia*, mar-too-**REE**-ah) means to affirm by testimony what one has seen, heard, experienced, or known. Therefore, John the Baptist had the prophetic duty of preparing the way for Jesus by preaching the testimonies of God.

The goal of John the Baptist was the same as the goal of John the apostle: to bring humanity to a place of faith in Jesus as Lord and Savior. The author is careful to specify that John the Baptist was not the genuine light, but that he came to "bear witness" (Gk. *martureo*, mar-too-**REH**-o), to testify of, or report on the One to come. This kind of witness would affirm by testimony what one has seen, heard, experienced, or known.

John the Baptist testified to the world of the nature and character of Jesus so that "all men through him might believe."

8 He was not that Light, but was sent to bear witness of that Light. 9 That was the true Light, which lighteth every man that cometh into the world.

The apostle John makes it clear that John the Baptist was not the Light. He was only to bear witness of the Light. Like the moon that does not shine its own light, but only reflects the light of the sun, so John the Baptist reflects the Light of Jesus Christ, the Son of God. Jesus would be the true Light that would light every person. The word "true" (Gk. *alethinos*, al-ay-thee-**NOS**) refers to that which is sincere or genuine. The apostle John is saying that John the Baptist pointed others to the light to come, and that Jesus Christ was the authentic Light. As we walk in the light, we learn to comprehend the things of God. It is our joy as believers to shine the light of Jesus to those around us.

10 He was in the world, and the world was made by him, and the world knew him not. 11 He came unto his own, and his own received him not.

Here, the Greek word for "world" is *kosmos* (**KOS**-mos). It can refer to the universe (both things and people), the inhabitants of the earth (i.e., humanity), and the evil world system alienated from God. Gnostics believed that the flesh and the material world were evil. The apostle John may have been refuting this heresy by making the statement that Jesus "was in the world." In other words, Jesus was not alienated from the material world and its inhabitants; this was the world that He had created (v. 3).

Even though Jesus was in the world that He had made, the world "knew him not" (v. 10). The Greek word for "knew" is *ginosko* (ghee-**NOCE**-ko) and refers to more than just head knowledge. It means "recognized or perceived" and carries the idea of knowing something intimately. John is conveying the real problem with humanity: The world should recognize its Creator. This recognition should motivate humanity to have a relationship with Jesus, but the world does not recognize Him, nor desire to have an intimate relationship with Him.

The rejection of Jesus by the world comes to a head in verse 11. There are two different meanings for the word "own" in this passage. First, He came to His "own" (Gk. *idios*, **EE**-dee-os), meaning "property" or "possessions" (i.e., homeland). Second, His "own" received Him not; the word is masculine in the Greek and refers to His own people, the Jews. For hundreds of years, the Jews had waited for the Messiah; now, when He came, they refused to receive Him as such.

While here on earth, Jesus preached to a mostly Jewish audience. They were not only blinded by their sin, but they were hindered by their religion and preconceived ideas. Their pride is more important to them than anything else, and they loathe admitting that they could be wrong.

The world belonged to Christ by virtue of His having created it, but the world did not know Him, would not enter into a relationship with Him, and refused to receive Him because they did not recognize Him for who He was. What a scathing commentary on the sinful condition of humanity!

12 But as many as received him, to them gave the power to become the sons of God, even to them that believe on his name: 13 Which were born, not of blood, nor of the will of the flesh, nor of the will of man, but of God.

But there is still hope for sinful humanity. Regardless of how bleak the situation may seem for humanity, God provides hope in the person of Jesus. There will be many who receive Jesus as Savior and Lord and recognize Him for who He is as the Creator of the universe. The word "received" (Gk. *paralambano*, pa-ra-lam-**BAN**-oh) means "took what was one's own, took to one's self, or made one's own." As used here, "received" is more than psychologically accepting or making some emotional assent to Jesus. Therefore, to receive Jesus means to take hold of everything that Jesus is (Lord, Savior, Creator, Redeemer, etc.) and make Him one's own so that His presence affects a person's goals, aims, plans, and desires.

Those who receive Jesus and allow Him to affect their goals, aims, and plans are given the "power to become the sons of God." The Greek word for "power" is *exousia* (ek-soo-**SEE**-ah) and is best translated as "power of authority (influence)" or "power to act." What John is saying is that whoever receives Jesus is given the power and authority to act in a way consistent with being a child of God, and that this power gives us access to all of the privileges that come through God's grace. This power is used when we become children of God. God's power must be at work in our lives in order for us to live and act in a way consistent with being a child of God (cf. John 1:13).

In verse 12, John goes on to say that the privileges of being children of God are bestowed on those who "believe" on (Gk. *pisteuo*, pist-**YOO**-oh) or have faith in His name. "Belief" here is more than simply something that happens in the mind. To believe on Jesus Christ means to place complete confidence in the nature, person, and character of Jesus Christ so that He influences the total being (goals, aims, plans, and desires). When you "received [Jesus]" and "believe on his name," John says, you entrusted Him with your life. Then this trust should lead to some sort of action, whereby you take hold of Jesus for yourself in order to be part of the family of God.

Johns tells us that this new birth did not come about "of blood" (Gk. *haima*, **HAH**-ee-mah), referring to the blood of humans or animals. Nor was it a result of "the will of the flesh" (Gk. *sarx*), meaning "carnal nature" or "passions." Rather, the new birth was a result of something supernatural (cf. John 3:5–6). When we receive Christ, we are adopted into the family of God (see 1 John 3:1). God's children are not born in the natural way of conception and birth. We are born of God spiritually. Like when humans adopt a child, He chooses us. It's not because of anything we have done to deserve it, but because of God's grace we can choose to believe and receive Jesus. We are not physical children, but spiritual children of our Father, God. Like children, we should strive to become like Him. We are frail humans, but when we receive the *logos*, we will begin to reflect the likeness of Him who is the Living Word.

14 And the Word was made flesh, and dwelt among us, (and we beheld his glory, the glory as of the only begotten of the Father,) full of grace and truth.

John 1:14 is one of the key verses in the New Testament that explains the Incarnation. "Incarnation" is defined as that act of grace whereby Christ took our human nature into union with His divine Person, becoming man. The Word was made flesh. Here, John brings our attention back to the divine Word, or *logos*. The Word, who is God, who created the universe and provided light to all humanity, became flesh. The word "made" here (Gk. *ginomai*, **GHIN**-oh-mahee) is the same word used in verse 3 and means "came into being." John is not saying that Jesus was some created, lesser god; he is affirming that Jesus existed in eternity past and took on a physical body through the Incarnation.

The divine Word not only took on a physical body, but also dwelt among us. The word "dwelt" (Gk. *skenoo*, skay-**NO**-oh) refers to abiding or living in a tabernacle (or tent). One cannot escape John's allusion to the Old Testament tabernacle, which was built as a temporary and mobile dwelling for God (see Exodus 36–40). The original tabernacle was a temporary meeting place. It had provisional status, anticipating the construction of the Temple in Jerusalem. In the Incarnation, when the Word was made flesh, humanity did not receive a temporary tabernacle; rather, God Himself in Jesus came to live among us. Dwelling with us was only a temporary solution, however. After His death and resurrection, Jesus gained a permanent spiritual body and went to dwell in heaven.

While He was here, John and the other disciples knew Jesus intimately as Teacher and Friend. They ate with Him, talked with Him, laughed with Him, and cried with Him. The disciples watched Jesus perform miracles, and they knew Him as the Messiah. The One who has always existed, the One who is God, become a human being (v. 14). Although He had always been omnipresent, Jesus had now come to be one of us.

The idea John is trying to communicate here is that the "glory" (Gk. *doxa*, **DOX**-ah, "perfection, honor, and praise") that we see in the incarnate Word is the glory of the Father in heaven. This is the strongest assertion of the deity of Christ that could be made. "Only begotten" is the Greek word *monogenes* (mo-no-geh-**NACE**) and means "unique, or one of a kind." While we can claim to be children of God in a general sense by receiving and believing in Christ, Jesus is the one and only unique Son of God.

And what is it that we see when we behold His glory? A revelation of God's preeminence and dignity, through Jesus, will reveal that He is "full of grace and truth." God's grace is a demonstration of His love. The word "grace"

(Gk. *charis*, **KHAR**-eece) is defined as "favor" or "that which affords pleasure." "Truth" (Gk. *aletheia*, ah-**LAY**-thi-ah) can be defined as "that which conforms to reality." Jesus is the one and only Son of God, and He conforms to the full reality of God in nature, character, and purpose (Colossians 2:9). The truth as it relates to the nature and character of Jesus Christ dispels any heresies that may rise concerning His divine character.

Sources:
Keener, Craig S. *The IVP Bible Background Commentary: New Testament*. Downers Grove, IL InterVarsity Press, 1993. 261.
Tenney, Merrill C. *Expositor's Bible Commentary* (John and Acts). Electronic edition. Edited by Frank E. Gaebelein. Grand Rapids, MI: Zondervan Publishing, 1992.
Vincent, Marvin R. *Vincent's Word Studies*, Vol. 2: The Writings of John. Electronic edition. Hiawatha, IA: Parsons Technology, 1998.

Say It Correctly

Incarnation. in-car-NA-shun.
Gnosticism. NOSS-tih-siz-um.

Daily Bible Readings

MONDAY
God Created the World
through Wisdom
(Proverbs 8:22–31)

TUESDAY
In Christ All Things Hold Together
(Colossians 1:13–17)

WEDNESDAY
Christ, the Head of All Things
(Colossians 1:18–22)

THURSDAY
God's Well-Ordered Creation
(Psalm 104:1–15)

FRIDAY
Praise God for Creation
(Psalm 104:24–35)

SATURDAY
The Son Reflects God's Glory
(Hebrews 1:1–4)

SUNDAY
The Word Became Flesh
(John 1:1–14)

Notes

Teaching Tips

Words You Should Know

A. Believing (John 4:48) *pisteuo* (Gk.)—To trust, have faith in

B. Amend (v. 52) *kompsoteron* (Gk.)—To be good, well, glad

Teacher Preparation

Unifying Principle—Never Too Far Away. When we or our loved ones are sick, we seek restoration and healing. When all efforts fail, what can we do? Jesus invites our active, faith-filled participation with His power to create new life through healing—even at a distance.

A. Read the Bible Background and Devotional Reading.

B. Pray for your students and lesson clarity.

C. Read the lesson Scripture in multiple translations.

O—Open the Lesson

A. Begin the class with prayer.

B. Ask participants to share stories about how they were willing to travel a great distance to see a person whose work they valued (e.g. a political figure, a medical specialist, an outstanding restaurateur). Lead into Bible study by saying that the Bible tells us about a man who went out of his way to find Jesus.

C. Have the students read the Aim for Change and the In Focus story.

D. Ask students how events like those in the story weigh on their hearts and how they can view these events from a faith perspective.

P—Present the Scriptures

A. Read the Focal Verses and discuss the Background and The People, Places, and Times sections.

B. Have the class share what Scriptures stand out for them and why, with particular emphasis on today's themes.

E—Explore the Meaning

A. Use In Depth or More Light on the Text to facilitate a deeper discussion of the lesson text.

B. Pose the questions in Search the Scriptures and Discuss the Meaning.

C. Discuss the Liberating Lesson and Application for Activation sections.

N—Next Steps for Application

A. Summarize the value of coming to God as a first response rather than as a last resort.

B. End class with a commitment to pray for healing for loved ones.

Worship Guide

For the Superintendent or Teacher
Theme: The Word Heals
Song: "There is a Balm in Gilead"

Handwritten note: I.P. THUR 7:30P (213) 338·8477 893 5948 4624

The Word Heals

Bible Background • JOHN 4:46–54
Printed Text • JOHN 4:46–54 | Devotional Reading • JOHN 4:31–34

Aim for Change

By the end of this lesson, we will UNDERSTAND the definition of faith and how Christ honors faithfulness, ACCEPT that faith in Christ strengthens the relationship between Christ and the believer, and TRUST Jesus, by faith and action, to do what we cannot do.

In Focus

Thomas, who was partially blind, walked into HOPE church on a Sunday afternoon. Visitors often walked in off the street at HOPE church. During this special time at HOPE, Pastor Hill was teaching on miracles. As Pastor Hill ended his teaching, he made the call for salvation, and Thomas walked to the front of the church. The pastor asked him his name as he was a visitor. He said, "My name is Thomas. I need food to feed my daughters; my wife died, and we are having a hard time."

Pastor Hill responded, "We have a food kitchen that will help you with food. Is there anything else we can do for you?" he asked.

Thomas responded, "Just pray for me!" Since Pastor Hill had been teaching on miracles, he prayed to God for a miracle on Thomas' behalf. The congregation had been seeing them manifest in their own lives. Their faith was activated to believe God for miracles.

Pastor Hill prayed specifically for Thomas' eyes, "Father, we know You are a miracle worker, You have restored sight to the blind, and that nothing is impossible for You. God, we believe that Thomas's eyes are healed. We believe by faith, that when he opens his eyes that he will be able to see."

When the pastor finished praying, the man opened his eyes. He began to cry and blink several times. Thomas said his eyes did not burn, and he could see. The congregation, pastor, and man all rejoiced because God had performed a miracle!

In today's lesson, believers testify that faith in God's Word produces healing. Can you recall your faith in God's Word producing healing in your life and others?

Keep in Mind

"So the father knew that it was at the same hour, in the which Jesus said unto him, Thy son liveth: and himself believed, and his whole house." (John 4:53, KJV)

"Then the father realized that that was the very time Jesus had told him, 'Your son will live.' And he and his entire household believed in Jesus." (John 4:53, NLT)

Focal Verses

KJV **John 4:46** So Jesus came again into Cana of Galilee, where he made the water wine. And there was a certain nobleman, whose son was sick at Capernaum.

47 When he heard that Jesus was come out of Judaea into Galilee, he went unto him, and besought him that he would come down, and heal his son: for he was at the point of death.

48 Then said Jesus unto him, Except ye see signs and wonders, ye will not believe.

49 The nobleman saith unto him, Sir, come down ere my child die.

50 Jesus saith unto him, Go thy way; thy son liveth. And the man believed the word that Jesus had spoken unto him, and he went his way.

51 And as he was now going down, his servants met him, and told him, saying, Thy son liveth.

52 Then enquired he of them the hour when he began to amend. And they said unto him, Yesterday at the seventh hour the fever left him.

53 So the father knew that it was at the same hour, in the which Jesus said unto him, Thy son liveth: and himself believed, and his whole house.

54 This is again the second miracle that Jesus did, when he was come out of Judaea into Galilee.

NLT **John 4:46** As he traveled through Galilee, he came to Cana, where he had turned the water into wine. There was a government official in nearby Capernaum whose son was very sick.

47 When he heard that Jesus had come from Judea to Galilee, he went and begged Jesus to come to Capernaum to heal his son, who was about to die.

48 Jesus asked, "Will you never believe in me unless you see miraculous signs and wonders?"

49 The official pleaded, "Lord, please come now before my little boy dies."

50 Then Jesus told him, "Go back home. Your son will live!" And the man believed what Jesus said and started home.

51 While the man was on his way, some of his servants met him with the news that his son was alive and well.

52 He asked them when the boy had begun to get better, and they replied, "Yesterday afternoon at one o'clock his fever suddenly disappeared!"

53 Then the father realized that that was the very time Jesus had told him, "Your son will live." And he and his entire household believed in Jesus.

54 This was the second miraculous sign Jesus did in Galilee after coming from Judea.

The People, Places, and Times

Capernaum. Located on the northwestern shore of the Sea of Galilee, Capernaum, a city in the Galilean province, was a central location for Jesus' earthly ministry. Jesus lived in Nazareth until He came to Galilee and was baptized by John the Baptist (Mark 1:9). After John the Baptist was imprisoned, Jesus returned to Galilee and resided in Capernaum (Matthew 4:12–16). Here, on the shore of the Sea of Galilee, the Lord called His first disciples—Peter, Andrew, James, and John (Matthew 4:18–22). Peter's home in Capernaum became the residence for Jesus and the apostles when they were not traveling (Mark 1:29; Luke 4:38). The Lord often preached in the synagogue in Capernaum (Mark 1:21; John 6:52–59) and performed many miracles in the city. These miracles included the healing of the centurion's servant (Matthew 8:5–13), the healing of the man with palsy (Mark 2:1–12), and the casting out of a demon in a man in the synagogue (Luke 4:31–36). Even though Jesus performed so many miracles in Capernaum, the people still had not repented (Matthew 11:23–24).

Why do people who have so much evidence of God's work refuse to see it?

Background

Cana of Galilee is the birthplace of miracles in Jesus' ministry. The healing of this nobleman's son is notable as Capernaum is approximately 16 miles away from Cana. This miracle is not only notable because of the geographic distance but because it marks Jesus' return to Galilee.

Prior to Jesus' arrival in Cana, Jesus had taken a journey through Judea and Galilee. Jesus was compelled to go to Samaria. Historically, the Samaritans were condemned by the Jewish people. Yet, Jesus needed to go to Samaria. Jesus encountered the Samaritan woman at Jacob's well (John 4:1-6). Jesus' natural thirst was used to fulfill the spiritual thirst of the Samaritan woman, leading Jesus and the Samaritan woman to have a life-altering, life-changing exchange.

Jesus revealed His identity to the Samaritan woman. The Samaritan woman found saving, believing faith in Jesus. Her encounter with Jesus caused a revival in Samaria. The Samaritan woman was the first recorded female evangelist in the Bible (John 4:39–42). Jesus was recognized as the Messiah and was honored accordingly.

Yet, Jesus' next journey was into Galilee. Jesus was received though not accepted or honored (John 4:43–45). In Galilee, belief was challenged, and miracles were hindered. The miracle healing of the nobleman's son was an announcement that Christ was in Cana and He was indeed the Messiah.

At-A-Glance

1. Flawed Believing Faith (John 4:46–47)
2. The Challenge of Faith (v. 48)
3. Dismantling Earthly Expectation (vv. 49–51)
4. The Healing Word of Jesus (vv. 52–54)

In Depth

1. Flawed Believing Faith (John 4:46–47)

The very existence of Jesus is a manifestation of the power of an unhindered and unrestrained spoken word. The nobleman was familiar with Jesus' miracles and believed in what Jesus could do. When the nobleman learned that Jesus was in Cana, he traveled for an entire day uphill to beckon Jesus to come to Capernaum to heal his son.

The nobleman had the faith to approach Jesus knowing He could heal his son, but his faith was flawed because he believed the healing required His presence, believing Jesus' authority and power was relegated to His bodily form. Oftentimes, our faith can be flawed in desperation indicating the need for the flaws to be worked by our faith being challenged.

Have you encountered times in your walk of faith, when your desperation revealed the flaws in your faith?

2. The Challenge of Faith (v. 48)

It is evident that the nobleman had believing faith, yet his faith was hindered by his thinking and experience. The nobleman believed the sickness of his son is what brought him to Jesus, but Jesus knew that the nobleman needed to be challenged in his faith to accept the reality of Him being Messiah and to demonstrate that His Word is as powerful as His presence when believed.

The nobleman's faith in Jesus was sparked by what he heard, but his faith needed to mature so that it could be strengthened by his own experience with Jesus. The challenge of his son's illness brought him to Jesus so that his reality of Jesus could be challenged.

How many times have we hindered God, because we were unwilling to allow God full access to move in a situation?

3. Dismantling Earthly Expectation (vv. 49–51)

Often crisis reveals our expectation of God. Jesus' encounters on earth were designed to shift our perspective from the earth to heaven. The nobleman had an earthly expectation of what Jesus could do: heal. It could only happen if Jesus came in person. Jesus needed the nobleman to understand that the power of God is unhindered by time or space. Jesus gave a direct order that dismantled the nobleman's expectation and increased his faith, "Go thy way; thy son liveth." The nobleman believed what Jesus said and obediently followed His directive (John 4:50).

The obedient response indicates that his faith increased. The nobleman journeyed to Capernaum and was met by his servant to confirm the words of Jesus, "Thy son liveth."

What can we do to dismantle our earthly expectations and exchange them for the answered prayer?

4. The Healing Word of Jesus (vv. 52–54)

The power embedded in the spoken word of Jesus shines out when the nobleman inquires at what time his son became well. The servants confirmed the exact timing of the word of healing that manifested for the son. The nobleman immediately recognizes the power in the healing word of Jesus, and the faith of the nobleman matured. The timing of healing words, "Thy son liveth" showed the nobleman the correlation between faith and miracles. He believed, his household believed, and his son lived.

Can you identify times when your faith and the word of God worked together to produce miracles?

Search the Scriptures

1. Why did Jesus challenge the nobleman regarding signs and wonders (John 4:48)?

2. Compare and contrast the centurion's (Matthew 8:5–13) and the nobleman's encounters with Jesus and the sending of the word to heal.

Discuss the Meaning

1. Why is it important to examine our expectation of healing?

2. How does what we believe impact what we receive from God?

Liberating Lesson

Many of us have had desperate situations when we needed God to heal us or someone that we love. Often times we have responded desperately to those needs and were often left defeated because we did not receive the answer we had hoped for. The result of unanswered prayers pushes believers into a posture of begging, even though God does not require that or even want that from us. God desires our prayers to be fervent and persistent which results in mature faith. Mature faith is what gives glory to God. Answered prayer also gives glory to God and serves as a testament to God's faithfulness to us. Not only does answered prayer witness God's faithfulness to us, but it also demonstrates to unbelievers the reality of God. God is trying to shift our expectation of Him. Earthly expectations of heavenly encounters would often weaken the demonstration of God's power in our lives.

Application for Activation

"Jesus heals" is an infallible truth. The Word's ability to heal is not bound by time, distance, circumstance, or the grave. We need to shift our perspective for the reality of these truths to manifest in our lives through Christ Jesus.

• Ask God to reveal to you areas of flawed faith.

• When you pray, are you begging or persisting in fervency?

• Discern whether your expectations of God are earthly focused or heavenly focused.

• Examine whether you are responding to God in obedience only or is your obedience coupled with faith and trust.

Follow the Spirit

What God wants me to do:

_____

_____

_____

_____

_____

Remember Your Thoughts

Special insights I have learned:

_____

_____

_____

_____

_____

More Light on the Text

John 4:46–54

The Bible provides the faithful accounts of Jesus' ministry, including His marvelous miracle working. Although most of the time He healed by touching the person, sometimes all He used was the power of His Word. With that Word, He created and ordered the world in the beginning, and with that Word, He could continue the work of bringing order to chaos.

This account of Jesus healing the nobleman's son has some similarities to Luke's account of Jesus healing a centurion's servant (Luke 7:1–10). Both occur in Galilee and feature Jesus curing people from a deadly illness without touching them. While there are similarities between these two healings there are substantial differences including where it occurred, who was requesting the miracle, and for whom the miracle was requested. John tells about the time Jesus healed a nobleman's son while in Cana. Luke tells about a different time that Jesus healed a centurion's servant in Capernaum. In Luke, Jesus goes toward the centurion's house, but is stopped from going inside, while in John Jesus makes no motion to go to the nobleman's house. Jesus is impressed by the centurion's faith, but chides the lacking faith of the nobleman and inhabitants of Cana.

While sometimes it is helpful to compare the way different Gospel writers share the same story of Jesus, it is also important to remember that, as John says at the end of his Gospel, no one would be able to record every one of the amazing things Jesus did. Usually when Gospel writers differ in their tellings of Jesus' actions, they differ only in the details or timing of events, not in such major elements and themes of the accounts. It is entirely possible—and as we have seen likely—that John and Luke are recording different events.

46 So Jesus came again into Cana of Galilee, where he made the water wine. And there was a certain nobleman, whose son was sick at Capernaum.

After a long time down in Jerusalem for Passover and a detour through Samaria, Jesus has returned to the area of Galilee. He does not go to his home in Nazareth, where He is not welcome (v. 44), but instead goes to Cana. This village is about 8 miles north of Nazareth and 12 miles west of the Sea of Galilee. He has already been in Cana before, where He performed His first public miracle by turning water into wine at a wedding (John 2:1–11). People are excited to see Him in the area again, hoping for more miracles (v. 45).

The Greek word for "nobleman" (v. 46) was *basilikos* (bah-see-lee-**KOCE**) and means "royal" or connected to the king. He has come all the way from Capernaum, where his son lays ill. Capernaum is a fishing town on the Sea of Galilee, about 15 miles from Cana. This man has traveled all that way, up into the Galilean hills, to see Jesus. He is wealthy or influential enough to have access to many things, except the one thing he wants—a cure for his son's failing health.

47 When he heard that Jesus was come out of Judaea into Galilee, he went unto him, and besought him that he would come down, and heal his son: for he was at the point of death.

After witnessing Jesus' first miracle in Galilee—turning water into wine—and the miracles He performed in Jerusalem during the Passover (2:23; 4:45), the Galileans were happy to receive Him again. The nobleman wasted no time presenting his request. The nobleman did not let his title or position keep him from going to and begging the One with a higher calling to heal his son. However, the nobleman's faith was limited by earthly thinking. With a son so close to death, he believed he needed Jesus closer. Thus, he asked Jesus to travel back down to his home in Capernaum. In all fairness, all of Jesus' miracles so far have been conducted onsite, and could have led the nobleman to believe that Jesus needed to be in his home in order to heal his son.

The nobleman was desperate because of his son's deadly sickness. He "besought" Jesus' aid. The Greek word here *erotao* (air-oh-**TAH**-oh) means "to ask," and is used when asking a person to do something. The nobleman is not asking for a thing, like health or a miracle. He is asking for Jesus to do something, to use His power. He knows he needs Jesus Himself.

Today, we know specific goods or services sometimes require us to go to specific people. You might have traveled miles to attend a certain event or meet a famous person. When the need is greater, our willingness to go further is greater too. We might feel desperate when a loved one is ill or in distress. God has provided us with many specialists to help problems, whether medical, financial, personal, or academic. He also provides Himself to us, to hear and respond to any request or worry we present to Him. Christians can feel confident that God will hear our prayers for healing of those close to them. Christians should also practice coming to God as a first response rather than a last resort during trials.

48 Then said Jesus unto him, Except ye see signs and wonders, ye will not believe.

As indicated by the use of "ye," Jesus was not only speaking to the nobleman but to those around him. If He had only been speaking to the nobleman, the King James English equivalent would have been "thee," the singular form of the second-person pronoun. This accurately translates the plural subject recorded in the Greek.

Contrasted with the faith of the Samaritans who readily believed after the testimony of one woman (see v. 39), the Galileans on the other hand, even after witnessing the first miracle needed to see more. Commentators point out that this is the only time that John used the words "signs and wonders" together, although the phrase is often seen elsewhere (Mark 13:22, Acts 4:30, Romans 15:19). The word "wonders" here is *teras* (Gk. **TEH**-ross) refers to extraordinary occurrences and unusual manifestations. John spends more time focused on Jesus' teaching and only includes a handful of miracles, so he does not discuss signs and wonders as often as the other Gospels. One commentator emphasized that Jesus' miracles are signs that show a glimpse of what heaven is like, of what God made the world to be, rather than just wonders whereby witnesses are awestruck.

Jesus challenged the people's faith with these words, "Except ye see signs and wonders, ye will not believe." It is natural for people to want further proof of a remarkable report. Those who trust in Jesus, however, know that a mature faith is more than mere affirmation of God's nature; it is a bold trust in God's power regardless of circumstances. John speaks of the importance of "believing" (Gk. *pisteuo*, peece-**TEW**-oh) far more than any of the other Gospel writers. Notably too, John only speaks of believing, and never of belief. For John, faith is an action—something you have to do—not a noun, something you can passively have. Instead of doing the work of going out on a limb and holding simply to faith itself as the evidence of things unseen, the people of Galilee want a different concrete example to cling to. They will believe Jesus if He proves Himself by performing miracles. Capernaum had become intoxicated with signs and wonders to prove the reality and deity of Jesus. The nobleman would be changed and his native Capernaum could see that signs and wonders should not dictate belief. Signs and wonders should be a by-product of belief (Acts 4:30), not a pre-condition for it. The focus should be the belief, not the miracles.

49 The nobleman saith unto him, Sir, come down ere my child die.

Adults know that distance from a source of power can decrease its potency. The nobleman fears that Cana's distance restricts Jesus' power. Even after Jesus issued the verbal rebuke, the nobleman still requests Jesus' presence in Capernaum. He believed that Cana's distance would restrict Jesus' power. This is what happens with normal physical powers. Voices are harder to hear from afar, words are harder to read, so the nobleman does not realize that Jesus' word would be so powerful even from 15 miles away.

Perhaps the nobleman had seen or heard about how patient Jesus could be with people, and felt the need to hurry Jesus along to his house. It is possible that Jesus was already two days later than one would expect for someone journeying from Judea to Galilee, as the Samaritans had urged him to stay with them for two more days (see v. 40). For the nobleman's son, time was of the essence and he repeated his request, "Sir, come down ere my child die." Thus, we find a man whose faith was not only limited by space, but also by time. Jesus later shows His mastery over sickness no matter the time when He waited to heal Lazarus until he had been dead for three days (John 11).

50 Jesus saith unto him, Go thy way; thy son liveth. And the man believed the word that Jesus had spoken unto him, and he went his way. 51 And as he was now going down, his servants met him, and told him, saying, Thy son liveth.

It must have been something about the way Jesus spoke those words that led the nobleman to believe. Upon hearing one sentence, he stopped trying to re-route Jesus, and changed his own direction. To walk away from faulty and religious thinking, and to renew his mind with just a few words was a major step in the right direction. To leave Jesus' side was the utmost demonstration of faith. Jesus had rebuked him and the other Galileans about their reticence to believe without miracles. Now the nobleman trusts Jesus enough now to leave and start his 15-mile journey back toward his son even before seeing any proof of this miracle. His faith was met with evidence when on his way home. His servants meet him and repeat Jesus' words almost exactly: "Thy son liveth." God's word never returns void.

The nobleman's expectation needed dismantling because it limited the healing power of Jesus to Capernaum. Now that he has seen the fulfillment of Jesus' healing word, his earthly expectation has indeed been dismantled. There may be areas today where God is trying to shift your expectation. Christians can trust Jesus' word and leading completely, knowing that He is able to do infinitely more than we could ever think or imagine!

52 Then enquired he of them the hour when he began to amend. And they said unto him, Yesterday at the seventh hour the fever left him. 53 So the father knew that it was at the same hour, in the which Jesus said unto him, Thy son liveth: and himself believed, and his whole house.

The nobleman is not anxious or afraid of time. In fact, he is seeking confirmation that time was on his side. This time stamp proved that the power he felt when Jesus spoke was the same power that healed his son in the selfsame hour. Jews of this time counted hours after sunrise, making the "seventh" hour around 2 o'clock in the afternoon. The Word of His power is not limited by time or space.

Everyone who was affected by the child's illness believed in Jesus because of the nobleman's testimony. There are several examples in the Bible of the entire family converting to the religion of the head of the household. All of the centurion Cornelius' relatives and servants became Christians along with Cornelius after they spoke in tongues by the power of the Holy Spirit (Acts 10). Likewise, the prison guard of Paul and Silas's cell in Philippi was just about to kill himself, when Paul stops him and shares the Gospel. Jesus' word brought healing, and the nobleman's word brought salvation (Acts 16).

54 This is again the second miracle that Jesus did, when he was come out of Judaea into Galilee.

It appears that John is taking readers on a journey, marked by the miracles and deep theology of Jesus. He emphasizes that this part of the journey is denoted by the second miracle. Commentators have used this verse to contrast the two miracles: the first miracle took place at a wedding—a joyous occasion, and was done to bless a husband and wife; on the other hand the second miracle demonstrated the complexity of life was related to a house of mourning and enacted on behalf of a father. Jesus was drawn to the second miracle by intercession, the beginning of someone else's faith, but his mother drew him to His first miracle, the beginning of His own ministry. One reason for John's inclusion of this miracle was for the audience to understand the progression of faith from its weak and sensuous stage, to a tested and strengthened stage, to a final crowned and rewarded stage.

One of the reasons Jesus came was to heal the sick. We limit His purpose in healing either because of flawed faith or flawed expectation. God promises that He will do exceedingly abundantly more than we can ask or think, through the power that works in us (Ephesians 3:20). We must strive to mature in faith, dismantle our earthly expectations, and ensure our expectations are congruent with heaven. We must ensure that we are both believing and obedient to all of God's orders in our lives.

Sources:

Full Life Holy Bible, King James Version. Grand Rapids, MI: Zondervan Publishing House. 1992. 802-804.

Guzik, David. *The Enduring Word Bible Commentary*. 2019.

MacLaren, A. Expositions of Holy Scriptures. https://biblehub.com/commentaries/john/4-54.htm (accessed September 17, 2020).

Nelson, Thomas. *New Spirit Filled Life Bible*. Nashville, TN: Thomas Nelson Publishers. 2002. 1519.

Perome, J. J. S. *The Cambridge Bible for schools and colleges*. https://biblehub.com/commentaries/john/4-48.htm (accessed September 17, 2020).

Radmacher, Earl D., ed. *Nelson's New Illustrated Bible Commentary: Spreading the Light of God's Word into Your Life*. Nashville, TN: Thomas Nelson Publishers, 1999. 1648-1653.

Spence-Jones, H. D. M. *The Pulpit Commentary*. https://biblehub.com/commentaries/john/4-53.htm (accessed September 17, 2020).

Say It Correctly

Cana. KAY-nah
Capernaum. kah-PER-nay-um.

Daily Bible Readings

MONDAY
Jesus Reveals His Glory
(John 2:1–11)

TUESDAY
O Lord, Heal Me!
(Psalm 6)

WEDNESDAY
Jesus Heals a Centurion's Servant
(Matthew 8:5–13)

THURSDAY
Jesus Heals a Paralyzed Man
(John 5:1–9)

FRIDAY
Jesus Heals a Blind Man
(John 9:1–7)

SATURDAY
God Heals Their Infirmities
(Psalm 41)

SUNDAY
Jesus Heals a Royal Official's Son
(John 4:46–54)

Notes

Teaching Tips

Words You Should Know

A. Raise again (John 11:24) *anistemi* (Gk.)—To stand up, raise up from sitting; to raise up from death

B. Believe (v. 27) *pisteuo* (Gk.)—To accept as true, be persuaded of, credit, or place confidence in

Teacher Preparation

Unifying Principle—Conquering the Ultimate Enemy. When people experience tragic situations, they long for comfort. Where can we find hope and strength for the future? Our faith in Jesus releases the power of God to bring resurrection and new life.

A. Read the Bible Background and Devotional Reading.

B. Pray for your students and lesson clarity.

C. Read the lesson Scripture in multiple translations.

O—Open the Lesson

A. Begin the class with prayer.

B. Before class, write several euphemisms for death (ex: passed away, bought the farm, gave up the ghost, kicked the bucket, six feet under, etc.) on individual index cards. Begin class by having volunteers draw a card and try to communicate the euphemism to the rest of the class in the style of the game Pictionary®. Lead into Bible study by asking why it is common to use such expressions.

C. Have the students read the Aim for Change and the In Focus story.

D. Ask students how events like those in the story weigh on their hearts and how they can view these events from a faith perspective.

P—Present the Scriptures

A. Read the Focal Verses and discuss the Background and The People, Places, and Times sections.

B. Have the class share what Scriptures stand out for them and why, with particular emphasis on today's themes.

E—Explore the Meaning

A. Use In Depth or More Light on the Text to facilitate a deeper discussion of the lesson text.

B. Pose the questions in Search the Scriptures and Discuss the Meaning.

C. Discuss the Liberating Lesson and Application for Activation sections.

N—Next Steps for Application

A. Summarize the value of looking forward to a future bodily resurrection of the dead.

B. End class with a commitment to pray for faith that they can face death confidently.

Worship Guide

For the Superintendent or Teacher
Theme: The Word Resurrects the Dead
Song: "When Grief is Raw"

The Word Resurrects the Dead

Bible Background • JOHN 11:17–44
Printed Text • JOHN 11:17–27, 38–44 | Devotional Reading • JOHN 3:18–21

Aim for Change

By the end of this lesson, we will EXPLORE Mary's and Martha's faith relationships with Jesus; EMBRACE with the confident expectation that Jesus has the power of God to save, heal, and raise people from the dead; and ENGAGE with Jesus honestly and faithfully, even when faced with impossible situations.

In Focus

Franklin hesitantly ascended the steps of the church. It had been a long time since he'd been in any church, but he couldn't stay away from DeShawn's funeral. He still couldn't believe that his friend had died so suddenly. He knew that DeShawn was in heaven, but that didn't help the ache in Franklin's heart.

The funeral started, and one by one, people shared how much DeShawn had meant to them. Franklin was touched when he heard the many testimonies of how DeShawn had shown God's love to others. His cousin said, "DeShawn lived his life in the certain hope that he had a place in heaven ready for him. But he also had hope that his mighty God could change this world too. That's why he fought so hard for change in our community."

Finally, the preacher came up to give the message. "Jesus said, 'I am the resurrection and the life.' Those of us who have believed in Jesus Christ as our Savior know that we will see DeShawn again. We do not mourn as those who have no hope! We do have hope, and His name is Jesus."

Franklin thought about the preacher's words for several days afterwards. It had been a long time since he had hope of any kind. Maybe now was the time to gain new hope—the hope of eternal life through Jesus Christ.

Because Jesus has conquered death, we have hope. What can we do to keep our hope vibrant in the face of impossible situations?

Keep in Mind

"Jesus said unto her, I am the resurrection, and the life: he that believeth in me, though he were dead, yet shall he live: And whosoever liveth and believeth in me shall never die. Believest thou this?" (John 11:25-26, KJV)

"Jesus told her, 'I am the resurrection and the life. Anyone who believes in me will live, even after dying. Everyone who lives in me and believes in me will never ever die. Do you believe this, Martha?'" (John 11:25-26, NLT)

Focal Verses

KJV **John 11:17** Then when Jesus came, he found that he had lain in the grave four days already.

18 Now Bethany was nigh unto Jerusalem, about fifteen furlongs off:

19 And many of the Jews came to Martha and Mary, to comfort them concerning their brother.

20 Then Martha, as soon as she heard that Jesus was coming, went and met him: but Mary sat still in the house.

21 Then said Martha unto Jesus, Lord, if thou hadst been here, my brother had not died.

22 But I know, that even now, whatsoever thou wilt ask of God, God will give it thee.

23 Jesus saith unto her, Thy brother shall rise again.

24 Martha saith unto him, I know that he shall rise again in the resurrection at the last day.

25 Jesus said unto her, I am the resurrection, and the life: he that believeth in me, though he were dead, yet shall he live:

26 And whosoever liveth and believeth in me shall never die. Believest thou this?

27 She saith unto him, Yea, Lord: I believe that thou art the Christ, the Son of God, which should come into the world.

38 Jesus therefore again groaning in himself cometh to the grave. It was a cave, and a stone lay upon it.

39 Jesus said, Take ye away the stone. Martha, the sister of him that was dead, saith unto him, Lord, by this time he stinketh: for he hath been dead four days.

40 Jesus saith unto her, Said I not unto thee, that, if thou wouldest believe, thou shouldest see the glory of God?

41 Then they took away the stone from the place where the dead was laid. And Jesus lifted up his eyes, and said, Father, I thank thee that thou hast heard me.

NLT **John 11:17** When Jesus arrived at Bethany, he was told that Lazarus had already been in his grave for four days.

18 Bethany was only a few miles down the road from Jerusalem,

19 and many of the people had come to console Martha and Mary in their loss.

20 When Martha got word that Jesus was coming, she went to meet him. But Mary stayed in the house.

21 Martha said to Jesus, "Lord, if only you had been here, my brother would not have died.

22 But even now I know that God will give you whatever you ask."

23 Jesus told her, "Your brother will rise again."

24 "Yes," Martha said, "he will rise when everyone else rises, at the last day."

25 Jesus told her, "I am the resurrection and the life. Anyone who believes in me will live, even after dying.

26 Everyone who lives in me and believes in me will never ever die. Do you believe this, Martha?"

27 "Yes, Lord," she told him. "I have always believed you are the Messiah, the Son of God, the one who has come into the world from God."

38 Jesus was still angry as he arrived at the tomb, a cave with a stone rolled across its entrance.

39 "Roll the stone aside," Jesus told them. But Martha, the dead man's sister, protested, "Lord, he has been dead for four days. The smell will be terrible."

40 Jesus responded, "Didn't I tell you that you would see God's glory if you believe?"

41 So they rolled the stone aside. Then Jesus looked up to heaven and said, "Father, thank you for hearing me.

42 And I knew that thou hearest me always: but because of the people which stand by I said it, that they may believe that thou hast sent me.

43 And when he thus had spoken, he cried with a loud voice, Lazarus, come forth.

44 And he that was dead came forth, bound hand and foot with graveclothes: and his face was bound about with a napkin. Jesus saith unto them, Loose him, and let him go.

42 You always hear me, but I said it out loud for the sake of all these people standing here, so that they will believe you sent me."

43 Then Jesus shouted, "Lazarus, come out!"

44 And the dead man came out, his hands and feet bound in graveclothes, his face wrapped in a headcloth. Jesus told them, "Unwrap him and let him go!"

The People, Places, and Times

Martha. Most scholars believe that Martha was the elder sister of Mary and Lazarus. This is because she is referred to as the owner of the house (Luke 10:38). In an earlier meeting with Jesus, it was Martha who became distraught when her sister Mary sat at Jesus' feet instead of helping her serve (Luke 10:39–42).

Bethany. This is a village on the eastern slope of the Mount of Olives, almost two miles east of Jerusalem. It appears that Jesus preferred to lodge there instead of in Jerusalem while He was in the area for the pilgrimage festivals of Passover, Tabernacles, and Pentecost. It was here in the house of Simon the Leper that Jesus was anointed days before his death. The name means "house of figs." Today, it is known as *el-Azariyeh* (i.e., "place of Lazarus").

Background

Only in the book of John do we find the recounting of Jesus raising Lazarus from the dead. This is a family that Jesus loved, and He was loved by them. When He needed a rest, He knew He could find it with these three adults.

At the start of John 11, Martha and Mary notify Jesus that their brother Lazarus is deathly sick (v. 3). But instead of rushing to Bethany, Jesus stays where He is for two more days. Therefore, by the time Jesus finally arrives in Bethany, Lazarus has been dead four days.

Obviously, Jesus was not in a rush to get to Bethany. He informs His disciples that Lazarus is in fact dead and that He is glad that He was not there to keep Lazarus from dying, so that they may believe (John 11:15). This statement shapes the theological heart of today's lesson.

At-A-Glance

1. Jesus Is in Control (John 11:17–20)
2. Jesus Is Always Right on Time (vv. 21–24)
3. Jesus Is the Resurrection and the Life (vv. 25–27)
4. Jesus Is Lord over Death (vv. 38-44)

In Depth

1. Jesus Is in Control (John 11:17–20)

When Jesus arrives in Bethany, Lazarus had already been dead four days. The professional mourners had arrived, and the situation looked hopeless to the human eye. Everything around Martha and Mary was telling them that it was time to give up hope—that there was nothing more to be done. Ultimately, Jesus is in complete control of the situation. His delay is for the benefit of His disciples and Lazarus' sisters, Martha and Mary, so they may come to trust in the Lord with all their hearts, instead of leaning on their own understanding (Proverbs 3:5).

Jesus wants us to put our complete confidence in Him because He is in control of all the affairs of life. When things look bad and we cannot see any way out, Jesus wants us to run to Him, like Martha, and place all of our trust in Him alone.

What benefit do we think we gain by handling things ourselves rather than trusting Jesus?

2. Jesus Is Always Right on Time (vv. 21–24)

Some scholars suggest Martha's first remarks to Jesus were ones of reproach instead of grief. In a positive light, however, we recognize Martha's faith in Jesus' ability to heal her brother is undiminished. She knows God will do whatever Jesus asks, which implies she believes Jesus is a righteous man for whom nothing is impossible.

When Jesus tells her, "thy brother shall rise again" (v. 23), Martha's response implies that she does not yet grasp Jesus' full implication. She understood that in the "last day" all would rise, but she does not expect an immediate miracle.

The way Martha addresses Jesus is similar to how we often address Him when things do not go the way we think they should. The Lord may not show up when we think He ought to, but we can be sure that He is always right on time.

How have you misunderstood God's meaning when He tries to comfort you?

3. Jesus Is the Resurrection and the Life (vv. 25–27)

When Jesus heard Martha's reply, He responded to her by stating emphatically, "I am the resurrection, and the life" (v. 25). In essence, Jesus was telling Martha, "You keep looking forward to some event in the future, but what you are looking for is standing right in front of you." Jesus challenged Martha to place her trust in Him as the One who holds the power of life and death in His hands. The Lord wants us to know that all power in heaven and on earth is in Jesus' hand (Matthew 28:18), and for this reason we should place all of our trust in Him.

Placing faith in Jesus has implications for the present and is not relegated to the afterlife. Jesus wants to effect change in our lives right now. As Christians, we must reach the point where our trust in Christ transcends our understanding of the world around us.

When has God surprised you when you thought the situation was beyond hope?

4. Jesus Is Lord over Death (vv. 38–44)

Mary comes to meet Jesus on the road and interacts with Him much as Martha did. Seeing the sorrow of the sisters and the mourners, Jesus is still upset when He comes to the grave. There, He begins to work a miracle. Martha still objects pragmatically, but Jesus insists.

Jesus' prayer to God here is largely for the benefit of those listening rather than for God Himself. Jesus will have it known that this miracle is to bring glory to God, above anything else. Then using only His voice, which created all things and therefore has authority over all things, He calls for Lazarus to come out.

Lazarus obediently comes out. He is still dressed as a corpse and must be freed from his wrappings, but his resurrection is a lasting testament to the power of Jesus' words.

Why do we, like Martha, object when God wants to work a miracle for us?

Search the Scriptures

1. How does Martha understand Jesus' words about her brother rising again (v. 24)?

2. What does Jesus say are the results of believing in Him (vv. 25–26)?

Discuss the Meaning

1. Jesus tells Martha, "Thy brother shall rise again" (from John 11:23), and raises him. Do you think that Jesus wants to demonstrate His resurrecting power in our lives even today? Give some examples of His power at work in your life.

2. What did Jesus mean when He said, "he that believeth in me, though he were dead, yet shall he live" (from v. 25)? How does this affect our lives right now?

Liberating Lesson

We have many euphemisms when discussing death. We care for our health, take security precautions, create safety devices, and so much more, because we fear our death. And when we are faced with death, we do not always know how to comfort others during times of grief. The whole situation makes us uncomfortable. This is largely because of all the uncertainty surrounding death.

Christians know, however, that Jesus is the Resurrection and the Life. He came to show us the way to an abundant life of bringing glory to God. We can trust Him to bring Christians a bodily resurrection and a heavenly home. The exact details of what that looks like are unclear, but the Christian's hope for eternal life frees us from fear of death.

Application for Activation

We have all been in situations that looked hopeless. Undoubtedly, we have been tempted to give up hope and count our losses. Think about some of the times that you have given up hope and the Lord came in and "resurrected" the situation. Think about the effect this had on you and what effect it should have on your faith. What would it look like for you to trust Jesus to resurrect the situation today?

Follow the Spirit

What God wants me to do:

_____

_____

_____

Remember Your Thoughts

Special insights I have learned:

_____

_____

_____

_____

More Light on the Text

John 11:17–27, 38–44

17 Then when Jesus came, he found that he had lain in the grave four days already. 18 Now Bethany was nigh unto Jerusalem, about fifteen furlongs off: 19 And many of the Jews came to Martha and Mary, to comfort them concerning their brother.

Lazarus had been dead and buried for four days. The KJV translates that Bethany is "about fifteen furlongs" from Jerusalem. A furlong is a unit of measure used in the medieval period, based on the length of a field, roughly equal to 220 yards. The Greek word translated as furlongs, however, is *stadion* (**STAY**-dee-on), which is the length of an ancient Greek race track, roughly 200 yards. Fifteen of them would be 9,000 feet, or 1.7 miles. John draws attention to this fact because it shows how close they were to Jerusalem. Therefore, there were many Jews from Jerusalem who had come to Bethany, who would witness the great miracle that was about to take place. Jewish custom provided for a 30-day period of mourning. To console the bereaved during this period of mourning was considered a pious act among the Jews.

These traveling visitors also call to question Jesus' delay in going to see Lazarus. He knows exactly what is taking place. But why does He linger and not rush to the scene? Could it be that He waited to demonstrate His power until all hope in human effort was exhausted?

20 Then Martha, as soon as she heard that Jesus was coming, went and met him: but Mary sat still in the house.

Upon hearing of Jesus' arrival, Martha hastened to meet Him, while Mary sat in the house. The different responses of Martha and Mary may indicate their personality types: Martha was the outgoing activist and Mary was the contemplative type. It can also be said that because Martha was the older of the two sisters, it was her duty to go out to meet Jesus. Martha rushes out to Jesus and leaves Mary in the house to continue the mourning rituals with the other mourners.

21 Then said Martha unto Jesus, Lord, if thou hadst been here, my brother had not died. 22 But I know, that even now, whatsoever thou wilt ask of God, God will give it thee.

Martha's words were a confession of her faith in the Lord; they were not intended as a reproach of Jesus, but were the response of a person in great grief. Martha believed that through Christ nothing was impossible with God. She firmly believed that Jesus would have saved Lazarus from death had He been present. But even now that Lazarus was dead, she believed that Jesus could still bring him back to life. In verse 22, the use of the phrase "thou wilt ask" (Gk. *aiteo*, eye-**TEH**-oh), which means "desire, call for, or crave," implies that she hoped that Jesus would and that He should pray for an immediate resurrection in spite of Lazarus' decomposing body.

23 Jesus saith unto her, Thy brother shall rise again. 24 Martha saith unto him, I know that he shall rise again in the resurrection at the last day.

The phrase "rise again" (Gk. *anistemi*, ah-**NEESE**-tay-mee) means to "stand up." Even though other writers often use this word in a

common way, John rarely uses it except to mean resurrection. The idea of resurrection, though, can have a double meaning. It relates to the recall of Lazarus from death to life that was about to take place, as well as to his final resurrection at the close of time. Martha seems to understand Jesus' words to mean that her brother will rise again during the last days. If she understood Jesus' words only in this sense, the assumption is that she had no thought of Lazarus' immediate resurrection (v. 22). Jesus had already taught some about the final Resurrection, which John will later write more about in Revelation. Some Jewish traditions also awaited a Resurrection, prophesied by Daniel (12:2) and Isaiah (26:19). This was understood as a time when the Messiah would recall all the faithful dead to eternal life during His blessed reign on earth in Jerusalem. Martha affirms that she holds to this basic tenet of Judaism, looking forward to the end of days but not hopeful for the present.

25 Jesus said unto her, I am the resurrection, and the life: he that believeth in me, though he were dead, yet shall he live: 26 And whosoever liveth and believeth in me shall never die. Believest thou this?

Like many Jews, Martha believed in the final resurrection of the dead and the coming rule of God. Therefore, when Jesus stated, "I am the resurrection, and the life," He was saying that the promise of resurrection and life is not only some future event, but also was immediately available. Lazarus' bodily resurrection in a few moments would be a sign that Jesus has the power which He claims. To Martha, this would have been a startlingly new revelation. Christ embodies the kingdom of blessings for humankind for which Martha and her people hoped. This revelation was an assurance of both a resurrection to the eschatological kingdom of God, and an abundant life in the present through Him who is Life (Gk. *zoe*, see below).

It was crucial that Martha grasp the full importance of what Christ was about to do for Lazarus. In Christ, death will never triumph over the believer. Moreover, Jesus was saying that the person who believes in Him, though they die, will live; and the person who lives and believes in Him will never die. This saying might have helped spur rumors like the one mentioned after Jesus' resurrection that the disciple John would not die (John 24:22–23). As John himself affirms there, however, Jesus does not mean that no Christian will ever suffer physical death. It means that Jesus has that sovereign power, but also that this life we experience now is nothing compared to the abundance of eternal life.

In verse 26, Jesus asks Martha a question that is the basis for determining her faith and the faith of all believers: "Believest thou this?" Jesus asks Martha if she has the faith to believe what He says. Did she believe that He (Jesus) is the Resurrection, and that He has the power of life over death? That is, does she believe in His sovereignty? Unless a person believes in Jesus and His Word, the eternal life He offers cannot be found.

27 She saith unto him, Yea, Lord: I believe that thou art the Christ, the Son of God, which should come into the world.

Here, Martha's reply is a full-fledged confession of her faith in Jesus. In her confession, Martha states, "I believe" (Gk. *pisteuo*, peese-**TEW**-oh), which means "to accept as true, be persuaded of, credit, or place confidence in." This is a belief that includes commitment. Martha was agreeing with Jesus' exposition about eternal life for those who believe in Him. Martha's magnificent confession contains some principal elements of the Person of Christ: Jesus is the Christ (God's anointed One) and the Son of God. In acknowledging Jesus as the coming Messiah, Martha also suggests that she believes

He will even now recall the dead to life, as the Messiah was to do during His reign.

When things look impossible from a human perspective, we cannot let this diminish our faith in the One who upholds "all things by the word of his power" (Hebrews 1:3). With just a word, Jesus can change anything. Jesus cares about the troubles of our lives, and more important than that, He has the power and desire to do something about it.

The word Jesus used for "life" is the Greek word *zoe* (dzo-**AY**), which speaks of life in the fullest sense. Jesus has the power to give life because He is Life itself. The power that Jesus has extends beyond merely the physical; He also holds the power to give life to the spiritually dead. Paul later explains this tenet of Christianity that we "were dead in trespasses and sins," and God "made us alive" or raised us from our spiritual death (Ephesians 2:1, 5). On another occasion, many Jews were angry that He claimed equality with God, Jesus explained, "For as the Father raiseth up the dead, and quickeneth them; even so the Son quickeneth whom he will" (John 5:21).

38 Jesus therefore again groaning in himself cometh to the grave. It was a cave, and a stone lay upon it. 39 Jesus said, Take ye away the stone. Martha, the sister of him that was dead, saith unto him, Lord, by this time he stinketh: for he hath been dead four days.

Jesus is moved deeply by all the sadness surrounding Lazarus's death. His friend is buried in a cave, as was common at the time. A stone was in front of the tomb, just as it would be in front of Jesus' tomb.

Jesus knows the kind of miracle He is about to implement, so He asks for the stone to be removed. Martha still does not fully understand. John's Gospel gives no indication that Jesus has done anything before for those who are already dead. Matthew, Mark, and

Luke all record Jesus' resurrection of Jairus' daughter, but she had only just died earlier that day. Luke also records Jesus' resurrection of the son of a widow in Nain (Luke 7:11–17), but as stated previously, Jewish burials happened soon after death. Even with knowledge of those miracles, one might not assume that Jesus could do anything after so much decay. While we all know today what Jesus can do, Martha can be excused for thinking only of the physical world she knows. Even though she believes Jesus is the long-awaited Christ, she also believes there is nothing to be done to reverse the decay that has already begun to consume her brother's body.

40 Jesus saith unto her, Said I not unto thee, that, if thou wouldest believe, thou shouldest see the glory of God?

Jesus has indeed recently spoke to Martha about those who believe in Him living and not dying. The verses we looked at so far did not mention seeing the glory of God. John writes this to remind his audience of Jesus' words to Martha about life, but also His words to His disciples earlier about how Lazarus' sickness would bring glory to God (John 11:4). When Jesus is first told that Lazarus is sick, He says, "This sickness is not unto death, but for the glory of God, that the Son of God might be glorified thereby." John's Gospel records much of when Jesus speaks of Himself in relationship with the Father. Jesus is clear all He does is for the Father's glory and by the Father's power and instruction. Because the Son and the Father are so entwined, however, whatever benefits the Father also benefits the Son (cf. John 10:30).

Jesus' insistence that Lazarus' sickness was for glorifying God shows us how God can use the evil things of this world for good. Even though Lazarus had to survive through a deadly illness, it ended up that Jesus used the opportunity to enact His greatest miracle yet:

resurrecting a long-dead person. When we go through similar trials, we ought to recognize that God can be glorified even in events that we see as wholly negative.

41 Then they took away the stone from the place where the dead was laid. And Jesus lifted up his eyes, and said, Father, I thank thee that thou hast heard me. 42 And I knew that thou hearest me always: but because of the people which stand by I said it, that they may believe that thou hast sent me.

Throughout the Gospel of John, Jesus urges those who hear Him to believe Him based on the evidence of His miracles. He knows He does not need to be near Lazarus to work this miracle, He does not need to say any magical words, He does not need the stone removed, He does not even need to pray beforehand. All that Jesus does in working this miracle is for the benefit of those who will see it, and hopefully believe in Him because of it.

Jesus here also models a helpful method of prayer. He begins with thanksgiving for a miracle He will do in the Father's power, but which He has not actually done yet. Even before the deed is done, He thanks God for hearing Him. Whenever we bring our concerns to God in prayer, remember to begin with thanksgiving. You can thank God for past miracles in your life, or for hearing all prayers, or anything else about God's constant nature. This will reframe your petition in your thoughts, calming you and reminding you that God is in control of everything. As the song says, "He's got the whole world in His hands." This is a simple message we learn early in our lives, but which we often forget when we grow older.

43 And when he thus had spoken, he cried with a loud voice, Lazarus, come forth. 44 And he that was dead came forth, bound hand and foot with graveclothes: and his face

was bound about with a napkin. Jesus saith unto them, Loose him, and let him go.

Here again we have foreshadowing of Jesus' burial. John mentioned the stone in front of Lazarus' grave (v. 38), and here mentions the "napkin" (Gk. *soudarion*, soo-**DAR**-ee-on) wrapped around his face, just like there will be a "napkin" as part of Jesus' graveclothes (John 20:7). No one who reads this Gospel should disbelieve that Jesus could raise from the dead, when there is already proof that He has performed such a similar miracle on another.

The graveclothes in Lazarus' resurrection offer an interesting contrast to Jesus' resurrection, too. Lazarus has to come out of his grave bound hand and foot, blinded and stifled by a cloth over his face. He needs others to come help him out of his restrictions. In Jesus' resurrection, on the other hand, His graveclothes are left behind, and His napkin neatly folded and placed to one side (John 20:7). Even in the way Jesus is resurrected, He shows His power over everything.

Sources:

Adeyemo, Tokunboh, ed. *Africa Bible Commentary*. Grand Rapids, MI: Zondervan, 2006.

Barclay, William. *The Gospel of John*. Vol. 2. Philadelphia, PA: The Westminster Press, 1956.

"Bethany." *Smith's Bible Dictionary*. Bible Study Tools.com. http://www.biblestudytools.com/dictionaries/smiths-bible- dictionary/bethany.html (accessed January 8, 2011).

Carson, D. A. *The Gospel According to John*. Grand Rapids, MI: William B. Eerdmans Publishing Company, 1991.

Strong's Exhaustive Concordance of the Bible. McLean, VA: MacDonald Publishing Company. n.d.

Say It Correctly

Furlongs. FUR-longs.
Eschatological. ess-ka-toe-LOG-ih-kal.

Daily Bible Readings

MONDAY
Awake, O Dead, and Sing!
(Isaiah 26:12–19)

TUESDAY
The Dead Shall Be Raised
(1 Corinthians 15:12–19)

WEDNESDAY
In Christ All Are Made Alive
(1 Corinthians 15:20–28)

THURSDAY
Wake Up!
(Daniel 12:1–4)

FRIDAY
The Dead Will Hear Christ's Voice
(John 5:25–29)

SATURDAY
Jesus Travels to Lazarus
(John 11:1, 3–16)

SUNDAY
The Raising of Lazarus
(John 11:20–27, 38–44)

Teaching Tips

Words You Should Know

A. Abide (John 12:46) *meno* (Gk.)—To stay, remain

B. Believe (v. 47) *phulaxe* (Gk.)—To guard or keep

Teacher Preparation

Unifying Principle—Bringing the Light. Most people acknowledge a sense of a higher, spiritual power that exceeds our human capabilities. How do we understand the mysteries of the universe, the world, and our lives? Jesus' mission is to save the world so that the world can live in an eternal relationship with His Father, God the Creator.

A. Read the Bible Background and Devotional Reading.

B. Pray for your students and lesson clarity.

C. Read the lesson Scripture in multiple translations.

O—Open the Lesson

A. Begin the class with prayer.

B. Play the song "The Revolution will not be Televised" by Gil Scott Heron from a CD or video– or music-sharing site. You may also wish to print out lyrics from a lyrics website. Discuss what this song says about changing the world. Lead into Bible study by saying that the Bible tells us how the world can be truly changed.

C. Have the students read the Aim for Change and the In Focus story.

D. Ask students how events like those in the story weigh on their hearts and how they can view these events from a faith perspective.

P—Present the Scriptures

A. Read the Focal Verses and discuss the Background and The People, Places, and Times sections.

B. Have the class share what Scriptures stand out for them and why, with particular emphasis on today's themes.

E—Explore the Meaning

A. Use In Depth or More Light on the Text to facilitate a deeper discussion of the lesson text.

B. Pose the questions in Search the Scriptures and Discuss the Meaning.

C. Discuss the Liberating Lesson and Application for Activation sections.

N—Next Steps for Application

A. Summarize the value of holding convictions based on the evidence that Jesus is who He says He is.

B. End class with a commitment to pray for encouragement in their mission to share the Gospel message with others.

Worship Guide

For the Superintendent or Teacher
Theme: The Word Saves
Song: "Here I am to Worship"

The Word Saves

Bible Background • JOHN 12:27–50
Printed Text • JOHN 12:44–50 | Devotional Reading • JOHN 5:19–24

—— Aim for Change ——

By the end of this lesson, we will RECOGNIZE that Jesus is God, DESIRE a closer relationship with God through choosing to follow Christ, and SHARE with others the opportunity to come into the light of Christ.

—— In Focus ——

Dr. Tiffany Garrett had been a physician for many years. She believed medicine was her calling and could not see herself doing anything else. In Tiffany's relationship with God, she viewed God's ways as truth and best. She often prayed, "God, let Your will be done in my life." However, as God began to reveal the light of His will, Dr. Garrett struggled with living out her prayer.

She wanted to obey what God was revealing to her through prayer, but she did not agree with God's plan. God was calling Tiffany to the mission field in Uganda. She would serve as a team member with the missionary team from her local church. She toiled within herself about what her parents, friends, colleagues, and everybody that knew her as a medical doctor would think. Dr. Garrett was divided in her heart about the decision. She could hear this Scripture in her head, "But all who reject me, and my message will be judged on the day of judgment by the truth I have spoken." Tiffany willingly surrendered.

Twenty years later, Tiffany reminisced on her struggle to follow the direction God revealed to her. She reflected on all the miracles God performed in her personal life, the people who received salvation. That one decision to follow God's will for that season of her life. She reminisced about all the times she wondered if she had made the right decision. Dr. Garrett concluded that trust, belief, and obedience to the Lord is never a mistake.

What miracles or divine opportunities are you missing out on because you are rejecting the directions of the Lord? Who might come to know Jesus if you say YES?

—— Keep in Mind ——

"I am come a light into the world, that whosoever believeth on me should not abide in darkness." (John 12:46, KJV)

"I have come as a light to shine in this dark world, so that all who put their trust in me will no longer remain in the dark." (John 12:46, NLT)

Focal Verses

KJV **John 12:44** Jesus cried and said, He that believeth on me, believeth not on me, but on him that sent me.

45 And he that seeth me seeth him that sent me.

46 I am come a light into the world, that whosoever believeth on me should not abide in darkness.

47 And if any man hear my words, and believe not, I judge him not: for I came not to judge the world, but to save the world.

48 He that rejecteth me, and receiveth not my words, hath one that judgeth him: the word that I have spoken, the same shall judge him in the last day.

49 For I have not spoken of myself; but the Father which sent me, he gave me a commandment, what I should say, and what I should speak.

50 And I know that his commandment is life everlasting: whatsoever I speak therefore, even as the Father said unto me, so I speak.

NLT **John 12:44** Jesus shouted to the crowds, "If you trust me, you are trusting not only me, but also God who sent me.

45 For when you see me, you are seeing the one who sent me.

46 I have come as a light to shine in this dark world, so that all who put their trust in me will no longer remain in the dark.

47 I will not judge those who hear me but don't obey me, for I have come to save the world and not to judge it.

48 But all who reject me and my message will be judged on the day of judgment by the truth I have spoken.

49 I don't speak on my own authority. The Father who sent me has commanded me what to say and how to say it.

50 And I know his commands lead to eternal life; so I say whatever the Father tells me to say."

The People, Places, and Times

The Trinity. One thing we know about God is that He is a God of relationship. In some ways God is a relationship. We can see this in God as Trinity. The Father relates to the Son. The Son relates to the Father. The Spirit relates to the Father and Son. They are a divine community so connected that they are one in essence. Although it is hard for our minds to comprehend, God is community and wants nothing less than for the people He created to dwell in community.

Background

Jesus gives His farewell sermon to the Jewish people six days before the Passover. Jesus had returned to Bethany, where He had performed one of the greatest miracles: raising Lazarus from the death. The chief priests had deep-seated issues with Jesus and because of that miracle. Too many people had come to a believing faith in Jesus. The Pharisees plotted to kill Jesus (John 11:45–48).

Jesus laments over the unbelief in the land. The people had witnessed Jesus perform countless miracles, yet they persisted in unbelief. There were those who believed Jesus but would not confess their belief because of fear of the Pharisees; they loved the praises of men rather than God (John 12:42). Jesus mourns within Himself over the rejection of the words He has spoken and their ultimate rejection of God. He commends those that accept the light that He bears, and the redemption provided to them because they believe (John 12:44).

At-A-Glance

1. Believing and Seeing Jesus
(John 12:44–45)
2. Jesus Is Light in Darkness (v. 46)
3. Jesus the Rejected Savior (vv. 47–48)
4. Jesus Speaks as the Father Speaks
(vv. 49–50)

In Depth

1. Believing and Seeing Jesus (John 12:44–45)

Jesus had been the miracle worker in the eyes of the people. He did not work miracles behind closed doors or in an obscure fashion. Jesus worked miracles where everyone could see Him. In His farewell address to the Jewish people, Jesus laments over their unbelief in Him and who sent Him. Jesus desperately desired for the people to believe on the God that sent Him.

Jesus mourned over their blindness to see Him and ultimately see the Father who sent hHim. Unbelief is regarded in Scripture as sin. It hinders salvation, deliverance, and the working of miracles in the lives of individuals but most importantly the lives of believers (John 8:24). The sin of unbelief severs the community of believers from God.

Jesus was brokenhearted because the people He was sent to save could not believe and see the goodness of God though it dwelt among them. Jesus could have demonstrated the power of God so much more and performed more miracles if only the people could see and believe. The Jewish people believed the prophecies that foretold of the coming of the Messiah and believed God would keep His word, but when God fulfilled the word of prophecy, the Jews were blinded to the excellence of Christ although He dwelt among them.

How much have you limited God's power from working in your life because you could not see or believe in Him?

2. Jesus Is Light in Darkness (v. 46)

Darkness is the absence of light and truth in the world. It can be embedded in the lives of people as an environment where sin festers and Satan has access to steal, kill, and destroy. God sent Jesus into the world to free mankind from the bondage of sin. Jesus is the light of the world (John 8:12). Jesus came so that people would not have to <u>succumb</u> to the darkness of this world. When Jesus is accepted as light, darkness must yield its grip so that we can live in freedom and live abundantly.

Jesus is the only source that provides light in dark circumstances. Jesus is the only way to God who is also light (1 John 1:5). Those who truly desire light will believe Jesus is the light of the world and will no longer live in darkness. Believing on Jesus means to accept Jesus as the Son of God and the Father who sent Him. Accepting Jesus as the light ensures power over the darkness of the world, and grants us fellowship with God the Father. Receiving Jesus as the light of the world means the power and blessing of salvation can be realized.

In what areas of your life does darkness permeate and the light of Christ need to dwell?

3. Jesus the Rejected Savior (vv. 47–48)

Jesus has been called the rejected cornerstone (Psalm 118:22). Jesus understood that His purpose for being sent into the world was to redeem humanity back to God. Jesus reminded the Jewish people that even if they rejected His words and staggered in unbelief, He did not judge them (John 12:47). Jesus affirms that He came to be salvation for the world. Jesus lamented over the rejection of the people not receiving the word of God, because the word of God was salvation.

Jesus needed those who rejected Him and His words to understand that there was a cost. Rejecting Jesus as Savior has the penalty of death. The judgment would come on the last day should rejection be their final decision. The penalty of death could be avoided by accepting Him.

Do you have a loved one that is rejecting Jesus as the Savior? What steps can you take to help them see and believe Jesus?

Norma

4. Jesus Speaks as the Father Speaks (vv. 49-50)

Throughout Jesus' ministry He reminds everyone that His purpose is only aligned to what the Father speaks and desires (John 5:19; 6:38). Every word that Jesus spoke came directly from God the Father. Every action Jesus performed is what the Father commanded.

God sent Jesus with a message to preach forgiveness of sin, the Gospel of salvation, and eternal life. Jesus spoke exactly what the Father said without deviation or flaw. Jesus proclaimed the Father's desire for everlasting life (John 12:50). Jesus came to fulfill His purpose of salvation from sin despite the rejection and persecution.

How has God commanded you share the Gospel of salvation? Have you followed the command?

Search the Scriptures

1. Why was it important that when people believe on Jesus and His words, they believe God (John 12:44)?

2. Why did Jesus emphasize salvation and not judgment although they rejected Him (v. 47)?

Discuss the Meaning

1. John 12 was ultimately Christ's message of salvation and His fulfilling the command to be a sin offering for humanity. Jesus lamented over the rejection of God's words through Him,

yet Jesus focused on the assignment to preach everlasting life. What relevance does Jesus' commitment to the Gospel of salvation have on our own evangelism?

2. Reflect on your life before salvation, do you remember how desperately you needed a Savior? Reminisce on your salvation experience and the impact salvation has had in your life. With whom could you share your testimony of salvation within your neighborhood?

Liberating Lesson

The most compelling way to convey the message of salvation is to share the purpose of Christ's coming. It is also important to express the benefits of external life granted by the light of Jesus Christ. There is so much darkness in the world, with global disease, the senseless killing of marginalized people, corrupted government, and a divided church. All of this darkness can cause people so much pain and grief. Jesus came to provide solutions for all of these issues.

When Christ is presented as Savior rather than a judge, more people freely see and believe God. Testimonies of salvation and conversion stories help make Christ reachable. As the church becomes more relatable, reachable, and tangible so does the message of Christ. Christ's message was simple and simple is what people need right now.

Application for Activation

• Individual believers must share their testimonies with unbelieving family members, friends, and neighbors. Pray for opportunities to share testimonies with unbelievers. Commit to individual evangelism.

• The Church must show how Christ has liberated them from darkness so that the world will know Christ's freedom. Create opportunities and forums to share about the good the Church has done, and the evils the Church used to permit but now has rejected.

Follow the Spirit

What God wants me to do:

_____

_____

_____

_____

Remember Your Thoughts

Special insights I have learned:

_____

_____

_____

_____

More Light on the Text

John 12:44-50

It is hard to fathom that some people today try to show a separation between Jesus and His Father. Some have gone so far as to say Jesus Himself was not certain He was the Messiah, suggesting He was hesitant in answering questions about His identity. This is not true of course, and in several instances in John's Gospel, including this passage before us, Jesus announces His deity and messiahship clearly.

The woman at the well mentioned that she knew the Messiah was coming—the prophesied One, He who is called Christ—and Jesus said, "I that speak unto thee am he" (John 4:26). To the Jews who asked Jesus to speak plainly about whether He was the Christ He said, "I and my Father are one" (John 10:30). They immediately tried to stone Him because they knew He was claiming to be equal to the Father. The Jews were hoping for a

conquering Messiah, but they had no concept of the Messiah being one with the Father, even though the Old Testament taught this (e.g., Isaiah 9:6). Later, when His own disciples asked about His identity, Jesus said, "He that hath seen me hath seen the Father...Believe me that I am in the Father and the Father is in me" (from John 14:9–11). Thus, no careful reading of the New Testament can seriously question that Jesus claimed to be the Messiah and that He was the Son of God.

44 Jesus cried and said, He that believeth on me, believeth not on me, but on him that sent me. 45 And he that seeth me seeth him that sent me.

John writes that Jesus "cried," which in Greek is *krazo* (**KRAD**-zo), meaning to call loudly, like a crow might. Jesus is speaking with loud solemnity. He is responding in kind to the faithless, those of the people who saw His miracles but "were not believing in Him," and the rulers who believed but "were not confessing Him, for fear they would be put out of the synagogue" (vv. 37, 42).Verse 36 said that Jesus had withdrawn from the people, so it is likely that these words in verses 44-50 were the apostle's summary of what Jesus said in this chapter, but also throughout His entire ministry. Jesus said simply *believe in me*. The Greek word *pisteuo* (peece-**TEU**-oo) and its derivative *pistis* (**PIS**-tis) are the most common New Testament words for "believe" or "faith." The meaning is to trust confidently, and in this context, to follow and declare Jesus as Lord.

Verse 45 repeats the declaration of Christ's deity, but also includes an important revelation: if we wish to understand God, we can see Him fully displayed in the incarnate Son. The word for "see" used in Greek comes from the root *theoreo* (theh-oh-**REH**-oh) which refers to studying something, rather than casually observing it. As we gaze intently on Christ—His person, His words, and His actions—we increasingly understand the Father (Romans 12:2; 2 Corinthians 3:18). Christianity is not a matter of personal opinions or political leanings, but is centered on the life of Christ.

46 I am come a light into the world, that whosoever believeth on me should not abide in darkness.

When we enter a dark room and flip the light switch, we have an immediate illustration for what illumination is. If we cannot see while writing in a dim environment, we begin looking for a light source (or our glasses). When we leave for a night drive, we will not reach the end of the driveway before we turn our headlights on. Jesus says in this verse that if we find ourselves groping in darkness, He is the only available light. We should look for Him. The very idea of light indicates that darkness is dispelled. In this case, Jesus is the antithesis of the fearfulness, ignorance, and deep dissatisfaction that are so evident in our society. What we have in Jesus is found nowhere else, and these words assure us that believing in Him brings life and joy. Christ offers more than just improved vision; He offers life abundant.

Each person must do something, however, and that is believe. When the word "darkness" is used in Scripture, as here, it usually is referring to Satan or his kingdom. By the grace of God, the believer steps out of the power of this palpable wickedness into the light of Jesus by trusting in Him and by accepting His sovereignty in their lives. It is alarming that people, who are made to be in the Light, would rather dwell in the joyless, hopeless, and devil-infused darkness. Nevertheless, some do. Those of us who have chosen the Light and have become followers of Christ should remember that these words apply to us as well—even after conversion. We may have accepted Him as our Savior, but we must

continually live each moment in the light of His presence. We can choose always to walk as those who are in the Light.

47 And if any man hear my words, and believe not, I judge him not: for I came not to judge the world, but to save the world.

Jesus was speaking clearly: *I am here to save.* It is incidental that He emphasizes He is not in the world to judge. Judgment is certain for those who refuse to listen (v. 48), but we should not lose sight of Jesus' main purpose of salvation. Jesus says when a person does not *phulaxe* (fu-**LAH**-ksay)—translated in the King James Version as "believe" but literally meaning to "guard"—he judges himself or herself. Later translations use the phrase "does not keep them" for "believe not," in an effort to render an accurate translation. We could rightly translate that such a person who does not "keep" Christ's words does not hold the words of the Lord closely, or does not "guard" them. As such, these people judge themselves by not holding to the Word.

The word "save" in Greek is *sozo* (**SODE**-zo), which can mean to heal a person from an illness or deliver them from peril. Jesus clearly announced the saving message of the Father, which had been in the works since the original fall of man. In popular teaching today, the idea of "the scarlet thread of redemption" is often used in reference to God's revelation of salvation. This "thread" begins in Genesis and goes through Revelation. (An example of this "type" is recorded in Joshua 2:17–24 when Rahab was instructed to let down a red thread from her window, and so her entire family was saved.) All of the books of the Bible connect to reveal God's loving-kindness and His desire that all would be saved and fellowship with Him (1 Timothy 2:4). Everything else is secondary, including judgment.

48 He that rejecteth me, and receiveth not my words, hath one that judgeth him: the word that I have spoken, the same shall judge him in the last day.

To reject Jesus is to declare Him invalid. Notice that a man or woman need not rail against Jesus to incur judgment; they only have to ignore Him. Sadly, our world today is filled with people who invalidate Jesus and His words. The first reference to "words" in this verse uses the word *rhemata* (rhe-ma-**TA**) in the Greek, and the second is *logos* (**LO**-gos). *Rhemata* appears in some modern translations as "my sayings," while *logos* is simply translated "word." Also, *rhemata* is more appropriately used for individual spoken or audible words, while *logos* refers to the truth in a more general and universal sense.

Jesus is referred to as the *Logos* (John 1:1), as He is the embodiment of the essence of the Father. It is a frightening possibility to reject what Jesus teaches *and* His incarnation of God's truth. The result is that His truth and our reaction to it will be our judge rather than Jesus Himself. In essence, Jesus has already laid out the law; it is up to each of us to accept His words and follow them. How a person reacts to Jesus shows what he really is. If he sees in Christ something attractive, believable, true to His word, then he has shown that his heart has been warmed to the Savior. On the other hand, if a person finds Jesus repulsive, rejects His words, considers those words false and unreliable, then he has shown he is not open to God, and has thus far judged himself. A conscious decision to accept Jesus is needed. Some call this section of Scripture the last sermon of Christ to Israel. Jesus had more to say to the disciples privately in the following chapters (the "Farewell Discourse," John 14–17), but these were His last public words in John's Gospel. Some of those who were standing nearby and listening to this final sermon were Jews, some

of whom were in the process of rejecting Christ. Jesus is warning them that there is no way to the Father except through Himself, because He is the embodiment of the Father on earth. No racial heritage, no great learning, and no societal standing will bring a person into the kingdom of God; only the Messiah can do that, and Jesus is identifying Himself as that One.

49 For I have not spoken of myself; but the Father which sent me, he gave me a commandment, what I should say, and what I should speak.

The question arises, what specifically is Jesus speaking about? He is referring first to His identity as the Son of God and therefore His purpose as completely entwined with the Father. This condition was continuous during Jesus' earthly sojourn; it was a symphony playing through all of His miraculous works and authoritative teaching. Nevertheless, there were times when it was made plain. God spoke of Jesus when John baptized Him in the Jordan. As Jesus came up out of the water God said, "This is my beloved Son, in whom I am well pleased" (Matthew 3:17). At the Transfiguration, the disciples heard the voice of God, "This is my beloved Son, in whom I am well pleased; hear ye him" (Matthew 17:5). In the verses before today's text we hear that when Jesus said, "Father, glorify thy name. Then came there a voice from heaven, saying, I have both glorified it, and will glorify it again" (John 12:28). Long before this, the prophets spoke of His coming, for example Isaiah said, "His name shall be called Wonderful, Counselor, The mighty God, The everlasting Father, The Prince of Peace" (Isaiah 9:6). Jesus was well attested by the Father.

This "commandment" given by the Father was an encompassing one that went with every word and action that Jesus took. The Greek word used, *entole* (en-to-**LAY**), refers to a single command (or a body of commands) that

546

is usually a commission given by a king. Jesus walked in the fullness of God and so carried forth His commands. We remember that Jesus said, "Verily, verily, I say unto you, The Son can do nothing of himself, but what he seeth the Father do: for what things soever he doeth, these also doeth the Son likewise" (John 5:19).

50 And I know that his commandment is life everlasting: whatsoever I speak therefore, even as the Father said unto me, so I speak.

Here the "commandment" is more clearly stated. This word "commandment," the same word used in verse 49, should be translated throughout these verses as something like "direction" or "commission," not as Moses would give a command, but as a way of thinking and being that would indicate how we should follow the Lord in Gospel living (see also John 13:34). This "life everlasting" is promised in the very essence of Jesus' life and deeds and not just in a single command. Other sayings of Jesus recorded in John's Gospel may help us here: "I am come that they may have life, and that they have it more abundantly" (from John 10:10); "For God so loved the world, that he gave his only begotten Son, that whosoever believeth in him should not perish, but have everlasting life. For God sent not his Son into the world to condemn the world; but that the world through him might be saved" (John 3:16–17). What Jesus brings to us is the salvation offered by God, and He does this with full assurance. He said, "I know" this life everlasting is offered! He happily brings this to anyone who would receive it. Sadly, this should remind us that if we put ourselves in opposition to His words we choose peril. On the other hand, if we choose Him, we follow His example and go about our gospel business with joy and purpose.

Jesus does not do this alone, for He reminds His listeners that His words carry the heft of the Father. Because of our knowledge of Jesus' place in the Trinity, which we know much more fully than those who were listening in that day, these words may seem unusual to us. It is as if He is including God to verify His words. In interpreting this and any of the words of Jesus while He was on earth, we must factor in the Incarnation. Though Jesus was fully God and had not lost any of His essence, He was not in His eternal position of glory. Here He was verifying that His words were given to Him by the Father, and so they carried the full weight of that authority. Knowing this, when Jesus said, "so I speak," the only acceptable response is, "we will heed."

Sources:
Barclay, William. *The Gospel of John*. The New Daily Study Bible. Philadelphia, PA: Westminster Press. Reprint, 1975. 2:135.
Criswell, W. H. *The Scarlet Thread through the Bible*. Nashville, TN: LifeWay Press, Reprint, 2014.
Gossip, Arthur John. *The Interpreter's Bible: The Gospel According to St. John (exposition)*. Nashville, TN: Abingdon Press. Reprint, 1980. 8:676.
Kittel, G., G. W. Bromiley, and G. Friedrich, eds. *Theological dictionary of the New Testament* (electronic ed., Vol. 3, p. 898). Grand Rapids, MI: Eerdmans.
Henry, Matthew. *Matthew Henry's Commentary on the Whole Bible*. Old Tappan, NJ: Fleming H. Revell, N.D. 5:1086.
Lenski, R. C. H. *Commentary on the New Testament: The Interpretation of St. John's Gospel*. Minneapolis, MN: Augsburg Publishing House, 1963. 4:895.

Say It Correctly

Transfiguration.
trans-FIG-yur-AH-shun.

Daily Bible Readings

MONDAY
You Must Be Born from Above
(John 3:1–8)

TUESDAY
Jesus Brings Eternal Life
(John 3:9–17)

WEDNESDAY
My Rock, Fortress, and Deliverer
(2 Samuel 22:2–7)

THURSDAY
Salvation Comes from God
(Psalm 62)

FRIDAY
Don't Neglect God's Message of Salvation
(Hebrews 2:1–9)

SATURDAY
Father, Glorify Your Name!
(John 12:27–36)

SUNDAY
Jesus, the Light of the World
(John 12:44–50)

Notes

_____

_____

_____

_____

Teaching Tips

Words You Should Know

A. Comforter (John 14:16) *parakleton* (Gk.)—One of the names of the Holy Spirit; one who is called to another's aid

B. World (v. 17) *kosmos* (Gk.)—The entire universe; the inhabitants of the earth; the unsaved

Teacher Preparation

Unifying Principle—Present Forever. People seek trustworthy guidance for their lives. How can we find guidance? Our love for Jesus, shown through our obedience to His words and the Holy Spirit's teachings, creates an incredible peace.

A. Read the Bible Background and Devotional Reading.

B. Pray for your students and lesson clarity.

C. Read the lesson Scripture in multiple translations.

O—Open the Lesson

A. Begin the class with prayer.

B. Write this common truism on the board: "Out of sight, out of mind." What does it say about long-distance relationships? Can participants tell about long-distance relationships that had difficulties? Note that Jesus made a provision that our relationship with Him will never be a long-distance one.

C. Have the students read the Aim for Change and the In Focus story.

D. Ask students how events like those in the story weigh on their hearts and how they can view these events from a faith perspective.

P—Present the Scriptures

A. Read the Focal Verses and discuss the Background and The People, Places, and Times sections.

B. Have the class share what Scriptures stand out for them and why, with particular emphasis on today's themes.

E—Explore the Meaning

A. Use In Depth or More Light on the Text to facilitate a deeper discussion of the lesson text.

B. Pose the questions in Search the Scriptures and Discuss the Meaning.

C. Discuss the Liberating Lesson and Application for Activation sections.

N—Next Steps for Application

A. Summarize the value of the Holy Spirit's indwelling to give Christians the presence, power, and counsel of God.

B. End class with a commitment to pray for a peace that is unaffected by the turmoil in the world.

Worship Guide

For the Superintendent or Teacher
Theme: The Word Gives Peace
Song: "Holy Spirit, Faithful Guide"

The Word Gives Peace

Bible Background • JOHN 14:15–31
Printed Text • JOHN 14:15–29 | Devotional Reading • JOHN 6:1–14

Aim for Change

By the end of this lesson, we will EXPLORE the relationship between God, Jesus, and the Holy Spirit; BE ENCOURAGED that Jesus offers us peace in the Holy Spirit, and COMMIT to obeying Christ rather than the prince of darkness.

In Focus

James and Trina had been experiencing tension in their marriage ever since their youngest had left the nest. Trina seemed less joyful lately. James asked if everything was OK. Trina insisted that she was fine. One night, James awoke to discover that Trina wasn't in bed. He noticed a light in the hallway. He listened closer and could hear muffled sobbing coming from their guest room. James' heart sank. He wanted to help fix it, but he didn't know how.

On his drive to work the next day, James prayed for Trina. James prayed that the Holy Spirit would show him what to do. That afternoon, James remembered the deep feeling of love and appreciation he had for Trina on their wedding day. *I wonder if she knows that?* he thought. He knew what he needed to do.

That night at dinner, James told Trina how much he still appreciated and loved her. "I want you to know that I see you. I see how you've always made sure the kids know they can still come by to be loved on by their Mama. I see how you work so hard at your job. I was thinking just this afternoon how lovely you were on our wedding day, and I think you're just as lovely today."

Trina's eyes filled with tears. "I didn't know you felt that way." Trina explained she'd been sad because it seemed that James loved her less now. They talked about how they could show love toward each other more often.

How have you felt the Holy Spirit communicate with you?

Keep in Mind

"And I will pray the Father, and he shall give you another Comforter, that he may abide with you for ever." (John 14:16, KJV)

"And I will ask the Father, and he will give you another Advocate, who will never leave you."
(John 14:16, NLT)

Focal Verses

KJV **John 14:15** If ye love me, keep my commandments.

16 And I will pray the Father, and he shall give you another Comforter, that he may abide with you for ever;

17 Even the Spirit of truth; whom the world cannot receive, because it seeth him not, neither knoweth him: but ye know him; for he dwelleth with you, and shall be in you.

18 I will not leave you comfortless: I will come to you.

19 Yet a little while, and the world seeth me no more; but ye see me: because I live, ye shall live also.

20 At that day ye shall know that I am in my Father, and ye in me, and I in you.

21 He that hath my commandments, and keepeth them, he it is that loveth me: and he that loveth me shall be loved of my Father, and I will love him, and will manifest myself to him.

22 Judas saith unto him, not Iscariot, Lord, how is it that thou wilt manifest thyself unto us, and not unto the world?

23 Jesus answered and said unto him, If a man love me, he will keep my words: and my Father will love him, and we will come unto him, and make our abode with him.

24 He that loveth me not keepeth not my sayings: and the word which ye hear is not mine, but the Father's which sent me.

25 These things have I spoken unto you, being yet present with you.

26 But the Comforter, which is the Holy Ghost, whom the Father will send in my name, he shall teach you all things, and bring all things to your remembrance, whatsoever I have said unto you.

27 Peace I leave with you, my peace I give unto you: not as the world giveth, give I unto you. Let not your heart be troubled, neither let it be afraid.

NLT **John 14:15** "If you love me, obey my commandments.

16 And I will ask the Father, and he will give you another Advocate, who will never leave you.

17 He is the Holy Spirit, who leads into all truth. The world cannot receive him, because it isn't looking for him and doesn't recognize him. But you know him, because he lives with you now and later will be in you.

18 No, I will not abandon you as orphans—I will come to you.

19 Soon the world will no longer see me, but you will see me. Since I live, you also will live.

20 When I am raised to life again, you will know that I am in my Father, and you are in me, and I am in you.

21 Those who accept my commandments and obey them are the ones who love me. And because they love me, my Father will love them. And I will love them and reveal myself to each of them."

22 Judas (not Judas Iscariot, but the other disciple with that name) said to him, "Lord, why are you going to reveal yourself only to us and not to the world at large?"

23 Jesus replied, "All who love me will do what I say. My Father will love them, and we will come and make our home with each of them.

24 Anyone who doesn't love me will not obey me. And remember, my words are not my own. What I am telling you is from the Father who sent me.

25 I am telling you these things now while I am still with you.

26 But when the Father sends the Advocate as my representative—that is, the Holy Spirit—he will teach you everything and will remind you of everything I have told you.

27 I am leaving you with a gift—peace of mind and heart. And the peace I give is a gift the world cannot give. So don't be troubled or afraid.

28 Ye have heard how I said unto you, I go away, and come again unto you. If ye loved me, ye would rejoice, because I said, I go unto the Father: for my Father is greater than I.

29 And now I have told you before it come to pass, that, when it is come to pass, ye might believe.

28 Remember what I told you: I am going away, but I will come back to you again. If you really loved me, you would be happy that I am going to the Father, who is greater than I am.

29 I have told you these things before they happen so that when they do happen, you will believe.

The People, Places, and Times

The Holy Spirit. The Holy Spirit is called by many names: the Holy Ghost, the Spirit of God, the Spirit of Christ, the Spirit of Truth, the Comforter or Counselor, and simply, the Spirit. The Holy Spirit is God. He is not a part of God, an influence from God, or an agent of God. He is God. God is Spirit (John 4:24). The distinction between God and "His Spirit" is an artificial one. It is our way of talking about God in motion. Strictly speaking, God does not move. He is everywhere. Therefore, He cannot go anywhere because He is already there. God does not move, but God moves things as a magnet draws things to it. When God causes motion, we speak of this power to move things not simply as God, but as God's Spirit. To distinguish between our *human* spirits and *evil* spirits, we speak of God as the *Holy* Spirit.

Background

The disciples were upset. Jesus' disciples were becoming both sad and scared. They were sad because over the past two to three years, they had come to love Jesus. True, they had not understood many of the things He had said and done, but through His love for them and their constant close association, a bond of respect and affection had grown between them. They did not want to break a friendship they had come to enjoy. They were scared because this same friendship meant they had an intimate identification with Jesus. They felt that if the authorities were after Jesus, the disciples' lives were also in danger. They were scared also because Jesus' death would mean they would be left alone in an extremely hostile environment.

It was to these sad and scared disciples that Jesus reaffirmed the active, powerful presence of God. Undoubtedly, the disciples felt better after Jesus' words of assurance (16:29, 30).

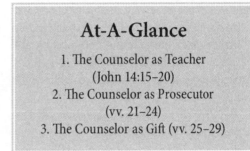

At-A-Glance

1. The Counselor as Teacher
(John 14:15–20)
2. The Counselor as Prosecutor
(vv. 21–24)
3. The Counselor as Gift (vv. 25–29)

In Depth

1. The Counselor as Teacher (John 14:15–20)

Jesus tells His disciples that the Counselor would reveal the truth about Jesus. Jesus was painfully aware that most of His contemporaries did not know who He truly was. Despite Peter's confession, not even His disciples really knew Him (John 14:7–12, 20). One denied Him. Another betrayed Him, and all the others ran and hid when He needed them most. But Jesus told them that after a while, they would know Him because the Counselor would throw the spotlight on Him and reveal to them who He really was.

They would know the deep beauty of His words and deeds and begin to understand the universal significance of His life and teachings.

They would know Him because God, the Holy Spirit, would make the real Jesus stand out in their experiences (John 14:20; 16:14, 15).

How can we let the Holy Spirit guide us?

2. The Counselor as Prosecutor (vv. 21–24)

Another of the Counselor's ministries was to convince people that Jesus was right and they were wrong. The Holy Spirit convinces unbelievers that: (1) Jesus was right about His Messianic claims, (2) they had been wrong in rejecting Him, and (3) if, like Satan, they deliberately chose to continue doing wrong in spite of their knowledge of right, then they would share Satan's fate (John 16:8-11).

God has been pictured as having two arms—one of love and the other of justice. Those who refuse the forgiveness and security of His arm of love are doomed to feel the crush of His arm of justice. The Counselor has both positive and negative ministries. For the believer, He is an Advocate; for those who refuse to believe, He is a Prosecutor.

What rewards have you experienced from keeping God's commandments?

3. The Counselor as Gift (vv. 25–29)

Jesus assures His disciples that the Holy Spirit will work as an Advocate for them, by teaching them and reminding them of Jesus' teaching. Not only will the Holy Spirit help the disciples remember all that happened in Jesus' ministry over the past three years, but the Spirit will also teach so that the disciples can more fully understand what they have seen.

This understanding grants them peace. This is a peace from God, and so it will always be available. Peace from the world comes and goes, but since God has sent the Holy Spirit to be with His followers all the time, they may have a peace that lasts.

How can we enjoy the Holy Spirit as our constant companion?

Search the Scriptures

1. What kind of warning did Jesus give His disciples before He left them (John 14:18–20)?

2. What else did Jesus promise His disciples before He left them (v. 27)?

Discuss the Meaning

1. Is the Holy Spirit's work confined only to the Church and the lives of believers, or is the Holy Spirit at work in the general society? How can we tell where the Holy Spirit is at work in the world?

2. The tearing down of the Berlin Wall, the collapse of Soviet Communism, and the ending of the "cold war"—were these events the work of the Holy Spirit in the world, or did these events result from the "strength of democracy," the military might of the United States, and/or an unusual stream of good luck?

Liberating Lesson

Many today will insist that we can never know certain things, especially events from long ago history. They say the Bible cannot be trusted to be an accurate account of Jesus' ministry.

As we learned in this week's lesson, however, Christians do not rely solely on the abilities of flawed humans to retain knowledge of God's Incarnation. Jesus assures the disciples that the Holy Spirit will help them remember all that happened. So when the disciples recorded Jesus' message, even though it was decades later, we can trust they did so with faithfulness according to the Spirit's guidance. Believers firmly trust the vital teachings of the church were kept unchanged throughout history because of the work of the Spirit.

Application for Activation

Look around this week in your community and find out where the Holy Spirit is at work empowering people to do the work of Jesus

(See Luke 4:18; Matthew 25:34–40). Ask the Lord for a way you can give your support to this group either by giving time, money, or other tangible resources (not just prayer). Share your experience in class next week.

Follow the Spirit

What God wants me to do:

_____

_____

_____

_____

Remember Your Thoughts

Special insights I have learned:

_____

_____

_____

_____

More Light on the Text

John 14:15–29

This section is a continuation of the discourse at the Passover table after the washing of the disciples' feet (chapter 13) and before their departure to the garden (14:31). In this chapter, Jesus gives them words of comfort and of hope for the future. He reveals to them God's plan for them after He is gone to the Father. These revelations include: the plan of eternal life (vv. 1–7), the true revelation of God (vv. 8–11), the unlimited power for the disciples (vv. 12–14), and revelation and promise of the coming of another Comforter, the Holy Spirit, who will remain with them forever. The

following verses under discussion constitute an important and fundamental doctrine in the Christian Church—the gift, purpose, and work of the Holy Spirit.

15 If ye love me, keep my commandments.
Jesus begins this segment of the discourse with a condition using the word "if" and ends with a command "keep my commandments." By using the word "if," does Jesus doubt their love for Him and, therefore, demand that they prove it by keeping His commandment? On the other hand, does He equate their love for Him with their keeping His commandment?

If the former is right, then the statement can be restated thus: "If you really [or, say you] love me then you [should] keep my commandments." If the latter is a better rendering, then it can be reworded thus, "Since you love [or because you love me], keep my commandments" (cf. Luke 11:13). Whichever is the case, Jesus is saying that the proof of their love for Him is the keeping of His commandment. He would repeat this in various ways both in this chapter (vv. 21, 23) and in several other passages (e.g. 15:10). John reiterates this also in his first epistle (1 John 5:3). It is a simple encapsulation of the Gospel. All that Jesus has been teaching them is summed up in this one commandment of love.

16 And I will pray the Father, and he shall give you another Comforter, that he may abide with you for ever;
The promise that follows seems to be directly linked with the preceding verse and the theme of loving obedience. It seems that His praying to the Father and the sending of the Comforter are conditional upon the apostles' relationship with Him, evidenced by keeping His commandment. This relationship would motivate him to pray to the Father on their behalf, and "he shall give you another Comforter."

The subject of the prayer is no doubt clear. That is, the sending of another Comforter. The Greek word translated "Comforter" (Gk. *parakletos*) has the idea of one called alongside to help. It has the idea of one who stands by another and exhorts or encourages. It is also translated "Advocate" (NLT) meaning one called by someone, particularly in a law court to plead one's case (1 John 2:1), not as a professional pleader but as a friend.

Here is the first of five times the function and activities of the Holy Spirit are mentioned in the discourse (also in 14:25–26; 15:26–27; 16:5–11; 16:12–15). The idea here is that since Jesus is about to leave them, He is going to plead or intercede on their behalf to the Father to send another Helper or Comforter who will "abide with [them] for ever." The duration of the presence of the Comforter on earth with the disciples and believers is not temporary as in Jesus' case, but permanent—forever.

We see here a picture of a discouraged group of people who are about to lose their Master through death, and their Master (Jesus) comes to encourage them. They are not going to be alone, He encourages them. He assures them that it is to their advantage that He depart so that the Holy Spirit would come and be with them permanently (16:7).

17 Even the Spirit of truth; whom the world cannot receive, because it seeth him not, neither knoweth him: but ye know him; for he dwelleth with you, and shall be in you.

This Paraclete is called "the Spirit of truth." This defines one of the functions of the Holy Spirit. The word "Spirit" used here translates the Greek *pneuma* (puh-**NEW**-mah), which means literally wind, the same word Jesus used to describe to Nicodemus the function of the Spirit in conversion (John 3:8).

Truth is one of the characteristics of the Holy Spirit. Truth is a recurrent theme in the Gospel of John (1:17). Jesus says earlier in this chapter that He is "the way, the truth, and the life" (14:6; cf. 8:32–36). From these and other passages, we learn that Christ is the embodiment of truth. Here the Spirit shares the same nature with Christ, and He communicates truth (15:26; 16:13), testifying about Christ.

Three times Jesus referred to the Holy Spirit as the Spirit of Truth (14:17; 15:26; 16:13). Perhaps this can be thought of as the Counselor's educative function. Jesus told His disciples many things that they did not understand. One of the Spirit's tasks was to bring these things back to their remembrance and help them understand their meaning (John 14:26; 16:4).

Jesus says the world (Gk. *kosmos*, koss-**MOSS**) cannot receive this Spirit. Although this word can refer to the entire universe, or to all the inhabitants of earth, here, context implies Jesus means the unsaved. He gives two reasons they cannot receive Him. Firstly, they do not see Him because they are spiritually blind (cf. 2 Corinthians 4:4). Secondly, they do not know Him because they refuse to believe or understand Him (cf. 1 Corinthians 2:14).

Talking about the sinful nature of the world, Christ says they prefer darkness rather than light (John 3:19), and calls them children of the devil who is a liar, for they desire to do their father's will (John 8:44). Only those who believe in the Gospel of Christ are able to receive and know the Spirit of truth (1 John 4:6). Peter says it is the work of faith (1 Peter 1:8; cf. John 20:29). In contrast to the world, the disciples know the Spirit or have experienced Him because He dwells in them, Jesus says. They have this privilege of knowing Him because of their belief and relationship with Christ.

The next point of interest in this verse is the use of the present and the future tenses, "for he lives with you and will be in you." Some interpret this as a continuation of the presence or indwelling of the Holy Spirit in the believer. This agrees with the previous verse: "that He may abide with you for ever." Another interpretation is that while the Spirit dwells with them in a measure now, they would receive the Spirit in greater measure when He comes into their lives in His fullness at the baptism of the Holy Spirit (John 3:34; cf. John 1:31–33). It is believed that this was fulfilled on the day of Pentecost in Acts.

18 I will not leave you comfortless: I will come to you. 19 Yet a little while, and the world seeth me no more; but ye see me: because I live, ye shall live also.

Jesus then assures His disciples of His continued presence. The word translated here "comfortless" is the Greek *orphanos* (or-**FON**-oce) from which we derive its English equivalent, orphan. Other renderings of this word include desolate or helpless. The next use of the word is found in James 1:27, where it is rendered fatherless.

It is common in African tradition, for example, to refer to an apprentice as the child of his master. The apprentice usually lives with the master's family and is generally regarded as part of the family. On many occasions, the apprentice shares in the inheritance of his master if his master dies while he is serving him. It is also believed that such happened in the Jewish tradition of Jesus' time. The disciples of a particular teacher were called his children, and if he died, they were considered orphans. Jesus has called His disciples children (John 13:33), and here He promises them that He will not leave them as orphans.

Jesus promises them further saying, "I will come to you." He could be referring to His immediate appearance after His resurrection, which happens approximately three days after this speech (John 20; Acts 1:3) On the other hand, it is also possible that He is talking about His coming in the person of the Holy Spirit, therefore carrying forward the same train of thought of verses 16 and 17. Or, again, He might be talking about His Second Coming, a thought which He started with in this chapter (vv. 1–3). All three are possible and all three might be inclusive in His thought.

20 At that day ye shall know that I am in my Father, and ye in me, and I in you. 21 He that hath my commandments, and keepeth them, he it is that loveth me: and he that loveth me shall be loved of my Father, and I will love him, and will manifest myself to him.

Jesus explains how after He appears to the disciples again—whether after the Resurrection, in the Person of the Holy Spirit, or at the Second Coming—the disciples will enjoy unity with Christ, and therefore unity with the Father. They will all share in the love and the presence of the Lord. To join in this great communion among the Persons of the Trinity, one need only keep Jesus' commandments (cf. v. 15). Again keeping the commandments is the sign and assurance that the disciples truly love Jesus. Since those commands from Jesus are ultimately from the Father, obeying them shows love for the Father too. Jesus also reciprocates the love shown Him by loving His disciples, and whomever He loves, the Father also loves.

22 Judas saith unto him, not Iscariot, Lord, how is it that thou wilt manifest thyself unto us, and not unto the world? 23 Jesus answered and said unto him, If a man love me, he will keep my words: and my Father will love him, and we will come unto him, and make our abode with him.

John never gives a complete list of Jesus' disciples. These lists are instead in Matthew, Mark, and Luke. While Matthew and Mark list a disciple named Thaddaeus (Matthew 10:3; Mark 3:18), Luke's list replaces Thaddaeus with

"Judas" who is related to James (Luke 6:16; Acts 1:13). We do not know if that is James the son of Zebedee, or James the son of Alpheus, or another James altogether. We also do not know precisely how Judas and James are related. The Greek is unclear and could mean Judas is James' son or his brother. Other translations write Judas' name as Jude so as to avoid confusion with Judas Iscariot (as John himself does in this verse). The name is based on the Hebrew name Judah, but since Greek does not have an "h" letter as Hebrew does, most Hebrew names ending in "h" are transliterated into Greek with an "s" at the end instead. This is the only action specifically ascribed to this Judas in John or Luke, and neither Matthew nor Mark mention Thaddaeus aside from their disciple lists.

He asks why Jesus only shows Himself as Messiah to His disciples but not just to everyone. God truly wishes that all would come to salvation, so Judas asks why He does not make it easier for everyone. Jesus' answer is not a direct explanation to Judas' query, but answers the question turned on its head. Instead of saying why some do not truly see and understand Jesus, He explains why some do see and understand Him. The reason is their love and obedience to Christ. Those who do this gain the presence of Christ and the Father.

The implication is that those who do not see Jesus' manifestation are those who do not follow Him or love Him anyway. It is all bundled up in a cycle. There are those who love God, who obey Him, and commune with Him; and there are those who do not love God, do not obey His commands, and do not enjoy His presence. There are only these camps and nothing in between or partially given.

24 He that loveth me not keepeth not my sayings: and the word which ye hear is not mine, but the Father's which sent me. 25

These things have I spoken unto you, being yet present with you.

Jesus goes back to the love motif again. Stating it negatively (cf. v. 15), Jesus reinforces the truth about loving Him and keeping His sayings (Gk. *logos*) or teaching. He says anyone who does not love Him cannot keep His teaching. This is akin to verse 17, where we learned that the world cannot receive the Holy Spirit because they do not know Him.

Jesus seems to be talking about rejection. In essence, he who rejects Christ will not even listen to His teachings, and in effect also rejects His Father since His teachings are the Father's (Luke 10:16; John 3:36; 13:20). Jesus refuses to take glory to Himself and says, "for all things that I have heard of my Father I have made known unto you" (John 15:15). The rejection of Christ and His teachings is, therefore, tantamount to rejection of God Himself.

"These things… spoken" include all Jesus' teachings. It is not limited to His immediate sayings, but to all His teachings from the beginning of His ministry. This verse serves as a transition to the next, which deals more with the Holy Spirit and His work. It goes with the tone with which He started the discourse, and that is comforting and encouraging in view of His imminent departure from them.

26 But the comforter, which is the Holy Ghost, whom the Father will send in my name, he shall teach you all things, and bring all things to your remembrance, whatsoever I have said unto you.

The conjunction "but" at the beginning of this verse clarifies the point of the previous verse. There Jesus seems to say, "Although I have been teaching you in person and will soon be leaving you, you are not losing anything, since you are about to receive the Comforter (Gk. *parakletos*), the Holy Spirit, whose work includes bringing to your remembrance all my teachings." Here

Christ mentions both the office and name of the Holy Spirit, both of which we have come across in the earlier verses of the chapter (vv. 16–18).

In verse 17, Jesus refers to Him as the Spirit of truth, but here He calls Him the Holy Spirit, intentionally distinguishing Him from any other spirit. As we have already noted in verse 16, the Holy Spirit is from the Father. The new thing here is that Jesus is the medium through ("in my name") whom the Holy Spirit will be sent.

The function of the Holy Spirit is to comfort, encourage, or communicate the truth. He also teaches. He will both teach and remind them of the teachings of Jesus. The work of the Holy Spirit is referred to here again in order to give the disciples confidence and encouragement to face Jesus' imminent departure. The Holy Spirit would have a dual function. He would both aid the disciples by recalling all that Jesus has taught them, and teach them Himself — which would include future events (cf. 16:13).

27 Peace I leave with you, my peace I give unto you: not as the world giveth, give I unto you. Let not your heart be troubled, neither let it be afraid. 28 Ye have heard how I said unto you, I go away, and come again unto you. If ye loved me, ye would rejoice, because I said, I go unto the Father: for my Father is greater than I. 29 And now I have told you before it come to pass, that, when it is come to pass, ye might believe.

Lastly, Jesus promises the disciples peace, His own peace, which will calm their hearts and fears. This peace is given differently than the world gives, that is, it is given completely, freely, and irrevocably. God's peace never ends, because Jesus' peace relies on the completed facts of Jesus' saving sacrifice and life-giving resurrection.

Jesus assures the disciples that even though they are sad there is reason for them to be happy. Jesus is going to the Father, who is full of glory even greater than Jesus'. Later Paul would similarly long for heaven, since it is "far better" (Philippians 1:23). This knowledge gives us hope, just as Jesus' departure gives us peace. Knowing that those who die in the Lord go to be with the Father, we do not have to mourn "as others which have no hope" (1 Thessalonians 4:13).

As we close this lesson (though Jesus' lesson to His disciples continues), Jesus explains that this promise of His return and the Spirit's coming was given so they will be even more sure of Jesus' identity when the Spirit does come. They knew that the test of a prophet was if his predictions always came true. Those who speak with the power of our omnipotent God will never prophesy incorrectly. The more Jesus told His disciples about the future, and the more they looked for the fulfillment of those words, the more sure they would become that Jesus is who He always claimed to be: the Son of God who comes to save the world.

Sources:
Henry, Matthew. *Matthew Henry's Commentary on the Whole Bible: New Modern Edition.* Vols. 1-6. Peabody, MA: Hendrickson Publishers, Inc., 2009.
Strong, James. *The New Strong's Exhaustive Concordance of the Bible.* Nashville, TN: Thomas Nelson, 2003.
Thayer, Joseph Henry. *A Greek-English Lexicon of the New Testament.* New York: American Book Company, 1889.

Say It Correctly

Paraklete. PARE-uh-kleet.
Thaddaeus. THAD-ee-us.

Daily Bible Readings

MONDAY
Seek Peace and Pursue It
(Psalm 34:4-14)

TUESDAY
Rest for the Weary
(Matthew 11:25-30)

WEDNESDAY
Jesus Has Conquered the World
(John 16:23-27, 32-33)

THURSDAY
Peace for the Upright
(Psalm 119:161-176)

FRIDAY
God's Unmoveable Covenant of Peace
(Isaiah 54:6-10)

SATURDAY
Don't Let Your Hearts Be Troubled
(John 14:1-4)

SUNDAY
Peace to the Disciples
(John 14:15-29)

Notes

A friendly reminder!

Pre-Order Your 2022-2023 Precepts For Living®

Order Today and Save 10% Off!
urbanministries.com/pfl
1-800-860-8642

Precepts for Living® is also Available Online!

Get downloadable, easy-to-follow lesson plans, Teaching Tips Videos and gain access to the Precepts for Living® Online Community Forum to discuss the lessons and share insights and more.

preceptsforliving.com

Teaching Tips

Words You Should Know

A. Dwell (Revelation 21:3) *skenoo* (Gk.)—To live in, especially in a tent

B. Fearful (v. 8) *deilos* (Gk.)—Timid, faithless

Teacher Preparation

Unifying Principle—No More Tears. People long for a place and time when life's stresses and death will not exist. Where can we find such a peaceful existence? The vision in Revelation 21 foretells that God will create a new heaven and earth where life's challenges will be banished forever.

A. Read the Bible Background and Devotional Reading.

B. Pray for your students and lesson clarity.

C. Read the lesson Scripture in multiple translations.

O—Open the Lesson

A. Begin the class with prayer.

B. Ask your participants what elements of a perfect society they have heard in lyrics. What other literary or mythological perfect societies have they heard about (Utopia, Shangri-La, El Dorado, etc.)? Explain that the Bible talks about a real perfect place coming at the end of the age.

C. Have the students read the Aim for Change and the In Focus story.

D. Ask students how events like those in the story weigh on their hearts and how they can view these events from a faith perspective.

P—Present the Scriptures

A. Read the Focal Verses and discuss the Background and The People, Places, and Times sections.

B. Have the class share what Scriptures stand out for them and why, with particular emphasis on today's themes.

E—Explore the Meaning

A. Use In Depth or More Light on the Text to facilitate a deeper discussion of the lesson text.

B. Pose the questions in Search the Scriptures and Discuss the Meaning.

C. Discuss the Liberating Lesson and Application for Activation sections.

N—Next Steps for Application

A. Summarize the value of living out one's new beginning now, confident that it will be fully realized in communion with God in heaven.

B. End class with a commitment to pray for confidence to face difficult times based on God's ultimate plan to bring everlasting peace.

Worship Guide

For the Superintendent or Teacher
Theme: A New Home
Song: "Oh, I Want to See You"

(213) 338·8477
893 5948 4624 ##

A New Home

Bible Background • REVELATION 21:1–8
Printed Text • REVELATION 21:1–8 | Devotional Reading • REVELATION 15:1–8

—————— Aim for Change ——————

By the end of this lesson, we will EXAMINE the unique genre of "apocalypse" that characterizes Revelation in order to discern how to understand its message, CONTEMPLATE the creation of a new heaven and a new earth for the hope that this vision holds for the faithful, and EMBRACE the peace of God that begins in this life with Jesus and continues in God's new creation.

—————— In Focus ——————

Randy's phone rang, and he buried his head in the hard hospital pillow. He didn't want to talk to anyone, even on his 50th birthday. He was too ashamed and too broken. He thought over the past few decades of his life. What had gone wrong?

His life had started out so promising—marrying his high school sweetheart, graduating from one of the country's best universities, landing his dream job. But then, the addictions took control of his life. Drugs, gambling, adultery—he had done them all. He sighed deeply. Now he was alone. He was just an old, broken, bitter man. If only he had never taken that first hit. If only he had never bet that first dollar. If only he had never cheated on Shari…if only…if only…

He let the tears come, rolling down his cheeks. "God, what I wouldn't give for a second chance," he prayed. "I've made such a mess of my own life. If You're really there, please help me. Help me!"

Now, Randy thinks of that day, a full decade ago, as the time when he really began to live. God heard his prayer and sent someone who shared the Gospel with him. God gave him the new beginning he had prayed for so desperately. God has restored Randy's family, and he thanks God every day with the assurance that he will one day dwell with God for all eternity.

Many people would like to have a new beginning. What is it like to begin anew? How can Robert's testimony demonstrate the hope of a new beginning to others?

—————— Keep in Mind ——————

"And God shall wipe away all tears from their eyes; and there shall be no more death, neither sorrow, nor crying, neither shall there be any more pain: for the former things are passed away." (Revelation 21:4, KJV)

"He will wipe every tear from their eyes, and there will be no more death or sorrow or crying or pain. All these things are gone forever." (Revelation 21:4, NLT)

Focal Verses

KJV **Revelation 21:1** And I saw a new heaven and a new earth: for the first heaven and the first earth were passed away; and there was no more sea.

2 And I John saw the holy city, new Jerusalem, coming down from God out of heaven, prepared as a bride adorned for her husband.

3 And I heard a great voice out of heaven saying, Behold, the tabernacle of God is with men, and he will dwell with them, and they shall be his people, and God himself shall be with them, and be their God.

4 And God shall wipe away all tears from their eyes; and there shall be no more death, neither sorrow, nor crying, neither shall there be any more pain: for the former things are passed away.

5 And he that sat upon the throne said, Behold, I make all things new. And he said unto me, Write: for these words are true and faithful.

6 And he said unto me, It is done. I am Alpha and Omega, the beginning and the end. I will give unto him that is athirst of the fountain of the water of life freely.

7 He that overcometh shall inherit all things; and I will be his God, and he shall be my son.

8 But the fearful, and unbelieving, and the abominable, and murderers, and whoremongers, and sorcerers, and idolaters, and all liars, shall have their part in the lake which burneth with fire and brimstone: which is the second death.

NLT **Revelation 21:1** Then I saw a new heaven and a new earth, for the old heaven and the old earth had disappeared. And the sea was also gone.

2 And I saw the holy city, the new Jerusalem, coming down from God out of heaven like a bride beautifully dressed for her husband.

3 I heard a loud shout from the throne, saying, "Look, God's home is now among his people! He will live with them, and they will be his people. God himself will be with them.

4 He will wipe every tear from their eyes, and there will be no more death or sorrow or crying or pain. All these things are gone forever."

5 And the one sitting on the throne said, "Look, I am making everything new!" And then he said to me, "Write this down, for what I tell you is trustworthy and true."

6 And he also said, "It is finished! I am the Alpha and the Omega—the Beginning and the End. To all who are thirsty I will give freely from the springs of the water of life.

7 All who are victorious will inherit all these blessings, and I will be their God, and they will be my children.

8 But cowards, unbelievers, the corrupt, murders, the immoral, those who practice witchcraft, idol worshipers, and all liars—their fate is in the fiery lake of burning sulfur. This is the second death."

The People, Places, and Times

John. John, whose name in Hebrew means "Jehovah is gracious," was one of Jesus' 12 disciples, and he is believed to be the author of the Gospel of John, three epistles, and the book of Revelation. The son of Zebedee and brother of James, he was one of the three in Jesus' inner circle (along with James and Peter) who witnessed the Transfiguration (Matthew 17:1), and he was present with Jesus in the Garden of Gethsemane right before His arrest (Mark 14:32–33). John is recorded as the only disciple present at the Crucifixion and was instructed by Jesus to care for His mother, Mary (John 19:25–27). Of all 12 disciples, he was the only one not martyred (according to tradition). However, he was imprisoned on the isle of Patmos for his faith. It was there that he wrote the book of Revelation.

Bride. The imagery of the bride is used widely in the Bible as a description of the people of God. In the Old Testament, the prophets presented Israel as a bride who had committed repeated adulteries (Jeremiah 3; Ezekiel 16; Hosea 3). The prophets also proclaimed that God was faithful to His unfaithful bride and would restore her (Isaiah 61:10). In the book of Revelation, bride imagery is used for the Church and her relationship to Christ. The bride belongs to Christ, who is the Bridegroom (Matthew 9:15). In Revelation, the Church, as the bride of the Lamb, has prepared herself for marriage by performing righteous deeds (19:7–8). In the last days a great wedding is portrayed with the Church prepared for her Bridegroom (21:2, 9). The bride pictured here has not earned her status through righteous deeds. These acts were the Church's obedient response to God's saving grace. The garments of righteousness were given to her.

Background

The book of Revelation records four visions of John. The first vision (1:12–3:22) is of Jesus and His messages to the seven churches. The second vision (4:1–13:18) depicts Jesus Christ at the Throne of God, the opening of the seven seals, and the seven trumpet blasts. The third vision (14:1–16:21) describes Christ on Mount Zion. Our lesson today opens with the beginning of the fourth vision, in which we will learn about the ultimate fulfillment of God's promise in Christ—the Holy City, the New Jerusalem.

At-A-Glance

1. The Presentation (Revelation 21:1–2)
2. The Proclamation (vv. 3–4)
3. The Promises (vv. 5–8)

In Depth

1. The Presentation (Revelation 21:1–2)

Genesis 1 gives us the account of the creation of the world. God divided the light from the darkness and the land from the seas. He created fish, birds, plants, animals and then He created humans. In Revelation 21, God reveals His creativity by first presenting the church, the Body of Christ, as the "bride." He then goes on to describe the place where the Bride will dwell—a new heaven and new earth. The old world will have passed away, with all of its problems, especially the chaotic sea. The new heaven and the new earth will be a fitting place for the Bride, the redeemed of the Lord, to dwell.

What kinds of images and feelings does "bride" bring to mind? Why are those helpful in understanding the relationship between Christ and the Church?

2. The Proclamation (vv. 3–4)

In the Garden of Eden, God came down and physically fellowshipped with Adam and Eve. They walked with Him and conversed with Him on a regular basis. But sin destroyed this fellowship. Now in verse 3, after presenting the New Jerusalem, God joyfully proclaims His intention to dwell with His people in the new city. In Scripture, the idea of God dwelling with His people and being their God is covenant language.

Perfect peace and joy result from God's eternal presence with His people. In God's perfect presence, there will be no more sorrow, no more pain, and no more suffering for all eternity. Verse 4 echoes Revelation 7:17; both verses promise that God Himself will tenderly care for His people, as a bridegroom cares for his bride. He will dry our tears and comfort us with the fact that the old has passed away. All is new. Never again will we experience the trials and tribulations of the old world.

Previously whenever a follower of God saw Him or was in His presence, it was a fearful thing (Exodus 20:18–19; Isaiah 6:5). What has changed that God dwelling with His Bride is now joyful?

3. The Promises (vv. 5–8)

God, seated on His throne, directs John to write down His words. God says He is even now working on our behalf, transforming us into the image of His dear Son (2 Corinthians 3:18) and readying us for the day when we will be completely new. Our hope for that day is certain, for God always finishes what He has begun. In the same sense that Jesus spoke the words, "It is finished" (from John 19:30), God announces that His plan is accomplished. All has proceeded according to His will and for His glory.

God promises abundant, life-giving water to all who are thirsty. For Middle Eastern people living in the desert, water was often a scarce and valuable commodity. This promise of plenteous water therefore symbolizes life and prosperity.

Those who overcome, who fight the good fight of faith, will enter the Holy City and be richly rewarded as God's heirs, entitled to all of the benefits of a son or daughter. Those who reject God, however, will experience a "second death" (v. 8). The first death is physical death on earth. The second death is an eternal dying—a perpetual burning in the lake of fire. Instead of dwelling with God, these people will be eternally separated from Him.

In what ways can the water of life be read figuratively or literally? In what ways is the lake of fire figurative or literal?

Search the Scriptures

1. What physical aspect of the new heaven and earth will be different from today's world (Revelation 21:1)?

2. To what was the Holy City compared (v. 2)?

Discuss the Meaning

1. What is the significance of the symbolism of New Jerusalem appearing as a bride?

2. Why did God want John to write down His words?

Liberating Lesson

What would it be like to be able to begin anew? People today are always longing for a fresh start—a new diet, a new job, a new house, a new school, a new marriage, etc. Some will take drastic measures to try to change their lives for the better. As Christians, we know that God offers the ultimate new beginning, which is salvation through Jesus Christ. When we are a new creation in Christ, we have the power to stop believing Satan's lies about ourselves and others, we have the power to think of others before ourselves, and we have the power to truly commune with God. We also understand that the joy and peace we experience briefly in this world is just a taste of what we will experience in God's presence forever.

Application for Activation

Remember that God's promises are sure. You can count on Him to keep every promise. As you live your life of faithfulness before God, you can be assured that He will complete what He started in you.

Others need to know this assurance as well. But people need to know they are sinners before they can recognize their thirst for what it is: a need for relationship with God. This week, pray for your unsaved loved ones and acquaintances. Pray that God will reveal to them their need for salvation. Pray that God will give you opportunities and wisdom to share the Good News of a true new beginning.

Follow the Spirit

What God wants me to do:

_____

_____

_____

_____

Remember Your Thoughts

Special insights I have learned:

_____

_____

_____

_____

More Light on the Text

Revelation 21:1–8

1 And I saw a new heaven and a new earth: for the first heaven and the first earth were passed away; and there was no more sea.

Revelation 21 and 22 present us with the Bible's longest and best portrait of what people commonly call "heaven," although what is actually shown is "a new heaven and a new earth" coming "down from God out of heaven" (21:1–2). Isaiah 65:17 also predicted "new heavens and a new earth."

Peter also wrote of a cosmic changeover or a total transformation (2 Peter 3:10–12). It describes a time when the current "heavens shall pass away" and be "dissolved" in fire, and "the earth…shall be burned up." This will make room for "new heavens and a new earth (2 Peter 3:13). This imagery indicates the magnitude of this renewal. We see a different angle in Paul's letter to the Roman church:

Creation "itself also shall be delivered from the bondage of corruption into the glorious liberty of the children of God" (Romans 8:21). This imagery indicates the continuity with the original creation even as it finally becomes what God always intended.

2 And I John saw the holy city, new Jerusalem, coming down from God out of heaven, prepared as a bride adorned for her husband.

Two key images used here are that of the holy city and of the bride. Paul introduces the idea of a "Jerusalem which is above" (Galatians 4:26) as part of his web of metaphors to explain the Christian's new freedom from the Law. Abraham's wife Hagar, a slave who bears a son who is not the child of promise, is compared to the current Jerusalem on Mount Zion, where the Temple stands, representing the Mosaic Law and the sacrificial system that tried to make it so God and His creation could be together. Abraham's wife Sarah, however, is a free woman who bears Isaac who inherits the covenant. She is likened to a heavenly Jerusalem, which is free and the mother of all those faithful to Jesus. In Hebrews, also, the writer contrasts Mount Sinai (of the Law) and the new Mount Zion (of Christ's grace). This new Jerusalem is filled with joy instead of terror as Sinai was. In it dwell "the general assembly and church," the justified saints, all the host of angels, and God and Jesus Himself (Hebrews 12:22–23).

Paul used imagery of the Church as Christ's bride (2 Corinthians 11:2; Ephesians 5:25–27), and John has already seen this terminology used previously in the vision (Revelation 19:7–8). Just as the groom wants to be with the bride, so Christ wants His church to be with Him. She has been made ready for Him. The word "adorned" (v. 2) in Greek is *kosmeo* (kos-**MEH**-o). This verb comes from the noun *kosmos* (**KOS**-mos), which is the Greek word for "the ordered world" and also means "ornament." From this Greek word, we get our word "cosmetics."

Those who are believers have received new life, as Christ begins the process of beautifying each Christian as a member of His Bride (Ephesians 5:25–32). We have been charged to walk in newness of life through the power of the Holy Spirit. We are to put aside our old ways of thinking, speaking, and living in order to fulfill God's plan for us. We must live with the goal of showing others the way to the new city of God.

3 And I heard a great voice out of heaven saying, Behold, the tabernacle of God is with men, and he will dwell with them, and they shall be his people, and God himself shall be with them, and be their God.

In Old Testament times, God localized and centralized His presence with His people at the tabernacle (Leviticus 26:11–13; Ezekiel 37:27). In New Testament times, God came in the form of a man, and He "dwelt among us" (John 1:14). The word "dwell" occurs in both Revelation 7:15 and 21:3. In Greek, "dwell" is *skenoo* (skay-**NO**-oh). This is literally the word for "to pitch a tent," reinforcing the connection between the Incarnation and the Tabernacle, which was a tent.

Here on the earth our sense of God's presence is often dimmed, interrupted, or obscured. God dwells with us through the Holy Spirit, and we perceive Him by faith. But in the Holy City, we will live in the full measure of God's physical presence. We will no longer accept His presence by faith alone. We will truly be with Him! What a glorious thought! When we are struggling through life here on earth, we can rejoice in the hope that one day we will live with our loving Creator, never to be parted from Him again.

Verse 3 restates Ezekiel 37:27, where God promises to one day dwell with His people in the fullest sense of the word. While on earth, we enjoy some of the blessings of being children of God: salvation, peace, joy, wisdom, and others. But when the New Jerusalem arrives, we will fully be His people and He will be our God, and we will dwell together. This reciprocal cadence is full of covenantal meaning. The sense here is of a prospective bride and groom who have been longing to consummate their marriage, to belong exclusively to one another, to have the right and the opportunity to live in each other's presence forever. God is exulting over His plan that has finally brought His redeemed, His beloved, to His side, never to be parted from her again.

4 And God shall wipe away all tears from their eyes; and there shall be no more death, neither sorrow, nor crying, neither shall there be any more pain: for the former things are passed away. 5 And he that sat upon the throne said, Behold, I make all things new. And he said unto me, Write: for these words are true and faithful.

God speaks directly at the beginning (1:8) and at the end (21:5) of the book of Revelation. Each of those who receives Christ in this life is already "a new creation" (2 Corinthians 5:17), but we live in a sinful world (Romans 8:19–22) until the time that it will become new. All the sad and terrible things of this present world will be no more in heaven. They are the result of sin, which has been cleared away.

"He that sat upon the throne" is the Father God, described in iconic detail in an earlier vision (Revelation 4:1–6). God calls out, "I make all things new" (v. 5). He means it! And He is doing it now! The present tense of the verb "make" assures us that God is even now creating His new world. This wording is also reminiscent of a prophecy from Isaiah. There, God says, "Behold, I will do a new thing" (Isaiah 43:19), which is providing abundantly for His people, even though they have not been faithful to Him. Isaiah shares how God will institute a new way of interacting with His people, by blessing His people again and using even people like Cyrus to be His instruments, simply so that they will know that Yahweh is the only God. In this section of Isaiah's prophecy, God also calls Himself "the first" and "the last" (Isaiah 44:6), which John will echo in his record of the following verse.

6 And he said unto me, It is done. I am Alpha and Omega, the beginning and the end. I will give unto him that is athirst of the fountain of the water of life freely.

God began everything by His will, and He will bring His plan to fruition. Just as Jesus said "It is finished" when His work which provided our salvation was complete (John 19:30), so also God will announce "It is done" at the end of human history (Revelation 21:6). Here, Christ is called the "Alpha and Omega." Alpha and omega are the first and last letters of the Greek alphabet. The author explains this first phrase by adding that Jesus is "the beginning and the end." Our sovereign God, the Alpha and the Omega, is the beginning and end of all things (Revelation 21:6).

The One who once offered a woman at a well "living water" (John 4:10) and said that "living water" could spring up inside of His people (John 7:37–38; cf. Zechariah 14:8) promises to give unto those who thirst of "the fountain of the water of life freely." This coming age, when we will see God's promises once and for all is portrayed in Scripture as flowing with abundant water (Isaiah 35:1–2; Ezekiel 47:1–12). Again, this promise echoes Isaiah's prophecy concerning the return from exile (Isaiah 44:3; 55:1). By these allusions, John hopes to communicate that God's people can think of the present world as captivity, and His coming as a return to our true home, where He will bless us abundantly.

Many people today do not lack physical water with which to quench their thirst, but they do lack what they need to quench their spiritual thirst. God created every human being to have a desire for the Creator. As believers, we are compelled to hold out the promise of living water to unbelievers, as Jesus did with the woman at the well (John 4:10). But even though we serve and love God here on earth, our thirst to know Him and to dwell in His presence is never fully quenched. Only when we reach that New City will our thirst for God be replaced with His eternal presence.

7 He that overcometh shall inherit all things; and I will be his God, and he shall be my son.

In Greek, the word for "overcometh" is *nikao* (nik-**AH**-o), which can mean "to be victorious." John often refers to those who "overcome" in Revelation, but does not directly say what it is they are overcoming. He uses the word often in his epistles, and there, we see the overcomer is the Christian who conquers the evil one (1 John 2:13–14), and the whole world (1 John 5:4–5). John says our faith is the victory we gain over the world, and our faith is that Jesus is the Son of God (1 John 5:4–5). A Christian is intended to be a world-conqueror, to hold fast to the belief that faith in Christ conquers temptations and persecutions.

Not only does God "make all things new" (21:5), but the Christian overcomer "shall inherit all things" (21:7). Indeed John's first audience had perhaps already heard Paul announce in a letter to the Corinthian Christians that "all things are yours" (1 Corinthians 3:21). We will belong to God as His children for all eternity (Revelation 21:7). We are His heirs.

8 But the fearful, and unbelieving, and the abominable, and murderers, and whoremongers, and sorcerers, and idolaters, and all liars, shall have their part in the lake which burneth with fire and brimstone: which is the second death.

This last, sobering verse tells us that not all will be overcomers. Not all are true followers of Jesus; those who are not will face eternal judgment. Unbelievers are found in many places, even in the church. These are those who have not put their trust in Jesus Christ as their Savior. Verses like this one compel us to tell others how to be saved. Hell is real. If we truly care about others, if we truly believe the truth of God's Word, we must share the Gospel, even with the dire warnings.

The Greek for "fearful" is *deilos* (dee-**LOS**), which means "timid" or "cowardly," but also implies faithless. If we consider the context of persecution under Rome, it helps us see that John was thinking of those who were too afraid to stand for Christ. During the time of trial, they were ashamed to say whose they were and whom they served. This word is not talking about the feeling of fear. Many exhibit true courage when they persevere in doing right even when they are actually afraid. What is condemned is letting fear keep us from standing up for our Lord.

The "abominable" are those who have allowed themselves to be saturated with the sinfulness of this world. Decadent ways of living were common in the days of the Roman Empire in which John lived, and who can deny the decadence of our world today? It's so easy to be polluted by the things that flash across our screens, by the celebrated lives of rap stars, by news, gossip, and entertainment offered night and day by mass media, and so on. We must make a concerted effort to keep our thoughts, our values, our words, and our actions clean before God.

Then we come to "murderers." John may have been thinking of those who persecuted Christians unto their deaths, but before we clear ourselves, we should remember that Jesus said, "Whosoever shall say, Thou fool, shall be in danger of hell fire" (from Matthew 5:22). We may congratulate ourselves because we never use the word "murderer" to describe ourselves, but think of the times we may have muttered, "You idiot!" under our breaths to the driver who just cut us off in traffic. Isn't this just the same?

"Whoremongers" are fornicators, those who have sexual relations outside of marriage. In our culture, it is common for unmarried couples to live together, but it is definitely against God's Word. The next to be thrown into the lake of fire are the sorcerers and idolaters. This describes the worship of anything other than the one true God, and most often some aspect of God's creation, from other human beings to superstitions to various material objects. Although we may not be in a context with idol worship as in Bible days, making material goods come before God is common. This is a case in which we need to examine our hearts to see where our priorities are.

The last in the list are the "liars." Included in this title are those who are insincere, those who lie by their silence, or those who practice any other kind of untruth. Those who claim to follow Christ but actually do not would also be included.

As we examine this list and ourselves, chances are that most of us know that we are guilty of some of these sins. If so, we need to repent and ask for God's forgiveness as well as for God's power through the Holy Spirit to make a more thorough progress in the path of sanctification. The point of this text is not that we earn salvation by works, but it does point out our responsibility for obedience and perseverance in the Christian life. God's Word gives us assurance that Christ's work saves us, but we are always commanded to live as those who are actively following Christ. If we do so, we can live in confident assurance that we will not be cast into the lake of fire at the last judgment.

Sources:

Henry, Matthew. *Matthew Henry's Commentary on the Whole Bible: New Modern Edition*. Vols. 1-6. Peabody, MA: Hendrickson Publishers, Inc., 2009.

NIV Study Bible, 1446.

Strong, James. *The New Strong's Exhaustive Concordance of the Bible*. Nashville, TN: Thomas Nelson, 2003.

Thayer, Joseph Henry. *A Greek-English Lexicon of the New Testament*. New York: American Book Company, 1889.

Say It Correctly

Zebedee. ZEH-beh-dee.
Gethsemane. Geth-SEH-mah-nee.
Omega. Oh-MAY-gah.

Daily Bible Readings

MONDAY
The Lord, Our Dwelling Place
(Psalm 90:1–12)

TUESDAY
To Love God Is to Know God
(1 John 2:12–17)

WEDNESDAY
Faith Is the Victory
(1 John 5:1–5)

THURSDAY
God Will Do a New Thing
(Isaiah 43:14–21)

FRIDAY
Come, You Who Thirst
(Isaiah 55:1–5)

SATURDAY
More Than Conquerors
(Romans 8:31–39)

SUNDAY
God Will Dwell with God's People
(Revelation 21:1–8)

Notes

_____

_____

_____

_____

Teaching Tips

Words You Should Know

A. Bride (Revelation 21:9) *numphe* (Gk.)—A betrothed or newly married young woman

B. Apostles (v. 14) *apostolos* (Gk.)—God's messengers who encountered Christ, planted churches, and ministered to the new church

Teacher Preparation

Unifying Principle—No Place Like It. It is difficult for people to imagine living in a place that is totally different from the one in which they presently live. What will the new place be like? Revelation 21 uses figurative language to describe the brilliant new city God will create.

A. Read the Bible Background and Devotional Reading.

B. Pray for your students and lesson clarity.

C. Read the lesson Scripture in multiple translations.

O—Open the Lesson

A. Begin the class with prayer.

B. When we plan a move we might make a packing list or to-do lists to prepare us for our new location. Work with class members to develop similar lists to prepare for our transition into the New Jerusalem.

C. Have the students read the Aim for Change and the In Focus story.

D. Ask students how events like those in the story weigh on their hearts and how they can view these events from a faith perspective.

P—Present the Scriptures

A. Read the Focal Verses and discuss the Background and The People, Places, and Times sections.

B. Have the class share what Scriptures stand out for them and why, with particular emphasis on today's themes.

E—Explore the Meaning

A. Use In Depth or More Light on the Text to facilitate a deeper discussion of the lesson text.

B. Pose the questions in Search the Scriptures and Discuss the Meaning.

C. Discuss the Liberating Lesson and Application for Activation sections.

N—Next Steps for Application

A. Summarize the value of knowing no joys on this earth can measure up to the joys awaiting us in heaven.

B. End class with a commitment to pray that the New Jerusalem would come soon.

Worship Guide

For the Superintendent or Teacher
Theme: A New City
Song: "Revelation Song"

A New City

Bible Background • REVELATION 21:9–27
Printed Text • REVELATION 21:9–21 | Devotional Reading • REVELATION 10:1–11

─────────── **Aim for Change** ───────────

By the end of this lesson, we will EXPLORE the possibility of living in a new place, IMAGINE the richness and serenity of living in the New Jerusalem, and CELEBRATE God's provision of a new city for believers throughout eternity.

─────────── **In Focus** ───────────

When Katheryn entered her new home, she had to fight back the tears. Everything was so beautiful. As she walked from room to room, she marveled at the softly colored walls, the hanging plants, and the lovely marble floors. Barry had painted all of the rooms in her favorite colors. The kitchen was large and airy, and she could tell that the windows had been replaced. Small containers of herbs planted in brightly-colored ceramic bowls lined the large kitchen window.

Katheryn and Barry had only been married seven days and were just returning from their honeymoon. She knew he had picked out a house for them, but she was unprepared for how wonderful her new home was. Barry's job had transferred him to California right after they had started dating, but he had flown home faithfully twice each month.

While Katheryn knew that she would miss her family and friends back in New Jersey, there was no doubt in her mind that her Barry loved her and wanted to make her happy in their new life together.

Some of Katheryn's friends had teased her about waiting so long to get married. "You'll be an old maid before you know it," they teased.

Katheryn understood now that she had done the right thing by waiting. It may have taken her longer to get married than her friends, but God had provided her with a godly man.

Christians, the bride of Christ, can look forward to a wonderful home prepared by our Lord. How does thinking about the Christian's heavenly home affect your daily outlook?

─────────── **Keep in Mind** ───────────

"And the wall of the city had twelve foundations, and in them the names of the twelve apostles of the Lamb." (Revelation 21:14, KJV)

"The wall of the city had twelve foundation stones, and on them were written the names of the twelve apostles of the Lamb." (Revelation 21:14, NLT)

Focal Verses

KJV **Revelation 21:9** And there came unto me one of the seven angels which had the seven vials full of the seven last plagues, and talked with me, saying, Come hither, I will shew thee the bride, the Lamb's wife.

10 And he carried me away in the spirit to a great and high mountain, and shewed me that great city, the holy Jerusalem, descending out of heaven from God,

11 Having the glory of God: and her light was like unto a stone most precious, even like a jasper stone, clear as crystal;

12 And had a wall great and high, and had twelve gates, and at the gates twelve angels, and names written thereon, which are the names of the twelve tribes of the children of Israel:

13 On the east three gates; on the north three gates; on the south three gates; and on the west three gates.

14 And the wall of the city had twelve foundations, and in them the names of the twelve apostles of the Lamb.

15 And he that talked with me had a golden reed to measure the city, and the gates thereof, and the wall thereof.

16 And the city lieth foursquare, and the length is as large as the breadth: and he measured the city with the reed, twelve thousand furlongs. The length and the breadth and the height of it are equal.

17 And he measured the wall thereof, an hundred and forty and four cubits, according to the measure of a man, that is, of the angel.

18 And the building of the wall of it was of jasper: and the city was pure gold, like unto clear glass.

19 And the foundations of the wall of the city were garnished with all manner of precious stones. The first foundation was jasper; the second, sapphire; the third, a chalcedony; the fourth, an emerald;

NLT **Revelation 21:9** Then one of the seven angels who held the seven bowls containing the seven last plagues came and said to me, "Come with me! I will show you the bride, the wife of the Lamb."

10 So he took me in the Spirit to a great, high mountain, and he showed me the holy city, Jerusalem, descending out of heaven from God.

11 It shone with the glory of God and sparkled like a precious stone—like jasper as clear as crystal.

12 The city wall was broad and high, with twelve gates guarded by twelve angels. And the names of the twelve tribes of Israel were written on the gates.

13 There were three gates on each side—east, north, south, and west.

14 The wall of the city had twelve foundation stones, and on them were written the names of the twelve apostles of the Lamb.

15 The angel who talked to me held in his hand a gold measuring stick to measure the city, its gates, and its wall.

16 When he measured it, he found it was a square, as wide as it was long. In fact, its length and width and height were each 1,400 miles.

17 Then he measured the walls and found them to be 216 feet thick (according to the human standard used by the angel).

18 The wall was made of jasper, and the city was pure gold, as clear as glass.

19 The wall of the city was built on foundation stones inlaid with twelve precious stones: the first was jasper, the second sapphire, the third agate, the fourth emerald,

20 the fifth onyx, the sixth carnelian, the seventh chrysolite, the eighth beryl, the ninth topaz, the tenth chrysoprase, the eleventh jacinth, the twelfth amethyst.

20 The fifth, sardonyx; the sixth, sardius; the seventh, chrysolyte; the eighth, beryl; the ninth, a topaz; the tenth, a chrysoprasus; the eleventh, a jacinth; the twelfth, an amethyst.

21 And the twelve gates were twelve pearls: every several gate was of one pearl: and the street of the city was pure gold, as it were transparent glass.

21 The twelve gates were made of pearls—each gate from a single pearl! And the main street was pure gold, as clear as glass.

The People, Places, and Times

New Jerusalem. The Israelites of old, along with all of God's people down through the ages, longed for the coming time when we will live in complete, eternal peace. The New Jerusalem (Revelation 21:1–2) was predicted even before the exile ended (Isaiah 65:17; 66:22). Devout Jews prayed regularly for the restoration of Jerusalem. Eventually, the idea of "New Jerusalem" came to symbolize hope for the Jewish nation. This new city would be a place built by God, where the righteous would dwell with Him in perfect peace forever. When speaking of a city, we are speaking of not only the physical infrastructure, but also the people who dwell in that city. In this sense, the new Holy City of Jerusalem is symbolic of the church as the redeemed Bride of Christ.

Background

After John's vision of the new heaven and the new Earth, the believer's final and eternal habitation, the angel, shows him a more specific picture: the church, here described as "the bride" (Revelation 21:9) and "the holy Jerusalem" (v. 10). The "new Jerusalem... prepared as a bride adorned for her husband" (21:2) is now shown to be a realm of perfect life, beauty, bounty, and wholeness. This passage explains in graphic detail the implications of that glorious statement, "the tabernacle of God is with men, and he will dwell with them" (v. 3). The rich imagery used here and elsewhere in the Scriptures seeks to portray in shimmering detail how great the believer's inheritance is: being with God Himself in all His glory! One might imagine the apostle Paul had this passage in mind when he said, "Eye hath not seen, nor ear heard, neither have entered into the heart of man, the things which God hath prepared for them that love him" (1 Corinthians 2:9).

At-A-Glance

1. Beautiful Bride (Revelation 21:9–11)
2. Beautiful Foundations (vv. 12–17)
3. Beautiful Walls (vv. 18–21)

In Depth

1. Beautiful Bride (Revelation 21:9–11)

The apostle John describes the church as the bride. What do we learn about the church's glorious identity from this term? If the church is Jesus' bride (for He indeed is the "husband" of v. 2), then she is bound and betrothed to Him in a holy and unbreakable covenant. This suggests that her duty is to love and respond to her husband, but more importantly it communicates the overwhelming love and commitment of Jesus Christ to His bride. If human beings consider themselves bound by the vows they take on their wedding day, how much more will Jesus consider Himself bound to His people, since in Him all God's promises are "yea" (2 Corinthians 1:20), and since He has sealed the covenant of marriage between God and His people with His own blood?

In the Old Testament, God's presence dwelt in Jerusalem and the people were blessed by His holiness and His favor. In the new heavens and the new earth, God will dwell in the midst of His people as never before. Christ, the great Mediator, will usher them into God's presence with robes of righteousness, and they will be thoroughly acceptable in His sight. How great is the love of the Father, and how secure is the identity of the saints!

What are the implications of the New Jerusalem, which is the bride and the church, descending out of heaven?

2. Beautiful Foundations (vv. 12–17)

The heavenly city that John saw is a picture of perfection. It has perfect dimensions, beautifully adorned with precious gems and gold. The heavenly city is protected with high, fortified walls. The 12 gates to the city are covered by 12 angels in order to ensure the city remains pure and unspoiled. The 12 gates echo the 12 gates in Ezekiel's new city, which represent the 12 tribes of Israel and the complete inclusion of God's people (Ezekiel 48:30–35).

However, one of the most interesting facts about the city is that it is built on 12 foundations, each one bearing the name of one of the 12 apostles, the first bearers of the Gospel. This is because only through the Gospel can one become a citizen of this heavenly city.

Why does the City of God need walls? To defend from attack? To exclude people from God's presence?

3. Beautiful Walls (vv. 18–21)

Twice in this small section of verses, John describes parts of the city both as being made of gold, and being clear as glass. As there is no such thing as transparent gold, we must assume John is using figurative language to try to describe just how amazing and wonderful this sight is. Here again, the number twelve is prominent, although John does not explicitly say what the number is to represent this time.

John describes the city's walls and gates, naming the beautiful precious stones that adorn them. The specific stones John names adorning the city's walls are meant to remind his audience of the twelve stones on the high priest's breastplate (Exodus 28:17–20). They are presented in a different order, and some names have changed, but the colors of the stones are consistent.

What is the purpose of sections of Scripture like this if they are figurative and not literal descriptions of heaven?

Search the Scriptures

1. How is John shown to be carried away to his vision of the New Jerusalem (Revelation 21:10)?

2. What is the significance of the tribes of Israel and of the apostles to the New Jerusalem?

Discuss the Meaning

It is easy to get lost in the details of this passage, and to wonder to what extent the prophecy will be fulfilled literally or figuratively. It is important to remember, though, that the point and goal of all Scripture is to reveal God to His people. What does this passage teach us about God? What kind of Person is He to make a city like this?

Liberating Lesson

Many of us seek to provide a good life for our families and loved ones. During times of economic and political uncertainty, that goal can seem far out of reach. We must understand that prosperity and peace are not the same thing. True stability and peace are found by relying on

God for guidance. The Word of God is a solid foundation that will allow us to find peace and build a good life both now and for eternity.

Application for Activation

The heavenly city had twelve gates that were always open. This image serves as a reminder of God's desire for everyone to come into His presence and have a relationship with Him. As we strive to build our lives on a solid foundation, let us not forget to reach out to someone else and let him or her know that God is welcoming them to also come into His presence with open arms.

Follow the Spirit

What God wants me to do:

_____

_____

_____

_____

_____

_____

Remember Your Thoughts

Special insights I have learned:

_____

_____

_____

_____

_____

More Light on the Text

Revelation 21:9–21

9 And there came unto me one of the seven angels which had the seven vials full of the seven last plagues, and talked with me, saying, Come hither, I will shew thee the bride, the Lamb's wife.

Here John is approached by one of the seven angels who had the seven vials full of the seven last plagues. We are first introduced to these angels when one of the four beasts in heaven gave them the seven golden vials full of the seven last plagues, which are also called the wrath of God (Revelation 15:1). A vial is a bowl; this term is translated from the Greek word *phiale* (fee-**AL**-ay).

After those plagues, John told us of the fall of Babylon the great (Revelation 17–18), the triumph of the heavenly army led by Christ (Revelation 19), the binding, incarceration, and final judgment of Satan (Revelation 20) and then the passing away (the transformation) of the first heaven and earth, which were replaced by a new heaven and earth (Revelation 21:1). After this renewal, John beholds the Holy City, the New Jerusalem (v. 2).

The angel who approaches John now is possibly the same angel who showed John the great harlot (Revelation 17:1). Commentators contrast the two sights: the great harlot sat on many waters—an indication of adultery or affections for many—while the holy city sat in one place, was able to be measured, and had undivided affection for her bridegroom. John saw the holy city in its entire splendor and likened it to a bride adorned for her husband (see v. 2). The angel came to John and bade him to follow so he could get a closer look.

In this verse, the angel invites John to come, proposing to show him the bride, the Lamb's wife. The Greek word *numphe* (noom-**FAY**) is translated "bride." It means a betrothed or newly married young woman. It signifies the close relationship between Christ and the church, also called the Lamb's wife. But as we shall find in the next verse, the name "bride" also refers to the holy Jerusalem, the City of God. Marriage imagery is used in the Old Testament to show a similar relationship between God and Israel; the word "bride" is one of the most important words used to refer to the Church. It normally signifies the relationship between Christ and the Church; here, however, we will see that "bride" is the Holy City of the New Jerusalem.

10 And he carried me away in the spirit to a great and high mountain, and shewed me that great city, the holy Jerusalem, descending out of heaven from God,

In the spirit, John had been taken to the wilderness to see the great harlot (see Revelation 17:3), but now he is taken to "a great and high mountain" to have an unobstructed view of the great city, namely the holy Jerusalem, descending out of heaven from God. This is similar to how Ezekiel is brought up to a "very high mountain" (Ezekiel 40:2) in his vision of a restored Jerusalem and Temple.

Both the body of believers and the city are referred to as the bride, the Lamb's wife. The fact is, in a sense, they are significantly alike. The holy Jerusalem is a city out of heaven; it is not heaven, but it possesses the features of heaven. It is the dwelling place of the resurrected bodies of the church (the redeemed bride), God, and Christ (Revelation 21:3; 22:3). The church is a holy nation (1 Peter 2:9); a human prefiguration of the heavenly Jerusalem, and the church makes up the City of God here on Earth (Hebrews 12:22). Therefore, the prepared bride (the Holy City) is a structure laid out as a city to provide a permanent dwelling place for the redeemed bride (the church), another structure in the image of God. One is in the form of a city, while the other is in human form, and both bear the presence of God.

Jesus promised to prepare a place for His followers in His Father's house (John 14:2–3; cf. Hebrews 11:10, 16). This city is undoubtedly the promised prepared place for the redeemed bride. Our bodies are our temporary habitations for our spirits and souls. The apostle Paul calls them "earthen vessels" (2 Corinthians 4:7). Our earthly homes are also temporary, but we have a final dwelling place. This is the Holy City, a wonderful place Jesus has prepared for us in heaven.

11 Having the glory of God: and her light was like unto a stone most precious, even like a jasper stone, clear as crystal;

Firstly, John's attention was drawn to the light of the city, whereby there was no darkness. The city housed the glory of God so much so that its illumination was like a most precious stone. In an attempt to put the preciousness into words, he writes that it is like a jasper stone. This is likely meant in terms of cost or rarity rather than color. Jasper stones come in many colors—red, yellow, and brown—but the author noted that the city's brightness was crystal clear.

12 And had a wall great and high, and had twelve gates, and at the gates twelve angels, and names written thereon, which are the names of the twelve tribes of the children of Israel: 13 On the east three gates; on the north three gates; on the south three gates; and on the west three gates.

Next to its brightness, John is struck by the details of the city's walls. He notes its height and thickness, and the security provided thereby. He counts and makes note of the number of gates, each guarded by an angel, and that each gate is inscribed with the names of the 12 tribes. The gates' angel guardians are reminiscent of the cherubim set to guard the way into the Garden of Eden (Genesis 3:24). There they guarded Adam and Eve from the Tree of Life, and here likewise, we will see the Tree of Life is also inside the city (Revelation 22:2, 14). One commentator surmised that the same arrangement used in the wilderness might have been used in the great city (Numbers 2). However, with the similarities between the prophet's mountaintop location, the enumeration of gates, walls, and their remarkable materials, it is more likely that John is calling on imagery from Ezekiel's vision of the restored city, which also had 12 gates named for the 12 tribes. Ezekiel even records which tribes' gates are on which wall of the city (Ezekiel 48:30–34).

The number 12 can signify human government; it is a perfect number, symbolizing God's power and authority. The number 12 is found 187 times in the Bible. The most prominent use is for the 12 tribes of Israel. Many other references to the number 12 are meant to directly or indirectly connect to the tribes, including the 12 apostles (Matthew 10:1), 12 memorial stones (Exodus 28:21), and 12 unleavened loaves in the Tabernacle (Leviticus 24:5–6).

14 And the wall of the city had twelve foundations, and in them the names of the twelve apostles of the Lamb.

The word "apostles" in this verse derives from the Greek word *apostolos* (ah-**POH**-stow-loce), which means "sent forth," referring to one who is sent forth with a message. An apostle can be specifically defined as one who: (1) has had an encounter with the resurrected Christ, (2) plants churches, and (3) and operates in the ministry with signs, wonders, and miracles. These twelve apostles are the twelve disciples (replacing Judas with either Matthias or Paul). Paul himself uses the image of an apostle as the foundation of the church in his letter to the Corinthians (1 Corinthians 3:10). There, however, Paul also asserts that Jesus Christ is the true foundation of the righteous (v. 11).

Paul explains that while the infrastructure and discipleship of New Covenant believers was built up by the apostles, the one true Rock is Christ. John is describing a vision of the Church itself rather than of Christian doctrine as a whole. Therefore, it is appropriate to say the Church's foundation was laid by the apostles. Since we speak of a building having a single foundation, it can be odd to hear of a place with 12 foundations. In ancient times, a foundation might be built up to the appropriate, level height by using several layers of carved stone. Each layer within the overall foundation could also be called a foundation.

15 And he that talked with me had a golden reed to measure the city, and the gates thereof, and the wall thereof. 16 And the city lieth foursquare, and the length is as large as the breadth: and he measured the city with the reed, twelve thousand furlongs. The length and the breadth and the height of it are equal. 17 And he measured the wall thereof, an hundred and forty and four cubits, according to the measure of a man, that is, of the angel.

Thirdly, John's attention was captured by the actions of the angel. The angel wasn't just taking John on a tour, but was measuring the city as they walked about it. Some commentators believe that the angel measured territory to ensure against enemy encroachment. Others believe that the angel measured the city simply as an exhibition of its beauty and proportion. The latter being supported by John's note of its largeness and perfect equal-ness. This measuring reed also recalls Ezekiel's Temple vision (Ezekiel 40:3). There, however, it was a simple normal measuring rod; here even such a common tool is made of gold.

The number 12 is again prominent: the city is a cube measuring 12,000 furlongs on each side, with walls that are 144 (which is 12 squared) cubits. A furlong (660 feet) is used to translate the Greek word *stadion* (607 feet), so this measurement for the city would total over 7 million feet or 1,380 miles. While the holy city in Ezekiel's Temple vision was roughly 12 furlongs to a side, this heavenly city is 1,000 times that size!

The cubic dimensions of the city are reminiscent of a key part of previous Temple architecture: the Holy of Holies. The Tabernacle's Holy of Holies was 10 cubits long, wide, and high. Solomon's Temple and Herod's Temple both enlarged this measurement to 20 cubits. This is also its size in Ezekiel's vision. Not only is this city larger by far, the note that all three of its dimensions are equal means this entire city is the Holy of Holies. Traditionally, only the high priest was allowed into this innermost sanctum of the Temple, and that only on one day of the year, the Day of Atonement. This spot was so holy because it was where heaven met earth. God declares it to be "the place of my throne and the place for the soles of my feet" (Ezekiel 43:7; cf. Revelation 22:3), the place where His presence is especially revealed to His righteous followers. As we can see from the Tabernacle's and the Temple's measurements, God has been expanding His presence among humanity since the beginning. Now on the Church Age, we are truly made one with Christ. The entire city, which is the Church, experiences the presence of God. None of the faithful are excluded from this most holy place. None have to travel to a specific spot to know Him. The entire city is filled with God's presence (cf. Revelation 21:3, 22).

18 And the building of the wall of it was of jasper: and the city was pure gold, like unto clear glass. 19 And the foundations of the wall of the city were garnished with all manner of precious stones. The first foundation was jasper; the second, sapphire; the third, a chalcedony; the fourth, an emerald; 20

The fifth, sardonyx; the sixth, sardius; the seventh, chrysolyte; the eighth, beryl; the ninth, a topaz; the tenth, a chrysoprasus; the eleventh, a jacinth; the twelfth, an amethyst.

Not only is John taken away by the splendor of the city wall's height and depth but he was struck by its décor. Previously, he wrote that light coming from the city was like jasper and then he noted that the wall was made of jasper, and the city was pure gold. The juxtaposition of the images of pure gold and clear glass show how overwhelming John's vision is. There are not words to adequately describe the glory of this heavenly city.

John takes the time to precisely name the stones of each foundational layer. The colors of each stone—reds, yellows, greens, and blues—are all arranged to mimic a rainbow. These specific stones are also reminiscent of the high priest's breastplate (Exodus 28:17–20). All the stones listed in the Septuagint translation of Exodus are listed here, though in a different order, except for three. John's list in Revelation lists those three as chalcedony (which is commonly red), chrysoprasus (which at the time referred to a yellowish-green gem), and jacinth (which at the time referred to a blueish stone). These still match up in color with Exodus' listings of carbuncle (red), ligure (yellowish-green), and agate (blue).

21 And the twelve gates were twelve pearls: every several gate was of one pearl: and the street of the city was pure gold, as it were transparent glass.

The city's wall and foundations were made from precious stones, and its streets are of pure gold—materials that could be hewn and fashioned as one saw fit. The city gates, however, are made of pearl, an item that does not need to be polished or cut. Even though pearls we know on earth are small—the largest one recorded is only two feet long and one foot wide—these pearls are big enough to carve out an entire city gate. This is where the image of heaven's "pearly gates" comes from. It is all one piece, complete, symbolizing the Church's purity.

Lastly, John remarks on the city's streets, which are "pure gold." The gold reminds us of how rich and extravagant all of heaven is. The purity, like the wholeness of the gates of pearl, reminds us of how Christ's Bride, the Church, the Holy City has been cleaned of all fault and blemish by the grace of God. This pure gold, however, is also transparent like glass, reminding John's audience of the brightness of God. Nothing in the Holy City will obscure God's brilliant glory.

Sources:

Cheyne, Thomas Kelly and J. Sutherland Black. *Encyclopaedia Biblica*. 1899.

Elliott, C. J. *Elliott's Commentary for English Readers*. https://biblehub.com/commentaries/revelation/21-12.htm (accessed September 17, 2020).

Jamieson, R., Fausset, A. R., & Brown, D. *Jamieson, Fausset & Brown's Commentary on the Whole Bible*. https://biblehub.com/commentaries/revelation/21-9.htm (accessed September 17, 2020).

McDonald, H.D. "Lamb of God." In *Evangelical Dictionary of Theology*, edited by Walter A. Elwell, 618–619. Grand Rapids, Mich.: Baker Book House, 1984.

Nelson, Thomas. *New Spirit Filled Life Bible*. Nashville, TN: Thomas Nelson Publishers. 2002. 1598.

Poole, M. Matthew. *Poole's Commentary on the Holy Bible*. https://biblehub.com/commentaries/revelation/21-18.htm. (accessed September 17, 2020).

Smith. C. *Sermon Notes for Revelation 21:9-27*. https://www.blueletterbible.org/Comm/smith_chuck/SermonNotes_Rev/Rev_57.cfm (accessed September 17, 2020).

Westcott, Ben. "Is this the world's largest pearl? It's been under a bed for 10 years." CNN. https://www.cnn.com/style/article/largest-pearl-philippines-amurao/index.html. Accessed November 27, 2020.

Say It Correctly

Chalcedony. kal-SHE-duh-nee.
Sardonyx. sar-DAW-nix
Sardius. SAR-dee-us.
Chrysolyte. KRIS-uh-lite.
Beryl. BER-el.
Chrysoprasus. KRIS-oh-pra-sus.
Jacinth. JAY-sinth.
Amethyst. AH-muh-thist.

Daily Bible Readings

MONDAY
You Shall Be Comforted in Jerusalem
(Isaiah 66:6–14)

TUESDAY
God's Glory Revealed in Jerusalem
(Isaiah 66:18–22)

WEDNESDAY
City of the Living God
(Hebrews 12:18–29)

THURSDAY
Jerusalem, Joy of All the Earth
(Psalm 48)

FRIDAY
The Faithful City, the Holy Mountain
(Zechariah 8:1–8)

SATURDAY
God, Who Dwells
in Unapproachable Light
(1 Timothy 6:11–16)

SUNDAY
The Holy City
(Revelation 21:9–21)

Teaching Tips

Words You Should Know

A. Fruit (Revelation 22:2) *karpos* (Gk.)—A product of plants or trees; figuratively, a product of work or effort, such as offspring, wages or moral attributes

B. Quickly (v. 7) *tachu* (Gk.)—Imminence ("soon") or suddenness ("quickly")

Teacher Preparation

Unifying Principle—No Better Refreshment. Rivers give life and nourishment to the things that exist around them. How do rivers nourish our lives? In God's new creation, God's power will be in the river, nourishing and healing people and nations in the New Jerusalem.

A. Read the Bible Background and Devotional Reading.

B. Pray for your students and lesson clarity.

C. Read the lesson Scripture in multiple translations.

O—Open the Lesson

A. Begin the class with prayer.

B. Before class, gather pictures or create a slideshow featuring beautiful landscapes with water and trees. Display the pictures or play the slideshow as class members arrive. Begin class by pointing out that one image of paradise is a lush garden scene.

C. Have the students read the Aim for Change and the In Focus story.

D. Ask students how events like those in the story weigh on their hearts and how they can view these events from a faith perspective.

P—Present the Scriptures

A. Read the Focal Verses and discuss the Background and The People, Places, and Times sections.

B. Have the class share what Scriptures stand out for them and why, with particular emphasis on today's themes.

E—Explore the Meaning

A. Use In Depth or More Light on the Text to facilitate a deeper discussion of the lesson text.

B. Pose the questions in Search the Scriptures and Discuss the Meaning.

C. Discuss the Liberating Lesson and Application for Activation sections.

N—Next Steps for Application

A. Summarize the value of responding to God's invitation to enter the fullness of God's kingdom.

B. End class with a commitment to pray for perfect peace that can only be achieved when God rules supreme.

Worship Guide

For the Superintendent or Teacher
Theme: The River of Life
Song: "Shall We Gather at the River"

The River of Life

Bible Background • REVELATION 22:1–7
Printed Text • REVELATION 22:1–7 | Devotional Reading • GENESIS 1:1–13

———————— **Aim for Change** ————————

By the end of this lesson, we will RESEARCH the biblical references to the "river of life" to learn its spiritual, symbolic, and material effect on creation, IMAGINE God's provisions to be found in the river of life, which will nourish and heal people and nations in the New Jerusalem, and RESPOND to the river of life through acceptance, faith, and entrance into the fullness of God's kingdom.

———————— **In Focus** ————————

Ms. Cattie knew growing old was a blessing. She had accumulated plenty of wisdom and experience throughout the years. However, growing old had its share of challenges too. Joints began to ache. Strength and speed diminished. Wrinkles and gray hair became her prominent features. One of the main problems with growing old, Ms. Cattie thought, was suffering a lot of loss. At 95 years old, Ms. Cattie had seen her share. She had buried both of her parents and two of her four children. Most of her closest friends had passed, and those who remained struggled to remember the great times they had together.

Most recently, she had lost her husband of 70 years. However, as God would allow it, she was eagerly preparing to celebrate the arrival of her first two great-great-grandsons. Twins! It was a tangible reminder that one day God would wipe away all tears and ease sorrows, replacing them both with all things new. These days, Ms. Cattie thought a lot about heaven. As grateful as she was for the life she lived, the experiences she had, and the family she had raised, she yearned for the day when all of the pain and heartache of this life would be left behind. She knew it was coming sooner rather than later. And she was ready. One day all things would become new.

In this lesson, we will learn about God's redemptive plan for heaven and earth. What is the thing you most look forward to in God's new heaven and new earth?

———————— **Keep in Mind** ————————

"And he shewed me a pure river of water of life, clear as crystal, proceeding out of the throne of God and of the Lamb." (Revelation 22:1, KJV)

"Then the angel showed me a river with the water of life, clear as crystal, flowing from the throne of God and of the Lamb." (Revelation 22:1, NLT)

Focal Verses

Background Andrea

KJV **Revelation 22:1** And he shewed me a pure river of water of life, clear as crystal, proceeding out of the throne of God and of the Lamb.

2 In the midst of the street of it, and on either side of the river, was there the tree of life, which bare twelve manner of fruits, and yielded her fruit every month: and the leaves of the tree were for the healing of the nations.

3 And there shall be no more curse: but the throne of God and of the Lamb shall be in it; and his servants shall serve him:

4 And they shall see his face; and his name shall be in their foreheads.

5 And there shall be no night there; and they need no candle, neither light of the sun; for the Lord God giveth them light: and they shall reign for ever and ever.

6 And he said unto me, These sayings are faithful and true: and the Lord God of the holy prophets sent his angel to shew unto his servants the things which must shortly be done.

7 Behold, I come quickly: blessed is he that keepeth the sayings of the prophecy of this book.

NLT **Revelation 22:1** Then the angel showed me a river with the water of life, clear as crystal, flowing from the throne of God and of the Lamb.

2 It flowed down the center of the main street. On each side of the river grew a tree of life, bearing twelve crops of fruit, with a fresh crop each month. The leaves were used for medicine to heal the nations.

3 No longer will there be a curse upon anything. For the throne of God and of the Lamb will be there, and his servants will worship him.

4 And they will see his face, and his name will be written on their foreheads.

5 And there will be no night there—no need for lamps or sun—for the Lord God will shine on them. And they will reign forever and ever.

6 Then the angel said to me, "Everything you have heard and seen is trustworthy and true. The Lord God, who inspires his prophets, has sent his angel to tell his servants what will happen soon."

7 "Look, I am coming soon! Blessed are those who obey the words of prophecy written in this book."

The People, Places, and Times

Lamb. In the book of Revelation, the designation "Lamb" occurs many times in symbolic reference to Christ and unites the two ideas of redemption and kingship. On one side are statements referring to a Lamb that has been slain (5:6, 12); those who "have washed their robes, and made them white in the blood of the Lamb" (7:14); and "they overcame him by the blood of the Lamb, and by the word of their testimony" (12:11). The stress here falls upon the redeeming work of Christ as the Lamb of God. On the other side, also connected with the title is the idea of sovereignty. It is the Lamb that

was slain that has power to take the book and loose its seals (5:6–7); there is reference to the wrath of the Lamb (6:16); and the Lamb is seen in the midst of the throne (7:17). In the general term, "Lamb," two ideas unite: victorious power and vicarious suffering. At the heart of God's sovereignty, there is sacrificial love.

Background

The first part of Revelation 22 portrays, in visions and images, the wonderful future awaiting God's people in the new heaven and the new earth. Drawing heavily on the book of Isaiah, John's vision concludes by showing the certainty of the promise. Just as the prophecies of the Old Testament have been fulfilled in Christ's first coming, so the prophecy of Revelation will be ultimately fulfilled through Christ's Second Coming. And just as Christ's first coming was great news for some (the poor in spirit who believed in Him) and bad news for others (the proud of heart who rejected Him), so also His unstoppable Second Coming will be wonderful news for those who belong to Christ, and woeful news for those who spurn the message of His Gospel. Revelation, like the Bible as a whole, is a book of both promise and warning. John's remarkable vision calls the Church to take comfort in the incomparable power and mercy of Christ, who comes for the redemption of His own.

At-A-Glance

1. God's Glorious People
(Revelation 22:1–2)
2. God's Glorious Presence (vv. 3–5)
3. God's Glorious Promise (vv. 6–7)

In Depth

1. God's Glorious People (Revelation 22:1–2)

The new heavens and new earth are a place of perfect abundance, a world fit for God and His people to reign. This is true, redeemed urban living! To paint a picture of the greatest possible abundance and blessing, John's vision returns to the place of God's original purpose: the Garden of Eden. Just as in Eden (Genesis 2:10), a life-giving river flows in the New Jerusalem. This "water of life" symbolizes the everlasting life given by Jesus through the Spirit (see John 7:37–39) and the "abundant life" He promised (John 10:10).

Just as the tree of life stood in Eden (Genesis 2:9), it will also stand in the New Jerusalem

amidst the river, represented by 12 trees (a number symbolizing divine government and completeness). Here, God will provide to heal and bind up all wounds—especially sin and spiritual brokenness (21:3–4), washed away as the nations partake of the water and the tree of life (22:2).

Humanity was not commanded to leave the earth as an untilled garden, but to work the ground and produce good things, thereby mirroring the creativity and benevolent reign of God over His creation. God brings about this purpose, redeeming not only His chosen remnant, but also the earth itself!

In what ways might the tree of life be used "for healing of the nations"?

2. God's Glorious Presence (vv. 3-5)

All this Edenic abundance is possible, because, like Eden, the New Jerusalem does not suffer from the curse anymore! The curse has been canceled out by the very presence of God. In the new city, God now dwells in perfect purity with a pure people.

Even as God exists in loving fellowship with Himself in three persons, so now all His people will be enfolded in that perfect triune love and communion. He claims us as His own with His name on our foreheads. Even though throughout the Scriptures, seeing the face of God had been a frightful thing, now we are pure enough to meet His gaze, which illuminates heaven.

Jesus is the light of the world, and of heaven. How have you seen His light in your life?

3. God's Glorious Promise (vv. 6-7)

God in His mercy frequently gives added testimony to the certainty of what He reveals. To call the Lord the "God of the holy prophets" (v. 6) is to show that these words, just like the prophets' words, are breathed out by God and cannot be false. Just as the prophets were able to say, "Thus says the LORD," so also the angel,

587

with the same authority, promises that these words are "faithful and true," and that these things "must shortly be done" (v. 6). Likewise, when John is commanded not to seal up the prophecy, but write it down, God shows us that the vision is true. The record of that vision is also inspired by Him, and utterly reliable.

The promise is also given a specific urgency. Christ promises to come quickly, signaling to the believer that the words of the book should be not only read but immediately obeyed. This admonishes all believers to expect Christ's return and the glorious fulfillment of God's promises.

How do we know that God's words are trustworthy and true?

Search the Scriptures

1. How will we benefit from the curse being removed from everything (Revelation 22:3)?

2. How would you evaluate your awareness and expectancy that Jesus is coming soon (v. 7)?

Discuss the Meaning

1. What did God mean by saying these things "must shortly be done" (v. 6), when this was recorded so long ago?

2. Why is it often hard to have a true longing for heaven?

Liberating Lesson

The human race continues to encounter injustice, oppression, and misery. In particular, the African American community possesses a history of oppression—one that continues today through racism and economic injustice. God provides opportunity to redress wrong and injustice through political or social means. Although we should act and live as God's agents for present change, social justice can become an idol; bitterness may ensue when cruelty and oppression continue. This passage reminds us that hope for a paradise on this earth is a misguided hope.

We will face setbacks and difficulties in trying to perfect systems run by flawed humans. We must not lose heart, though. We do what we can now, and trust that in the end, God will fix everything better than we ever could manage ourselves. The Christian's hope is set immeasurably high. In the new heavens and new earth, God's bride, the Church, becomes as perfectly radiant as the New Jerusalem; there will true healing take place.

Application for Activation

Think about circumstances or relationships in your life that leave you feeling bitter or resentful because of the way you've been treated. How do you respond when you feel slighted? Does a focus on making things right in this world keep you from longing for the next? Take this opportunity to repent of your misplaced hope and turn to Christ for forgiveness. In light of the incredible promises of God about your identity and your abundant inheritance, take time each day to intentionally rejoice and give thanks for the glory that awaits you in God's presence.

Follow the Spirit

What God wants me to do:

_____

_____

_____

Remember Your Thoughts

Special insights I have learned:

_____

_____

_____

More Light on the Text

Revelation 22:1-7

1 And he shewed me a pure river of water of life, clear as crystal, proceeding out of the throne of God and of the Lamb.

John's vision in the Spirit continues (cf. Revelation 21:10). He is given a panoramic view of the Holy City. He is shown a pure river containing the water of life. The Greek word translated "river" is *potamos* (poh-tah-MOCE), which means running water, like a stream, flood, or river. The Sons of Korah spoke prophetically of this river: "There is a river, the streams whereof shall make glad the city of God, the holy place of the tabernacles of the most High" (Psalm 46:4). It is the water of life that brings the life of God.

This river had been foreshadowed by the river in the Garden of Eden (Genesis 2:10), watering the plants and animals so they can flourish in the garden paradise. The river from the millennial Temple (Ezekiel 47:1–12) also foreshadows this river. Ezekiel's river grew ever deeper as it flowed from the Temple and brought life to all creatures wherever it flowed, even as it filled and purified the Dead Sea. Zechariah also prophesied the issuing out of "living waters" from Jerusalem (Zechariah 14:8). A figurative reference to this river that Jesus makes describes one of the greatest spiritual realities of the Christian faith: the outpouring, deposit, and flow of the Holy Spirit in the life of the believer (John 7:38–39). In each of these descriptions of the heavenly river, its source is the presence of God. God Himself is the life-giving stream, and Jesus is the "living water" with which it flows (John 4:7–15).

2 In the midst of the street of it, and on either side of the river, was there the tree of life, which bare twelve manner of fruits, and yielded her fruit every month: and the leaves of the tree were for the healing of the nations.

The Bible metaphorically calls four things the tree of life: wisdom (Proverbs 3:18), the fruit of righteousness (Proverbs 11:30), fulfilled desire (Proverbs 13:12), and a wholesome tongue (Proverbs 15:4). These things are all described as giving life to those who partake of them. The same can be said of this tree in Revelation, except that the life that this tree gives is eternal.

The New Jerusalem is prefigured by the Garden of Eden, the first place where humans lived in their innocence. Both have rivers, and Eden is the first place where the tree of life was mentioned. Everything in the Holy City is of the greatest proportion, being the most perfect reality compared to other references or similarities in the Bible, which are mere foreshadowings. For instance, the Bible talks about one tree of life in the middle of the Garden of Eden, but here numerous trees abound on both sides of the river.

The tree of life conferred immortality on anyone who ate its fruit, hence its name (Genesis 3:22). In Ezekiel's vision, he revealed that the fruit of the tree of life was meant for food and healing (Ezekiel 47:12). Here John tells us the same thing: The fruit and leaves are for the healing of the nations. This tree is said to bear 12 kinds of fruit every month. As a tree of life, it bears fruit to confer immortality on its eater and maintain life in the Holy City. The monthly harvest of fruit from the tree of life and the availability of its leaves to heal the nations (see Revelation 21:24, 26) indicate that the blessings of the New Jerusalem have neither chronological nor geographical limitations. God's people do not have to wait for a specific harvest season, but can enjoy a bountiful crop at any time of year. The leaves are available not just to those who happen to live near the Temple, but to all the nations.

3 And there shall be no more curse: but the throne of God and the Lamb shall be in it:

and his servants shall serve him: 4 And they shall see his face; and his name shall be in their foreheads.

The worst thing a person can say to someone else is a curse. The Greek word translated "curse" here is *katanathema* (kah-tah-**NAH**-theh-mah), meaning a wish that evil may befall a person. Curses served as protective and punitive measures against violating the terms of a treaty; they were intended to doom a person to calamity or destruction. Linguistically there is no indication as to which curse is no longer at play. However, the statement about the absence of a curse or accursed thing immediately follows mention of the tree of life. Since Adam and Eve were barred from the tree of life (Genesis 3:22–24) immediately after curses were pronounced for consumption of the fruit of the tree of the knowledge of good and evil, the audience is primed to think of the first and greatest curse on humanity. The Curse in the Garden of Eden was a divine judgment against humankind's disobedience. But in the Holy City, even that Curse has no place. The occupants of this city are not objects of divine wrath and punishment, so no disaster can come upon them. They are the redeemed who have qualified as occupants of the New Jerusalem by their faith in Christ and have distinguished themselves with lives above sin, curse, and calamity. The New Jerusalem will offer ultimate bliss to the believer, the greatest rewards and privileges that are not available in our present world. The throne of God and Christ will be there, bringing the habitation, presence, and direct government of God to the redeemed.

John notes that the throne is shared by both God and the Lamb. Here again is an element of Johannine theology that permeates his Gospel, his epistles, and his apocalypse: Jesus is God. The Son and the Father are one and the same. Revelation shows many scenes of worshipers around the throne of God. Once the Lamb is introduced in the visions, however, praise is always given to both the one on the throne and to the Lamb. With this in mind, John is also told twice in his visions to worship only God, and not the angel who is showing these things to him. With the repeated instruction only to worship God and the repeated worship of the Lamb, one can only conclude that Jesus, the Lamb who was slain, is God.

Most blessedly of all, the divine prohibition will end God's order that forbids humanity from seeing His face will no longer exist. This Old Testament order, communicated by God to Moses, stated: "Thou canst not see my face: for there shall no man see me, and live" (from Exodus 33:20). Over the ages, the physical sight of God had been denied to humans, because the consequence was death. But in the New Jerusalem, there will be a new order: God's servants will serve Him, and they will see His face and behold Him physically. This is because those who live in the Holy City will be completely transformed to be like God (1 John 3:2). They will be absent of sin, and their bodies will be changed (1 Corinthians 15:51–53).

His name will be on their foreheads as a seal of allegiance. When 144,000 of the tribes of Israel are sealed (Revelation 7), God's mark is placed on their foreheads. These people are then protected from the judgment of the fifth trumpet, which is a swarm of locusts from the abyss under a king named Apollyon (9:1–11). God's mark on His elects' foreheads is in contrast to the marks the Beast forces people to take either in their hands or their foreheads (13:16). Those who avoid taking the Beast's mark are those who reign with Jesus during the millennial reign (20:4).

Two seals on the forehead are significant in this context from the Old Testament as well. First, the high priest wore a medallion across his forehead sealing him as "HOLINESS TO THE LORD" (Exodus 28:36). This mark let the priest take Israel's sin on himself and absolve them before God, so that the people could commune with the Lord (v. 38). Second, John perhaps has another vision of Ezekiel's in mind (Ezekiel 9). In this one, God is angered by the idolatry being practiced in Israel and even in the Temple itself. He sends one servant throughout Jerusalem to mark the foreheads of those who have not partaken of the rampant idolatry. That faithful remnant is spared as six other divine servants follow after the first servant and slaughter all whom he does not mark, that is, all the idolaters. This vision's resonances with the Passover cannot be missed. God's mark on one's forehead labels you as His own faithful servant and protects you from His judgment.

5 And there shall be no night there; and they need no candle, neither light of the sun; for the Lord God giveth them light: and they shall reign forever and ever.

Both water and sunlight are necessary for the growth of trees and other forms of plant life. John has already noted the water source in heaven, and now he tells about the light source. In the beginning, God created light. On day four, the sun and moon were specifically given their functions to bring about day and night (Genesis 1:14). Here the passage says there shall be no night. Figuratively, the night stands for various periods and conditions in human life: a time of ignorance and helplessness (Micah 3:6), the depraved condition of humankind (1 Thessalonians 5:5–7), and also a time of inactivity or death (John 9:4). In the Holy City, there will be no ignorance, the depraved conditions of humankind will not exist, and death will be no more. Here we see the fulfillment of Christ's teaching that He is the Light of the world (John 8:12).

6 And he said unto me, These sayings are faithful and true: and the Lord God of the holy prophets sent his angel to shew unto his servants the things which must shortly be done.

This is the second time the angel used the words "faithful" and "true" (21:5; 22:6), which also are applied directly to Christ (Revelation 3:14; 19:11) As Christ is faithful and true, so are His words sent via prophets or angels also faithful and true. The apparent redundancy here must indicate the special importance to the church of these particular words—even while underscoring that God always has, in the same trustworthy manner, revealed the future through His prophets. The phrase translated as "the Lord God, who inspires his prophets" in the NLT literally means that the prophets' very breath and spirit (Gk. *pneuma*, puh-NEW-mah; breath, spirit) comes from God. (KJV's reading of "holy prophets" is based on a different set of manuscripts that exchange *pneuma* with *hagion*, **HAH**-gee-on, holy. Those that read *pneuma* are older and more reliable.) This points to the authority of John's vision, connecting John's prophecy to the prophets of the past as originating from God

The hinge phrase "must shortly be done" (v. 6) has been translated many ways, yet all clearly concur that the Greek word *tachos* (**TAH**-khos) means quickness or speed. The original Greek did not intend "quickly" as commonly understood. Few would say 2,000 years is "quickly," but "suddenly" could happen at any time, even the distant future. This rendering also agrees with other verses that describe His coming as a thief in the night, taking a self-indulgent, self-absorbed world by surprise (Matthew 24:38–41; 1 Thessalonians 5:4).

Ever since John penned his vision, these words of imminent hope have been available for all to see and react to as they choose When Christ finally does return, no one will be able to claim total surprise, and they also will have no one to blame if His coming isn't welcome.

7 Behold, I come quickly: blessed is he that keepeth the sayings of the prophecy of this book.

After reinforcing this element of surprise, the angel encourages believers, but subtly implies that those who do not "keep the sayings of the prophecy in this book" will not be "blessed" at Jesus' sudden appearance In this Revelation beatitude, believers will be blessed, more likely ecstatic, as our time of vindication and the completion of our redemption will have come at long last. In stark contrast, the unbelieving world will be judged and condemned. Here translated "sayings" but generally translated "words," John uses the Greek word *logos* (**LOW**-goce), a word he used multiple times in 36 verses of his Gospel, to refer to the entire Word of God (see especially John 1).

Each succeeding generation must anticipate, prepare, watch, and be ready for Jesus' return. Nothing in our present world can give us enduring comfort and eternal joy; we must place all our hopes on Jesus Christ, serving Him wholeheartedly. He has prepared a wonderful and glorious future for those who put their trust in Him.

Sources: Henry, Matthew. *Matthew Henry's Commentary on the Whole Bible: New Modern Edition*. Vols. 1-6. Peabody, MA: Hendrickson Publishers, Inc., 2009.

Strong, James. *The New Strong's Exhaustive Concordance of the Bible*. Nashville, TN: Thomas Nelson, 2003.

Thayer, Joseph Henry. *A Greek-English Lexicon of the New Testament*. New York: American Book Company, 1889.

Say It Correctly

Johannine. joe-HAH-nine.
Apollyon. ah-PAH-lee-on.

Daily Bible Readings

MONDAY
My Soul Thirsts for You
(Psalm 63)

TUESDAY
Living Waters Shall Flow
from Jerusalem
(Zechariah 14:6–11)

WEDNESDAY
Jesus Promises Living Water
(John 4:4–14)

THURSDAY
Worship God in Spirit and Truth
(John 4:15–26)

FRIDAY
Rivers of Living Water
(John 7:37–40)

SATURDAY
Water on the Thirsty Land
(Isaiah 44:1–8)

SUNDAY
For the Healing of the Nations
(Revelation 22:1–7)

Teaching Tips

Words You Should Know

A. Prophecy (Revelation 22:10) *propheteia* (Gk.)—A revelation from God given through the mouth of a prophet; may or may not deal with the future directly

B. Rewards (v. 12) *misthos* (Gk.)—Wages or payment for services

P—Present the Scriptures

A. Read the Focal Verses and discuss the Background and The People, Places, and Times sections.

B. Have the class share what Scriptures stand out for them and why, with particular emphasis on today's themes.

Tea...

Ev...
the...
Re...
and...

Rea...

...
tran...

O—
A
B
final
shar...
abou...
by as...
C.
Chan...
D.
story
view...

Keep in Mind

"For I testify unto every man that heareth the words of the prophecy of this book, If any man shall add unto these things, God shall add unto him the plagues that are written in this book: And if any man shall take away from the words of the book of this prophecy, God shall take away his part out of the book of life, and out of the holy city, and from the things which are written in this book" (Revelation 22:18–19, KJV)

594

"For I testify unto every man that heareth...

"Yea...
"That's...
"Now I go...
just finished the...

"You started with...
always read the endin...
of-the-world horrors, wh...
you do that?" Chris asked.

"Nobody told me where to s...
come out. You know, to see if the...

Chris tried to explain, "But Genes...
heard Jason howling in laughter.

"Don't worry, the ending told me what...
want to know more about how and why."

*In the book of Revelation, Christians are as...
triumphal procession with Christ! How does this joy...*

Come and Enjoy

Bible Background • REVELATION 22:8–21
Printed Text • REVELATION 22:10–21 | Devotional Reading • GENESIS 1:26–31

———————— **Aim for Change** ————————

By the end of this lesson, we will SURVEY the biblical references to the "second coming" in order to see the importance of this hoped-for reality, REJOICE that the invitation from Jesus to be a part of the new creation continues through the end of all things, and EMBRACE the call to become part of God's kingdom.

———————————— **In Focus** ————————————

Chris laughed along with the audience as he listened to his friend, Jason, a popular comedian, ...eliver his punch lines with ease. A phone call interrupted him in mid-laughter. It was Jason. "...re you watching the show I did last week?" Jason asked.

"...h, I told you I would. Pretty funny stuff. I can never figure out where you're headed." "...the secret of a good punch line." He chuckled.

"...a good one for you. I told you I would start reading the Bible; today I have ...last chapter," Jason said.

"...the last chapter?" Chris asked nervously. It wasn't that unusual. Jason ...g before considering any book. But Chris was thinking of the end-...ich might be too much for a new Christian. "Jason, why would

...tart, so I figured I'd find out how everything was going to ...nding was worth it," Jason replied.

...is and the walk of Christ." Before he could finish, he

...I needed to know. We win in the end! Now I

...*sured of the ultimate happy ending—a*
...*ful knowledge affect your life?*

...of this book, If any man shall ...ten in this book: And if any ...ll take away his part out ...ritten in this book."

"And I solemnly declare to everyone who hears the words of prophecy written in this book: If anyone adds anything to what is written here, God will add to that person the plagues described in this book. And if anyone removes any of the words from this book of prophecy, God will remove that person's share in the tree of life and in the holy city that are described in this book."
(Revelation 22:18–19, NLT)

Focal Verses

KJV **Revelation 22:10** And he saith unto me, Seal not the sayings of the prophecy of this book: for the time is at hand.

11 He that is unjust, let him be unjust still: and he which is filthy, let him be filthy still: and he that is righteous, let him be righteous still: and he that is holy, let him be holy still.

12 And, behold, I come quickly; and my reward is with me, to give every man according as his work shall be.

13 I am Alpha and Omega, the beginning and the end, the first and the last.

14 Blessed are they that do his commandments, that they may have right to the tree of life, and may enter in through the gates into the city.

15 For without are dogs, and sorcerers, and whoremongers, and murderers, and idolaters, and whosoever loveth and maketh a lie.

16 I Jesus have sent mine angel to testify unto you these things in the churches. I am the root and the offspring of David, and the bright and morning star.

17 And the Spirit and the bride say, Come. And let him that heareth say, Come. And let him that is athirst come. And whosoever will, let him take the water of life freely.

18 For I testify unto every man that heareth the words of the prophecy of this book, If any man shall add unto these things, God shall add unto him the plagues that are written in this book:

19 And if any man shall take away from the words of the book of this prophecy, God shall take away his part out of the book of life, and out of the holy city, and from the things which are written in this book.

20 He which testifieth these things saith, Surely I come quickly. Amen. Even so, come, Lord Jesus.

21 The grace of our Lord Jesus Christ be with you all. Amen.

NLT **Revelation 22:10** Then he instructed me, "Do not seal up the prophetic words in this book, for the time is near.

11 Let the one who is doing harm continue to do harm; let the one who is vile continue to be vile; let the one who is righteous continue to live righteously; let the one who is holy continue to be holy.

12 Look, I am coming soon, bringing my reward with me to repay all people according to their deeds.

13 I am the Alpha and the Omega, the First and the Last, the Beginning and the End."

14 Blessed are those who wash their robes. They will be permitted to enter through the gates of the city and eat the fruit from the tree of life.

15 Outside the city are the dogs—the sorcerers, the sexually immoral, the murderers, the idol worshipers, and all who love to live a lie.

16 "I, Jesus, have sent my angel to give you this message for the churches. I am both the source of David and the heir to his throne. I am the bright morning star."

17 The Spirit and the bride say, "Come." Let anyone who hears this say, "Come." Let anyone who is thirsty come. Let anyone who desires drink freely from the water of life.

18 And I solemnly declare to everyone who hears the words of prophecy written in this book: If anyone adds anything to what is written here, God will add to that person the plagues described in this book.

19 And if anyone removes any of the words from this book of prophecy, God will remove that person's share in the tree of life and in the holy city that are described in this book.

20 He who is the faithful witness to all these things says, "Yes, I am coming soon!" Amen! Come, Lord Jesus!

21 May the grace of the Lord Jesus be with God's holy people.

The People, Places, and Times

Alpha and Omega. Alpha and omega are, respectively, the first and last letters in the Greek alphabet. Jesus claims the title "Alpha and Omega" at the very beginning of the vision He reveals to John (Revelation 1:11), here at the revelation of the Church, and one last time near the very end of the vision (22:13). By referring to Himself as "Alpha and Omega," God is making it clear that He is the source of everything. He is the Beginning and the End; He is sovereign, reigning over every aspect of His creation.

Background

Revelation 21 and the first part of chapter 22 portray, in visions and images, the wonderful future awaiting God's people in the new heaven and the new earth. And just as Christ's first coming was great news for some (the poor in spirit, who believed in Him) and bad news for others (the proud of heart, who rejected Him), so also His unstoppable Second Coming will be wonderful news for those who belong to Christ, and woeful news for those who spurn the message of His Gospel. Revelation, like the Bible as a whole, is both a book of promise and a book of warning. John's remarkable vision calls the church to examine itself, to "give diligence to make [its] calling and election sure" (2 Peter 1:10), and to take comfort in the incomparable power and mercy of Christ, who comes for His own and for their redemption.

At-A-Glance

1. Christ Is Coming Certainly and
   Quickly (Revelation 22:10–11)
2. Christ Is Coming as King and Lord
   (vv. 12–16)
3. Christ Is Coming for the Faithful Who
   Belong to Him (vv. 17–21)

In Depth

1. Christ Is Coming Certainly and Quickly (Revelation 22:10–11)

An angel guiding John through his vision warns John not to close up the record of this revelation, because it will all soon take place. It is almost not worth a person changing their actions, because there is that little time to repent, so the angel encourages the unjust and the filthy to continue in their sinful ways. A significant amount of narrative space is taken up in Revelation by opening the seals of another book, so John leaving his own record open is significant. With it open, anyone is allowed to read it. Everyone may be encouraged to read it, to see the fate that awaits the faithful and the unfaithful, and mend their ways.

What may we imply about the character of God since He does not want people stopped from hearing this prophecy?

2. Christ Is Coming as King and Lord (22:12–16)

Hear the powerful, kingly language of Jesus as He promises His coming! Only a king would speak this way, promising a "reward" (v. 12) and daring to examine and understand the fullness of a person's deeds. In the language of Isaiah (Isaiah 44:6; 48:12), Christ's voice thunders in testimony to His preeminence. In the Old Testament, this kind of language beginning and ending, first and last (v. 13)—could apply to Yahweh alone. Can there be any doubt that Jesus is laying claim to the same divine status? He sends His angel to do His will (v. 16). He lays claim to David's lineage (v. 16) and the promises concerning the eternal King to come (Isaiah 11:1). This testimony matters greatly to the Christian not only that Christ might be rightly worshiped, but also that the believer may know the certainty of His coming! When Christ comes as King and Lord, He will "give every man according as his work shall be" (v. 12). Each person acts according to his true nature and the state of his heart toward Christ, and each person is judged by the fruit of that nature.

Why is it important that Jesus announces His identity in verses 13–16? How does His identity relate to the hope of the Christian?

3. Christ Is Coming for the Faithful Who Belong to Him (vv. 17–21)

The book of Revelation, with all its vivid imagery and difficult symbolism, is simply a letter. It begins like a letter, with a greeting and a blessing to the seven churches (Revelation 2–3); and it ends like a letter, with a benediction (22:21). Fittingly, this letter concludes with an invitation: in light of the sure coming of Christ as King and Lord, will you be found to belong to Him? Verse 17 reminds us of the full, free offer of Christ in the Gospel. The Holy Spirit extends the invitation to accept Christ as Lord, and even the bride, the true church, is pictured urging all to come unto Christ. Echoing Jesus' invitation during His ministry (John 7:37–39), John beseeches those in the seven churches and beyond to recognize and satisfy their thirst by receiving the water of eternal life in the Gospel.

This closing passage pictures a great law court with four faithful witnesses: the angel, John, the Holy Spirit, and finally Jesus Himself (v. 20). And where there is a law court, there is accountability and justice; all who hear are accountable to respond to the message! John demonstrates the beautiful, simple response of faith: "Amen. Even so, come, Lord Jesus."

Why do you think the gracious invitation of verse 17 and the stern warning of verses 18–19 are put next to each other?

Search the Scriptures

1. For what purpose does Jesus say He will return quickly (v. 12)?

2. To whom does Jesus give the message of Revelation (v. 16)?

Discuss the Meaning

1. How is this last part of Revelation a happy ending? What do you find surprising or unexpected about this ending?

2. How does this passage help you understand the book of Revelation as a whole?

Liberating Lesson

Throughout church history, countless individuals and communities have predicted with confidence the exact date on which Jesus will return. Without exception, they have been wrong. As a result, the whole idea of expecting a miraculous return of Christ has been largely discredited in the minds of many. The book of Revelation, when it focuses on the return of Christ, does not list a series of mysterious hints that the church is left to decode. Nor does it merely tell us what we want to hear, flattering us by sparing any sense of accountability and judgment at Christ's return. Before a world that mocks its expectation as "pie in the sky" and a church that often misunderstands its message as a riddle to solve, the book of Revelation focuses on the faithfulness and preeminence of Christ. Because Jesus is the first and the last, the King of kings, and the true descendant of David, the Christian can rest in His promises. Thanks be to God for His indescribable gift!

Application for Activation

If you could have written the last chapter of the Bible, how would you have written it? Often the Spirit uses the parts of the Bible we find most surprising to drive home the Word's significance. Read through these last few verses of Revelation and write down the parts you find unexpected. Think through what each surprising part means for the church and for you individually, and resolve to make that meaning part of your regular prayers and conversation with others in the church.

Follow the Spirit

What God wants me to do:

_____

_____

_____

_____

Remember Your Thoughts

Special insights I have learned:

_____

_____

_____

_____

More Light on the Text
Revelation 22:10–21

The context of the last chapter of the last book of Scripture brings human history to a close. Like ultimate bookends of man's inimitable story, our beginning and our end are contrasted and captured by authors Moses and John. In Genesis, the serpent tempts the first Adam, he falls, and Paradise is lost. In Revelation, the serpent is destroyed, the second Adam is victorious, and Paradise is restored. The significant elements of the garden Paradise were two people, the tree of life, and a river that watered the garden (Genesis 2:9–10). In the New Jerusalem the fountain of life flows from the throne of God (Revelation 22:1–2; 4:6), and lining both sides of the river are many trees of life (22:14) that are not only freely accessible, but ever fruitful for the enjoyment and healing of many nations (Psalm 46:4). In Eden, one tree was forbidden; in Paradise, nothing is forbidden.

This succinct picture of our final Paradise supersedes the original, in particular, because of the absence of temptation, death, and evil.

10 And he saith unto me, Seal not the sayings of the prophecy of this book: for the time is at hand. 11 He that is unjust, let him be unjust still: and he which is filthy, let him be filthy still: and he that is righteous, let him be righteous still: and he that is holy, let him be holy still.

In one of his visions, Daniel is given the command to "shut thou up the vision" and not yet reveal what the Lord says (Daniel 8:26). Even in a different part of John's apocalyptic vision, he is instructed not to record the sayings he hears (Revelation 10:4). But now the message or "saying" is given for publication.

While the imagery of Revelation and the final chapters of Daniel are similar, their relationship is disputed by scholars. Some believe both are dealing with the same end times events. Others believe they describe separate events occurring closer to the time of the writers. While we cannot be sure of how these apocalyptic prophecies relate to each other, Christians can all affirm the significance of the second coming of Christ, even though they may differ in interpreting the details of it.

"At hand" is the Greek term *eggus* (eng-GOOS), which means near, nigh, or ready. This is breaking news the church needs to hear, so it can begin to watch and pray for Christ's second coming. This is an evangelistic word for the church, the Gospel of Christ is to be revealed, proclaimed, and told to all who will hear, for all too soon there will be no more opportunity to repent and receive the grace of God. While urgent, the message is still positive because it implies that right up until the end of life, there is still time to choose (Hebrews 9:27).

12 And, behold, I come quickly; and my reward is with me, to give every man according as his work shall be.

It is difficult to translate the Greek word *tachu* here, but King James translators chose "quickly" over the possibly more literal rendering of "suddenly." Both, as a result, intend for the church, the bride of Christ, to prepare herself and be ready at any time for the return of her beloved Bridegroom. Whether He returns "quickly" or "suddenly," both achieve the intended result of urging believers to be prepared for Christ's return because no one really knows when it will happen. The main point, repeated over and over in Scripture, is to be ready for Christ's return whenever it happens.

Christ here says He is bringing a reward with Him to give to everyone "according as his work shall be." Each of us is familiar with being rewarded for a job well done. Christians can look forward to being rewarded with eternity in the presence of God. Some might point to this verse to suggest a works based salvation, but this is to take this verse out of context. First, this verse alludes to two passages (Isaiah 40:10; 62:11), both of which use the same word ("reward," or "recompense") and both of which refer to God coming to bring salvation (not to reward good behavior). Second, the New Testament elsewhere makes clear that God brings salvation to His people on the grounds of Christ's righteousness alone (Titus 3:8; James 2:20). They receive that righteousness by faith, not by works. So in what sense does Christ reward each one according to His works? Verse 11 reveals the key: each person acts according to his true nature and the state of his heart toward Christ. Even in light of Christ's decisive second coming, only those God called will persevere to the end, through the faith the Spirit has given them. This verse is not intended to make a doctrinal statement, but rather was an exhortation to preparedness, which includes an ever ready, healthy, fruitful (works producing) faith. A positive take on the verse is that Jesus will come with "rewards" (Gk. *misthos*, mis-**THOS**), like wages or payment for services, for those who have been faithful. While no one is saved by works, those who are saved will be rewarded according to their "works" (Gk. *ergon*, **ER**-gon, employment or labor).

13 I am Alpha and Omega, the beginning and the end, the first and the last.

Alpha is the first letter of the 22-letter Greek alphabet and Omega is the last, thus the connection to the beginning and the end, and the first and the last. If Genesis and Revelation are the bookends of human history, Jesus is the holder of the bookends both preexisting and post-existing our temporal time frame. This is true not only in the sense of existence, but in character and holiness, without beginning or end, and without change (Malachi 3:6). Alpha and Omega, moreover, is one of many self-proclaimed images of Christ found in Scripture. The same names are applied to God and here are specifically applied to Christ. Jesus often applies to Himself titles elsewhere applied to God: Alpha and Omega (cf. 1:8; 21:6), first and last (cf. Isaiah 41:4; 44:6; 48:12; Revelation 1:17; 2:8), beginning and end (21:6). This gives another insurmountable argument for His deity. God is from "everlasting to everlasting" (Psalm 90:2), and He is the same "yesterday, and to day, and for ever" (Hebrews 13:8).

Knowing this identity of Christ gives the Christian peace. If Jesus is the faithful and true King, on par with the perfections of Yahweh, how could He fail to come through on behalf of His beloved ones?

14 Blessed are they that do his commandments, that they may have right to the tree of life, and may enter in through the gates into the city. 15 For without are

dogs, and sorcerers, and whoremongers, and murderers, and idolaters, and whosoever loveth and maketh a lie.

These verses remind the audience of what is at stake: eternal blessing in the City of God, or exclusion from it. We might fear how exactly the world will end. Will humankind bring about the end of the world through selfishness or carelessness? Believers do not have to worry about this though, but can accept that just as God brought the universe into being, God will bring this age to a close. We know to avoid the company of dangerous and disreputable people, and instead urgently offer others Jesus' invitation to enter the Kingdom.

While dogs are a favorite pet today, dogs in this time were denigrated. While hunting dogs could be useful, most dogs are simply strays. The word for "dogs" (Gk. *kunes*) is used in the New Testament to denote spiritual scavengers and predators who work to undermine the saving faith of others (Matthew 7:6; Philippians 3:2; 2 Peter 2:22). When referring to a pet or puppy, the diminutive (Gk. *kunarion*) is used (Matthew 15:26–27; Mark 7:27–28). In addition to these street scavengers, the city also excludes many of the same kinds of people just mentioned in the last chapter (Revelation 21:8): sorcerers, whoremongers, murderers, idolaters, and liars. This listing clarifies that the liars excluded from the heavenly kingdom are those who love lying.

16 I Jesus have sent mine angel to testify unto you these things in the churches. I am the root and the offspring of David, and the bright and morning star.

Jesus places His stamp of approval on the testimony of the message of Revelation to the church (the word "you" in the Greek is plural), which includes our present age. No mortal could be both root (the Creator) and offspring (Isaiah 11:1); Jesus is both the Lord of David and the son of David (Matthew 22:42–45).

The fallen angel, Lucifer, once called a morning star (Isaiah 14:12), has from the beginning lied to mankind and falsely presented himself as an angel of light (2 Corinthians 11:14). Jesus affirms that He alone is the true Morning Star. Here two ordinary Greek words are combined to form a unique metaphor: *orthrinos* (or- thrin-**OS**) for "morning" and *aster* (as-**TARE**) for "star." The Greek word *phosphoros* (foce-**FOR**-os) means light bearing, and is translated both "daystar" and "morning star." It is used only once in the rest of the New Testament (2 Peter 1:19) and is applied to Christ both there and in Revelation. The Morning Star will continue to shine, as He always has shone for eternity.

17 And the Spirit and the bride say, Come. And let him that heareth say, Come. And let him that is athirst come. And whosoever will, let him take the water of life freely.

Both the Spirit of God, who indwells God's church, and the bride of Christ (the church, believers) are invited. Those who have yet to decide for Christ are also invited to come to the water of life! We, along with the Spirit, wait expectantly but we also serve as a testimony that the human heart is satisfied by coming to Jesus, and any who comes to Him may freely drink of the water of life (John 7:37–39; Revelation 22:1), both now and forever.

18 For I testify unto every man that heareth the words of the prophecy of this book, If any man shall add unto these things, God shall add unto him the plagues that are written in this book: 19 And if any man shall take away from the words of the book of this prophecy, God shall take away his part out of the book of life, and out of the holy city, and from the things which are written in this book.

This invitation is strengthened and complemented by the following warning: no one must add or take away from the words of Revelation (vv. 18–19). John's stern words call to mind Deuteronomy 29:19–20, John urges the people of God to spurn false teaching and idolatry. The seven churches (indeed, the whole church) receives so much through this prophecy, this peek into God's plan for the ages! The church's faithfulness is demanded in return—a faithfulness springing from true faith.

Adults want important stories and accounts to be relayed correctly. Although the warnings of verse 18 seem to be applied only to John's vision, the warning not to add to or subtract from God's Word is found elsewhere to apply to all of Scripture (Deuteronomy 4:2; 12:32; Proverbs 30:5–6). God will judge appropriately offenders for their violation of His *logos*. The clearly promised curse balances the previous promised blessing offered to the faithful (v. 12) and together retain a familiar blessing/curse theme from the Old Testament as the New Testament closes.

20 He which testifieth these things saith, Surely I come quickly. Amen. Even so, come, Lord Jesus.

Christ's parting words are filled with mercy and hope. When Jesus ascended after His resurrection, He promised to be with them by His Spirit; now He promises He will soon return. The Greek word for "testify" is *martureo* (mar-too-**REH**-oh) and means to give or bear witness, just as the apostles were eye-witnesses who became those who testified throughout the New Testament. His coming will be fulfilled as completely as the fulfillment of sending the Holy Spirit, the Comforter and Teacher of the church. The primary message for the church is to be and remain ready.

The book of Revelation started with the Spirit (1:10), the church lives and exists because of the Spirit, and individual believers are raised to newness of life only through being born of the Spirit (John 3:5, 8; Galatians 4:29). The heartbeat of every Christian (the body and bride of Christ) is the Spirit. The Spirit has been our teacher of truth, always leading us toward Christ. The Spirit within you will confirm these words, "that when I come, whatever the day and year, it will seem to happen suddenly, and will take many by surprise." All born again believers, will be ready because of the Spirit and will wait expectantly, no matter how long it takes.

21 The grace of our Lord Jesus Christ be with you all. Amen.

It is no coincidence that both the book and the Word end with a word of grace. The only other time John uses this word, actually, is at the very beginning of his record of the revelation, wishing "grace" (Gk. *charis*, **KHAR**-eese) on all the seven churches receiving letters from his first vision (Revelation 1:4). This was a common greeting at the time, which helps to center the speaker's and the hearer's thoughts on Christ. Christ came to bring us grace. By His grace, we can grow more and more into His image as His beautiful Church.

When Christ's work on earth was finished, He left to prepare a place for us, and as surely as He came according to His promise, He will return as promised for His bride. Until we are perfected in Him, we can find no better comfort, stronger peace, or more enduring hope, than the presence of His grace to sustain us until His return.

Sources:

Beale, Gregory K. *Revelation: A Commentary on the Greek Text.* Grand Rapids, Mich.: Eerdmans, 1998.

Henry, Matthew. "Commentary on Revelation 22." In *Matthew Henry's Commentary on the Whole Bible.* Peabody, Mass.: Henderson Publishers, 1991.

Say It Correctly

Apocalyptic. ah-pah-kah-LIP-tic.

Daily Bible Readings

MONDAY
Invited to the Heavenly Banquet
(Luke 14:16–24)

TUESDAY
Preparing for God to Appear
(Exodus 19:9–15)

WEDNESDAY
The Alpha and Omega
(Revelation 1:3–8)

THURSDAY
The Ending Declared from
the Beginnings
(Isaiah 46:8–13)

FRIDAY
God Is Your Husband
(Isaiah 54:1–5)

SATURDAY
God's Steadfast Love Never Ceases
(Lamentations 3:21–31)

SUNDAY
Come, Lord Jesus!
(Revelation 22:10–21)

Notes

A

Abomination: A foul and detestable thing

Affliction: Anguish, burden, persecution, tribulation, or trouble

Angel: A messenger of God, not eternal or all-knowing; specific types include cherubim and seraphim

Ascension: Raising up in authority or physical place. Can especially refer to the event forty days after Jesus' death, burial, and Resurrection, when He returned to heaven to sit at the right hand of the Father (Acts 1:9–11)

Atone: To propitiate, satisfy the demands of an offended holy God; or reconcile to a holy God after sin

B

Baptize: To dip, immerse, or submerge

Blameless: Irreproachable, faultless, flawless

Blessedness: Happiness, joy, or prosperity, to be well spoken of by God or others

Bless the Lord: To bend the knee in praise to God

Blood of the Lamb: The blood that Jesus shed on the Cross that redeems humanity

Bowels: To ancient Middle Easterners, the place of emotion, distress, or love

C

Called by God: Appointed or commissioned to fulfill a task

Charge: Admonish, order, command

Chosen: To be approved and selected by God

Christ: The Anointed One, the expected Messiah the Jews hoped for and whom Christians believe came as Jesus of Nazareth

Commandments: God's mandates; the entire body of Laws issued by God through Moses for Israel

Conduct: Manner of living

Confess: To acknowledge or fully agree

Consider: To determine or make out

Covenant: An agreement or promise between God and humanity based on God's character, strength, and grace

Crucifixion: A method of Roman execution in which a criminal was hung on a cross

D

Decalogue: From "ten words" in Greek; the Ten Commandments

Desolation: The state of being deserted or uninhabited

Disciples: Learners, students, followers

Dominion: Rule or reign

Dwelling place: A person's refuge or home

E

El: The Hebrew word for "god" or "mighty one"

Evil: Bad, unpleasant, or displeasing things

Evil doer: A malefactor, wrongdoer, criminal, troublemaker

Evil spirits: Messengers and ministers of the devil

Exalt: To raise up to the highest degree possible

Exhortation: Giving someone motivation to change his or her behavior either by rebuke or encouragement

F

Faithfulness: Steadfastness, steadiness

Fear of the Lord: Reverence or awe of who God is, resulting in obedience to Him and abstaining from evil

G

Glory: Splendor, unparalleled honor, dignity, or distinction; praise and worship

God's bride: The Church

God's own hand: God's strength, power

Gospel: The Good News of Jesus the Messiah's arrival and presence of His kingdom

Graven image: An idol cut (often from stone, wood, or metal) and worshiped as a god

Great Tribulation: A time of great suffering that has not been experienced since the world began (Matthew 24:21, Revelation 7:14)

H

Hallowed: Consecrated, dedicated, or set apart

Hear: Listen to, yield to, or obey

Hearken: Pay attention to, give attention to

Heart: The figurative place of emotion and passion

Heathens: The Gentiles, all those who are not a part of the people of God

Holy: Anything consecrated and set aside for sacred use; set apart from sin

Honor: To revere or value

Host: An army or a vast number

I

Idolatry: The worship of anything other than God

Infidel: One who is unfaithful, unbelieving, and not to be trusted

Iniquity: Perversity, depravity, guilt, sin

I

Just: Righteous, that which is right and fair

Justice: Righteousness in government

K

Kingdom of Christ: The rule and reign of Christ as King both now and in the age to come

L

Law: Either the Mosiac Law or any human law; synonyms include commandments, ordinances, statutes, legal regulations, authoritative instructions, and teachings

Logos (LOW-goce): (Gk.) Word; the Word of God, either the Bible or Jesus

M

Manna: Food from heaven baked into a kind of bread, which God miraculously gave to the Israelites in the wilderness

Messiah: The Anointed One

Minister: A servant, an attendant, one who executes the commands of another

Mosiac Law: The law passed down by Moses from God to the Hebrew people at Mt. Sinai

O

Omnipotent: All-powerful

Omnipresent: All-present, being everywhere

Omniscient: All-knowing

Ordained: Established and founded by God; founded, fixed, or appointed

P

Parousia (par-oo-SEE-ah): (Gk.) presence, appearing; Christ's Second Coming

Peace: Wholeness, quietness, contentment, health, prosperity; more than an absence of conflict or problems, but every part of life being blessed

Pentateuch: The first five books of the Old Testament

Power: Boldness, might, or strength, especially God's

Prophets: People filled with the Spirit of God and under the authority and command of God, who pleaded His cause and urged humanity to be saved

Profit: To gain or benefit to succeed, especially in Spiritual things; to move forward or succeed in one's efforts

Prosper: Examined, tested, tried

Psalm: A piece of music or a melody, especially one dedicated to God or a god

Purity: Sinlessness, without blemish spiritually

R

Ransom: To buy back or pay a price for a person, buying their freedom

Redeem: To ransom or purchase

Refuge: A shelter from rain, storm, or danger; stronghold or fortress; a place to run to and be secure when the enemy threatens

Repent: To turn back from sin and turn to God in faith

Righteous: To be declared not guilty

Righteousness: Justness, rightness, especially God's, which He works as a gift in His people; the right way to live as opposed to a lifestyle that treats others unfairly or unjustly

S

Sabbath: From "ceasing (from work)" in Hebrew; the day set aside to worship God

Sanctuary: The holy place, either in the Tabernacle or the Temple

Salvation: Rescue, safety, or deliverance, especially from eternal punishment

Satan: A fallen angel who is opposed to God and His people

Savior: Defender, rescuer, or deliverer; a term applied to Christ as the rescuer of those who are in bondage to sin and death

Scribes: Secretaries, recorders, men skilled in the Law during Jesus' day

Selah (SEH-lah): (Heb.) A pause in singing to allow for an instrumental musical interlude or silent meditation

Septuagint: "Seventy" in Latin; the Greek translation of the Hebrew Old Testament made by 70 Jewish scholars beginning in the third century BC

Servant: A slave, subject, or worshiper

Shalom (sha-LOME): (Heb.) Peace, prosperity, blessing

Shekinah Glory: The awesome presence of the Lord; His honor, fame, and reputation

Shofar (sho-FAR): (Heb.) A ram's horn; commonly used in celebration, as well as in signaling armies or large groups of people in civil assembly

Soul: The immaterial part of a person (what leaves the body after death), or the whole being, the self, one's life

Stiffnecked: Obstinate and difficult

Strengthen: To secure, make firm

Strive: To struggle, to exert oneself

Supplication: Seeking, asking, entreating, pleading, imploring, or petitioning

T

Tabernacle: A tent; the name of the portable temple constructed by Moses and the people of Israel

Tetragrammaton: YHWH; the four consonants of God's name, as the Jews would often write it

Torah: (Heb.) Law, instrument, or direction; the first five books of the Old Testament

Transfiguration: A change or transformation. Often refers to Jesus' transformation while on the Mount of Olives with His disciples Peter, James, and John, when His face shone like the sun and His clothing was white as snow (Matthew 17:2; Mark 9:2; Luke 9:29)

Transgression: Sin, rebellion, breaking God's Law

Try: In the sense of a test, to refine or purify

Trumpet: A ram's horn or simple metal tube used in celebration as well as in signaling armies or large groups of people in civil assembly

V

Vanity (vain): A waste, a worthless thing, or simply emptiness

W

Wisdom: Prudence, an understanding of ethics

Woe: Grief or sorrow

Worship: Bow down deeply, show obedience and reverence

Wrath: Burning anger, rage

Y

Yahweh: God's name, often spelled with consonants only (see Tetragrammaton)

Notes

you will never have obedient life if
you don't have obedient mind
Roman 1
2 cor 10:3-4   Power- dumis
ochuruma stronghold

Notes

INTERNATIONAL AFRICAN AMERICAN MUSEUM

OPENING 2022
in Charleston,
South Carolina

Houses of worship, faith-based organizations, schools or seminaries —learn about ways to join us on our journey at **IAAMuseum.org/Faith** or contact Reverend DeMett Jenkins at **djenkins@iaamuseum.org.**

TO HONOR THE UNTOLD STORIES OF THE AFRICAN AMERICAN JOURNEY AT ONE OF OUR COUNTRY'S MOST SACRED SITES.

A JOURNEY
OF CENTURIES

THIS MUSEUM IS ABOUT A JOURNEY
that began centuries ago in Africa, and still continues.
It is about the journey of millions of Africans, captured
and forced across the Atlantic in the grueling and
inhumane Middle Passage, who arrived at Gadsden's
Wharf in Charleston, South Carolina and other ports
in the Atlantic World.

The journey will
challenge, illuminate,
inspire and, ultimately
will move people
to action.

With resilience, resistance, ingenuity, and intelligence, they
and their descendants shaped every aspect of our world.

The museum will sit on the shoulders of 18 strong columns.
On the ground level, the African Ancestors Memorial Garden will
highlight the original shoreline—the exact spot where so many
captive Africans first set foot in America. There will be gardens
for quiet contemplation, as well as space for performances
and programs.

Connections across the African diaspora, the spread of African
American culture and influence, and the movements or justice
and equality. The Center for Family History will enable visitors
to trace their genealogy, while changing exhibitions and special
events will keep the museum energized. Educational programs
will provide lifelong learning opportunities for visitors both young
and old.

The museum strives to foster empathy and understanding,
empowering visitors with the knowledge of the past.
The journey will challenge, illuminate, inspire and, ultimately,
will move people to action.

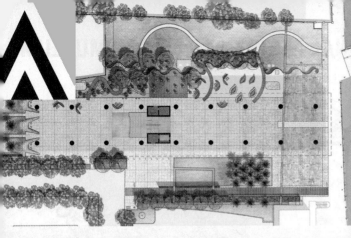

THE AFRICAN ANCESTORS MEMORIAL GARDEN

The African Ancestors Memorial Garden will commemorate one of our country's most sacred sites. It will be a place to reflect on the historic

significance of the site, experience botanical gardens, artistic installations, a huge infinity fountain on the edge of the original wharf, a soundscape that explores diverse African languages, performances, programs, and more. It will be free and open to the public.

isitors will learn bout seeds and lants that came ong with African ncestors at this ethnobotanical garden.

At the Tide Tribute, visitors will reflect on the courage and the fate of those men, women, and children who endured and died during the Middle Passage.

"The idea is to draw your eyes out to the Atlantic and have that moment where you feel the hallowed ground and that connection back across."

~Acclaimed Landscape Architect, Walter Hood, Hood Design Studio

Granite mirrors offer an opportunity for reflection.

They sit atop the site of a former storehouse where enslaved Africans awaited the slave market. In 1806–1807, while waiting for the market price to increase, upwards of 700 enslaved Africans died here as a result of harsh weather, close confinement, and insufficient food.

The five kneeling statues represent "rice negroes," enslaved people, often times children, who were forced to work in the rice fields.

THE LEGACY OF PEI COBB FREED AND HARRY COBB

Pei Cobb Freed & Partners is the design architect for the museum. Some of the firm's best-known work includes the crystalline extension to the Louvre in Paris, the JFK Presidential Library in Boston, and the Bank of China Tower in Hong Kong. Harry Cobb, one of the founding partners, describes the museum as "a purposefully unrhetorical work of architecture quietly affirming the power of place, as it shelters and frames a richly articulated work of landscape art."

EXHIBITIONS AT THE MUSEUM

Visitors will engage with dynamic exhibits featuring historic figures, events, and experiences from slavery through the 20th-century civil rights movement and into the present. Ralph Appelbaum Associates works with the museum on exhibit design. The company's portfolio includes many of the world's most important museums.

Galleries:

Transatlantic Experience
South Carolina Connections
Atlantic Worlds
African Roots/African Routes
Carolina Gold
Gullah Geechee
American Journeys
Changing Exhibition

THE CENTER FOR FAMILY HISTORY

The Center for Family History is a one of a kind, unprecedented research center with a special focus on African American genealogy. Our goal is to help individuals and their families gain a greater understanding of their families' history and the role their ancestors played in helping to shape American history. Although the museum opens in 2022, you can enjoy our online offerings and digital archives now.

The Center for Family History will serve as a groundbreaking resource for the study and advancement of African American genealogy with connections to Africa and the African diaspora.

FAITH-BASED PROGRAMS

The museum offers innovative and engaging programming. Our programs have ranged from community conversations to presentations by lauded scholars like Henry Louis Gates, David Blight, and Lonnie Bunch. We've developed a range of faith-based programs highlighting the central role of faith, spirituality, and religion in the African American experience. Educational programs will provide lifelong learning opportunities for young and old. We're busy creating K-12 curriculum, field-trip experiences, digital content, professional development programs, and more!

Images:

(1) Awakening of the Ancestors Through Music Program
(2) Clergy Members at Groundbreaking Worship Service
(3) Allison Creek Presbyterian Church

LEARN MORE

Houses of worship, faith-based organizations, schools or seminaries —learn about ways to join us on our journey at **IAAMuseum.org/Faith** or contact Reverend DeMett Jenkins at **djenkins@iaamuseum.org**.